Easy to Read

Accurate Literal Translation

of the

HOLY BIBLE

The Complete New Testament
with a Treasure of Old Testament Passages

The New Authorized Version in Present-Day English™

AV7 closely follows the time-honored traditional English text commonly known as the Authorized Version or KJV, with recognized errors corrected, obsolete and archaic words and phrases updated to present-day English, and with many refinements and enhancements.

AV7 The New Authorized Version of the New Testament in Present-Day English™

All Scripture texts contained herein are the gift of Almighty God to mankind and may be freely copied for any non-commercial use* with only three stipulations:

1. For the benefit of readers, the source of any quotations from this text should be identified as ***AV7***.
2. No changes may be made in ***AV7*** or in any New Authorized Version Foundation text without written consent.
3. *Commercial use is defined as any reproduction of the ***AV7*** text for which any fee is charged. Commercial use requires an appropriate license from the copyright holder.

Compiled and published by Communication Architects
for the New Authorized Version Foundation

Printed in the USA in cooperation with Barbour Publishing

ISBN numbers:

1-59789-446-X (Burgundy) 1-59789-447-8 (Green)
1-59789-448-6 (Clouds) 1-59789-449-4 (Youth)

For additional information, please visit: www.***AV7***.org

Introduction

The greatest wisdom, truth, and practical guidance for living a successful life are found within the pages of the Bible. It is the most inspiring, the most trustworthy, and the most widely published and distributed source of wisdom and truth ever compiled.

The Bible is the best-selling book of all time. No other best-seller has ever come even close to it. It is, without rival, the most widely read and studied, and the most extensively researched, verified, and validated document in the history of mankind.

Regrettably however, among the great number of different versions of the Bible in print, many use interpretive paraphrasing that may dilute, diminish, or misrepresent the full truth of the Word of God. While a paraphrase may be helpful to some readers, it is important to realize that paraphrasing is not a literally accurate source of truth. Some versions have taken great liberties in the changes they have made. Therefore, readers would be wise to compare any non-literal version to an accurate literal translation.

It is important to understand that there can never be such a thing as different versions of the truth. Every deviation from literal accuracy increases the risk of moving farther and farther away from trustworthy truth. Many Bible publishers have sponsored or created their own unique "All rights reserved" versions and paraphrases of the Bible. All of these very different versions cannot possibly be equally reliable and trustworthy.

AV7 is different. It is not a product of commercial sponsorship or the result of any individual's or committee's interpretation of what the Word of God says. Instead, ***AV7*** is a present-day English update of the traditional English text that stood for more than 300 years as the most widely accepted, literally accurate English language translation of the Bible. ***AV7*** closely follows that text.

Therefore, you can now read, study, and rightly divide the Word of Truth with a trustworthy, literally accurate version of the Bible that is easy to read in present-day English.

AV7

The New Authorized Version of the Bible
in Present-Day English TM

Table of Contents

The Ten Commandments are the foundation of all truth 4
The Most Essential Truth in the Bible — An overview 6

The Gospel as written by **John** 15
The Gospel as written by **Matthew** 45
The Gospel as surveyed by **Mark** 84
The Gospel as surveyed by **Luke** for Theophilus 107

Pastoral letters written by some of the first eyewitnesses
to the life and teachings of the Word of God
to encourage new believers in their faith:

A letter written by Luke to Theophilus called **Acts** . . 147
A series of letters written by Paul:
A letter to the **Romans** 184
Two letters to the **Corinthians** 200
A letter to the **Galatians** 225
A letter to the **Ephesians** 230
A letter to the **Philippians** 235
A letter to the **Colossians** 239
Two letters to the **Thessalonians** 242
Two letters to **Timothy** 247
A letter to **Titus** 254
A letter to **Philemon** 256
An unsigned letter to the **Hebrews** 256
A letter written by **James** 268
Two letters written by **Peter** 272
Three letters written by **John** 278
A letter written by **Jude** 283
The Revelation as recorded by John 285

A Treasure of **Old Testament** wisdom 303
Features and Benefits of the ***AV7*** presentation 313
Description of how the ***AV7*** text was prepared 314

A cordial invitation to join the family of God 318

The Ten Commandments are the foundation of all truth

The Ten Commandments are the most readily recognizable of all truths. They are unique in many ways, one of which is that when God established these Ten Commandments, that was the first time that He is reported to have spoken directly to all of mankind, rather than to and through certain individuals one at a time.

The Ten Commandments are further distinguished by the fact that this was the only time in all of recorded history that God ever wrote a message to mankind by His own hand. And it is significant that He wrote this message as an engraving carved in stone.

Ever since that event some 3,300 years ago, the Ten Commandments have been almost universally acknowledged and accepted as the foundation of all truth by people who believe in God.

Very few people who acknowledge that there is a God will ever dispute the relevance, common sense, reasonableness, viability, practicality, and appropriateness of the Ten Commandments as wise words to live by and to govern and be governed by.

Some people have claimed that the Ten Commandments were given only to the Jews, or that they were only meant for the ancient time and place in which they were given. Consequently, they say that only Jews are required to obey them. Some others suggest that God's Ten Commandments are no longer applicable today.

However, as you read these Ten Commandments, it will surely be very apparent that God meant what He said and that He fully intended for these Ten Commandments to remain in effect for all people and for all time.

Please note: The ***AV7*** Bible text uses reduced-size italics to identify words that have been interpolatively added to otherwise literally translated words to improve clarity, readability, and understandability. For example, in the verse: "I *am* the Lord your God" (see #1 on the facing page), the word "am" is an interpolatively added word. The ***AV7*** text also uses key word flags to identify significant word revisions from the traditional English text. For example, the word "murder+" (see #6 on the facing page) is a more accurate translation than the traditional translation "kill."

The 10 Commandments

Exodus 20:1-17

#1 [v1-3] God spoke … saying: I *am* the Lord your God … You shall have no other gods before me.

#2 [v4] You shall not make for yourself any graven image or any likeness *of any thing* that *is* in heaven above or that *is* in the earth beneath or that *is* in the water under the earth. [5] You shall not bow yourself down to them nor serve them, for I the Lord your God *am* a jealous God, visiting the iniquity of the fathers upon the children to the third and fourth *generation* of those who hate me [6] and showing mercy to thousands of those who love me and keep my commandments.

#3 [v7] You shall not take the name of the Lord your God in vain, for the Lord will not hold those guiltless who take His name in vain.

#4 [v8] Remember the Sabbath day to keep it holy. [9] Six days shall you labor and do all your work, [10] but the seventh day *is* the Sabbath of the Lord your God. *In it,* you shall not do any work: You nor your son nor your daughter, your servant nor your maid, nor your cattle, nor your visitor[+] who *is* within your gates. [11] For *in* six days the Lord made heaven and earth, the sea, and all that *is* in them, and *He* rested *on* the seventh day. Therefore the Lord blessed the Sabbath day and hallowed it.

#5 [v12] Honor your father and your mother *so* that your days may be long upon the land which the Lord your God has given *to* you.

#6 [v13] You shall not murder[+].

#7 [v14] You shall not commit adultery.

#8 [v15] You shall not steal.

#9 [v16] You shall not bear false witness against your neighbor.

#10 [v17] You shall not covet your neighbor's house *and* you shall not covet your neighbor's wife nor his manservant nor his maidservant nor his ox nor his ass nor any thing that *is* your neighbor's.

The Most Essential Truth

All of the words and messages presented in the Bible are of great importance and great value, and no part of the Bible should be omitted, ignored, or disregarded. However, all of the words and messages in the Bible are not equal in importance.

Some words and messages, such as the Ten Commandments, establish never-to-be-changed laws as benchmarks of bedrock importance. Other portions include historical narratives, eye-witness accounts of supernatural events, genealogical records, biographical data, personal testimonies, prophetic allegories, and various other types and categories of content.

Interspersed among the 790,391 words in 31,089 verses in the 66 books in the Bible, there are certain key verses — **universal truths and declarative instructions** — that God communicates to mankind. Sometimes He speaks with His own voice, sometimes through the mouths of prophets, and in certain places, God specifically speaks as "**the Word of God**." The first words in the Book of John identify and introduce the Word of God in this way:

"In the beginning was the Word,
and the Word was with God,
and the Word was God."
(and then in verse 14)
"... and the Word became flesh and lived+ among us."

Only one person in all of recorded history has ever qualified for that name and title. The words that He spoke out of His own mouth are far more significant and more important than any other words ever spoken or written.

A book entitled ***The Most Essential Truth in the Bible*** (ISBN 978-0-935597-02-7) features 249 passages in which the Word of God proclaims the most essential of all universal truths and declarative instructions. In the 7 pages that follow, you can quickly read 98 of these key passages. While it takes more than 66 hours to read the entire Bible, you can read these key passages in less than 10 minutes. For more information visit: www.MostEssential.com

You can also enjoy refreshing inspiration and encouragement every day by frequently re-reading and meditating on these key passages from the incomparable wisdom of the Word of God.

If anyone has ears that can hear let them listen.

#11 It is written:
Mankind shall not live
by bread alone,
but by every word that proceeds
out of the mouth of God.

#12 Again it is written: You shall not tempt the Lord your God.

#13 You shall worship
the Lord your God
and Him only shall you serve.

#14 Truly, truly, I say to you: Unless a person is born again, they cannot see the kingdom of God.

#15 Truly, truly, I say to you: Unless a person is born of water and *of* the Spirit, they cannot enter into the kingdom of God. *Those* who are born of flesh are flesh, and *those* who are born of the Spirit are spirit. Do not marvel that I said: You must be born again.

#17 God so loved the world,
that He gave
His Only Begotten Son,
so that whoever believes in Him
should not perish,
but have eternal life.

#18 God did not send His Son into the world to condemn the world, but *so* that the world through Him might be saved. *Those* who believe in Him are not condemned, but *those* who do not believe are condemned already, because they have not believed in the name of the Only Begotten Son of God.

#20 *The Word of God said:* Whoever drinks of the water that I give will never thirst. Instead, the water that I give will become a well of water within them springing up into eternal life.

#21 God *is* Spirit. *Those* who worship Him must worship *Him* in spirit and in truth.

#23 Repent. For the kingdom of heaven is *very* near.

#24 Follow me and I will make you fishers of men.

#25 Sin no more, lest a worse thing come to you.

#27 Truly, truly, I say to you: *Those* who hear my Word and believe in Him who sent me have eternal life and will not come into condemnation, but *they* are passed from death to life.

#28 *Those* who have done good will come forth to the resurrection of life, and *those* who have done evil to the resurrection of damnation.

#29 Search the Scriptures.
For in them
you think you have eternal life,
and they testify of me.

#30 Blessed *are* the poor in spirit, for theirs is the kingdom of heaven.

#31 Blessed *are those* who mourn, for they shall be comforted.

#32 Blessed *are* the meek, for they shall inherit the earth.

#33 Blessed *are those* who do hunger and thirst after righteousness, for they shall be filled.

#34 Blessed *are* the merciful, for they shall obtain mercy.

#35 Blessed *are* the pure in heart, for they shall see God.

#36 Blessed *are* the peacemakers, for they shall be called children of God.

#37 Blessed *are those* who are persecuted for righteousness' sake, for theirs is the kingdom of heaven.

#38 Blessed are you when *people* revile you and persecute *you* and say all kinds of evil against you falsely for my sake.

#39 Rejoice and be exceedingly glad. For great *is* your reward in heaven. For so *likewise did* they persecute the prophets who were before you.

#40 You are the salt of the earth, but if salt has lost its savor, with what will it be salted? It is thereafter good for nothing but to be cast out and trampled under foot.

#41 You are the light of the world. A city that is set on a hill cannot be hid. Nor do people light a candle and put it under a bushel, but on a candlestick *so that* it gives light to all who are in the house.

#42 Let your light so shine before *people* that they may see your good works and glorify your Father in heaven.

#43 Do not think that I have come to destroy the law or the prophets. I have not come to destroy, but to fulfill. For truly I say to you: Until heaven and earth pass, one jot or one smallest mark shall in no way pass from the law until all is fulfilled.

#44 Whoever therefore shall break one of these least commandments and shall teach people *to do* so shall be called the least in the kingdom of heaven. But whoever shall do *them* and teach *them*, the same shall be called great in the kingdom of heaven.

#53 You have heard that it has been said: You shall love your neighbor and hate your enemy. But I say to you:

Love your enemies.
Bless *those* who curse you.
Do good to *those* who hate you.
And pray for *those*
who despitefully use you
and persecute you
so that you may be the children
of your Father in heaven.

#57 Pray in this manner:

Our Father in heaven,
Holy is your name.
Your kingdom come.
Your will be done,
on earth as *it is* in heaven.

Give us this day our daily bread.
And forgive us *for* our debts
as we forgive our debtors.

Lead us *so that we will* not
yield to temptation,
but deliver us from evil.

For the kingdom is yours,
and the power and the glory,
forever. Amen.

#58 If you forgive others *for* their trespasses *then* your heavenly Father will also forgive you. But if you do not forgive others *for* their trespasses *then* neither will your Father forgive your trespasses.

#61 Do not lay up for yourselves treasures on earth where moth and rust corrupt and where thieves break through and steal. Lay up for yourselves treasures in heaven where neither moth nor rust corrupt and where thieves do not break through or steal.

#62 Do not be afraid, little flock. For it is your Father's good pleasure to give the kingdom *of God* to you.

#65 No one can serve two masters. For either they will hate the one and love the other, or else they will hold to the one and despise the other.

You cannot serve God
and *worldly* treasures.

#66 Take heed and beware of covetousness. For one's life *is* not *to be found* in the abundance *of things* one possesses.

#73 Seek first the kingdom of God and His righteousness and all these things will be added to you.

#75 Do not judge *so* that you *will* not be judged. For with what judgment you judge, you will be judged. With what gauge you measure, it will be measured to you again.

#76 Give and it will be given to you: Good measure, pressed down, shaken together, and running over. Others will give to your innermost *needs*. For with the same gauge with which you measure it will be measured to you again.

#80 Ask and it will be given
to you. Seek and you will find.
Knock and it will be
opened to you.
For everyone who asks receives
and *those* who seek *will* find
and to *those* who knock
it will be opened.

#82 - - - *The Golden Rule* - - -

Therefore all things whatsoever you would that others should do to you, you do to them. For this is *the sum of* the law and the prophets.

#84 Beware of false prophets who come to you in sheep's clothing, but inwardly they are greedy wolves. You will know them by their fruits.

#86 Not everyone who says to me: Lord, Lord, will enter into the kingdom of heaven, but *only those* who do the will of my Father in heaven.

#91 Go and learn what *this* means: I will have mercy and not sacrifice. For I have not come to call the righteous but sinners to repentance.

#92 Do not be afraid.
Only believe.

#95 As you go, proclaim *the Word*, say: The kingdom of heaven is *very* near.

#106 … there is nothing covered that will not be revealed and *nothing* hidden that will not be known.

#109 Whoever will confess me before people, I will confess before my Father in heaven. But whoever will deny me before people, I will deny before my Father in heaven.

#114 Come to me
all *you* who labor
and are heavily burdened.
I will give you rest.
Take my yoke upon you
and learn of me.
For I am meek and lowly
in heart. You will find
rest for your souls.
For my yoke *is* easy
and my burden is light.

#115 You are overly anxious and troubled about *too* many things. But one thing is necessary: *giving heed to the Word of God* …

#118 Every kingdom divided against itself is brought to desolation. Every city or house divided against itself will not stand.

#119 *Those* who are not with me are against me. *Those* who do not gather with me scatter.

#122 … out of the abundance of the heart the mouth speaks. A good person out of good treasure of the heart brings forth good things. An evil person out of evil treasure brings forth evil things.

#123 … *for* every idle word that people speak, they will give *an* account of it on the day of judgment.

For by your words
you will be justified
and by your words
you will be condemned.

#124 … blessed *are those* who hear the Word of God and keep it.

#125 … whoever does the will of my Father in heaven, the same is my brother and sister and mother.

#130 Be of good cheer. I am *with you*. Do not be afraid.

#132 This is the work of God: That you believe in *the one* whom He has sent.

#137 Truly truly I say to you:

Those who believe in me
have eternal life.

#141 If anyone has ears to hear, let them hear. Out of the heart proceed evil thoughts, murders, adulteries, fornications, thefts, false witness, covetousness, wickedness, deceit, filthiness, an evil eye, blasphemy, pride, *and* foolishness. These are *the things* that defile a person …

#142 If anyone will come after me, let them deny themselves and take up their cross and follow me. For whoever would save their life will lose it and whoever would lose their life for my sake will find it. For what is anyone to profit if they gain the whole world and lose their own soul? Or what shall anyone give in exchange for their soul?

#143 If you can believe, all things *are* possible to *those* who believe.

#156 If anyone thirsts, let them come to me and drink. As the Scripture has said *of those* who believe in me: Out of their innermost being will flow rivers of living water.

#157 If you continue
in my Word *then*
you are indeed
my disciples.
You shall know the truth
and the truth
will make you free.

#159 Truly, truly, I say to you: If anyone keeps my Word, they will never see death.

#161 I am the door. If anyone enters in through me, they will be saved …

#162 … I have come *so* that they *might* have life and have *it* more abundantly.

#177 I am the resurrection and the life. *Those* who believe in me, though they were dead, yet shall they live.

Whoever lives and believes
in me will never die.
Do you believe this?

#182 Have you not read that He who made *them* at the beginning made them male and female and said: For this reason a man shall leave father and mother and cleave to his wife and they two shall be one flesh. Therefore they are no longer two but one flesh. Therefore what God has joined together do not let anyone separate.

#186 If you will enter into life, keep the commandments. You shall do no murder. You shall not commit adultery. You shall not steal. You shall not bear false witness. Honor your father and *your* mother. And, you shall love your neighbor as yourself.

#189 … With God
all things are possible.

#196 Truly I say to you: If you have faith and do not doubt, but say to this mountain: Be removed and be cast into the sea, it will be done. All things whatsoever you ask in prayer believing, you will receive.

#200 You err *by* not knowing the Scriptures or the power of God.

#201 What is written in the law?
How do you read *it*?
You shall love the Lord
your God with all your heart
and with all your soul
and with all your mind.
Do this and you will live.
This is the first
and great commandment.

#202 The second *is* like it:
You shall love your neighbor
as yourself.
On these two commandments
hang all the law and the prophets.

#204 Do not be called Rabbi. For one is your Master, Christ. All *of* you are family.

#205 Do not call any *man* your father on the earth, for one is your Father, who is in heaven. Neither *should* you be called masters. For one is your Master, Christ. But one who is greatest among you shall be your servant.

#206 Whoever exalts themselves will be humbled and *those* who humble themselves will be exalted.

#207 Take heed *so* that no one deceives you.

#211 Heaven and earth will pass away but my words will not pass away.

#223 A new commandment
I give to you:
That you love one another.
As I have loved you,
that you also love one another.
By this all *people* will know
that you are my disciples:
If you have love
toward one another.

#225 Do not let your heart be troubled. You believe in God. Believe also in me.

#226 I am the way,
the truth, and the life.
No one comes to the Father,
but by me.

#229 If you love me,
keep my commandments.

#230 *Those* who have my commandments and keep them are the ones who *truly* love me. *Those* who love me will be loved by my Father and I will love them and will reveal myself to them. If anyone loves me, they will keep my words and my Father will love them and we will come to them and live within them.

#232 Peace I leave with you. My peace I give to you. I do not give to you as the world gives. Do not let your heart be troubled *and do not* let it be afraid.

#235 I have spoken these things to you *so* that my joy might remain in you and *so that* your joy might be full.

#236 This is my commandment:
That you love one another
as I have loved you.

#237 Greater love has no one than this, that one lay down one's *own* life for one's friends.

#242 I have spoken these things to you *so* that in me you might have peace. In the world you will have tribulation. But be of good cheer. I have overcome the world.

#243 Watch and pray *so* that you do not enter into temptation. The spirit indeed *is* willing, but the flesh *is* weak.

#244 Peace to you. As *my* Father has sent me, even so I *now* send you.

#245 Receive *the* Holy Spirit.

#246 Follow me.

#247 Go therefore
and teach all nations,
baptizing them
in the name of the Father
and of the Son
and of the Holy Spirit,
teaching them to observe
all things whatsoever
I have commanded you.
Behold I am with you always,
even to the end of the world.

#248 *Those* who believe and are baptized will be saved, but *those* who do not believe will be damned.

#249

--- *The Invitation* ---

Behold, I stand at the door and knock.

If anyone *will* hear my voice
and open the door,

I will come in to them
and dine+ with them
and they with me.

The Complete **AV7** *New Testament*

with the most essential passages highlighted.

Jesus Christ is the most amazing person who ever lived and He is the central figure of the entire Bible. While the Old Testament is very important in setting the stage for and foretelling His arrival, we begin with the New Testament because it presents four accounts of His life on earth and a written record of the most important words that He spoke as the Word of God.

While most Bibles have traditionally presented the first four books of the New Testament (called "The Gospels") in the sequence Matthew, Mark, Luke, and John, this presentation begins with the book of John, followed by Matthew, Mark, and Luke. Some of the reasons for beginning with John should become apparent as you begin to read.

The Gospel of Jesus Christ as written by John

Chapter 1

1 In the beginning was the Word
and the Word was with God
and the Word was God. *Genesis 1:1*

2 He+ was, in the *very* beginning, with
God.
3 Everything+ *came into* existence+
through Him. Without Him nothing
would have come+ into existence.
4 In Him was life and the life was the
light of men.
5 The light shines in darkness and the
darkness does not overtake+ it.
6 *Now* there was a man sent from God
whose name *was* John.
7 *John* came as a witness to testify+ of
the Light *so* that through Him everyone
might believe.
8 *John* was not that Light, but *was sent* to
testify+ of that Light.
9 *This* was the true Light, that enlightens+
everyone+ who comes into the world.
10 He was in the world and the world was
made by Him and *yet* the world did not
know Him.
11 He came to His own and His own did
not receive Him. *Isaiah 53:3*
12 But *to* all+ *who* received Him, He gave
authority+ *and power* to become the
children+ of God, *even* to *those* who
believe on His name,
13 *to those* who were born not of blood
nor of the will of the flesh nor of the will
of man, but of God.

14 And the Word was made flesh
and lived+ among us

and we beheld His glory: Glory as of the
Only Begotten of the Father, full of
grace and truth.
15 John testified+ about Him, and called+
out saying: This was He of whom I
spoke. He who comes after me is preferred before me because He was before
me.
16 Of His fullness we *have* all received,
and grace *for everyone* instead+ of grace
for a favored few.
17 For the law was given by Moses, *but*
grace and truth came by Jesus Christ.
18 No one has seen God at any time. The
Only Begotten Son who is in the bosom
of the Father has declared *Him.*
19 This is the testimony+ of John when
the Jews sent priests and Levites from
Jerusalem to ask him: Who are you?

20 He confessed and did not deny, but
confessed: I am not the Christ.
21 They asked him: What then? Are you
Elijah? He said: I am not. Are you that
prophet? He answered: No.
22 Then they said to him: Who are you?
Tell us so that we may give an answer to
those who sent us. What do you say of
yourself?
23 He said: I *am* the voice of one crying
in the wilderness: Make straight the
way of the Lord, as the prophet Isaiah
said. *Isaiah 40:3*
24 *Those* who were sent *to John* were of
the Pharisees.
25 They asked him and said to him: Why
do you baptize then? If you are not the
Christ or Elijah or that prophet?
26 John answered them saying: I baptize
with water but there stands one among
you whom you do not know.
27 It is He, who, coming after me, is
preferred before me. I am not *even*
worthy to loosen His sandal[+] straps.[+]
28 These things were done in Bethabara
beyond Jordan where John was baptizing.
29 The next day John saw Jesus coming
to him and *he* said:

Behold the Lamb of God
who takes away
the sin of the world.

30 This is He of whom I said: After me
comes a man who is preferred before
me, because He was before me.
31 I did not know Him, but I came
baptizing with water *so* that He might be
made known[+] to Israel.
32 *Then* John testified[+] saying: I saw the
Spirit descending from heaven like a
dove, and it *came to* reside[+] on Him.
33 I did not know Him, but He who sent
me to baptize with water said to me: *The
one* upon whom you shall see the Spirit
descending and remaining on Him is *the
One* who baptizes with the Holy Spirit.

34 I saw and testify[+]
that this is the Son of God.

35 Again the next day, after John stood
with two of his disciples
36 looking at Jesus as He walked *by*, he
said: Behold the Lamb of God.
37 The two disciples heard him say this
and they followed Jesus.
38 Then Jesus turned, saw them following, and said to them: What are you
seeking? They said to Him: Rabbi,
meaning[+] Master. Where do you live?
39 He said to them: Come and see. *So*
they went *with Him* and saw where He
lived[+] and stayed[+] with Him that day,
for it was about four *in the afternoon*.
40 One of the two who heard John *speak*
and followed *Jesus* was Andrew, Simon
Peter's brother.
41 He first found his own brother Simon
and said to him: We have found the
Messiah who is called[+] the Christ.
42 *Andrew* brought *his brother* to Jesus and
when Jesus saw[+] him He said: You are
Simon the son of Jonah. You shall be
called Cephas. That is translated[+] Peter,[+] *which means a steadfast stone*.
43 The next[+] day, Jesus went[+] to Galilee, found Philip, and said to him:
Follow me.
44 Now Philip was from Bethsaida, the
same city as Andrew and Peter.
45 Philip found Nathanael and said to him:
We have found Him of whom Moses in
the law and the prophets wrote: Jesus of
Nazareth, the son of Joseph.
46 Nathanael said to him: Can any good
thing come out of Nazareth? Philip said
to him: Come and see.
47 Jesus saw Nathanael coming to Him
and said of him: Behold an Israelite
indeed in whom is no guile.
48 Nathanael said to *Jesus*: From where do
you know me? Jesus answered and said to
him: Before Philip called you, when you
were under the fig tree, I saw you.
49 Nathanael answered and said to Him:
Rabbi, you are the Son of God. You are
the King of Israel.
50 Jesus answered and said to him: Because I said to you *that* I saw you under
the fig tree you believe? You shall see
greater things than these.

51 *Then Jesus* said to him: Truly,[+] truly,
I say to you: Hereafter you will see
heaven open and the angels of God
ascending and descending upon the Son
of man.

John Chapter 2

1 *On* the third day, there was a marriage
in Cana of Galilee and Jesus' mother
was there.
2 Both Jesus and His disciples were
invited[+] to the marriage.
3 When they *ran* out[+] *of* wine, Jesus'
mother said to Him: They have no wine.
4 Jesus said to her: What *is this* to you
and to me, woman? My hour has not yet
come.
5 His mother said to the servants: *Do*
whatever He may say to you.
6 *Now* there were six stone water pots
standing[+] there of the kind *used* by the
Jews for purifying, each[+] *able to* hold[+]
nearly twenty to thirty gallon.[+]
7 Jesus said to them: Fill the water pots
with water. And they filled them up to
the brim.
8 *Then* He said to them: Draw *some* out
now and take[+] *it* to the host[+]. They
took[+] *it as Jesus said.*
9 When the host[+] tasted the water that
was made *into* wine, *he* did not understand[+] where it had *come* from. But the
servants who drew the water knew. The
host[+] called the bridegroom
10 and said to him: Everyone[+] at the
beginning sets forth good wine. When
the guests have drunk well, then what is
lower[+] *quality is set out. But* you have
kept the good wine until now.
11 This beginning of miracles Jesus did
in Cana of Galilee, and manifested forth
His glory, and His disciples believed in
Him.
12 After this, *Jesus* went to Capernaum,
He and His mother and His brothers and
His disciples, and they stayed[+] there
though not many days.
13 The Jews' Passover was at hand and
Jesus went up to Jerusalem.
14 In the temple, *He* found *those* who sold
oxen and sheep and doves, and *also* the
money changers sitting *there*. *Malachi 3:1*
15 *So* He made a whip[+] of small cords,
and He drove them all out of the temple,
along with the sheep and oxen, and *He*
poured out the changers' money and
overthrew the tables. *Malachi 3:2,3*
16 To *those* who sold doves, *He* said:
Take these things away.[+] Do not make
my Father's house a house of merchandise.
17 And His disciples remembered that it
was written: The zeal of your house has
eaten me up. *Psalm 69:9*
18 Then the Jews answered and said to
Him: What sign *can* you show us *to*
demonstrate your authority for these things
that you do?
19 Jesus answered and said to them:
Destroy this temple and in three days I
will raise it up.
20 Then the Jews said: *It took* forty six
years to build this temple and you *claim*
that you can raise[+] it up in three days?
21 But *Jesus* was speaking of the temple
of His body.
22 Therefore, when He was risen from
the dead, His disciples remembered that
He had said this to them, and they
believed the Scripture and the Word that
Jesus had said.
23 Now when He was in Jerusalem at the
Passover in the feast *day*, many believed
in His name when they saw the miracles
that He did.
24 But Jesus did not commit Himself to
their *testimony* because He knew all *men*
25 and *He* did not need any *of them* to
testify concerning[+] man, for He knew
what was in man.

John Chapter 3

1 *Now* there was a man of the Pharisees
named Nicodemus, a ruler of the Jews.
2 He came to Jesus by night and said to
Him: Rabbi, we know that you are a
teacher come from God, for no one can
do these miracles that you do, unless[+]
God is with them.
3 Jesus answered and said to him:

> Truly,[+] truly, I say to you:
> Unless[+] a person[+] is born again,
> they cannot see
> the kingdom of God.

4 Nicodemus said to Him: How can anyone[+] be born when they are old? Can they enter a second time into their mother's womb and be born?

5 Jesus answered: Truly,[+] truly, I say to you: Unless[+] a person[+] is born of water and *of* the Spirit, they cannot enter into the kingdom of God.

6 *Those* who are born of flesh are flesh, and *those* who are born of the Spirit are spirit.

7 Do not marvel that I said to you: You must be born again.

8 The wind blows where it will[+] and you hear the sound of it, but *you* cannot tell from where it comes and where it goes. So *it* is *with* everyone who is born of the Spirit.

9 Nicodemus answered and said to Him: How can these things be?

10 Jesus answered and said to him: Are you a master of Israel and do not understand[+] these things?

11 Truly,[+] truly, I say to you: We speak what we know and testify *about* what we have seen, but you do not receive our witness.

12 If I have told you earthly things and you do not believe, how will you believe if I tell you *about* heavenly things?

13 No one has ascended up to heaven except[+] He who came down from heaven, *even* the Son of man who is in heaven.

14 *Just* as Moses lifted up the serpent in the wilderness, even so the Son of man must be lifted up

15 *so* that whoever believes in Him should not perish, but have eternal life. *Proverbs 8:35*

> 16 For God so loved the world,
> that He gave
> His Only Begotten Son,
> *so* that whoever believes in Him
> should not perish,
> but have eternal[+] life.

17 For God did not send His Son into the world to condemn the world, but *so* that the world through Him might be saved.

18 *Those* who believe in Him are not condemned, but *those* who do not believe are condemned already, because they have not believed in the name of the Only Begotten Son of God.

19 And this is the condemnation: That light has come into the world, but people[+] *have* loved darkness rather than light, because their deeds were evil.

20 For everyone who does evil hates the light and does not come to the light, lest their deeds should be proved[+] *evil*.

21 But *those* who do truth come to the light *so* that their deeds may be made known,[+] that they are worked[+] in God.

22 After these things, Jesus and His disciples went[+] into the land of Judea, and He stayed[+] there with them and baptized.

23 John was also baptizing in Aenon near Salim, because there was much water there and *the people* came and were baptized.

24 For John had not yet been cast into prison.

25 Then a question arose between *some* of John's disciples and the Jews about purifying.

26 They came to John and said to him: Rabbi, the one who was with you beyond Jordan, to whom you bear witness, behold He is baptizing and everyone[+] is going[+] to Him.

27 John answered and said: A person[+] can receive nothing unless[+] it is given *to* them from heaven.

28 You yourselves *can* testify[+] that I said: I am not the Christ, but that I am sent before Him.

29 One who has a bride is a bridegroom, but the friend of the bridegroom who stands and hears him, rejoices greatly because of the bridegroom's voice. Therefore, my joy is fulfilled in this.

30 He must increase but I *must* decrease.

31 He who comes from above is above all. *Those* who are of the earth are earthly and speak *about* earthly *things*. He who comes from heaven is above all.

32 He testifies *about* what He has seen and
heard, but no one receives His testimony.
33 *Those* who have received His testimony have *given their* seal *of affirmation*
that God is true.
34 For He whom God has sent speaks the
words of God, for God does not give the
Spirit *in a limited* measure. *Matthew 4:4*
35 The Father loves the Son and has
given all things into His hand.
36 *Those* who believe in the Son have
eternal+ life. *Those* who do not believe
the Son shall not see life, but the wrath
of God remains+ on them.

John Chapter 4

1 Therefore, when the Lord knew that
the Pharisees had heard that Jesus made
and baptized more disciples than John,
2 although Jesus Himself did not baptize, but His disciples *did*,
3 He left Judea and departed again into
Galilee.
4 But He needed to go through Samaria
on the way.
5 *So*, He came to a city of Samaria called
Sychar, near the parcel of ground that
Jacob gave to his son Joseph.
6 Now Jacob's well was there. Therefore Jesus, being tired+ from *His* journey, sat *down* on the well. It was about
twelve o'clock+ *noon*.
7 *Then* a woman from Samaria came to
draw water, and Jesus said to her: Give
me a drink.
8 For His disciples had gone to the city
to buy food.+
9 Then the woman from Samaria said to
Him: How is it that you, being a Jew,
ask me, a woman from Samaria, *for a*
drink? For the Jews have no dealings
with the Samaritans.
10 Jesus answered and said to her: If you
knew the gift of God and who it is that
says to you: Give me a drink, you would
have asked of Him and He would have
given you living water.
11 The woman said to Him: Sir, you have
nothing with *which* to draw and the well
is deep. From where then have you
obtained living water?
12 Are you greater than our father Jacob,
who gave us this well and drank from it
himself, and his children and his cattle?
13 Jesus answered and said to her: Whoever drinks of this water will thirst
again.

14 But whoever drinks
of the water that I give
will never thirst.
However, the water that I give
will become a well of water
within+ them springing up
into eternal+ life.

15 The woman said to Him: Sir, give me
this water *so* that I will not thirst nor *need*
to come here to draw *water*.
16 Jesus said to her: Go. Call your husband and come here.
17 The woman answered and said: I have
no husband. Jesus said to her: You have
well said: I have no husband.
18 For you have had five husbands, and
he whom you now have is not your
husband. In this, you spoke the truth.
19 The woman said to Him: Sir, I perceive
that you are a prophet.
20 Our fathers worshiped in this mountain, but you say that in Jerusalem is the
place where people+ ought to worship.
21 Jesus said to her: Woman, believe me.
The hour is coming when you will not
worship the Father either in this mountain or in Jerusalem.
22 You do not understand+ what you
worship. We know what we worship,
for salvation *comes* through+ the Jews.
23 But the hour is coming, and is now
here, when the true worshipers will
worship the Father in spirit and in truth,
for the Father seeks such to worship
Him.

24 God *is* Spirit.
Those who worship Him
must worship *Him*
in spirit and in truth.

25The woman said to Him: I know that
the Messiah is coming who is called
Christ. When He has come, He will tell
us everything.+
26Jesus said to her: I who speak to you
am *He*.
27At this point,+ *Jesus'* disciples came,
and *they* marveled that He talked with
the woman. Yet no one said: What were
you seeking? Or: Why were you talking
with her?
28*Then* the woman left her water pot and
went into the city and said to the people+:
29Come *and* see a man who told me
everything that I ever did. Is this not the
Christ?
30Then *the people* came out of the city
and came to Him.
31Meanwhile, His disciples urged+ Him
saying: Master, eat.
32But He said to them: I have food+ to
eat that you do not *yet* understand+.
33Therefore the disciples said to one
another: Has anyone brought *anything*
to Him to eat?
34Jesus said to them: My food+ is to do
the will of Him who sent me and to
finish His work.
35Do you not say: There are yet four
months and *then* the harvest *time comes*?
Behold I say to you: Lift up your eyes
and look at the fields, for they are white,
ready to harvest.
36*Those* who reap receive wages and
gather fruit to eternal life *so* that both
those who sow and *those* who reap may
rejoice together.
37Herein is that saying true: One sows
and another reaps.
38I sent you to reap that on which you
bestowed no labor. Others labored and
you have *now* entered their labors.
39Many of the Samaritans of that city
believed in Him because of the words+
of the woman who testified: He told me
everything+ that I ever did.
40So when the Samaritans came to Him,
they begged+ Him that He would stay+
with them, and He stayed+ there two days.
41And many more believed because of
His Word.
42*They* said to the woman: Now we
believe, not because of *what* you said,
but because we have heard *Him* ourselves and *we* know that this is indeed
the Christ, the Savior of the world.
43Now after two days, *Jesus* departed
from there+ and went to Galilee.
44For Jesus Himself testified, that a prophet
has no honor in his own country.
45Then when He had come into Galilee,
the Galileans received Him, having seen
all the things that He did at Jerusalem at
the feast, for they also went to the feast.
46So Jesus came again into Cana of
Galilee, where He *had* made the water
into wine. And there was a certain
nobleman *there*, whose son was sick in
Capernaum.
47When he heard that Jesus had come
out of Judea into Galilee, he went to
Jesus and begged+ Him that He would
come down and heal his son, for he was
at the point of death.
48Then Jesus said to him: Unless+ you see
signs and wonders, you will not believe.
49The nobleman said to Him: Sir, come
down before+ my child dies.
50Jesus said to him: Go. Your son lives.
And the man believed the word that Jesus
had spoken to him and he went away.+
51As he was going, his servants met him
and told *him* saying: Your son lives.
52Then he inquired of them the hour
when *his son* began to recover.+ They
said to him: Yesterday at one o'clock+
in the afternoon the fever left him.
53So the father knew that *it was* at the
same hour in which Jesus said to him:
Your son lives. *Then both* he and his
entire+ household+ believed.
54This *was* the second miracle *that* Jesus
did when He had come out of Judea into
Galilee.

John Chapter 5

1 After this, there was a feast of the
Jews, and Jesus went up to Jerusalem.
2 Now there is a pool with five porches
near the sheepgate+ in Jerusalem. In
Hebrew, *this place* is called Bethesda.

3 *Within* these *porches* a large+ number+
of disabled+ people+ lay: blind,
crippled,+ *and* withered, waiting for the
water to move.
4 From time to time,+ an angel went
down into the pool and stirred+ the
water. After this stirring,+ whoever
stepped into the water first was healed+
of whatever disease they had.
5 *Now* a certain man there, had an infirmity *for* thirty eight years.
6 When Jesus saw him lying *there* and
knew that he had been *there* a long time,
He said to him: Do you want+ to be
made whole?
7 The disabled+ man answered Him:
Sir, when the water is stirred,+ I have no
one to put me into the pool. While I am
coming, another steps down before me.
8 Jesus said to him: Rise, take up your
bed and walk.
9 Immediately the man was made whole
and took up his bed and walked. And
that day was the Sabbath.
10 Then the Jews said to the one who was
cured: It is the Sabbath day. It is not
lawful for you to carry *your* bed.
11 He answered them: The one who
made me well+ said to me: Take up your
bed and walk.
12 Then they asked him: Who is the man who
said to you: Take up your bed and walk?
13 The *man* who had been healed did not
know+ who it was, for Jesus had *quietly*
moved+ away, a multitude being in *that*
place.
14 Afterward Jesus found *the man* in the
temple and said to him: Behold, you are
made whole.

Sin no more,
lest a worse thing come to you.

15 *Then* the man departed and told the Jews
that it was Jesus who had made him whole.
16 Therefore, the Jews persecuted Jesus
and sought to slay Him because He had
done these things on the Sabbath day.
17 But Jesus answered them: My Father
is working until now+ and I am working.
18 Therefore the Jews sought *all* the more
to kill Him, not only because He had
broken the Sabbath, but also *because He*
said that God was His Father, making
Himself equal with God.
19 Then Jesus answered and said to them:
Truly,+ truly, I say to you: The Son can do
nothing by Himself, but *only* what He sees
the Father do. For what things+ He does,
these also the Son does in like manner+.
20 For the Father loves the Son and shows
Him all things that *He* Himself does, and
He will show Him greater works than
these, *so* that you may marvel.
21 For as the Father raises up the dead
and gives life+ *to them*, even so the Son
will give life+ *to* whomever He chooses+.
22 For the Father judges no one, but has
committed all judgment to the Son,
23 *so* that all *people* should honor the Son,
even as they honor the Father. Anyone
who does not honor the Son does not
honor the Father who has sent Him.
24 Truly,+ truly, I say to you:

Those who hear my Word
and believe in Him who sent me
have eternal+ life and will not
come into condemnation,
but are passed from death to life.

25 Truly,+ truly, I say to you: The hour
is coming, and now is, when the dead
will hear the voice of the Son of God,
and *those* who hear will live.
26 For as the Father has life in Himself,
so *He* also gave to the Son to have life in
Himself.
27 *He* has given Him authority to execute
judgment also, because He is the Son of
man.
28 Do not marvel at this. For the hour is
coming in which all who are in the
graves will hear His voice
29 and will come forth.

Those who have done good
to the resurrection of life,
and *those* who have done evil
to the resurrection of damnation.

30 *By* my own self *alone*, I can do nothing.
As I hear, I judge, and my judgment is
just because I do not seek my own will
but the will of the Father who has sent me.
31 If I *alone* bear witness of myself, my
witness is not *confirmed as* true.
32 There is another who bears witness of
me, and *we* know that the testimony *of*
this witness for me is true.
33 You sent to John and he testified[+] to
the truth.
34 But I do not receive testimony from
man, but I say these things *so* that you
might be saved.
35 *John* was a burning and shining light,
and you were willing to rejoice in his
light for a season.
36 But I have the greater testimony[+] than
that of John. For the works that the
Father has given me to finish, the same
works that I do bear witness of me, that
the Father has sent me.
37 The Father Himself who sent me has
borne witness of me. You have neither heard
His voice at any time nor seen His shape.
38 You do not have His Word abiding in
you. For you do not believe the one
whom He has sent.

> 39 Search the Scriptures.
> For in them you think
> you have eternal life,
> and they[+] testify of me.
> *Jeremiah 29:13*

40 But you will not come to me *so* that you
might have life.
41 I do not receive honor from people[+].
42 But I know you, that you do not have
the love of God in you.
43 I have come in my Father's name and you
do not receive me. If another shall come in
his own name, you will receive him.
44 How can you believe, *you* who receive
honor from[+] one another but[+] do not
seek the honor that *comes* from God
alone[+]?
45 Do not think that I will accuse you to
the Father. There is *one* who accuses
you, *even* Moses in whom you trust.
46 *If* you had believed Moses, *then* you
would have believed me, because[+] he
wrote about[+] me.
47 But if you do not believe his writings,
then how will you believe my words?

John Chapter 6

1 After these things, Jesus went over the
sea of Galilee *by* Tiberias.
2 A great multitude followed Him *be-*
cause they saw the miracles that He
worked[+] for the afflicted.[+]
3 Jesus went up on a mountain and sat
down there with His disciples.
4 *Now* the Passover, a feast of the Jews,
was near.
5 When Jesus lifted up *His* eyes and saw
a great multitude[+] coming to Him, He
said to Philip: Where shall we buy bread
so that these may eat?
6 *Jesus* said this to test[+] *Philip*, for He
already knew what He was going[+] to do.
7 Philip answered Him: *A half year wages*
worth[+] of bread is not sufficient for them
if everyone of them receives[+] a little.
8 One of His disciples, Andrew, Simon
Peter's brother, said to Him:
9 There is a lad here who has five barley
loaves and two small fish, but what are
they among so many?
10 Jesus said: Have[+] the people[+] sit
down. *For* there was much grass in that
place. So the people[+] sat down, about
five thousand men *and their families*.
11 *Then* Jesus took the loaves and when
He had given thanks He distributed to
the disciples and the disciples *gave* to
those *who were* sitting[+] *there*. In like
manner[+] *they distributed portions* of the
fish, as much as *they* wanted.[+]
12 When they were filled, He said to His
disciples: Gather up the fragments that
remain *so* that nothing is lost.
13 Therefore they gathered together and
filled twelve baskets with the fragments
of the five barley loaves that remained
over and above from *those* who had eaten.
14 When the people[+] had seen the miracle
that Jesus did, *they* said: This truly is the
Prophet who is to come into the world.
Psalm 110:4

15 Therefore, when Jesus perceived that they would come and take Him by force to make Him king, He departed to the mountain again *to be* alone.
16 When *the* evening came, His disciples went down to the sea,
17 entered a boat, and went over the sea toward Capernaum. It was now dark and Jesus had not come to them.
18 *Then* the sea rose up+ *because* of a great wind that blew.
19 When they had rowed about three and a half miles, they saw Jesus walking on the sea and drawing near to the boat, and they were afraid.
20 But He said to them: I Am+ *with you*. Do not be afraid.
21 Then they willingly received Him into the boat, and immediately the boat *arrived* at the land where they were going.+
22 The next day, the people who stood on the other side of the sea saw that there was no other boat there, except+ the one in which His disciples had entered, and that Jesus did not leave+ with His disciples in the boat, but *that* His disciples had left+ alone.
23 However, other boats had come from Tiberias near the place where they ate bread after the Lord had given thanks.
24 Therefore, when the people saw that Jesus was not there, nor His disciples, they also got into boats and came to Capernaum seeking Jesus.
25 When they found Him on the other side of the sea, they said to Him: Rabbi, when did you come here?
26 Jesus answered them and said: Truly,+ truly, I say to you: You seek me, not because you saw the miracles, but because you ate of the loaves and were filled.
27 Do not labor for food+ that perishes, but for that food+ that endures to eternal+ life, which the Son of man will give to you, for God the Father has set *His* seal *on* Him. *Proverbs 9:5*
28 Then they said to Him: What shall we do *so* that we might work the works of God?
29 Jesus answered and said to them:

> This is the work of God:
> That you believe
> in *the one* whom He has sent.

30 Therefore, they said to Him: What sign will you show *us* then *so* that we may see and believe you? What work *will you perform*?
31 Our fathers ate manna in the desert. As it is written: He gave them bread from heaven to eat. *Exodus 16:4*
32 Then Jesus said to them: Truly,+ truly, I say to you: Moses did not give you the bread from heaven, but my Father gives you the true bread from heaven.
33 For the bread of God is *the One* who comes down from heaven and gives life to the world.
34 Then they said to Him: Lord, give us this bread always+ *forevermore*.
35 Jesus said to them: I am the bread of life. *Those* who come to me will never hunger. *Those* who believe in me will never thirst.
36 But *as* I said to you, you have seen me and *yet you* do not believe.
37 All whom+ the Father gives *to* me will come to me, and *those* who come to me I will in no way+ cast out.
38 For I came down from heaven not to do my own will, but *to do* the will of *the one* who sent me.
39 This is the will of the Father who sent me: That of all He has given me I should not lose any+ but should raise them+ up again at the last day.
40 This is the will of Him who sent me: That everyone who sees the Son and believes in Him may have eternal+ life. I will raise them+ up at the last day.
41 Then the Jews complained+ about+ Him because He said: I am the bread come down from heaven.
42 They said: Is this not Jesus the son of Joseph whose father and mother we know? How is it then that He says: I came down from heaven?

43 Therefore Jesus answered and said to
them:

Do not complain+
among yourselves.

44 No one can come to me unless+ the
Father who has sent me draws them,
and I will raise them up at the last day.
45 It is written in the prophets: And they
shall all be taught by God. Therefore
everyone who has heard and has learned
of the Father comes to me. *cf Isaiah 2:3,*
Isaiah 54:13, Jeremiah 31:33, and Micah 4:2
46 Not that anyone has seen the Father
except+ *the One* who is from God. He
has seen the Father.
47 Truly+ truly I say to you:

Those who believe in me
have eternal+ life.

48 I am the bread of life.
49 Your fathers ate manna in the wilderness and are dead.
50 This is the bread come down from
heaven. Anyone+ may eat of *this bread*
and not die.
51 I am the living bread come down from
heaven. If anyone eats of this bread,
they will live forever. The bread I will
give is my flesh, *and* I will give *myself*
for the life of the world.
52 Therefore, the Jews argued+ among
themselves saying: How can this man
give us *His* flesh to eat?
53 Then Jesus said to them: Truly,+
truly, I say to you: Unless+ you eat the
flesh of the Son of man *which is the bread*
of life, the Word of God, and drink His
blood *which is to be filled with the Holy*
Spirit, you have no life in you.
54 Whoever eats my flesh and drinks my
blood has eternal life, and I will raise
them up at the last day.
55 For my flesh truly is *to* eat+ and my
blood truly is *to* drink.
56 *Those* who eat my flesh and drink my
blood dwell in me and I in them.
57 As the living Father has sent me, and
I live by the Father, so also *those* who
eat me, *my Word*, shall live by me.
58 This is that bread come down from
heaven: Not as your fathers ate manna
and are dead, *but those* who eat of this
bread will live forever.
59 *Jesus* said these things in the synagogue as He taught in Capernaum.
60 Therefore when His disciples heard
this, many *of them* said: This is a diffi-
cult+ saying *to understand*. Who is able+
to hear *and comprehend* it?
61 When Jesus knew in Himself that His
disciples complained+ about+ this,+ He
said to them: Does this offend you?
62 *What* then+ if you see the Son of man
ascend up *to* where He was before?
63 It is the Spirit who gives life.+ The
flesh profits nothing. The words that I
speak to you are Spirit and *they* are life.
64 But there are some of you who do not
believe. For Jesus knew from the beginning who they were who did not believe,
and who would betray Him.
65 *Then* He said: Therefore I said to you
that no one can come to me unless+ it is
given to them by my Father.
66 After that, many of His disciples went
back and did not walk with Him *any* more.
67 Then Jesus said to the twelve: Will
you also go away?
68 Simon Peter answered Him: Lord, to
whom shall we go? You have the words
of eternal life.
69 We believe and are sure that you are
the Christ, the Son of the living God.
70 Jesus answered them: Have I not chosen
you twelve? And *yet* one of you is a devil.
71 He spoke of Judas Iscariot, *the son* of
Simon. For it was *Judas* who would betray
Jesus, *even* being one of the twelve.

John Chapter 7

1 After these things, Jesus walked in
Galilee, for He would not walk in Judea+
because the Jews sought to kill Him.
2 Now the Jews' Feast of Tabernacles
was at hand.
3 Therefore His brothers said to Him:
Depart from here+ and go into Judea *so*

that your disciples may also see the
works that you do.
4 For no one does anything in secret and
seeks *thereby* to be *known* openly. If you
are doing these things, show yourself to
the world.
5 For *even* His brothers did not believe
in Him.
6 Then Jesus said to them: My time has not
yet come, but your time is always ready.
7 The world cannot hate you, but it hates
me because I testify about[+] it, that its
works are evil.
8 You go *on* to this feast. I am not going
to this feast yet because it is not yet my
time *to be* fulfilled[+].
9 When He had said these words to
them, He stayed[+] in Galilee.
10 But when His brothers had left,[+] then
Jesus also went up to the feast, not
openly, but as in secret.
11 Then the Jews sought Him at the feast
and said: Where is He?
12 And there was much murmuring
among the people concerning Him. Some
said: He is a good man. Others said: No,
He deceives the people.
13 However, no one spoke openly about[+]
Him for fear of the Jews.
14 Now about midway[+] *through* the feast,
Jesus went into the temple and taught.
15 The Jews marveled saying: How does this
man know letters, *with* no education[+]?
16 Jesus answered them and said: My
doctrine is not mine but His who sent me.
17 If anyone will do *God's* will, they will
know about this doctrine, whether it is from
God or *whether* I speak *only* from[+] myself.
18 *Those* who speak for[+] themselves seek
their own glory. But He who seeks the
glory of the one who sent Him is true
and *there* is no unrighteousness in Him.
19 Did not Moses give you the law, and
yet none of you keeps the law? Why do
you seek[+] to kill me?
20 The people answered and said: You have
a demon.[+] Who is seeking[+] to kill you?
21 Jesus answered and said to them: I
have done one work and you all marvel.
22 Moses gave circumcision to you, not
that it was from Moses but from the
patriarch fathers, and therefore you circumcise men *even* on the Sabbath day.
23 If a man receives circumcision on the
Sabbath day *so* that the law of Moses
should not be broken, *why* are you angry
at me, because I have made a man
completely[+] whole on the Sabbath day?
24 Do not judge according to appearance,
but judge *with* righteous judgment.
25 Then some of them from[+] Jerusalem
said: Is this not He whom they seek to
kill?
26 But behold, He speaks boldly and they
say nothing to Him. Surely[+] the rulers
must know that this truly[+] is the Christ.
27 However we know this man *and*
where He *comes* from, but when Christ
comes, no one *will* know where He
has come from.
28 Then Jesus cried *out* in the temple as He
taught saying: You both know me and you
know where I am from. And I have not
come of myself, but He who sent me is
true, *He* whom you do not know.
29 But I know Him for I am from Him
and He has sent me.
30 Then they sought to take Him, but no
one laid hands on Him because His hour
had not yet come.
31 Many of the people believed in Him
and said: When Christ comes, will He
do more miracles than what this *man*
has done?
32 The Pharisees heard that the people
murmured such things concerning Him
and *so* the Pharisees and the chief priests
sent officers to take Him.
33 Then Jesus said to them: Yet a little
while *longer* I am *to be* with you, and
then I *must* go to Him who sent me.
34 You will seek me and will not find *me*,
for where I am *going* you *will* not be
able[+] to come.
35 Then the Jews said among themselves:
Where will He go that we will not find
Him? Will He go to *those* dispersed
among the Greeks[+] and teach the Greeks?
36 *And* what *kind of* saying is this that He
said: You will seek me and will not find
me for where I am *going* you *will* not be
able[+] to come.

37 *Then* on the last day, the great *day* of
the feast, Jesus stood *up* and cried *out*
saying:

> If anyone thirsts,
> let them come to me and drink.
> *Proverbs 8:17*

38 As the Scripture has said *of those*
who believe in me: Out of their innermost being[+] will flow rivers of living
water. *Isaiah 58:11*
39 *Jesus* spoke this about[+] the Spirit
whom those believing in Him were
about[+] to receive. For the Holy Spirit
was not yet *being given* because Jesus
was not yet glorified.
40 Therefore, when they heard this
Word,[+] many of the people said: Truly
this is the Prophet. *Deuteronomy 18:18*
41 Others said: This is the Christ. But
some said: Will Christ come out of
Galilee?
42 Has the Scripture not said that Christ
comes through[+] the seed of David and
from[+] the town of Bethlehem, where
David was? *Jeremiah 23:5 Micah 5:2*
43 So, there was a division among the
people because of *Jesus*.
44 Some of them would have taken Him
right then, but no one laid hands on Him.
45 Then the officers came to the chief
priests and Pharisees who[+] said to *the*
officers: Why have you not brought
Him *to us*?
46 The officers answered: No *one* ever
spoke like this man.
47 Then the Pharisees answered them:
Are you also deceived?
48 Have any of the rulers believed in
Him, or *any* of the Pharisees?
49 But this *crowd of* people who do not
know the law are cursed.
50 *Then* Nicodemus who had come to
Jesus by night, being one of them, said
to them:
51 Does our law judge *any* man before
hearing from Him first[+] and knowing
what He has done?
52 They answered and said to him: Are
you from[+] Galilee also? Search and
see[+] that[+] no prophet arises out of
Galilee.
53 *Then* everyone went to their own house.

John Chapter 8

1 Jesus went to the Mount of Olives.
2 And early in the morning He came into
the temple again, and all the people came
to Him, and He sat down and taught them.
3 *Then* the scribes and Pharisees brought
a woman to Him *who had been* caught[+]
in adultery. When they had set her in the
midst,
4 they said to Him: Master, this woman
was caught[+] in adultery, in the very act.
5 Now Moses, in the law, commanded
us that such *offenders* should be stoned.
But what do you say?
6 They said this, testing[+] Him, *so* that
they might have *grounds* to accuse Him.
But Jesus stooped down and wrote on
the ground with *His* finger *as though He*
had not heard them.
7 When they continued asking Him, He
lifted Himself up and said to them: Let
whoever is without sin among you cast
the first stone at her.
8 And again, He stooped down and
wrote on the ground.
9 *Those* who heard *this*, being convicted
by *their own* conscience, went out one by
one, beginning at the eldest *even* to the
last. Jesus was left alone *with* the woman
standing in the midst.
10 When Jesus had lifted Himself up and
saw no one but the woman, He said to
her: Woman, where are those accusers?
Has no one condemned you?
11 She said: No one Lord. Jesus said to
her: Neither do I condemn you. Go and
sin no more.
12 Then Jesus spoke again to them saying: I am the light of the world. *Those*
who follow me will not walk in darkness
but will have the light of life.
13 Therefore, the Pharisees said to Him:
You bear witness[+] of yourself. Your
witness[+] *alone* is not true *by itself*.
14 Jesus answered and said to them: *Even*
though I bear witness[+] of myself, my

witness[+] is true for I know where I came
from and where I *am* going, but you
cannot tell where I *have* come from and
where I *am* going.
15 You judge after the flesh. I *am* judging
no one.
16 *Yet* if I *should* judge, my judgment
would be true for I am not alone, but I
and the Father who sent me.
17 It is also written in your law that the
testimony of two people[+] is true.
Deuteronomy 17:6, Deuteronomy 19:15
18 I am one who bears witness of myself.
And the Father who sent me *also* bears
witness of me.
19 Then they said to Him: Where is your
Father? Jesus answered: You do not
know me or my Father. If you had
known me, you would have known my
Father also.
20 Jesus spoke these words in the treasury as He taught in the temple. And no
one laid hands on Him for His hour had
not yet come.
21 Then Jesus said to them, *once* again: I
am going away,[+] and you will seek me
and *you* will die in your sins, *for* where
I am *going*, you cannot come.
22 Then the Jews said: Will He kill
Himself? Because He said: Where I am
going, you cannot come.
23 He said to them: You are from beneath. I am from above. You are of this
world. I am not of this world.
24 Therefore, I said to you that you will
die in your sins. For if you do not believe
that I am, you will die in your sins.
25 Then they said to Him: Who are you?
Jesus said to them: *From* the beginning,
I have told you.
26 I have many things to say and to judge
of you, but He who sent me is true. I
speak to the world those things that I
have heard from[+] Him.
27 They did not understand that He spoke
to them of the Father.
28 Then Jesus said to them: When you
have lifted up the Son of man, then you
will know that I am, and *that* I do nothing
of myself, but *only* as my Father has
taught me *do* I speak these things.
29 He who sent me is with me. The
Father has not left me alone, for I
always do those things that please Him.
30 As He spoke these words, many
believed in Him.
31 Then Jesus said to those Jews who
believed in Him:

> If you continue in my Word
> *then* you are indeed my disciples.

32 You shall know the truth and the truth
will make you free.
33 They answered Him: We are
Abraham's seed and *we* were never in
bondage to anyone. How *is it that* you
say: You will be made free?
34 Jesus answered them: Truly,[+] truly I
say to you: Whoever commits sin is the
servant of sin.
35 The servant does not stay[+] in the
house forever, *but* the Son remains[+]
forever[+].
36 Therefore, if the Son makes you free,
then you will truly[+] be free.
37 I know that you are Abraham's seed,
but you seek to kill me because my
Word has no place in you.
38 I speak what I have seen with my
Father. You do what you have seen with
your father.
39 They answered and said to Him:
Abraham is our father. Jesus said to
them: If you were Abraham's children,
you would do the works of Abraham.
40 But now you seek to kill me, a man who
has told you the truth that I have heard
from[+] God. Abraham did not do this.
41 You do the deeds of your father. Then
they said to Him: We are not born of
fornication. We have one Father: God.
42 Jesus said to them: If God were your
Father, you would love me. For I proceeded forth and came from God. I did
not come on my own,[+] but He sent me.
43 Why do you not understand my
speech? Because you are not able[+] to
hear my Word.
44 You are of *your* father the devil, and you
desire[+] to do the lusts of your father.

He was a murderer from the beginning
and did not abide in the truth because
there is no truth in him. When he speaks
a lie, he speaks of his own, for he is a liar
and the father of it.
45 And because I speak the truth, you do
not believe me.
46 Who among[+] you convicts[+] me of
sin? And if I speak[+] the truth, why do
you not believe me?
47 *Those* who are *transformed* by God
hear God's words. You therefore do
not hear *them* because you are not
transformed by God.
48 Then the Jews answered and said to
Him: Do we not say correctly[+] that you
are a Samaritan and have a demon[+]?
49 Jesus answered: I do not have a
demon,[+] but I honor my Father. And
you dishonor me.
50 I do not seek my own glory. There
is one who seeks and judges.
51 Truly,[+] truly, I say to you:

> If anyone[+] keeps my Word,[+]
> they will never see death.

52 Then the Jews said to Him: Now we
know that you have a demon.[+] Abraham
and the prophets are dead. *But* you say:
If anyone keeps my Word,[+] they will
never taste of death, forever.[+]
53 Are you greater than our father Abraham
who died? And the prophets *who* died.
Whom do you make yourself *to be*?
54 Jesus answered: If I honor myself, my
honor is nothing. It is my Father who
honors me. *He* of whom you say that He
is your God.
55 Yet you have not known Him. But I
know Him. If I should say I do not know
Him, I would[+] be a liar like you. But I
know Him and keep His Word[+].
56 Your father Abraham rejoiced to see
my day, and he saw *it* and was glad.
57 Then the Jews said to Him: You are
not yet fifty years old and have you seen
Abraham?
58 Jesus said to them: Truly,[+] truly, I say
to you: Before Abraham was, I Am.
59 Then they took up stones to throw[+] at
Him, but Jesus hid Himself and went out
of the temple, going through the midst
of them and passing *right by them*.

John Chapter 9

1 As *Jesus* passed by, He saw a man *who*
was blind from birth.
2 His disciples asked Him saying:
Master, who sinned? This man or his
parents? *Considering* that he was born
blind.
3 Jesus answered: *It was* not *that* this
man sinned, or his parents. But *this*
occurred so that the works of God should
be made manifest in him.
4 I must work the works of Him who
sent me while it is day, *because* the night
is coming when no one can work.
5 As long as I am in the world, I am the
light of the world.
6 When He had thus spoken, He spit on
the ground, made *some soft* clay with it,[+]
and He anointed the eyes of the blind
man with the clay.
7 *Then Jesus* said to him: Go. Wash in the
pool of Siloam. *The name Siloam* means[+]
sent. Therefore *the man* went away,[+]
washed, and came *back* seeing.
8 *Then* the neighbors and *those* who had
previously[+] seen that he was blind said:
Is this not the *blind man* who sat and
begged?
9 Some said: This is he. Others *said*: He
is like *the blind man*. *But* he said: I am *the*
same man.
10 Therefore they said to him: How were
your eyes opened?
11 He answered and said: A man who is
called Jesus made clay and anointed my
eyes and said to me: Go to the pool of
Siloam and wash. *So* I went and washed
and I received sight.
12 Then they said to him: Where is He?
He said: I do not know.
13 They brought him who previously[+]
was blind to the Pharisees.
14 *Now* it was the Sabbath day when
Jesus made the clay and opened *the*
blind man's eyes.

15 Therefore+ the Pharisees *once* again
asked him how he had received his
sight. He said to them: *Jesus* put clay on
my eyes, and I washed and *now I can* see.
16 Therefore, some of the Pharisees said:
This man is not of God, because He does
not keep the Sabbath day. Others said:
How can a man who is a sinner do such
miracles? There was division among them.
17 Again, they said to the blind man: What
do you say about+ Him who opened
your eyes? He said: He is a prophet.
18 But the Jews did not believe, concerning him, that he had been blind
and received his sight, until they called
the parents of him who had received
his sight.
19 They asked *the parents* saying: Is this
your son whom you say was born blind?
How then does he now see?
20 His parents answered them and said:
We know that this is our son and that he
was born blind.
21 But by what means he now sees, we do
not know. Or who has opened his eyes,
we do not know. He is of age. Ask him
and he will speak for himself.
22 *The blind man's* parents spoke these
words because they feared the Jews. For
the Jews had already agreed that if any-
one+ confessed that *Jesus* was Christ,
they should be put out of the synagogue.
23 Therefore his parents said: He is of
age. Ask him.
24 Then, *yet* again, they called the man
who was blind and said to him: Give
God the praise. We know that this man
is a sinner.
25 He answered and said: Whether He is
a sinner *or not* I do not know. One thing
I know: That, whereas I was blind, now
I see.
26 Then they said to him again: What did
He *do* to you? How did He open your
eyes?
27 He answered them: I have told you
already and you did not hear. Would
you therefore hear *it* again? Will you
also be His disciples?
28 Then they reviled him and said: You are
His disciple, but we are Moses' disciples.
29 We know that God spoke to Moses.
As for this *fellow*, we do not know
where He is from.
30 The man answered and said to them:
Well, this is marvelous: That you do not
know where He is from, and *yet* He has
opened my eyes.
31 Now we know that God does not hear
sinners, but if anyone is a worshiper of
God and does His will, He hears them.
32 Since the world began, it has never+
been heard that anyone opened the eyes
of one who was born blind.
33 If this man were not of God, He could
do nothing.
34 They answered and said to him: You
were born altogether in sins, and do you
teach us? *Then* they cast him out.
35 Jesus heard that they had cast him out,
so when He found *the man*, He said to
him: Do you believe in the Son of God?
36 He answered and said: Who is He
Lord, *so* that I might believe in Him?
37 Jesus said to him: You have both seen
Him and it is He who talks with you.
38 *Then* he said: Lord I believe. And he
worshiped Him.
39 Jesus said: For judgment I have come
into this world, *so* that *those* who do not
see might see, and *so* that *those* who see
might be made blind.
40 *Some* of the Pharisees who were with
Him heard these words and said to Him:
Are we blind also?
41 Jesus said to them: If you were blind,
you would have no sin. But now you say:
We see. Therefore your sin remains.

John Chapter 10

1 Truly,+ truly, I say to you: Anyone
who does not enter into the sheepfold by
the door, but climbs up some other way,
the same is a thief and a robber.
2 But one+ who enters by the door is the
shepherd of the sheep.
3 The doorkeeper+ opens to *the shepherd*
and the sheep hear his voice and he
calls his own sheep by name and leads
them out.
4 When he puts forth his own sheep, he

goes before them and the sheep follow
him, for they know his voice.
5 They will not follow a stranger but
will flee from him, for they do not know
the voice of strangers.
6 Jesus spoke this parable to them, but
they did not understand what it[+] was
that He spoke to them.
7 Then Jesus said to them again: Truly,[+]
truly, I say to you: I am the door of the
sheep.
8 All who ever came before me are
thieves and robbers, but the sheep did
not hear them.

> 9 I am the door.
> If anyone enters in through[+] me,
> they will be saved

and will go in and out and find pasture.
10 The thief does not come, except[+] to
steal, kill, and destroy.

> I have come
> *so* that they *might* have life
> and have *it* more abundantly.
> *Jeremiah 29:11*

11 I am the good shepherd. The good
shepherd gives His life for the sheep.
12 But one who is a hired hand[+] and not
the shepherd, *in other words* the sheep
are not his *very* own, sees the wolf
coming and leaves the sheep and runs
away.[+] And the wolf catches *some* and
scatters the sheep.
13 The hired hand[+] runs away[+] because
he is a hired hand[+] and does not care
about the sheep.
14 I am the good shepherd and know my
sheep and am known by my *own*.
15 As the Father knows me, even so I
know the Father and I lay down my life
for the sheep.
16 I also have other sheep, not of this
fold. I must bring them *in* also. They
will hear my voice and there will be one
fold *and* one shepherd.
17 For this reason,[+] my Father loves me.
Because I lay down my life *so* that I
might take it again.
18 No one takes it from me, but I lay it
down of myself. I have authority[+] *and*
power to lay it down and I have authority[+]
and power to take it again. This commandment I have received from[+] my Father.
19 Therefore, there was *once* again, a
division among the Jews because[+] of
these words.[+]
20 Many of them said: He has a demon[+]
and is mad. Why do you listen[+] *to* Him?
21 Others said: These are not the words of
one[+] who has a demon.[+] Can a demon[+]
open the eyes of the blind?
22 *Now* it was at the Feast of Dedication,
and it was winter.
23 And Jesus walked in Solomon's porch
in the temple.
24 Then the Jews came around[+] Him and
said to Him: How long *will you keep* us
in suspense[+]? If you are the Christ, tell
us plainly.
25 Jesus answered them: I told you and you
did not believe. The works that I do in my
Father's name, they bear witness of me.
26 But you do not believe because you are
not of my sheep, as I said to you.
27 My sheep hear my voice and I know
them and they follow me.
28 I give eternal life to them and they will
never perish, nor will anyone[+] pluck
them out of my hand.
29 My Father who gave *them to* me is
greater than all. No *one* is able to pluck
them out of my Father's hand.
30 I and *my* Father are one.
31 Then the Jews took up stones again to
stone Him.
32 Jesus answered them: I have shown[+]
you many good works from my Father.
For which of those works do you
stone me?
33 The Jews answered Him saying: We
do not stone you for a good work, but for
blasphemy. Because you, being a man,
make yourself God.
34 Jesus answered them: Is it not written in your law: I said: You are gods?
Psalm 82:6
35 If He called them gods to whom the
Word of God came, and the Scripture
cannot be broken,

36 do you say of Him whom the Father
has sanctified and sent into the world:
You blaspheme, because I said: I am
the Son of God?
37 If I do not *do* the works of my Father,
then do not believe me.
38 But if I do, *even* though you do not
believe me, believe the works *so* that
you may know and believe that the
Father *is* in me and I *am* in Him.
39 Therefore they sought again to take
Him, but He escaped out of their hand
40 and went away again beyond Jordan to
the place where John at first baptized,
and He stayed[+] there.
41 Many came[+] to Him and said: John
did no miracle, but all things that John
spoke of this man were true.
42 And many believed in Him there.

John Chapter 11

1 Now a certain *man named* Lazarus was
sick *in* Bethany, the town of Mary and
her sister Martha.
2 It was Mary who had anointed the
Lord with ointment and wiped His
feet with her hair, whose brother
Lazarus was sick.
3 Therefore the sisters sent *word* to
Jesus saying: Lord, behold *Lazarus*
whom you love is sick.
4 When Jesus heard *that*, He said:
This sickness is not to death, but for
the glory of God *so* that the Son of
God might be glorified by it[+].
5 Now Jesus loved Martha and her
sister and Lazarus.
6 *Yet* when He heard that *Lazarus* was
sick, He still stayed[+] two days in the
same place where He was.
7 Then, after that, He said to *His*
disciples: Let us go to Judea again.
8 *His* disciples said to Him: Master, the
Jews have recently[+] sought to stone
you. Do you *intend* to go there again?
9 Jesus answered: Are there not twelve
hours in the day? If anyone walks in the
day*light*, they will not stumble, because
they see the light of this world.
10 But if people[+] walk in the night, they
stumble because there is no light in them.
11 He said these things, and after that He
said to them: Our friend Lazarus sleeps,
but I *am* going *to him so* that I may
awaken him out of sleep.
12 Then His disciples said: Lord, if he
sleeps, he will do well.
13 However Jesus spoke of *Lazarus's*
death. But they thought that He had
spoken of rest in *normal* sleep.
14 Then Jesus said to them plainly:
Lazarus is dead.
15 I am glad for your sakes that I was
not there, *so* that you may believe.
Nevertheless let us go to him.
16 Then Thomas who is called Didymus
said to his fellow disciples: Let us go
also *so* that we may die with *Jesus*.
17 Then when Jesus came, He found that
Lazarus had *been* in the grave four days
already.
18 Now Bethany was near Jerusalem,
about two miles[+] away.[+]
19 Many of the Jews had come to Martha
and Mary to comfort them concerning
their brother.
20 As soon as Martha heard that Jesus
was coming, she went and met Him, but
Mary was *still* sitting in the house.
21 Then Martha said to Jesus: Lord, if
you had been here my brother *would* not
have died.
22 But I know that, even now, whatever
you will ask of God, God will give *it
to* you.
23 Jesus said to her: Your brother will
rise again.
24 Martha said to Him: I know that he
will rise again in the resurrection at the
last day.
25 Jesus said to her:

> I am the resurrection
> and the life.
> *Those* who believe in me,
> though they were dead,
> yet shall they live.

26 Whoever lives and believes in me will
never die. Do you believe this?

27 She said to Him: Yes Lord. I believe
that you are the Christ, the Son of God
who has come to the world.
28 When she had said this, she went away
and called her sister Mary secretly
saying: The Master has come and is
calling for you.
29 As soon as *Mary* heard *that*, she arose
quickly and came to Him.
30 Now Jesus had not yet come into the
town, but was in that place where Martha
met Him.
31 Then the Jews who were with her in
the house and comforted her, when they
saw that Mary rose up hastily and went
out, *they* followed her saying: She *is*
going to the grave to weep there.
32 When Mary came where Jesus was
and saw Him, she fell down at His feet
saying to Him: Lord, if you had been
here, my brother *would* not have died.
33 Therefore, when Jesus saw *Mary*
weeping, and the Jews who came with
her also weeping, He groaned in the
spirit and was troubled.
34 *He* said: Where have you laid *Lazarus*?
They said to Him: Lord, come and see.
35 Jesus wept.
36 Then the Jews said: Behold how He
loved *Lazarus*.
37 Some of them said: Could not this man
who opened the eyes of the blind, also
have caused *Lazarus* not to have died?
38 Therefore, Jesus groaned within
Himself *and* came to the grave. It was
a cave and a stone lay upon it.
39 Jesus said: Take away the stone. Martha,
the sister of *Lazarus* who had died,[+] said to
Jesus: Lord, by this time he *surely* smells[+]
very bad for he has been *dead* four days.
40 Jesus said to her: Did I not say to you
that if you would believe you would see
the glory of God?
41 Then they took away the stone *from the
place* where the dead *man* was laid, and
Jesus lifted up *His* eyes and said: Father,
I thank you that you have heard me.
42 I knew that you always hear me, but
because of the people who stand by I
said *this so* that they may believe that you
have sent me.
43 When He had thus spoken, He cried *out*
with a loud voice: Lazarus, come forth.
44 *Then Lazarus* who had been dead came
forth, bound hand and foot with grave
clothes and his face wrapped[+] with a
cloth.[+] Jesus said to them: Loose him
and let him go.
45 Then many of the Jews who had come
to Mary and had seen the things that
Jesus did, believed in Him.
46 But some of them went away[+] to the
Pharisees and told them what Jesus
had done.
47 Then the chief priests and Pharisees
gathered a council and said: What *shall*
we do? For this man does many miracles.
48 If we leave[+] Him alone, all *people*
will believe in Him, and the Romans
will come and take away both our
place and nation.
49 One of them *named* Caiaphas, being
the high priest that year, said to them:
You know nothing *at all*.
50 Nor *do you* consider that it is expedient
for us, that one man should die for the
people *so* that the whole nation does
not perish.
51 And he did not say[+] this from[+] himself
only, but being high priest that year, he
unwittingly prophesied that Jesus would
die for that nation.
52 And not for that nation only, but that
He would also gather together in one,
the children of God who were scattered.
53 Then from that day forth, they took
counsel together to put *Jesus* to death.
54 Therefore, Jesus no longer[+] walked
openly among the Jews, but went from
there[+] to a country near the wilderness,
to a city called Ephraim, and continued
there with His disciples.
55 *Now* the Jews' Passover was *very* near,
and many went out of the country *and* up
to Jerusalem before the Passover, to
purify themselves.
56 *And* they sought Jesus and spoke among
themselves as they stood in the temple,
saying: What do you think? That He will
come to the feast *or* not?
57 Now both the chief priests and the
Pharisees had given a commandment,

that if anyone knew where He was,
they should show *it so* that they might
take Him.

John Chapter 12

1 Six days before the Passover, Jesus
came to Bethany where Lazarus was,
the one who had been dead *but* whom
Jesus had raised from the dead.
2 They made a supper *for Jesus* there,
and Martha served, and Lazarus was
one of *those* who sat at the table with
Him.
3 Then Mary took a pound of ointment
of spikenard, very costly, and anointed
the feet of Jesus and wiped His feet with
her hair. And the house was filled with
the aroma[+] of the ointment.
4 Then one of *Jesus'* disciples, Judas
Iscariot, Simon's *son, the one* who would
betray *Jesus* said:
5 Why was this ointment not sold for *a
year's wages*[+] and given to the poor?
6 He said this, not that he cared for the
poor, but because he was a thief and had
carried the *money* bag and *he often* took[+]
what was put in it.
7 Then Jesus said: Let her alone. *It was*
for[+] the day of my burial[+] *that* she had
kept this.
8 For you always have the poor with
you. But you will not always have me.
9 Many of the Jews knew that He was
there, but they did not come only for
Jesus' sake, but *so* that they might see
Lazarus also, whom He had raised from
the dead.
10 But the chief priests consulted *so* that
they might put Lazarus to death also,
11 *for it was because of Lazarus* that many
of the Jews went *away* and believed in
Jesus.
12 On the next day, many people who had
come to the feast, when they heard that
Jesus was coming to Jerusalem,
13 took branches of palm trees and
went forth to meet Him, and cried
out: Hosanna! Blessed *is He* who comes
in the name of the Lord, the King of
Israel.
14 When He had found a young donkey,[+]
Jesus sat on it. As it is written:
15 Do not be afraid, daughter of Zion.[+]
Behold your King comes sitting on a
donkey[+]'s colt. *Zechariah 9:9*
16 *Jesus'* disciples did not understand
these things at first, but when Jesus was
glorified, then they remembered that
these things were written of Him and
that they had done these things to Him.
17 Therefore, the people who were with
Him when He called Lazarus out of his
grave and raised him from the dead
testified[+] *and spread the Word.*
18 For this reason[+] the people *came to*
meet Him, because[+] they heard that He
had done this miracle.
19 Therefore, the Pharisees said among
themselves: Do you see[+] that[+] *we are*
gaining[+] nothing? Behold the world has
gone after Him.
20 *Now* there were certain Greeks among
those who came up to worship at the feast.
21 They came to Philip, who was from
Bethsaida in Galilee, and asked[+] him
saying: Sir, we would *like to* see Jesus.
22 Philip came and told Andrew *and*
Andrew and Philip told Jesus.
23 Jesus answered them saying: The
hour has come for the Son of man to
be glorified.
24 Truly,[+] truly, I say to you: Unless[+] a
grain[+] of wheat falls to the ground and
dies, it remains[+] alone. But if it dies, it
brings forth much fruit.
25 *Those* who love their life will lose it,
but *those* who hate their life in this world
will keep it to eternal life.
26 If anyone *will* serve me, let them
follow me, and where I am, my servant
will be there also. If anyone *will* serve
me, *my* Father will honor them.
27 Now my soul is troubled, and what
shall I say? Father, save me from this
hour? But *it is* for this reason[+] *that* I
came to this hour.
28 Father, glorify your name. Then there
came a voice from heaven *saying*: I have
glorified *it* and will glorify *it* again.
29 Therefore the people who stood by
and heard *this* said that it thundered.

Others said: An angel spoke to Him.
30 Jesus answered and said: This voice
did not come because of me, but for
your *benefit*.
31 Now is the judgment of this world. Now
the prince of this world will be cast out.
32 *When* I am lifted up from the earth *and*
exalted, I will draw all *people* to me.
33 He said this signifying *by* what death
He would *soon* die.
34 The people answered Him: We have
heard out of the law that Christ *will*
remain+ forever. How *is it that* you say:
The Son of man must be lifted up? Who
is this Son of man?
35 Then Jesus said to them: Yet a little
while is the light with you. Walk *in the*
light while you have the light, lest
darkness come upon you. For *those*
who walk in darkness do not know
where they *are* going. *Proverbs 4:19*
36 While you have light, believe in the
light *so* that you may be the children of
light. Jesus spoke these things and *then*
departed and hid Himself from them.
37 But though He had done so many
miracles before them, they *still* did not
believe in Him.
38 This fulfilled the words of the prophet
Isaiah who said: Lord, who has believed
our report? And to whom has the arm
of the Lord been revealed?
39 For this reason+ they could not
believe. Because Isaiah said again:
40 He has blinded their eyes and hardened their heart *so* that they would not
see with *their* eyes or understand with
their heart and be converted and I would
heal them. *Isaiah 6:9,10*
41 Isaiah said these things when he saw
Jesus glory and spoke of Him.
42 Nevertheless, many among the chief
rulers also believed in *Jesus*, but
because of the Pharisees they did not
confess *Him*, lest they should be put
out of the synagogue.
43 For they loved the praise of men more
than the praise of God.
44 *Then* Jesus cried *out* and said: *Those*
who believe in me do not believe in me,
but in Him who sent me.
45 *Those* who see me see Him who sent me.
46 I have come *as* a light into the world *so*
that whoever believes in me will+ not
remain+ in darkness.
47 If anyone hears my words, and does
not believe, I do not judge them. For I
did not come to judge the world, but to
save the world.
48 *Those* who reject me and do not receive
my words, have one who judges them.
The Word that I have spoken, that+ will
judge them in the last day.
49 For I have not spoken from+ myself,
but the Father who sent me gave me a
commandment: What I should say and
what I should speak.
50 I know that His commandment is
eternal+ life. Therefore, whatever I speak,
even as the Father said to me, so I speak.

John Chapter 13

1 Now before the Feast of the Passover,
when Jesus knew that His hour had
come that He would depart out of this
world to the Father, having loved His
own who were in the world, He loved
them to the end.
2 During+ *the last* supper, the devil had
already+ put *it* into the heart of Judas
Iscariot, Simon's *son*, to betray *Jesus*.
3 *Now* Jesus knew that the Father had
given all things into His hands and that
He had come from God and *would be*
returning+ to God.
4 *So,* He arose from supper, laid aside
His garments, took a towel, and
wrapped+ *it around* Himself.
5 After that, He poured water into a
basin and began to wash the disciples'
feet and to wipe *them* with the towel with
which He was wrapped.+
6 Then He came to Simon Peter, and
Peter said to Him: Lord, are you
washing my feet?
7 Jesus answered and said to him: What
I *am* doing, you do not understand+ now.
But you will understand+ after this.
8 Peter said to Him: You shall never
wash my feet. Jesus answered him: If I
do not wash you, you have no part with me.

9 Simon Peter said to Him: Lord, *then*
not my feet only, but also *my* hands
and *my* head.
10 Jesus said to him: *Those* who are
bathed[+] do not need *more* than to wash
the feet, but *they* are completely[+] clean.
You are clean. But not all *of you*.
11 For He knew who would betray Him.
Therefore He said: You are not all clean.
12 So, after He had washed their feet and
had taken His garments and sat down
again, He said to them: Do you know
what I have done to you?
13 You call me Master and Lord, and
You say well, for *so* I am.
14 If I then, *your* Lord and Master, have
washed your feet, *then* you also ought to
wash the feet of one another.
15 For I have given you an example *so*
that you should do as I have done to you.
16 Truly,[+] truly, I say to you: The
servant is not greater than his lord. Nor
are those who are sent greater than *one*
who sent them.
17 If you know these things, blessed[+] are
you if you do them.
18 I do not speak of you all. I know whom
I have chosen. But *so* the Scripture may
be fulfilled, one[+] who eats bread with
me has lifted up his heel against me.
Psalm 41:9
19 Now I tell you *this* before it comes, *so*
that when it has come to pass, you may
believe that I am.
20 Truly,[+] truly, I say to you: *Those* who
receive whomever I send receive me
and *those* who receive me receive Him
who sent me.
21 When Jesus had said these things, He
was troubled in spirit and testified and
said: Truly,[+] truly, I say to you that one
of you will betray me.
22 Then the disciples looked at one another,
perplexed[+] about whom He spoke.
23 Now one of Jesus' disciples whom *He*
loved was leaning on His chest.[+]
24 Therefore, Simon Peter signaled[+] to
him that he should ask who it might[+] be
of whom He spoke.
25 Then the one[+] leaning[+] on Jesus'
chest[+] said to Him: Lord, who is it?
26 Jesus answered: It is *the* one[+] to whom
I shall give a morsel[+] when I have
dipped *it*. And when He had dipped
the morsel,[+] He gave *it* to Judas
Iscariot, *the son* of Simon.
27 After the morsel,[+] Satan entered
Judas. Then Jesus said to him: What
you *must* do, do quickly.
28 But[+] no one at the table knew why[+]
Jesus said this to *Judas*.
29 Some thought *that* since[+] Judas had
the *money* bag, Jesus had said to him:
Buy what[+] *things* we need for[+] the feast.
Or, that He should give something to the
poor.
30 Therefore, having received the morsel,[+] *Judas* immediately went out. And
it was night.
31 When he was gone, Jesus said: Now is
the Son of man glorified and God is
glorified in Him.
32 If God be glorified in Him, God will
also glorify *the Son of man* in Himself and
will glorify Him immediately[+].
33 Little children, yet a little while I am
with you. *Then* you will seek me and as
I said to the Jews: Where I *am* going you
cannot come. So now I say to you:

34 A new commandment
I give to you:
That you love one another.
As I have loved you,
that you also love one another.

35 By this all *people* will know that you
are my disciples: If you have love
toward one another.
36 Simon Peter said to Him: Lord where
are you going[+]? Jesus answered him:
Where I *am* going you cannot follow
me now, but you shall follow me
afterwards.
37 Peter said to Him: Lord, why can I not
follow you now? I will lay down my life
for your sake.
38 Jesus answered him: Will you lay
down your life for my sake? Truly,[+]
truly, I say to you: The cock will not
crow until you have denied me three
times.

John Chapter 14

1 Do not let your heart
be troubled.
You believe in God.
Believe also in me.

2 In my Father's house are many man-
sions. If *it were* not*so*, I would have told
you. *Now* I *am* going to prepare a place
for you.
3 And if I go and prepare a place for
you, I will come again and receive you
to myself *so* that where I am, *there* you
may be also.
4 You know where I *am* going,[+] and you
know the way.
5 Thomas said to Him: Lord, we do not
know where you *are* going. How can we
know the way?
6 Jesus said to him:

I am the way,
the truth, and the life.
No one comes to the Father,
but by me.

7 If you had known me, you would have
known my Father also. From henceforth
you know Him and have seen Him.
8 Philip said to Him: Lord show us the
Father and it *will be* sufficient[+] *for* us.
9 Jesus said to him: Have I been so long
a time with you and yet have you not
known me, Philip? *Those* who have seen
me have seen the Father. How *is it that*
you say *then*: Show us the Father?
10 Do you not believe that I am in the
Father and the Father *is* in me? The
words that I speak to you I do not speak
of myself, but the Father who dwells in
me does the works.
11 Believe me that I *am* in the Father and
the Father *is* in me. Or else believe me
because[+] of the very works themselves[+].
12 Truly,[+] truly, I say to you: *Those* who
believe in me will also do the works that
I do, and greater *works* than these will
they do because I go to my Father.
13 Whatever you ask in my name, that
I will do *so* that the Father may be
glorified in the Son.
14 If you ask anything in my name, I
will do *it*.

15 If you love me,
keep my commandments.

16 I will *pray and* ask[+] the Father and He
will give you another Comforter *so* that
He may stay[+] with you forever.
17 *That comforter is* the Spirit of Truth
whom the world cannot receive because
it does not see or know Him. But you
know Him for He dwells with you and
will be in you.
18 I will not leave you orphaned.[+] I will
come to you. *Deuteronomy 31:6*
19 Yet a little while and the world *will* see
me no more. But you *will* see me.
Because I live, you will also live.
20 At that day, you will know that I *am*
in my Father and you *are* in me and I
am in you.

21 *Those* who have
my commandments
and keep them[+] are the ones
who *truly* love me.
Those who love me
will be loved by my Father
and I will love them
and will reveal[+] myself to them.
Proverbs 8:17

22 *Then* Jude, not *Judas* Iscariot, said to
Him: Lord, how is it that you will manifest yourself to us and not to the world?
23 Jesus answered and said to him: If
anyone[+] loves me, they will keep my
words and my Father will love them
and we will come to them and live[+]
within them.
24 *Those* who do not love me do not keep
my Word.[+] The Word that you hear is
not mine, but the Father's who sent me.
25 I have spoken these things to you *while*
I am still present with you.
26 But the Comforter *is* the Holy Spirit

whom the Father will send in my name. *He will* teach you all and remind[+] you *of* all that I have said to you.

> 27 Peace I leave with you.
> My peace I give to you.
> I do not give to you
> as the world gives.
> Do not let your heart be troubled
> *and do not* let it be afraid.

28 You have heard how I said to you: I *am* going away and *I will* come to you *again*. If you loved me, you would rejoice because I said: I *am* going to the Father. For my Father is greater than I.

29 Now I have told you before it comes to pass, *so* that when it has come to pass, you might believe.

30 Hereafter I will not talk with you *very* much *more*. For the prince of this world *is* coming and *he* has nothing in me.

31 But *so* that the world may know that I love the Father, as the Father has commanded me, even so I do. *Now* arise. Let us go from here.

John Chapter 15

1 I am the true vine and my Father is the grower[+].

2 Every branch in me that does not bear fruit He takes away. Every *branch* that bears fruit, He purges *so* that it may bring forth more fruit.

3 Now you are clean through the Word that I have spoken to you.

4 Abide in me and I *will abide* in you. Because[+] the branch cannot bear fruit by[+] itself unless[+] it remains[+] *and abides* in the vine. Nor[+] can you, unless[+] you abide in me.

5 I am the vine. You *are* the branches. *Those* who stay[+] *and abide* in me and I in them bring forth much fruit. For without me you can do nothing.

6 If anyone[+] does not stay[+] *and abide* in me, *they will be* cast out[+] like[+] a *broken* and withered branch, and these *are* gathered and thrown[+] into a fire and burned.

7 If you abide in me and my words abide in you, *then you shall* ask whatever[+] you will and it will be done *for* you.

8 Herein is my Father glorified: That you become[+] my disciples and bear much fruit.

9 As the Father has loved me, so have I loved you. *Now continue* to abide[+] in my love.

10 If you keep my commandments, you will abide in my love, even as I have kept my Father's commandments and abide in His love.

> 11 I have spoken these things
> to you *so* that my joy
> might remain in you
> and *so that* your joy
> might be full.

> 12 This is my commandment:
> That you love one another
> as I have loved you.

> 13 Greater love
> has no one than this,
> that one[+] lay down
> one's *own* life for one's friends.

14 You are my friends if you do whatever I command you.

15 Henceforth I will not call you servants, for the servant does not understand what his lord does. But I have called you friends, for all things that I have heard from[+] my Father I have made known to you.

16 You have not chosen me but I have chosen you and ordained you *so* that you should go and bring forth fruit and *so that* your fruit should remain and *so* that whatever you ask of the Father in my name, He may give it *to* you.

17 *And* these things I command you: That you love one another.

18 If the world hates you, know that it hated me before *it hated* you.

19 If you were of the world, the world would love its own. But because you are not of the world, but I have chosen you out of the world, therefore the world hates you.

20 Remember the Word that I said to
you: The servant is not greater than his
lord. If they have persecuted me, they
will also persecute you. If they have kept
my Word,[+] they will keep yours also.
21 But they will do all these things to you
because of my name, because they do
not know Him who sent me.
22 If I had not come and spoken to them,
they *would* not have had sin, but now
they have no covering[+] for their sin.
23 *Those* who hate me hate my Father also.
24 If I had not done among them the
works that no one[+] *else ever* did, they
would not have had sin, but now *they*
have seen *my works* and *even so* hated me
and my Father.
25 But this fulfills the word written in
their law: They hated me without a
cause. *Psalm 69:4 Psalm 35:19*
26 Yet[+] when the Comforter is come,
whom I will send to you from the
Father, *the one who is* the Spirit of Truth
who proceeds from the Father, He will
testify of me.
27 And you also will bear witness, because you have been with me from the
beginning.

John Chapter 16

1 I have spoken these things to you *so*
that you would not be offended *and
fall away*.
2 They will put you out of the synagogues. Yes, the time *is* coming when[+]
whoever kills you will think that they
do a service *to* God.
3 They will do these things to you because they have not known *either* the
Father or me.
4 But I have told you these things *so*
that when the time comes, you may
remember that I told you of them. I
did not say these things to you at the
beginning because I was with you.
5 But now I *am* going away[+] to Him who
sent me, and none of you asks me:
Where *are* you going[+]?
6 But because I have said these things to
you, sorrow has filled your hearts.
7 Nevertheless I tell you the truth: It is
expedient for you that I go away. For if
I do not go away, the Comforter will not
come to you. But if I depart, I will send
Him to you.
8 When He comes, He will convince[+]
the world of sin, and of righteousness,
and of judgment.
9 Of sin, because they do not believe
in me.
10 Of righteousness, because I *am* going to
my Father and you *will* see me no more.
11 Of judgment, because the prince of
this world is judged.
12 I still[+] have many *more* things to say to
you, but you cannot bear them now.
13 However, when the Spirit of Truth
has come, He will guide you into all
truth. For He will not speak from[+]
Himself, but whatever He hears *from
God* He will speak, and He will show
you things to come.
14 He will glorify me, for He will receive
of mine and declare[+] *that* to you.
15 All things that the Father has are mine.
Therefore I said that He will take of
mine and declare[+] *that* to you.
16 A little while and you will not see me,
and again a little while and you will see
me, because I *am* going to the Father.
17 Then *some* of *Jesus'* disciples said
among themselves: What is this that He
says to us: A little while and you will not
see me, and again a little while and you
will see me. And: Because I go to the
Father?
18 Therefore, they said: What is this that
He says: A little while? We cannot tell
what He is saying.
19 Now Jesus knew that they desired[+] to
ask Him *about this*, and *so He* said to
them: Do you inquire among yourselves
about what I said: A little while and you
will not see me, and again a little while
and you will see me?
20 Truly,[+] truly, I say to you: That you
will weep and mourn,[+] but the world
will rejoice. You will be sorrowful, but
your sorrow will be turned into joy.
21 When a woman is in labor,[+] she has
grief[+] *and pain* because her hour has

come, but as soon as she has delivered the child, she no longer[+] remembers the anguish, because[+] of *her* joy that a child[+] is born into the world.

22 Therefore, you now have grief,[+] but I will see you again and your heart will rejoice and no one will take away your joy from you.

23 In that day, you will ask nothing of me. Truly,[+] truly, I say to you: Whatever you ask the Father in my name, He will give *it to* you.

24 Before this,[+] you have asked nothing in my name. *Now* ask and you shall receive *so* that your joy may be full.

25 I have spoken these things to you in proverbs, but the time is coming when I will no longer[+] speak to you in proverbs, but I will show you plainly of the Father.

26 At that day, you shall ask in my name. I do not say to you that I will *pray and* ask[+] the Father for you.

27 For the Father Himself loves you because you have loved me and have believed that I came forth[+] from God.

28 I came forth from the Father and have come into the world. *Now* I *am* leaving the world again and *I am* going *back* to the Father.

29 His disciples said to Him: Behold, now you speak plainly and speak no proverb.

30 Now are we sure that you know all things and *we* do not need anyone *to* ask you *any more*. By this we believe that you came forth from God.

31 Jesus answered them: Do you now believe?

32 Behold the hour is coming,[+] yes *it* has now come, that you will be scattered, everyone[+] to their own, and will leave me alone. Yet I am not alone because the Father is with me.

33 I have spoken these things to you *so* that in me you might have peace. In the world you will have tribulation. But

Be of good cheer.
I have overcome the world.

John Chapter 17

1 Jesus spoke these things[+] and *then* lifted up His eyes to heaven and said: Father, the hour has come. Glorify your Son *so* that your Son may glorify you, also.

2 You have given Him authority[+] *and power* over all flesh, *so* that He could give eternal life to all[+] whom you have given *to* Him.

3 And this is eternal life: That they might know you, the only true God, and Jesus Christ whom you have sent.

4 I have glorified you on the earth. I have finished the work you gave me to do.

5 Now Father, glorify me *along* with yourself with the glory I had with you before the world was.

6 I have manifested your name to *those* whom you gave *to* me out of the world. They were yours and you gave them *to* me. And they have kept your Word.

7 Now they know that all things whatsoever you have given *to* me are from[+] you.

8 For I have given to them the words you gave *to* me and they received *them*. *Now they* truly[+] *do* know that I came forth[+] from you and they believe that you sent me.

9 I pray for them. I do not pray for the world, but for *those* whom you have given *to* me. For they are yours.

10 All mine are yours and yours are mine. And I am glorified in them.

11 Now, I am *to be* in the world no more, but these are in the world and I *am* coming to you. Holy Father, through your name, keep *those* whom you have given *to* me *so* that they may be one as we *are one*.

12 While I was with them in the world, I kept them in your name. I have kept *those* whom you gave *to* me and not one of them has perished,[+] except[+] the son of damnation[+] *so* the Scripture might be fulfilled. *Psalm 41:9*

13 And now, I *am* coming to you, and I *am* speaking these things in the world *so* that they might have my joy fulfilled within[+] themselves.

14 I have given them your Word. The world has hated them because they are not of the world, even as I am not of the world.

15 I do not pray that you should take them out of the world, but that you keep them from + evil.

16 They are not of the world, even as I am not of the world.

17 Sanctify them through your truth. Your Word is truth.

18 *Just* as you have sent me into the world, I have also sent them into the world.

19 I *have* sanctified myself for them+ *so* that they might also be sanctified in+ truth.

20 *And* I do not pray for these alone, but also for *those* who will believe in me through their word.

21 *I do this so* that all may be one *just* as you, Father, *are* in me and I *am* in you, *so* that they may be one in us also *and so* that the world may believe that you have sent me.

22 I have given *to* them the glory you gave *to* me, *so* that they may be one even as we are one:

23 I in them and you in me. *So* that they may be made perfect in one, and *so* that the world may know that you have sent me and have loved them *just* as you have loved me.

24 Father, *it is my desire and* will that *those* whom you have given *to* me also be with me where I am, *so* that they may behold my glory that you have given *to* me. For you *have* loved me *since* before the foundation of the world.

25 O righteous Father: The world has not known you, but I have known you and these *now* know that you have sent me.

26 I have made+ your name known+ to them, and *I* will *make it* known+ that the love with which you have loved me can+ be in them, and I *myself will be* in them.

John Chapter 18

1 When Jesus had spoken these words, He went forth with His disciples over the brook *of* Kedron, where *there* was a garden into which He and His disciples entered.

2 Judas who betrayed Him also knew the place, for Jesus often went there with His disciples.

3 Then Judas, having received a company+ *of soldiers* and officers from the chief priests and Pharisees, went+ there with lanterns and torches and weapons.

4 Therefore, knowing all things that would come upon Him, Jesus went forth and said to them: Whom do you seek?

5 They answered Him: Jesus of Nazareth. Jesus said to them: I Am. And Judas who betrayed Him also stood with them.

6 Then as soon as *Jesus* had said to them: I Am. They went backward and fell to the ground.

7 Then He asked them again: Whom do you seek? And they said: Jesus of Nazareth.

8 Jesus answered: I have told you that I Am. Therefore if you seek me, let these *others* go.

9 *He said this so* that the Word+ He *had* spoken would be fulfilled: I have not lost one of those you gave *to* me.

10 Then Simon Peter, having a sword, drew it and struck+ the high priest's servant and cut off his right ear. The servant's name was Malchus.

11 Then Jesus said to Peter: Put *away* your sword into the sheath. *This is* the cup that my Father has given *to* me. Shall I not drink it?

12 Then the company+ *of soldiers* and the captain and officers of the Jews took Jesus, bound Him,

13 and led Him away to Annas first, for he was father in law to Caiaphas who was the high priest that year.

14 *Now* it was Caiaphas who had given counsel to the Jews that it was expedient that one man should die for the people.

15 Simon Peter and another disciple followed Jesus. That *other* disciple was known to the high priest and *he* entered with Jesus into the palace of the high priest.

16 But Peter stood at the door outside.+ Then that other disciple who was known to the high priest went out and spoke to

the doorkeeper+ and brought in Peter.
17 Then the girl+ who kept the door said
to Peter: Are you not also *one* of this
man's disciples? He said: I am not.
18 The servants and officers who had
made a fire of coals stood there, for it
was cold. They warmed themselves and
Peter stood with them and warmed
himself.
19 The high priest then asked Jesus about+
His disciples and about+ His doctrine.
20 Jesus answered him: I spoke openly
to the world. I always+ taught in the
synagogue and in the temple where
the Jews always come together,+ and
I have said nothing in secret.
21 Why ask me? Ask *those* who heard me
what I have said to them. Behold, they
know what I said.
22 When He had said these things, one of
the officers who stood by struck Jesus
with the palm of his hand saying: Do
you answer the high priest in this way+?
23 Jesus answered him: If I have spoken
evil, testify+ of the evil. But if well,
why do you strike+ me?
24 Now Annas had sent *Jesus* bound to
Caiaphas the high priest.
25 And Simon Peter stood *by the fire*
and warmed himself. Therefore, they
said to him: Are you not also *one* of
Jesus' disciples? *Peter* denied *it* and
said: I am not.
26 *Then* one of the servants of the high
priest, being a relative+ of *the one* whose
ear Peter had cut off, said: Did I not see
you in the garden with Him?
27 Peter then denied again, and immediately the cock crowed.+
28 Then they led Jesus from Caiaphas to
the hall of judgment, and it was early.
They themselves did not go+ into the
judgment hall lest they should be defiled,
but *so* that they might eat the Passover.
29 Pilate then went out to them and said:
What accusation do you bring against
this man?
30 They answered and said to him: If He
were not an evil doer,+ we would not
have delivered Him up to you.
31 Then Pilate said to them: You take
Him and judge Him according to your
law. Then the Jews said to him: It is not
lawful for us to put anyone to death.
32 *They said this so* that the Word+ Jesus
spoke signifying *by* what death He was
about+ to die would be fulfilled.
33 Then Pilate entered the judgment hall
again, called Jesus, and said to Him:
Are you the King of the Jews?
34 Jesus answered him: Do you say this
of yourself or did others tell it *to* you
about+ me?
35 Pilate answered: Am I a Jew? Your own
nation and the chief priests have delivered
you to me. What have you done?
36 Jesus answered: My kingdom is not of
this world. If my kingdom were of this
world, then my servants would fight *so*
that I would not be delivered to the
Jews. But my kingdom is not of this
world+.
37 Therefore, Pilate said to Him: Are
you a king then? Jesus answered: You
say that I am a king. *It is* to this *end that*
I was born. And, *it is* for this reason+
that I came into the world: That I should
testify+ to the truth. Everyone who is of
the truth hears my voice.
38 Pilate said to Him: What is truth? And
when he had said this, he went out again
to the Jews and said to them: I find no
fault in Him.
39 But you have a custom that I should
release one to you at the Passover.
Therefore, do you want+ me to release
the King of the Jews to you?
40 Then they all cried *out* again saying:
Not this man, but Barabbas. Now
Barabbas was a robber.

John Chapter 19

1 Therefore Pilate then took Jesus and
flogged+ *Him*.
2 And the soldiers made+ a crown of
thorns and put *it* on His head and they
put a purple robe on Him
3 and said: Hail King of the Jews. And
they struck+ Him with their hands.
4 Pilate then+ went out+ to them again
and said: Behold I bring Him out+ to

you *so* that you may know that I find no
fault in Him.
5 Then Jesus came out[+] wearing the
crown of thorns and the purple robe. And
Pilate said to them: Behold the man.
6 Therefore, when the chief priests and
officers saw Him, they cried out saying:
Crucify *Him*. Crucify *Him*. Pilate said to
them: You take Him and crucify *Him*,
for I find no fault in Him.
7 The Jews answered *Pilate*: We have a
law, and by our law He ought to die
because He made Himself the Son of
God.
8 Therefore, when Pilate heard that
word, he was *even* more afraid
9 and went into the judgment hall again
and said to Jesus: Where are you *from*?
But Jesus gave him no answer.
10 Then Pilate said to Him: Do you not
speak to me? Do you not know that I
have authority[+] *and power* to crucify you
and authority[+] *and power* to release you?
11 Jesus answered: You could have no
authority[+] *or power at all* against me
unless[+] it was given *to* you from above.
Therefore he who delivered me to you
has the greater sin.
12 From that time on[+] Pilate sought to
release *Jesus*. But the Jews cried out
saying: If you let this man go, you are
not Caesar's friend. Whoever makes
himself a king speaks against Caesar.
13 Therefore, when Pilate heard that
word, he brought Jesus out[+] and *he* sat
on the judgment seat in a place that is
called *the* Pavement, or in Hebrew,
Gabbatha.
14 It was the *day of* preparation for[+] the
Passover, and about twelve o'clock[+] *noon*
He said to the Jews: Behold your King.
15 But they cried out: Away. Away.
Crucify Him. Pilate said to them: Shall
I crucify your King? The chief priests
answered: We have no king but Caesar.
16 Therefore *Pilate* then delivered *Jesus*
to them to be crucified. And they took
Jesus and led *Him* away.
17 *Then*, bearing His cross, *Jesus* went to
a place called *the place* of a skull. In
Hebrew, *the place* is called Golgotha.
18 They crucified Him there, and two
others with Him, one on either side
and Jesus in the middle[+] *between them*.
Isaiah 53:12
19 Pilate wrote a title and put *it* on the
cross, and the writing was: Jesus of
Nazareth the King of the Jews.
20 Many of the Jews then read this
title. For the place where Jesus was
crucified was near the city. It was
written in Hebrew, Greek, *and* Latin.
21 Then the chief priests of the Jews
said to Pilate: Do not write: The King
of the Jews, but that He said: I am
King of the Jews.
22 Pilate answered: What I have written I have written.
23 When the soldiers had crucified
Jesus, they took His garments and
made four parts, *giving* a part to each[+]
soldier. *They* also *took His* coat. *But*
His coat was seamless,[+] woven from
the top throughout.
24 Therefore they said among themselves: Let us not tear[+] it, but cast
lots for it *to decide* whose it shall be.
They did this so that the Scripture might
be fulfilled that says: They divided[+]
my clothing[+] among them and for my
coat[+] they cast lots. Therefore the
soldiers did these things. *Psalm 22:18*
25 Now Jesus' mother stood there by
the cross, *along with* His mother's
sister Mary, the *wife* of Cleophas, and
Mary Magdalene.
26 When Jesus saw His mother and the
disciple standing by whom He loved,
He said to His mother: Woman behold your son.
27 Then He said to the disciple: Behold
your mother. From that hour, that
disciple took *Jesus'* mother to *be* his
own.
28 After this, knowing that all things
were now accomplished *so* the Scripture might be fulfilled, Jesus said: I
thirst. *Psalm 22:15*
29 Now a vessel full of vinegar was
setting there. *So* they filled a sponge
with vinegar and put *it* upon *a* hyssop
branch and put *it* to His mouth.

30 When Jesus had thus[+] received the
vinegar, He said: It is finished. And
He bowed His head and yielded[+] up
His spirit.[+]
31 Because it was *the day of* preparation
for that great Sabbath day, *and so* that
the bodies might not remain on the cross
on the Sabbath, the Jews therefore
begged[+] Pilate that their legs might be
broken and *the bodies* taken away.
32 *So* the soldiers came and broke the
legs of the first *man* and of the other
man who was crucified with *Jesus*.
33 But when they came to Jesus and
saw that He was already dead, they
did not break His legs. *Psalm 34:20*
34 But one of the soldiers pierced His
side with a spear and immediately[+]
blood and water came out. *Zechariah 12:10*
35 Now, one who saw *this occur has*
testified[+] and his record is true. *This*
witness knows that *what* he *has* said *is*
true, *so* that you might believe.
36 For these things were done *so* the
Scripture would be fulfilled *that says*:
Not *one* of His bones shall be broken.
Psalm 34:20
37 Again another Scripture says: They
shall look upon Him whom they
pierced. *Zechariah 12:10*
38 After this, Joseph of Arimathaea,
being a disciple of Jesus but secretly
for fear of the Jews, begged[+] Pilate
that he might take away Jesus' body.
And Pilate allowed[+] *him to do so*.
Therefore *Joseph* came and took *away*
Jesus' body.
39 Nicodemus also came *forward. He had*
at first come to Jesus by night, *but now*
he brought a mixture of myrrh and
aloes, about a hundred pound *weight*.
40 Then they took Jesus' body and
wrapped it in linen cloths with the
spices, as it is the Jews manner to bury.
41 Now in the place where He was
crucified there was a garden, and in
the garden a new tomb[+] in which no
one[+] had yet been laid.
42 So[+] they laid Jesus there because of
the Jewish preparation *day*, for the
tomb[+] was nearby.[+]

John Chapter 20

1 *On* the first *of* the week, early *when it*
was yet dark, Mary Magdalene came to
the tomb[+] and saw *that* the stone *had*
been taken away from the tomb.[+]
2 Therefore[+] *Mary* ran[+] to Simon Peter
and to the other disciple whom Jesus
loved and said to them: They have taken
the Lord from[+] the tomb and we do not
know where they have laid Him.
3 Then Peter[+] and that other disciple
went[+] *quickly* to the tomb.[+]
4 The two[+] ran together and the other
disciple outran Peter and came to the
tomb[+] first.
5 Stooping down *to look in*, he saw the
linen clothes lying *there*, yet he did
not go in.
6 Then Simon Peter came following
him and went into the tomb[+] and saw the
linen clothes lying *there*.
7 The cloth[+] that had been around[+] *Jesus'*
head *was* not lying with the linen clothes,
but *was* folded[+] in a place by itself.
8 Then the other disciple who came to
the tomb[+] first also went in and saw *all*
these things and believed.
9 For as yet they did not understand[+] the
Scripture that *Jesus* must rise again from
the dead. *Psalm 16:10*
10 Then the disciples went away again to
their *own homes*.
11 But Mary stood outside[+] the tomb[+]
weeping. As she wept, she stooped
down *and looked* into the tomb.[+]
12 *She* saw two angels in white sitting.
One *sat* at the head and the other at the
feet where Jesus' body had lain.
13 They said to her: Woman, why are
you weeping? She said to them: Because
they have taken away my Lord and I do
not know where they have laid Him.
14 When she had thus said, she turned
back, and saw Jesus standing, but did
not understand[+] that it was Jesus.
15 Jesus said to her: Woman, why do you
weep? Whom do you seek? Supposing
Him to be the gardener, she said to Him:
Sir, if you have moved[+] Him from here,

tell me where you have laid Him and I will take Him away.

16 Jesus said to her: Mary. She turned *and* said to Him: Rabboni. Which is to say, Master.

17 Jesus said to her: Do not touch me *now*. For I have not yet ascended to my Father. But go to my brothers and say to them: I *am now* ascending to my Father and your Father, *to* my God and your God.

18 *Then* Mary Magdalene went+ *to* the disciples *and* told *them* that she had seen the Lord and *that* He had spoken these things to her.

19 Therefore, *it* being evening of that day, the first *of* the week, and the doors where the disciples were assembled having been shut for fear of the Jews, Jesus came *forth* and stood in the midst and said to them: Peace to you.

20 When He had said this, He showed them His hands and side. Then the disciples were glad when they saw *that it was* the Lord.

21 Then Jesus said to them again:

> Peace to you.
As *my* Father has sent me,
even so I *now* send you.

22 When He had said this, He breathed on *them* and said to them:

> Receive *the* Holy Spirit.

23 Those+ sins *you* forgive+ are forgiven+ *to* them *and* those+ you retain, are retained.

24 *Now* one of the twelve, Thomas *also* called Didymus, was not with them when Jesus came.

25 Therefore, the other disciples said to him: We have seen the Lord. But He said to them: Unless+ I see the print of the nails in His hands and put my finger into the print of the nails and thrust my hand into His side, I will not believe.

26 After eight days, *Jesus'* disciples were again inside+ *the room* and Thomas with them. *Although* the doors were shut, Jesus came and stood in the midst and said: Peace to you.

27 Then He said to Thomas: Bring+ your finger here and behold my hands. Bring your hand and thrust *it* into my side. Do not be faithless, but believing. *Psalm 22:16*

28 Thomas answered and said to Him: My Lord and my God.

29 Jesus said to him: Thomas, you have believed because you have seen me. Blessed *are those* who have not seen and *yet* have believed.

30 And indeed,+ Jesus did many other signs in the presence of His disciples that are not written in this book.

31 But these are written *so* that you might believe that Jesus is the Christ, the Son of God, *so* that *by* believing you might have life through His name.

John Chapter 21

1 After *all* these things, Jesus showed Himself to the disciples again at the sea of Tiberias, and He showed *Himself* in this way+:

2 Simon Peter, Thomas called Didymus, Nathanael of Cana in Galilee, the *sons* of Zebedee, and two others of *Jesus'* disciples were together.

3 And Simon Peter said to them: I am going fishing. They said to Him: We *will* go with you, also. *So* they went forth and entered a boat immediately and that night they caught nothing.

4 But when morning came, Jesus stood on the shore, but the disciples did not understand+ that it was Jesus.

5 Then Jesus said to them: Children, have you any food+? They answered Him: No.

6 He said to them: Cast the net on the right side of the boat and you will find. Therefore they cast *in their nets* and now they were not able to draw it *in* for the large+ *catch* of fish.

7 Therefore that disciple whom Jesus loved said to Peter: It is the Lord. Now when Simon Peter heard that it was the Lord, he *put on his* fisher's coat, for he was naked, and threw+ himself into the sea.

8 The other disciples came in a little boat dragging the net with fish for they were not far from land but *only* about+ a hundred yards *out*.

9 As soon as they came to land, they saw a fire of coals and fish laying+ *on it* and bread.

10 Jesus said to them: Bring *some* of the fish you just+ caught.

11 Simon Peter went over+ and pulled+ the net full of big+ fish to land, a hundred and fifty three *to be exact*, and *although* there were so many, the net was not broken.

12 Jesus said to them: Come *and* dine. None of the disciples dared+ to ask Him: Who are you? *For they* knew that it was the Lord.

13 Then Jesus came and took bread and gave *it to* them, and fish likewise.

14 This is now the third time that Jesus showed Himself to His disciples after He was risen from the dead.

15 So when they had dined, Jesus said to Simon Peter: Simon *son* of Jonah, do you *truly* love me? More than these? *Peter* said to Him: Yes Lord. You know that I love you. *Jesus* said to him: Feed my lambs.

16 *Then* He said to *Peter* again the second time: Simon *son* of Jonah, *do* you *truly* love me? *Peter* said to Him: Yes Lord. You know that I love you. *Jesus* said to him: Feed my sheep.

17 *And* He said to *Peter* the third time: Simon *son* of Jonah, do you + love me? Peter was grieved because *Jesus had* said to him the third time: Do you+ love me? And he said to *Jesus*: Lord, you know all things. You know that I + love you. Jesus said to him: Feed my sheep.

18 Truly,+ truly, I say to you: When you were young, you *seized* life+ *unto* yourself and walked wherever you wanted+ *to go*. But when you become+ old, you will stretch forth your hands and another will support+ you and carry *you* where you do not want+ *to go*.

19 *Jesus* spoke this *to* signify by what death *Peter* would glorify God. And when He had spoken this, He said to *Peter*: Follow me.

20 Peter then turned around+ *and* saw the disciple whom Jesus loved following. *This was the one* who leaned on *Jesus'* chest+ at supper and said: Lord, who is *the one* who betrays you?

21 *Upon* seeing *that disciple*, Peter said to Jesus: Lord and what *about* this man?

22 Jesus said to him: If I will that he stay+ until I come, what *is that* to you? You follow me.

23 This word+ went among *all* the family+ *of believers*, that this disciple would not die. But+ Jesus did not say to him: He will not die. *Instead, He said*: If I will that he stay+ until I come, what *is that* to you?

24 This *eyewitness* was the *same* disciple who *now* testifies+ of these things and *has* written+ these things. And we know that his testimony is true.

25 There are also many other things that Jesus did, which, if every+ *detail* was written *down*, I suppose that even the world itself could not contain the books that would be written. Amen.

The Gospel of Jesus Christ as written by Matthew

Chapter 1

1 *This* book *lists* the generations of Jesus Christ the son of David the son of Abraham: *Genesis 12:3*

2 Abraham fathered+ Isaac. Isaac fathered Jacob. Jacob fathered Judah and his brothers. *Genesis 17:19 Numbers 24:17*

3 Judah fathered Perez and Zerah by Tamar. Perez fathered Hezron. Hezron fathered Ram.

4 Ram fathered Amminadab. Amminadab fathered Nahshon. Nahshon fathered Salmon.

5 Salmon fathered Boaz by Rahab. Boaz fathered Obed by Ruth. Obed fathered Jesse.

6 Jesse fathered David the king. David the king fathered Solomon by *the wife* of Uriah. *Isaiah 11:1*

7 Solomon fathered Rehoboam.
Rehoboam fathered Abijah. Abijah
fathered Asa.
8 Asa fathered Jehoshaphat. Jehoshaphat
fathered Joram. Joram fathered Uzziah.
9 Uzziah fathered Jotham. Jotham
fathered Ahaz. Ahaz fathered
Hezekiah.
10 Hezekiah fathered Manasseh.
Manasseh fathered Amon. Amon
fathered Josiah.
11 Josiah fathered Jeconiah and his
brothers, about the time they were
carried away to Babylon.
12 After they were brought to Babylon,
Jeconiah fathered Shealtiel. Shealtiel
fathered Zerubbabel.
13 Zerubbabel fathered Abiud. Abiud
fathered Eliakim. Eliakim fathered Azor.
14 Azor fathered Zadoc. Zadoc fathered
Achim. Achim fathered Eliud.
15 Eliud fathered Eleazar. Eleazar
fathered Matthan. Matthan fathered
Jacob.
16 Jacob fathered Joseph the husband of
Mary from whom Jesus who is called
Christ was born.
17 So all the generations from Abraham
to David *are* fourteen generations. From
David until the carrying away into
Babylon *are* fourteen generations. From
the carrying away into Babylon to Christ
are fourteen generations. *Isaiah 11:1*
18 Now the birth of Jesus Christ *came
about* this way.+ When His mother Mary
was espoused to Joseph, before they
came together she was found with child
by the Holy Spirit.+
19 Then Joseph her husband, being a
righteous+ *man* and not willing to make
her a public example, was of a mind+ to
put her away privately.+
20 But while he thought on these things,
behold the angel of the Lord appeared to
him in a dream saying: Joseph, son of
David, do not fear to take Mary *as* your
wife. For what is conceived in her is of
the Holy Spirit.
21 She will bring forth a son and you shall
call His name Jesus, for He will save
His people from their sins.
22 Now all this was done to fulfill what
was spoken of the Lord by the prophet
who said:
23 Behold a virgin shall be with child and
shall bring forth a son and they shall call
His name Emmanuel, which means+:
God with us. *Isaiah 7:14*
24 Then Joseph, being raised from sleep,
did as the angel of the Lord had directed+
him and took *Mary to be* his wife.
25 *However, he* did not know her *as his wife*
until she had brought forth her firstborn
son. And *they* called His name Jesus.

Matthew Chapter 2

1 Now when Jesus was born in
Bethlehem of Judea in the days of Herod
the king, behold wise men came from
the east to Jerusalem *Micah 5:2*
2 saying: Where is He who is born King
of the Jews? For we have seen His star
in the east and have come to worship
Him. *Psalm 72:10,11*
3 When Herod the king had heard *these
things*, he was troubled, and all Jerusalem
with him.
4 When he had gathered all the chief
priests and scribes of the people together,
he demanded of them where Christ
would be born.
5 They said to him: In Bethlehem of
Judea, for thus it is written by the prophet:
6 You Bethlehem *in* the land of Judah
are not the least among the princes of
Judah. For out of you will come a
Governor who will rule my people
Israel. *Micah 5:2*
7 Then Herod, when he had privately+
called the wise men, inquired of them
diligently what time the star appeared.
8 He sent them to Bethlehem and said:
Go and search diligently for the young
child. When you have found *Him*, bring
word to me *so* that I may come and
worship Him also.
9 When they had heard the king, they
departed. And behold, the star that they
saw in the east went before them until it
came and stood over where the young
child was.

10 When they saw the star, they rejoiced
with exceedingly great joy.
11 And when they came into the house,
they saw the young child with Mary His
mother and *they* fell down and worshiped
Him. Then they opened their treasures
and presented gifts to Him: gold and
frankincense and myrrh.
12 *Then* being warned by God in a dream
that they should not return to Herod,
they departed to their own country
another way.
13 After they left, behold the angel of the
Lord appeared to Joseph in a dream
saying: Arise and take the young child
and His mother and flee into Egypt and
stay there until I bring word to you. For
Herod will seek the young child to
destroy Him.
14 Then he arose *and* took the young child
and His mother by night and went to Egypt.
15 *They stayed* there until the death of
Herod, thus fulfilling what was spoken
of the Lord by the prophet *who* said: Out
of Egypt have I called my Son. *Hosea 11:1*
16 Then Herod, when he saw that he was
mocked by the wise men, was exceedingly angry[+] and sent forth and killed[+]
all the *male* children in Bethlehem and
in all the borders[+] thereof, from two
years old and under, according to the
time learned[+] from the wise men.
17 This fulfilled what was spoken by the
prophet Jeremiah *who* said:
18 In Ramah there was a voice heard:
lamentation, weeping, and great mourning. Rachel weeping *for* her children
and *she* would not be comforted because
they are no *more*. *Jeremiah 31:15*
19 But when Herod was dead, behold an
angel of the Lord appeared in a dream to
Joseph in Egypt
20 saying: Arise and take the young child
and His mother and go into the land of
Israel. For *those* who sought the young
child's life are *now* dead.
21 He arose and took the young child and His
mother and came into the land of Israel.
22 But when he heard that Archelaus
reigned in Judea in the room of his father
Herod, he was afraid to go there. Even
so,[+] being warned by God in a dream, he
turned aside into a part of Galilee.
23 He came and lived[+] in a city called
Nazareth, thus fulfilling what was
spoken by the prophets: He shall be
called a Nazarene. *Judges 13:5*

Matthew Chapter 3

1 In those days, John the Baptist came
proclaiming[+] in the wilderness of Judea,
2 saying:

> Repent.
> For the kingdom of heaven
> is *very* near.[+]

3 For this is *the one* who was spoken of
by the prophet Isaiah *who* said: The
voice of one crying in the wilderness:
Prepare the way of the Lord. Make His
paths straight. *Isaiah 40:3*
4 This same John had his clothing[+] of
camel's hair and a leather belt[+] around[+]
his waist.[+] His food[+] was locusts and
wild honey.
5 Then went out to him Jerusalem and
all Judea and all the region around[+]
the Jordan.
6 *They* were baptized by him in *the*
Jordan, confessing their sins.
7 But when he saw many of the Pharisees
and Sadducees come to his baptism, he
said to them: O generation of vipers,
who has warned you to flee from the
wrath to come?
8 Bring forth therefore fruits worthy[+]
of repentance.
9 Do not think to say within yourselves:
We have Abraham as *our* father. For I
say to you: God is able from these stones
to raise up children to Abraham.
10 Now also the axe is laid to the root of
the trees. Therefore, every tree that
does not bring forth good fruit is *to be*
cut[+] down and cast into the fire.
11 I indeed baptize you with water for
repentance, but He who is coming after
me is mightier than I. I am not worthy
to carry[+] *His* sandals.[+] He will baptize
you with the Holy Spirit and *with* fire.

[12]*His* fan *is* in His hand and He will
thoroughly purge His floor and gather His
wheat into the barn.+ But He will burn
up the chaff with unquenchable fire.
[13]Then Jesus came from Galilee to
Jordan to John, to be baptized by him.
[14]But John forbad Him saying: I need to
be baptized by you, and you come to me?
[15]Jesus answering said to him: Allow
it to be so now. For thus it becomes us
to fulfill all righteousness. Then he
allowed+ Him.
[16]When He was baptized, Jesus came up
immediately+ out of the water and lo the
heavens were opened to Him and He
saw the Spirit of God descending like a
dove and coming+ upon Him. *Isaiah 11:2*
[17]And behold, a voice from heaven said:
This is my beloved Son in whom I am
well pleased. *Psalm 2:7*

Matthew Chapter 4

[1] Then Jesus was led up by the Spirit
into the wilderness to be tempted by the
devil.
[2] When He had fasted forty days and
forty nights, afterward He was hungry.
[3] And then the tempter came to Him
and said: If you are the Son of God,
command that these stones be made
bread.
[4] But *Jesus* answered and said:

> It is written:
> Mankind+ shall not live
> by bread alone,
> but by every word that proceeds
> out of the mouth of God.
> *Deuteronomy 8:3*

[5] Then the devil took Him up to the holy
city and sat Him on a pinnacle of the
temple
[6] and said to Him: If you are the Son of
God, cast yourself down. For it is
written: He will give His angels charge
over+ you. In *their* hands they will bear
you up lest at any time you dash your
foot against a stone. *Psalm 91:11,12*
[7] Jesus said to him: Again it is written:

> You shall not tempt
> the Lord your God.
> *Deuteronomy 6:16*

[8] Again, the devil took Him up to an
exceedingly high mountain and showed
Him all the kingdoms of the world and
the glory of them.
[9] And *he* said to Him: All these things
will I give you if you will fall down and
worship me.
[10]Then Jesus said to him: Get*away* from
here Satan. For it is written:

> You shall worship
> the Lord your God
> and Him only shall you serve.
> *Exodus 34:14, Deuteronomy 10:20*

[11]Then the devil left Him and behold
angels came and ministered to Him.
[12]Now when Jesus heard that John was
cast into prison, He went to Galilee.
[13]Leaving Nazareth, He came and lived+
in Capernaum on the sea coast in the
borders of Zabulon and Nephthalim.
Isaiah 9:1
[14]This fulfilled what the prophet Isaiah
had said:
[15]The land of Zabulon and the land of
Nephthalim *by* the way of the sea
beyond Jordan, Galilee of the Gentiles.
Isaiah 9:1
[16]The people who sat in darkness saw
great light. To *those* who sat in the
region and shadow of death, light is
sprung up. *Isaiah 9:2*
[17]From that time *on* Jesus began to
proclaim+ *the Word* and to say:

> Repent. For the kingdom
> of heaven is *very* near+.

[18]*Then* Jesus, walking by the sea of
Galilee, saw two brothers, Simon called
Peter and Andrew his brother casting a net
into the sea, for they were fishermen.+
[19]He said to them: Follow me and I will
make you fishers of men.

20 Immediately,[+] they left *their* nets and followed Him.

21 Going on from there,[+] He saw another two brothers, James *the son* of Zebedee and John his brother, in a boat with Zebedee their father mending their nets. He called them

22 and immediately they left the boat and their father and followed Him.

23 *Then* Jesus went all around[+] Galilee teaching in their synagogues, proclaiming[+] the Gospel of the kingdom, and healing all kinds[+] of sickness and all kinds[+] of disease among the people. *Isaiah 35:5*

24 His reputation[+] went throughout all Syria. They brought to Him all *kinds of* sick people who were taken with many different[+] diseases and torments and those *who were* demon[+] possessed and *those* who were lunatics and *those* who had paralysis[+] and He healed them. *Isaiah 35:5*

25 Great multitudes of people followed Him from Galilee and Decapolis and Jerusalem and Judea and *from* beyond Jordan.

Matthew Chapter 5

1 Seeing the multitudes, *Jesus* went up into a mountain and when He sat *down* His disciples came to Him.

2 And He opened His mouth and taught them saying:

3 Blessed *are* the poor in spirit, for theirs is the kingdom of heaven.

4 Blessed *are those* who mourn, for they shall be comforted.

5 Blessed *are* the meek, for they shall inherit the earth. *Psalm 37:11*

6 Blessed *are those* who do hunger and thirst after righteousness, for they shall be filled.

7 Blessed *are* the merciful, for they shall obtain mercy. *Proverbs 11:17*

8 Blessed *are* the pure in heart, for they shall see God.

9 Blessed *are* the peacemakers, for they shall be called the children of God.

10 Blessed *are those* who are persecuted for righteousness' sake, for theirs is the kingdom of heaven. *Isaiah 8:12*

11 Blessed are you when *people* revile you and persecute *you* and say all kinds[+] of evil against you falsely for my sake.

12 Rejoice and be exceedingly glad. For great *is* your reward in heaven. For so *likewise did* they persecute the prophets who were before you. *2 Chronicles 36:16*

13 You are the salt of the earth, but if salt has lost its savor, with what will it be salted? It is thereafter[+] good for nothing but to be cast out and trampled[+] under foot[+].

14 You are the light of the world. A city that is set on a hill cannot be hid.

15 Nor do people[+] light a candle and put it under a bushel, but on a candlestick*so that* it gives light to all who are in the house.

16 Let your light so shine before *people* that they may see your good works and glorify your Father in heaven.

17 Do not think that I have come to destroy the law or the prophets. I have not come to destroy, but to fulfill.

18 For truly[+] I say to you: Until heaven and earth pass, one jot or one smallest mark[+] shall in no way[+] pass from the law until all is fulfilled.

19 Whoever therefore shall break one of these least commandments and shall teach people[+] *to do* so shall be called the least in the kingdom of heaven. But whoever shall do *them* and teach *them*, the same shall be called great in the kingdom of heaven.

20 For I say to you: Unless[+] your righteousness shall exceed *the righteousness* of the scribes and Pharisees, you shall in no case enter into the kingdom of heaven.

21 You have heard that it was said of old[+]: You shall not kill and whoever shall kill shall be in danger of the judgment. *Exodus 20:13*

22 But I say to you: Whoever is angry with *one of* the family[+] *of God* without a *just* cause shall be in danger of the judgment. Whoever says to *one of* the family[+]: Raca, *to offend,* shall be in danger of the council. But whoever says: You fool, shall be in danger of hell fire.

23 Therefore if you bring your gift to the altar and there remember that *one of* your family[+] has anything[+] against you,

24 leave your gift there before the altar and go first *to* be reconciled to your family[+] and then come and offer your gift.

25 Agree with your adversary quickly while you are on the way with them, lest at any time the adversary deliver you to the judge and the judge deliver you to the officer and you be cast into prison. *Proverbs 25:8*

26 Truly[+] I say to you: You shall by no means come out from there[+] until you have paid the *very* last[+] penny[+].

27 You have heard that it was said of old[+]: You shall not commit adultery. *Exodus 20:14*

28 But I say to you that whoever looks upon a woman to lust after her has committed adultery with her already in his heart. *Proverbs 6:25*

29 If your right eye causes[+] you *to sin,* pluck it out and cast *it* from you. For it is *more* profitable for you that one of your members should perish and not *that* your whole body should be cast into hell.

30 If your right hand causes[+] you *to sin,* cut it off and cast *it* from you. For it is *more* profitable for you that one of your members should perish and not *that* your whole body should be cast into hell.

31 It has been said: Whoever shall put away his wife, let him give her a written divorce[+]. *Deuteronomy 24:1*

32 But I say to you that whoever shall put away his wife, except[+] for the cause of fornication, causes them[+] to commit adultery. And whoever shall marry *one who is thus* divorced commits adultery. *Deuteronomy 24:1*

33 Again, you have heard that it was said of old[+]: You shall not perjure[+] yourself but shall perform your oaths to the Lord. *Numbers 30:2*

34 But I say to you: Do not swear *oaths* at all. Not by heaven for it is God's throne

35 nor by the earth for it is His footstool. And not by Jerusalem for it is the city of the great King.

36 Nor shall you swear by your head, because you cannot make one hair black or white.

37 But let your communication be *simply* yes *for* yes *and* no *for* no. For whatever is more than these comes of evil.

38 You have heard that it has been said: An eye for an eye and a tooth for a tooth. *Exodus 21:24*

39 But I say to you: Do not stand against[+] evil *with force*, but whoever shall strike[+] you on your right cheek, turn to them the other also. *Proverbs 24:29*

40 If anyone will sue you at the law and take away your coat, let them have *your* vest[+] also.

41 Whoever shall compel you to go a mile, go with them two.

42 Give to *those* who ask you and from *those* who would borrow from you do not turn away. *Proverbs 19:17*

43 You have heard that it has been said: You shall love your neighbor and hate your enemy. *Leviticus 19:18*

44 But I say to you:

> Love your enemies.
> Bless *those* who curse you.
> Do good to *those* who hate you.
> And pray for *those*
> who despitefully use you
> and persecute you
> *Proverbs 16:7*

45 *so* that you may be the children of your Father in heaven. For He makes His sun to rise on the evil and on the good and *He* sends rain on the righteous[+] and on the unrighteous[+].

46 For if you love *those* who love you, what reward will you have? Do not even worldly[+] people the same?

[47]And if you greet+ your family+ only,
what do you *do* more*than others*? Do not
even worldly+ people so?
[48]Therefore be perfect even as your
Father in heaven is perfect. *Leviticus 19:2*

Matthew Chapter 6

[1] Take heed that you do not give your
alms before people+ to be seen by them.
Otherwise you *will* have no reward from
your Father in heaven.
[2] Therefore when you give+ alms, do
not sound a trumpet before you as the
hypocrites do in the synagogues and in
the streets *so* that they may have glory
from people.+ Truly+ I say to you: They
have their reward.
[3] But when you give+ alms, do not let
your left hand know what your right
hand does
[4] *so* that your alms may be in secret and
your Father who sees in secret will
reward you openly.

[5] When you pray,
do not be
as the hypocrites *are*.

For they love to pray standing in the
synagogues and on the corners of the
streets *so* that they may be seen by
people.+ Truly+ I say to you: They have
their reward.
[6] But when you pray, enter into your
closet and when you have shut your
door, pray to your Father in secret and
your Father who sees in secret will
reward you openly. *Isaiah 26:20*

[7] When you pray,
do not use vain repetitions
as the heathen *do*.

For they think that they will be heard for
their much speaking.
[8] Therefore do not be like them, for

your Father knows
what things you need
before you ask Him.

[9] Therefore pray in this manner:
Our Father in heaven,
Holy+ is your name.
[10] Your kingdom come.
Your will be done,
on earth as *it is* in heaven.

[11] Give us this day
our daily bread.

[12] And forgive us *for* our debts
in which we have done wrong to others
as we forgive our debtors,
those we feel have done wrong to us.

[13] Lead us, *so that we will*
not *yield* to temptation,
but deliver us from evil.
For the kingdom is yours,
and the power and the glory,
forever. Amen.

[14] For if you forgive others
for their trespasses
then your heavenly Father
will also forgive you.
[15] But if you do not forgive others
for their trespasses
then neither will your Father
forgive your trespasses.

[16]Moreover when you fast, do not be like
the hypocrites of a sad countenance. For
they disfigure their faces *so* that they
will appear to people+ to fast. Truly+ I
say to you: They have their reward.
[17]But you, when you fast, anoint your
head and wash your face
[18]*so* that you do not appear to people+ to
fast but*only* to your Father in secret, and
your Father who sees in secret will
reward you openly.

[19] Do not lay up for yourselves
treasures on earth
where moth and rust corrupt
and where thieves
break through and steal.

> 20 Lay up for yourselves
> treasures in heaven
> where neither moth nor rust
> corrupt and where thieves
> do not break through or steal.
> 21 For where your treasure is,
> there will your heart be also.
> *Proverbs 23:7*

22 The light of the body is the eye. Therefore if your eye is single *then* your whole body will be full of light.

23 But if your eye is evil, your whole body will be full of darkness. Therefore if the light that is in you is darkness, how great *is* that darkness.

> 24 No one can serve two masters.
> For either they will hate the one
> and love the other,
> or else they will hold to the one
> and despise the other.
> You cannot serve
> God and *worldly* treasures+.

25 Therefore I say to you: Take no thought for your life, what you will eat or what you will drink. Nor for your body, what you will put on. Is not life more than food+ and the body *more* than clothing+?

26 Behold the birds+ of the air, for they do not sow nor do they reap or gather into barns. Yet your heavenly Father feeds them. Are you not much better than they?

27 Who among+ you by taking thought can add one cubit to your stature?

28 Why do you take thought for clothing+? Consider the lilies of the field, how they grow. They do not toil nor do they spin.

29 Yet I say to you that even Solomon in all his glory was not arrayed like one of these.

30 Therefore if God so clothes the grass of the field, which is *here* today and tomorrow is cast into the oven, *will He* not much more *clothe* you, O you of little faith?

31 Therefore take no thought saying: What shall we eat? Or what shall we drink? Or how will we be clothed?

32 For after all these things do the Gentiles seek. But your heavenly Father knows that you have need of all these things.

> 33 But seek first
> the kingdom of God
> and His righteousness
> and all these things
> will be added to you.

34 Therefore take no thought for tomorrow, for tomorrow will take thought for the things of itself. Sufficient to the day *is* the evil thereof.

Matthew Chapter 7

> 1 Do not judge *so* that
> you *will* not be judged.

2 For with what judgment you judge, you will be judged. With what gauge+ you measure, it will be measured to you again.

3 Why do you notice+ the speck+ that is in your brother's *or sister's* eye, but do not consider the beam that is in your own eye?

4 How can+ you say to your brother *or sister*: Let me pull out the speck+ from your eye when behold a beam *is* in your own eye?

5 You hypocrite. First cast out the beam from your own eye. Then you will see clearly to cast the speck+ from your brother's *or sister's*, eye.

6 Do not give what is holy to the dogs or cast your pearls before swine lest they trample them under their feet and turn again and tear+ you.

> 7 Ask and it will be
> given *to* you.
> Seek and you will find.
> Knock and it will be
> opened to you.

8 For everyone who asks receives and *those* who seek *will* find and to *those* who knock it will be opened.

9 Or who is there among you, if *your* son asks *for* bread will give him a stone?

10 Or if he asks *for* a fish will give him a serpent?

11 If you then being wicked+ know how to give good gifts to your children, how much more will your Father in heaven give good things to *those* who ask Him?

--- The Golden Rule ---

12 Therefore all things whatsoever
you would that others
should do to you,
you do to them.
For this is *the sum*
of the law and the prophets.

13 Enter in at the strait gate, for wide *is* the gate and broad *is* the way that leads to destruction and there are many who go in that way+

14 Because strait *is* the gate and narrow *is* the way that leads to life and there are few who find it.

15 Beware of false prophets
who come to you in sheep's
clothing, but inwardly
they are greedy+ wolves.

16 You will know them by their fruits. Do people+ gather grapes from thorns or figs from thistles? *Proverbs 20:11*

17 Even so, every good tree brings forth good fruit but a corrupt tree brings forth evil fruit.

18 A good tree cannot bring forth evil fruit nor *can* a corrupt tree bring forth good fruit.

19 Every tree that does not bring forth good fruit is cut+ down and cast into the fire.

20 Therefore by their fruits you will know them.

21 Not everyone who says to me: Lord, Lord, will enter into the kingdom of heaven, but *only those* who do the will of my Father in heaven.

22 Many will say to me in that day: Lord, Lord, have we not prophesied in your name? And in your name cast out demons+? And in your name done many wonderful works?

23 Then I will profess to them: I never knew you. Depart from me, you who work iniquity. *Psalm 6:8*

24 Therefore whoever hears these sayings of mine and does them I will compare+ to a wise man who built his house upon a rock.

25 The rain descended and the floods came and the winds blew and beat upon that house, but it did not fall for it was founded upon a rock.

26 Everyone who hears these sayings of mine and does not do them shall be compared+ to a foolish man who built his house on the sand.

27 The rain descended and the floods came and the winds blew and beat upon that house and it fell. And great was the fall of it.

28 *Then* it came to pass, when Jesus had ended these sayings, the people were astonished at His doctrine.

29 For He taught them as *one* having authority and not as the scribes.

Matthew Chapter 8

1 When He had come down from the mountain, great multitudes followed Him.

2 And behold a leper came worshiping Him saying: Lord, if you will, you can make me clean.

3 Jesus put forth *his* hand and touched him saying: I will. Be clean. And immediately his leprosy was cleansed.

4 Jesus said to him: See *that* you tell no one, but go+ *and* show yourself to the priest and offer the gift that Moses commanded as a testimony to them. *Leviticus 14:2*

5 When Jesus entered Capernaum, a centurion came to Him beseeching Him

6 and saying: Lord, my servant lies at home sick with paralysis+ *and* grievously tormented.

7 Jesus said to him: I will come and heal him.

8 The centurion answered and said: Lord, I am not worthy that you should come under my roof, but speak the word only and my servant will be healed.

9 For I am a man under authority having soldiers under me *and* I say to this *man*: Go and he goes, and to another: Come and he comes, and to my servant: Do this and he does *it*.

10 When Jesus heard *this*, He marveled and said to *those* who followed: Truly+ I say to you: I have not found so great *a* faith, no, not in Israel.

11 I say to you that many will come from the east and west and will sit down with Abraham and Isaac and Jacob in the kingdom of heaven,

12 but the children of the kingdom will be cast out into *the* outer darkness *and* there will be weeping and gnashing of teeth.

13 *Then* Jesus said to the centurion: Go.

> As you have believed,
> *so* be it done to you.

And his servant was healed in the same hour.

14 When Jesus came to Peter's house, He saw *Peter's* wife's mother laying *down* and sick with a fever.

15 *Jesus* touched her hand and the fever left her and she arose and ministered to them.

16 When the evening+ had come, they brought to Him many *who were* demon+ possessed and He cast out the spirits with *His* word and healed all who were sick.

17 This fulfilled what the prophet Isaiah had said: He took our infirmities and bore *our* sicknesses. *Isaiah 53:4*

18 Now when Jesus saw great multitudes around+ Him, He gave instructions+ to depart to the other side.

19 *Then* a certain scribe came and said to Him: Master, I will follow you wherever you go.

20 Jesus said to him: The foxes have holes and the birds of the air *have* nests, but the Son of man does not have anywhere to lay *His* head.

21 *Then* another of His disciples said to Him: Lord, allow+ me first to go and bury my father.

22 Jesus said to him:

> Follow me.

Let the dead bury their dead.

23 *Then* when He entered a boat, His disciples followed Him

24 and behold a great storm+ arose in the sea so that the boat was covered by the waves. But *Jesus* was asleep.

25 His disciples came to *Him* and awoke Him saying: Lord, save us *or* we *will* perish.

26 He said to them: Why are you fearful, O you of little faith? Then He arose and rebuked the winds and the sea and there came a great calm.

27 But the men marveled saying: What kind+ of man is this that even the winds and the sea obey Him.

28 *Then* when He came to the other side, to the country of the Gergesenes, there met Him two *who were* demon+ possessed coming out of the tombs exceedingly fierce so that no one might pass by that way.

29 And behold they cried out saying: What do we have to do with you Jesus, you Son of God? Have you come here to torment us before the time?

30 *Now* there was, a good way off from them, a herd of many swine feeding,

31 so the demons+ begged+ Him saying: If you cast us out, allow+ us to go into the herd of swine.

32 *Jesus* said to them: Go. And when they came out, they went into the herd of swine and behold the whole herd of swine ran violently down a steep place into the sea and perished in the waters.

33 *Those* who kept them fled and went into the city and told everything, and what had befallen the *one who was* demon+ possessed.

34 And behold the whole city came out to meet Jesus. When they saw Him, they begged+ *Him* to depart out of their borders.+

Matthew Chapter 9

1 *Then* He entered a boat and crossed[+]
over *the sea* and came to His own city.
2 And behold they brought to Him a man
sick with paralysis[+] lying on a bed.
Seeing their faith, Jesus said to the *one*
sick with paralysis[+]: Son, be of good
cheer. Your sins are forgiven.
3 And behold some of the scribes said
within themselves: This *man* blasphemes.
4 Knowing their thoughts, Jesus said:
Why do you think evil in your hearts?
5 For which[+] is easier to say: *Your* sins
are forgiven. Or to say: Arise and walk.
6 But *this is done so* that you may know
that the Son of man has authority[+] *and*
power on earth to forgive sins. Then He
said to the *one* sick with paralysis[+]:
Arise, take up your bed and go to your
house.
7 And he arose and departed to his
house.
8 When the multitude saw *this*, they
marveled and glorified God who had
given such authority[+] *and power* to men.
9 As Jesus passed forth from there,[+] He
saw a man named Matthew sitting at the
tax office[+] and He said to him: Follow
me. And he arose and followed Him.
10 And it came to pass, as Jesus sat *down*
to eat[+] in the house, behold many
worldly[+] people and sinners came and
sat down with Him and His disciples.
11 When the Pharisees saw *this*, they said
to His disciples: Why does your Master
eat with worldly[+] people and sinners?
12 But when Jesus heard *that*, He said to
them: *Those* who are whole do not need
a physician, but *those* who are sick *do*.

13 Go and learn what *this* means:
I will have mercy
and not sacrifice.
For I have not come
to call the righteous
but sinners to repentance.
Hosea 6:6

14 Then the disciples of John came to Him
saying: Why do we and the Pharisees fast
often, but your disciples do not fast?
15 Jesus said to them: Can the children of
the bride chamber mourn as long as the
bridegroom is with them? But the days
will come when the Bridegroom will be
taken from them and then they will fast.
16 No one puts a piece of new cloth onto
an old garment, for what is put in to fill
it up takes from the garment and the
tear[+] is made worse.
17 Nor do people[+] put new wine into old
wineskins[+] *or* else the wineskins[+] break
and the wine runs out and the wineskins[+] perish. But they put new wine
into new wineskins[+] and both are
preserved.
18 While He spoke these things to them,
behold there came a certain ruler and
worshiped Him saying: My daughter is
even now dead, but come and lay your
hand upon her and she will live.
19 Jesus arose and followed him and *so*
did His disciples.
20 And behold a woman who was diseased
with an issue of blood *for* twelve years
came behind *Him* and touched the hem
of His garment.
21 For she said within herself: If I may
but touch His garment, I will be whole.
22 But Jesus turned around[+] and when
He saw her He said: Daughter, be of
good comfort. Your faith has made you
whole. And the woman was made whole
from that hour.
23 When Jesus came into the ruler's
house and saw the minstrels and the
people making a noise,
24 He said to them: Withdraw.[+] For the
maid is not dead but *is* sleeping. And
they laughed *at* Him *scornfully*.
25 But when the people were sent out,[+]
Jesus went in and took her by the hand
and the maid arose.
26 The report[+] of this[+] went throughout[+]
all that land.
27 When Jesus departed from there,[+]
two blind men followed Him, crying
and saying: Son of David, have mercy
on us.

28 When He had come into the house, the blind men came to Him and Jesus said to them: Do you believe that I am able to do this? They said to Him: Yes Lord.
29 Then He touched their eyes saying: According to your faith be it to you.
30 Their eyes were opened *but* Jesus strictly+ charged them saying: See *that* no one knows *about this*.
31 But when they went away,+ they spread His reputation+ widely+ *throughout* all that country.
32 As they went out, behold they brought to Him a speechless+ demon+ possessed man.
33 When the demon+ was cast out, the speechless+ *man* spoke and the multitudes marveled saying: It was never so seen in Israel *before*.
34 But the Pharisees said: He casts out demons+ through the prince of the demons.+
35 Jesus went to all the cities and villages, teaching in their synagogues, proclaiming+ the Gospel of the kingdom, and healing every sickness and every disease among the people.
36 But when He saw the multitudes, He was moved with compassion on them because they fainted and were scattered widely+ like sheep having no shepherd.
37 Then He said to His disciples: The harvest truly *is* plentiful, but the laborers *are* few.
38 Pray therefore *to* the Lord of the harvest, *so* that He will send forth laborers into His harvest.

Matthew Chapter 10

1 When He had called His twelve disciples, He gave them authority+ *and power against* unclean spirits, to cast them out, and to heal all kinds+ of sickness and all kinds+ of disease.
2 Now the names of the twelve apostles are these: The first, Simon who is called Peter and Andrew his brother, James *the son* of Zebedee and John his brother,
3 Philip and Bartholomew, Thomas and Matthew the worldly+ person, James *the son* of Alphaeus, and Lebbaeus whose surname was Thaddaeus,
4 Simon the Canaanite and Judas Iscariot who also betrayed Him.
5 These twelve Jesus sent forth and instructed+ them saying: Do not go into the way of the Gentiles and do not enter into *any* city of the Samaritans,
6 but go instead to the lost sheep of the house of Israel.

7 As you go,
proclaim+ *the Word*, saying:
The kingdom of heaven
is *very* near+.
8 Heal the sick. Cleanse the
lepers. Raise the dead.
Cast out demons.+
Freely you have received,
freely give.

9 Provide neither gold nor silver nor brass in your purses,
10 nor *a provision* bag+ for *your* journey nor two coats nor sandals+ nor staves. For the worker+ is worthy of his food+.
11 Into whatever city or town you enter, inquire who in it is worthy and stay+ there until you go *on* from there+.
12 When you come into a house, greet+ it.
13 If the house is worthy let your peace come upon it, but if it is not worthy let your peace return to you. *1 Samuel 25:6*
14 Whoever will not receive you or hear your words, when you depart out of that house or city, shake off the dust from your feet.
15 Truly+ I say to you: It will be more tolerable for the land of Sodom and Gomorrah in the day of judgment than for that city.
16 Behold I send you forth like sheep in the midst of wolves. Therefore be *as* wise as serpents and *as* harmless as doves.
17 But beware of people,+ for they will deliver you up to the councils and they will flog+ you in their synagogues.
18 You will be brought before governors and kings for my sake for a testimony against them and the Gentiles.

19 When they deliver you up, take no
thought how or what you shall speak,
for it will be given *to* you in that same
hour what you shall speak. *Proverbs 16:1*
20 For it is not you who *will be* speaking
but the Spirit of your Father who speaks
in you.
21 Brother will deliver up brother to
death and the father *his* child. Children
will rise up against parents and cause
them to be put to death. *Micah 7:6*
22 You will be hated by all for my name's
sake, but *those* who endure to the end
will be saved.
23 But when they persecute you in this
city, flee to another. For truly+ I say
to you: You will not have gone to *all*
the cities of Israel until the Son of
man has come.
24 The disciple is not above *his* master
nor the servant above his lord.
25 It is enough for the disciple that he be
like his master and the servant like his
lord. If they have called the master of
the house Beelzebub, how much more
will they call those of his household?
26 Therefore do not be afraid of them, for

there is nothing covered
that will not be revealed
and *nothing* hid
that will not be known.

27 What I tell you in darkness, speak in
light. What you hear in the ear, proclaim+
from the housetops.
28 Do not fear *those* who kill the body but
are not able to kill the soul. Instead,+
fear *Him who* is able to destroy both soul
and body in hell.
29 Are not two sparrows sold for a penny+?
And not one of them will fall to the
ground without your Father *knowing it*.
30 The very hairs of your head are all
numbered.
31 Therefore, do not be afraid. You are
of more value than many sparrows.
32 Whoever therefore will confess me
before people,+ I will confess also before my Father in heaven.
33 But whoever will deny me before
people,+ I will also deny before my
Father in heaven.
34 Do not think that I have come to send
peace on earth. I did not come to send
peace, but a sword.
35 For I have come to set a man at
contention+ against his father and the
daughter against her mother and the
daughter in law against her mother in
law. *Micah 7:6*
36 A man's foes *will be* those of his own
household.
37 *Those* who love father or mother more
than me are not worthy of me. *Those*
who love son or daughter more than me
are not worthy of me.
38 *Those* who do not take *up* their cross and
follow after me are not worthy of me.
39 *Those* who find their life will lose it.
Those who lose their life for my sake will
find it.
40 *Those* who receive you receive me and
those who receive me receive Him who
sent me.
41 *Those* who receive a prophet in the
name of a prophet will receive a prophet's
reward. *Those* who receive a righteous
man in the name of a righteous man will
receive a righteous man's reward.
42 Whoever will give a drink to one of
these little ones, *even* a cup of cold *water*
only in the name of a disciple, truly+ I
say to you: They shall in no way+ lose
their reward.

Matthew Chapter 11

1 Now+ it came to pass, when Jesus
had made an end of commanding His
twelve disciples, He departed from
there+ to teach and to proclaim+ *the*
Word in their cities.
2 When John, in prison, heard *about*
the works of Christ, he sent two of his
disciples
3 and said to Him: Are you the *one who was*
to come or should+ we look for another?
4 Jesus answered and said to them: Go
and show John again those things that
you hear and see.

[5] The blind receive their sight, the lame walk, the lepers are cleansed, the deaf hear, the dead are raised up, and the poor have the Gospel proclaimed+ to them. *Isaiah 35:5*
[6] Blessed are *those* who will not be offended *and disbelieve* in me.
[7] As they departed, Jesus began to say to the multitudes, concerning John: What did you go out into the wilderness to see? A reed shaken with the wind?
[8] But what did you go out to see? A man clothed in soft clothing+? Behold *those* who wear soft *clothing* are in kings' houses.
[9] But what did you go out to see? A prophet? Yes, I say to you, and more than a prophet.
[10] For this is *he* of whom it is written: Behold I send my messenger before your face who will prepare your way before you. *Malachi 3:1*
[11] Truly+ I say to you: Among *those* who are born of women, there has not risen *one* greater than John the Baptist. Even so+ *those* who are least in the kingdom of heaven are greater than he.
[12] From the days of John the Baptist until now the kingdom of heaven suffers violence and the violent take it by force,
[13] for all the prophets and the law prophesied until John.
[14] If you will receive *it*, this is Elijah who was to come.
[15] *Those* who have ears to hear, let them hear.
[16] But to what shall I compare+ this generation? It is like children sitting in the market *places* and calling to their fellows
[17] and saying: We have piped to you and you have not danced. We have mourned to you and you have not grieved+.
[18] For John came neither eating nor drinking and they say: He has a demon+.
[19] The Son of man came eating and drinking and they say: Behold a gluttonous man and a wine drinker,+ a friend of worldly+ people and sinners. But wisdom is justified by her children.
[20] Then He began to upbraid the cities in which most of His mighty works were done because they did not repent.
[21] Woe to you, Chorazin. Woe to you, Bethsaida. For if the mighty works that were done in you had been done in Tyre and Sidon, they would have repented long ago in sackcloth and ashes.
[22] But I say to you: It will be more tolerable for Tyre and Sidon at the day of judgment than for you.
[23] You Capernaum, *being* exalted to heaven, will be brought down to hell. For if the mighty works that have been done in you had been done in Sodom, it would have remained until this day.
[24] But I say to you that it shall be more tolerable for the land of Sodom in the day of judgment than for you.
[25] *Then* at that time, Jesus answered and said: I thank you O Father, Lord of heaven and earth, because You have hid these things from the wise and prudent and have revealed them to babes.
[26] Even so Father, for so it seemed good in your sight.
[27] All things are delivered to me by my Father. No one knows the Son but the Father. Nor does anyone know the Father except+ the Son and *those* to whom the Son will reveal *Him*.

[28] Come to me
all *you* who labor
and are heavily burdened+
and I will give you rest.
Jeremiah 31:25

[29] Take my yoke upon you and learn from me. For I am meek and lowly in heart, and you will find rest for your souls. *Jeremiah 6:16*
[30] For my yoke *is* easy and my burden is light.

Matthew Chapter 12

[1] At that time, Jesus went through a corn *field* on the Sabbath day. His disciples were hungry and began to pluck the ears of corn and eat.

2 When the Pharisees saw *this*, they said to Him: Behold your disciples do what is not lawful to do on the Sabbath day.

3 But *Jesus* said to them: Have you not read what David did when he was hungry, and *those* who were with him?

4 How he entered the house of God and ate the show bread that was not lawful for him to eat, nor for *those* who were with him, but only for the priests?

5 Or have you not read in the law that on the Sabbath days the priests in the temple profane the Sabbath and are blameless?

6 But I say to you: In this place is *one* greater than the temple.

7 But if you had known what *this* means: I will have mercy and not sacrifice, you would not have condemned the innocent+. *Hosea 6:6*

8 For the Son of man is Lord even of the Sabbath day.

9 When He departed from there,+ He went into their synagogue.

10 And behold there was a man who had *a* withered hand and they asked Him saying: Is it lawful to heal on the Sabbath days? *They did this so* that they might accuse Him.

11 *Jesus* said to them: What man shall there be among you who shall have one sheep and, if it fall into a pit on the Sabbath day, will he not lay hold on it and lift *it* out?

12 *And* how much then is a man better than a sheep? Therefore it is lawful to do good+ on the Sabbath days.

13 Then He said to the man: Stretch forth your hand. And he stretched *it* forth and it was restored whole like the other.

14 Then the Pharisees went out and held a council against Him, *to decide* how they might destroy Him.

15 But when Jesus knew *this*, He withdrew from there.+ Great multitudes followed Him and He healed them all.

16 And *He* charged them to not make Him known.

17 This fulfilled what the prophet Isaiah had said:

18 Behold my servant whom I have chosen, my beloved in whom my soul is well pleased. I will put my spirit upon Him and He will show judgment to the Gentiles. *Isaiah 42:1*

19 He will not strive or cry. Nor will anyone hear His voice in the streets. *Isaiah 42:2*

20 A bruised reed He will not break and smoking flax He will not quench until He sends forth judgment to victory. *Isaiah 42:3*

21 In His name will the Gentiles trust. *Isaiah 42:4*

22 Then one *who was* demon+ possessed was brought to Him, blind and speechless.+ *Jesus* healed him so that the blind and speechless+ *one* both spoke and saw.

23 All the people were amazed and said: Is this not the son of David?

24 But when the Pharisees heard *this* they said: This *fellow* does not cast out demons+ except+ by Beelzebub the prince of the demons.+

25 Jesus knew their thoughts and said to them:

> Every kingdom
> divided against itself
> is brought to desolation.
> Every city or house divided
> against itself will not stand.
> *Proverbs 11:29*

26 If Satan casts out Satan, he is divided against himself. How then will his kingdom stand?

27 And if I cast out demons+ by Beelzebub, *then* by whom do your children cast *them* out? Therefore they shall be your judges.

28 But if I cast out demons+ by the Spirit of God, then the kingdom of God has come to you.

29 Or else how can one enter into a strong man's house and spoil his goods, unless+ he first bind the strong man, and then he will spoil his house.

> 30 *Those* who are not with me
> are against me. *Those* who
> do not gather with me scatter.

31 Therefore I say to you: All kinds[+] of
sin and blasphemy will be forgiven to
people,[+] but blasphemy *against* the *Holy*
Spirit will not be forgiven to people[+].
32 Whoever speaks a word against the
Son of man, it will be forgiven them.
But whoever speaks against the Holy
Spirit, it will not be forgiven them. Not
in this world or in the *world* to come.
33 Either make the tree good and its fruit
good, or else make the tree corrupt and
its fruit corrupt. For the tree is known
by *its* fruit.
34 O generation of vipers, how can you,
being evil, speak good things?

For out of the abundance
of the heart the mouth speaks.
35 A good person[+]
out of the good treasure
of the heart
brings forth good things.
An evil person[+]
out of evil treasure
brings forth evil things.
Psalm 19:14, Proverbs 10:11

36 But I say to you
that *for* every idle word
that people[+] speak,
they will give *an* account of it
on the day of judgment.
37 For by your words
you will be justified
and by your words
you will be condemned.

38 Then some of the scribes and of the
Pharisees answered saying: Master, we
would *like to* see a sign from you.
39 But He answered and said to them: An
evil and adulterous generation seeks
after a sign. There shall no sign be given
to it but the sign of the prophet Jonah.
40 For as Jonah was three days and three
nights in the belly of the whale, so will
the Son of man be three days and three
nights in the heart of the earth. *Jonah 1:17*
41 The men of Nineveh will rise in
judgment with this generation and
will condemn it because they repented at
the proclaiming[+] of Jonah. And behold
one greater than Jonah *is* here. *Jonah 3:5*
42 The queen of the south will rise up in
the judgment with this generation and
will condemn it. For she came from the
ends[+] of the earth to hear the wisdom of
Solomon, and behold *one* greater than
Solomon *is* here. *1 Kings 10:1*
43 When the unclean spirit is gone out of
someone, he walks through dry places
seeking rest and finds none.
44 So he says: I will return to my house from
which I came out, and when he comes, he
finds *it* empty, swept, and put in order[+].
45 Then he goes and takes with him seven
other spirits more wicked than himself
and they *all* enter in and dwell there. *So*
the last *state* of that person[+] is worse
than the first. Even so shall it be also to
this wicked generation.
46 While He yet talked to the people,
behold *His* mother and His brothers stood
outside[+] desiring to speak with Him.
47 Then one said to Him: Behold your
mother and your brothers stand outside[+] desiring to speak with you.
48 But He answered and said to the one
who spoke[+] *to* Him: Who is my mother?
And who are my brothers?
49 *Then* He stretched forth His hand
toward His disciples and said: Behold
my mother and my brothers.

50 For whoever does the will
of my Father in heaven,
the same is my brother
and sister and mother.

Matthew Chapter 13

1 The same day Jesus went out of the
house and sat by the seaside.
2 Great multitudes were gathered
together to Him so that He went into
a boat and sat, and the whole multitude
stood on the shore.
3 He spoke many things to them in
parables saying: Behold a sower went
forth to sow.

4 When he sowed, some fell by the wayside and the birds[+] came and devoured them up.

5 Some fell on stony places where they did not have much earth. Immediately[+] they sprang up because they had no depth of earth,

6 and when the sun was up, they were scorched, and because they had no root, they withered away.

7 Some fell among thorns and the thorns sprang up and choked them.

8 But other *seed* fell into good ground and brought forth fruit: some a hundredfold, some sixtyfold, *and* some thirtyfold.

9 Who has ears to hear, let them hear.

10 *Then* the disciples came and said to Him: Why do you speak to them in parables?

11 *Jesus* answered and said to them: Because it is given to you to know the mysteries of the kingdom of heaven, but to them it is not given.

12 For whoever has, to them will *more* be given and they will have more abundance. But whoever has nothing, from them will be taken away even what they have. *Proverbs 9:9*

13 Therefore I speak to them in parables, because seeing they do not see and hearing they do not hear, nor do they understand. *Jeremiah 5:21*

14 In them, the prophecy of Isaiah is fulfilled that says: By hearing you will hear and not understand. Seeing you will see and not perceive. *Isaiah 6:9*

15 For the hearts of these people are calloused.[+] *Their* ears are dull of hearing and they have closed their eyes, lest at any time they should see with *their* eyes and hear with *their* ears and should understand with *their* hearts and should be converted, and I should heal them. *Isaiah 6:10*

16 But blessed *are* your eyes for they see and your ears for they hear.

17 For truly[+] I say to you that many prophets and righteous *people* have desired to see what you see but have not seen *it* and to hear what you hear but have not heard *it*.

18 Hear therefore the parable of the sower:

19 When anyone hears the Word of the kingdom and does not understand *it*, then the wicked *one* comes and catches away what was sown in their heart. This is the one who received seed by the wayside.

20 But the one who received the seed into stony places, the same is *like those* who hear the Word and immediately[+] receive it with joy.

21 Yet they have no root in themselves *and therefore they* endure *only* for a while. For when tribulation or persecution arises because of the Word, immediately[+] they are offended *and disbelieve*

22 And the one who received seed among the thorns is *like those* who hear the Word but the cares of this world and the deceitfulness of riches choke the Word and they become unfruitful.

23 But the one who received seed into the good ground is *like those* who hear the Word and understand *it* and who also bear fruit and bring forth, some a hundredfold, some sixty, *and* some thirty.

24 *Then* another parable He put forth to them saying: The kingdom of heaven is compared[+] to a man who sowed good seed in his field.

25 But while people[+] slept, his enemy came and sowed tares among the wheat and went away[+].

26 But when the blade was sprung up and brought forth fruit, then the tares appeared also.

27 So the servants of the property owner[+] came and said to him: Sir, did you not sow good seed in your field? From where then does it have tares?

28 He said to them: An enemy has done this. The servants said to him: Do you want[+] us to go and gather them up?

29 But he said: No, lest while you gather up the tares you also root up the wheat with them.

30 Let both grow together until the harvest. In the time of harvest I will say to the reapers: Gather together first the tares and bind them in bundles to burn them, but gather the wheat into my barn.

31 Another parable He put forth to them
saying: The kingdom of heaven is like a
grain of mustard seed that a man sowed
in his field.
32 Indeed *it* is the least of all seeds, but
when it is grown, it is the greatest
among herbs and becomes a tree so that
the birds of the air come and lodge in its
branches. *Psalm 104:12*
33 *Then* He spoke another parable to
them: The kingdom of heaven is like
leaven that a woman hid in three
measures of meal until the whole was
permeated+.
34 All these things Jesus spoke to the
multitude in parables and without a
parable He did not speak to them.
35 This fulfilled what the prophet had
said: I will open my mouth in parables.
I will utter things that have been kept
secret from the foundation of the world.
Psalm 78:2
36 Then Jesus sent the multitude away
and went into the house, and His
disciples came to Him saying: Declare
to us the parable of the tares of the field.
37 He answered and said to them: He
who sows the good seed is the Son of
man.
38 The field is the world and the good
seed are the children of the kingdom.
But the tares are the children of the
wicked *one*.
39 The enemy that sowed them is the
devil. The harvest is the end of the
world and the reapers are the angels.
40 Therefore as the tares are gathered
and burned in the fire, so shall it be in
the end of this world.
41 The Son of man will send forth His
angels and they will gather out of His
kingdom all things that offend *and
cause people to sin* and *all those* who do
iniquity *Zephaniah 1:3*
42 and cast them into a furnace of fire and
there will be wailing and gnashing of
teeth.
43 Then the righteous will shine forth as
the sun in the kingdom of their Father.
Who has ears to hear, let them hear.
Daniel 12:3
44 Again, the kingdom of heaven is like
treasure hid in a field. When someone+
has found *it*, they hide *it* and with *great*
joy go and sell all that they have and buy
that field.
45 Again, the kingdom of heaven is like
a merchant seeking fine+ pearls.
46 When he found one pearl of great
price, *he* sold all that he had and
bought it.
47 Again, the kingdom of heaven is like
a net that was cast into the sea and
gathered of every kind.
48 When it was full, they drew *it* to shore
and sat down and gathered the good into
vessels but cast the bad away.
49 So shall it be at the end of the world.
The angels will come forth and sever the
wicked from among the righteous+
50 and *they* will cast *the wicked* into the
furnace of fire and there will be wailing
and gnashing of teeth.
51 Jesus said to them: Have you understood all these things? They said to Him:
Yes Lord.
52 Then He said to them: Therefore every scribe *who is* instructed about the
kingdom of heaven is like a property
owner+ who brings forth out of his
treasure *things* new and old.
53 And it came to pass when Jesus had
finished these parables He departed from
there.+
54 And when He had come into His
own country, He taught them in their
synagogue so that they were astonished
and said: From where has this *man
acquired* this wisdom and *these* mighty
works?
55 Is this not the carpenter's son? Is not
His mother called Mary and His brothers
James, Joses, Simon, and Jude?
56 And His sisters, are they not all with
us? From where then has this *man
acquired* all these things?
57 They were offended by Him *and disbe-
lieved*, but Jesus said to them: A prophet
is not without honor, save in his own
country and in his own house.
58 *Therefore* He did not *do* many mighty
works there because of their unbelief.

Matthew Chapter 14

1 At that time, Herod the tetrarch heard
of the reputation+ of Jesus
2 and*he* said to his servants: This is John
the Baptist. He is risen from the dead
and therefore mighty works *are shown* at
work by him.
3 For Herod had seized+ John and bound
him and put *him* in prison for the sake of
Herodias, his brother Philip's wife *whom
Herod stole and married*.
4 For John *had* said to him: It is not
lawful for you to have her.
5 And when *Herod* would have put *John*
to death, *he did not because* he feared the
multitude because they counted *John* as
a prophet.
6 But *then* when Herod's birthday was
kept, the daughter of Herodias danced
before them and pleased Herod.
7 Therefore he promised with an oath to
give her whatever she would ask.
8 And she, having been instructed by
her mother, said: Give me here John the
Baptist's head on a platter.+
9 The king was sorry, nevertheless because
of his oath and *those* who sat with him to
eat,+ he commanded *it* to be given *to her*
10 and he sent and beheaded John in the
prison
11 and *John's* head was brought on a
platter+ and given to the girl+ and she
gave+ *it* to her mother.
12 *Then John's* disciples came and took
away the body and buried it and *then*
went and told Jesus.
13 When Jesus heard *about it*, He departed
from there+ by boat to a deserted+ place
apart. When the people heard *about this*,
they followed Him on foot out of the cities.
14 Jesus went forth and saw a great multitude and was moved with compassion
toward them and He healed their sick.
15 When it was evening, His disciples
came to Him saying: This is a deserted+
place and the time is now past. Send
the multitude away *so* that they may
go into the villages and buy food+ *for*
themselves.
16 But Jesus said to them: They do not need
to go away.+ You give them *food* to eat.
17 They said to Him: We have here only+
five loaves and two fish.
18 He said: Bring them here to me.
19 *Then* He commanded the multitude to
sit down on the grass and *He* took the
five loaves and the two fish and looking
up to heaven, He blessed and broke *them*
and gave the loaves to *His* disciples and
the disciples to the multitude.
20 They all ate and were filled and of the
fragments that remained they took up
twelve baskets full.
21 *Those* who had eaten were about five
thousand men plus+ women and children.
22 Immediately+ *after that* Jesus directed+
His disciples to get into a boat and go
ahead+ of Him to the other side while
He sent the multitudes away.
23 And when He had sent the multitudes
away, He went up into a mountain apart
to pray and when the evening had come
He was there alone.
24 But the boat was now in the midst of
the sea *and* tossed with waves, for the
wind was contrary.
25 *Then* in the fourth watch of the night
sometime after three o'clock in the morning
Jesus went to them, walking on the sea.
26 When the disciples saw Him walking
on the sea, they were troubled and said:
It is a spirit, and they cried out for fear.
27 But immediately+ Jesus spoke to them
saying:

> Be of good cheer.
> I am+ *with you*.
> Do not be afraid.

28 Peter answered Him and said: Lord, if
it is you, bid me come to you on the water.
29 *Jesus* said: Come. And when Peter had
come down out of the boat, he walked
on the water to go to Jesus.
30 But when he saw the wind boisterous
he was afraid and beginning to sink he
cried *out* saying: Lord save me.
31 Immediately, Jesus stretched forth *His*
hand, caught him, and said to him: O
you of little faith. Why did you doubt?

32 When they entered[+] the boat, the wind stopped.

33 Then *those* who were in the boat came and worshiped Him saying: Truly, you are the Son of God.

34 When they had crossed[+] over *the sea*, they came to the land of Gennesaret.

35 When the people[+] of that place recognized[+] Him, they sent *word* all around[+] that country and brought to Him all who were diseased.

36 *They* begged[+] Him that they might only touch the hem of His garment, and all[+] *who* touched *Him* were made perfectly whole.

Matthew Chapter 15

1 Then scribes and Pharisees from Jerusalem came to Jesus saying:

2 Why do your disciples transgress the tradition of the elders? For they do not wash their hands when they eat bread.

3 But He answered and said to them: Why do you also transgress the commandment of God by your tradition?

4 For God commanded saying: Honor your father and mother. And: Anyone who curses father or mother, let them die the death. *Exodus 20:12, Exodus 21:17*

5 But you say: Whoever says to *their* father or mother: *It is* a gift, by whatever you might be profited by me;

6 and does not honor their father or their mother, *they shall be free*. Thus you have made the commandment of God of no effect by your tradition.

7 *You* hypocrites. Well did Isaiah prophesy of you saying:

8 These people draw near to me with their mouths and honor me with *their* lips but their hearts are far from me. *Isaiah 29:13*

9 However, *it is* in vain *that* they worship me, teaching *as* doctrines the commandments of men. *Isaiah 29:13*

10 *Then* He called the multitude and said to them: Hear and understand.

11 *It is* not what goes into the mouth *that* defiles, but what comes out of the mouth that defiles.

12 Then His disciples came and said to Him: Do you know that the Pharisees were offended after they heard this saying?

13 But He answered and said: Every plant that my heavenly Father has not planted will be rooted up. *Proverbs 2:22*

14 Let them alone. They are blind leaders of the blind, and if the blind lead the blind both will fall into the ditch.

15 Then Peter answered and said to Him: Declare to us this parable.

16 Jesus said: Are you also yet without understanding?

17 Do you not yet understand that whatever enters in at the mouth goes into the belly and is then purged[+]?

18 But the *words* spoken[+] by the mouth come from the heart and they defile a person[+].

19 For out of the heart proceed evil thoughts, murders, adulteries, fornications, thefts, false witness, *and* blasphemies.

20 These are *the things* that defile a person,[+] but to eat with unwashed hands does not defile a person[+].

21 Then Jesus went from there[+] to the borders[+] of Tyre and Sidon.

22 And behold a woman of Canaan came out of the same borders[+] and cried *out* to Him saying: Have mercy on me O Lord, son of David. My daughter is grievously oppressed[+] with a demon[+].

23 But He answered her not a word, and His disciples came and begged[+] Him saying: Send her away for she cries *out* after us.

24 But He answered and said: I was not sent but to the lost sheep of the house of Israel.

25 Then she came and worshiped Him saying: Lord help me.

26 But He answered and said: It is not good[+] to take the children's bread and cast *it* to dogs.

27 And she said: True Lord, yet the dogs eat of the crumbs that fall from their masters' table.

28 Then Jesus answered and said to her: O woman, great *is* your faith. Be it to

you even as you will. And her daughter
was made whole from that very hour.
29 Jesus *then* departed from there,[+] came
near the sea of Galilee, and went up into
a mountain and sat down there.
30 Great multitudes came to Him, having
with them *those who were* lame, blind,
speechless,[+] maimed, and many others,
and cast them down at Jesus' feet and He
healed them; *Isaiah 35:5*
31 so that the multitude wondered when
they saw the speechless[+] to speak, the
maimed to be whole, the lame to walk,
and the blind to see and they glorified
the God of Israel. *Isaiah 35:5*
32 Then Jesus called His disciples and
said: I have compassion on the multitude because they have continued with
me now three days and have nothing to
eat. I will not send them away fasting
lest they faint on the way.
33 His disciples said to Him: From where
should we get[+] *so much* bread in the wilderness as to fill so great a multitude?
34 Jesus said to them: How many loaves
do you have? They said: Seven and a
few little fish.
35 *Then Jesus* commanded the multitude
to sit down on the ground
36 and He took the seven loaves and the
fish and gave thanks and broke *them* and
gave to His disciples and the disciples
gave to the multitude.
37 They all ate and were filled and they
took up, of the broken *pieces* that were
left, seven baskets full.
38 *Those* who ate were four thousand men
plus[+] women and children.
39 *Then Jesus* sent away the multitude and
took a boat into the borders[+] of Magdala.

Matthew Chapter 16

1 The Pharisees and Sadducees came
testing[+] *and* asked Him if He would
show them a sign from heaven.
2 He answered and said to them: When
it is evening, you say: *It will be* fair
weather for the sky is red.
3 And in the morning: *It will be* foul
weather today for the sky is red and
threatening.[+] O *you* hypocrites. You
can discern the face of the sky, but can
you not *discern* the signs of the times?
4 A wicked and adulterous generation
seeks after a sign, *but* no sign will be
given to it except[+] the sign of the
prophet Jonah. And He left them and
departed.
5 When His disciples had come to the other
side, they had forgotten to take bread.
6 Then Jesus said to them: Take heed
and beware of the leaven of the Pharisees
and of the Sadducees.
7 They reasoned among themselves
saying: *It is* because we have taken no
bread.
8 When Jesus perceived *their thoughts*
He said to them: O you of little faith.
Why do you reason among yourselves
saying it is because you have brought no
bread?
9 Do you not yet understand or remember the five loaves of the five thousand
and how many baskets you took up?
10 Nor the seven loaves of the four
thousand and how many baskets you
took up?
11 How is it that you do not understand
that I did not speak to you concerning
bread *but so* that you should beware of
the leaven of the Pharisees and of the
Sadducees?
12 Then they understood that He did not
tell *them to* beware of the leaven of bread
but of the doctrine of the Pharisees and
of the Sadducees.
13 When Jesus came into the borders[+] of
Caesarea Philippi, He asked His disciples saying: Who do men say that I the
Son of man am?
14 They said: Some *say that you are* John
the Baptist, some *say* Elijah, *and* others
say Jeremiah[+] or one of the prophets.
15 He said to them: But who do you say
that I am?
16 Simon Peter answered and said: You
are the Christ, the Son of the living God.
17 Jesus answered and said to him: Blessed
are you Simon Barjona for flesh and
blood have not revealed *this* to you, but
my Father in heaven.

18 I say also to you that you are *now* Peter
and upon this rock I will build my
church and the gates of hell will not
prevail against it.
19 I will give to you the keys of the
kingdom of heaven. Whatever you bind
on earth will be *already* bound in heaven
and whatever you loose on earth will be
already loosed in heaven.
20 Then He charged His disciples that
they should tell no one that He was Jesus
the Christ.
21 From that time forth Jesus began to
show His disciples that He must go to
Jerusalem and suffer many things by
the elders, chief priests, and scribes
and be killed and be raised again the
third day.
22 Then Peter took Him *aside* and began
to rebuke Him saying: Far be it from
you, Lord. This shall not be to you.
23 But *Jesus* turned and said to Peter:
Get behind me Satan. You are an
offense to me for you do not savor the
things that are of God, but those that
are of men.
24 Then Jesus said to His disciples:

If anyone[+] will come after me,
let them deny themselves
and take up their cross
and follow me.

25 For whoever would[+] save their life
will lose it and whoever would[+] lose
their life for my sake will find it.
Proverbs 13:7
26 For what is anyone to profit if they
gain the whole world and lose their own
soul? Or what shall anyone give in
exchange for their soul?
27 For the Son of man will come in the
glory of His Father *and* with His
angels, and then He will reward everyone[+] according to their deeds[+].
Jeremiah 17:10
28 Truly[+] I say to you: There are some
standing here who will not taste of death
until they see the Son of man coming in
His kingdom.

Matthew Chapter 17

1 After six days, Jesus took Peter, James,
and John his brother up to a high
mountain apart
2 and *He* was transfigured *right there* before
them. His face did shine like[+] the sun and
His clothing[+] was *as* white as the light.
3 And behold there appeared to them
Moses and Elijah talking with Him.
4 Then Peter answered and said to Jesus:
Lord, it is good for us to be here. If
you will, let us make three tabernacles
here. One for you, one for Moses, *and*
one for Elijah.
5 While he spoke, behold a bright cloud
overshadowed them and behold a voice
out of the cloud said: This is my
beloved Son in whom I am well
pleased. Hear Him. *Psalm 2:7*
6 When the disciples heard *this* they fell
on their faces and were greatly[+] afraid.
7 Jesus came and touched them and
said: Arise and do not be afraid.
8 When they lifted up their eyes, they
saw no one except[+] Jesus.
9 *Then* as they came down from the
mountain, Jesus charged them saying:
Tell the vision to no one until the Son of
man is risen from the dead.
10 His disciples asked Him saying: Why
then do the scribes say that Elijah
must come first?
11 Jesus answered and said to them:
Elijah truly will come first and restore
all things. *Malachi 4:6*
12 But I say to you that Elijah has already
come and they did not know him, but
have done to him whatever they desired.[+] Likewise will the Son of man
also suffer by them. *Malachi 4:5*
13 Then the disciples understood that He
spoke to them of John the Baptist.
14 When they had come to the multitude,
a *certain* man came to Him, kneeling
down to Him and saying:
15 Lord have mercy on my son for he is
a lunatic and greatly[+] oppressed,[+] for
often times he falls into the fire and
often into the water.

16 I brought him to your disciples and they could not cure him.

17 Then Jesus answered and said: O faithless and perverse generation. How long shall I be with you? How long shall I endure[+] you? Bring him here to me.

18 Jesus rebuked the demon[+] and he departed out of him and the child was cured from that very hour.

19 Then the disciples came to Jesus privately[+] and said: Why could we not cast him out?

20 Jesus said to them: *It was* because of your unbelief. For truly[+] I say to you: If you have faith as a grain of mustard seed, you shall say to this mountain: Move from here to there[+] and it will move. Nothing will be impossible to you.

21 However this kind does not go out but by prayer and fasting.

22 While they abode in Galilee Jesus said to them: The Son of man will be betrayed into the hands of men.

23 They will kill Him and the third day He will be raised again. And they were exceedingly sorry.

24 When they had come to Capernaum, *those* who received tribute *money* came to Peter and said: Does your master not pay tribute?

25 He said: Yes. And when he had come into the house, Jesus preceded[+] him saying: What do you think, Simon? From[+] whom do the kings of the earth take custom or tribute? From[+] their own children or from[+] strangers?

26 Peter said to Him: From[+] strangers. Jesus said to him: Then the children are free.

27 Nevertheless, lest we should offend them, go to the sea, throw[+] *in* a hook, and take up the first fish that comes up. When you have opened its mouth you will find a piece of money. Take that and give it to them for me and *for* you.

Matthew Chapter 18

1 At the same time the disciples came to Jesus saying: Who is the greatest in the kingdom of heaven?

2 Jesus called a little child to Himself and sat him *down* in the midst of them

3 and said: Truly[+] I say to you: Unless[+] you be converted and become as little children, you will not enter into the kingdom of heaven.

4 Whoever therefore will humble themselves as this little child, the same is greatest in the kingdom of heaven.

5 Whoever will receive one such little child in my name receives me.

6 But whoever offends *and sins against* one of these little ones who believe in me, it would be better for them if[+] a millstone were hung around[+] their neck and *if* they were drowned in the depth of the sea.

7 Woe to the world because of offenses. For it must be that offenses come, but woe to those through whom the offenses come.

8 Therefore if your hand or your foot causes[+] you *to sin*, cut them off and cast *them* from you. It is better for you to enter into life crippled[+] or maimed rather than having two hands or two feet to be cast into everlasting fire.

9 If your eye causes[+] you *to sin*, pluck it out and cast *it* from you. It is better for you to enter into life with one eye rather than having two eyes to be cast into hell fire.

10 Take heed that you do not despise one of these little ones. For I say to you: In heaven their angels do always behold the face of my Father in heaven.

11 For the Son of man has come to save *those* who were lost.

12 What do you think? If a man had a hundred sheep and one of them was gone astray, would he not leave the ninety nine and go into the mountains and seek what is gone astray?

13 And if he finds it, truly[+] I say to you: He rejoices more over that *one* than over[+] the ninety nine that did not go astray.

14 Even so, it is not the will of your Father in heaven that one of these little ones should perish.

15 If *one of* your family[+] sins[+] against you, go and warn[+] them *about their error* between you and them alone. If *they* will hear you, *then* you *will* have rescued[+] your family[+] *member*.

16 But if they will not hear, *then* take with you one or two more *so* that by the mouth of two or three witnesses every word may be established. *Deuteronomy 19:15*

17 And if they will neglect to hear them, *then* tell *it* to the church. But if they neglect to hear the church *then* let them be to you as a heathen and a worldly+ person.

18 Truly+ I say to you: Whatever you bind on earth will *already* be bound in heaven and whatever you loose on earth will *already* be loosed in heaven.

19 Again I say to you: If two of you agree on earth as touching anything that they ask, it will be done for them by my Father in heaven.

20 For where two or three are gathered together in my name, there I am in the midst of them.

21 Then Peter came to Him and said: Lord, how often shall my brother sin against me and I forgive him? Until seven times?

22 Jesus said to him: I do not say to you until seven times but until seventy times seven.

23 The kingdom of heaven *may be* compared+ to a certain king who wanted to take account of his servants.

24 When he had begun the review,+ one was brought to him who owed him ten thousand talents.

25 But since+ he had nothing *with which* to pay, his lord commanded him to be sold and his wife and children and all that he had, and payment to be made.

26 The servant therefore fell down and worshiped him saying: Lord have patience with me and I will pay you all.

27 Then the lord of that servant was moved with compassion and released+ him and forgave him the debt.

28 But the same servant went out and found one of his fellow servants who owed him *four months wages*+ and he laid hands on him and took *him* by the throat saying: Pay me what you owe.

29 His fellow servant fell down at his feet and begged+ Him saying: Have patience with me and I will pay you all.

30 He would not, but went and cast him into prison until he should pay the debt.

31 So when his fellow servants saw what was done, they were very sorry and came and told their lord all that was done.

32 Then his lord, after he had called him, said to him: O you wicked servant. I forgave you all that debt because you begged+ me.

33 Should you not also have had compassion on your fellow servant even as I had pity on you?

34 And his lord was angry+ and delivered him to the torturers+ until he should pay all that was due to him.

35 So likewise will my heavenly Father do also to you if you do not, from your hearts, forgive everyone *of the* family+ *of God for* their trespasses.

Matthew Chapter 19

1 It came to pass *that* when Jesus had finished these sayings He departed from Galilee and came into the borders+ of Judea beyond Jordan.

2 Great multitudes followed Him and He healed them there.

3 The Pharisees also came to Him, testing+ Him and saying to Him: Is it lawful for a man to put away his wife for every cause?

4 He answered and said to them: Have you not read that

He who made *them*
at the beginning
made them male and female
Genesis 1:27

5 and said: For this reason+
a man shall leave father
and mother and cleave to his wife
and they two shall be one flesh.
Genesis 2:24

6 Therefore they are
no longer+ two, but one flesh.
Therefore
what God has joined *together*,
mankind+ *must* not separate+.

7 They said to Him: Why then did Moses command to give a written divorce+ and to put her away? *Deuteronomy 24:1*
8 He said to them: Because of the hardness of your hearts Moses allowed+ you to put away your wives. But from the beginning it was not *to be* so.
9 I say to you: Whoever shall put away his wife, except *it be* for fornication, and shall marry another commits adultery. And whoever marries *one who* is *thus* put away commits adultery. *Matthew 5:32*
10 His disciples said to Him: If the case of the man be so with *his* wife it is not good to marry.
11 But *Jesus* said to them: All *people* cannot receive this saying, *but* only+ *those* to whom it is given.
12 For there are some eunuchs who were so born from *their* mother's womb. There are some eunuchs who were made eunuchs by men. There are eunuchs who have made themselves eunuchs for the kingdom of heaven's sake. *Those* who are able to receive *this*, let them receive *it*.
13 Then *some* little children there were brought to Him *so* that He *might* lay *His* hands on them and pray, but the disciples rebuked them.
14 But Jesus said: Allow *the* little children and do not forbid them to come to me. For of such is the kingdom of heaven.
15 He laid *His* hands on them; and *then* departed from there.+
16 Behold one came and said to Him: Good Master what good thing shall I do *so* that I may have eternal life?
17 *Jesus* said to him: Why do you call me good? *There is* none good but one *who is* God. But

> if you will enter into life,
> keep the commandments.
> *Leviticus 18:5*

18 *The man* said to Him: Which? Jesus said: You shall do no murder. You shall not commit adultery. You shall not steal. You shall not bear false witness. *Exodus 20:13,14,15,16*
19 Honor your father and *your* mother. And, you shall love your neighbor as yourself. *Exodus 20:12, Leviticus 19:18*
20 The young man said to Him: All these things have I kept from my youth up. What do I yet lack?
21 Jesus said to him: If you will be perfect, go *and* sell your possessions+ and give to the poor and you will have treasure in heaven, and come *and* follow me.
22 But when the young man heard that saying, he went away sorrowful for he had great possessions.
23 Then Jesus said to His disciples: Truly+ I say to you that a rich person+ shall hardly *be able to* enter into the kingdom of heaven. *Proverbs 11:28*
24 Again I say to you: It is easier for a camel to go through the eye of a needle than for a rich person+ to enter into the kingdom of God.
25 When His disciples heard *this* they were exceedingly amazed saying: Who then can be saved?
26 But Jesus looked+ at *them and* said to them: With people+ this is impossible, but

> with God
> all things are possible.
> *Jeremiah 32:17*

27 Then Peter answered and said to Him: Behold we have forsaken all and followed you. What shall we have therefore?
28 Jesus said to them: Truly+ I say to you that you who have followed me, in the regeneration when the Son of man shall sit on the throne of His glory, you also shall sit upon twelve thrones judging the twelve tribes of Israel.
29 Everyone who has forsaken houses or brothers or sisters or father or mother or wife or children or lands for my name's sake shall receive a hundredfold and shall inherit eternal+ life.
30 But many *who are* first will be last and the last *will be* first.

Matthew Chapter 20

1 The kingdom of heaven is like a
property owner+ who went out early
in the morning to hire laborers into
his vineyard.
2 When he had agreed with the laborers
for a day's wages+ he sent them into
his vineyard.
3 *Then* he went out about the third hour,
about nine o'clock+ in the morning
and saw others standing idle in the
marketplace
4 and said to them: Go also into the
vineyard and whatever is right I will
give you. And they went.
5 Again he went out about the sixth and
ninth hour and did likewise.
6 And about the eleventh hour he went
out and found others standing idle and
said to them: Why do you stand here all
the day idle?
7 They said to him: Because no one has
hired us. He said to them: Go also into
the vineyard and whatever is right you
will receive.
8 So when evening+ had come, the lord
of the vineyard said to his steward: Call
the laborers and give them *their* wages+
beginning from the last to the first.
9 When they who *were hired* about the
eleventh hour came, everyone+ received
a day's wages+.
10 But when the first came, they supposed
that they should have received more, but
they each+ also+ received a day's wages+.
11 When they had received *it*, they com-
plained+ against the head+ of the house
12 saying: These last have worked+ *but*
one hour and you have made them equal
to us who have borne the burden and
heat of the day.
13 But he answered one of them and said:
Friend I do you no wrong. Did you not
agree with me for a day's wages+.
14 Take *what is* yours and go. + I will give
to this last even as to you.
15 Is it not lawful for me to do what I will
with my own? Is your eye evil because
I am good?
16 So the last shall be first and the first last,
for many are called but few chosen.
17 *Then* Jesus went+ up to Jerusalem *and*
He took the twelve disciples aside+ on
the way and said to them:
18 Behold we are *now* going up to
Jerusalem *where* the Son of man will
be betrayed to the chief priests and to
the scribes and they will condemn
Him to death. *Psalm 22, Isaiah 53*
19 *They* will deliver Him to the Gentiles
to mock and to flog+ and to crucify *Him*,
and the third day He will rise again.
20 Then the mother of Zebedee's children
with her sons came to Him worshiping
Him and desiring a certain thing of Him.
21 He said to her: What will you *have*? She
said to Him: Grant that these my two
sons may sit, the one on your right hand
and the other on the left, in your kingdom.
22 But Jesus answered and said: You do
not know what you ask. Are you able to
drink of the cup of which I shall drink
and be baptized with the baptism with
which I shall be baptized? They said to
Him: We are able.
23 He said to them: You shall indeed
drink of my cup and be baptized with
the baptism with which I shall be
baptized, but to sit at my right hand
and at my left is not mine to give, but
it shall be given to them for whom it is
prepared by my Father.
24 When the ten heard *this* they were
moved with indignation against the
two brothers.
25 But Jesus called them *to Himself* and
said: You know that the princes of the
Gentiles exercise dominion over them
and *those* who are great exercise authority
upon them.
26 But it shall not be that way+ among
you. But whoever will be great among
you, let them be your servant+.
27 Whoever will be chief among you, let
them be your servant.
28 Even as the Son of man did not come
to be ministered to, but to minister and
to give His life a ransom for many.
29 As they departed from Jericho, a great
multitude followed Him.

30 And behold two blind men sitting by
the wayside, when they heard that Jesus
passed by, cried out saying: Have mercy
on us, O Lord, son of David.
31 The multitude rebuked them *saying*
that they should be silent.+ But they
cried *out all* the more saying: Have
mercy on us, O Lord, son of David.
32 Jesus stood still and called them and
said: What do you want me to do to you?
33 They said to Him: Lord that our eyes
may be opened.
34 So Jesus had compassion *on them*
and touched their eyes and immediately
their eyes received sight and they
followed Him.

Matthew Chapter 21

1 When they drew near to Jerusalem
and had come to Bethphage to the Mount
of Olives, then Jesus sent two disciples
2 saying to them: Go into the village
before+ you and immediately+ you will
find a donkey+ tied and a colt with her.
Loose *it* and bring *it* to me.
3 If anyone+ says anything+ to you, you
shall say: The Lord has need of them,
and immediately+ they will send them.
4 All this was done to fulfill what was
spoken by the prophet *who* said:
5 Tell the daughter of Zion+: Behold
your King comes to you meek and
sitting upon a donkey+ and a colt, the
foal of a donkey. *Isaiah 62:11, Zechariah 9:9*
6 The disciples did as Jesus commanded
them.
7 *They* brought the donkey+ and the colt
and put their clothes on them and *Jesus*
sat *on the colt*.
8 A very great multitude spread their
garments along+ the way. Others cut
down branches from the trees and
spread+ *them* along+ the way.
9 The multitudes who went before and
those who followed cried *out* saying:
Hosanna to the son of David. Blessed *is*
He who comes in the name of the Lord.
Hosanna in the highest. *Psalm 118:26*
10 When He had come into Jerusalem, all
the city was moved saying: Who is this?
11 The multitude said: This is Jesus the
prophet of Nazareth of Galilee.
12 *Then* Jesus went into the temple of God
and cast out all *those* who bought and
sold in the temple and *He* overthrew the
tables of the money changers and the
seats of *those* who sold doves
13 and said to them: It is written: My
house shall be called the house of prayer,
but you have made it a den of thieves.
Isaiah 56:7, Jeremiah 7:11
14 The blind and the lame came to Him in
the temple and He healed them. *Isaiah 35:5*
15 When the chief priests and scribes saw
the wonderful things that He did and the
children crying in the temple and saying: Hosanna to the son of David, they
were greatly+ displeased.
16 *They* said to Him: Hear what these
people+ say? Jesus said to them: Yes.
Have you never read: Out of the mouth
of babes and nursing infants+ you have
perfected praise? *Psalm 8:2*
17 *Then* He left them and went out of the
city to Bethany and He lodged there.
18 Now in the morning as He returned to
the city He was hungry.
19 When He saw a fig tree on the way, He
came to it and found nothing on it
except+ leaves and said to it: Let no fruit
grow on you henceforth forever. And
immediately+ the fig tree withered away.
20 When the disciples saw *this*, they marveled saying: How soon the fig tree has
withered away.
21 Jesus answered and said to them:
Truly+ I say to you:

If you have faith
and do not doubt,
you will not only do this
to the fig tree, but also
if you say to this mountain:
Be removed and be cast
into the sea, it will be done.

22 All things whatsoever
you ask in prayer believing,
you will receive.

23 When He had come into the temple, the chief priests and the elders of the people came to Him as He was teaching and said: By what authority do you *do* these things? And who gave you this authority?

24 Jesus answered and said to them: I will also ask you one thing. If you tell me, I in like wise will tell you by what authority I do these things.

25 The baptism of John, from where was it *authorized*? From heaven, or from[+] men? They reasoned with themselves saying: If we say: From heaven, He will say to us: Why did you not then believe him?

26 But if we say: From men, we fear the people for all hold John as a prophet.

27 They answered Jesus and said: We cannot tell. And He said to them: *Then* neither will I tell you by what authority I do these things.

28 But what do you think *of this*? A *certain* man had two sons. He came to the first and said: Son, go work today in my vineyard.

29 *The son* answered and said: I will not, but afterward he repented and went.

30 He came to the second and said likewise. And *the second son* answered and said: I *will go* sir, *but he* did not go.

31 *Now* which of them did the will of *his* father? They said to Him: The first. Jesus said to them: Truly[+] I say to you that the worldly[+] people and harlots *will* go into the kingdom of God before you.

32 For John came to you in the way of righteousness and you did not believe him, but the worldly[+] people and the harlots believed him. You, when you had seen *it*, did not repent afterward *so* that you might believe him.

33 *Now* hear another parable: There was a certain property owner[+] who planted a vineyard and built a fence[+] around it, dug a wine press in it, built a tower, let it out to *tenant* farmers,[+] and went into a far country. *Isaiah 5:2*

34 When the time of the fruit drew near, he sent his servants to the *tenant* farmers[+] *so* that they might receive the fruits of it.

35 *But* the *tenant* farmers[+] took his servants, beat one, killed another, and stoned another.

36 Again, he sent other servants more than the first and they did to them likewise.

37 But last of all he sent his son to them saying: *Surely* they will reverence my son.

38 But when the *tenant* farmers[+] saw the son, they said among themselves: This is the heir. Come, let us kill him and let us seize his inheritance.

39 *So* they caught him and cast *him* out of the vineyard and killed[+] *him*.

40 *Now then* when the lord of the vineyard comes, what will he do to those *tenant* farmers[+]?

41 They said to Him: He will miserably destroy those wicked men and will lease[+] *his* vineyard to other *tenant* farmers[+] who will render *to* him the fruits in their seasons.

42 Jesus said to them: Did you never read in the Scriptures: The stone that the builders rejected has become the head of the corner. This is the Lord's doing and it is marvelous in our eyes. *Psalm 118:22*

43 Therefore I say to you: The kingdom of God will be taken from you and given to a nation bringing forth the fruits thereof.

44 Whoever falls on this stone will be broken. But on whomever it falls, it will grind them to powder.

45 When the chief priests and Pharisees had heard His parables, they perceived that He spoke of them.

46 But when they sought to lay hands on Him, they feared the multitude because they took Him for a prophet.

Matthew Chapter 22

1 *Now* Jesus answered and spoke to them again by parables and said:

2 The kingdom of heaven is like a certain king who made a marriage for his son.

3 *He* sent forth his servants to call *those* who were invited[+] to the wedding *but* they would not come.

4 Again, he sent forth more[+] servants
saying: Tell *those* who are invited[+]:
Behold I have prepared my dinner.
My oxen and *my* fatted calves[+] *are*
killed and all things *are* ready. Come
to the marriage.
5 But they made light of *it* and went their
separate ways: one to his farm, another
to his merchandise.
6 The rest[+] took his servants, treated
them spitefully, and killed[+] *them*.
7 When the king heard *about this*, he was
angry.[+] He sent forth his armies and
destroyed those murderers and burned
up their city.
8 Then he said to his servants: The
wedding is ready but *those* who were
invited[+] were not worthy.
9 Go therefore into the highways and
invite[+] everyone[+] you find to the
marriage.
10 So those servants went out into the
highways and gathered together everyone,[+] as many as they *could* find[+] both
good and bad, and the wedding was
furnished with guests.
11 *Now* when the king came in to see the
guests, he saw there a man who did not
have on a wedding garment.
12 He said to him: Friend, how did you
come in here not having a wedding
garment? And he was speechless.
13 Then the king said to the servants:
Bind him hand and foot and take him
away and cast *him* into outer darkness
and there will be weeping and gnashing
of teeth.
14 For many are called but few *are* chosen.
15 Then the Pharisees left[+] and took
counsel how they might entangle Him in
His talk.
16 They sent their disciples with the
Herodians out to Him saying: Master,
we know that you are true and teach the
way of God in truth. Nor do you *take*
special care for any *one person over*
another, for you do not regard the positions[+] people[+] *hold*.
17 Tell us therefore: What do you think?
Is it lawful to give tribute to Caesar or
not?
18 But Jesus perceived their wickedness
and said: Why do you test[+] me *you*
hypocrites?
19 Show me the tribute money. They
brought a coin[+] to Him.
20 He said to them: Whose image and
title[+] *is* this?
21 They said to Him: Caesar's. Then
He said to them: Render therefore to
Caesar the things that are Caesar's
and to God the things that are God's.
22 When they had heard *these words*, they
marveled and left Him and went away.[+]
23 The same day, the Sadducees who say
that there is no resurrection came to
Him and asked Him
24 saying: Master, Moses said if a man
die having no children, *then* his brother
shall marry his wife and raise up seed to
his brother. *Deuteronomy 25:5*
25 Now there were with us seven brothers and the first, when he had married a
wife, died[+] and having no issue, left his
wife to his brother.
26 Likewise the second also and the third
to the seventh.
27 Last of all the woman died also.
28 Therefore in the resurrection, of the
seven, whose wife will she be? For they
all had her.
29 Jesus answered and said to them:

> You err
> *by* not knowing the Scriptures
> or the power of God.

30 For in the resurrection they neither
marry nor are given in marriage but are
as the angels of God in heaven.
31 But as touching the resurrection of the
dead, have you not read what was
spoken to you by God saying:
32 I am the God of Abraham and the God
of Isaac and the God of Jacob. God is not
the God of the dead but of the living.
Exodus 3:6
33 When the multitude heard *this*, they
were astonished at His doctrine.
34 But when the Pharisees had heard that
He had put the Sadducees to silence,
they were gathered together.

35 Then one of them *who was* a lawyer asked
Him a question, testing[+] Him and saying:
36 Master, which *is* the great commandment in the law?
37 Jesus said to him:

> You shall love the Lord
> your God with all your heart
> and with all your soul
> and with all your mind.
> *Deuteronomy 6:5*
> 38 This is the first
> and great commandment.

> 39 The second *is* like it:
> You shall love your neighbor
> as yourself.
> *Matthew 19:19*

40 On these two commandments hang all
the law and the prophets.
41 While the Pharisees were gathered
together, Jesus asked them
42 saying: What do you think of Christ?
Whose son is He? They said to Him: *The
son* of David.
43 He said to them: How then does David
in spirit call Him Lord saying:
44 The Lord said to my Lord: Sit at my
right hand until I make your enemies
your footstool? *Psalm 110:1*
45 If David then called Him Lord, how is
He his son?
46 No one was able to answer Him a
word *and* from that day forth no one[+]
dared[+] ask Him any more *questions*.

Matthew Chapter 23

1 Then Jesus spoke to the multitude and
to His disciples
2 saying: The scribes and the Pharisees
sit in Moses' seat.
3 Therefore everything[+] whatsoever they
instruct[+] you *to* observe, observe and do
that, but do not follow[+] their works, for
they say and do not *do as they say*.
4 They bind heavy burdens grievous to
be borne and lay *them* on people's
shoulders, but they *themselves* will not
use one of their fingers *to* move with.
5 But they do all their works to be seen
by people.[+] They make broad their
phylacteries and enlarge the borders of
their garments. *Deuteronomy 6:8*
6 *They* love the uppermost rooms at feasts
and the chief seats in the synagogues
7 and greetings in the market*places* and
to be called Rabbi, Rabbi by people.[+]

> 8 Do not be called Rabbi.
> For one is your Master, Christ.
> All *of* you are family[+].
> 9 Do not call any[+] *man*
> your father on the earth,
> for one is your Father,
> who is in heaven.
> 10 Neither *should* you
> be called masters.
> For one is your Master, Christ.
> 11 But one who is greatest
> among you
> shall be your servant.
> 12 Whoever exalts themselves
> will be humbled[+] and
> *those* who humble themselves
> will be exalted.
> *Proverbs 25:6*

13 But woe to you scribes and Pharisees.
Hypocrites. For you shut up the kingdom
of heaven against men for you neither
go in*yourselves*, nor do you allow[+] *those*
who are entering to go in.
14 Woe to you scribes and Pharisees.
Hypocrites. For you devour widows'
houses and for a pretence make long
prayer. Therefore you will receive the
greater damnation.
15 Woe to you scribes and Pharisees.
Hypocrites. For you travel[+] sea and
land to make one convert[+] and when he
is made you make him twofold more the
child of hell than yourselves.
16 Woe to you blind guides who say:
Whoever swears by the temple, *that* is
nothing; but whoever swears by the
gold of the temple is a debtor.
17 *You* fools and blind. Which[+] is
greater, the gold, or the temple that
sanctifies the gold?

18 And *you say*: Whoever swears by the
altar, it is nothing but whoever swears
by the gift that is upon it, is guilty.
19 *You* fools and blind. Which+ *is* greater,
the gift or the altar that sanctifies the gift?
20 Whoever therefore swears by the altar,
swears by it and by all things upon it.
21 And whoever swears by the temple,
swears by it and by Him who dwells
therein.
22 Anyone+ who swears by heaven,
swears by the throne of God and by Him
who sits upon it.
23 Woe to you scribes and Pharisees.
Hypocrites. For you pay tithe of mint
and anise and cummin and have omitted the weightier *matters* of the law:
judgment, mercy, and faith. These
small things you ought to have done,
but not to leave the other undone.
24 *You* blind guides who strain at a gnat
and swallow a camel.
25 Woe to you scribes and Pharisees.
Hypocrites. For you make clean the
outside of the cup and of the platter
but within they are full of extortion
and excess.
26 *You* blind Pharisee. First clean the
inside+ of the cup and platter, and then
the outside of them may be clean also.
27 Woe to you scribes and Pharisees.
Hypocrites. For you are like white-
washed+ tombs+ that look+ beautiful *on
the* outside+ but *on the* inside+ are full of
dead *men's* bones and of all uncleanness.
28 Even so you also appear outwardly *to
be* righteous to people+ but inside+ you
are full of hypocrisy and iniquity.
29 Woe to you scribes and Pharisees.
Hypocrites. Because you build the tombs
of the prophets and decorate+ the tombs+
of the righteous
30 and say: If we had lived+ in the days
of our fathers, we would not have been
partakers with them in the blood of the
prophets.
31 Therefore you are witnesses to yourselves that you are the children of *those*
who killed the prophets.
32 Fill yourselves+ up, then, the measure
of your fathers.
33 *You* serpents. *You* generation of vipers.
How can you escape the damnation of
hell?
34 Therefore behold I send to you
prophets and wise men and scribes.
Some of them you will kill and crucify
and *some* of them you will flog+ in your
synagogues and persecute from city
to city.
35 *So* that upon you may come all the
righteous blood shed upon the earth
from the blood of righteous Abel to the
blood of Zechariah son of Berechiah
whom you killed+ between the temple
and the altar. *Genesis 4:8, 2 Chronicles 24:20,21*
36 Truly+ I say to you: All these things
will come upon this generation.
37 O Jerusalem, Jerusalem. *You* who kill
the prophets and stone *those* who are
sent to you. How often would I have
gathered your children together even as
a hen gathers her chicks+ under *her*
wings, but you would not *come*.
38 Behold your house is left to you desolate. *Jeremiah 22:5*
39 For I say to you: You will not see me
henceforth until you say: Blessed *is* He
who comes in the name of the Lord.
Psalm 118:26

Matthew Chapter 24

1 *Then* Jesus went out and departed from
the temple and His disciples came to
Him to show Him the buildings of the
temple.
2 Jesus said to them: Do you not see all
these things? Truly+ I say to you: There
will not be left here stone upon stone
that will not be thrown down.
3 As He sat upon the Mount of Olives,
the disciples came to Him privately
saying: Tell us. When will these things
be? And what *will be* the sign of your
coming and of the end of the world?
4 Jesus answered and said to them:

> Take heed
> *so* that no one deceives you.
> *Jeremiah 29:8*

5 For many will come in my name saying: I am Christ and will deceive many.
6 You will hear of wars and rumors of
wars. See that you are not troubled for
all *these things* must come to pass but the
end is not yet.
7 For nation will rise against nation
and kingdom against kingdom. There
will be famines and pestilences and
earthquakes in many different[+] places.
2 Chronicles 15:6, Isaiah 19:2
8 All these *are* the beginning of sorrows.
9 Then they will deliver you up to be
afflicted and *to* kill you. You will be
hated by all nations for my name's sake.
10 Then many will be offended *and fall*
from faith and will betray one another
and hate one another.
11 Many false prophets will arise and
deceive many.
12 Because iniquity will abound, the love
of many will grow[+] cold.
13 But *those* who endure to the end, the
same will be saved.
14 And this Gospel of the kingdom will be
proclaimed[+] in all the world for a witness
to all nations and then the end will come.
15 Therefore, let whoever reads *this*
understand: When you see the abomination of desolation spoken of by
Daniel the prophet stand in the holy
place *Daniel 11:31*
16 then let *those* who are in Judea flee into
the mountains.
17 Let one who is on the housetop not
come down to take anything out of their
house,
18 nor *those* who are in the field return
back to take their clothes.
19 Woe to *those* who are with child and to
those who are nursing[+] in those days.
20 But pray that your flight not be in the
winter or on the Sabbath day.
21 For then *there* will be great tribulation
such as has not *occurred* since the beginning of the world to this time. No, nor
ever shall be *again*. *Daniel 12:1*
22 Unless[+] those days should be shortened, there would no flesh be saved. But
for the sake of the elect those days will
be shortened.
23 Then if anyone says to you: Lo here *is*
Christ or there. Do not believe *it*.
24 For there will arise false Christs and
false prophets *who* will show great signs
and wonders so that, if *it were* possible,
they will deceive the very elect.
25 Behold I have told you before.
26 Therefore if they say to you: Behold
He is in the desert, do not go forth and
behold *He is* in the secret chambers, do
not believe *it*.
27 For as the lightning comes out of the
east and shines even to the west, so also
will the coming of the Son of man be.
28 For wherever the carcass is, there will
the eagles be gathered together.
29 Immediately after the tribulation of
those days, the sun will be darkened,
the moon will not give her light, the
stars will fall from heaven, and the
powers of the heavens will be shaken.
Isaiah 13:10, Joel 2:10
30 Then the sign of the Son of man will
appear in heaven and then all the tribes
of the earth will mourn and they will see
the Son of man coming in the clouds of
heaven with power and great glory.
Daniel 7:13
31 He will send His angels with a great
sound of a trumpet and they will gather
together His elect from the four winds,
from one end of heaven to the other.
Zechariah 9:14
32 Now learn a parable of[+] the fig tree.
When its branch is yet tender, and
puts forth leaves, you know that summer
is near.
33 So likewise you, when you see all these
things, know that it is near at the doors.
34 Truly[+] I say to you: This generation
will not pass until all these things are
fulfilled.

35 Heaven and earth
will pass away
but my words
will not pass away.

36 But of that day and hour no *one* knows.
No, not *even* the angels of heaven, but
only my Father.

37 But as the days of Noah *were*, so also
will the coming of the Son of man be.
Genesis 6:5
38 For in the days before the flood, they
were eating, drinking, marrying, and
giving in marriage until the day that
Noah entered the ark. *Genesis 7:7*
39 And *they* did not understand+ until the
flood came and took them all away. So
also will the coming of the Son of man be.
40 Then *as* two are in the field, one will
be taken and the other left.
41 *As* two *are* grinding at the mill, one
will be taken and the other left.
42 Watch, therefore, for you do not know
at what hour your Lord is coming+.
43 But know this: If the head+ of the
house had known in what watch the thief
would come, he would have watched
and would not have suffered his house to
be broken up.
44 Therefore be ready. For the Son of man
will come in an hour you do not expect+.
45 Who then is a faithful and wise servant
whom his lord has set+ over his household to give them food+ in due season?
46 Blessed *is* that servant whom his lord will
find doing *as instructed* when he comes.
47 Truly+ I say to you that he will set+
that servant over all his goods.
48 But if that evil servant says in his
heart: My lord delays his coming
49 and begins to strike+ *his* fellow servants
and to eat and drink with drunks,
50 the lord of that servant will come in a
day when he is not looking for *him* and
in an unknown+ hour.
51 and shall cut him in half+ and appoint
his portion with the hypocrites and there
will be weeping and gnashing of teeth.

Matthew Chapter 25

1 Then the kingdom of heaven shall
be compared+ to ten virgins who took
their lamps and went forth to meet the
bridegroom.
2 Five of them were wise and five *were*
foolish.
3 *Those* who *were* foolish took their
lamps and took no oil with them.
4 But the wise took oil in their vessels
with their lamps.
5 While the bridegroom tarried, they all
slumbered and slept.
6 At midnight there was a cry: Behold
the Bridegroom is coming.+ Go out to
meet Him.
7 Then all those virgins arose and
trimmed their lamps.
8 The foolish said to the wise: Give us
some of your oil for our lamps have
gone out.
9 But the wise answered saying: *No*.
Lest there not be enough for us and you.
But rather go to *those* who sell and buy
for yourselves.
10 While they went to buy, the Bridegroom came. *Those* who were ready
went in with Him to the marriage and
the door was shut.
11 Afterward the other virgins also came
saying: Lord, Lord, open to us.
12 But He answered and said: Truly+ I
say to you: I do not know you.
13 Watch, therefore. For you do not
know either the day or the hour in which
the Son of man is coming.
14 For *the kingdom of heaven is* like+ a man
traveling to a far country *who* called his
servants and gave+ his goods to them.
15 To one he gave five talents. To another two. And to another one. To
everyone+ according to their several
abilities, and *then* immediately+ took his
journey.
16 Then the one who had received the
five talents traded with the same and
earned+ another five talents.
17 Likewise the one who *had received* two
also gained another two.
18 But the one who had received one
talent dug in the earth and hid the
lord's money.
19 After a long time, the lord of those
servants came and examined+ *their accounts* with them.
20 So the one who had received five
talents brought another+ five talents
saying: Lord, you delivered to me
five talents. Behold I have gained five
talents more.

[21]His lord said to him: Well done good
and faithful servant. You have been
faithful over a few things, I will set+ you
over many things. Enter into the joy of
your lord.
[22]Likewise, the one who had received
two talents said: Lord, you delivered to
me two talents. Behold I have gained
two more talents.
[23]His lord said to him: Well done good
and faithful servant. You have been
faithful over a few things, I will set+ you
over many things. Enter into the joy of
your lord.
[24]Then the one who had received one
talent said: Lord, I knew that you are
a hard man, reaping where you have
not sown and gathering where you
have not spread+.
[25]I was afraid and hid your talent in the
earth. Lo *there* you have *what is* yours.
[26]The lord answered and said: *You* wicked
and lazy+ servant. You knew that I reap
where I did not sow and gather where I
have not spread+.
[27]Therefore you should have put my
money with the bankers+ and *then* at my
coming I should have received my own
with interest+.
[28]Therefore take the talent from *the
lazy+ servant* and give *it* to *the* one who
has ten talents.
[29]For to everyone who has will *more* be
given and they will have abundance. But
from *those* who have nothing, even what
they have will be taken away.
[30]Cast the unprofitable servant into outer
darkness *where* there will be weeping
and gnashing of teeth.
[31]When the Son of man comes in His glory
and all the holy angels with Him, then
He will sit upon the throne of His glory.
[32]Before Him will be gathered all nations and He will separate them one
from another as a shepherd divides *the*
sheep from the goats. *Ezekiel 34:17,20*
[33]He will set the sheep at His right hand,
but the goats at the left.
[34]Then the King will say to those at His
right hand: Come, you blessed by my
Father. Inherit the kingdom prepared
for you from the foundation of the world.
[35]For I was hungry and you gave me
food.+ I was thirsty and you gave me
drink. I was a stranger, and you took me
in. *Isaiah 58:7*
[36]*I was* naked and you clothed me. I was
sick and you visited me. I was in prison
and you came to me. *Isaiah 58:7*
[37]Then the righteous will answer Him
saying: Lord, when did we see you
hungry and fed *you*? Or thirsty and gave
you drink?
[38]When did we see you a stranger and
took *you* in? Or naked and clothed *you*?
[39]Or when did we see you sick or in
prison and came to you?
[40]The King will answer and say to them:
Truly+ I say to you: Inasmuch as you
have done *it* to one of the least of these
my brothers, you have done *it* to me.
Proverbs 19:17
[41]Then He will also say to them on the
left hand: Depart from me you cursed
into everlasting fire prepared for the
devil and his angels.
[42]For I was hungry and you gave me
no food.+ I was thirsty and you gave
me no drink.
[43]I was a stranger and you did not take me
in. Naked and you did not cloth me. Sick
and in prison and you did not visit me.
[44]Then they will also answer Him saying: Lord, when did we see you hungry
or thirsty or a stranger or naked or sick
or in prison and did not minister to you?
[45]Then He will answer them saying:
Truly+ I say to you: Inasmuch as you
did not do *it* to one of the least of these,
you did not do *it* to me.
[46]*Therefore* these shall go away into
everlasting punishment. But the righteous into eternal life. *Daniel 12:2*

Matthew Chapter 26

[1] Now+ it came to pass when Jesus had
finished all these sayings, He said to His
disciples:
[2] You know that after two days is *the
Feast of* the Passover and the Son of man
is betrayed to be crucified.

3 Then the chief priests, the scribes, and
the elders of the people assembled
together at[+] the palace of the high
priest who was called Caiaphas.
4 *They* consulted *so* that they might take
Jesus by deceit[+] and kill *Him*.
5 But they said: Not on the feast *day*, lest
there be an uproar among the people.
6 Now when Jesus was in Bethany in the
house of Simon the leper
7 A woman having an alabaster box of
very precious ointment came to Him and
poured it on His head as He sat *to eat*[+].
8 But when His disciples saw *this*, they
were indignant and said: To what
purpose *is* this waste?
9 For this ointment might have been
sold for much and given to the poor.
10 When Jesus understood *it* He said to
them: Why do you trouble the woman?
For she has done[+] a good work upon
me.
11 For you always have the poor with
you, but you will not always have me.
12 For she has poured this ointment on
my body for my burial.
13 Truly[+] I say to you: Wherever this
Gospel shall be proclaimed[+] in the
whole world, what this woman has done
will also be told as a memorial of her.
14 Then one of the twelve called Judas
Iscariot went to the chief priests
15 and said *to them*: What will you give
me and I will deliver Him to you? And
they agreed[+] with him for thirty pieces
of silver. *Zechariah 11:12*
16 From that time, he sought opportunity
to betray Him.
17 Now the first *day* of the *Feast of* Unleavened Bread, the disciples came to
Jesus saying to Him: Where do you
want us to prepare for you to eat the
Passover? *Exodus 12:14*
18 He said: Go into the city to such a
man and say to him: The Master says:
My time is *very* near.[+] I will keep the
Passover at your house with my disciples.
19 The disciples did as Jesus had
directed[+] them and they made preparations[+] *for* the Passover.
20 Now when the evening[+] had come,
He sat down with the twelve.
21 As they ate He said: Truly[+] I say to
you that one of you will betray me.
22 They were exceedingly sorrowful and
began, everyone of them, to say to Him:
Lord, is it me?
23 He answered and said: He who dips
his hand with me in the dish, the same
will betray me.
24 The Son of man goes as it is written of
Him. But woe to that man by whom the
Son of man is betrayed. It *would* have
been good for that man if he had not
been born.
25 Then Judas who betrayed Him answered and said: Master, is it me? He
said to him: You have said.
26 As they were eating, Jesus took
bread and blessed, broke *it*, and gave
it to the disciples and said: Take. Eat.
This is my body.
27 *Then* He took the cup, gave thanks,
and gave *it* to them saying: Drink of
it, all *of you*.
28 For this is my blood of the new covenant,[+] which is shed for many for the
remission of sins.
29 But I say to you: I will not drink
henceforth of this fruit of the vine until
that day when I drink it new with you in
my Father's kingdom.
30 When they had sung a hymn, they
went out to the Mount of Olives.
31 Then Jesus said to them: All *of* you
will be offended because of me this
night. For it is written: I will strike[+] the
shepherd and the sheep of the flock will
be scattered. *Zechariah 13:7*
32 But after I am risen again, I will go
before you into Galilee.
33 Peter answered and said to Him:
Though all *people* will be offended
because of you, I will never be
offended.
34 Jesus said to him: Truly[+] I say to you
that this night, before the cock crows,
you will deny me three times.
35 Peter said to Him: Though I should die
with you, I will not deny you. Likewise
all the disciples said *the same* also.

36 Then Jesus went[+] with them to a
place called Gethsemane and said to
the disciples: Sit here while I go and
pray *over* there[+].
37 He took Peter with Him, and the two
sons of Zebedee, and *He* began to be
sorrowful and very heavy.
38 Then He said to them: My soul is
exceedingly sorrowful, even unto death.
Stay[+] here and watch with me.
39 He went a little farther and fell on His
face and prayed saying: O my Father. If
it be possible, let this cup pass from me.
Nevertheless, not as I will, but as you *will*.
40 *Then* He came to the disciples, found
them asleep, and said to Peter: What?
Could you not watch with me one hour?

> 41 Watch and pray
> *so* that you do not
> enter into temptation.
> The spirit indeed *is* willing,
> but the flesh *is* weak.

42 *Then* He went away again the second
time and prayed saying: O my Father. If
this cup may not pass away from me
unless[+] I drink it, your will be done.
43 And *then* He came and found them
asleep again, for their eyes were heavy
44 and He left them and went away again
and prayed the third time saying the
same words.
45 Then He came to His disciples and
said to them: Sleep on now and take *your*
rest. Behold the hour is *very* near[+] and
the Son of man is betrayed into the
hands of sinners.
46 Rise. Let us be going. Behold he who
betrays me is near[+].
47 While He spoke, behold, Judas, one of
the twelve, came. With him *came* a
great multitude with swords and staves,
coming from the chief priests and elders
of the people.
48 Now he who betrayed Him gave them
a sign saying: Whomever I shall kiss,
that same is He. Hold Him fast. *Psalm 41:9*
49 Immediately[+] he came to Jesus and
said: Hail Master, and kissed Him.
50 Jesus said to him: Friend, why[+] have
you come? Then they came and laid
hands on Jesus and took Him. *Psalm 41:9*
51 And behold one of *those* who were
with Jesus stretched out *his* hand and
drew his sword and struck a servant of
the high priest and cut[+] off his ear.
52 Then Jesus said to him: Put up your
sword into its place, for all *those* who take
up the sword shall perish by[+] the sword.
53 Do you think that I cannot now pray to
my Father and He would[+] immediately[+]
give me more than twelve legions of
angels?
54 But how then would[+] the Scriptures
be fulfilled? So[+] it must be *done* in
this way.
55 In that same hour, Jesus said to the
multitudes: Have you come out as against
a thief with swords and staves to take
me? I sat daily with you teaching in the
temple and you laid no hold on me.
56 But all this was done *so* the Scriptures
of the prophets might be fulfilled. Then
all the disciples left[+] Him and fled.
Zechariah 13:7
57 *Those* who had seized[+] Jesus led *Him*
away to Caiaphas the high priest where
the scribes and the elders were assembled.
58 But Peter followed Him *from* a
distance[+] to the high priest's palace and
went in and sat with the servants to see
the end.
59 Now the chief priests and elders and
all the council sought false testimony[+]
against Jesus to put Him to death.
60 But *they* found none. Yes, though
many false witnesses came, *yet* they
found none. At last, two false witnesses
came *Psalm 27:12, Psalm 35:11*
61 and said: This *fellow* said: I am able to
destroy the temple of God and to build
it in three days.
62 The high priest arose and said to Him:
Do you answer nothing? What *is it that*
these witness against you?
63 But Jesus *remained* silent.[+] And the
high priest answered and said to Him: I
beg[+] you by the living God that you tell
us whether you are the Christ, the Son
of God. *Isaiah 53:7*

64 Jesus said to him: You have said.
Nevertheless I say to you: Hereafter
you will see the Son of man sitting at the
right hand of power and coming in the
clouds of heaven. *Psalm 110:1, Daniel 7:13*
65 Then the high priest tore+ his clothes
saying: He has spoken blasphemy.
What further need do we have of
witnesses? Behold, now you have
heard His blasphemy.
66 What do you think? They answered
and said: He is guilty of death.
67 Then they spit in His face and buffeted
Him. Others struck+ *Him* with the palms
of their hands, *Isaiah 50:6*
68 saying: Prophesy to us, you Christ.
Who is he who struck+ you?
69 Now Peter sat outside+ in the palace.
A girl+ came to him saying: You also
were with Jesus of Galilee.
70 But *Peter* denied *it* before *them* all saying: I do not know what you are saying.+
71 *Then* when he went+ out to the porch,
another saw him and said to *those* who
were there: This *fellow* was also with
Jesus of Nazareth.
72 Again he denied with an oath: I do not
know the man.
73 After a while *those* who stood by came
and said to Peter: Surely you also are *one*
of them, for your speech betrays you.
74 Then he began to curse and to swear
saying: I do not know the man. And
immediately the cock crowed.+
75 And Peter remembered the words of
Jesus who had said to him: Before the
cock crows you will deny me three times.
And he went out and wept bitterly.

Matthew Chapter 27

1 When the morning had come, all the
chief priests and elders of the people
took counsel against Jesus to put Him
to death.
2 When they had bound Him, they led
Him away and delivered Him to Pontius
Pilate the governor.
3 Then Judas, who had betrayed Him,
when he saw that He was condemned,
repented and took+ the thirty pieces of
silver to the chief priests and elders
4 saying: I have sinned in that I have
betrayed innocent blood. They said:
What *is that* to us? You live+ *with that*.
5 And he threw+ down the pieces of
silver in the temple and went *out* and
hung himself. *Zechariah 11:13*
6 The chief priests took the silver
pieces and said: It is not lawful to put
them into the treasury because it is the
price of blood.
7 *So* they took counsel and with them
bought the potter's field in which to
bury strangers.
8 Therefore that field was called: The
field of blood. *And it is* to this day.
9 This fulfilled what was spoken by the
prophet Jeremiah *who* said: And they
took the thirty pieces of silver, the price
and value set+ by the sons+ of Israel,
Jeremiah 32:7, Zechariah 11:12
10 and gave them for the potter's field, as
the Lord directed+ me. *Zechariah 11:13*
11 *When* Jesus stood before the governor,
the governor asked Him saying: Are
you the King of the Jews? And Jesus
said to him: You say.
12 When He was accused by the chief
priests and elders, He answered nothing.
13 Then Pilate said to Him: Do you not
hear how many things they witness
against you?
14 *Jesus* answered not a word; so that the
governor marveled greatly. *Isaiah 53:7*
15 Now at *the* feast, it was the custom+
for the governor to release a prisoner to
the people, whomever+ they wanted.+
16 And they had then a notable prisoner
called Barabbas.
17 Therefore when they were gathered
together, Pilate said to them: Whom do
you want+ me to release to you? Barabbas
or Jesus who is called Christ?
18 For he knew that *it was* for envy they
had delivered Him.
19 *Now* when he was seated+ on the
judgment seat, his wife sent to him
saying: Have nothing to do with that
righteous+ man, for I have suffered
many things this day in a dream because
of Him.

20 But the chief priests and elders persuaded the multitude that they should
ask *for* Barabbas and destroy Jesus.
21 The governor answered and said to
them: Which[+] of the two do you want[+]
me to release to you? They said:
Barabbas.
22 Pilate said to them: What shall I do then
with Jesus who is called Christ? *They* all
said to him: Let Him be crucified.
23 The governor said: Why? What evil
has He done? But they cried out *all* the
more saying: Let Him be crucified.
24 When Pilate saw that he could not
prevail, but *that* rather a tumult was
made, he took water and washed *his*
hands before the multitude saying: I am
innocent of the blood of this righteous[+]
person. See *to it*.
25 Then all the people answered and said:
His blood *be* on us and on our children.
26 Then he released Barabbas to them
and when he had flogged[+] Jesus, he
delivered *Him* to be crucified.
27 Then the soldiers of the governor took
Jesus into the common hall and gathered
to Him the whole company[+] *of soldiers*.
28 They stripped Him and put a scarlet
robe on Him.
29 And when they had made[+] a crown of
thorns, they put *it* on His head and a reed
in His right hand. *Then* they bowed the
knee before Him and mocked Him saying: Hail, King of the Jews.
30 They spit on Him and took the reed
and struck[+] Him on the head. *Isaiah 50:6*
31 After they had mocked Him, they took
the robe off of Him and put His own
clothing[+] on Him and led Him away to
crucify *Him*. *Psalm 22:7*
32 As they came out, they found a man of
Cyrene by the name of Simon and they
compelled him to bear *Jesus'* cross.
33 When they had come to a place called
Golgotha, that is to say a place of a skull
34 they gave Him vinegar to drink mingled
with gall. When He had tasted *it*, He
would not drink. *Psalm 69:21*
35 *Then* they crucified Him and divided[+]
His garments *by* casting lots, thus fulfilling what was spoken by the prophet:
They divided[+] my garments among
them and upon my coat[+] they cast
lots. *Psalm 22:18*
36 And, sitting down, they watched Him
there
37 and set up over His head *the* written
accusation: This is Jesus The King of
the Jews.
38 There were two thieves crucified with
Him: One on the right side[+] and another
on the left. *Isaiah 53:12*
39 *Those* who passed by reviled Him,
shaking[+] their heads *Psalm 109:25*
40 and saying: You who *would* destroy
the temple and rebuild[+] *it* in three days,
save yourself. If you are the Son of God,
come down from the cross.
41 Likewise also the chief priests mocked
Him with the scribes and elders, saying:
Psalm 22:7
42 He saved others. He cannot save
Himself. If He is the King of Israel,
let Him come down from the cross
now and we will believe Him.
43 He trusted in God, let *God* deliver Him
now, if He will have Him, for He said:
I Am the Son of God. *Psalm 22:8*
44 The thieves also, who were crucified
with Him, reviled[+] Him. *Psalm 109:25*
45 Now from twelve o'clock[+] *noon*, there
was darkness over all the land until[+]
three[+] *in the afternoon*.
46 About three[+] *in the afternoon* Jesus
cried *out* with a loud voice saying:
Eli, Eli, lama sabachthani. That is to
say: My God, my God, why have you
forsaken me? *Psalm 22:1*
47 Some of *those* who stood there, when they
heard *that*, said: This *man* calls for Elijah.
48 Immediately[+] one of them ran and
took a sponge, filled *it* with vinegar, put
it on a reed, and gave *it to* Him to drink.
49 The rest said: Let *Him* be. Let us see
whether Elijah will come to save Him.
50 When Jesus had cried *out* again with a
loud voice, He yielded up the spirit.[+]
51 And behold the veil of the temple was
torn[+] in two from the top to the bottom,
the earth quaked,[+] and the rocks broke.[+]
52 Graves were opened and many bodies
of saints who slept arose

53 and came out of the graves after His
resurrection and went into the holy city
and appeared to many.
54 Now when the centurion and *those*
who were with him watching Jesus saw
the earthquake and those things that
were done, they feared greatly, saying:
Truly this was the Son of God.
55 Many women who *had* followed Jesus
from Galilee ministering to Him were
there watching+ *from* a distance.+
56 Among them were Mary Magdalene,
Mary the mother of James and Joses,
and the mother of Zebedee's children.
57 When the evening+ had come, there
came a rich man of Arimathaea named
Joseph, who also himself was Jesus'
disciple. *Isaiah 53:9*
58 He went to Pilate and asked+ *for* Jesus'
body. Then Pilate commanded the body
to be delivered.
59 When Joseph had taken the body, he
wrapped it in a clean linen cloth
60 and laid it in his own new tomb that he
had cut+ out in the rock. *Then* he rolled
a great stone to the door of the tomb+
and departed. *Isaiah 53:9*
61 And there were Mary Magdalene and
the other Mary sitting over by+ the tomb.+
62 Now the next day that followed the
day of the preparation, the chief priests
and Pharisees came together to Pilate
63 saying: Sir, we remember that that
deceiver said, while He was yet alive:
After three days I will rise again.
64 Therefore command that the tomb+ be
made sure until the third day, lest His
disciples come by night and steal Him
away and say to the people *that* He is
risen from the dead. So, the last error
will be worse than the first.
65 Pilate said to them: You have guards.+
Go *and* make *it* as sure as you can.
66 So they went and made the tomb+
sure, sealing the stone and setting
guards.+

Matthew Chapter 28

1 At the end of the Sabbath, as it began
to dawn toward the first of the week,
Mary Magdalene and the other Mary
came to see the tomb.+
2 And behold there was a great earthquake, for the angel of the Lord
descended from heaven, came and
rolled back the stone from the door,
and sat upon it.
3 His countenance was like lightning
and his clothing+ white as snow.
4 For fear of him, the keepers shook and
became like+ dead *people*.
5 The angel answered and said to the
women: Do not be afraid, for I know
that you seek Jesus who was crucified.
6 He is not here, for He is risen as He
said. Come. See the place where the
Lord had lain.+ *Psalm 16:10, Psalm 49:15*
7 Go quickly and tell His disciples that He
is risen from the dead, and behold He
goes before you into Galilee. You will
see Him there. Behold I have told you.
8 They departed quickly from the tomb+
with fear and great joy and ran to bring
word to His disciples.
9 As they went to tell His disciples,
behold Jesus met them saying: All hail.
And they came and held Him by the feet
and worshiped Him.
10 Then Jesus said to them: Do not be
afraid. Go tell my brothers to go into
Galilee and they will see me there.
11 Now when they were going, behold
some of the guards+ came into the city
and showed the chief priests all the
things that were done.
12 When they were assembled with the
elders and had taken counsel, they gave
large *sums of* money to the soldiers,
13 saying: Say *that* His disciples came by
night and stole Him *away* while we slept.
14 If this comes to the governor's ears,
we will persuade him and secure you.
15 So they took the money and did as
they were taught, and this saying is
commonly reported among the Jews
even until this day.
16 Then the eleven disciples went away
into Galilee, to a mountain where Jesus
had directed+ them *to go*.
17 When they saw Him, they worshiped
Him. But some doubted.

18 *Then* Jesus came and spoke to them
saying: All authority+ is given to me in
heaven and in earth.

19 Go therefore
and teach all nations,
baptizing them in the name
of the Father and of the Son
and of the Holy Spirit,
20 teaching them to observe
all things whatsoever
I have commanded you.
Behold I am with you always,
even to the end of the world.
Amen.

The Gospel of Jesus Christ as surveyed by Mark

Chapter 1

1 The beginning of the Gospel of Jesus
Christ the Son of God.
2 As it is written in the prophets: Behold
I send my messenger before your face
who will prepare your way before you.
Matthew 11:10
3 The voice of one crying in the wilderness: Prepare the way of *the* Lord.
Make His paths straight. *Matthew 3:3*
4 John baptized in the wilderness and
proclaimed+ the baptism of repentance
for the remission of sins.
5 All *those in* the land of Judea and those
of Jerusalem went to him and were all
baptized by him in the Jordan river
confessing their sins.
6 John was clothed with camel's hair
with a leather+ belt+ around+ his waist+
and he ate locusts and wild honey.
7 And *he* proclaimed+: One is coming
after me *who* is mightier than I, the
straps+ of whose sandals+ I am not
worthy to stoop down and loosen.
8 I indeed have baptized you with water
but He will baptize you with the Holy
Spirit.
9 Now+ it came to pass in those days *that*
Jesus came from Nazareth of Galilee and
was baptized by John in *the* Jordan *river*.
10 Immediately+ *after* coming up out of
the water, He saw the heavens opened
and the Spirit descending like a dove
upon Himself.
11 And there came a voice from heaven
saying: You are my beloved Son in
whom I am well pleased.
12 *Then* immediately *after that* the Spirit
drove Him into the wilderness.
13 He was there in the wilderness forty
days tempted by Satan. And *He* was
with the *wild* beasts. And the angels
ministered to Him.
14 Now after John was put in prison,
Jesus came into Galilee proclaiming+
the Gospel of the kingdom of God
15 and saying: The time is fulfilled and
the kingdom of God is *very* near.+
Repent and believe the Gospel.
16 Now as He walked by the sea of
Galilee, He saw Simon and Andrew his
brother casting a net into the sea, for
they were fishermen.+
17 Jesus said to them: Come after me and
I will make you to become fishers of men.
18 Immediately+ they left+ their nets and
followed Him.
19 When He had gone a little farther from
there,+ He saw James the *son* of Zebedee
and John his brother who also *were* in a
boat mending their nets.
20 Immediately+ He called them and they
left their father Zebedee in the boat with
the hired servants and followed+ Him.
21 *From there* they went to Capernaum
and immediately+ on the Sabbath day
Jesus entered the synagogue and taught.
22 They were astonished at His doctrine
for He taught them as one who had
authority and not as the scribes.
23 In their synagogue there was a man
with an unclean spirit and he cried out
24 saying: Let *us* alone. What do we have
to do with you Jesus of Nazareth? Have
you come to destroy us? I know who you
are: the Holy One of God.
25 Jesus rebuked him saying: Be still+
and come out of him.

26 When the unclean spirit had shaken+ him and cried *out* with a loud voice, *it* came out of him.
27 They were all amazed so that they questioned among themselves saying: What is this? What new doctrine *is* this? For He commands with authority, even the unclean spirits, and they obey Him.
28 Immediately His reputation+ spread widely+ throughout all the region around+ Galilee.
29 As soon as they came+ out of the synagogue, *Jesus* entered the house of Simon and Andrew with James and John.
30 Simon's wife's mother lay *sick* with a fever and immediately+ they spoke to Him about her.
31 He came *to her*, took her *by the* hand and lifted her up, and immediately the fever left her and she ministered to them.
32 Evening+ having come, when the sun had set, they brought to Him all who were diseased and those *who were* demon+ possessed.
33 All the city was gathered together at the door.
34 He healed many who were sick *with* various+ diseases and cast out many demons.+ But *He* did not allow+ the demons+ to speak because they knew Him.
35 In the morning, rising up a great while before day *break*, He went out and departed to a solitary place and prayed there.
36 Simon and the others who were with Him followed after Him.
37 When they found Him they said to Him: All *the people* are seeking you.
38 He said to them: Let us go to the next towns *so* that I can proclaim+ *the Word* there also, because *it is* for this *purpose that* I have come.
39 *Then* He proclaimed+ *the Word* in their synagogues throughout all Galilee and cast out demons.+
40 A leper came to Him beseeching Him, kneeling down to Him, and saying to Him: If you will you can make me clean.
41 Moved with compassion, Jesus put forth *His* hand and touched him and said to him: I will. Be clean.
42 As soon as He had spoken, immediately the leprosy departed from him and he was cleansed.
43 *Jesus* strictly+ warned+ him and immediately+ sent him away
44 saying to him: See *that* you say nothing to anyone. But go+ and show yourself to the priest and *make an* offering+ for your cleansing *according to* those things that Moses commanded, as a testimony to them.
45 But he went out and began to tell+ many+ *people* and spread+ the matter widely+ so that Jesus could no longer+ enter the city openly, but was outside+ in deserted+ places. And *yet the people still* came to Him from everywhere.+

Mark Chapter 2

1 After *some* days, *Jesus* entered Capernaum again and it was *quickly* reported+ that He was in the house.
2 Immediately+ many gathered together so that there was no room to receive *them all*. No, not even+ near+ the door; and He proclaimed+ the Word to them.
3 They came to Him bringing one sick with paralysis+ who was carried+ by four *others*.
4 When they could not get near Him because of the crowd,+ they uncovered the roof where He was. When they had broken *it* up, they let down the bed in which the *one* sick with paralysis+ lay.
5 When Jesus saw their faith, He said to the *one* sick with paralysis+: Son, your sins are forgiven.
6 But there were some of the scribes sitting there and reasoning in their hearts:
7 Why does this *man* speak such blasphemies? Who can forgive sins, but God only?
8 Immediately when Jesus perceived in His spirit that they so reasoned within themselves, He said to them: Why do you reason these things in your hearts?

9 Which+ is easier to say to *someone* sick with paralysis+: *Your* sins are forgiven; or to say: Arise and take up your bed and walk.

10 But *so* that you may know that the Son of man has authority+ *and power* on earth to forgive sins, He said to the *one* sick with paralysis+:

11 I say to you: Arise. Take up your bed and go+ to your house.

12 Immediately he arose, took up the bed, and went forth before them all so that they were all amazed and glorified God saying: We never saw *anything like* this *before*.

13 *Then Jesus* went to the seaside again and all the multitude came+ to Him and He taught them.

14 As He passed by, He saw Levi the *son* of Alphaeus sitting at the tax office+ and said to him: Follow me. And he arose and followed Him.

15 Now+ it came to pass, as *Jesus* sat *down* to eat+ in *Levi's* house, many worldly+ people and sinners sat with Jesus and His disciples, for there were many and they followed Him.

16 When the scribes and Pharisees saw Him eat with worldly+ people and sinners, they said to His disciples: How is it that He eats and drinks with worldly+ people and sinners?

17 When Jesus heard *this*, He said to them: *Those* who are whole have no need of a physician but *those* who are sick *do*. I did not come to call the righteous but sinners to repentance.

18 *Now* the disciples of John and of the Pharisees used to fast *so* they came and said to Him: Why do the disciples of John and of the Pharisees fast but your disciples do not fast?

19 Jesus said to them: Can the children of the bride chamber fast while the bridegroom is with them? As long as they have the bridegroom with them, they cannot fast.

20 But the days will come when the Bridegroom will be taken away from them and then they will fast in those days.

21 No one sews a piece of new cloth on an old garment, *or* else the new piece that fills it up takes away from the old and the tear+ is made worse.

22 And no one puts new wine into old wineskins,+ *or* else the new wine will burst the wineskins+ and the wine is spilled and the wineskins+ will be destroyed.+ But new wine must be put into new wineskins+.

23 Now+ it came to pass that *Jesus* went through the corn fields on the Sabbath day and His disciples began to pluck the ears of corn as they went.

24 The Pharisees said to Him: Behold why do they, on the Sabbath day, *do* what is not lawful?

25 *Jesus* said to them: Have you never read what David did when he had need and was hungry, he and *those* who were with him,

26 how he went into the house of God in the days of Abiathar the high priest and ate the show bread that is not lawful for *anyone* but the priests to eat, and *he* also gave *some* to *those* who were with him.

27 He said to them: The Sabbath was made for people+ and not people for the Sabbath.

28 Therefore the Son of man is Lord also of the Sabbath.

Mark Chapter 3

1 *Then Jesus* entered the synagogue again, and there was a man there who had a withered hand.

2 *The Pharisees* watched Him *to see* whether He would heal him on the Sabbath day *so* that they might accuse Him.

3 *Jesus* said to the man who had the withered hand: Stand forth.

4 And He said to them: Is it lawful to do good on the Sabbath days or to do evil? To save life or to kill? But they *remained* silent.+

5 When He had looked around+ at them with anger, being grieved for the hardness of their hearts, He said to the man: Stretch forth your hand, and he stretched *it* out and his hand was restored whole as the other.

6 *Then* the Pharisees went forth and immediately[+] took counsel with the Herodians against Him, *to decide* how they might destroy Him.

7 But Jesus withdrew to the sea with His disciples and a great multitude from Galilee followed Him, and from Judea

8 and from Jerusalem and from Idumaea and *from* beyond Jordan. And those from Tyre and Sidon, a great multitude, when they had heard what great things He did, *they also* came to Him.

9 He told His disciples that a small boat should wait for Him because of the multitude, lest they should overcrowd[+] Him.

10 For He had healed many so that all[+] *who* had plagues pressed *in* upon Him to touch Him.

11 Unclean spirits, when they saw Him, fell down before Him and cried *out* saying: You are the Son of God.

12 And He strictly[+] charged them to not make Him known.

13 *Then* He went up into a mountain and called *those* whom He wanted[+] and they came to Him.

14 He appointed[+] twelve to[+] be with Him, *so* that He might send them forth to proclaim[+] *the Word*

15 and to have authority[+] *and power* to heal sicknesses and to cast out demons.[+]

16 Simon He surnamed Peter.

17 James the *son* of Zebedee and John the brother of James He surnamed Boanerges, which is: the sons of thunder.

18 *The others were* Andrew, Philip, Bartholomew, Matthew, Thomas, James the *son* of Alphaeus, Thaddaeus, Simon the Canaanite,

19 and Judas Iscariot who also betrayed Him. *Then* they went into a house

20 and the multitude came together again so that they could not so much as eat bread.

21 When His friends heard *about it*, they went out to lay hold on Him, for they said: He is beside Himself.

22 *Then* the scribes who came down from Jerusalem said: He has Beelzebub and by the prince of the demons[+] He casts out demons.[+]

23 *Jesus* called them *to Himself* and said to them in parables: How can Satan cast out Satan?

24 If a kingdom is divided against itself, that kingdom cannot stand.

25 If a house is divided against itself, that house cannot stand.

26 If Satan rise up against himself and is divided, he cannot stand but has *met his* end.

27 No one can enter into a strong man's house and spoil his goods unless[+] he first bind the strong man. Then he will spoil his house.

28 Truly[+] I say to you: All sins will be forgiven to the children[+] of people,[+] and blasphemies with which [+] they blaspheme;

29 but *those* who blaspheme against the Holy Spirit will have no forgiveness but are in danger of eternal damnation.

30 *He said this* because they said: He has an unclean spirit.

31 Then His brothers and mother came and, standing outside,[+] *they* sent for Him *by* calling *out to* Him.

32 The multitude sat around[+] Him and said to Him: Behold your mother and your brothers outside[+] seek you.

33 He answered them saying: Who are my mother or my brothers?

34 And He looked around[+] at *those* who sat around[+] Him and said: Behold my mother and my brothers.

35 For whoever does the will of God, the same is my brother and my sister and mother.

Mark Chapter 4

1 *Then Jesus* began again to teach by the seaside. There was gathered to Him a great multitude so that He entered a boat and sat *out* upon the sea, and the whole multitude was on the land by the sea.

2 He taught them many things by parables and said to them in His doctrine:

3 Listen.[+] Behold a sower went out to sow.

4 Now[+] it came to pass as he sowed *that* some fell by the wayside and the birds[+] of the air came and devoured it up.

5 Some fell on stony ground where it did not have much earth. Immediately it sprang up, because it had no depth of earth.

6 But when the sun was up, it was scorched and because it had no root, it withered away.

7 Some fell among thorns and the thorns grew up and choked it and it yielded no fruit.

8 Other fell on good ground and yielded fruit that sprang up and increased and brought forth: some thirty, some sixty, and some a hundred *times more*.

9 He said to them: *Those* who have ears to hear, let them hear.

10 *Later,* when He was alone, *those* who were around[+] Him with the twelve asked Him about the parable.

11 He said to them: Unto you it is given to know the mystery of the kingdom of God, but for *those* who are outside,[+] all *these* things are done in parables

12 *so* that seeing they may see and not perceive, and hearing they may hear and not understand, lest at any time they should be converted and *their* sins should be forgiven them. *Matthew 13:14*

13 He said to them: Do you not understand[+] this parable? How then will you understand[+] all *the other* parables?

14 The sower sows the Word *of God*.

15 These are the *ones* by the wayside where the Word is sown, but when they have heard, Satan comes immediately and takes away the Word that was sown in their hearts.

16 These are likewise sown on stony ground and when they hear the Word, *they* immediately receive it with gladness

17 but *they* have no root in themselves and so *they* endure only for a time. *Then* later,[+] when affliction or persecution arises because of the Word, immediately they are caused[+] *to sin*.

18 These are the *ones* who are sown among thorns, such as hear the Word

19 but the cares of this world and the deceitfulness of riches and the lusts of other things enter in and choke the Word and it becomes unfruitful.

20 These are the *ones* who are sown on good ground, such as hear the Word and receive *it* and bring forth fruit: some thirtyfold, some sixty, and some a hundred *times more*.

21 He said to them: Is a candle brought to be put under a bushel or under a bed and not to be set on a candlestick?

22 There is nothing hid that will not be revealed.[+] Neither has anything *been* kept secret but that it should *eventually* become known[+]. *Matthew 10:26*

23 If anyone has ears to hear, let them hear.

24 He said to them: Take heed what you hear. With what gauge[+] you measure, it will be measured to you. To you who hear, more will be given.

25 For to *those* who have will *more* be given and from *those* who have nothing, from them will be taken *away* even what they have.

26 *Then* He said: The kingdom of God is like this: If a man should cast seed into the ground

27 and should sleep and rise night and day and the seed should spring and grow up, he does not understand[+] how.

28 For the earth brings forth fruit by herself: First the blade, then the stalk,[+] *and* after that the full ear of corn.

29 But when the fruit is brought forth, *the farmer* immediately puts in the sickle because the harvest *time* has come.

30 *Then* He said: To what shall we compare[+] the kingdom of God? Or with what illustration[+] shall we compare it?

31 *It is* like a grain of mustard seed which, when it is sown in the earth, is the smallest[+] *of* all the seeds in the earth.

32 But when it is sown, it grows up and becomes greater than all herbs and shoots out great branches so that the birds[+] of the air may lodge under the shadow of it.

33 With many such parables He spoke the Word to them, as they were able to hear *it*.

34 But without a parable He did not speak to them, and when they were alone, He expounded everything to His disciples.

35 The same day when the evening[+] had
come, He said to them: Let us go[+] over
to the other side.
36 When they had sent away the multitude,
they took Him as *He* was in the boat.
And there were other little boats with
Him also.
37 *Then* a great windstorm[+] arose and the
waves beat into the boat so that it was
now full.
38 *Jesus* was in the aft[+] of the boat asleep
on a pillow. They awakened Him and
said to Him: Master, do you not care
that we *might* perish?
39 He arose and rebuked the wind and said
to the sea: Peace. Be still. And the wind
stopped[+] and there was a great calm.
40 He said to them: Why are you so
fearful? How is it that you have no faith?
41 And they were exceedingly fearful
and said to one another: What kind[+] of
man is this that even the wind and the sea
obey Him?

Mark Chapter 5

1 *Then* they came over to the other side
of the sea to the country of the Gadarenes.
2 When *Jesus* had come out of the boat,
immediately *coming* out of the tombs, a
man with an unclean spirit met Him.
3 *This man* had *his* dwelling *place* among
the tombs and no one could bind him.
No, not with chains.
4 He had often been bound with shackles[+] and chains, and the chains had
been pulled apart[+] by him, and the
shackles[+] broken in pieces. No one
could subdue[+] him.
5 Always, night and day, he was in the
mountains and in the tombs, crying and
cutting himself with stones.
6 But when he saw Jesus *from* a distance,[+]
he ran and worshiped Him
7 and cried *out* with a loud voice and
said: What have I to do with you Jesus,
Son of the most high God? I beg[+] you by
God that you not torment me.
8 For *Jesus* said to him: Come out of the
man *you* unclean spirit.
9 *Jesus* asked him: What *is* your name?
He answered saying: My name *is*
Legion for we are many.
10 And *they* begged[+] *Jesus* greatly[+] that
He would not send them away out of the
country.
11 Now a large herd of swine was there
on the mountain feeding.
12 And all the demons[+] begged[+] Him
saying: Send us into the swine *so* that we
may enter into them.
13 Immediately[+] Jesus allowed[+] them to
go[+] and the unclean spirits left[+] and
entered the swine, and the *entire* herd of
about two thousand ran violently down
a steep place into the sea and were
choked in the sea.
14 *Those* who fed the swine fled and told
all about this in the city and in the
country, and the *people* went out to see
what it was that was done.
15 And they came to Jesus and saw the
one who had been demon[+] possessed
and had the legion, dressed[+] and sitting
still, in his right mind, and they were
afraid.
16 *Those* who saw *it* told what had happened[+] to the one who had been demon[+]
possessed, and concerning the swine,
17 and they began to beg[+] Him to depart
out of their borders.[+]
18 When *Jesus* had come into the boat,
the one who had been demon[+] possessed begged[+] Him that he might stay
with Him.
19 However Jesus did not allow him,
but said to him: Go home to your
friends and tell them how much[+] the
Lord has done for you, *that He* has had
compassion on you.
20 *So* he departed and began to tell[+]
everyone in Decapolis how much[+] Jesus
had done for him, and all *the people*
marveled.
21 When Jesus crossed[+] over *the sea*
again by boat to the other side, many
people gathered to Him, and He was
near the sea.
22 And behold one of the rulers of the
synagogue, Jairus by name, came *to*
Him, and when he saw Him, he fell at
His feet

23 and begged+ Him greatly saying: My little daughter lies at the point of death. *I beg+ you to* come and lay your hands on her *so* that she may be healed, and she will live.
24 *Jesus* went with him and many people followed Him and crowded+ in upon Him.
25 *Now* a certain woman had an issue of blood twelve years
26 and had suffered many things by many physicians. *She* had spent all that she had and was no better, but rather grew worse.
27 *So,* when she heard about Jesus, *she* came in the crowd+ *and from* behind touched His garment.
28 For she said: If I may touch but His clothes, I will be whole.
29 Immediately+ the flow+ of her blood was dried up and she felt in *her* body that she was healed of that plague.
30 Jesus, immediately knowing in Himself that virtue had gone out of Him, turned around+ in the crowd+ and said: Who touched my clothes?
31 His disciples said to Him: You see the multitude crowding+ *in upon* you and you say: Who touched me?
32 And He looked around+ to see who had done this.
33 But the woman, fearful and trembling knowing what was done in her, came and fell down before Him and told Him all the truth.
34 He said to her: Daughter, your faith has made you whole. Go in peace and be healed+ of your plague.
35 While He spoke, someone+ came from *the house of* the ruler of the synagogue who said: Your daughter is dead. Why trouble the Master any further?
36 As soon as Jesus heard the word that was spoken, He said to the ruler of the synagogue:

> Do not be afraid.
> Only believe.

37 He allowed+ no one to follow Him except+ Peter, James, and John the brother of James.
38 He came to the house of the ruler of the synagogue and saw the tumult and *those* who wept and wailed greatly.
39 When He had come in, He said to them: Why do you make this fuss+ and weep? The girl+ is not dead, but sleeps.
40 They laughed *at* Him *scornfully*, but when He had sent+ them all out, He took the father and the mother of the girl+ and *those* who were with Him and entered in where the girl+ was lying.
41 He took the girl+ by the hand and said to her: Talitha cumi, which means+: *Little* girl+ I say to you: Arise.
42 Immediately+ the girl+ arose and walked for she was twelve years *old*. They were astonished with great amazement.+
43 *Jesus* charged them strictly+ that no one should know *about* this, and commanded that something should be given to her to eat.

Mark Chapter 6

1 *Then Jesus* went from there+ to His own country, and His disciples followed Him.
2 When the Sabbath day had come, He began to teach in the synagogue. Many hearing *Him* were astonished saying: From where has this *man acquired* these things? What wisdom *is* this given to Him *so* that even such mighty works are worked+ by His hands?
3 Is this not the carpenter, the son of Mary, the brother of James and Joses and of Jude and Simon? Are His sisters not here with us? And they were offended by Him.
4 But Jesus said to them: A prophet is not without honor, except in his own country and among his own relatives+ and in his own house.
5 He could do no mighty works there except that He laid His hands on a few sick people+ and healed *them*.
6 He marveled because of their unbelief. And He went *all* around+ the villages teaching.
7 *Then* He called the twelve and began to send them forth two *by* two and gave them authority+ *and power* over unclean spirits.

8 *He* commanded them to take nothing
for *their* journey except a staff only: No
provision bag,+ no bread, *and* no money
in *their* purse.
9 But *to* wear sandals, but not *to* put on
two coats.
10 He said to them: In whatever place +
you enter into a house, stay+ there until
you depart from that place.
11 Whoever will not receive you or
hear you, when you depart from there+
shake off the dust under your feet for
a testimony against them. Truly+ I
say to you: It will be more tolerable
for Sodom and Gomorrah in the day
of judgment than for that city.
12 *So* they went forth+ and proclaimed+
that people+ should repent.
13 They cast out many demons+ and
anointed many with oil who were sick
and healed *them*.
14 *When* king Herod heard *about Jesus*
because His name was spread widely,+
he said that John the Baptist was risen
from the dead and therefore mighty
works do show forth themselves in him.
15 Others said: It is Elijah. And others
said: It is a prophet or *someone* like one
of the prophets.
16 But when Herod heard *about it* he said:
It is John whom I beheaded. He is risen
from the dead.
17 For Herod himself had sent forth and
seized+ John and bound him in prison
for the sake of Herodias, his brother
Philip's wife, for he had married her.
18 For John had said to Herod: It is not
lawful for you to have your brother's
wife.
19 Therefore Herodias had a quarrel
against *John* and would have killed him.
But she could not.
20 For Herod feared John, knowing that
he was a righteous+ and holy man,
therefore Herod protected+ him. When
Herod heard *John*, he did many things
and heard *John* gladly.
21 When a convenient day had come,
Herod made *his* birthday supper for
his lords, high captains, and chief
estates of Galilee.
22 And when the daughter of Herodias
came in and danced and pleased Herod
and *those* who sat with him, the king said
to the girl+: Ask of me whatever you
will and I will give *it to* you.
23 He swore to her: Whatever you ask of
me, I will give *it to* you, to the half of
my kingdom.
24 She said to her mother: What shall I
ask? Her *mother* said: The head of John
the Baptist.
25 *So* she came in to the king immediately+
and with haste and asked saying: I desire+
that you give me the head of John the
Baptist on a platter+ immediately.+
26 The king was exceedingly sorry, *but*
because of his oath and for the sake of *those*
who sat with him, he would not reject her.
27 *Therefore* the king immediately sent an
executioner and commanded *John's*
head to be brought, and *the executioner*
beheaded him in the prison.
28 *Then he* brought *John's* head on a
platter+ and gave it to the girl+ and
the girl+ gave it to her mother.
29 When *John's* disciples heard *about it*,
they came and took *away* his body+ and
laid it in a tomb.
30 *Then* the apostles gathered themselves
together to Jesus and told Him everything, both what they had done and what
they had taught.
31 *Jesus* said to them: Come + apart to a
deserted+ place and rest a while. For
there were many coming and going and
they had no time+ *even* to eat.
32 *So* they went to a deserted+ place by
boat privately.
33 The people saw them departing and
many knew Him and ran on foot there
out of all cities and outran them and
came together to Him.
34 When Jesus came, He saw many people
and was moved with compassion toward
them because they were like sheep not
having a shepherd. *So* He began to teach
them many things.
35 When the hour+ was late,+ *Jesus'*
disciples came to Him and said: This
is a deserted+ place and now the
hour+ *is* late.+

36 Send them away *so* that they may go into the country *all* around^{+} and into the villages and buy bread *for* themselves, for they have nothing to eat.
37 *Jesus* answered and said to them: You give them *food* to eat. And they said to Him: Shall we go and buy *a half a year wages worth*$^{+}$ of bread and give them to eat?
38 He said to them: How many loaves do you have? Go and see. When they knew, they said: Five, and two fish.
39 *Then Jesus* directed^{+} them all *to* sit down group^{+} *by* group on the green grass.
40 And they sat down in groups^{+} of hundreds and fifties.
41 When He had taken the five loaves and the two fish, He looked up to heaven and blessed and broke the loaves and gave *them* to His disciples to set before them and the two fish He *also* divided among them all.
42 And they all ate and were filled.
43 *Afterward* they took up twelve baskets full of the fragments and of the fish.
44 *Those* who ate of the loaves were about five thousand men.
45 Immediately^{+} *after that Jesus* directed^{+} His disciples to get into the boat and to go before *Him* to the other side, to Bethsaida, while He sent away the people.
46 When He had sent them away, He went to a mountain to pray.
47 *Then* when evening^{+} had come, the boat was in the midst of the sea and *Jesus was* alone on the land.
48 He saw them toiling in rowing for the wind was contrary to them. About the fourth watch of the night *sometime after three o'clock in the morning Jesus* came to them walking upon the sea, and would have passed by them.
49 But when they saw Him walking upon the sea, they supposed it had been a spirit and cried out.
50 For they all saw Him and were troubled. And immediately He talked with them and said to them: Be of good cheer. I am^{+} *with you*. Do not be afraid.
51 *Then* He went up to them in the boat and the wind stopped.$^{+}$ They were greatly^{+} amazed within themselves beyond measure and wondered.
52 For they did not understand^{+} *the miracle* of the loaves because their heart was hardened.
53 When they had crossed^{+} over *the sea*, they came to the land of Gennesaret and drew to the shore.
54 And when they had come out of the boat, immediately^{+} the *people* recognized^{+} Him
55 and ran through that whole region *all* around^{+} and began to carry *those* who were sick in bed to where they heard He was.
56 Wherever He entered into villages or cities or country, they laid the sick in the streets and begged^{+} Him that they might touch, if it were *possible*, even *just* the border of His garment. As many as touched Him were made whole.

Mark Chapter 7

1 Then the Pharisees came together to Him, and *also* some^{+} of the scribes who came from Jerusalem.
2 When they saw some of His disciples eat bread with defiled, that is to say with unwashed hands, they found fault.
3 For holding *to* the tradition of the elders, the Pharisees and all the Jews do not eat unless they wash *their* hands often.
4 And *when they come* from the market, they do not eat unless they wash; and there are many other things that they have received to hold, *such as* the washing of cups and pots, brazen vessels, and tables.
5 Then the Pharisees and scribes asked Him: Why do your disciples not walk according to the tradition of the elders, but eat bread with unwashed hands?
6 He answered and said to them: Well has Isaiah prophesied of you hypocrites, as it is written: This people honors me with *their* lips, but their hearts are far from me. *Matthew 15:8*

7 However, in vain do they worship me, teaching *as* doctrines the commandments of men. *Matthew 15:9*

8 For laying aside the commandment of God, you hold the traditions of men: *such as* the washing of pots and cups and many other *things* like such you do.

9 *Then* He said to them: Full well you reject the commandment of God *so* that you may keep your own tradition.

10 For Moses said: Honor your father and your mother. And whoever curses father or mother, let them die the death.

11 But you say: If a person+ says to their father or mother: Whatever benefit+ *you might have received* from me *was given as* Corban, that is a *temple* gift,

12 and you allow+ them to do no more for their father or their mother,

13 *by doing this, you are* making the Word of God of no effect through your tradition which you have delivered. Many *things* like such you do.

14 When He had called all the people, He said to them: Listen+ to me everyone *of you* and understand:

15 There is nothing outside+ *of* a person,+ which *by* entering into them can defile them. But the things that come out of them, those are the things that defile a person+.

16 If anyone has ears to hear, let them hear.

17 When *Jesus* went into a house *away* from the people, His disciples asked Him about+ the parable.

18 He said to them: Are you so without understanding also? Do you not perceive that whatever thing from outside+ enters into a person+ cannot defile them.

19 Because it does not enter into their heart but into the belly and *then* into the discard+ *it* goes, purging all foods+.

20 He said: *It is* what comes out of a person+ that defiles them.

21 For from within, out of the hearts of people+ proceed evil thoughts, adulteries, fornications, murders, *Matthew 15:19*

22 thefts, covetousness, wickedness, deceit, filthiness,+ an evil eye, blasphemy, pride, *and* foolishness. *Matthew 15:19*

23 All these evil things come from within and defile a person+.

24 From there+ *Jesus* arose and went into the borders of Tyre and Sidon. *He* entered a house and wanted+ no one *to* know *it*, but He could not be hid.

25 For a *certain* woman whose young daughter had an unclean spirit heard of Him and came and fell at His feet.

26 The woman was a Greek of Syrophenician *or mixed race* nationality.+ She begged+ *Jesus* to cast the demon+ out of her daughter.

27 But Jesus said to her: Let the children first be filled, for it is not good+ to take the children's bread and to cast *it* to the dogs.

28 She answered and said to Him: Yes Lord. Yet the dogs under the table eat of the children's crumbs.

29 He said to her: For this saying, Go.+ The demon+ is gone out of your daughter.

30 When she had come to her house, she found the demon+ gone and her daughter laying on the bed.

31 *Then* again departing from the borders+ of Tyre and Sidon, *Jesus* came to the sea of Galilee, through the midst of the borders+ of Decapolis.

32 They brought to Him one who was deaf and had an impediment in his speech and they asked+ Him to put His hand upon him.

33 *Jesus* took him aside from the multitude and put His fingers into his ears and He spit *on His finger* and touched his tongue.

34 *Then* looking up to heaven He sighed and said to him: Ephphatha. That is: Be opened.

35 Immediately+ his ears were opened and the string of his tongue was loosed and he spoke plainly.

36 *Jesus* charged him that he should tell no one, but the more He charged them, so much more broadly+ they published *it*.

37 *Everyone* was astonished beyond measure saying: He has done all things well. He makes both the deaf to hear and the speechless+ to speak.

Mark Chapter 8

1 In those days, the multitude being very large+ and having nothing to eat, Jesus called His disciples and said to them:
2 I have compassion on the multitude because they have now been with me three days and have nothing to eat.
3 If I send them away fasting to their own houses, they will faint by the way, for many of them came from far *away*.
4 His disciples answered Him: From where can anyone+ satisfy these *people* with bread here in the wilderness?
5 He asked them: How many loaves do you have? They said: Seven.
6 He directed+ the people to sit down on the ground. *Then* He took the seven loaves, gave thanks, broke *them* and gave *them* to His disciples to set before *them*. And they sat *them* before the people.
7 They also had a few small fish and He blessed and commanded to set them also before *them*.
8 So they *all* ate and were filled. And of the broken *pieces* that were left, they took up seven baskets *full*
9 *Those* who had eaten were about four thousand. *Then* He sent them away.
10 Immediately+ He entered a boat with His disciples and came into the parts of Dalmanutha.
11 *Then* the Pharisees came and began to question Him, seeking a sign from heaven from Him, testing+ Him.
12 He sighed deeply in His spirit and said: Why does this generation seek after a sign? Truly+ I say to you: No sign will be given to this generation.
13 *Then* He left them and, entering the boat again, *He* departed to the other side.
14 Now *the disciples* had forgotten to take bread and they did not have in the boat with them more than one loaf.
15 *Jesus* charged them saying: Take heed. Beware of the leaven of the Pharisees and the leaven of Herod.
16 They reasoned among themselves saying: *It is* because we have no bread.
17 Jesus knew *their thoughts and* said to them: Why do you reason because you have no bread? Do you not yet perceive or understand? Have you hardened your hearts, still+?
18 Having eyes, do you not see? And having ears, do you not hear? And do you not remember?
19 When I broke the five loaves among five thousand, how many baskets full of fragments did you take up? They said to Him: Twelve.
20 When *I broke* the seven among four thousand, how many baskets full of fragments did you take up? They said: Seven.
21 He said to them: How is it that you do not understand?
22 *Then Jesus* came to Bethsaida and they brought a blind man to Him and begged+ Him to touch *the man*.
23 *So,* He took the blind man by the hand and led him out of the town. When He had spit on his eyes and put His hands upon him, He asked him if he saw anything.+
24 *The man* looked up and said: I see people+ like trees walking.
25 After that, *Jesus* put *His* hands upon his eyes again and made him look up, and he was restored and saw everyone+ clearly.
26 *Then Jesus* sent him away to his house saying: Do not go into the town or tell anyone in the town.
27 *Then* Jesus and His disciples went to the towns of Caesarea Philippi. Along+ the way, He asked His disciples saying to them: Who do people+ say that I am?
28 They answered: John the Baptist. But some *say* Elijah. *And* others *say* one of the prophets.
29 He said to them: But who do you say that I am? Peter answered and said to Him: You are the Christ.
30 *But* He charged them that they should tell no one about Him.
31 He began to teach them that the Son of man must suffer many things and be rejected by the elders and the chief priests and scribes and be killed, and after three days rise again.

32 *Jesus* spoke the Word+ openly. *But then* Peter took Him *aside* and began to rebuke Him.

33 But when He had turned around+ and looked at His disciples, He rebuked Peter saying: Get behind me Satan. For you do not savor the things that are of God but the things that are of men.

34 *Then* when He had called the people *together* with His disciples, He said to them: Whoever will come after me, let them deny themselves and take up their cross and follow me.

35 For whoever would+ save their life will lose it, but whoever would+ lose their life for my sake and *for* the Gospel, the same will save it.

36 For what will it profit anyone if they gain the whole world and lose their own soul?

37 Or what shall anyone+ give in exchange for their soul?

38 Whoever therefore is ashamed of me and of my words in this adulterous and sinful generation, the Son of man will be ashamed of them also when He comes in the glory of His Father with the holy angels.

Mark Chapter 9

1 *Then* He said to them: Truly+ I say to you that there are some of *those* who stand here who will not taste of death until they have seen the kingdom of God come with power.

2 After six days, Jesus took Peter, James, and John, and led them up into a high mountain apart by themselves and He was transfigured *right there* before them.

3 His clothing+ became shining *and* exceedingly white as snow, like no cleaner+ on earth could whiten them.

4 *Then* Elijah with Moses appeared to them and they were talking with Jesus.

5 Peter answered and said to Jesus: Master, it is good for us to be here. Let us make three tabernacles. One for you and one for Moses and one for Elijah.

6 For he did not know what to say for they were greatly+ afraid.

7 There was a cloud that overshadowed them and a voice came out of the cloud saying: This is my beloved Son. Hear Him.

8 Suddenly, when they had looked around,+ they saw no one any more, except+ Jesus *still* with them.

9 As they came down from the mountain, *Jesus* charged them that they should tell no one what things they had seen, until the Son of man was risen from the dead.

10 *So* they kept that word to themselves, questioning with one another what the rising from the dead could+ mean.

11 *Then* they asked *Jesus* saying: Why do the scribes say that Elijah must come first?

12 *Jesus* answered and told them: Elijah truly+ comes first *and* restores all things, and how is it written of the Son of man: that He must suffer many things and be rejected+. *Matthew 17:11*

13 But I say to you that Elijah has indeed come and they have done to him whatever they desired,+ as it is written about+ him. *Matthew 17:12*

14 *Then* when *Jesus* came to *His* disciples, He saw a great multitude around+ them and the scribes questioning with them.

15 Immediately+ all the people, when they saw+ Him, were greatly amazed and running to *Him* greeted+ Him.

16 He asked the scribes: What were you questioning with them?

17 One of the multitude answered and said: Master, I have brought to you my son who has a spirit *making him* unable to speak.+

18 Wherever he *goes* it tears him and he foams *at the mouth* and gnashes with his teeth and withers+ *away*. I spoke to your disciples *to ask* if they could cast it out and they could not.

19 *Jesus* answered saying: O faithless generation. How long shall I be with you? How long shall I endure+ you? Bring him to me.

20 They brought *the boy* to *Jesus* and when he saw Him, immediately+ the spirit convulsed+ him and he fell on the ground and rolled+ *around* foaming *at the mouth.*

21 *Jesus* asked his father: How long ago
is it since this came to him? He said:
Since childhood.
22 Often times it has cast him into the fire
and into the water to destroy him. But if
you can do anything, have compassion
on us and help us.
23 Jesus said to him:

> If you can believe,
> all things *are* possible
> to *those* who believe.

24 Immediately[+] the father of the child
cried out and said with tears: Lord, I
believe. Help my unbelief.
25 When Jesus saw that the people came
running together, He rebuked the foul
spirit saying to it: *You evil* spirit *blocking*
speech and hearing, I charge you: Come
out of him and enter no more into him.
26 *The spirit* cried *out* and convulsed[+] him
greatly[+] and came out of him, and *the*
boy was like one dead, so that many
said: He is dead.
27 But Jesus took him by the hand and
lifted him up and he arose.
28 *Then* when *Jesus* had come into the
house, His disciples asked Him privately:
Why could we not cast him out?
29 He said to them: This kind can come
forth by nothing but by prayer and
fasting.
30 *Then* they departed from there[+] and
passed through Galilee and He would
not *allow* that anyone should know *it*.
31 For He taught His disciples and said to
them: The Son of man is delivered into
the hands of men and they will kill Him.
After He is killed, He will rise the
third day.
32 But they did not understand that saying
and were afraid to ask Him.
33 *Then* He came to Capernaum and *when*
they were[+] in the house He asked them:
What was it that you disputed among
yourselves by the way?
34 But they *remained* silent[+] for on the way
they had disputed among themselves
who *would be* the greatest.
35 *Then Jesus* sat down and called the
twelve and said to them: If anyone
desires to be first, *the same* will be last
of all and *the* servant of all.
36 He took a child and set him in the
midst of them, and when He had taken
him in His arms, He said to them:
37 Whoever will receive one of such
children in my name receives me. And
whoever will receive me does not
receive me but Him who sent me.
38 John answered Him saying: Master,
we saw someone casting out demons[+] in
your name who does not follow us. *So*
we forbad him because he does not
follow us.
39 But Jesus said: Do not forbid him, for
there is no one who does a miracle in my
name who can lightly speak evil of me.
40 For whoever is not against us is for us.
41 For whoever will give you a cup of
water to drink in my name because you
belong to Christ, truly[+] I say to you:
They will not lose their reward.
42 *But* whoever offends *and sins against*
one of *these* little ones who believe in
me, it would be better for them if[+] a
millstone were hung around[+] their neck
and they were thrown[+] into the sea.
43 If your hand causes[+] you *to sin*, cut it
off. It is better for you to enter into life
maimed than having two hands to go
into hell, into the fire that will never be
quenched,
44 where the *flesh eating* worms never die
and the fire is never[+] quenched.
45 If your foot causes[+] you *to sin*, cut it
off. It is better for you to enter crippled[+]
into life, than having two feet to be cast
into hell, into the fire that will never be
quenched,
46 where the *flesh eating* worms never die
and the fire is never[+] quenched.
47 If your eye causes[+] you *to sin*, pluck it
out. It is better for you to enter into the
kingdom of God with one eye, than
having two eyes to be cast into hell fire,
48 where the *flesh eating* worms never die
and the fire is never[+] quenched.
49 For everyone will be salted with fire and
every sacrifice will be salted with salt.

50 Salt *is* good, but if the salt has lost its
saltness with what will you season it?
Have salt in yourselves and have peace
with one another.

Mark Chapter 10

1 *Then Jesus* arose from there[+] and went[+]
into the borders[+] of Judea on the other[+]
side of Jordan, and the people went[+] to
Him again. And, as it was His custom,
He taught them again.
2 The Pharisees came to Him and asked
Him: Is it lawful for a man to put away
his wife? *They said this to* test[+] Him.
3 He answered and said to them: What
did Moses command you?
4 They said: Moses allowed[+] *us* to write
a written divorce[+] to put *them* away.
5 Jesus answered and said to them: He
wrote this precept because of the hardness of your hearts.
6 But from the beginning of the creation
God made them male and female.
Matthew 19:4
7 For this reason[+] a man shall leave his
father and mother and cleave to his wife
Matthew 19:5
8 and they two shall be one flesh. So
then, they are no longer[+] two but one
flesh. *Matthew 19:6*
9 Therefore what God has joined
together, mankind[+] *must* not separate[+].
Matthew 19:6
10 *Later*, in the house, *Jesus'* disciples asked
Him again about[+] the same *matter*.
11 He said to them: Whoever shall put
away his wife and marry another commits adultery against her.
12 And if a woman shall put away her
husband and be married to another, she
commits adultery.
13 *Then* they brought young children to
Him *so* that He could[+] touch them,
but *His* disciples rebuked *those* who
brought *them*.
14 But when Jesus saw *this*, He was
much displeased and said to them:
Allow the little children to come to
me and do not forbid them, for of such
is the kingdom of God.
15 Truly[+] I say to you: Whoever will not
receive the kingdom of God as a little
child will not enter in.
16 *Then* He took them up in His arms, put
His hands upon them and blessed them.
17 When He went forth into the way, one
came running, knelt *down* to Him and
asked Him: Good Master, what shall I
do that I may inherit eternal life?
18 Jesus said to him: Why do you call me
good? No one *is* good but one. God.
19 You know the commandments: Do
not commit adultery. Do not kill. Do not
steal. Do not bear false witness. Do not
dcfraud. Honor your father and mother.
20 He answered and said to Him: Master,
all these have I observed from my
youth.
21 Then Jesus, beholding him, loved him
and said to him: One thing you lack. Go
and sell whatever you have and give to
the poor, and you will have treasure in
heaven. *Then* come, take up the cross
and follow me.
22 But at that word he became[+] sad and
went away grieved, for he had great
possessions.
23 *Then* Jesus looked around[+] and said to
His disciples: *Those* who have riches
will hardly *be able to* enter into the
kingdom of God.
24 The disciples were astonished at His
words, but Jesus answered again saying
to them: Children, how hard is it for
those who trust in riches to enter into the
kingdom of God.
25 It is easier for a camel to go through the
eye of a needle than for a rich person[+]
to enter into the kingdom of God.
26 They were astonished beyond[+]
measure and said among themselves:
Who then can be saved?
27 Jesus looking upon them said: With
people[+] *it is* impossible, but not with
God. For with God, all things are
possible.
28 Then Peter began to say to Him:
Behold, we have left all and have
followed you.
29 Jesus answered and said: Truly[+] I say
to you: There is no one who has left

house or brothers or sisters or father or
mother or wife or children or lands for
my sake and the Gospel's
30 but will receive a hundredfold now
in this time, houses and brothers and
sisters and mothers and children and
lands, *along* with persecutions; and in
the world to come, eternal life.
31 But many *who are* first will be last and
the last first.
32 *Then as* they were on the way *again*
going up to Jerusalem, Jesus went
before them and they were amazed.
As they followed, they were afraid.
But *Jesus* took the twelve again and
began to tell them what things would
happen to Him.
33 *He said*: Behold we are going to Jerusalem and the Son of man will be delivered
to the chief priests and to the scribes and
they will condemn Him to death and
deliver Him to the Gentiles. *Matthew 20:18*
34 They will mock Him and flog[+] Him
and spit on Him and kill Him, and the
third day He will rise again.
35 *Then* James and John the sons of
Zebedee came to Him saying: Master,
we would *ask* that you do for us
whatever we desire.
36 He said to them: What do you want me
to do for you?
37 They said to Him: Grant to us that we
may sit, one at your right hand and the
other at your left hand, in your glory.
38 But Jesus said to them: You do not
know what you ask. Can you drink of
the cup from which I *shall* drink? And be
baptized with the baptism with which I
am *to be* baptized?
39 They said to Him: We can. And Jesus
said to them: You will indeed drink of
the cup from which I *shall* drink and
with the baptism with which I am baptized, you will be baptized.
40 But to sit at my right hand and at my
left hand is not mine to give, but *it will
be given to them* for whom it is prepared.
41 When the ten heard *this*, they began to
be much displeased with James and John.
42 But Jesus called them and said to
them: You know that *those* who are
accounted to rule over the Gentiles
exercise lordship over them and their
great ones exercise authority upon them.
43 But it shall not be so among you. But
whoever will be great among you, shall
be your servant[+].
44 Whoever of you will be the chief, will
be servant of all.
45 For even the Son of man did not come
to be ministered to, but to minister and
to give His life *as* a ransom for many.
46 *Then* they came to Jericho, and as
Jesus went out of Jericho with His
disciples and a great number of people,
blind Bartimaeus the son of Timaeus,
sat by the wayside begging.
47 When he heard that it was Jesus of
Nazareth, he began to cry out and say:
Jesus son of David, have mercy on me.
48 Many charged him *saying* that he should
be silent.[+] But he cried *out all* the more:
Son of David, have mercy on me.
49 *Then* Jesus stopped[+] and asked[+] for
him to be called. *So* they called the blind
man, saying to him: Be encouraged.[+]
Rise. *Jesus* is calling for you.
50 And he, casting away his garment,
rose and came to Jesus.
51 Jesus answered and said to him: What
do you want me to do to you? The blind
man said to Him: Lord, that I might
receive my sight.
52 Jesus said to him: Go. Your faith has
made you whole. And immediately he
received his sight and followed Jesus in
the way.

Mark Chapter 11

1 When they came near to Jerusalem,
to Bethphage and Bethany at the Mount
of Olives, *Jesus* sent forth two of His
disciples
2 and said to them: Go into the village
before[+] you. As soon as you enter it,
you will find a colt tied on which no one
has *ever* sat. Loose *it* and bring *it to me.*
3 If anyone says to you: Why are you
doing this? Say that the Lord has need of
it and immediately[+] he will send it here.
4 *So* they went away and found the colt

tied by the door outside+ in a cross-
way,+ and they loose it.
5 Certain of *those* who stood there said
to them: What are you doing, loosing
the colt?
6 *The disciples* said to them as Jesus had
commanded, and they let them go.
7 *Then* they brought the colt to Jesus and
cast their garments on it and He sat upon
it. *Matthew 21:5*
8 Many spread their garments in the
way. Others cut down branches off the
trees and spread+ *them* in the way.
9 *Those* who went before and *those* who
followed cried *out* saying: Hosanna.
Blessed *is* He who comes in the name of
the Lord.
10 Blessed *be* the kingdom of our father
David that comes in the name of the
Lord. Hosanna in the highest.
11 Jesus entered Jerusalem and *went* into
the temple. When He had looked around+
upon everything+ and *now that* the hour
was already late, He went out to Bethany
with the twelve.
12 On the next day, when they had come
from Bethany, *Jesus* was hungry.
13 Seeing a fig tree with leaves *at a*
distance,+ He came *closer to see* if
perhaps+ He might find anything on
it. When He came to it, He found
nothing but leaves, for the time for
figs was not *yet*.
14 *But* Jesus answered and said to it: No
one *shall* eat fruit from you hereafter
forever. His disciples heard *this*.
15 *Then* they came to Jerusalem and Jesus
went into the temple and began to cast
out *those* who bought and sold in the
temple, and overthrew the tables of the
money changers and the seats of *those*
who sold doves.
16 *He* would not allow+ anyone to carry
any vessel through the temple.
17 *Then* He taught them saying: Is it not
written: My house shall be called the
house of prayer by all nations? But
you have made it a den of thieves.
Matthew 21:13
18 The scribes and chief priests heard
this and sought how they might destroy
Him, for they feared Him because all the
people were astonished at His doctrine.
19 *Then*, when evening+ had come, He
went out of the city.
20 In the morning as they passed by, they
saw the fig tree dried up from the roots.
21 Peter remembering+ *what occurred*
earlier said to Him: Master, behold the fig
tree that you cursed has withered away.
22 Jesus answering said to them: Have
faith in God.
23 For truly+ I say to you that whoever
says to this mountain: Be removed and
be cast into the sea, and does not doubt
in their heart, but believes that those
things that they said shall come to pass,
they shall have whatever they say.
24 Therefore I say to you: What things
+ you desire, when you pray, believe
that you receive *them* and you shall
have *them*.
25 And when you stand praying: Forgive,
if you have anything+ against anyone+
so that your Father also who is in heaven
may forgive your trespasses.
26 But if you do not forgive, neither will
your Father in heaven forgive your
trespasses.
27 *Then* they came again to Jerusalem and
as He was walking in the temple, the
chief priests and the scribes and the
elders came to Him
28 and said to Him: By what authority do
you *do* these things? And who gave you
this authority to do these things?
29 Jesus answered and said to them: I will
also ask of you one question. Answer
me and I will tell you by what authority
I do these things.
30 The baptism of John: Was *it* from
heaven or of men? Answer me.
31 They reasoned among+ themselves
saying: If we say: From heaven, He will
say: Why then did you not believe him?
32 But if we say: Of men, they feared the
people for all *the people* considered+ that
John was indeed a prophet.
33 *So* they answered and said to Jesus:
We cannot tell. And Jesus answering
said to them: *Then* neither will I tell you
by what authority I do these things.

Mark Chapter 12

1 *Then Jesus* began to speak to them in
parables: A *certain* man planted a
vineyard, set a hedge about *it*, dug *a*
place for the wine vat, built a tower,
let it out to *tenant* farmers,[+] and went
into a far country.
2 At the season he sent a servant to the
tenant farmers[+] *so* that he might receive
from the farmers[+] of the fruit of the
vineyard.
3 *But* they caught *him* and beat him and
sent *him* away empty *handed*.
4 Again he sent to them another servant
but they cast stones at him, wounded
him in the head, and sent *him* away
shamefully treated[+].
5 Again he sent another, but they killed
him and many others, beating some and
killing some.
6 Therefore, having only[+] one son, his
beloved, at last he sent *his only son* to
them, saying: *Surely* they will reverence
my son.
7 But those *tenant* farmers[+] said among
themselves: This is the heir. Come.
Let us kill him and the inheritance
will be ours.
8 *So* they took him and killed *him* and
cast *him* out of the vineyard.
9 Therefore what will the lord of the
vineyard do? He will come and destroy
the *tenant* farmers[+] and will give the
vineyard to others.
10 Have you not read this Scripture: The
stone that the builders rejected has become the head of the corner. *Matthew 21:42*
11 This was the Lord's doing and it is
marvelous in our eyes.
12 *So* they sought to lay hold on Him, but
they feared the people for they knew that
He had spoken the parable against them.
So they left Him and went away.[+]
13 *Then* they sent some of the Pharisees
and of the Herodians to Him to catch
Him in *His* words.
14 When they had come, they said to
Him: Master, we know that you are true
and do not *have special* care for any *one*
person over another, for you do not regard the positions[+] people[+] *hold*, but
teach the way of God in truth. Is it
lawful to give tribute to Caesar or not?
15 Shall we give or shall we not give? But
knowing their hypocrisy, *Jesus* said to
them: Why do you test[+] me? Bring a
coin[+] to me *so* that I may see *it*.
16 They brought *it* and He said to them:
Whose *is* this image and title[+]? They
said to Him: Caesar's.
17 *So* Jesus answering said to them:
Render to Caesar the things that are
Caesar's and to God the things that
are God's. They marveled at Him.
18 Then the Sadducees who say there is
no resurrection came to Him and they
asked Him saying:
19 Master, Moses wrote to us: If a man's
brother die and leave *his* wife and leave
no children, that his brother should take
his wife and raise up seed to his brother.
20 Now there were seven brothers. The
first took a wife and dying left no seed.
21 *Then* the second took her and died and he
also left no seed. And the third likewise.
22 The seven had her and left no seed.
Last of all the woman also died.
23 Therefore in the resurrection when
they rise, whose wife will she be? For
the seven had her as *their* wife.
24 Jesus answering said to them: Do you
not therefore err because you do not
know the Scriptures or the power of
God?
25 For when they rise from the dead, they
neither marry nor are given in marriage
but are like[+] the angels in heaven.
26 And *regarding* the dead, that they rise:
Have you not read in the book of Moses,
how in the bush God spoke to him
saying: I *am* the God of Abraham and
the God of Isaac and the God of Jacob.
27 He is not the God of the dead but the
God of the living. You therefore do
greatly err.
28 *Then* one of the scribes came and,
having heard them reasoning together
and perceiving that He had answered
them well, asked Him: Which is the first
commandment of all?

29 Jesus answered him: The first of all the commandments *is this*: Hear O Israel. The Lord our God is one Lord. *Deuteronomy 6:4*

30 You shall love the Lord your God with all your heart and with all your soul and with all your mind and with all your strength. This *is* the first commandment. *Matthew 22:37*

31 And the second *is* like this: You shall love your neighbor as yourself. There is no other commandment greater than these. *Matthew 19:19*

32 The scribe said to Him: Well *said* Master. You have spoken the truth. For there is one God and there is no other but He.

33 To love Him with all the heart and with all the understanding and with all the soul and with all the strength and to love neighbor as oneself[+] is more than all burnt offerings and sacrifices.

34 When Jesus saw that he answered *with an* understanding mind,[+] He said to him: You are not far from the kingdom of God. No one after that dared[+] ask Him *any question*.

35 While *He was* teaching in the temple, Jesus answering said: How *is it* that the scribes say that Christ is the son of David?

36 For David himself said by the Holy Spirit: The Lord said to my Lord: Sit at my right hand until I make your enemies your footstool.

37 Therefore David himself calls Him Lord. How[+] *then* is He *David's* son? And the common people heard Him gladly.

38 *Then* He said to them in His doctrine: Beware of the scribes who love to go in long clothing and *love* salutations in the marketplaces,

39 the chief seats in the synagogues and the uppermost rooms at feasts,

40 who devour widows' houses and for a pretence make long prayers. They will receive greater damnation.

41 *Then* Jesus sat near[+] the treasury and saw[+] how the people cast money into the treasury. Many who were rich cast in much.

42 *But then* a certain poor widow came and threw in two mites, which were *worth about* a penny.[+]

43 *Jesus* called His disciples and said to them: Truly[+] I say to you that this poor widow has cast more in than all *those* who have cast into the treasury.

44 For *they* all cast in *out* of their abundance, but she *even out* of her lack[+] cast in everything[+] that she had, *even* all her *means of* livelihood[+].

Mark Chapter 13

1 As *Jesus* went out of the temple, one of His disciples said to Him: Master, see what manner of stones and what buildings *are here*.

2 Jesus answering said to him: See these great buildings? There will not be left stone upon stone that will not be thrown down.

3 *Later* as He sat on the Mount of Olives near[+] the temple, Peter, James, John, and Andrew asked Him privately:

4 Tell us when will these things be? And what *will be* the sign when all these things will be fulfilled?

5 Jesus answering them began to say: Take heed lest anyone[+] deceive you.

6 For many will come in my name saying: I am *Christ* and will deceive many.

7 When you hear of wars and rumors of wars, do not be troubled for *such things* need to be, but the end *will* not *be* yet.

8 For nation will rise against nation and kingdom against kingdom. There will be earthquakes in many different[+] places and there will be famines and troubles. These *are* the beginnings of sorrows.

9 But take heed to yourselves, for they will deliver you up to councils. In the synagogues you will be beaten. You will be brought before rulers and kings for my sake, for a testimony against them.

10 *But* the Gospel must first be published among all nations.

11 But when they take[+] *you away* and deliver you up, take no thought beforehand what you shall speak *and* do not premeditate. But whatever shall be given

to you in that hour, that you *shall* speak.
For it is not you who *will be* speaking,
but the Holy Spirit.
12 Now brother will betray brother to
death and father *betray* child. Children
will rise up against *their* parents and
cause them *to be* put to death.
13 You will be hated by all for my name's
sake, but *those* who endure to the end,
the same will be saved.
14 Let *those* who read *this* understand:
When you see the abomination of desolation spoken of by Daniel the prophet
standing where it should not, then let *those*
who are in Judea flee to the mountains.
15 Let *those* who are on the housetop not
go down into the house nor enter *there*
to take anything out of their house.
16 Let *those* who are in the field not turn
back again to take up their garments.
17 But woe to *those* who are with child and
to *those* who are nursing+ in those days.
18 Pray that your flight not be in the
winter.
19 For *in* those days *there* will be affliction
such as has not *occurred* from the beginning of the creation which God created
to this time, nor shall *there* be *ever again*.
20 Unless+ the Lord shortened those days,
no flesh would be saved. But for the
sake of the elect whom He has chosen,
He has shortened the days.
21 Then if anyone says to you: Behold
here *is* Christ. Or behold *He is* there, do
not believe *them*.
22 For false Christs and false prophets
will arise and will show signs and
wonders to deceive,+ if *it were* possible,
even the elect.
23 But take heed. Behold, I have foretold
all *these* things *to* you *before they occur*.
24 But in those days, after that tribulation, the sun will be darkened and the
moon will not give its light.
25 The stars of heaven will fall and the
powers that are in heaven will be shaken.
26 Then they will see the Son of man
coming in the clouds with great power
and glory.
27 And then He will send His angels and
gather together His elect from the four
winds, from the ends+ of the earth to the
ends+ of heaven.
28 Now learn a parable from the fig tree.
When its branch is yet tender and puts
forth leaves, you know that summer
is near.
29 So in like manner, when you see these
things come to pass, know that it is near,
even at the doors.
30 Truly+ I say to you, that this generation will not pass, until all these
things are done.
31 Heaven and earth will pass away, but
my words will not pass away.
32 But of that day and *that* hour no one
knows. No, not *even* the angels in heaven
nor the Son, but the Father *only*.
33 Take heed, watch, and pray. For you
do not know when the time is *to be*.
34 *For the Son of man is* like+ a man taking
a far journey who left his house and
gave authority to his servants, to every
person+ their work, and *then* commanded
the doorkeeper+ to watch.
35 Watch, therefore. For you do not
know when the master of the house is
coming: In the evening,+ at midnight, at
the cock crowing, or in the morning,
36 lest coming suddenly, he find you
sleeping.
37 And what I say to you, I say to all:
Watch.

Mark Chapter 14

1 After two days was *to be the Feast of* the
Passover and of unleavened bread. The
chief priests and the scribes sought how
they might take Him by craft and put
Him to death.
2 But they said: Not on the feast *day*, lest
there be an uproar of the people.
3 *Now* as *Jesus* sat *down* to eat+ in the
house of Simon the leper in Bethany, a
woman came *to Him* with an alabaster
box of ointment of spikenard, very
precious. And she broke the box and
poured *the contents* on His head.
4 *But* there were some who had indignation
within themselves and said: Why was
this waste of the ointment made?

5 For it might have been sold for more
than *a year's wages*[+] and given to the poor.
And they complained[+] against her.
6 Jesus said: Let her alone. Why do
you trouble her? She has done[+] a
good work on me.
7 For you have the poor with you
always, and whenever you will you
may do good *to them*. But you will not
always have me.
8 She has done what she could. She
has come beforehand to anoint my
body for burial[+].
9 Truly[+] I say to you: Wherever this
Gospel shall be proclaimed[+] throughout
the whole world, *this* also that she has
done will be spoken of for a memorial
of her.
10 *Then* Judas Iscariot, one of the twelve,
went to the chief priests to betray Him
to them.
11 When they heard *this*, they were glad
and promised to give him money. *So
Judas* sought how he might conveniently
betray Him.
12 The first day of *the Feast of* Unleavened
Bread when they killed the Passover
lamb, His disciples said to Him: Where
do you want us to go and prepare *so* that
you may eat the Passover?
13 He sent forth two of His disciples and
said to them: Go into the city and there
a man bearing a pitcher of water will
meet you. Follow him.
14 Wherever he goes in, say to the head[+]
of the house: The Master asks: Where is
the guest chamber where I shall eat the
Passover with my disciples?
15 He will show you a large upper room
furnished *and* prepared. Make ready for
us there.
16 *So* His disciples went forth and came
into the city and found as He had said to
them, and they made preparations[+] *for*
the Passover.
17 *Then* in the evening, He came with the
twelve.
18 As they sat and ate, Jesus said: Truly[+]
I say to you: One of you who eats with
me will betray me.
19 They began to be sorrowful and to say
to Him one by one: *Is* it me? And
another *said: Is* it me?
20 He answered and said to them: *It is*
one of the twelve who dips with me in
the dish.
21 The Son of man indeed goes as it is
written of Him. But woe to that man by
whom the Son of man is betrayed. It
would be good for that man if he had
never been born.
22 As they ate, Jesus took bread, blessed,
broke *it*, gave to them, and said: Take.
Eat. This is my body.
23 *Then* He took the cup, and when He
had given thanks, He gave *it* to them and
they all drank of it.
24 He said to them: This is my blood of
the new covenant,[+] which is shed for
many.
25 Truly[+] I say to you: I will drink no
more of the fruit of the vine until the day
that I drink it new in the kingdom of
God.
26 *Then* when they had sung a hymn, they
went out to the Mount of Olives.
27 And Jesus said to them: All *of* you
will be offended because of me this
night. For it is written: I will strike[+]
the shepherd and the sheep will be
scattered. *Matthew 26:31*
28 But after I am risen, I will go before
you into Galilee.
29 But Peter said to Him: Although all
will be offended, yet I *will* not.
30 Jesus said to him: Truly[+] I say to you:
That this day, *even* in this night before
the cock crows twice, you will deny me
three times.
31 But *Peter* spoke *all* the more forcefully[+]: If I should die with you, I will not
deny you in any way.[+] And they all
spoke[+] in the same manner.[+]
32 *Then* they came to a place named
Gethsemane and He said to His disciples:
Sit here while I pray.
33 And He took Peter, James, and John
with Him and began to be greatly[+]
amazed and to be very heavy.
34 He said to them: My soul is exceedingly sorrowful unto death. Stay[+] here
and watch.

35 *Then* He went forward a little, fell on
the ground, and prayed that, if it were
possible, the hour might pass from Him.
36 He said: Abba, Father, all things *are*
possible to you. Take away this cup
from me. Nevertheless not what I will
but what you will.
37 *Then* He came and found them sleeping and said to Peter: Simon, are you
sleeping? Could you not watch one
hour?
38 Watch and pray lest you enter into
temptation. The spirit truly *is* ready but
the flesh *is* weak.
39 Again He went away and prayed and
spoke the same words.
40 When He returned, He found them
asleep again, for their eyes were
heavy. *And* they did not know how+ to
answer Him.
41 *Then* He came the third time and said
to them: Sleep on now and take *your*
rest. It is enough. The hour has come.
Behold the Son of man is betrayed into
the hands of sinners.
42 Rise up. Let us go. Behold, he who
betrays me is near+.
43 Immediately, while He spoke, Judas,
one of the twelve, came. With him *came*
a great multitude with swords and staves,
coming from the chief priests and the
scribes and the elders.
44 He who betrayed *Jesus* had given them
a token saying: Whomever I kiss, that
same is He. Take Him and lead *Him*
away safely.
45 As soon as *Judas* had come, he went
to *Jesus* immediately+ and said: Master,
Master. And kissed Him. *Matthew 26:48*
46 *Then* they laid their hands on Him and
took Him.
47 One of *those* who stood by drew a
sword and struck+ a servant of the high
priest and cut off his ear.
48 Jesus answered and said to them:
Have you come out as against a thief
with swords and *with* staves to take me?
49 I was with you daily in the temple
teaching and you did not take me. But
the Scriptures must be fulfilled.
50 *Then* they all left+ Him and fled.
51 Now a certain young man followed
Jesus. *He had only* a linen cloth around+ *his*
naked *body*. The young men seized+ him
52 *but* he left the linen cloth and fled from
them naked.
53 *So* they led Jesus away to the high
priest. With Him were assembled all the
chief priests and the elders and the scribes.
54 Peter followed Him *from* a distance,+
even into the palace of the high priest.
He sat with the servants and warmed
himself at the fire.
55 The chief priests and all the council
sought *a* witness against Jesus to put
Him to death, *but they* found none.
56 For many bore false testimony+ against
Him, but their testimonies+ did not
agree.
57 *Then* certain *ones* arose and bore false
testimony+ against Him saying:
58 We heard Him say: I will destroy this
temple that is made with hands and
within three days I will build another
made without hands. *Matthew 26:61*
59 But neither did their testimonies+
agree.
60 *Then* the high priest stood up in the
midst and asked Jesus saying: Do you
not answer? What *is it that* these witness
against you?
61 But *Jesus remained* silent+ and answered
nothing. Again the high priest asked
Him and said to Him: Are you the
Christ, the Son of the Blessed?
62 Jesus said: I Am. You will see the Son
of man sitting at the right hand of power
and coming in the clouds of heaven.
63 Then the high priest tore+ his clothes
and said: What need do we have for any
further witnesses?
64 You have heard the blasphemy. What
do you think? And they all condemned
Him to be guilty of death.
65 Some began to spit on Him and to
cover His face and to buffet Him and
to say to Him: Prophesy. And the
servants struck Him with the palms of
their hands.
66 *Meanwhile* Peter was in the court+
below.+ One of the maids of the high
priest came

67 and when she saw Peter warming
himself, she looked at him and said:
And you also were with Jesus of
Nazareth.
68 But *Peter* denied *it* saying: I do not
know or understand what you say. *Then*
he went out into the porch and the cock
crowed.+
69 *Then* a maid saw him again and began
to say to *those* who stood by: This is *one*
of them.
70 *Peter* denied it again. And a little after,
those who stood by said again to Peter:
Surely you are *one* of them for you are a
Galilaean and your speech is like+ *that*.
71 But *Peter* began to curse and to swear
saying: I do not know this man of whom
you speak.
72 *Then* the second time the cock crowed,+
Peter called to mind the word that Jesus
said to him: Before the cock crows
twice, you will deny me three times.
When he thought about this, he wept.

Mark Chapter 15

1 Immediately+ in the morning, the chief
priests held a consultation with the elders
and scribes and the whole council. *Then*
they bound Jesus, carried *Him* away, and
delivered *Him* to Pilate.
2 Pilate asked Him: Are you the King of
the Jews? And He answering said to
him: You say *it*.
3 The chief priests accused Him of many
things, but He answered nothing.
4 Pilate asked Him again saying: Do
you not answer? Behold how many
things they witness against you.
5 But Jesus still+ answered nothing, so
that Pilate marveled. *Matthew 27:14*
6 Now at *the* feast *Pilate was to* release
one prisoner to them, whomever they
desired.
7 And there was *one* named Barabbas
who laid bound with *those* who had made
insurrection with him, *and Barabbas* had
committed murder in the insurrection.
8 Now the multitude began to cry aloud
asking+ *Pilate to do* as he had always+
done for them.
9 But Pilate answered them saying: Do
you want me *to* release the King of the
Jews to you?
10 For he knew that the chief priests had
delivered *Jesus* because+ of envy.
11 But the chief priests stirred *up* the
people *so* that *Pilate* would release
Barabbas to them instead.
12 Pilate answered and said to them again:
Then what do you want me to do *to Him*
whom you call the King of the Jews?
13 They cried out again: Crucify Him.
14 Then Pilate said to them: Why? What
evil has He done? And they cried out *all*
the more exceedingly: Crucify Him.
15 *So* Pilate, choosing+ to satisfy+ the
people, released Barabbas to them and
delivered Jesus, when he had flogged+
Him, to be crucified.
16 The soldiers led Him away into the hall
called Praetorium, and they called together the whole company+ *of soldiers*.
17 They clothed Him with purple and
made+ a crown of thorns and put it
around+ His *head*.
18 And *they* began to salute Him *saying*:
Hail, King of the Jews.
19 They struck+ Him on the head with a
reed and spit on Him and bowing *their*
knees worshiped Him.
20 When they had mocked Him, they
took the purple off of Him, put His own
clothes on Him, and led Him out to
crucify Him.
21 *Then* they compelled one *called* Simon,
a Cyrenian who passed by coming out of
the country, the father of Alexander and
Rufus, to bear His cross.
22 They brought Him to the place *called*
Golgotha, which means+: The place of
a skull.
23 They gave Him wine mingled with
myrrh to drink, but He did not accept+ *it*.
24 When they had crucified Him, they
divided+ His garments, casting lots upon
them *to decide* what each one+ would+
take. *Matthew 27:35*
25 It was nine o'clock+ *in the morning*
when+ they crucified Him.
26 The title+ of His accusation was
written over *Him*: The King of the Jews.

27 And they crucified two thieves with Him: One at His right hand and the other at His left. *Matthew 27:38*

28 *Thus* the Scripture was fulfilled that says: He was numbered with the transgressors. *Isaiah 53:12*

29 *Those* who passed by railed at Him, shaking+ their heads and saying: Ah, you who *would* destroy the temple and build *it again* in three days: *Matthew 27:41*

30 Save yourself and come down from the cross.

31 Likewise also the chief priests, mocking, said among themselves with the scribes: He saved others, *but* He cannot save Himself. *Matthew 27:42*

32 Let Christ the King of Israel descend now from the cross *so* that we may see and believe. And *those* who were crucified with Him reviled Him.

33 When twelve o'clock+ *noon* came, there was darkness over the whole land until three *in the afternoon*.

34 At three o'clock+ *in the afternoon*, Jesus cried *out* with a loud voice saying: Eli, Eli, lama sabachthani. That means+: My God, my God. Why have you forsaken me?

35 Some of *those* who stood by, when they heard *this*, said: Behold He calls Elijah.

36 One ran and filled a sponge full of vinegar and put *it* on a reed and gave *it to* Him to drink saying: Let *Him* alone. Let us see whether Elijah will come to take Him down.

37 *Then* Jesus cried *out* with a loud voice and expired.+

38 And the veil of the temple was torn+ in two from the top to the bottom.

39 When the centurion who stood near+ Him saw that He cried out and expired,+ he said: Truly this man was the Son of God.

40 There were also women looking on *from* a distance.+ Among them were Mary Magdalene, Mary the mother of James the less and of Joses, and Salome.

41 *This Salome was the one* who, when He was in Galilee, followed Him and ministered to Him, *along with* many other women who came up with Him to Jerusalem.

42 Now when the evening+ had come, because it was the preparation, that is, the day before the Sabbath,

43 Joseph of Arimathaea, an honorable counselor who also waited for the kingdom of God, went in boldly to Pilate and asked+ *for* Jesus' body.

44 Pilate wondered+ if *Jesus* was already dead and, calling the centurion, he asked him whether He had been dead for long.+

45 When he knew *it* from the centurion, he gave the body to Joseph.

46 *Joseph* bought fine linen, took *Jesus* down and wrapped Him in the linen, laid Him in a tomb+ cut+ out of a rock, and rolled a stone to the door of the tomb.+

47 And Mary Magdalene and Mary *the mother* of Joses saw+ where He was laid.

Mark Chapter 16

1 When the Sabbath was past, Mary Magdalene and Mary the *mother* of James and Salome bought sweet spices *so* that they might come and anoint Him.

2 Very early + *on* the first *of the* week, they came to the tomb+ at the rising of the sun.

3 They said among themselves: Who will roll away the stone from the door of the tomb+ *for* us?

4 *But* when they looked, they saw that the stone was rolled away, for it was very large.+

5 Entering the tomb,+ they saw a young man sitting on the right side clothed in a long white garment, and they were frightened.+

6 He said to them: Do not be frightened.+ You seek Jesus of Nazareth who was crucified. He is risen. He is not here. Behold the place where they laid Him. *Matthew 28:6*

7 But go+ *and* tell His disciples and Peter that He has gone before you into Galilee. There you will see Him, as He said to you.

8 *So* they went out quickly and fled from

the tomb,+ for they trembled and were amazed. Nor did they say anything to anyone,+ for they were afraid.

9 *Now* having risen early, *the* first *of the* week *Jesus* appeared first to Mary Magdalene out of whom He had cast seven demons.+

10 She went and told *those* who had been with Him as they mourned and wept.

11 When they heard that He was alive and had been seen by her, they did not believe.

12 After that, He appeared in another form to two of them as they walked and went into the country.

13 They went and told *it* to the rest+ and *they* did not believe them either.

14 Afterward He appeared to the eleven as they sat *down* to eat+ and *He* upbraided them for their unbelief and hardness of heart because they did not believe *those* who had seen Him after He was risen.

15 He said to them: Go into all the world and proclaim+ the Gospel to all creation+.

> 16 *Those* who believe
> and are baptized will be saved,
> but *those* who do not believe
> will be damned.

17 These signs will follow *those* who believe: In my name they will cast out demons.+ They will speak with new tongues.

18 They will take up serpents and if they drink any deadly thing it will not hurt them. And they will lay hands on the sick and they will recover.

19 So then after the Lord had spoken to them, He was received up into heaven and sat at the right hand of God. *Psalm 68:18*

20 And they went forth and proclaimed+ *the Word* everywhere, the Lord working with *them* and confirming the Word with signs following. Amen.

The Gospel of Jesus Christ as surveyed by Luke

Chapter 1

1 Having observed+ *that* many *others* have taken *it* upon themselves+ to set forth a declaration of those things that are most surely believed among us,

2 as *those* who were eyewitnesses and ministers of the Word have delivered *those things* to us,

3 it seemed good to me also, having diligently+ *sought* understanding of everything+ from the very first, to write to you an orderly+ *account*, most excellent Theophilus,

4 *so* that you might know the certainty of those things in which you have been instructed.

5 *Now* there was, in the days of Herod the king of Judea, a certain priest named Zacharias of the course of Abijah. His wife *was* of the daughters of Aaron and her name *was* Elisabeth.

6 They were both righteous before God, walking in all the commandments and ordinances of the Lord, blameless.

7 They had no child because Elisabeth was barren, and *now* they were both well advanced+ in years.

8 Now+ it came to pass, that while *Zacharias* executed the priest's office before God in the order of his course,

9 according to the custom of the priest's office, his lot was to burn incense when he went into the temple of the Lord.

10 The whole multitude of the people were praying outside+ at the time of incense.

11 *Then* an angel of the Lord appeared to him standing on the right side of the altar of incense.

12 When Zacharias saw *this*, he was troubled and fear fell upon him.

13 But the angel said to him: Do not be afraid Zacharias, for your prayer is heard. Your wife Elisabeth will bear a son to you and you shall call his name John.

14 And you will have joy and gladness, and many will rejoice at his birth.
15 For he will be great in the sight of the Lord. *He* will not drink either wine or strong drink, and he will be filled with the Holy Spirit, even from his mother's womb.
16 He will turn many of the children of Israel to the Lord their God.
17 He will go before *the Lord* in the spirit and power of Elijah, to turn the hearts of the fathers to the children and the disobedient to the wisdom of the righteous,+ to make ready a people prepared for the Lord.
18 Zacharias said to the angel: How+ can I understand+ this? For I am an old man and my wife *is* well advanced+ in years.
19 The angel answering said to him: I am Gabriel who stands in the presence of God. *I* am sent to speak to you and to show you these glad tidings.
20 And behold *now* you shall be speechless+ and not able to speak until the day that these things shall be performed, because you did not believe my words that *surely* will be fulfilled in their season.
21 *Meanwhile* the people waited for Zacharias and marveled that he stayed+ so long in the temple.
22 *Then* when he came out he could not speak to them. They perceived that he had seen a vision in the temple, for he signaled+ to them, but remained speechless.
23 Now+ it came to pass that as soon as the days of his service+ were fulfilled,+ he departed to his own house.
24 After those days his wife Elisabeth conceived and hid herself five months saying:
25 Thus has the Lord dealt with me in the days in which He looked upon *me* to take away my reproach among men.
26 *Meanwhile* in *Elisabeth's* sixth month, the angel Gabriel was sent from God to a city of Galilee named Nazareth
27 to a virgin espoused to a man whose name was Joseph of the house of David. The virgin's name *was* Mary.
28 The angel came to her and said: Hail, *O highly* favored, the Lord *is* with you. Blessed *are* you among women.
29 When *Mary* saw *him*, she was troubled by what he said and wondered+ in her mind what kind+ of greeting+ this might+ be.
30 The angel said to her: Do not be afraid Mary, for you have found favor with God.
31 Behold you will conceive in your womb and bring forth a son, and shall call His name Jesus. *Isaiah 7:14*
32 He will be great and will be called the Son of the Highest and the Lord God will give to Him the throne of His father David,
33 and He will reign over the house of Jacob forever. Of His kingdom there will be no end. *Isaiah 9:7*
34 Then Mary said to the angel: How shall this be since+ I have not known+ a man?
35 The angel answered and said to her: The Holy Spirit will come upon you and the power of the Highest will overshadow you. And therefore, that Holy One+ who will be born of you shall be called the Son of God.
36 And behold your cousin Elisabeth has also conceived a son in her old age and this is the sixth month with her who was called barren.
37 For with God nothing will be impossible.
38 Mary said: Behold the handmaid of the Lord. Be it to me according to your word. And the angel departed from her.
39 *Then* Mary arose in those days and went with haste into the hill country to a city of Judah.
40 *She* entered the house of Zacharias and greeted+ Elisabeth.
41 And it came to pass that when Elisabeth heard Mary's greeting, the babe in her womb leaped and Elisabeth was filled with the Holy Spirit.
42 *Then* she spoke out with a loud voice and said: Blessed *are* you among women and blessed *is* the fruit of your womb.
43 Why *has* this *honor come* to me, that the mother of my Lord should come to me?
44 For behold, as soon as the voice of your greeting+ sounded in my ears, the babe in my womb leaped for joy.

45 Blessed *is* she who believed, for there
will be a performance of those things
that were told *to* her from the Lord.
46 Mary said: My soul magnifies the
Lord.
47 My spirit rejoices in God my Savior.
48 For He has regarded the low estate of
His handmaiden. For behold, from
henceforth all generations will call
me blessed.
49 For He who is mighty has done great
things to me. Holy *is* His name.
50 His mercy *is* on *those* who fear Him
from generation to generation.
51 He has shown strength with His arm.
He has scattered the proud in the
imagination of their hearts.
52 He has put down the mighty from *their*
seats and exalted those of low degree.
53 He has filled the hungry with good
things and He has sent *the* rich away
empty.
54 He has helped[+] His servant Israel in
remembrance of *His* mercy,
55 as He spoke to our fathers, to Abraham
and to his seed forever.
56 Mary stayed[+] with *Elisabeth* about
three months and *then* returned to her
own house.
57 Now Elisabeth fulfilled[+] the time *in*
which[+] she should give birth[+] and she
brought forth a son.
58 Her neighbors and her cousins heard
how the Lord had shown great mercy
upon her and they rejoiced with her.
59 And it came to pass that on the eighth
day they came to circumcise the child
and they called him Zacharias after the
name of his father.
60 But[+] his mother answered and said:
No. He shall be called John.
61 They said to her: *But* there is no one in
your family[+] who is called by this name,
62 and they made signs to his father *asking*
what he would have *the child* called.
63 *Zacharias* asked for a writing table and
wrote saying: His name is John. And
they all marveled.
64 Immediately, his mouth was opened
and his tongue *loosed* and he spoke and
praised God.
65 Fear came upon all who lived[+]
around[+] them and all these things[+]
were reported[+] throughout all the hill
country of Judea.
66 All who heard *these things* laid *them*
up in their hearts saying: What kind[+]
of child will this be? And the hand of
the Lord was with him.
67 Now *John's* father Zacharias was
filled with the Holy Spirit and prophesied
saying:
68 Blessed *be* the Lord God of Israel,
for He has visited and redeemed His
people.
69 *He* has raised up a horn of salvation
for us in the house of His servant
David,
70 *just* as He spoke by the mouth of His
holy prophets who have been *with us*
since the world began,
71 *so* that we should be saved from our
enemies and from the hand of all who
hate us,
72 to perform the mercy *promised* to our
fathers and to remember His holy
covenant.
73 *Remember* the oath that He swore to
our father Abraham,
74 that He would grant *deliverance* to us
so that we, *by* being delivered out of the
hand of our enemies, might serve Him
without fear,
75 in holiness and righteousness before
Him all the days of our life.
76 *Then Zacharias said:* You, child, shall
be called the prophet of the Highest. For
you shall go before the face of the Lord
to prepare His ways,
77 to give knowledge of salvation to
His people by the remission of their
sins
78 through the tender mercy of our God
from whom the Dayspring from on high
has visited us,
79 to give light to *those* who sit in
darkness and *in* the shadow of death
and to guide our feet into the way of
peace.
80 The child grew and *became* strong in
spirit, and was in the deserts until the
day of his showing to Israel.

Luke Chapter 2

1 Now+ it came to pass in those days *that* a decree went out from Caesar Augustus that all the world should be registered.+ *Daniel 9:25*

2 This census+ was first made when Cyrenius was governor of Syria

3 and all went to be registered,+ everyone to their own city.

4 Joseph also went up from Galilee out of the city of Nazareth to Judea to the city of David called Bethlehem, because he was of the house and family+ of David. *Micah 5:2*

5 *He went* to be registered+ with Mary his espoused wife *who was great* with child.

6 So it was that, while they were there, the days were fulfilled+ that she should give birth,+

7 and she brought forth her firstborn son and wrapped Him in swaddling clothes and laid Him in a manger, because there was no room for them in the inn.

8 Now+ in the same country, there were shepherds abiding in the field, keeping watch over their flock by night.

9 And behold, the angel of the Lord came upon them and the glory of the Lord shone around+ them and they were greatly+ afraid.

10 The angel said to them: Do not be afraid, for behold I bring to you good tidings of great joy that will be *for* all people.

11 For unto you is born this day in the city of David, a Savior who is Christ the Lord.

12 This *shall be* a sign to you: You will find the babe wrapped in swaddling clothes, lying in a manger.

13 And suddenly there was with the angel a multitude of the heavenly host praising God and saying:

14 Glory to God in the highest. And on earth peace *and* good will toward *all* mankind.+

15 *Now* it came to pass, as the angels had gone away from them into heaven, the shepherds said to one another: Let us now go to Bethlehem and see the *fulfillment of* this word that the Lord has made known to us.

16 *So* they went+ with haste and found Mary and Joseph, and the babe lying in a manger.

17 When they had seen *this*, they made widely+ known the things+ that were told *to* them concerning this child.

18 All *those* who heard *this* wondered at those things that were told *to* them by the shepherds.

19 But Mary kept all these things in her heart and pondered *them*.

20 *Then* the shepherds returned, glorifying and praising God for all the things that they had heard and seen, as it was told to them.

21 When eight days were fulfilled+ *and the time came* for circumcising the little+ child, His name was called Jesus, which is the name *He* was called+ by the angel before He was conceived in the womb.

22 When the days of *Mary's* purification were accomplished, according to the law of Moses, they took Him to Jerusalem to present *Him* to the Lord.

23 As it is written in the law of the Lord: Every male who opens the womb shall be called holy to the Lord. *Exodus 13:2, Exodus 13:12, Exodus 22:29, Numbers 3:13, Numbers 8:16-17, Numbers 18:15*

24 *So the child was brought* to offer a sacrifice according to what is said in the law of the Lord: A pair of turtledoves or two young pigeons.

25 And behold, there was a man in Jerusalem whose name *was* Simeon. *He was* righteous+ and devout, waiting for the consolation of Israel, and the Holy Spirit was upon him.

26 It was revealed to him by the Holy Spirit that he should not see death before he had seen Christ+ the Lord.

27 *So* He came by the Spirit into the temple. When the parents brought in the child Jesus to do for Him according *to* the custom of the law,

28 *Simeon* took *Jesus* up in his arms and blessed God and said:

29 Lord, now let your servant depart in peace, according to your Word.

30 For my eyes have seen your salvation

31 that you have prepared in the presence+ of all the people,

32 a light for *the* revelation+ *of* the Gentiles and *for* the glory of your people Israel.

33 Joseph and His mother marveled at those things that were spoken of Him.

34 Simeon blessed them and said to Mary His mother: Behold this *child* is appointed+ for the fall and rising again of many in Israel and *also for* a sign *that will be* spoken against.

35 Yes. A sword will pierce through your own soul also *so* that the thoughts of many hearts may be revealed.

36 *Then came* one *called* Anna, a prophetess, the daughter of Phanuel of the tribe of Asher. She was *well* advanced+ *in years* and had lived with a husband seven years from her virginity

37 but+ *then had been* a widow for about eighty four years. *During that time* she had not departed from the temple but served *God* with fastings and prayers night and day.

38 Now she also came in that same hour *and* gave thanks to the Lord and spoke about *Jesus* to all *those* who looked for redemption in Jerusalem.

39 When they had performed all things according to the law of the Lord, they returned to Galilee, to their own city Nazareth.

40 And the child grew and became+ strong in spirit *and* filled with wisdom, and the grace of God was upon Him.

41 Now every year at the Feast of the Passover, His parents went to Jerusalem.

42 And when He was twelve years old, they went up to Jerusalem according+ *to* the custom of the feast.

43 And when they had fulfilled the days, as they returned, the young+ Jesus stayed+ behind in Jerusalem, but+ Joseph and His mother did not know *about this*.

44 But supposing Him to be in the company, they went a day's journey, and sought Him among *their* relatives+ and acquaintance.

45 When they did not find Him, they returned+ to Jerusalem seeking Him.

46 Now+ it came to pass that after three days they found Him in the temple, sitting in the midst of the teachers,+ both hearing them and asking them questions.

47 All who heard Him were astonished at His understanding and answers.

48 When *Joseph and His mother* saw Him, they were amazed and His mother said to Him: Son, why have you done+ this to us? Behold your father and I have *been much* distressed+ seeking+ you.

49 He said to them: How is it that you sought me? Did you not know that I must be about my Father's business?

50 But+ they did not understand the words He spoke to them.

51 *Then* He went down with them and came to Nazareth and was subject to them, but His mother kept all these things+ in her heart.

52 And Jesus increased in wisdom and stature and in favor with God and *with* people.+ *Isaiah 11:2*

Luke Chapter 3

1 Now in the fifteenth year of the reign of Tiberius Caesar, Pontius Pilate was governor of Judea, Herod was tetrarch of Galilee and his brother Philip tetrarch of Ituraea and of the region of Trachonitis, and Lysanias *was* the tetrarch of Abilene.

2 Annas and Caiaphas were the high priests. *Then* the Word of God came to John the son of Zacharias in the wilderness.

3 And *John* went+ into all the country around+ Jordan proclaiming+ the baptism of repentance for the remission of sins.

4 As it is written in the book of the words of the prophet Isaiah *who* said: The voice of one crying in the wilderness: Prepare the way of the Lord. Make His paths straight. *Matthew 3:3*

5 Every valley shall be filled and every mountain and hill shall be brought low. The crooked shall be made straight and the rough ways *shall be* made smooth.

6 All flesh will see the salvation of God.
7 Then he said to the multitude that
came forth to be baptized by him: O
generation of vipers, who has warned
you to flee from the wrath to come?
8 Bring forth therefore fruits worthy of
repentance and do not begin to say
within yourselves: We have Abraham
as *our* father. For I say to you that God
is able to raise up children to Abraham
from these stones.
9 Now also the axe is laid to the root of
the trees. Therefore, every tree that
does not bring forth good fruit is *to be*
cut[+] down and cast into the fire.
10 *Then* the people asked him saying:
What shall we do then?
11 He answered saying to them: *If* anyone
has two coats, let them give[+] to one who
has none. And *those* who have food,[+] let
them do likewise.
12 Then worldly[+] people also came to be
baptized and said to him: Master, what
shall we do?
13 He said to them: Exact no more than
what is appointed *to* you.
14 The soldiers also[+] asked[+] him saying:
And what shall we do? He said to them:
Do violence to no one. Do not accuse *anyone*
falsely. And be content with your wages.
15 Since[+] all the people were in expectation, everyone[+] reasoned[+] in their hearts
about[+] John, *wondering* whether he
might[+] be the Christ or not.
16 John answered saying to *them* all: I
indeed baptize you with water, but one
is coming *who is* mightier than I, the
straps[+] of whose sandals[+] I am not
worthy to loosen. He will baptize you
with the Holy Spirit and with fire.
17 *His* fan *is* in His hand and He will
thoroughly purge His floor and will gather
the wheat into His barn,[+] but the chaff He
will burn with unquenchable fire.
18 And *John* proclaimed[+] many other
things in his exhortation to the people.
19 But Herod the tetrarch, having been
reproved by *John* because[+] of Herodias
his brother Philip's wife *whom Herod*
stole and married and for all the evils
Herod had done,
20 added yet this above all, that he shut up
John in prison.
21 Now when all the people were baptized,
it came to pass that Jesus also being
baptized and praying, the heaven was
opened
22 and the Holy Spirit descended upon
Him in a bodily shape like a dove and
a voice came from heaven saying:
You are my beloved Son. In you I am
well pleased.
23 *Then* Jesus Himself began *His ministry*
when He was about thirty years of age. *It*
was supposed *that He was* the son of
Joseph *who was the descendant* of Heli
24 of Matthat of Levi of Melchi of Janna
of Joseph
25 of Mattathiah of Amos of Nahum of
Esli of Naggai
26 of Maath of Mattathiah of Semei of
Joseph of Judah
27 of Johanan of Rhesa of Zerubbabel of
Shealtiel of Neri
28 of Melchi of Addi of Cosam of
Elmodam of Er
29 of Jose of Eliezer of Jorim of Matthat
of Levi
30 of Simeon of Judah of Joseph of Jonan
of Eliakim
31 of Melea of Menan of Mattatha of
Nathan of David
32 of Jesse of Obed of Boaz of Salmon of
Nahshon
33 of Amminadab of Ram of Hezron of
Perez of Judah *Genesis 49:10*
34 of Jacob of Isaac of Abraham of Terah
of Nahor *Genesis 17:19*
35 of Saruch of Ragau of Phalec of Heber
of Sala
36 of Cainan of Arphaxad of Sem of
Noah of Lamech
37 of Methuselah of Enoch of Jared of
Mahalaleel of Cainan
38 of Enos of Seth of Adam of God.

Luke Chapter 4

1 Now[+] Jesus, being full of the Holy
Spirit, returned from Jordan and was
led by the Spirit into the wilderness.
2 *For* forty days, *He was* tempted by the

devil. In those days, He ate nothing and after they were ended, He was hungry.

3 *Then* the devil said to Him: If you are the Son of God, command this stone that it be made bread.

4 Jesus answered him saying: It is written that mankind[+] shall not live by bread alone, but by every Word of God. *Matthew 4:4*

5 *Then* the devil took[+] *Jesus* up to a high mountain *and* showed to Him all the kingdoms of the world in a moment of time.

6 And the devil said to Him: I will give you authority[+] *and power over* all these, and the glory of them, for that is delivered to me and to whomever I will, I *can* give it.

7 Therefore, if you will worship me, all *this* shall be yours.

8 Jesus answered and said to him: Get behind me Satan. For it is written: You shall worship the Lord your God and Him only shall you serve. *Matthew 4:10*

9 *Then Satan* took *Jesus* to Jerusalem, sat Him on a pinnacle of the temple, and said to Him: If you are the Son of God, cast yourself down from here.

10 For it is written: He will give His angels charge over you to keep you. *Matthew 4:6*

11 In *their* hands they will bear you up, lest at any time you dash your foot against a stone. *Matthew 4:6*

12 Jesus answering said to him: It is said: You shall not tempt the Lord your God. *Matthew 4:7*

13 When the devil had ended all the temptation, he departed from *Jesus* for a season.

14 *Then* Jesus returned in the power of the Spirit to Galilee, and His reputation[+] went all around[+] the region.

15 He taught in their synagogues, being honored[+] by everyone.[+]

16 *Then* He came to Nazareth where He had been brought up. And, as His custom was, He went into the synagogue on the Sabbath day and stood up to read.

17 The book of the prophet Isaiah was delivered to Him, and when He had opened the book, He found the place where it was written:

18 The Spirit of the Lord *is* upon me because He has anointed me to proclaim[+] the Gospel to the poor. He has sent me to heal the broken hearted, to proclaim[+] deliverance to the captives and recovering of sight to the blind, to set at liberty *those* who are bruised, *Isaiah 61:1*

19 to proclaim[+] the acceptable year of the Lord … *Isaiah 61:2*

20 *Then* He closed the book, gave *it back* to the attendant,[+] and sat down. And the eyes of all who were in the synagogue were fastened on Him.

21 He began to say to them: This day this Scripture is fulfilled in your ears.

22 All bore witness *to* Him and wondered at the gracious words that came out of His mouth. And they said: Is this not Joseph's son?

23 He said to them: You will surely say to me this proverb: Physician, heal yourself. Whatever we have heard done in Capernaum, do also here in your country.

24 He said: Truly[+] I say to you: No prophet is accepted in his own country.

25 But truly I say to you: Many widows were in Israel in the days of Elijah when the heaven was shut up three years and six months, when great famine was throughout all the land.

26 But Elijah was not sent to any of them except[+] to Sarepta, *a city* of Sidon, to a woman *who was* a widow.

27 Many lepers were in Israel in the time of Elisha the prophet and none of them was cleansed except[+] Naaman the Syrian.

28 When they heard these things, all those in the synagogue were filled with wrath

29 and rose up and thrust Him out of the city and led Him to the brow of the hill on which their city was built *so* that they might cast Him down headlong.

30 But passing through the midst of them, *Jesus* went away[+]

31 and came down to Capernaum, a city of Galilee, and taught them on the Sabbath days.

32 They were astonished at His doctrine,
for His Word was with authority+ *and*
power.
33 Now+ there was a man in the synagogue who had a spirit of an unclean
demon+ and cried out with a loud
voice
34 saying: Let *us* alone. What do we
have to do with you Jesus of Nazareth?
Have you come to destroy us? I know
who you are: The Holy One of God.
35 Jesus rebuked him saying: Be still+
and come out of him. And when the
demon+ had thrown him in the midst, he
came out of him and did not hurt him.
36 They were all amazed and spoke among
themselves saying: What a Word this *is*.
For He commands the unclean spirits
with authority and power and they
come out.
37 *So* His reputation+ went into every
place in the country *all* around.+
38 *Then* He arose out of the synagogue
and entered Simon's house *where*
Simon's wife's mother was taken with
a great fever, and they prayed *to* Him
for her.
39 He stood over her and rebuked the
fever *and* it left her and immediately she
arose and ministered to them.
40 Now when the sun was setting, all
those who had any sick *ones* with many
different+ diseases brought them to Him
and He laid His hands on everyone of
them and healed them.
41 Demons+ also came out of many,
crying out and saying: You are Christ
the Son of God. But+ He rebuked *them*
and did not allow them to speak, for they
knew that He was Christ.
42 When it was day, He departed and
went into a deserted+ place. But+ the
people sought Him *out* and came to Him
and detained+ him *so* that He could+ not
depart from them.
43 He said to them: I must proclaim+
the kingdom of God to other cities
also, because *it is* for that *purpose* I
have been sent.
44 And He proclaimed+ *the Word* in the
synagogues of Galilee.

Luke Chapter 5

1 Now+ it came to pass that as the
people pressed *in* upon *Jesus* to hear the
Word of God, He stood by the lake of
Gennesaret
2 and saw two boats standing by the
lake. But the fishermen were gone out
of them and were washing *their* nets.
3 *So,* He entered one of the boats, which
was Simon's, and asked+ him if he
would thrust out a little from the land,
and *then* He sat down and taught the
whole crowd+ *of people* from+ the boat.
4 When He finished+ speaking *to them,*
He said to Simon: Launch out into the
deep and let down your nets for a
catch+.
5 Simon answering said to Him: Master,
we have toiled all night and have taken
nothing. Nevertheless at your word I
will let down the net.
6 When they had done this, they caught+
a large+ number+ of fish, *so many that*
their net broke.
7 *So* they signaled+ to *their* partners
who were in the other boat that they
should come and help them, and they
came and filled both the boats so that
they began to sink.
8 When Simon Peter saw *this*, he fell
down at Jesus' knees saying: Depart
from me for I am a sinful man, O Lord.
9 For *Peter* and all who were with him
were astonished at the catch+ of the fish
they had taken.
10 So also *were* James and John the sons
of Zebedee who were partners with
Simon. But+ Jesus said to Simon: Do
not be afraid. From henceforth you will
catch men.
11 And when they had brought their boats
to land, they left+ everything+ *behind*
and followed Him.
12 Now+ it came to pass when *Jesus*
was in a certain city, behold a man
full of leprosy *came to Him. Upon*
seeing Jesus he fell on *his* face and
begged+ Him saying: Lord, if you
will you can make me clean.

13 *Jesus* put forth *His* hand and touched
him saying: I will. Be clean. And
immediately the leprosy departed from
him.
14 *But then Jesus* charged him to tell no
one but *He said:* Go and show yourself
to the priest and *make an* offering+ for
your cleansing as Moses commanded,
for a testimony to them.
15 But *because of this, all* the more His
reputation+ went *all* around,+ and
great multitudes came together to hear
and to be healed of their infirmities by
Him.
16 *Then* He withdrew into the wilderness
and prayed.
17 Now+ it came to pass on a certain
day as He was teaching, that there
were Pharisees and teachers+ of the
law sitting by, who had come from+
every town of Galilee, Judea, and
Jerusalem. And the power of the Lord
was *present* to heal them.
18 And behold men brought a man in a
bed who was paralyzed+ and they
sought to bring him in and lay *him*
before *Jesus*.
19 When they could not find by what
way they might bring him in because
of the multitude, they went upon the
housetop and let him down through
the *roof* tiles+ with *his* bed+ into the
midst before Jesus.
20 When *Jesus* saw their faith, He said
to *the sick man*: Man, your sins are
forgiven.
21 *Then* the scribes and the Pharisees
began to reason saying: Who is this who
speaks blasphemies? Who can forgive
sins but God alone?
22 But when Jesus perceived their
thoughts, He answering said to them:
What are you thinking+ in your hearts?
23 Which+ is easier to say: Your sins
are forgiven. Or to say: Rise up and
walk.
24 But *so* that you may know that the Son
of man has authority+ *and power* on earth
to forgive sins, *Jesus* said to the *one* sick
with paralysis+: I say to you: Arise and
take up your bed+ and go to your house.
25 Immediately he rose up before them
and took up that on which he *had been*
laying+ and departed to his own house,
glorifying God.
26 They were all amazed and glorified
God and were filled with fear saying:
We have seen astonishing+ things today.
27 After these things *Jesus* went forth and
saw a worldly+ person named Levi
sitting at the tax office+ and He said to
him: Follow me.
28 Therefore,+ he left everything,+ rose
up, and followed *Jesus*.
29 Levi made a great feast *for Jesus* in
his own house and there was a great
multitude+ of worldly+ people and of
others who sat down with them.
30 But their scribes and Pharisees com-
plained+ against His disciples saying:
Why do you eat and drink with
worldly+ people and sinners?
31 Jesus answering said to them: *Those*
who are whole do not need a physician,
but *those* who are sick *do*.
32 I did not come to call the righteous but
sinners to repentance.
33 *Then* they said to Him: Why do the
disciples of John fast often and make
prayers, and likewise *the disciples* of the
Pharisees, but yours eat and drink?
34 He said to them: Can you make the
children of the bride chamber fast while
the bridegroom is with them?
35 But the days will come when the Bridegroom will be taken away from them
and then they will fast in those days.
36 Then He spoke a parable to them:
No one puts a piece of a new garment
on an old garment, or else the new
makes a tear+ and the piece that was
taken out of the new does not agree
with the old.
37 No one puts new wine into old wine-
skins+ *or* else the new wine will burst
the wineskins+ and be spilled and the
wineskins+ will perish.
38 But new wine must be put into new
wineskins+ *so* both are preserved.
39 No one having drunk old *wine* imme-
diately+ desires new, for he says: The
old is better.

Luke Chapter 6

1 Now[+] it came to pass on the second
Sabbath after the first, that *Jesus* walked[+]
through the corn fields, and His disciples
plucked the ears of corn and ate,
rubbing *them* in *their* hands.
2 Certain of the Pharisees said to them:
Why do you *do* what is not lawful to do
on the Sabbath days?
3 Jesus answering them said: Have you
not even read what David did when he
himself and *those* who were with him
were hungry?
4 How he went into the house of God
and took and ate the show bread, which
it is not lawful for anyone[+] except[+] the
priests alone *to eat*? And *he* also gave
some to *those* who were with him.
5 *Then Jesus* said to them: The Son of
man is Lord also of the Sabbath.
6 Now[+] it came to pass on another
Sabbath that *Jesus* entered the synagogue
and taught, and there was a man whose
right hand was withered.
7 The scribes and Pharisees watched
Jesus to see whether He would heal on
the Sabbath day *so* that they might find
an accusation against Him.
8 But He knew their thoughts and said to
the man who had the withered hand:
Rise up and stand forth in the midst.
And he arose and stood forth.
9 Then Jesus said to them: I will ask you
one thing: Is it lawful on the Sabbath
days to do good or to do evil? To save
life or to destroy *it*?
10 Looking around[+] upon them all, He
said to the man: Stretch forth your hand.
And he did so and his hand was restored
whole as the other.
11 *The scribes and Pharisees* were filled with
rage[+] and conferred[+] with one another
to decide what they might do to Jesus.
12 *Then* it came to pass in those days that
Jesus went to a mountain to pray and
continued all night in prayer to God.
13 When it was day, He called His disciples,
and from[+] *among* them He chose twelve
whom He also named apostles:
14 Simon, whom He also named Peter,
and Andrew his brother, James and
John, Philip and Bartholomew,
15 Matthew and Thomas, James the *son*
of Alphaeus and Simon called Zelotes,
16 Jude *the brother* of James, and Judas
Iscariot, who also became[+] the traitor.
17 *Jesus* came down with them and stood
in the plain *with* a multitude[+] of His
disciples and *also* a great multitude of
people out of all Judea and Jerusalem
and from the sea coast of Tyre and
Sidon, who came to hear Him and to be
healed of their diseases,
18 *including those* who were oppressed[+]
with unclean spirits, and they were healed.
19 The whole multitude sought to touch
Him, for virtue went out of Him and
healed *them* all.
20 He lifted up His eyes to His disciples
and said: Blessed *are you who are* poor
for the kingdom of God is yours.
21 Blessed *are you* who hunger now for
you shall be filled. Blessed *are you* who
weep now for you shall laugh.
22 Blessed are you when people[+] shall
hate you and when they shall separate
you *from their company* and reproach *you*
and cast out your name as evil, because[+]
of the Son of man.
23 Rejoice in that day and leap for joy,
for behold, your reward *will be* great in
heaven, for in like manner did their
fathers *treat* the prophets.
24 But woe to you who are rich, for you
have received your consolation.
25 Woe to you who are full, for you shall
hunger. Woe to you who laugh now, for
you shall mourn and weep.
26 Woe to you, when everyone[+] speaks
well of you, for so did their fathers
speak to the false prophets.
27 But I say to you who hear: Love your
enemies. Do good to *those* who hate
you. *Matthew 5:44*
28 Bless *those* who curse you. And pray
for *those* who use you despitefully.
29 To one who strikes[+] you on the cheek
offer also the other, and *if* anyone takes
away your vest[+] do not forbid *them to
take your* coat also.

30 Give to everyone+ who asks of you.
Of anyone who takes away your goods,
do not ask to take *them* back.
31 As you would *have* others+ do to you,
you also do to them likewise.
32 For if you love *those* who love you,
what grace+ have you *shown*? For
sinners also love *those* who love them.
33 And if you do good to *those* who do
good to you, what grace+ have you
shown? For sinners also do the same.
34 And if you lend *to those* from whom
you hope to receive, what grace+ have
you *shown*? For sinners also lend to
sinners to receive as much again.
35 *Instead, I say to you:* Love your enemies
and do good and lend, hoping for
nothing again, and your reward will
be great and you shall be the children
of the Highest. For He is kind to the
unthankful and *to* the evil.
36 Therefore, be merciful as your Father
also is merciful.
37 Do not judge and you will not be
judged. Do not condemn and you will
not be condemned. Forgive and you will
be forgiven.

> 38 Give and it will be given
> to you: Good measure,
> pressed down, shaken together,
> and running over,
> others+ will give
> to your innermost+ *needs*.
> For with the same gauge+
> with which you measure+
> it will be measured to you again.

39 *Then Jesus* spoke a parable to them:
Can the blind lead the blind? Will they
not both fall into the ditch?
40 The disciple is not above his master,
but everyone who is perfect will be
like+ their master.
41 Why do you notice+ the speck+ that is
in your brother's *or sister's* eye, but do not
notice+ the beam that is in your own eye?
42 How can you say to your brother:
Brother, let me pull out the speck+ that
is in your eye, when you yourself do not
notice+ the beam that is in your own
eye? You hypocrite. First cast the beam
out of your own eye and then you will
see clearly to pull out the speck+ that is
in your brother's eye.
43 For a good tree does not bring forth
corrupt fruit. Nor does a corrupt tree
bring forth good fruit.
44 For every tree is known by its own
fruit. People+ do not gather figs from
thorn *bushes*. Nor do they gather grapes
from a thorn+ bush.
45 A good person brings forth what is
good out of the good treasure in their
heart. An evil person brings forth what
is evil out of the evil treasure *that is in*
their heart. For the mouth speaks *out* of
the abundance of the heart.
46 Why do you call me: Lord, Lord, and
do not *do* the things that I say?
47 Whoever comes to me and hears my
sayings and does them: I will show you
to whom they are *to be* compared+:
48 They are like a person who built a house
and dug deep and laid the foundation on
a rock. When the flood arose, the stream
beat forcefully+ upon that house, and could
not shake it for it was founded upon a rock.
49 But *those* who hear and do not *follow
through* are like a person+ who built a house
upon the earth without a foundation,
against which the stream beat force-
fully+ and immediately it fell, and the
ruin of that house was great.

Luke Chapter 7

1 Now when *Jesus* had ended all His
words+ to the people, He entered
Capernaum.
2 *There* a certain centurion's servant
who was dear to him, was sick and
ready to die.
3 When *the centurion* heard about Jesus,
he sent the elders of the Jews to Him,
beseeching Him that, having come, He
would heal his servant.
4 When *the elders* came to Jesus, they
begged+ Him diligently,+ saying that
the centurion for whom He should do this
was worthy.

5 For *they said:* He loves our nation and he has built a synagogue *for* us.

6 Then Jesus went with them and when He was not far from the house, the centurion sent friends to Him saying: Lord, do not trouble yourself. For I am not worthy that you should come+ under my roof.

7 Nor, for that reason+ did I think myself worthy to come to you. But *if you would just* speak a word, my servant will be healed.

8 For I also am a man set under authority, having soldiers under me. I say to one: Go. And he goes. To another: Come. And he comes. To my servant: Do this. And he does *it*.

9 When Jesus heard these things, He marveled at him and *He* turned around+ and said to the people who followed Him: I say to you: I have not found such+ great faith *before,* even in Israel.

10 *Upon* returning to the house, *those* who had been sent found the servant who had been sick *now* well.+

11 And it came to pass on the next+ *day* that *Jesus* went to a city called Nain, and many of His disciples went with Him and many people *followed*.

12 Now when He came near to the gate of the city, behold a dead man was being carried out, the only son of his mother, and she was a widow. Many people from the city were with her.

13 When the Lord saw her, He had compassion on her and said to her: Do not weep.

14 *Then* He came and touched the casket+ and *those* who carried+ *it* stopped.+ He said: Young man, I say to you: Arise.

15 The dead *man* sat up and began to speak. And *Jesus* gave+ him to his mother.

16 Fear seized+ everyone+ and they glorified God saying: A great prophet has risen up among us. And, God has visited His people.

17 The report+ of this went throughout all Judea and throughout the region all around.+

18 The disciples of John told+ him about+ all these things,

19 and John called two of his disciples *and* sent *them* to Jesus saying: Are you the *one who was to* come, or should we look for another?

20 When the men had come to *Jesus*, they said: John the Baptist has sent us to you saying: Are you the *one who was to* come, or should we look for another?

21 In that same hour, *Jesus* cured many of *their* infirmities and plagues, and of evil spirits. And to many *who were* blind He gave sight.

22 Then Jesus answering said to *John's disciples*: Go and tell John what things you have seen and heard: That the blind see, the lame walk, the lepers are cleansed, the deaf hear, the dead are raised, *and* the Gospel is proclaimed+ to the poor.

23 Blessed are *those* who will not be offended *and disbelieve* in me.

24 *After* the messengers from John departed, *Jesus* began to speak to the people concerning John: What did you go out into the wilderness to see? A reed shaken with the wind?

25 But what did you go out to see? A man clothed in soft clothing+? Behold *those* who are gorgeously appareled and live luxuriously+ are in kings' courts.

26 But what did you go out to see? A prophet? Yes, I say to you, and much more than a prophet.

27 This is *the one* of whom it is written: Behold I send my messenger before your face, who shall prepare your way before you. *Matthew 11:10*

28 For I say to you: Among *all* those born of women, there is not a greater prophet than John the Baptist, but *those* who are least in the kingdom of God are greater than he.

29 All the people who heard *Jesus*, and the worldly+ people, justified God, being baptized with the baptism of John.

30 But the Pharisees and lawyers rejected the counsel of God against themselves, not being baptized by him.

31 *Then* the Lord said: To what then shall I compare+ the people+ of this generation? What are they like?

32 They are like children sitting in the
marketplace, calling to one another,
and saying: We have piped to you and
you have not danced. We have mourned
to you and you have not wept.
33 For John the Baptist came neither
eating bread nor drinking wine, and you
say: He has a demon+.
34 *Now*, the Son of man has come eating
and drinking, and you say: Behold a
gluttonous man, a wine drinker,+ a
friend of worldly+ people and sinners.
35 But wisdom is justified by all her
children.
36 *Then* one of the Pharisees asked+ *Jesus*
to eat with him. *So* He went to the
Pharisee's house and sat down to eat.
37 And behold a woman in the city who
was a sinner, when she knew that *Jesus*
sat *down* to eat+ in the Pharisee's house,
brought an alabaster box of ointment
38 and stood at His feet behind *Him*
weeping and began to wash His feet
with tears and wipe *them* with the hair
of her head and kissed His feet and
anointed *them* with the ointment.
39 Now when the Pharisee who had
invited+ Him saw *this*, he spoke within
himself saying: If this man was a prophet,
He would have known who and what
kind+ of woman *this is* who touches
Him, for she is a sinner.
40 Jesus answering said to him: Simon, I
have something+ to say to you. He said:
Master, say on.
41 There was a certain creditor who had
two debtors. One owed *nearly two year's*
wages+ and the other *two month's wages*+.
42 When they had nothing *with which* to
pay, he frankly forgave them both. Tell
me therefore: Which of them will love
him most?
43 Simon answered and said: I suppose that
the one to whom he forgave most. *Jesus*
said to him: You have judged correctly+.
44 *Then* He turned to the woman and said
to Simon: See this woman? I entered
your house *and* you gave me no water
for my feet, but she has washed my feet
with tears and wiped *them* with the hair
of her head.
45 You gave me no kiss, but since the
time I came in, this woman has not
stopped+ kissing my feet.
46 You did not anoint my head with oil,
but this woman has anointed my feet
with ointment.
47 Therefore I say to you: Her sins,
which are many, are forgiven. For she
loved much. But *those* to whom little is
forgiven, love *but* little.
48 *Then Jesus* said to her: Your sins are
forgiven.
49 *Those* who sat *down* to eat+ with Him
began to say within themselves: Who is
this that forgives sins also?
50 He said to the woman: Your faith has
saved you. Go in peace.

Luke Chapter 8

1 Now+ after *this*, it came to pass that
Jesus went throughout every city and
village, proclaiming+ *the Word* and
showing the glad tidings of the kingdom
of God. And the twelve *disciples went*
with Him.
2 Also, certain women who had been
healed of evil spirits and infirmities,
Mary called Magdalene out of whom
went seven demons,+
3 Joanna the wife of Chuza, Herod's
steward, Susanna, and many others
ministered to Him from their substance.
4 When many people had gathered
together, having come to Him out of
every city, He spoke *to them* by a
parable:
5 A sower went out to sow his seed. As
he sowed, some fell by the wayside and
it was trampled+ down and the birds+ of
the air devoured it.
6 Some fell upon a rock and as soon as
it had sprung up, it withered away
because it lacked moisture.
7 Some fell among thorns and the thorns
sprang up with it and choked it.
8 Other *seed* fell on good ground and
sprang up and bore fruit a hundredfold.
And when He had said these things, He
cried *out*: *Those* who have ears to hear,
let them hear.

9 *Then* His disciples asked Him saying:
What might this parable be?
10 *Jesus* said: Unto you it is given to know
the mysteries of the kingdom of God.
But to others *I speak* in parables, that
seeing they might not see and hearing
they might not understand.
11 Now the parable is this: The seed is the
Word of God.
12 Those by the wayside are *those* who
hear, *and* then the devil comes and takes
away the Word out of their hearts, lest
they should believe and be saved.
13 Those on the rock *represent those* who,
when they hear, receive the Word with
joy *but* they have no root *and so* they
believe *only* for a time,[+] and in *a* time
of trials[+] *they* fall away.
14 *The seed* that fell among thorns are
those who, when they have heard, go
forth and are choked with *the* cares and
riches and pleasures of *this* life, and
bring no fruit to perfection.
15 But that on the good ground are *those*
who, in an honest and good heart,
having heard the Word, keep *it* and
bring forth fruit with patience.
16 No one, having lit a candle, covers it
with a vessel or puts *it* under a bed, but
sets *it* on a candlestick *so* that *those* who
enter in may see the light.
17 For nothing is secret, that will not be
made manifest. Nor *is anything* hid, that
will not come to light[+] and become
known[+].
18 Therefore, take heed how you hear,
for whoever has, to them *more* will be
given, and whoever has nothing, from
them will be taken even what they seem
to have.
19 Then His mother and brothers came to
Him, but were not able to get *close to*
Him because of the crowd.[+]
20 *Someone* told Him *about this*, saying:
Your mother and your brothers are
standing outside[+] desiring to see you.
21 He answered and said to them: My
mother and my brothers *and sisters*
are these who hear the Word of God
and do it.
22 Now it came to pass on a certain day
that *Jesus* got into a boat with His
disciples, and He said to them: Let us go
over to the other side of the lake. And
they launched forth.
23 But as they sailed, *Jesus* fell asleep.
Then a windstorm[+] came down on the
lake and they were filled *with water* and
were in jeopardy.
24 *His disciples* came to Him and awoke
Him saying: Master, master, we *are*
perishing. Then He arose and rebuked
the wind and the raging of the water,
and they stopped[+] and there was a calm.
25 He said to them: Where is your faith?
They were afraid, and wondered, and
said to one another: Who is this *man*?
For He commands even the winds and
water and they obey Him.
26 *Then* they arrived in the country of the
Gadarenes near[+] Galilee.
27 When He went forth to land, a certain
man out of the city met Him. *This man*
had demons[+] for a long time and wore
no clothes *and* did not live[+] in *a* house
but among the tombs.
28 When he saw Jesus, he cried out and
fell down before Him and with a loud
voice said: What do I have to do with
you Jesus, Son of God most high? I
beseech you, do not torment me.
29 For *Jesus* commanded the unclean spirit
to come out of the man, for often times
it had seized[+] him. He had been kept
bound with chains and shackles,[+] but he
broke the bands and was driven into the
wilderness by the demon.[+]
30 Jesus asked him saying: What is your
name? He said: Legion. Because many
demons[+] had entered him.
31 *The demons* begged[+] *Jesus* to not
command them to go into the bottomless pit.[+]
32 *Now* there was a herd of many swine
there feeding on the mountain and they
begged[+] Him that He allow them to
enter into the *swine*, and He allowed[+]
them *to do so*.
33 Then the demons[+] went out of the man
and entered the swine and the herd ran
violently down a steep place into the
lake and were choked.

34 When *those* who fed *them* saw what
was done, they fled and told *it* in the city
and in the country.
35 Then the *people* went out to see what
was done. *They* came to Jesus and found
the man out of whom the demons+ had
departed, sitting at the feet of Jesus,
clothed and in his right mind. And they
were afraid.
36 *Those* who had seen *it* told *the others*
who came later how *Jesus* healed the
man+ who had been demon+ possessed.
37 Then the whole multitude from the
country around+ the Gadarenes begged+
Jesus to depart from them, for they were
taken with great fear. *So Jesus* got into
the boat and returned back again.
38 Now the man from+ whom the
demons+ were gone+ begged+ *Jesus* to
be *taken* with Him, but Jesus sent him
away saying:
39 Return to your own house and
declare+ all+ *the great things* God has
done to you. *So* he went away+ and
published throughout the whole city
all+ *the great things* Jesus had done *for*
him.
40 And it came to pass that when Jesus
returned, the people *gladly* received
Him, for they were all waiting for Him.
41 Behold a man named Jairus, a ruler of
the synagogue, came and fell down at
Jesus' feet and begged+ Him to come to
his house,
42 for he had only one daughter, about
twelve years of age, and she was+
dying. As *Jesus* went, the people
crowded+ *in upon* Him,
43 and a woman *who* had been bleeding
for twelve years and had spent all her
means of livelihood+ on physicians, but
could not be healed by any *of them*
44 came behind *Him* and touched the
border of His garment. Immediately her
bleeding stopped.+
45 Jesus said: Who touched me? When
everyone+ denied *it*, Peter and *those*
who were with Him said: Master, the
multitude is overcrowding+ you and
pressing *you* and do you say: Who
touched me?
46 Jesus said: Somebody touched me,
for I perceive that virtue has gone out
of me.
47 When the woman saw that she was not
hidden,+ she came trembling. Falling
down before Him, she declared to Him,
before all the people, the reason+ she
had touched Him and how she was
immediately healed.
48 *Jesus* said to her: Daughter, be of good
comfort. Your faith has made you whole.
Go in peace.
49 While He spoke, one came from *the*
house of the ruler of the synagogue,
saying to him: Your daughter is dead.
Do not trouble the Master.
50 But when Jesus heard *this*, He answered him saying: Do not be afraid.
Only believe and she will be made
whole.
51 When *Jesus* went+ into the house, He
allowed+ no one to go in except+ Peter,
James, John, and the father and mother
of the girl.+
52 Everyone wept and mourned for her,
but *Jesus* said: Do not weep. She is not
dead but *is* sleeping.
53 They laughed at Him *scornfully*,
knowing that she was dead.
54 *Then* Jesus sent+ them all out and took
her by the hand and called *to her* saying:
Child, arise.
55 Her spirit came again and she arose
immediately,+ and *Jesus* directed+ *them*
to give her *something* to eat.
56 Her parents were astonished, but He
charged them that they should tell no
one what was done.

Luke Chapter 9

1 Then *Jesus* called His twelve disciples
together and gave them power and authority over all demons,+ and to cure
diseases.
2 And He sent them to proclaim+ the
kingdom of God and to heal the sick.
3 He said to them: Take nothing for *your*
journey: not staves nor *provision* bag+
nor bread nor money. And do not have
two coats apiece.

4 Whatever house you enter, stay+ there,
and from there+ depart.
5 Whoever will not receive you, when
you go out of that city, shake off the very
dust from your feet for a testimony
against them.
6 *So* they departed and went through the
towns, proclaiming+ the Gospel and
healing everywhere.
7 Now Herod the tetrarch heard about+
all that was done by *Jesus* and he was
perplexed. Because, it was said by some
that John had been raised from the dead,
8 by some that Elijah had appeared, and
by others that one of the old prophets
was risen again.
9 Herod said: I have beheaded John, but
who is this of whom I hear such things?
And he desired to see Him.
10 When the apostles returned, they
told *Jesus* all that they had done. *Then*
He took them away+ privately to a
deserted+ place belonging to the city
called Bethsaida.
11 When the people knew *about this*, they
followed Him and He received them
and spoke to them about+ the kingdom
of God, and *He* healed *those* who had
need of healing.
12 When the day began to wear away, the
twelve came and said to Him: Send the
multitude away *so* that they may go into
the towns and country *all* around+ to
lodge and get food,+ for we are in a
deserted+ place.
13 But He said to them: You give them *food*
to eat. They said: We have no more than
five loaves and two fish, unless+ we go
and buy food+ for all these people.
14 Now there were about five thousand
men. *Jesus* said to His disciples: Make
them sit down in groups+ of fifty.
15 They did so and made them all sit
down.
16 Then He took the five loaves and the
two fish, and looking up to heaven, He
blessed them and broke and gave to the
disciples to set before the multitude.
17 They all ate and were filled, and of the
fragments that remained, they took up
twelve baskets.
18 *Now* it came to pass, as He was alone
praying, His disciples came+ *to* Him
and He asked them saying: Who do the
people say that I am?
19 They answering said: John the Baptist.
But some *say* Elijah. Others *say* that one
of the old prophets is risen again.
20 He said to them: But who do you say
that I am? Peter answering said: The
Christ of God.
21 And He strictly+ charged and directed+
them to tell this *to* no one,
22 saying: The Son of man must suffer
many things and be rejected by the
elders and chief priests and scribes, and
be slain, and be raised the third day.
23 *Then* He said to *them* all: If anyone+
will come after me, let them deny
themselves and take up their cross daily
and follow me.
24 For whoever would+ save their life
will lose it, but whoever would+ lose
their life for my sake, will save it.
25 For what is a person+ benefited+ if
they gain the whole world and lose
themselves or be destroyed+?
26 For whoever is ashamed of me and
of my words, of them will the Son of
man be ashamed when He comes in
His own glory and *in His* Father's and
of the holy angels.
27 But in truth I say to you: There are
some standing here who will not taste
death until they see the kingdom of
God.
28 *Then* it came to pass about eight days
after these sayings, *Jesus* took Peter,
John, and James, and went up into a
mountain to pray.
29 As He prayed, the appearance of His
face changed+ and His clothing+ *became*
white *and* radiant.+
30 And behold two men talked with Him,
+ Moses and Elijah,
31 who appeared in glory and spoke of His
exodus+ that would *soon* be accomplished
in Jerusalem.
32 But Peter and *those* who were with him
were heavy with sleep. When they were
awake, they saw His glory and the two
men who stood with Him.

33 *Then* it came to pass as *Moses and Elijah*
departed from *Jesus*, Peter said to Him:
Master, it is good for us to be here. Let
us make three tabernacles. One for you,
one for Moses, and one for Elijah. *Peter*
did not know what he was saying.
34 As *Peter* spoke, a cloud came and
overshadowed them and they *became*
fearful as they entered the cloud.
35 *Then* a voice came out of the cloud
saying: This is my beloved Son. Hear
Him.
36 As the voice occurred,[+] Jesus was
found alone. And they kept *this matter*
silent[+] and told no one in those days any
of those things that they had seen.
37 It came to pass on the next day, when
they had come down from the mountain,[+]
many people met Him.
38 And behold a man in the multitude[+]
cried out saying: Master I beseech you:
Look upon my son for he is my only
child.
39 And behold, a spirit takes him and he
suddenly cries out. It convulses[+] him *so*
that he foams *at the mouth*, bruising him
and it will hardly leave[+] him.
40 I begged[+] your disciples to cast him
out and they could not.
41 Jesus answering said: O faithless and
perverse generation. How long shall I
be with you and endure[+] you? Bring
your son here.
42 Even[+] as *the boy* was coming, the
demon[+] threw him down and convulsed[+]
him. Jesus rebuked the unclean spirit
and healed the child and gave[+] him to
his father.
43 They were all amazed at the mighty
power of God. While everyone marveled[+] at everything Jesus did, He said
to His disciples:
44 Let these words[+] sink down into your
ears, for the Son of man will *soon* be
delivered into the hands of men.
45 But they did not understand this saying.
It was hidden from them *so* that they did
not perceive it, and they were afraid to
ask Him about[+] that saying.
46 Then a discussion[+] arose among them
as to who might[+] be *the* greatest.
47 Perceiving the thoughts in their hearts,
Jesus took a child and sat *the child* down
by Him
48 and said to them: Whoever will receive
this child in my name receives me.
Whoever will receive me receives Him
who sent me. For *those* who are least
among you all, the same shall be great.
49 John answered and said: Master, we
saw one casting out demons[+] in your
name and we forbad him because he
does not follow us.
50 Jesus said to *John*: Do not forbid him.
For whoever is not against us is for us.
51 *Then* it came to pass that the time had
come when *Jesus* was to be received up,
and He steadfastly set His face to go to
Jerusalem.
52 *He* sent messengers before His *own*
presence[+] and they entered a village of
the Samaritans to make ready for Him.
53 But they did not receive Him because
His face was *set* to go to Jerusalem.
54 When His disciples James and John
saw *this*, they said: Lord, do you want
us to command fire to come down
from heaven and consume them even
as Elijah did?
55 But *Jesus* turned and rebuked them and
said: You do not understand[+] what
manner of spirit you are *to be*.
56 For the Son of man did not come to
destroy people's[+] lives, but to save
them. *Then* they went to another village.
57 *Now* it came to pass that as they went
in the way, a certain *man* said to *Jesus*:
Lord, I will follow you wherever you
go.
58 Jesus said to him: Foxes have holes
and birds of the air *have* nests, but the
Son of man does not have anywhere to
lay *His* head.
59 *Then* He said to another: Follow me.
But he said: Lord, allow me to go and
bury my father first.
60 Jesus said to him: Let the dead bury
their dead. You go and proclaim[+] the
kingdom of God.
61 Another also said: Lord, I will follow
you, but first let me bid farewell to *those*
who are at my house.

62 Jesus said to him: No one, having put
their hand to the plow and *then* looking
back, is fit for the kingdom of God.

Luke Chapter 10

1 After these things, the Lord appointed
another seventy also and sent them by
twos[+] before His *own* presence[+] into
every city and place where He Himself
would come.
2 He said to them: The harvest truly *is*
great but the laborers *are* few. Therefore,
pray *to* the Lord of the harvest *so* that He
will send forth laborers into His harvest.
3 *Now* go. Behold I send you forth as
lambs among wolves.
4 Do not carry a purse nor *provision*
bag[+] nor sandals,[+] and do not *stop to*
salute anyone along[+] the way.
5 Into whatever house you enter, first
say: Peace to this house.
6 If a son of peace is there, your peace
shall rest upon *that house*. If not, it shall
return[+] to you.
7 Remain in the same house, eating and
drinking such things as they provide,[+]
for workers[+] are worthy of their wages.[+]
Do not go from house to house.
8 Into whatever city you enter and they
receive you, eat such things as are set
before you.
9 Heal the sick who are there and say to
them: The kingdom of God has come
near to you.
10 But into whatever city you enter and
they do not receive you, go[+] out into the
streets of the same and say:
11 Even the very dust of your city that
clings[+] on us, we wipe off against you.
Even so[+] know that the kingdom of God
has come near to you.
12 But I say to you, that it will be more
tolerable for Sodom in that day *of
judgment*, than for that city.
13 Woe to you Chorazin. Woe to you
Bethsaida. For if the mighty works that
have been done in you had been done
in Tyre and Sidon, they would have
repented a great while ago, sitting in
sackcloth and ashes.
14 But it shall be more tolerable for Tyre
and Sidon at the judgment, than for you.
15 You Capernaum, *being* exalted to
heaven, will be thrust down to hell.
16 *Those* who hear you, hear me. *Those*
who despise you, despise me. *Those* who
despise me, despise Him who sent me.
17 *Later*, the seventy returned again with
joy saying: Lord, even the demons[+] are
subject to us through your name.
18 He said to them: I saw[+] Satan fall
from heaven like[+] lightning.
19 Behold I give you authority[+] *and power*
to tread on serpents and scorpions and
over all the power of the enemy. Nothing shall by any means hurt you.
20 Even so, do not rejoice that the spirits
are subject to you, but rather rejoice
because your names are written in heaven.
21 In that hour, Jesus rejoiced in spirit
and said: I thank you, O Father, Lord
of heaven and earth, that you have hid
these things from the wise and prudent
and have revealed them to babes.
Even so, Father, for so it seemed
good in your sight.
22 All things are delivered to me by my
Father. No one knows who the Son is
but the Father, and who the Father is but
the Son and *those* to whom the Son will
reveal *Him*.
23 *Then* He turned to *His* disciples and
said privately: Blessed *are* the eyes that
see the things that you see.
24 For I tell you that many prophets and
kings have desired to see what you see
but have not seen *it*, and to hear what
you hear but have not heard *it*.
25 *Then* behold, a certain lawyer stood up
and tested[+] *Jesus* saying: Master, what
shall I do to inherit eternal life?
26 *Jesus* said to him: What is written in
the law? How do you read *it*?
27 *The lawyer* answering said: You
shall love the Lord your God with all
your heart and with all your soul and
with all your strength and with all your
mind; and your neighbor as yourself.
Matthew 22:37
28 *Jesus* said to him: You have answered
correctly.[+] Do this and you will live.

29 But *the lawyer*, wanting to justify
himself, said to Jesus: And who is my
neighbor?
30 Jesus answering said: A certain *man*
went down from Jerusalem to Jericho
and fell among thieves who stripped
him of his clothing,[+] wounded *him*, and
departed, leaving *him* half dead.
31 *About the same time* a certain priest came
down that way, and when he saw *the injured
man*, he passed by on the other side.
32 Likewise a Levite came by the *same*
place, looked *at the injured man*, and
passed by on the other side.
33 But *then* a certain Samaritan, as he was
traveling[+] by, saw *the injured man*, had
compassion *on him*,
34 went to *him*, bound up his wounds,
poured *soothing* oil *on him, gave him* wine,
set him on his own beast, *and* brought
him to an inn and took care of him.
35 On the next day when he departed, *the
Samaritan* took out two coins[+] and gave
them to the host and said to him: Take
care of him. Whatever more you spend,
I will repay you when I come again.
36 Which now of these three do you
think, was *a good* neighbor to the one
who fell among the thieves?
37 *The lawyer* said: He who showed mercy
on him. Then Jesus said to him: Go and
do likewise.
38 Now it came to pass as they went, that
Jesus entered a certain village and a
certain woman named Martha received
Him into her house.
39 *Martha* had a sister named[+] Mary who
sat at Jesus' feet and heard His Word.
40 But Martha was distracted[+] by much
busyness in serving, and *she* came to Him
and said: Lord, do you not care that my
sister has left me to serve alone? Speak[+]
to her *so* that she *will* help me.
41 Jesus answered and said to her:
Martha, Martha.

> You are overly anxious[+]
> and troubled
> about *so* many things.
> 42 But one thing is necessary[+]

and Mary has chosen that good part *and*
that will not be taken from her.

Luke Chapter 11

1 *Now* it came to pass that as *Jesus* was
praying in a certain place, when He
stopped,[+] one of His disciples said to
Him: Lord, teach us to pray, as John
also taught his disciples.
2 *Jesus* said to them: When you pray,
say: Our Father in heaven, Holy[+] is
your name. Your kingdom come. Your
will be done, on earth as *it is* in heaven.
3 Give us each[+] day our daily bread.
4 And forgive us *for* our sins, for we also
forgive everyone *who is* indebted to us.
And lead us *so that we* not *yield* to
temptation, but deliver us from evil.
5 *Then* He said to them: Who among[+]
you shall have a friend and shall go to
him at midnight and say to him: Friend,
lend me three loaves.
6 For a friend of mine in his journey has
come to me and I have nothing to set
before him.
7 And from inside[+] *your friend* shall
answer and say: Do not trouble me *now,
for* the door is shut and *both I and* my
children are in bed *and* I cannot arise
now and give you *anything*.
8 I say to you: Though he will not arise
and give *anything to* him because he is his
friend, yet because of his persistence[+]
he will rise and give him all[+] he needs.
9 I say to you: Ask and it will be given
to you. Seek and you will find. Knock
and it will be opened to you.
10 For everyone who asks receives, and
those who seek *will* find, and to *those*
who knock it will be opened.
11 If a son asks *for* bread from[+] any of
you who are fathers, will *you* give him
a stone? Or if *he asks for* a fish, will *you*
give him a serpent?
12 Or if he asks *for* an egg, will *you* offer
him a scorpion?
13 If you then, being wicked,[+] know how to
give good gifts to your children, how much
more shall *your* heavenly Father give the
Holy Spirit to *those* who ask Him?

14 *Later on, Jesus* was casting out a demon[+]
that had caused a man to be speechless.[+]
And it came to pass, when the demon[+]
was gone out, the speechless[+] *man* spoke.
And the people marveled.[+]
15 But some of them said: He casts out
demons[+] through Beelzebub the chief
of the demons.[+]
16 Others, testing[+] *Him*, sought from[+]
Him a sign from heaven.
17 But knowing their thoughts, He said to
them: Every kingdom divided against
itself is brought to desolation. A house
divided against a house falls.
18 If Satan also is divided against himself,
how shall his kingdom stand? Because
you say that I cast out demons[+] through
Beelzebub,
19 *well* if I cast out demons[+] by Beelzebub,
then by whom do your sons cast *them*
out? Therefore shall they be your judges.
20 But if I cast out demons[+] with the
finger of God, *then* no doubt the kingdom
of God has come upon you.
21 When an armed strong man keeps his
palace *guarded*, his possessions[+] are in
peace.
22 But when *one* stronger than he comes
upon him and overcomes him, *the
overcomer* takes from *the strong man* all
his armor in which he trusted, and
divides his spoils.
23 *Those* who are not with me are against
me. *Those* who do not gather with me
scatter.
24 When the unclean spirit is gone out of
a person,[+] *that unclean spirit* walks
through dry places seeking rest. Finding
none, he says: I will return to my house
from which I came.
25 When he comes, he finds *it* swept and
put in order[+].
26 Then he goes and takes seven other
spirits more wicked than himself and they
enter in and dwell there. And the last *state*
of that person[+] is worse than the first.
27 *Now* it came to pass, as *Jesus* spoke
these things: A certain woman in the
crowd[+] lifted up her voice and said to
Him: Blessed *is* the womb that bore you
and the breasts[+] that nursed[+] you.
28 But He said: Yes rather,

> Blessed *are those* who hear the
> Word of God and keep it.
> *Proverbs 8:32*

29 When the people were gathered close[+]
together, He began to say: This is an
evil generation. They seek a sign, but
there shall not be *any* sign given *to* it
except[+] the sign of Jonah the prophet.
Matthew 12:39
30 For as Jonah was a sign to the Ninevites,
so also will the Son of man be to this
generation. *Matthew 12:40*
31 The queen of the south will rise up in the
judgment with the people[+] of this generation and condemn them. For she came
from the ends[+] of the earth to hear the
wisdom of Solomon. And behold *one*
greater than Solomon *is* here. *Matthew 12:42*
32 The men of Nineveh shall rise up in
the judgment with this generation and
shall condemn it, for they repented at
the proclaiming[+] of Jonah. And behold,
one greater than Jonah *is* here.
33 No one, having lit a candle, puts *it* in
a secret place or under a bushel, but on
a candlestick *so* that *those* who come in
may see the light.
34 The light of the body is the eye.
Therefore when your eye is single *then*
your whole body is also full of light. But
when *your eye* is evil, *then* your body also
is full of darkness.
35 *Therefore*, take heed that the light *that
is* in you is not darkness.
36 If your whole body therefore *is filled
with* light, having no part dark, *then* the
whole *truly* will be light as when a
brightly shining light[+] illuminates[+] you.
37 As He spoke, a certain Pharisee asked[+]
Jesus to dine with him. *So*, He went in
and sat down to eat.
38 When the Pharisee saw that *Jesus*
did not wash first, before dinner, he
wondered[+] *at that*.
39 The Lord said to him: Now you
Pharisees make the outside of the cup
and platter clean, but your inward part
is full of greed[+] and wickedness.

40 *You* fools. Did not He who made what
is outside[+] also make what is inside[+]?
41 But *rather* give alms *of* lasting[+] *value*
and behold, all things are clean to you.
42 But woe to you Pharisees. For you
tithe *of* mint and rue and all kinds[+] of
herbs, but *you* bypass[+] justice[+] and the
love of God. These you ought to do, but
not to leave the other undone.
43 Woe to you Pharisees. For you love
the uppermost seats in the synagogues
and greetings in the market *places*.
44 Woe to you scribes and Pharisees.
Hypocrites. For you are like[+] unmarked[+]
graves and those[+] who walk over *them*
are not aware *of them*.
45 Then one of the lawyers answered and
said to Him: Master, saying these things,
you insult[+] us, also.
46 He said: Woe to you lawyers, also.
For you saddle[+] people[+] with grievous
burdens and you yourselves do not touch
the burdens with one of your fingers.
47 Woe to you. For you build the tombs[+]
of the prophets, and your fathers
killed them.
48 Truly you bear witness that you consent[+] *to* the deeds of your fathers. For
they indeed killed them, and you build
their tombs[+].
49 Therefore the wisdom of God *has* also
said: I will send prophets and apostles *to*
them, and they will persecute and slay
some of them,
50 *so* that the blood of all the prophets
that was shed from the foundation of
the world, may be required of this
generation,
51 from the blood of Abel to the blood
of Zacharias, who perished between
the altar and the temple. Truly[+] I say
to you: It shall be required of this
generation.
52 Woe to you lawyers. For you have
taken away the key of knowledge. You
did not enter in yourselves and you
hindered *those* who were entering.
53 As He said these things to them, the
scribes and the Pharisees began to
forcefully[+] press and provoke Him to
speak of many things,
54 laying in wait for Him, seeking to
catch some *statement* out of His mouth
so that they might accuse Him.

Luke Chapter 12

1 Meanwhile,[+] *as* a large[+] crowd[+]
gathered so *close together* that they
stepped[+] on one another, *Jesus* began
to say to His disciples: First, beware
of the leaven of the Pharisees, which
is hypocrisy.
2 For there is nothing covered that will
not be revealed, nor hid that will not
become[+] known. *Matthew 10:26*
3 Therefore, whatever you have spoken
in darkness will be heard in the light and
what you have spoken in the ear in
closets will be proclaimed from[+] the
housetops.
4 I say to you my friends: Do not be
afraid of *those* who kill the body and
after that have no more that they can do.
5 But I will forewarn you whom you
shall fear: Fear Him who, after He has
killed, has authority[+] *and power* to cast
into hell. Yes, I say to you: Fear Him.
6 Are not five sparrows sold for two
pennies,[+] and not one of them is
forgotten before God?
7 But even the very hairs of your head
are all numbered. Therefore, do not be
afraid. You are of more value than
many sparrows.
8 I also say to you:

> Whoever will confess me
> before people,[+] the Son of man
> will also confess them
> before the angels of God.

9 But *those* who deny me before people[+]
will be denied before the angels of God.
10 Whoever speaks a word against the
Son of man may be forgiven. But *anyone*
who blasphemes against the Holy Spirit
will not be forgiven.
11 When they bring you to the synagogues
and highest officials[+] and powers, take
no thought how or what you shall answer
or what you shall say.

12 For the Holy Spirit will teach you in
that same hour what you ought to say.
13 Someone+ in the crowd+ said to Him:
Master, tell+ my brother *to* divide the
inheritance with me.
14 *Jesus* said to him: Man, who made me
a judge or a divider over you?
15 And He said to them:

Take heed
and beware of covetousness.
For one's life *is* not *to be found*
in the abundance *of things*
one possesses.

16 *Then* He spoke a parable to them
saying: The ground of a certain rich
man brought forth plentifully.
17 He thought within himself saying:
What shall I do, because I have no room
to store+ *all* my fruits?
18 *Then* he said: This *is what* I will do: I will
pull down my barns and build larger+
ones, and there I will store+ all my fruits
and my possessions+. *Proverbs 27:1*
19 I will say to my soul: Soul, you have
many goods stored+ up for many
years. *Now* take your ease: Eat, drink,
and be merry.
20 But God said to him: *You* fool. This
night your soul will be required of you.
Then whose shall those things be that
you have prepared+ *for yourself*?
21 So *it is with those* who lay up treasure for
themselves and are not rich toward God.
22 He said to His disciples: Therefore I
say to you: Take no thought for your life
and what you shall eat, nor what *clothes*
to put on *your* body.
23 Life is more than food+ and the body
more than clothes+.
24 Consider the ravens. They neither sow
nor reap nor have storehouses or barns,
and God feeds them. *Yet* how much
more value+ you *are* than the birds+.
25 Who among you, by taking thought,
can add one cubit to their stature?
26 Therefore, if you are not able *to do*
even the smallest+ *thing*, why give thought
to the rest?
27 Consider how the lilies grow. They do
not toil. They do not spin. Yet I say to
you that Solomon in all his glory was not
arrayed like one of these.
28 Therefore, if God so clothes the grass,
which is in the field today and tomorrow
is cast into the oven, how much more
will he clothe you, O you of little faith?
29 Do not seek what you shall eat or what
you shall drink, and do not be of *a*
doubtful mind.
30 For all the nations of the world seek
after these things, and your Father knows
that you have need of these things.
31 But rather, you *just* seek the kingdom
of God, and all these things will be
added to you.

32 Do not be afraid, little flock.
For it is your Father's
good pleasure to give
the kingdom *of God* to you.

33 Sell what you have and give alms.
Make+ *provision* bags *for* yourselves that
will not grow+ old, a treasure in the
heavens that will not fail, where no thief
approaches nor moth corrupts.
34 For where your treasure is, there will
your heart be also. *Matthew 6:21*
35 Let your waist+ be belted+ up and *your*
lights burning.
36 *Be* like people waiting+ for their lord,
so that whenever he returns from the
wedding, when he comes and knocks,
you may open to him immediately.
37 Blessed *are* those servants whom the
lord, when he comes, finds watching.
Truly+ I say to you that he will prepare+
himself and seat+ them *to be served* and
he will come forth and serve them.
38 Blessed are those servants if he comes
in the second watch or in the third watch
and finds *them watching*.
39 And know this: If the head+ of the house
had known what hour the thief would
come, he would have watched and not
allowed+ his house to be broken through.
40 Therefore, you also *must be* ready. For
the Son of man will come at an hour
when you do not expect+ *Him*.

41 Then Peter said to Him: Lord, are you speaking this parable to us, or to everyone[+]?

42 The Lord said: Who then is that faithful and wise steward whom *the* lord will set over his household to give *them their* portion[+] in due season?

43 Blessed *is* that servant whom the lord shall find working[+] when he comes.

44 Truly I say to you, that he will set *such a servant* over all that he has.

45 But if that servant says within their heart: My lord delays his coming, and begins to beat the servants and maids and to eat and drink and to be drunk,

46 *then* the lord of that servant will come in a day when not expected[+] and in an unknown[+] hour, and will cut him in two[+] and will appoint *that servant's* portion *to be* with the unbelievers.

47 That servant who knew the lord's will and did not prepare nor do according to his will shall be beaten with many *stripes*.

48 But *those* who do not *know his will* and did commit things worthy of stripes shall be beaten with few *stripes*. For to whomever much is given, much will be required from them; and to whom much was committed, more will be asked of them.

49 I have come to send fire on the earth and what I desire[+] *is* if it already be started[+].

50 But I have a baptism with which to be baptized and how constrained[+] I am until it be accomplished.

51 Did you think[+] that I came to give peace on earth? I tell you: No, but rather division.

52 For from henceforth, there will be five in one house divided three against two and two against three.

53 The father will be divided against the son and the son against the father. The mother against the daughter and the daughter against the mother. The mother in law against her daughter in law and the daughter in law against her mother in law.

54 *Then* He said to the people: When you see a cloud rise out of the west, immediately[+] you say: A *rain* shower is coming, and so it is.

55 When *you see* the south wind blow you say: There will be heat, and it comes to pass.

56 *You* hypocrites. You can discern the face of the sky and of the earth, but how is it that you do not discern this time?

57 Yes, and why even of yourselves do you not judge what is right?

58 When you go with your adversary to the magistrate, *as you are* on the way, diligently *do everything you can so* that you may be freed[+] from him, lest he drag[+] you to the judge and the judge deliver you to the officer and the officer cast you into prison.

59 I tell you: You will not depart from there[+] until you have paid the *very* last penny[+].

Luke Chapter 13

1 At that same time,[+] some who were there told Him about the Galilaeans, whose blood Pilate had mingled with their sacrifices.

2 Jesus answering said to them: Do you suppose that these Galilaeans were sinners above all the Galilaeans, because they suffered such things?

3 I tell you: No. But unless[+] you repent, you will all likewise perish.

4 Or *consider* those eighteen upon whom the tower in Siloam fell and killed[+] them. Do you think that they were sinners above all *other* people[+] who lived[+] in Jerusalem?

5 I tell you: No. But unless[+] you repent, you will all likewise perish.

6 *Then Jesus* spoke this parable also: A certain *man* had a fig tree planted in his vineyard. He came and sought fruit upon it and found none.

7 Then he said to the dresser of his vineyard: Behold *for* three years I have come seeking fruit on this fig tree and have found none. Cut it down. Why *allow it* to burden[+] the ground?

8 *The vine dresser* answering said to *his master*: Lord, let it alone this year also until I can dig around[+] it and fertilize[+] *it*.

9 If it bears fruit, *good*. If not, *then* after that cut it down.

10 *Later on, Jesus* was teaching in one of the synagogues on the Sabbath.

11 And behold there was a woman who had a spirit of infirmity eighteen years and was bent over[+] and unable[+] to lift up *herself*.

12 When Jesus saw her, He called *to her* and said: Woman, you are loosed from your infirmity.

13 He laid *His* hands on her and immediately she was made straight and glorified God.

14 Since[+] Jesus had healed on the Sabbath day, the ruler of the synagogue answered with indignation and said to the people: There are six days in which people[+] ought to work. Therefore, come in those *days* and be healed, and not on the Sabbath day.

15 Then the Lord answered him and said: *You* hypocrite. Does not each one of you on the Sabbath loose his ox or *his* donkey[+] from the stall and lead *it* to water?

16 Should not this woman, being a daughter of Abraham whom Satan has bound, behold, eighteen years, be loosed from this bond on the Sabbath day?

17 When He had said these things, all His adversaries were ashamed and all the people rejoiced for all the glorious things that were done by Him.

18 Then He said: What is the kingdom of God like? To what shall I compare[+] it?

19 It is like a grain of mustard seed that a man cast into his garden, and it grew and became[+] a large[+] tree and the birds[+] of the air lodged in its branches.

20 Again He said: To what shall I compare[+] the kingdom of God?

21 It is like leaven that a woman hid in three measures of meal until the whole was permeated[+].

22 *Then* He went throughout the cities and villages, teaching, and journeying toward Jerusalem.

23 Then someone said to Him: Lord, are there few who are being[+] saved? He said to them:

24 *Earnestly* endeavor[+] to enter in through[+] the strait gate. For I say to you *that* many will seek to enter in and will not be able.

25 Once the master of the house has risen and shut the door, and you begin to stand outside[+] and to knock at the door saying: Lord, Lord, open to us. He will answer and say to you: I do not know you where you are.

26 Then you will begin to say: We ate and drank in your presence and you taught in our streets.

27 But He will say: I tell you, I do not know you where you are. Depart from me all you workers of iniquity.

28 And there will be weeping and gnashing of teeth when you see Abraham, Isaac, Jacob, and all the prophets in the kingdom of God, and you *yourselves* thrust out.

29 They will come from the east and west and from the north and south and will sit down in the kingdom of God.

30 And behold, there are *some who come in* last who will be first and there are *some who came in* first who will be last.

31 The same day some of the Pharisees came and said to Him: Get out and depart from here, for Herod will kill you.

32 *Jesus* said to them: Go and tell that fox: Behold I cast out demons[+] and I do cures today and tomorrow, and the third *day* I will be perfected.

33 Nevertheless, I must proceed[+] today and tomorrow and the *day* following, for it cannot be that a prophet shall perish outside[+] of Jerusalem.

34 O Jerusalem, Jerusalem, you kill the prophets and stones *those* who are sent to you. How often would I have gathered your children together as a hen *gathers* her brood under *her* wings, and you would not *come*.

35 *Now* behold your house is left to you desolate. Truly[+] I say to you: You will not see me until *the time* comes when you will say: Blessed *is* He who comes in the name of the Lord.

Luke Chapter 14

1 *Now* it came to pass, as *Jesus* went into
the house of one of the chief Pharisees
to eat bread on the Sabbath day, that
they watched Him.
2 And behold, there was a certain man
before Him who had a serious illness.+
3 Jesus answering spoke to the lawyers
and Pharisees saying: Is it lawful to heal
on the Sabbath day?
4 They *remained* silent.+ *So Jesus* took
hold+ *of him*, healed him, and released+
him.
5 *Then He* answered them saying: Who
among+ you shall have a donkey+ or an
ox fall into a pit and will not immediately+
pull it out on the Sabbath day?
6 Again, they could not answer Him
about these things.
7 *So, Jesus* put forth a parable to *those*
who were invited,+ remarking+ how
they chose out the chief rooms *for
themselves*, and saying to them:
8 When you are invited+ to a wedding,
do not sit down in the highest place+ lest
someone+ more honorable than you be
invited+ by *the host*,
9 and *then the host* who invited+ you *both
might* come and say to you: Give *your*
place to this man, and you then, with
shame, must+ take the lowest place+.
10 But when you are invited,+ go and sit
down in the lowest place+ *so* that when
the one who invited you comes, he might
say to you: Friend, go up higher. Then
you shall be honored+ in the presence of
those who sit *down* to eat+ with you.
11 For whoever exalts themselves will be
humbled+ and *those* who humble themselves will be exalted. *Matthew 23:12*
12 Then He said to the one who invited+
Him: When you make a dinner or a
supper, do not call your friends or your
brothers or your relatives+ or *your* rich
neighbors lest they also invite+ you *back*
again and repayment+ be made *to* you.
13 But when you make a feast, call the
poor, the maimed, the lame, *and* the
blind
14 and you will be blessed, for they
cannot repay+ you. You will be repaid+
at the resurrection of the righteous+.
15 When one of *those* who sat *down* to
eat+ with Him heard these things, *Jesus*
said to him: Blessed *are those* who shall
eat bread in the kingdom of God.
16 Then *Jesus* said to him: A certain man
made a great supper and invited+ many
people.
17 *Then he* sent his servant at supper time
to say to *those* who were invited+:
Come. For all things are now ready.
18 But they all with one *consent* began to
make excuses. The first said to him: I
have bought a piece of ground and I need
to go and see it. I beg+ you *to* excuse me.
19 Another said: I have bought five yoke
of oxen and I am going to examine+
them. I ask+ you *to* excuse me.
20 Another said: I have married a wife
and therefore I cannot come.
21 So that servant came and reported+
these things to his lord. Then the master
of the house, being angry, said to his
servant: Go out quickly into the streets
and lanes of the city and bring in the
poor, the maimed, the crippled,+ and
the blind.
22 The servant said: Lord, it has been
done as you have commanded, and yet
there is room.
23 The lord said to the servant: Go out
into the highways and hedges and
compel *them* to come in *so* that my house
may be filled.
24 For I say to you, that none of *those* who
were invited+ shall taste of my supper.
25 Great multitudes went with *Jesus* and
He turned and said to them:
26 If anyone+ comes to me and does not
hate father and mother and wife and
children and brothers and sisters and
yes, *even* their own life also, they cannot
be my disciple. *Matthew 10:37*
27 Whoever does not bear their cross and
come after me cannot be my disciple.
28 For who among+ you, intending to
build a tower, does not sit down first and
count the cost, *to see* whether *you* have
sufficient to finish *it*?

29 Lest perhaps+ after having laid the
foundation and not being able to finish
it, all who see+ *this* begin to mock
30 saying: This person+ began to build
and was not able to finish.
31 Or what king, going to make war
against another king, does not sit down
first and take counsel *to know* whether he
might be able, with ten thousand, to meet
one who comes against him with twenty
thousand?
32 Otherwise,+ while the *enemy* is yet a
great way off, he *might* send an ambassador *to* ask for peace.
33 So likewise, whoever does not forsake
all that they have cannot be my disciple.
34 Salt *is* good. But if salt has lost its
savor, with what shall it be seasoned?
35 *Otherwise* it is not fit for the land or for
the dunghill, *but just* to be cast out. *Those*
who have ears to hear, let them hear.

Luke Chapter 15

1 Then all the worldly+ people and
sinners drew near to *Jesus* to hear Him.
2 But the Pharisees and scribes com-
plained+ saying: This man receives
sinners and eats with them.
3 *Then Jesus* spoke this parable to them
saying:
4 What man among+ you having a
hundred sheep, if he lost one of them,
would not leave the ninety nine in the
wilderness and go after what is lost,
until he finds it?
5 And when he has found *it*, lays *it* on his
shoulders, rejoicing;
6 and coming home, calls together
friends and neighbors saying to them:
Rejoice with me, for I have found my
sheep that was lost.
7 I say to you, that likewise *there* will
be *more* joy in heaven over one sinner
who repents than over ninety nine
righteous+ persons who do not need
repentance.
8 Or, what woman, having ten pieces of
silver, if she loses one piece, does not
light a lamp,+ sweep the house, and
seek diligently until she finds *it*?
9 And when she has found *it*, *does she not*
call *her* friends and neighbors together
saying: Rejoice with me, for I have
found the piece that I had lost.
10 Likewise, I say to you: there is joy in
the presence of the angels of God over
one sinner who repents.
11 *Then* He said: A certain man had two
sons.
12 The younger of them said to *his* father:
Father, give me the portion of *your*
property+ that will fall *to me*. So, *his*
father divided *his worldly* possessions+ to
his sons.
13 Not many days later,+ the younger son
gathered everything+ together and went
away+ to a far country and there wasted
all his possessions+ with riotous living.
14 *After* he had spent everything+ *he had*,
a mighty famine arose in that land and
he began to be in want.
15 *So,* he joined a citizen of that country
who sent him into his fields to feed swine.
16 *The foolish son* would gladly+ have
filled his belly with the husks that the
swine ate but no one gave him *any*.
17 When he came to himself, he said:
How many of my father's hired servants
have bread enough and to spare, and I
am perishing with hunger.
18 I will arise and go to my father and will
say to him: Father, I have sinned against
heaven and before you.
19 *I* am no longer+ worthy to be called
your son. Make me as one of your hired
servants.
20 *So* he arose and went+ to his father,
but when he was yet a great distance+
away, his father saw him, had compassion, ran *to him*, embraced+ his
neck, and kissed him.
21 The son said to him: Father, I have
sinned against heaven and in your sight
and am no longer+ worthy to be called
your son.
22 But the father said to his servants:
Bring forth the best robe and put *it* on
him. Put a ring on his hand and sandals+
on *his* feet.
23 Bring the fatted calf here and kill *it*.
Let us eat and be merry.

24 For this my son was dead but *now* is alive again. He was lost but *now* is found. And they began to be merry.

25 Now *the father's* elder son was in the field, and as he came near the house, he heard music and dancing.

26 *So,* he called one of the servants and asked what these things meant.

27 *The servant* said to him: Your brother has come *home* and your father has killed the fatted calf because he has received him safe and sound.

28 *The older brother* was angry and would not go in. Therefore his father came out and pleaded+ *with* him.

29 He answering said to *his* father: Behold, these many years I have served you *and* not at any time transgressed your commandment. Yet you never gave me a *young* goat *so* that I might make merry with my friends.

30 But *now,* when this son *of* yours has come, *one* who has devoured your livelihood+ with harlots, you have killed the fatted calf for him.

31 *The father* said to him: Son, you are always+ with me and all that I have is yours.

32 It was fitting+ that we should make merry and be glad, for this your brother was dead and *now* is alive again. *He* was lost, but *now* is found.

Luke Chapter 16

1 *Then Jesus* said to His disciples: There was a certain rich man who had a steward. The same was accused to him that he had wasted his goods.

2 *So, the man* called *his steward* and said to him: How is it that I hear this of you? Give an account of your stewardship, for you cannot+ be *my* steward *any* longer.

3 Then the steward said within himself: What shall I do? For my lord *now* takes the stewardship away from me. I cannot dig and I am ashamed to beg.

4 I know+ what I will do, *so* that when I am removed+ from the stewardship *position*, they may receive me into their houses.

5 So he called everyone of his lord's debtors and said to the first: How much do you owe to my lord?

6 He said: A hundred measures of oil. *The steward* said to him: Take your bill and sit down quickly and write fifty.

7 Then he said to another: How much do you owe? He said: A hundred measures of wheat. *The steward* said to him: Take your bill and write eighty.

8 The lord commended the unrighteous+ steward because he had done shrewdly.+ For the children of this world are, in their generation, *more* shrewd+ than the children of light.

9 I say to you: *If you* make yourselves friends with the *worldly* treasures+ of unrighteousness, *then* when you fail, *they will* receive you into *their* eternal+ dwellings+.

10 *Those* who are faithful in the smallest+ *matters* are also faithful in much and *those* who are unrighteous+ in the smallest+ *matters* are also unrighteous in much.

11 Therefore, if you have not been faithful in the unrighteous *worldly* treasures,+ who will commit to your trust the true *riches*?

12 If you have not been faithful in what is another's, who will give you your own?

13 No servant can serve two masters. For either *a servant* will hate the one and love the other, or else hold to the one and despise the other. You cannot serve God and *worldly* treasures+. *Matthew 6:24*

14 Now the Pharisees, who were covetous, also heard all these things and they ridiculed+ Him.

15 He said to them: You + justify yourselves before people,+ but God knows your hearts. For what is highly esteemed among people+ is *an* abomination in the sight of God.

16 The law and the prophets *were* until John. Since that time, the kingdom of God is proclaimed+ and everyone+ presses into it.

17 It is easier for heaven and earth to pass, than one smallest mark+ of the law to fail.

18 Whoever puts away his wife and marries
another, commits adultery. Whoever
marries one who is put away from *her*
husband commits adultery. *Matthew 19:9*
19 There was a certain rich man who was
clothed in purple and fine linen and *lived*
in luxury+ and merrymaking+ every day.
20 And, there was a certain beggar named
Lazarus who laid at *the rich man's* gate,
full of sores,
21 desiring to be fed with the crumbs that
fell from the rich man's table. Moreover the dogs came and licked his sores.
22 *Now* it came to pass that the beggar
died and was carried by the angels into
Abraham's bosom. *Then* the rich man
also died and was buried.
23 In hell, being in torments, *the rich*
man lifted up his eyes and saw Abraham
at a far distance,+ and Lazarus in his
bosom.
24 And he cried *out* and said: Father
Abraham, have mercy on me and send
Lazarus *so* that he may dip the tip of his
finger in water and cool my tongue, for
I am tormented in this flame.
25 But Abraham said: Son, remember
that in your lifetime you received your
good things and likewise Lazarus evil
things. But now he is comforted and you
are tormented.
26 Above+ all this, there is a great chasm+
fixed between you and us so that
whoever *might* want+ to go+ from
here+ to you cannot. Nor *can* anyone+
from there come+ to us.
27 Then *the rich man* said: I beg+ you
therefore, father, that you would send
him to my father's house.
28 For I have five brothers, *and I pray* that
he might testify to them, lest they also
come into this place of torment.
29 Abraham said to him: They have Moses
and the prophets. Let them hear them.
30 He said: No, father Abraham, but if
one went to them from the dead, they
will repent.
31 *Abraham* said to him: If they do not
hear Moses and the prophets, neither
will they be persuaded, *even* though one
rose from the dead.

Luke Chapter 17

1 Then *Jesus* said to the disciples: It is
impossible but that offenses will come.
But woe *to those* through whom they
come.
2 It would be better for them if+ a
millstone were hung around+ their neck
and they were cast into the sea, than that
they should offend *or cause sin to come to*
one of these little ones.
3 Take heed to yourselves. If *one of* your
family+ trespasses against you, rebuke
them. If they repent, forgive them.
4 If *one* trespasses against you seven
times in a day, and seven times in a day
turn again to you saying: I repent, you
shall forgive them.
5 The apostles said to the Lord: Increase
our faith.
6 The Lord said: If you had faith as a
grain of mustard seed, you might say to
this fig+ tree: Be plucked up by the root
and be planted in the sea, and it should
obey you.
7 Who among+ you, having a servant
plowing or feeding cattle, will say to
him immediately+ when he comes *in*
from the field: Go and sit down to eat?
8 Will *you* not rather say to him: Make
ready *that* with which I may dine+ and
prepare+ yourself *to* serve me until I
have eaten and drunk, and afterward
you shall eat and drink.
9 Does he thank that servant because he
did the things that were commanded *to*
him? I think not.
10 So likewise you, when you have done
all those things that you are commanded
to do, say: We are unprofitable servants.
We have done what was our duty to do.
11 *Now* it came to pass, as *Jesus* went to
Jerusalem, that He passed through the
midst of Samaria and Galilee.
12 As He entered a certain village, ten men
who were lepers met Him, standing+ *at*
a distance.+
13 They lifted up *their* voices and said:
Jesus, Master, have mercy on us.
14 When He saw *them*, He said to them:

Go *and* show yourselves to the priests.
And it came to pass that as they went,
they were cleansed.
15 One of them, when he saw that he was
healed, turned back and with a loud
voice glorified God.
16 *He* fell face *down* at *Jesus'* feet, giving
Him thanks. And he was a Samaritan.
17 Jesus answering said: Were there not
ten cleansed? But where *are* the nine?
18 There are none found that returned to
give glory to God, except+ this stranger.
19 *Jesus* said to him: Arise and go. Your
faith has made you whole.
20 When the Pharisees asked Him when
the kingdom of God should come, He
answered them and said: The kingdom
of God does not come with observation.
21 Nor shall they say: Behold here. Or,
behold there. For behold, the kingdom
of God is within you.
22 *Then* He said to the disciples: The days
will come when you will desire to see
one of the days of the Son of man and
you will not see *it*.
23 They will say to you: See here. Or:
See there. Do not go after *them* or follow
them.
24 For as the lightning that illuminates+
out of one *part* under heaven shines to
the other *part* under heaven, so also will
the Son of man be in His day.
25 But first He must suffer many things
and be rejected by this generation.
26 As it was in the days of Noah, so will
it also be in the days of the Son of man.
27 They ate, they drank, they married
wives, and they were given in marriage
until the day that Noah entered the ark and
the flood came and destroyed them all.
28 Likewise also as it was in the days of
Lot. They ate, they drank, they bought,
they sold, they planted, and they built.
29 But the same day that Lot went out of
Sodom, it rained fire and brimstone
from heaven and destroyed *them* all.
30 Even thus shall it be in the day when
the Son of man is revealed.
31 In that day, *if* someone is up on the
housetop with their goods+ in the house,
let them not come down to take it away.
And *those* who are in the field, let them
likewise not return back.
32 Remember Lot's wife.
33 Whoever will seek to save their life
will lose it, and whoever would+ lose
their life will preserve it.
34 I tell you: In that night there will be
two *people* in one bed. The one will be
taken and the other will be left.
35 Two will be grinding together. One
will be taken and the other left.
36 *Two will be in the field. One will be taken*
and the other left.
37 They answered and said to Him: Where
Lord? And He said to them: Wherever
the body *is*, there the eagles will be
gathered together.

Luke Chapter 18

1 *Then Jesus* spoke a parable to them *to*
this end: That people+ should always
pray, and not faint *or give up*.
2 *He* said: There was a judge in a city who
did not fear God or regard anyone+.
3 There was also a widow in that city,
and she came to *the judge* saying: Avenge
me of my adversary.
4 For a while, *the judge* would not
respond. But afterward he said within
himself: Although I do not fear God or
regard man,
5 yet because this widow troubles me, I
will avenge her, lest by her continual
coming she weary me.
6 The Lord said: Hear what the un-
righteous+ judge said.
7 Will God not *also* avenge His own
elect who cry day and night to Him,
even though He bear with them *for* a
long *while*.
8 I tell you: He will avenge them speedily.
Nevertheless when the Son of man
comes, will He find faith on the earth?
9 *Jesus* spoke this parable to certain *ones*
who trusted in themselves, *believing* that
they were righteous, and despised
others:
10 Two men went up into the temple to
pray. The one a Pharisee and the other
a worldly+ person.

11 The Pharisee stood and prayed thus
with himself: God, I thank you that I am
not as other men *are*: extortioners,
unrighteous,+ adulterers, or even as this
worldly+ person.
12 I fast twice in the week *and* I give tithes
of all that I possess.
13 The worldly+ person, standing *at a*
distance+ *away*, would not so much as
lift up *his* eyes to heaven, but beat+ upon
his *own* breast saying: God be merciful
to me a sinner.
14 I tell you: This man went down to his
house justified *rather* than the other. For
everyone who exalts themselves will be
humbled+ and *those* who humble themselves will be exalted. *Matthew 23:12*
15 *Then* they brought infants to *Jesus*, *so*
that He would touch them. But when *His*
disciples saw *this*, they rebuked them.
16 But Jesus called *to* them and said:
Allow little children to come to me and
do not forbid them. For of such is the
kingdom of God.
17 Truly+ I say to you: Whoever will not
receive the kingdom of God as a little
child shall in no way+ enter therein.
18 A certain ruler asked Him saying: Good
Master, what shall I do to inherit eternal life?
19 Jesus said to him: Why do you call me
good? No one *is* good except+ one. God.
20 You know the commandments: Do
not commit adultery. Do not kill. Do not
steal. Do not bear false witness. Honor
your father and your mother.
21 *The ruler* said: All these I have kept
from my youth.
22 Now when Jesus heard these things, He
said to him: Yet you lack one thing. Sell
all *the things* that you have and distribute
to the poor and you shall have treasure
in heaven. And come, follow me.
23 When he heard this, he was very
sorrowful, for he was very rich.
24 When Jesus saw that he was very
sorrowful, He said: How hard+ *it is for*
those who have riches *to* enter into the
kingdom of God.
25 It is easier for a camel to go through an
eye of a needle than for a rich man to
enter into the kingdom of God.
26 *Those* who heard *this* said: Who then
can be saved?
27 *Jesus* said: The things that are impossible with people+ are possible with God.
28 Then Peter said: Behold, we have left
all and followed you.
29 *Jesus* said to them: Truly+ I say to you:
There is no one who has left house or parents
or brothers or wife or children for the
sake of the kingdom of God *Matthew 19:29*
30 who will not receive many times+
more in this present time, and in the
world to come, eternal+ life.
31 Then *Jesus* took the twelve and said to
them: Behold, we *shall now* go up to
Jerusalem and all things that are written
by the prophets concerning the Son of
man will be accomplished. *Matthew 20:18*
32 For He will be delivered to the
Gentiles *to* be mocked and spitefully
treated and spit on.
33 They will flog+ *Him* and put Him to death,
and the third day He will rise again.
34 *The disciples* did not understand these
things. This saying was hid from them
and they did not know *the meaning of* the
things that *Jesus now* spoke *to them*.
35 *Now* it came to pass that as *Jesus* had
come near Jericho, a certain blind man
sat by the wayside begging.
36 Hearing the multitude pass by, *the*
blind man asked what it meant.
37 They told him that Jesus of Nazareth
is passing by.
38 *So* he cried *out* saying: Jesus son of
David, have mercy on me.
39 *Those* who went before rebuked him,
saying that he should be silent.+ But he
cried *out* so much the more: Son of
David, have mercy on me.
40 Jesus stopped+ and directed+ *the blind*
man to be brought to Him. When he had
come near, *Jesus* asked him
41 saying: What do you want me to do to you?
He said: Lord, that I may receive my sight.
42 Jesus said to him: Receive your sight.
Your faith has saved you.
43 Immediately he received his sight and
followed *Jesus*, glorifying God. And
when they saw *this*, all the people gave
praise to God.

Luke Chapter 19

1 *Then Jesus* entered and passed through Jericho.

2 And behold *there was* a man named Zacchaeus who was a chief among the worldly[+] people, and he was rich.

3 He sought to see Jesus, *to see* who He was, but *he* could not *see* because of the crowd,[+] because he was small[+] in stature.

4 *So* he ran ahead[+] and climbed up into a sycamore tree to see *Jesus*, for He was to pass that *way*.

5 When Jesus came to the place, He looked up and saw him and said to him: Zacchaeus, come down quickly.[+] For today I must stay[+] at your house.

6 *So* he came down quickly[+] and received *Jesus* joyfully.

7 When they saw *this* everyone[+] complained[+] saying: He has gone to stay[+] with a man who is a sinner.

8 *Then* Zacchaeus stood and said to the Lord: Behold Lord, half of my goods I *am* giving to the poor, and if I have taken anything from anyone by false accusation, I *will* restore *them* fourfold.

9 Jesus said to him: This day salvation has come to this house, since[+] *Zacchaeus* also is a son of Abraham.

10 For the Son of man has come to seek and to save *those* who were lost.

11 As they heard these things, *Jesus* spoke another[+] parable *to them* because He was near Jerusalem and because they thought that the kingdom of God *was going to* appear immediately.

12 Therefore He said: A certain nobleman went into a far country to receive for himself a kingdom, and *then* to return.

13 He called his ten servants, gave[+] ten pounds to them, and said to them: Occupy until I come.

14 But his citizens hated him and sent a message after him saying: We will not have this *man* to reign over us.

15 *Now* it came to pass that when he had returned, having received the kingdom, he then commanded those servants to be called to him to whom he had given the money *so* that he might know how much each one[+] had gained[+].

16 The first came saying: Lord, your pound has gained ten pounds.

17 *The nobleman* said to him: Well *done* good servant. Because you have been faithful in a very little, you *shall now* have authority over ten cities.

18 The second came saying: Lord, your pound has gained five pounds.

19 *The nobleman* likewise said to him: You also *shall* be over five cities.

20 *Then* another came saying: Lord, behold *here is* your pound that I have kept wrapped[+] up in a cloth[+].

21 For I feared you because you are an austere man. You take up what you have not laid down and reap what you did not sow.

22 *The nobleman* said to him: Out of your own mouth I will judge you, *you* wicked servant. You knew that I was an austere man, taking up what I did not lay down and reaping what I did not sow.

23 Why then did you not give my money to the bank *so* that at my coming I might have received[+] *what was mine* with interest[+]?

24 *Then* he said to *those* who stood by: Take the pound from him and give *it* to the one who has ten pounds.

25 They said to him: Lord, he has ten pounds.

26 I say to you, that to everyone who has will *more* be given, but from *those* who have nothing, even what they have will be taken away from them.

27 But those *who were* my enemies, *those* who were unwilling[+] *for* me to reign over them, bring here and slay *them* before me.

28 After[+] *Jesus* had said these things, He went, *as He had started* before, going[+] up to Jerusalem.

29 *Now* it came to pass, when He had come near Bethphage and Bethany at the mount called *the Mount* of Olives, He sent two of His disciples

30 saying: Go into the village near[+] *you*. Upon[+] entering, you will find a colt tied, on which no one has ever sat. Loosen it and bring *it here*.

31 If anyone asks you: Why do you
loosen *it*? You shall say this: Because
the Lord has need of it.
32 *Those* who were sent went and found *it*
just[+] as He had said to them.
33 As they were loosing the colt, the
owners said to them: Why are you
loosening the colt?
34 They said: The Lord has need of it.
35 *Then* they brought it to Jesus and they
cast their garments upon the colt and sat
Jesus upon[+] *it*.
36 And as He went, they spread their
clothes in the way. *Zechariah 9:9*
37 When He had come near, even now at
the descent of the Mount of Olives, the
whole multitude of the disciples began
to rejoice and praise God with a loud
voice for all the mighty works that they
had seen,
38 saying: Blessed *be* the King who comes
in the name of the Lord. Peace in heaven
and glory in the highest. *Psalm 118:26*
39 Some of the Pharisees from among the
multitude said to Him: Master, rebuke
your disciples.
40 He answered and said to them: I tell
you that if these should *remain* silent[+]
the stones would *immediately* cry out.
41 As *Jesus* came near, He saw[+] the city
and wept over it
42 saying: If you had *only* known, even
you, at least in this your day, the things
that are for your peace. But now they are
hid from your eyes.
43 For the days will come upon you *in
which* your enemies will cast a blockade[+]
around[+] you and surround[+] you and
keep you in on every side
44 and *knock you* to the ground, and
your children within you. They will
not leave in you stone upon stone
because you did not understand[+] the
time of your visitation.
45 *Then Jesus* went into the temple and
began to cast out *those* who bought and
sold therein,
46 saying to them: It is written: My house
is the house of prayer. But you have
made it a den of thieves. *Matthew 21:13*
47 *Jesus* taught in the temple daily, but the
chief priests and the scribes and the chief
of the people sought to destroy Him.
48 But *they* could not find what they might
do, for all the people were very attentive
to hear Him.

Luke Chapter 20

1 *Now* it came to pass, *that* on one of
those days as *Jesus* taught the people in
the temple and proclaimed[+] the Gospel,
the chief priests and the scribes came
with the elders
2 and spoke to Him saying: Tell us.
By what authority do you *do* these
things? Or who is He who gave you
this authority?
3 *Jesus* answered and said to them: I will
also ask you one thing. Answer me.
4 The baptism of John, was it from
heaven, or of men?
5 They reasoned with themselves saying: If we say: From heaven, He will
say: Why then did you not believe him?
6 But if we say: Of men. All the people
will stone us for they are persuaded that
John was a prophet.
7 They answered that they could not tell
from where *it came*.
8 Jesus said to them: *Then* neither will I
tell you by what authority I do these
things.
9 Then He began to speak this parable to
the people: A certain man planted a
vineyard, leased[+] it to *tenant* farmers,[+]
and went into a far country for a long
time.
10 At the *harvest* season, he sent a servant
to the *tenant* farmers[+] *so* that they should
give him *his portion* of the fruit of the
vineyard. But the farmers[+] beat him and
sent *him* away empty *handed*.
11 Again he sent another servant, and they
beat him also and treated *him* shamefully and sent *him* away empty *handed*.
12 Again he sent a third, and they wounded
him also and cast *him* out.
13 Then the lord of the vineyard said:
What shall I do? I will send my beloved
son. Perhaps[+] when they see *him* they
will respect[+] him.

14 But when the *tenant* farmers[+] saw
him, they reasoned among themselves
saying: This is the heir. Come, let us kill
him *so* that the inheritance may be ours.
15 So they cast him out of the vineyard,
and killed *him*. What therefore will the
lord of the vineyard do to them?
16 He will come and destroy these
tenant farmers[+] and give the vineyard
to others. When they heard *this*, they
said: *God* forbid.
17 *Then Jesus* looked[+] at them and said:
What is this then that is written: The stone
that the builders rejected has become
the head of the corner. *Matthew 21:42*
18 Whoever falls upon that stone will be
broken, but on whomever it falls, it will
grind them to powder.
19 *In* that same hour, the chief priests and
the scribes sought to lay hands on Him,
but they feared the people, for they
perceived that He had spoken this
parable against them.
20 *So* they watched *Him* and sent forth
spies who pretended[+] *to be* righteous[+]
men *so* that they might take hold of Him
as He was speaking, to deliver Him to the
power and authority of the governor.
21 They asked Him saying: Master, we
know that you say and teach rightly *and*
you do not accept *any other* person's
authority, but teach the way of God truly.
22 Is it lawful for us to give tribute to
Caesar, or not?
23 But He perceived their craftiness and
said to them: Why are you testing[+] me?
24 Show me a coin.[+] Whose image and
title[+] does it have? They answered and
said: Caesar's.
25 *Then* He said to them: Therefore, render
to Caesar the things that are Caesar's
and to God the things that are God's.
26 *So* they could not catch[+] Him in His words
before the people, but *instead* they marveled
at His answer and *remained* silent.[+]
27 Then some of the Sadducees who deny
that there is any resurrection came and
asked Him,
28 saying: Master, Moses wrote to us: If
any man's brother die having a wife and
he die without children, that his brother
should take his wife and raise up *children*
as seed to his brother.
29 *Once* there were seven brothers.
The first took a wife and died without
children.
30 The second took her as *his* wife and he
died childless.
31 The third took her and in like manner
the seven also, and they *all* left no
children and died.
32 Last of all the woman died also.
33 Therefore, in the resurrection whose
wife of them is she? For seven had her
as *their* wife.
34 Jesus answering said to them: The
children of this world marry and are
given in marriage,
35 but *those* who shall be accounted
worthy to obtain that world and the
resurrection from the dead, neither
marry nor are given in marriage.
36 Nor can they die any more, for they
are equal to the angels and are the
children of God, being the children of
the resurrection,
37 now that the dead are raised, even *as*
Moses showed at the bush when he
called the Lord the God of Abraham and
the God of Isaac and the God of Jacob.
38 For He is not a God of the dead, but of
the living, for all live to Him.
39 Then some of the scribes answering
said: Master, you have well said.
40 After that they did not dare[+] ask Him
any *more questions*.
41 *Then Jesus* said to them: How can they
say that Christ is David's son?
42 In the book of Psalms, David himself
said: The Lord said to my Lord: Sit at
my right hand
43 until I make your enemies your footstool.
44 Therefore, if David calls Him Lord,
how is He then his son?
45 Then in the audience of all the people
He said to His disciples:
46 Beware of the scribes who desire to
walk in long robes and love greetings
in the market *places* and the highest
seats in the synagogues and the chief
room at feasts,

47 who devour widows' houses and for a show make long prayers. These shall receive greater damnation.

Luke Chapter 21

1 *Then Jesus* looked up and saw the rich men casting their gifts into the treasury.

2 And He also saw a certain poor widow casting in there two mites, *worth about a penny*.

3 He said: Truly I say to you, that this poor widow has cast in more than all *of* them.

4 For all these have cast into the offerings of God *out* of their abundance, but she, *even out* of her poverty,[+] has cast in all the *means of* livelihood[+] that she had.

5 *Later* as some spoke about the temple, how it was adorned with fine[+] stones and gifts, *Jesus* said:

6 *As for* these things that you behold, the days will come in which there will not be left stone upon stone that will not be thrown down.

7 *Then* they asked Him saying: Master, but when shall these things be? And what sign *will there be* when these things shall come to pass?

8 He said: Take heed *so* that you are not deceived. For many will come in my name saying: I am *Christ*, and the time draws near. Do not go after them.

9 When you hear about wars and commotions, do not be terrified. For these things must come to pass first, but the end *is* not immediately[+].

10 Then He said to them: Nation will rise against nation and kingdom against kingdom.

11 Great earthquakes will be in many different[+] places, and famines and pestilences. Fearful sights and great signs from heaven will occur[+].

12 But before all these, they will lay their hands on you and persecute *you*, delivering *you* up to the synagogues and into prisons, *and* bringing *you* before kings and rulers for my name's sake.

13 But this will turn to you for a testimony.

14 Therefore, *be* settled in your hearts to not meditate before *hand* what *or how* you will answer.

15 For I will give you a mouth and wisdom that all your adversaries will not be able to speak against[+] nor stand against[+].

16 You will be betrayed by both parents and brothers and *close* relatives[+] and friends, and they will *even* put to death *some* from among[+] you.

17 You will be hated by all because of my name.

18 But not a hair of your head will perish.

19 In your patience, possess your souls.

20 When you see Jerusalem surrounded[+] with armies, then know that *its* desolation is near.

21 Then let *those* who are in Judea flee to the mountains. Let *those* who are in the midst of it depart. And do not let *those* who are in *other* countries enter into there.

22 For these are the days of vengeance *so* that all *the* things that are written may be fulfilled. *Isaiah 61:2*

23 But woe to *those* who are with child and to *those* who are nursing[+] in those days. For there will be great distress in the land and wrath upon this people.

24 They will fall by the edge of the sword and be led away captive into all nations. Jerusalem will be trampled[+] down by the Gentiles until the times of the Gentiles are fulfilled.

25 There will be signs in the sun and in the moon and in the stars. And upon the earth, distress of nations, with perplexity. The sea and the waves *will* roar.

26 Men's hearts *will* fail them for fear and for expectation[+] of those things that are coming upon the world.[+] For the powers of heaven will be shaken.

27 Then they will see the Son of man coming in a cloud with power and great glory.

28 When these things begin to come to pass, look up and lift up your heads. For your redemption draws near.

29 *Then Jesus* spoke a parable to them: Behold the fig tree and all the trees.

30 When they shoot forth, you see and
know of yourselves that summer is now
very near[+].
31 So likewise when you see these things
come to pass, know that the kingdom of
God is *very* near.
32 Truly[+] I say to you: This generation
will not pass away until all be fulfilled.
33 Heaven and earth will pass away, but
my words will not pass away.
34 Take heed to yourselves, lest at any
time your hearts be overburdened[+] with
excesses[+] and drunkenness and *the* cares
of this life *so* that *judgment* day comes
upon you unexpectedly[+].
35 For it will come like[+] a snare upon
all *those* who dwell on the face of the
whole earth.
36 Therefore watch and pray always *so*
that you may be accounted worthy to
escape all these things that will come to
pass and to stand before the Son of man.
37 In the daytime *Jesus* taught in the
temple. At night He went out and stayed[+]
on the mountain that is called *the Mount*
of Olives.
38 And all the people came to Him early
in the morning to hear Him in the
temple.

Luke Chapter 22

1 Now the Feast of Unleavened Bread
called the Passover drew near.
2 And the chief priests and scribes sought
how they might kill *Jesus*, because they
feared the people.
3 Then Satan entered into Judas surnamed Iscariot *who* was *one* of the twelve.
4 *Judas* went away[+] and conferred[+]
with the chief priests and captains *to*
determine how he might betray *Jesus*
to them.
5 They were delighted[+] and agreed[+] to
give him money.
6 *So Judas* promised and sought opportunity to betray *Jesus* to them, in the
absence of the multitude.
7 Then the day of unleavened bread
came, when the Passover *lamb* must be
killed.
8 *Jesus* sent Peter and John saying: Go
and prepare the Passover *for* us *so* that
we may eat.
9 They said to Him: Where do you want
us to prepare?
10 He said to them: Behold, when you
have entered the city, there a man will
meet you bearing a pitcher of water.
Follow him into the house where he
enters.
11 Say to the head[+] of the house: The
Master says to you: Where is the guest
chamber where I shall eat the Passover
with my disciples?
12 He will show you a large, furnished
upper room. Make ready there.
13 *So* they went and found *it* as *Jesus*
had said to them, and they made
preparations[+] *for* the Passover.
14 When the hour had come, *Jesus* sat down
and the twelve apostles *sat* with Him.
15 He said to them: *It is* with *a burning*
desire *that* I have desired to eat this
Passover with you before I suffer.
16 For I say to you: I will not any more
eat thereof, until it is fulfilled in the
kingdom of God.
17 *Then Jesus* took the cup, gave thanks,
and said: Take this and divide *it* among
yourselves.
18 For I say to you: I will not drink of the
fruit of the vine until the kingdom of
God comes.
19 *Then Jesus* took *the* bread, gave thanks,
broke *it*, and gave *it* to them saying:
This is my body, given for you. Do
this in remembrance of me.
20 Likewise, after supper *He took* the cup
and said: This cup *represents* the new
covenant[+] in my blood, shed for you.
21 But, behold the hand of the one who
betrays me *is* with me on the table.
22 Truly the Son of man goes as it was
determined. But woe to that man by
whom He is betrayed.
23 *Then* they began to inquire among
themselves who among them it was that
should do this thing.
24 And there was also a dispute[+] among
them *regarding* who among them should
be considered[+] the greatest.

25 *But Jesus* said to them: The kings of the
Gentiles exercise lordship over them,
and *those* who exercise authority upon
them are called benefactors.
26 But you *shall* not *be* that way.+ Let
those who are *to be* greatest among you
be like the younger, and *those* who lead+
be as *those* who serve.
27 For who+ *is* greater? *Those* who sit
down to eat+ or *those* who serve? *Is it* not
those who sit *down* to eat+? But I am
among you as one who serves.
28 You are the ones who have continued
with me in my trials+.
29 And I appoint to you a kingdom, as my
Father has appointed to me.
30 *So* that you may eat and drink at my
table in my kingdom and sit on thrones
judging the twelve tribes of Israel.
31 *Then* the Lord said: Simon, Simon.
Behold, Satan has desired *to have* you *so*
that he may sift *you* as wheat.
32 But I have prayed for you, that your
faith not fail. When you are converted,
strengthen the family+ *of God*.
33 *Peter* said to Him: Lord, I am ready to
go with you, both into prison and to death.
34 *Jesus* said: I tell you Peter, the cock
will not crow this day before you deny
three times that you know me.
35 He said to them: When I sent you
without purse and *provision* bag+ and
sandals,+ did you lack anything? They
said: Nothing.
36 Then He said to them: But now, let *those*
who have a purse take *it*, and likewise
take a provision bag.+ Let *those* who have
no sword sell their clothes and buy one.
37 For I say to you, that this that is written
must yet be accomplished in me: He
was numbered+ among the transgressors. For the things concerning me have
an end. *Isaiah 53:12*
38 They said: Lord, behold here *are* two
swords. He said to them: It is enough.
39 *Then* going forth, as it was *His* custom,+ He went to the Mount of Olives,
and His disciples also followed Him.
40 When He was at the place, He said to
them: Pray *so* that you do not enter into
temptation.
41 *Then Jesus* withdrew about a stone's
throw+ *away* from them and knelt down
and prayed
42 saying: Father, if you are willing,
remove this cup from me. Nevertheless
not my will, but yours be done.
43 *Then* an angel appeared to Him from
heaven, strengthening Him.
44 Being in agony, *Jesus* prayed *even*
more earnestly, and His sweat became+
like+ great drops of blood falling down
to the ground.
45 When He rose up from prayer and had
come to His disciples, He found them
sleeping, *exhausted* from sorrow.
46 *Jesus* said to them: Why are you
sleeping? Rise and pray lest you enter
into temptation.
47 While He spoke, behold a multitude
came forth, and the one who was called
Judas, one of the twelve, went before
them. And *Judas* drew near to Jesus to
kiss Him.
48 But Jesus said to him: Judas, are you
betraying the Son of man with a kiss?
Matthew 26:48
49 When *those* who were around+ *Jesus*
saw what would follow, they said to
Him: Lord, shall we strike+ with the
sword?
50 And one of them struck+ the servant of
the high priest and cut off his right ear.
51 Jesus answered and said: Do you *really*
condone+ this? And He touched *the*
servant's ear and healed him.
52 Then Jesus said to the chief priests,
captains of the temple, and the elders
who had come to Him: Have you come
out as against a thief with swords and
staves?
53 When I was with you daily in the
temple, you stretched forth no hands
against me. But this is your hour and the
power of darkness.
54 Then they took *Jesus*, led *Him away*,
and brought Him to the high priest's
house. And Peter followed *from* a
distance.+
55 When they had started+ a fire in the
midst of the courtyard+ and *everyone* sat
down together, Peter sat among them.

56 *Then* a certain maid saw[+] *Peter* as he
sat by the fire, peered[+] *intently* at him,
and said: This man was also with *Jesus*.
57 *But Peter* denied *Jesus* saying: Woman,
I do not know Him.
58 After a little while another noticed[+]
Peter and said: You are also of them.
And Peter said: Man, I am not.
59 About one hour later,[+] another confidently affirmed saying: Truly this *fellow*
also was with Him, for he is a Galilaean.
60 Peter said: Man, I do not know what
you say. And immediately, while *Peter*
spoke, the cock crowed.[+]
61 *Then* the Lord turned and looked upon
Peter, and Peter remembered the word
of the Lord, how He had said to him:
Before the cock crows, you will deny
me three times.
62 And Peter went out and wept bitterly.
63 *Then* the men who held Jesus mocked
Him and struck[+] *Him*.
64 When they had blindfolded Him, they
struck Him on the face and asked Him
saying: *Now* prophesy. Who is it that
struck[+] you?
65 And they spoke many other things to
Him blasphemously.
66 As soon as it was day, the elders of the
people and the chief priests and the
scribes came together and led *Jesus* into
their council *chambers*, saying:
67 Are you the Christ? Tell us. He said to
them: If I tell you, you will not believe.
68 If I also ask *you*, you will not answer
me or let *me* go.
69 Hereafter the Son of man will sit at the
right hand of the power of God.
70 Then they all said: Are you then the
Son of God? And He said to them: You
say that I am.
71 And they said: What further witness
do we need? For we ourselves have
heard *Him* from[+] His own mouth.

Luke Chapter 23

1 *Then* the whole multitude of them
arose and led *Jesus* to Pilate.
2 And they began to accuse Him saying:
We found this *fellow* corrupting[+] the
nation and forbidding to give tribute
to Caesar, saying that He Himself is
Christ a King.
3 Pilate asked Him saying: Are you the
King of the Jews? *Jesus* answered *Pilate*
and said: You say *it*.
4 Then Pilate said to the chief priests and
to the people: I find no fault in this man.
5 But they were more *fiercely* insistent,[+]
saying: He stirred up the people, teaching
throughout all Judea,[+] beginning from
Galilee to this place.
6 When Pilate heard *the name* Galilee,
he asked if the man was a Galilaean.
7 As soon as he knew that *Jesus* belonged to
Herod's jurisdiction, he sent Him to Herod,
who was in Jerusalem at that time.
8 When Herod saw Jesus, he was exceedingly glad, for he had desired to see Him
for a long *time* because he had heard
many things about Him and he hoped to
see some miracle done by Him.
9 Then *Herod* questioned with Him in
many words, but *Jesus* answered nothing.
10 The chief priests and scribes *then*
stood and forcefully[+] accused *Jesus*.
11 *Then* Herod, with his soldiers,[+]
belittled[+] *Jesus* and mocked *Him* and
dressed[+] Him in a gorgeous robe and
sent Him back[+] to Pilate.
12 *That* same day, Pilate and Herod
were made friends together, for before
that they had been at enmity between
themselves.
13 *Then* Pilate, when he had called together
the chief priests and the rulers and the
people,
14 said to them: You have brought this
man to me as one who corrupts[+] the
people. But behold, I have examined
Him before you *and I* have found no fault
in this man touching those things of
which you accuse Him.
15 No, nor yet Herod. For I sent you to
him and behold, *Herod and I agree that*
nothing worthy of death is done by Him.
16 Therefore, I will chastise Him and
release *Him*.
17 For *tradition had made it* necessary that
Pilate must release one *prisoner* to them
at the feast.

18 *Then* they all cried out at once saying:
Away with this *man*, and release to us
Barabbas.
19 *It was* for a certain sedition made in the
city and for murder *that Barabbas* had
been cast into prison.
20 Therefore Pilate, *being* willing to
release Jesus, spoke again to them.
21 But *the people* cried *out* saying:
Crucify *Him*. Crucify Him.
22 *Pilate* said to them the third time:
Why? What evil has He done? I have
found no cause of death in Him. Therefore, I will chastise Him and let *Him* go.
23 But they were insistent+ with loud
voices, requiring that *Jesus* be crucified,
and their voices, and *those* of the chief
priests prevailed.
24 *So* Pilate gave *the* sentence that it
should be as they required,
25 and he released to them *Barabbas* who,
for sedition and murder was cast into
prison, whom they had desired. But he
delivered Jesus *according* to their will.
26 As they led Him away, they laid hold
upon one Simon, a Cyrenian coming out
of the country, and they laid the cross on
him *so* that he might carry+ *it* for Jesus.
27 A great multitude+ of people followed
Jesus, *including many* women who cried+
and grieved+ *for* Him.
28 But Jesus turning to them said:
Daughters of Jerusalem, do not weep
for me but weep for yourselves and for
your children.
29 For behold the days are coming in
which they will say: Blessed *are* the
barren and the wombs that never gave
birth+ and the breasts+ that never nursed+.
30 Then they will begin to say to the
mountains: Fall on us. And to the hills:
Cover us.
31 For if they do these things in a green
tree, what will be done in the dry?
32 *Now* there were also two others,
criminals,+ led *away* with *Jesus* to be put
to death.
33 When they had come to the place
called Calvary, there they crucified Him
and the criminals,+ one on the right
side+ and the other on the left. *John 19:18*
34 Then Jesus said: Father, forgive
them. For they do not know what they
are doing. *The soldiers then* divided+
up His clothing+ and cast lots *for it*.
Psalm 109:4, Matthew 27:35
35 And the people stood beholding, and
the rulers also with them ridiculed+ *Him*
saying: He saved others. Let Him save
Himself, if He is Christ, the chosen of
God. *Matthew 27:41*
36 The soldiers also mocked Him, coming
to Him and offering Him vinegar,
37 saying: If you are the king of the Jews,
save yourself.
38 A title+ was also written over Him in
letters of Greek and Latin and Hebrew
reading: This is the king of the Jews.
39 One of the criminals+ who was hung
there beside Jesus railed at Him saying:
If you are Christ, save yourself and
us.
40 But the other answering rebuked him
saying: Do you not fear God, seeing you
are in the same condemnation?
41 We indeed justly *deserve this*, for we
receive the due reward of our deeds. But
this man has done nothing amiss.
42 And he said to Jesus: Lord, remember
me when you come into your kingdom.
43 Jesus said to him: Truly+ I say to you:
Today you will be with me in paradise.
44 *When* it was about twelve o'clock+
noon, there was a darkness over all the
earth until three *in the afternoon*.
45 The sun was darkened and the veil of
the temple was torn+ *down* the middle.+
46 And when Jesus had cried *out* with a
loud voice, He said: Father, into your
hands I commend my spirit. And having
said that, He expired.+
47 Now when the centurion saw what
was done, he glorified God saying:
Certainly this was a righteous man.
48 And all the people who came together
to that sight, beholding the things that
were done, beat+ *on* their breasts, and
returned.
49 All *those* who knew+ *Jesus*, and the
women who followed Him from Galilee,
stood *at a* distance+ *away*, beholding
these things.

50 And behold, *there was* a man named
Joseph, a counselor *and* a good and
righteous[+] man,

51 *one who* had not consented to the
counsel and deed *of the rest* of them.
Joseph was from Arimathaea, a city of
the Jews *and* he himself also was waiting for the kingdom of God.

52 This *Joseph* went to Pilate and asked[+]
for Jesus' body.

53 He took it down, wrapped it in linen,
and laid it in a tomb[+] that was cut[+] in
stone, *one* in which no one before had
ever been laid.

54 That day was the preparation and the
Sabbath drew on.

55 The women also who came with Him
from Galilee, followed after and saw[+] the
tomb[+] and how His body was laid *in it*.

56 *Then* they returned and prepared spices
and ointments and rested the Sabbath
day according to the commandment.

Luke Chapter 24

1 *Now* upon the first of the week *at*
early twilight,[+] they came to the tomb[+]
bringing the spices they had prepared,
and certain *others came* with them.

2 They found the stone rolled away
from the tomb.[+]

3 *Upon* entering *the tomb*, they did not
find the body of the Lord Jesus.

4 *Now* it came to pass, as they were
much perplexed about this,[+] behold two
men in shining garments stood by them.

5 *The women* were frightened[+] and bowed
down *their* faces to the earth. *But the men
in shining garments* said to them: Why do
you seek the living among the dead?

6 *Jesus* is not here, but *He* is risen.
Remember how He spoke to you when
He was yet in Galilee

7 saying: The Son of man must be
delivered into the hands of sinful men
and be crucified, and the third day rise
again.

8 *Then* they remembered His words

9 and returned from the tomb[+] and told
all these things to the eleven and to all
the rest.

10 It was Mary Magdalene, Joanna, Mary
the mother of James, and other *women
who were* with them who told these
things to the apostles.

11 But their words seemed to *the apostles*
like[+] idle tales and they did not believe them.

12 Then Peter got up[+] and ran to the
tomb[+] and, stooping down, he saw[+] the
linen clothes laid by themselves. *Then he*
left,[+] wondering within himself at what
had come to pass.

13 And behold, on that *same* day, two of
them went to a village called Emmaus,
which was *about* seven miles[+] from
Jerusalem.

14 And they talked together about all
these things that had taken place.[+]

15 *Now* it came to pass that, while they
conversed and reasoned *together*, Jesus
Himself drew near *to them* and went
along with them.

16 But their eyes were held[+] *so* that they
should not know Him.

17 *Then Jesus* said to them: What kind of
conversation[+] *is* this that you have with
one another as you walk and are sad?

18 One of them, whose name was
Cleopas, answering said to Him: Are
you only a stranger in Jerusalem and
have not known the things that have
come to pass there in these *last few* days?

19 *Jesus* said to them: What things?
And they said to Him: Concerning
Jesus of Nazareth, who was a prophet
mighty in deed and word before God
and all the people.

20 *Have you not heard* how the chief
priests and our rulers delivered Him
to be condemned to death and have
crucified Him?

21 We trusted that it was *Jesus* who
would have redeemed Israel. But yet
today is the third day since these
things were done.

22 Yes, and certain women also of our
company made us astonished, having
been to the tomb[+] early.

23 When they did not find His body,
they came saying that they had also
seen a vision of angels who said that
Jesus is alive.

24 Some of *those* who were with us went to the tomb+ and found *it just* as the women had said, but they did not see *Jesus*.

25 Then *Jesus* said to them: O fools and slow of heart to believe all that the prophets have spoken.

26 Was it not necessary+ *that Christ should* suffer these things and *then* to enter into His glory?

27 *Then*, beginning with Moses and all the prophets, *Jesus* expounded to them in all the Scriptures the things concerning Himself.

28 *As* they drew near to the village, where they were going,+ *Jesus* appeared+ as though He would have gone further.

29 But they constrained Him saying: Stay+ with us, for it is toward evening and the day is far spent. *So Jesus* went in to stay+ with them.

30 *Now* it came to pass, as He sat *down* to eat+ with them, He took bread and blessed, broke *it*, and gave *it* to them.

31 *Then* their eyes were opened and they knew Him, and He vanished out of their sight.

32 And they said to one another: Did our hearts not burn within us while He talked with us on the way and while He opened the Scriptures to us?

33 *Then* they got up+ that same hour and returned to Jerusalem and found the eleven gathered together, and *those* who were with them,

34 saying: The Lord is risen indeed and has appeared to Simon.

35 They told what things *were done* in the way and how He was known by them in *the* breaking of bread.

36 *Then* as they spoke *of* these *things*, Jesus Himself stood in the midst of them and said to them: Peace to you.

37 But they were terrified and frightened+ and supposed that they had seen a spirit.

38 *Jesus* said to them: Why are you troubled? And why do thoughts arise in your hearts?

39 Behold my hands and my feet, that it is I myself. Touch+ me and see. For a spirit does not have flesh and bones as you see me have.

40 After+ *Jesus* had said these things, He showed them *His* hands and *His* feet.

41 While they yet did not believe, for joy, and wondered, He said to them: Do you have anything to eat+.

42 They gave Him a piece of a broiled fish and a honeycomb.

43 He took *it* and ate before them.

44 *Then* He said to them: These *are* the words that I spoke to you while I was yet with you: All things must be fulfilled that were written in the law of Moses and *in* the prophets and *in* the psalms, concerning me.

45 Then He opened their understanding *so* that they might understand the Scriptures.

46 He said to them: Thus it is written and thus it was essential+ for Christ to suffer and to rise from the dead the third day,

Psalm 22:12-18, Isaiah 50:6

47 so that repentance and remission of sins should be proclaimed+ in His name among all nations, beginning at Jerusalem.

48 You are witnesses of these things.

49 And behold I send the promise of my Father upon you. But stay+ in the city of Jerusalem until you are endowed+ with power from on high.

50 *Then* He led them out as far as to Bethany and He lifted up His hands and blessed them.

51 And it came to pass while He blessed them *that* He was taken+ from them and carried up to heaven.

52 And they worshiped Him and returned to Jerusalem with great joy.

53 And *they* continued praising and blessing God in the temple. Amen.

This concludes
the four Gospel accounts
of the life and teachings
of Jesus Christ,
the Word of God.

*Following are 23
letters and accounts
written by early followers
of Jesus Christ
to encourage faith in Him.*

Acts Chapter 1

1 The first+ record+ *that* I made,
Theophilus, *was about all* that Jesus
began to do and teach
2 until the day in which He was taken up.
After that, through the Holy Spirit,
He gave instructions+ to the apostles
whom He had chosen.
3 After He had suffered+ *death*, He also
showed Himself to *them* alive by many
infallible proofs. *For* forty days, He was
seen by them and spoke *to them* about the
things pertaining to the kingdom of God.
4 Being assembled together with *them*,
He commanded them to not depart from
Jerusalem, but *to*: Wait for the promise
of the Father that you have heard me
proclaim.
5 For John indeed+ baptized with water,
but you shall be baptized with the Holy
Spirit, not many days from now.
6 Therefore, when they came together,
they asked of Him saying: Lord, will
you at this time restore again the
kingdom to Israel?
7 He said to them: It is not for you to
know the times or the seasons the Father
has put under+ His own authority+.

8 Yet after the Holy Spirit
has come upon you,
you shall receive power

and you shall be witnesses to me both in
Jerusalem and in all Judea and in Samaria
and to the ends+ of the earth.
9 When He had spoken these things,
while they observed,+ He was taken
up and a cloud received Him out of
their sight.
10 While they looked steadfastly toward
heaven as He went up, behold, two men
stood by them in white apparel.
11 *They* said: Men of Galilee, why do you
stand gazing up into heaven? This same
Jesus who is taken up from you into
heaven, will come *back* in like manner
as you have seen Him go into heaven.
12 Then they returned to Jerusalem from
the mountain called Olivet, which is a
Sabbath day's journey from Jerusalem.
13 When they entered+ *the city*, they went
into an upper room where *they* were
staying+: Peter, James, John, Andrew,
Philip, Thomas, Bartholomew, Matthew,
James *the son* of Alphaeus, Simon
Zelotes, and Jude *the brother* of James.
14 These all continued with one accord in
prayer and supplication, *along* with the
women and Mary the mother of Jesus,
and with His brothers.
15 In those days, Peter stood up in the
midst of the disciples and spoke.+ The
number of names together was about a
hundred and twenty.
16 *Peter said:* Men *and* family+: This
Scripture needed to be fulfilled. The
Holy Spirit spoke through the mouth of
David before concerning Judas *Iscariot*
who was *the* guide to *those* who took
Jesus. *Psalm 109:7*
17 For he was numbered with us and had
obtained part of this ministry.
18 Now this man purchased a field with
the reward of iniquity, and falling headlong, he burst apart+ in the midst and all
his insides+ gushed out.
19 *This fact* became+ known to all who
live in Jerusalem, so that field is *now*
called in their own language+:
Aceldama. That is: The Field of Blood.
20 For it is written in the book of Psalms:
Let his habitation be desolate and let no
one dwell therein. Let another take his
office.+ *Psalm 109:8*
21 Therefore, *from among* these men who
have joined+ with us all the time that the
Lord Jesus went in and out among us,
22 beginning from the baptism of John to

that day *in* which He was taken up from us, one *must be selected* to be a witness with us of *Jesus'* resurrection.

23 *So* they put forth[+] two *names*: Joseph called Barsabas, who was surnamed Justus, and Matthias.

24 *Then* they prayed and said: You Lord, know the hearts of all *people*. Show which[+] of these two you have chosen

25 *so* that he may take part of this ministry and apostleship from which Judas *Iscariot* fell by transgression*so* that he might go to his own place.

26 And they gave forth their lots and the lot fell upon Matthias, and he was numbered with the*other* eleven apostles.

Acts Chapter 2

1 When the day of Pentecost had come, they were all with one accord in one place.

2 Suddenly there came a sound from heaven, like a rushing mighty wind, and it filled all the house where they were sitting.

3 And there appeared to them divided[+] tongues like fire, both[+] *of which* sat down upon each of them,

4 and they were all filled with the Holy Spirit and began to speak with other tongues as the Spirit gave them utterance.

5 Now *at that time* there were Jews living[+] in Jerusalem, devout men from every nation under heaven.

6 And when this was reported,[+] the multitude came together and were confounded, because everyone[+] heard them speaking in their own language.

7 They were all amazed and marveled, saying to one another: Behold, are these who speak not all Galileans?

8 How *is it that* we hear everyone[+] in our own tongue in which we were born?

9 Parthians, Medes, Elamites, and *those who* live in Mesopotamia, Judea, Cappadocia, Pontus, Asia,

10 Phrygia, Pamphylia, Egypt, and in the parts of Libya around Cyrene, also strangers of Rome, Jews and proselytes,

11 Cretans, and Arabians. *We all* hear them speaking in our tongues *about* the wonderful works of God.

12 They were all amazed and perplexed[+] *and* said to one another: What does this mean?

13 Others, mocking, said: These men are full of new wine.

14 But Peter, standing with the eleven, raised[+] his voice and said to them: You men of Judea and all *of you* who dwell in Jerusalem: Let this be known to you and listen carefully[+] to my words:

15 These *people* are not drunk as you suppose, since it is *only* about nine o'clock[+] *in the morning*.

16 But this is what was spoken by the prophet Joel:

17 God has declared[+]: It will come *to pass* in the last days *that* I will pour out of my Spirit upon all flesh. Your sons and your daughters will prophesy. Your young men will see visions. And your old men will dream dreams. *Joel 2:28*

18 In those days, I will pour out of my Spirit on my servants and on my handmaidens and they will prophesy. *Joel 2:29*

19 I will show wonders in heaven above and signs on the earth below,[+] *with* blood and fire and vapor of smoke. *Joel 2:30*

20 The sun will be turned into darkness and the moon to *the color of* blood before that great and notable day of the Lord comes. *Joel 2:31*

> 21 And it will come *to pass that* whoever will call on the name of the Lord will be saved. *Joel 2:32*

22 Men of Israel, hear these words: Jesus of Nazareth *was* a man proved[+] by God among you, by miracles and wonders and signs that God did through Him in the midst of you, as you yourselves also know.

23 *Jesus* was delivered by the predetermined[+] purpose[+] and foreknowledge of God *and* you have taken *Him* by wicked hands *and* crucified and slain *Him*.

[24] *But* God raised *Him* up, having loosed
the pains of death, because it was not
possible that He could be held+ by it.
[25] For David spoke concerning Him: I
foresaw the Lord continuously+ before
me. For He is at my right hand *so* that
I would not be shaken.+ *Psalm 16:8*
[26] Therefore my heart rejoiced and my
tongue was glad. Moreover, my flesh
will rest in hope. *Psalm 16:9*
[27] Because, you will not leave my soul in
Hades. Nor will you allow+ your Holy
One to see corruption. *Psalm 16:10*
[28] You have made the ways of life known
to me. You will make me full of joy with
your countenance. *Psalm 16:11*
[29] Men *and* family,+ let *me* speak freely
to you about the patriarch David. He is
dead and buried, and his tomb+ is with
us to this day.
[30] Therefore, being a prophet, he knew
that God had sworn to him with an oath
that, from the fruit of his loins according
to the flesh, He would raise up Christ to
sit on his throne.
[31] *David* foresaw+ this *and* spoke about
the resurrection of Christ: That His soul
was not left in Hell nor did His flesh see
corruption. *Psalm 16:10*
[32] God has raised up this Jesus, *and* we
all are witnesses of this *fact*.
[33] Therefore, being exalted to the right
hand of God, and having received the
promise of the Holy Spirit from the
Father, He has poured+ out this that you
now see and hear.
[34] For David is not ascended into the
heavens. But he himself said: The Lord
said to my Lord: Sit at my right hand
Psalm 110:1
[35] until I make your enemies+ your footstool. *Psalm 110:1*
[36] Therefore, let all *of* the house of Israel
know assuredly, that God has made that
same Jesus whom you have crucified,
both Lord and Christ.
[37] Now when they heard *this*, they were
pierced+ in their hearts and said to Peter
and to the rest of the apostles: Men *and*
family,+ what shall we do?
[38] Then Peter said to them:

Repent and be baptized,
everyone of you,
in the name of Jesus Christ
for the remission of sins,
and you will receive
the gift of the Holy Spirit.

[39] For the promise is to you and to your
children and to all who are far away,+
to all+ *whom* the Lord our God calls.
[40] With many other words *Peter* testified
and exhorted saying: Be saved from this
corrupt+ generation.
[41] Then *those* who gladly received his
word were baptized. The same day there
were added, about three thousand souls.
[42] And they continued steadfastly in the
apostles' doctrine and fellowship and in
breaking bread and in prayers.
[43] Fear came upon every soul and many
wonders and signs were done by the
apostles.
[44] All who believed were together and
had everything+ common.
[45] *They* sold their possessions and goods
and divided+ them to all as everyone+
had need.
[46] And they continued daily in one
accord, in the temple and breaking
bread from house to house. *They* ate
their food+ with gladness and singleness
of heart,
[47] praising God and having favor with
all the people. And the Lord added to
the assembly+ daily *those* who were
being saved.

Acts Chapter 3

[1] Now Peter and John went together into
the temple at the hour of prayer, the ninth
hour, or three o'clock in the afternoon.
[2] A certain man *who had been* lame from
his mother's womb was carried *and* laid
daily at the gate of the temple called
Beautiful to ask for alms from *those* who
entered the temple.
[3] *Upon* seeing Peter and John about to go
into the temple, *the lame man* asked *them*
for alms.

4 Fastening his eyes upon *the man* Peter, with John, said: Look at us.
5 *The man* gave heed to them, waiting[+] *expectantly* to receive something from them.
6 Then Peter said: Silver and gold I do not have. But such as I have, I give to you. In the name of Jesus Christ of Nazareth, rise up and walk.
7 *Then Peter* took *the lame man* by the right hand and lifted *him* up, and immediately his feet and ankle bones received strength.
8 *The man* jumped[+] up, stood and walked and entered with them into the temple, walking and leaping and praising God.
9 All the people saw him walking and praising God.
10 They knew that it was *the lame man* who *had* sat *asking* for alms at the Beautiful gate of the temple and they were filled with wonder and amazement at what had happened to him.
11 As the lame man who was healed held Peter and John, all the people ran together to them in the porch called Solomon's, greatly wondering.
12 When Peter saw *this*, he answered the people: Men of Israel, why *do* you marvel at this? Why *do* you look so earnestly at us as though by our own power or holiness we had made this man to walk?
13 The God of Abraham and of Isaac and of Jacob, the God of our fathers has glorified His Son Jesus whom you delivered up and denied in the presence of Pilate when *Pilate* was determined to let *Jesus* go.
14 But you denied the Just and Holy One and desired a murderer be granted to you.
15 *You* killed the Prince of life, whom God has raised from the dead, of which we are witnesses.
16 *It is Jesus* name, through faith in His name, *that* has made this man, whom you see and know, strong. Yes, faith *in Jesus* has given *this man* perfect soundness in the presence of you all.
17 Now family,[+] I know[+] that *it was* through ignorance *that* you *and* your rulers *did what you did*.
18 But those things that God *long* before had shown by the mouths of all His prophets that Christ would suffer, *Jesus* has *indeed* fulfilled.

> 19 Therefore, repent and be converted *so* that your sins may be blotted out *and so* that times of refreshing will come from the presence of the Lord.

20 *God* will send Jesus Christ who was proclaimed[+] to you before.
21 *Meanwhile, Jesus* must *be* received *in* heaven until the times of restoration[+] of all things that God has spoken by the mouth of all His holy prophets since the world began.
22 For Moses truly said to the fathers: The Lord your God will raise up a prophet to you, like me, from *among* your family.[+] You shall hear Him in everything[+] He shall say to you. *Deuteronomy 18:15*
23 And it shall come to pass, *that* every soul who will not hear that prophet will be destroyed from among the people. *Deuteronomy 18:19*
24 Yes, and all the prophets from Samuel and *all* those *who* followed after, all[+] *who* have spoken have likewise foretold of these days.
25 You are the children of the prophets and of the covenant that God made with our fathers, saying to Abraham: And in your descendants,[+] all the families[+] of the earth will be blessed. *Genesis 18:18*
26 To you first, God raised up His Son Jesus *and* sent Him to bless you in turning everyone of you away from your iniquities.

Acts Chapter 4

1 As *Peter and John* spoke to the people, the priests and the captain of the temple and the Sadducees came upon them.
2 They were upset[+] that they taught the people and proclaimed[+] through Jesus the resurrection from the dead.
3 *So* they laid hands on them and put *them* in holding until the next day. For it was now evening.

4 However, many of *those* who heard the Word believed. The number of the men was about five thousand.

5 On the next day, the rulers, elders, and scribes,

6 Annas the high priest, Caiaphas, John, Alexander, and all[+] *who* were of the family[+] of the high priest, gathered together at Jerusalem.

7 They stood[+] *Peter and John* before them *and* asked, By what power or by what name have you done this?

8 Then Peter, filled with the Holy Spirit, said to them: You rulers of the people and elders of Israel,

9 If we this day are *being* examined for the good deed done to the disabled[+] man, by what means he is made whole,

10 *May* it be known to you all and to all the people of Israel that *it is* by the name of Jesus Christ of Nazareth whom you crucified *and* whom God raised from the dead, *it is* by Him that this man stands here before you whole.

11 This is the stone that was rejected[+] by you builders and *it* has become the head of the corner. *Psalm 118:22*

12 There is no salvation in any other, for there is no other name under heaven given among men by which we must be saved.

13 When they saw the boldness of Peter and John and perceived that they were uneducated[+] and unsophisticated[+] men, they marveled, for they knew that they had been with Jesus.

14 Seeing the man who was *now* healed standing with them, they could say nothing against it.

15 But then they commanded them to go aside *away* from the council *and* they conferred among themselves.

16 *They* said: What shall we do to these men? For indeed a notable miracle has been done by them. *It is* known[+] to all who dwell in Jerusalem and we cannot deny *it*.

17 But *so* that it spreads no further among the people, let us strictly[+] threaten them *so* that they *will* not speak, hereafter, to anyone in this name.

18 *So* they called them and commanded them to not speak at all or teach in the name of Jesus.

19 But Peter and John answered and said to them: Whether it is right in the sight of God to listen to you more than to God, you judge.

20 For we cannot but speak the things that we have seen and heard.

21 So, after they further threatened them, they let them go, finding no *basis* for punishing them. For all *people* glorified God for what had been done.

22 For the man on whom this miracle of healing was shown was more than forty years old.

23 Being let go, they went to their own company and reported all that the chief priests and elders had said to them.

24 When they heard that, they raised[+] their voices to God with one accord and said: Lord, you *are* God who has made heaven and earth and the sea and all that in them is.

25 By the mouth of your servant David, you have said: Why did the heathen rage and the people imagine vain things? *Psalm 2:1*

26 The kings of the earth stood up and the rulers were gathered together against the Lord and against His Christ. *Psalm 2:2*

27 For truly against your holy child Jesus, whom you have anointed, both Herod and Pontius Pilate, with the Gentiles and the people of Israel were gathered together

28 to do whatever your hand and your counsel determined before to be done.

29 Now Lord, behold their threatenings. Grant to your servants that with all boldness they may speak your Word.

30 Stretch forth your hand to heal *so* that signs and wonders may be done by the name of your holy child Jesus.

31 When they had prayed, the place was shaken where they were assembled together. They were all filled with the Holy Spirit and they spoke the Word of God with boldness.

32 The multitude of *those* who believed were of one heart and of one soul. None

of them said that any of the things that they possessed was their own, but they had everything[+] *in* common.

33 With great power, the apostles gave witness of the resurrection of the Lord Jesus. Great grace was upon them all.

34 Neither was there any among *them* who lacked, for all[+] *who* were possessors of lands or houses sold them and brought the prices of the things that were sold

35 and laid *them* down at the apostles' feet, and distribution was made to everyone[+] as they had need.

36 Joses, who was surnamed Barnabas by the apostles, *as that name* means[+] son of consolation, a Levite from the country of Cyprus,

37 had *some* land, sold *it*, and brought the money and laid *it* at the apostles' feet.

Acts Chapter 5

1 *Then* a certain man named Ananias, with Sapphira his wife, sold a possession

2 and kept back *part* of the price. His wife was also aware[+] *of this. Ananias* brought a certain part and laid *it* at the apostles' feet.

3 Peter said: Ananias, why has Satan filled your heart to lie to the Holy Spirit and to keep back *part* of the price of the land?

4 While it remained *unsold*, was it not your own? And *even* after it was sold, was it not *still* under your own authority[+]? Why have you conceived this thing in your heart? You have not lied to people,[+] but to God.

5 *Upon* hearing these words, Ananias fell down and died[+] and great fear came upon all who heard these things.

6 The young men arose, covered[+] him up, carried *him* out, and buried *him*.

7 It was about three hours later *when* his wife also came in, not knowing what had been done.

8 Peter answered her: Tell me if you sold the land for so much? She said: Yes, for so much.

9 Then Peter said to her: How is it that you have agreed together to test[+] the Spirit of the Lord? Behold the feet of *those* who have buried your husband *are* at the door and will *now* carry you out.

10 Then she immediately[+] fell down at his feet and died.[+] *Then* the young men came in, found her dead, and carried *her* out and buried *her* by her husband.

11 Great fear came upon all the assembly[+] and upon all[+] *who* heard these things.

12 By the hands of the apostles, many signs and wonders were worked[+] among the people and they were all with one accord in Solomon's porch.

13 Among the rest, no one dared[+] to join them, but the people *highly* regarded[+] them.

14 *Many* more believers were added to the Lord, multitudes of both men and women.

15 So much so that they brought forth the sick into the streets and laid *them* on beds and couches *so* that at the least shadow of Peter passing by might overshadow some of them.

16 There also came a multitude from the cities *all* around[+] to Jerusalem, bringing sick folks and *those* who were oppressed[+] with unclean spirits and they healed everyone.

17 Then the high priest and all those of the sect of the Sadducees who were with him rose up, filled with indignation.

18 *They* laid their hands on the apostles and put them into the common prison.

19 But the angel of the Lord *came* at night, opened the prison doors, brought them forth, and said:

20 Go, stand and speak all the words of life to the people in the temple.

21 When they heard *that*, they entered the temple early in the morning and taught, but the high priest and *those* who were with him came and called the council and all the senate of the children of Israel together, and sent to the prison to have *Peter and John* brought *to them*.

22 But when the officers did not find them in the prison, they returned and told *of this*

23 saying: We found the prison shut with all safety and the keepers standing

outside+ before the doors. But when we
opened *the doors*, we found no one inside.
24 Now when the high priest and the
captain of the temple and the chief priests
heard these things, they they wondered+
how *big* this *story* would grow.
25 Then someone came and told them:
Behold the men you put in prison are
standing in the temple and teaching the
people.
26 Then the captain went with the officers
and brought *Peter and John* without
violence, for they feared the people, lest
they should be stoned.
27 When they had brought them, they set
them before the council and the high
priest asked them:
28 Did we not strictly+ command you
to not teach in this name? And behold
you have filled Jerusalem with your
doctrine and intend to bring this man's
blood upon us.
29 Then Peter and the *other* apostles
answered and said: We must+ obey God
rather than men.
30 The God of our fathers raised up Jesus,
whom you killed+ and hung on a tree.
31 This *is the one* whom God exalted *to*
be Prince and Savior *having* the right
to give repentance to Israel and forgiveness *of* sins.
32 We are His witnesses of these things.
So also *is* the Holy Spirit, whom God
has given to *those* who obey Him.
33 When they heard *this*, they were cut *to*
the heart and took counsel to slay them.
34 Then in the council a Pharisee named
Gamaliel stood up, a teacher+ of the law
who had a *good* reputation among all the
people. *He* commanded *them* to allow+
the apostles a little space.
35 *He* said to them: Men of Israel, take
heed to yourselves what you intend to do
concerning these men.
36 Before these days *one named* Theudas
rose up, boasting himself to be somebody. A number of men, about four
hundred, joined themselves to him. *But*
eventually he was killed+ *and* all, as
many as obeyed him, were scattered
and brought to nothing.
37 After this a man *named* Judas of
Galilee rose up in the days of the taxing
and drew away many people after him.
He also perished and all, as many as
obeyed him, were dispersed.
38 Now I say to you: Refrain from these
men and let them alone. For if this
counsel or this work be of men, it will
come to nothing.
39 But if it be of God, you cannot overthrow it lest perhaps+ you be found even
to fight against God.
40 *So* they *all* agreed with *Gamaliel*. Then
they called the apostles, beat *them*,
commanded that they should not speak
in the name of Jesus, and let them go.
41 *The apostles* then departed from the
presence of the council, rejoicing that
they were counted worthy to suffer
shame for His name.
42 *After that* every day in the temple and
in every house, they did not stop+
teaching and proclaiming+ Jesus Christ.

Acts Chapter 6

1 In those days, when the number of the
disciples was multiplied, there arose
complaints+ from the Greeks against
the Hebrews because their widows were
neglected in the daily distribution.+
2 Therefore the twelve called the multitude of the disciples *together* and said: It
is not reasonable+ that we should leave
the Word of God and serve tables.
3 Therefore family,+ select+ seven men
of honest report, full of the Holy Spirit
and wisdom, from among you whom we
may appoint over these needs,+
4 and we will give ourselves continually
to prayer and to the ministry of the
Word.
5 The saying pleased the whole multitude. They chose Stephen, a man full of
faith and of the Holy Spirit, and Philip,
and Prochorus, and Nicanor, and Timon,
and Parmenas, and Nicolas a convert+
from Antioch.
6 These they set before the apostles, and
when they had prayed, they laid *their*
hands on them *to commission them*.

7 The Word of God increased and the
number of the disciples greatly multiplied
in Jerusalem, and a great multitude[+] of
the priests were obedient to the faith.
8 Stephen, full of faith and power, did
great wonders and miracles among the
people.
9 Then there arose certain *detractors*
from the synagogue of the Libertines,
and Cyrenians, and Alexandrians, and
of those of Cilicia and of Asia, disputing
with Stephen.
10 They were not able to stand against[+]
the wisdom and the Spirit by which he
spoke.
11 So they *secretly* induced[+] men to say:
We have heard Him speak blasphemous
words against Moses and *against* God.
12 They stirred up the people and the
elders and the scribes, and came upon
him and caught him and brought *him* to
the council.
13 *They* set up false witnesses who said:
This man does not stop[+] speaking
blasphemous words against this holy
place and the law.
14 For we have heard him say that this
Jesus of Nazareth will destroy this place
and will change the customs that Moses
delivered *to* us.
15 All who sat in the council looked
steadfastly at him *and* saw his face *become radiant* as *though* it had become[+]
the face of an angel.

Acts Chapter 7

1 Then the high priest said: Are these
things so?
2 *In reply, Stephen* said: Men, family,[+]
and fathers, listen carefully.[+] The God
of glory appeared to our father Abraham
when he was in Mesopotamia, before he
lived[+] in Haran,
3 and said to him: Get out of your
country and from your family[+] and
come into the land that I will show you.
Genesis 12:1
4 Then *Abraham* came out of the land of
the Chaldeans and lived[+] in Haran.
From there,[+] when his father was dead,
he moved into this land in which you
now dwell.
5 *God* gave *Abraham* no inheritance in it.
No, not *so much as* to set his foot on. Yet
He promised that He would give it to
him for a possession, and to his seed
after him, *even* when he did not *yet* have
a child.
6 God spoke in this way *knowing* that
Abraham's seed would journey[+] into a
strange land that would bring them into
bondage and mistreat[+] *them with* evil *for*
four hundred years.
7 The nation to whom they shall be in
bondage I will judge, said God. After
that, they shall come forth and serve me
in this place. *Genesis 15:14*
8 *Then God* gave the covenant of circumcision *to Abraham* and *he* fathered[+] Isaac
and circumcised him *on* the eighth day.
Then Isaac *fathered* Jacob and Jacob
fathered the twelve patriarchs.
9 The patriarchs, moved with envy,
sold Joseph into Egypt. But God was
with him.
10 *God* delivered *Joseph* out of all his
afflictions and gave him favor and
wisdom in the sight of Pharaoh, king of
Egypt, *who* made *Joseph* governor over
Egypt and all his house.
11 Now a famine[+] came over all the land
of Egypt and Canaan, a great affliction,
and our fathers found no sustenance.
12 But when Jacob heard that there was
corn in Egypt, *at* first, he sent out our
fathers.
13 At a second *time*, Joseph was made
known to his family[+] and Joseph's
family[+] was made known to Pharaoh.
14 Then Joseph summoned[+] *and* sent *for*
his father Jacob and all his family,[+]
seventy five souls.
15 So Jacob went down into Egypt and
died. He and our fathers
16 were carried into Sychem and laid in
the tomb[+] that Abraham bought for a
sum of money from the sons of Emmor
the father of Sychem.
17 But when the time of the promise that
God had sworn to Abraham drew near,
the people grew and multiplied in Egypt,

18 until another king arose who did not
know Joseph.
19 That *king* oppressed+ our ancestors+
and treated our fathers wickedly so that
they cast out their young children, to the
end they might not live.
20 During this time, Moses was born and
he was *very* fair to God. *He was* nurtured+
in his father's house *for* three months.
21 When he was cast out, Pharaoh's
daughter took him and nurtured+ him as
her own son.
22 Moses was educated+ in all the wisdom
of the Egyptians and *he* was mighty in
words and deeds.
23 When he was forty years old, it came
into his heart to visit his family,+ the
children of Israel.
24 Seeing one *of them* suffer wrong, he
defended and avenged *the one* who was
oppressed and struck+ *down* an Egyptian.
25 *Moses* thought+ *that* his brothers would
have understood that God, by his hand,
would deliver them. But they did not
understand.
26 The next day, he appeared+ to them
as they argued+ and *he* tried to set
them at peace+ saying: Sirs, you are
brothers. Why do you *do* wrong to one
another?
27 But *the one* who did his neighbor
wrong, pushed+ *Moses* away saying:
Who made you a ruler and a judge over
us? *Exodus 2:14*
28 Will you kill me as you did the Egyptian yesterday? *Exodus 2:14*
29 At this saying, Moses fled and became
a stranger in the land of Midian where
he fathered+ two sons.
30 After forty years passed,+ an angel
of the Lord appeared to him in the
wilderness of Mount Sinai in a flame
of fire in a bush.
31 When Moses saw *this*, he wondered at
the sight. As he drew near to behold *it*,
the voice of the Lord came to him
32 *saying*: I *am* the God of your fathers,
the God of Abraham and the God of
Isaac and the God of Jacob. Then Moses
trembled and did not dare+ *to* behold.
Exodus 3:6
33 Then the Lord said to him: Take
your sandals+ off of your feet, for the
place where you stand is holy ground.
Exodus 3:5
34 I have seen the suffering+ of my
people in Egypt and I have heard their
groaning and *I* have come down to
deliver them. Now come, I will send
you into Egypt. *Exodus 2:24*
35 This Moses whom they refused saying: Who made you a ruler and a judge?
The same did God send *to be* a ruler and
a deliverer by the hand of the angel who
appeared to him in the bush.
36 He brought them out after he had
shown wonders and signs in the land of
Egypt, and in the Red sea, and in the
wilderness forty years.
37 This is that Moses who said to the
children of Israel: The Lord your God
will raise up for you a prophet from
among your brothers, like me. You shall
hear Him. *Deuteronomy 18:15*
38 This is *the man* who was in the
assembly+ in the wilderness with the
angel who spoke to him on Mount Sinai,
and *with* our fathers. *It was he* who
received the living+ oracles to give to us.
39 *But* our fathers would not obey *him*.
Instead, they thrust *him away* from them
and in their hearts turned back again to
Egypt.
40 *They* said to Aaron: Make gods *for* us
to go before us. For *as for* this Moses
who brought us out of the land of Egypt,
we do not know+ what has become of
him. *Exodus 32:23*
41 They made a calf in those days and
offered sacrifice to the idol and rejoiced
in the works of their own hands.
42 But God turned and gave them up to
worship the host of heaven. As it is
written in the book of the prophets: *O*
house of Israel, did you offer to me slain
beasts and sacrifices *for* forty years in
the wilderness? *Amos 5:25*
43 And you *also* took up the tabernacle of
Moloch and the star of your god
Remphan, *with* figures that you made to
worship. I will carry you away beyond
Babylon. *Amos 5:26,27*

44 Our fathers had the tabernacle of witness in the wilderness, as *God* who spoke to Moses instructed,[+] *so* he would make it according to the pattern[+] he had seen.

45 Our fathers who came after brought *this* in with Joshua[+] into the possession of the Gentiles whom God drove out before the face of our fathers, until the days of David.

46 *But then David* found favor before God and desired to find a tabernacle for the God of Jacob.

47 But *then it was* Solomon *who* built a house *for God*.

48 However the most High does not dwell in temples made with hands. As the prophet said:

49 Heaven *is* my throne and earth *is* my footstool. What house will you build *for* me? says the Lord. Or what place of my rest? *Isaiah 66:1*

50 Has not my hand made all these things? *Isaiah 66:2*

51 You stiff necked and uncircumcised in heart and ears. You always resist the Holy Spirit. As your fathers *did*, so you *do*.

52 Which of the prophets have your fathers not persecuted? And they have slain *those* who foretold[+] of the coming of the Just One of whom you have now been the betrayers and murderers.

53 You have received the law by the disposition of angels but have not kept *it*.

54 When they heard these things, they were cut to the heart and gnashed their teeth at him.

55 But *Stephen*, being full of the Holy Spirit, looked up steadfastly into heaven and saw the glory of God and Jesus standing at the right hand of God.

56 *He* said: Behold I see the heavens opened and the Son of man standing at the right hand of God.

57 Then they cried out with a loud voice and stopped their ears and ran upon him with one accord.

58 *They* cast *Stephen* out of the city and stoned *him* and the witnesses laid down their clothes at the feet of a young man whose name was Saul.

59 They stoned Stephen *as he* called upon *God* saying: Lord Jesus, receive my spirit.

60 Then he knelt down and cried *out* with a loud voice: Lord, do not lay this sin to their charge. When he had said this, he fell asleep.

Acts Chapter 8

1 Saul consented to *Stephen's* death. At that time there was a great persecution against the assembly[+] at Jerusalem and all except the apostles were scattered throughout the regions of Judea and Samaria.

2 Devout men carried Stephen *to his burial* and grieved[+] greatly over him.

3 As for Saul, he made havoc of the assembly,[+] entering every house and dragging[+] *away* men and women, committing *them* to prison.

4 *Those* who were scattered went everywhere proclaiming[+] the Word.

5 Then Philip went down to the city of Samaria, and proclaimed[+] Christ to them.

6 With one accord, the people gave heed to the things that Philip spoke, hearing and seeing the miracles that he did.

7 For unclean spirits crying *out* with loud voices came out of many who were possessed *with them* and many afflicted[+] with palsies and *many* who had been lame were healed.

8 There was great joy in that city.

9 But there was a man called Simon who in the past[+] in the same city used sorcery and bewitched the people of Samaria, suggesting[+] that *he* himself was great.

10 All from the least to the greatest gave heed to him, saying: This man is the great power of God.

11 They *highly* regarded *this Simon* because for a long time he had bewitched them with sorceries.

12 But now they believed Philip *who was* proclaiming[+] the things concerning the kingdom of God and the name of Jesus Christ, and both men and women were baptized.

13 Then Simon himself also believed
and when he was baptized, he continued
with Philip and *was* amazed[+] as he
saw the miracles and signs that were
done.
14 Now when the apostles in Jerusalem
heard that Samaria had received the
Word of God, they sent Peter and John
to them.
15 So they came down and prayed for
them, *so* that they might receive the
Holy Spirit.
16 For as yet, *the Holy Spirit* had not come
upon any of them but only *upon* those
who had been baptized in the name of
the Lord Jesus.
17 *So Peter and John* laid *their* hands upon
the new believers and then they received
the Holy Spirit.
18 When Simon saw that *it was* through
the laying on of the apostles' hands *that*
the Holy Spirit was given, he offered
them money,
19 saying: Give me also this authority[+] *so*
that on whomever I lay hands, they may
receive the Holy Spirit.
20 But Peter said to him: *May* your
money perish with you, because you
have thought that the gift of God could
be purchased with money.
21 You have no part or share[+] in this, for
your heart is not right in the sight of
God.
22 Therefore, repent of your wickedness
and pray *to* God that the thoughts in
your heart may be forgiven.
23 For I perceive that you are in the gall
of bitterness and *in* the bond of iniquity.
24 Then Simon answered and said: Pray
to the Lord for me, that none of these
things that you have spoken *will* come
upon me.
25 After *Peter and John* had testified and
proclaimed[+] the Word of the Lord, they
returned to Jerusalem and proclaimed[+]
the Gospel in many villages of the
Samaritans.
26 Then the angel of the Lord spoke to
Philip saying: Arise and go toward the
south on the desert road[+] that goes from
Jerusalem to Gaza.
27 *So Philip* arose and went and behold *he met*
a man from Ethiopia, a eunuch with great
authority under Candace queen of the Ethiop-
ians who had the charge of all her treasure.
He had come to Jerusalem to worship.
28 *Now, he* was returning and sitting in his
chariot reading the prophet Isaiah.
29 Then the Spirit said to Philip: Go near
and join yourself to this chariot.
30 *So* Philip ran to *the eunuch*, heard him
reading the prophet Isaiah, and said: Do
you understand what you *are* reading?
31 *The eunuch* said: How can I, unless
someone should guide me? And he asked
Philip to come up and sit with him.
32 The place in the Scripture that he read was
this: He was led like a sheep to the slaughter
and like a lamb silent[+] before its shearer,
He did not open His mouth. *Isaiah 53:7*
33 In *Jesus'* humiliation, justice[+] was
taken away *and denied to Him*. Who *then*
shall declare His generation? *Who can*
count how long it will last? For His life has
been taken from the earth. *Isaiah 53:8*
34 The eunuch answered Philip and said:
I beg[+] you: About whom is the prophet
speaking *in* this? About himself? Or
about some other man?
35 Then Philip opened his mouth and
began at the same Scripture and proclaimed[+] Jesus to him.
36 As they went on *their* way, they came
to a certain *body of* water and the eunuch
said: See, *here is* water. What hinders
me from being baptized?
37 Philip said: If you believe with all your
heart, you may. *The eunuch* answered
and said: I believe that Jesus Christ is
the Son of God.
38 *Then the eunuch* commanded the chariot
to stop[+] and Philip and the eunuch both
went down into the water and *Philip*
baptized him.
39 When they came up out of the water,
the Spirit of the Lord caught Philip away
so that the eunuch no longer[+] saw him,
but he went on his way rejoicing.
40 Philip was *later* found at Azotus.
Passing through *there* he proclaimed[+]
the Gospel in all the cities until he came
to Caesarea.

Acts Chapter 9

1 While *Saul was still* breathing out
threatenings and slaughter against the
disciples of the Lord, he went to the high
priest
2 and requested[+] letters from him to the
synagogues in Damascus *so* that if he
found any of this way, *followers of Christ*,
whether they were men or women, he
might bring them bound to Jerusalem.
3 As he journeyed, he came near
Damascus and suddenly a light from
heaven shined *down* on[+] him.
4 He fell to the ground and heard a voice
saying to him: Saul, Saul, why do you
persecute me?
5 He said: Who are you, Lord? The
Lord said: I am Jesus whom you
persecute. *It is* hard for you to kick
against the pricks.
6 Trembling and astonished, *Saul* said:
Lord, what will you have me to do?
The Lord *said* to him: Arise and go
into the city and it will be told *to* you
what you must do.
7 The men who traveled with him stood
speechless, hearing a voice, but seeing
no one.
8 Saul arose from the ground and when
he opened his eyes he saw no one, *for he
was blind* but they led him by the hand
and took *him* to Damascus.
9 He was three days without sight and
neither ate nor drank.
10 There was a certain disciple at
Damascus named Ananias. In a vision,
the Lord said to him: Ananias. And he
said: Behold I *am here*, Lord.
11 The Lord *said* to him: Arise, and go to
the street called Straight and inquire in
the house of Judas for *one* called Saul of
Tarsus. For behold, he is praying *there*.
12 In a vision, *he* has seen a man named
Ananias coming in and putting *his* hand
on him *so* that he might receive his sight.
13 Then Ananias answered: Lord, I have
heard from many *people* about this man,
how much evil he has done to your
saints at Jerusalem.
14 Here he has authority from the chief
priests to bind all who call on your
name.
15 But the Lord said to him: Go *to him*,
for he is a chosen vessel to me, to bear
my name before the Gentiles and kings
and the children of Israel.
16 For I will show him what *great things*
he must suffer for my name's sake.
17 *So,* Ananias went away[+] and entered
the house. Putting his hands on *Saul, he*
said: Brother Saul, the Lord Jesus who
appeared to you on the way as you came
has sent me *so* that you might receive
your sight and be filled with the Holy
Spirit.
18 Immediately *something like* scales fell
from *Saul's* eyes and he received sight
immediately[+] and arose and was baptized.
19 Then he received *some* food[+] and was
strengthened and *he remained* a few days
with the disciples at Damascus.
20 Immediately[+] he proclaimed[+] Christ
in the synagogues, *confidently declaring*
that *surely Jesus* is the Son of God.
21 But all who heard *him* were amazed and
said: Is this not the one who destroyed
those who called on *Jesus* name in Jerusalem? And *did he not* come here intending
to take them bound to the chief priests?
22 Yet Saul increased *all* the more in
strength and confounded the Jews who
lived[+] at Damascus, *thus* proving that
this *surely* is *the work of the* very Christ.
23 After many days were fulfilled, the
Jews took counsel *together* to kill *Saul*.
24 Saul knew that they were waiting and
that they watched the gates day and night
for an opportunity to kill him.
25 So the disciples took *Saul* by night and
let *him* down by the wall in a basket.
26 When Saul had *first* come to Jerusalem,
he tried[+] to join himself to the disciples,
but they were all afraid of him and did not
believe that he was a disciple.
27 But Barnabas brought *Saul* to the
apostles, and declared to them how he
had seen the Lord in the way and that He
had spoken to him and how he had
boldly proclaimed[+] the name of Jesus in
Damascus.

28 He was with them coming in and going out at Jerusalem.

29 He spoke boldly in the name of the Lord Jesus and disputed against the Greeks, but they went about to slay him.

30 When the brothers knew *about* this, they brought *Saul* down to Caesarea and sent him forth to Tarsus.

31 Then the assemblies[+] throughout all Judea and Galilee and Samaria were *at* rest and edified. Walking in the fear of the Lord, and in the comfort of the Holy Spirit, were multiplied.

32 *Now* it came to pass, as Peter passed throughout all *quarters*, he came to the saints who lived[+] at Lydda.

33 There he found a certain man named Aeneas who had stayed in bed *for* eight years and was sick with paralysis.[+]

34 Peter said to him: Aeneas, Jesus Christ makes you whole. Arise and make your bed. And he arose immediately.

35 All who lived[+] at Lydda and Saron saw him, and turned to the Lord.

36 Now at Joppa, there was a certain disciple named Tabitha who was *also* known[+] *as* Dorcas. This woman was full of good works and alms deeds that she did.

37 *But* it came to pass in those days that she *became* sick and died. After they washed *her*, they laid *her* in an upper chamber.

38 Since[+] Lydda was near to Joppa, and the disciples had heard that Peter was there, they sent two men to him to ask that he come to them without delay.

39 Then Peter arose and went with them. When he arrived, they took him into the upper chamber. All the widows stood by him weeping and showing the coats and garments that Dorcas made while she was with them.

40 But Peter sent them all out *of the room* and knelt down and prayed. Turning to the body *he* said: Tabitha, arise. She opened her eyes and when she saw Peter, she sat up.

41 He gave her *his* hand and lifted her up, and when he had called the saints and widows, *he* presented her alive.

42 *All* this was *made* known throughout all Joppa and many believed in the Lord.

43 *Then* it came to pass that he stayed many days in Joppa with Simon, a tanner.

Acts Chapter 10

1 There was a certain man in Caesarea called Cornelius, a centurion of the company[+] *of soldiers* called the Italian *company*.

2 *Cornelius was a* devout *man* who revered[+] God, with all his house. *He* gave many alms to the people and prayed to God always.

3 About three o'clock[+] *in the afternoon*, in a vision he clearly[+] saw an angel of God coming in to him and saying to him: Cornelius.

4 When *Cornelius* looked at *the angel*, he was afraid and said: What is it, Lord? *The angel* said to him: Your prayers and your alms have come up for a memorial before God.

5 Now send men to Joppa and call for Simon whose surname is Peter.

6 He is staying[+] with Simon the tanner whose house is by the seaside. He will tell you what you ought to do.

7 After the angel who spoke to Cornelius departed, he called two of his household servants and a devout soldier *who faithfully* served him.

8 After he explained all *these* things to them, he sent them to Joppa.

9 On the next day as they went on their journey and drew near to the city, Peter went up on the housetop to pray about twelve o'clock[+] *noon*.

10 He became very hungry and would have eaten, but while they made ready, he fell into a trance.

11 *He* saw heaven opened and a vessel like a large sheet knit at the four corners descending to him and let down to the ground.

12 In this *sheet* were all kinds[+] of four footed beasts of the earth and wild beasts and creeping things and birds[+] of the air.

13 Then a voice came to him *saying*: Rise, Peter. Kill and eat.

14 But Peter said: *Surely* not, Lord, for
I have never eaten anything that is
common or unclean.
15 The voice *spoke* to him again a second
time, *saying*: What God has cleansed,
you *must* not call common.
16 This was done three times and the
vessel was received up again into heaven.
17 Now while Peter pondered+ what this
vision that he had seen should mean,
behold the men who were sent from
Cornelius had made inquiry for Simon's
house and stood before the gate.
18 *They* called and asked if Simon who
was surnamed Peter was staying+ there.
19 While Peter thought about this vision,
the Spirit said to him: Behold three men
seek you.
20 Therefore arise. Get down and go
with them, doubting nothing. For I have
sent them.
21 Then Peter went down to the men who
were sent to him from Cornelius and
said: Behold I am *he* whom you seek.
What *is* the reason+ *that* you have come?
22 They said: Cornelius the centurion, a
righteous+ man, one who fears God and
is of good report among all the nation of
the Jews, was warned from God by a
holy angel to send for you *and ask you to*
come to his house and to hear words
from you.
23 Then *Peter* invited+ them in and lodged
them. On the next day, Peter went away
with them and certain brothers from
Joppa accompanied him.
24 The next day, + they entered Caesarea.
Cornelius *was* waiting for them and *he*
had called together his relatives+ and
close friends.
25 As Peter was coming in, Cornelius
met him and fell down at his feet and
worshiped *him*.
26 But Peter lifted+ him up saying: Stand
up. I myself am also a man.
27 As *Peter* talked with *Cornelius*, he
went in and found many who had
come together.
28 He said to them: You know that it is an
unlawful thing for a man who is a Jew
to keep company or come to one of
another nation. But God has shown me
that I should not call anyone common or
unclean.
29 Therefore I came *to you* without
dispute+ as soon as I was sent for. I ask
therefore, for what intent have you sent
for me?
30 Cornelius said: Four days ago, I was
fasting until this hour. At three o'clock+
in the afternoon, I prayed in my house and
behold, a man stood before me in bright
clothing.
31 *He* said: Cornelius, your prayer is
heard and your alms are remembered in
the sight of God.
32 Therefore, send to Joppa and call
Simon whose surname is Peter *to come*
here. He is staying at the house of Simon
the tanner by the seaside. When he
comes, *he* will speak to you.
33 Therefore, I immediately sent for you.
You have done well *to* have come.
Therefore we are now all here, present
before God, to hear all things that are
commanded *to* you by God.
34 Then Peter opened *his* mouth and said:
Truly I perceive that God is not *a*
discriminating respecter of persons.
35 But in every nation, *those* who fear Him
and work righteousness are accepted
by Him.
36 The Word that *God* sent to the children
of Israel proclaiming+ peace by Jesus
Christ who is Lord of all,
37 that Word you know. It was published
throughout all Judea, beginning in
Galilee after the baptism that John
proclaimed+:
38 God anointed Jesus of Nazareth with
the Holy Spirit and with power. *He* went
about doing good and healing all who
were oppressed by the devil. For God
was with Him. *Matthew 3:16*
39 We are witnesses of everything+ *that*
He did, both in the land of the Jews and
in Jerusalem. *It was this Jesus* they killed+
and hung on a tree.
40 *But* God raised Him up the third day
and showed Him openly.
41 Not to all the people, but to witnesses
chosen before by God, *even* to *those of* us

who ate and drank with Him after He
rose from the dead.
42 He commanded us to proclaim[+] *the*
Word to the people and to testify that it
is He who was ordained by God *to be* the
Judge of *the* quick and *the* dead.
43 All the prophets gave witness to Him,
that through His name, whoever believes
in Him shall receive remission of sins.
44 While Peter spoke these words, the
Holy Spirit fell on all who heard the
Word.
45 Those of the circumcision who believed
were astonished, *including* all[+] *who*
came with Peter, because the gift of
the Holy Spirit was poured out on the
Gentiles also.
46 For they heard them speak with tongues
and magnify God. Then Peter answered:
47 Can anyone forbid water, *so* that these
who have received the Holy Spirit as
well as we *have* should not be baptized?
48 And he commanded them *all* to be
baptized in the name of the Lord. Then
they asked[+] him to stay[+] *with them for* a
few days.

Acts Chapter 11

1 The apostles and family[+] in Judea *soon*
heard that the Gentiles had also received
the Word of God.
2 *So* when Peter came up to Jerusalem,
those of the circumcision contended with
him,
3 saying: You went in to uncircumcised
men and ate with them.
4 But Peter reviewed *the matter with them*
from the beginning and explained[+] *it* to
them in detail[+] saying:
5 I was in the city of Joppa praying. In
a trance I saw a vision *of* a certain vessel
like a great sheet descend, let down
from heaven by four corners. It came
directly to me.
6 When I fastened my eyes on it, I
looked[+] *inside* and saw four footed
beasts of the earth and wild beasts and
creeping things and birds[+] of the air.
7 *Then* I heard a voice say to me, Arise,
Peter. Slay and eat.
8 But I said: *Surely* not, Lord, for nothing common or unclean has *ever* entered
my mouth at any time.
9 But the voice answered again from
heaven, *saying*: What God has cleansed,
do not call common.
10 This was done three times. *Then*
everything[+] was drawn up again into
heaven.
11 And behold immediately there were
three men *who had* already come to the
house where I was *staying*, sent from
Caesarea to me.
12 The Spirit told me *to* go with them, not
doubting *anything*. These six brothers
also accompanied me and we entered
the man's house.
13 He told[+] us how he had seen an angel
in his house, who stood and said to him:
Send men to Joppa and call for Simon
whose surname is Peter.
14 *Peter* will tell you words by which you
and all your house will be saved.
15 As I began to speak, the Holy Spirit
fell upon them, as *it did* upon us at the
beginning.
16 Then I remembered the Word of the
Lord, that He said: John indeed baptized
with water, but you shall be baptized
with the Holy Spirit.
17 Since[+] God gave them the same[+] gift
as *He did* to us who believed on the Lord
Jesus Christ, who was I that I could
withstand God?
18 When they heard these things, they
remained silent[+] and glorified God
saying: Then God has also granted repentance to *eternal* life to the Gentiles.
19 Now *those* who were scattered *because*
of the persecution that arose about
Stephen traveled as far as Phoenicia,
Cyprus, and Antioch, proclaiming[+] the
Word, but only to the Jews *and* to no
one *else*.
20 Some of them were men of Cyprus
and Cyrene, who, when they had
come to Antioch, spoke to the Greeks,
proclaiming[+] the Lord Jesus.
21 The hand of the Lord was with them
and a great number believed and turned
to the Lord.

22 Then news+ of *all* this came to the assembly+ in Jerusalem and they sent forth Barnabas to go as far as Antioch.

23 When he came and saw the grace of God, *he* was glad and exhorted them all, that with purpose of heart they should *be* joined+ *close* to the Lord.

24 For *Barnabas* was a good man, full of the Holy Spirit and faith and many people were added to the Lord.

25 Then Barnabas went to Tarsus to look for Saul.

26 When he found him, he brought him *back* to Antioch, and it came to pass that *for* a whole year they joined+ with the assembly+ *of believers* there and taught many people. And the disciples were called Christians first *there* in Antioch.

27 In these days, prophets came from Jerusalem to Antioch.

28 One of them named Agabus stood up and signified by the Spirit that there would be *a* great famine+ throughout all the world. This *soon* came to pass in the days of Claudius Caesar.

29 Therefore, the disciples determined *that* everyone, according to their ability, should send relief to the family+ who lived+ in Judea.

30 *So* they did *this* and sent it to the elders by the hands of Barnabas and Saul.

Acts Chapter 12

1 Now about that time, Herod the king stretched forth *his* hands to harass+ some of the assemblies+ *of believers*.

2 He killed James the brother of John with the sword.

3 When he saw *that* this pleased the Jews, he proceeded further to take Peter also. This *occurred during* the days *known as the Feast* of Unleavened Bread. *Exodus 12:18*

4 After *Herod* apprehended *Peter*, he put *him* in prison and sent four squads+ of soldiers to keep him *there*, intending to bring him forth to the people after Passover.+

5 While Peter was kept in prison, the assembly+ *of believers* prayed to God without ceasing for him.

6 *On* the night when Herod *had intended* to bring him forth, Peter was sleeping between two soldiers, bound with two chains *and* keepers by the door kept the prison *secure*.

7 But *then* behold, the angel of the Lord came upon *Peter* and a light shined in the prison. *The angel* touched+ Peter on the side and raised him up saying: Arise up quickly. *Instantly*, *Peter's* chains fell from *his* hands.

8 The angel said to him: Prepare+ yourself and put+ on your sandals. And so he did. *Then the angel* said to *Peter*: Put+ on your garment and follow me.

9 *Peter* followed *the angel*, but *he* did not understand+ that what was done by the angel was real.+ *He* thought *that* he had seen a vision.

10 After they went past the first and the second ward, they came to the iron gate that leads to the city. It opened for them of its own accord and they went out and passed by one street. Then+ the angel departed from him.

11 When Peter came to himself, he said: Now I know with certainty+ that the Lord sent His angel and delivered me out of the hand of Herod and *from* all the expectations of the Jews.

12 After he had considered *this*, he went to the house of Mary the mother of John, whose surname was Mark where many *believers* had gathered together praying.

13 As Peter knocked at the door of the gate, a girl+ named Rhoda came to listen carefully+ *to see who was there*.

14 When she recognized+ Peter's voice, she did not open the gate but in *her* excitement+ *she* ran in and told *the others* that Peter was standing at the gate.

15 They said to her: You *must be* mistaken.+ But she constantly affirmed that it was true.+ Then they said: It is his angel.

16 But Peter continued knocking *and* when they opened *the door* and saw him, they were astonished.

17 *Peter* signaled+ to them with his hand to *remain* silent+ *and he* described+ to them how the Lord had brought him out of the prison. Then he said: Go *and*

report[+] these things to James and to the
family.[+] And he departed and went to
another place.
18 Now as soon as it was day, there was no
small stir among the soldiers, *wondering*
what had become of Peter.
19 When Herod sought *Peter* and did not
find him, he questioned[+] the keepers
and *then* commanded that *they* should be
put to death. *Then* he went from Judea
down to Caesarea and stayed *there*.
20 Now, *during this time* Herod was highly
displeased with the *people* of Tyre and
Sidon. But they came to him with one
accord and sought[+] peace *with him*. *They*
had *already* made Blastus the king's
chamberlain their friend because their
country was supplied[+] *with food* by the
king's *country*.
21 *Therefore* on the appointed[+] day, Herod
dressed[+] in *his* royal apparel, sat upon
his throne, and made an oration to them.
22 The people gave a shout, *saying: It is*
the voice of *a* god and not *of a* man.
23 Immediately, the angel of the Lord
struck[+] *Herod down* because he did not
give God the glory, and he died[+] and
was eaten by worms.
24 But the Word of God grew and
multiplied.
25 *Meanwhile*, when Barnabas and Saul
had fulfilled *their* ministry, they returned
from Jerusalem and *they* took John,
whose surname was Mark, with them.

Acts Chapter 13

1 In the assembly[+] *of believers* at Antioch,
there were certain prophets and teachers
including Barnabas, Simeon who was
called Niger, Lucius of Cyrene, Manaen,
who had been brought up with Herod the
tetrarch, and Saul.
2 As they ministered to the Lord and
fasted, the Holy Spirit said: Separate
Barnabas and Saul for the work to which
I have called them.
3 *Therefore*, after they fasted and prayed,
they laid hands on them *and* sent *them on*
their way.
4 Being *thus* sent forth by the Holy
Spirit, they departed to Seleucia, *and*
from there[+] they sailed to Cyprus.
5 While they were in Salamis, they
proclaimed[+] the Word of God in the
synagogues of the Jews. They also had
John as *their* minister *there*.
6 As they went through the island[+] of
Paphos, they encountered[+] sorcerer *and*
a false prophet, a Jew whose name
was Barjesus.
7 *He* was with the deputy of the country,
Sergius Paulus, a prudent man who
called for Barnabas and Saul and desired
to hear the Word of God.
8 But Elymas the sorcerer as his name is
interpreted, opposed[+] them, seeking to
turn the deputy away from the faith.
9 Then Saul, who *is now also called*
Paul, filled with the Holy Spirit, set
his eyes on him,
10 and said: *You* child of the devil, *you*
enemy of righteousness, *you are* full of
deceit[+] and mischief. Will you not stop[+]
perverting the right ways of the Lord?
11 Now behold, the hand of the Lord *is*
upon you and you shall be blind *and*
you will not see the sun for a season.
Immediately a mist and a darkness fell
on him *and* he went around seeking
some to lead him by the hand.
12 When the deputy saw what was done,
he believed *and* was astonished at the
doctrine of the Lord.
13 Now when Paul and his company left[+]
Paphos, they went to Perga in Pamphylia
and John left[+] them *and* returned to
Jerusalem.
14 When they left[+] Perga, they went to
Antioch in Pisidia, and went into the
synagogue on the Sabbath day and sat
down.
15 After the reading of the law and the
prophets, the rulers of the synagogue
said to them: Men *and* family,[+] if you
have any word of exhortation for the
people, speak *freely*.
16 Then Paul stood up and, signaling[+]
with *his* hand, *he* said: Men of Israel and
you who fear God, *please* listen.
17 The God of this people of Israel chose
our fathers and exalted the people when

they lived+ as strangers in the land of
Egypt, and with a high arm He brought
them out of it.
18 For forty years, He endured+ their
behavior+ in the wilderness.
19 After He destroyed seven nations in
the land of Canaan, He divided that land
to them by lot.
20 After that He gave *them* judges for
four hundred and fifty years, until Samuel
the prophet.
21 Then they wanted a king, *so* God gave
God gave to them Saul the son of Kish,
a man of the tribe of Benjamin, for forty
years. *1 Samuel 9:17*
22 When *God* removed *Saul*, He *then*
raised up David for them to be their
king. And to *David* He gave *this* testimony and said: I have found David the
son of Jesse *to be* a man after my own
heart, *someone* who will fulfill all *of* my
will. *1 Samuel 13:14*
23 From this man's seed, God has raised
up to Israel a Savior, Jesus *Christ* according to *His* promise. *Psalm 132:11*
24 Before *Christ* came, John first pro-
claimed+ the baptism of repentance to
all the people of Israel. *Matthew 3:2*
25 As John fulfilled his course, he said:
Who do you think that I am? I am not *the
Messiah*. But behold, one is coming after
me the sandals+ of whose feet I am not
worthy to loosen. *Matthew 3:11*
26 Men *and* family,+ children of the stock
of Abraham, and whoever among you
fears God: The Word of this salvation is
now sent to you.
27 But *those* who live in Jerusalem and
their rulers, because they did not know
Jesus or the voices of the prophets who are
read every Sabbath day, they fulfilled
those prophets' words by condemning *Him*.
28 Although they found no cause *in Him*
for death, yet *even so* they wanted Pilate
to execute+ Him.
29 *Then* when they had fulfilled all that was
written about Him, they took *Him* down
from the tree and laid *Him* in a tomb.+
30 But God raised Him from the dead.
31 He was seen *for* many days by *those*
who came up with Him from Galilee to
Jerusalem *and* they are His witnesses to
the people.
32 *Now* we declare to you *the* glad
tidings, that the promise that was
made to the fathers,
33 God has fulfilled to us, their children,
in that He has raised up Jesus again, as
it is also written in the second psalm:
You are my Son. This day I have
begotten you. *Psalm 2:7*
34 Now concerning *the fact* that *God* raised
Jesus up from the dead, no longer+ to
return to *the decay and* corruption *of this
world*, *God* said this: I will give you the
sure mercies of David. *Isaiah 55:3*
35 And, in another *psalm* He also said:
You will not allow+ your Holy One to
see corruption *and decay*. *Psalm 16:10*
36 After David had served his own generation according+ to the will of God, *he*
fell asleep and was laid to *rest with* his
fathers, and saw corruption *and decay*.
37 But *Jesus* whom God raised again saw
no corruption *or decay*.
38 Therefore be it known to you, men *and*
family,+ that through this man, forgiveness of sins is proclaimed+ to you.
39 All who believe *in Jesus* are justified
from all things. From *all of this*, you could
not be justified by the law of Moses.
40 *Therefore* take heed+ so that what was
spoken by the prophets does not come
upon you.
41 Behold you despisers and wonder and
perish. For I *will* work a work in your
days, a work that you will not+ believe,
even though a man declare it to you.
Habakkuk 1:5
42 After the Jews left the synagogue, the
Gentiles begged+ that these words might
be proclaimed+ to them the next Sabbath.
43 When the congregation was concluded,+ many of the Jews and worship-
ing+ converts+ followed Paul and
Barnabas, speaking with them *and*
encouraging+ them to continue in the
grace of God.
44 *On* the next Sabbath day almost the
whole city came together to hear the
Word of God.
45 But when the Jews saw the multitudes,

they were filled with envy and spoke
against those things that were spoken by
Paul, contradicting and blaspheming.
46 Then Paul and Barnabas grew[+] bold
and said: It was necessary that the Word
of God should first have been spoken to
you, but since you put it *away* from you
and judge yourselves unworthy of eternal[+] life, behold, we turn to the Gentiles.
47 For the Lord has commanded us,
saying: I have set you to be a light to the
Gentiles, *so* that you should be *proclaiming* salvation to the ends of the earth.
Isaiah 49:6
48 When the Gentiles heard this, they
were glad and glorified the Word of the
Lord. And many believed *and were*
ordained to eternal life.
49 The Word of the Lord was *then* published throughout all the region.
50 But the Jews stirred up the prominent[+]
religious[+] women and chief men of the
city and inflamed[+] persecution against
Paul and Barnabas and expelled them
out of their borders.[+]
51 But they shook off the dust from their
feet against them and went to Iconium.
52 *And* the disciples were filled with joy
and with the Holy Spirit.

Acts Chapter 14

1 *While* in Iconium, *Paul and Barnabas*
went into the synagogue of the Jews and
spoke so that a great multitude of both
Jews and Greeks believed.
2 But the unbelieving Jews stirred up the
Gentiles and *caused them to have* evil
thoughts[+] against *Paul and Barnabas*.
3 Yet they stayed[+] *there for* a long time,
speaking boldly in the Lord. This
testified to the Word of *God's* grace
and *He* granted signs and wonders to
be done by their hands.
4 But the multitude of the city was
divided. Part held with the Jews and part
with the apostles.
5 Then an assault *was planned* by both
the Gentiles and the Jews *and* their
rulers, to mistreat[+] *them* and stone them.
6 *Paul and Barnabas* were aware of *this*
and *so they* fled to Lystra and Derbe, cities
of Lycaonia, and to the surrounding[+]
region
7 *and* proclaimed[+] the Gospel there.
8 In Lystra, a disabled[+] man sat *by the
way*. His feet had been crippled from his
mother's womb *and he* had never walked.
9 As this *man* heard Paul speak, *Paul*
looked at him steadfastly and perceived
that he had faith to be healed.
10 *So Paul* said with a loud voice: Stand
upright on your feet. And *the crippled
man* leaped *up* and walked.
11 When the people saw what Paul had
done, they raised[+] their voices, saying
in the speech of Lycaonia: The gods
have come down to us in the likeness of
men.
12 They called Barnabas, Jupiter *and*
Paul, Mercurius, because he was the
chief speaker.
13 Then the priest of Jupiter, *whose temple*
was near[+] their city, brought oxen and
garlands to the gates, and wanted[+] to
make[+] a sacrifice with the people.
14 When the apostles Barnabas and Paul,
heard *this*, they tore[+] their clothes and
ran in among the people, crying out,
15 saying: Sirs, why do you *do* these
things? We also are men of like passions
with you, and *we* proclaim[+] to you to
turn *away* from these vain *things* to the
living God who made heaven and earth
and the sea and everything that is therein.
16 In times past, *God* allowed[+] all nations
to walk in their own ways.
17 Nevertheless He did not leave Himself
without a witness in that He did good
and gave us rain from heaven and fruitful seasons, filling our hearts with food
and gladness.
18 But saying these *things* scarcely restrained the multitudes[+] *to* not *make a*
sacrifice to them.
19 Then *certain* Jews from Antioch and
Iconium came and persuaded the
people, and after *they* stoned Paul,
they dragged[+] *him* out of the city,
supposing *that* he was dead.
20 However, as the disciples stood
around[+] *Paul*, he rose up and went *back*

into the city. The next day he departed
with Barnabas to Derbe.
21 After they had proclaimed+ the Gospel
to that city and taught many, they returned again to Lystra and *to* Iconium
and Antioch.
22 *They* reassured+ the souls of the
disciples *and* exhorted them to continue
in the faith, *telling them* that *often* we
must *go* through much tribulation *in
order to* enter into the kingdom of God.
23 After they had ordained elders in
every assembly+ *of believers* and prayed
with fasting, they commended them to
the Lord in whom they believed.
24 *And then*, after they had passed throughout Pisidia, they came to Pamphylia.
25 When they had proclaimed+ the Word
in Perga, they went down into Attalia.
26 From there+ *they* sailed *back* to Antioch,
from where they had been recommended
to the grace of God for the work that
they fulfilled.
27 When they returned,+ they gathered
the assembly+ together *and* reviewed+
all that God had done through+ them and
how He had opened the door of faith to
the Gentiles.
28 And they stayed+ with the disciples
there *for* a long time.

Acts Chapter 15

1 Certain men *then* came down from
Judea *and* taught the family+ *saying*:
Unless+ you are circumcised after the
manner of Moses, you cannot be saved.
2 *This brought great* dissension and therefore Paul and Barnabas had no small
dispute with them. *So*, they decided+
that Paul and Barnabas and certain others of them should go to Jerusalem to the
apostles and elders about this question.
3 *So*, the assembly+ *of believers* sent
them on. *As* they passed through
Phoenicia and Samaria, *they* described
the conversion of the Gentiles *and this*
caused great joy to all the family.+
4 When they arrived+ at Jerusalem,
they were received by the assembly+
and *by* the apostles and elders, and they
reported+ all *the* things that God had
done through+ them.
5 But some of the Pharisees who *had
become* believers stood+ *up* and said that
they believed that it was necessary+ to
circumcise them and to instruct+ *them* to
keep the law of Moses.
6 *So* the apostles and elders came together
to consider this matter.
7 After there had been much disputing,
Peter rose up and said to them: Men *and*
family,+ you know that a good while
ago God made *a* choice among us, that
from my mouth, the Gentiles should hear
the Word of the Gospel and believe.
8 God, who knows the hearts, bore witness *of* them *by* giving them the Holy
Spirit, even as *He did* to us.
9 *He* made no difference between them
and us, purifying their hearts by faith.
10 Therefore, why do you now test+
God, by putting a yoke upon the neck of
the disciples, which neither our fathers
nor we were able to bear?
11 But we believe that *it is* through the
grace of the Lord Jesus Christ *that* we will
be saved, even as they *surely have been*.
12 Then all the multitude kept silent and
gave *their* attention+ to Barnabas and
Paul *who* described+ *the many* miracles
and wonders *that* God had worked+
among the Gentiles through them.
13 After they stopped+ speaking,+ James
answered saying: Men *and* family,+
listen carefully+ to me.
14 Simon *Peter* has declared how God
first visited the Gentiles to take from
among them a people for His name.
15 To this the words of the prophets
agree. As it is written:
16 After this I will return and will build
again the tabernacle of David, which is
fallen down. I will build again from
those ruins and I will set it up. *Amos 9:11*
17 Thereby *all* the rest+ of mankind+
might *also* seek the Lord, *including* all
the Gentiles who are called by my
name. *Thus* spoke the Lord *Himself* who
does all these things. *Amos 9:12*
18 *Surely* God knows *about* all His works
from the beginning of the world.

19 Therefore my judgment+ is that we should not trouble *those* who have turned to God from among the Gentiles.

20 But we *should* write to *instruct* them that they *must* abstain from*the* pollutions of idols and *from* fornication and *from* things strangled and *from* blood.

21 For *many* long generations,+ Moses has had in every city *those* who proclaim+ his *writings as they are* read in the synagogues every Sabbath day.

22 Then it seemed good+ to the apostles and elders *and* with the whole assembly+ to send chosen men of their own company to Antioch with Paul and Barnabas, *namely* Jude surnamed Barsabas and Silas, *who were* leading+ men in the family.+

23 They wrote this *letter to send with them: The apostles, elders, and family+ here send* greetings to the family+ of Gentiles in Antioch, Syria, and Cilicia.

24 Since+ we have heard, that certain *ones* who came *to you* from us have troubled you with *their* words, subverting your souls *by* saying *that you must* be circumcised and keep the law, *we want to inform you that* we gave no *such* commandment.

25 It seemed good to us, being assembled with one accord, to send *these* chosen men to you *along* with our beloved Barnabas and Paul.

26 *These* men have risked+ their lives for the name of our Lord Jesus Christ.

27 Therefore we have sent Jude and Silas who will also tell*you* the same things by *their own* mouths.

28 For it seemed good to the Holy Spirit and to us to lay upon you no greater burden than these necessary things:

29 Abstain from meats offered to idols and from blood and from things strangled and from fornication. If you keep yourselves from these, you will do well. Fare well.

30 So when they were dismissed, they went to Antioch *and* when they had gathered the multitude together, they delivered the epistle.

31 When it was read, they *all* rejoiced for the consolation.

32 Jude and Silas, also being prophets, exhorted the family+ with many words, and confirmed *them*.

33 After they stayed *there for* a while, they returned+ in peace to the apostles.

34 *But* Silas decided+ to remain there.

35 Paul and Barnabas also continued teaching and proclaiming+ the Word of the Lord in Antioch, *along* with many others.

36 Some days later, Paul said to Barnabas: Let us go again and visit our family+ in every city where we have proclaimed+ the Word of the Lord, *and see* how they are doing.

37 Barnabas decided+ to take John, whose surname was Mark, with them.

38 But Paul thought *it would* not *be* good to take *Mark* with them, *because* he had left+ them in Pamphylia and did not go with them to *finish* the work.

39 The disagreement+ between them was so sharp that they parted+ from one another. So Barnabas took Mark and sailed to Cyprus.

40 Paul chose Silas and left,+ being recommended by the family+ to the grace of God.

41 He went through Syria and Cilicia, confirming the assemblies+ *of believers*.

Acts Chapter 16

1 Then *Paul* went to Derbe and Lystra. And behold a certain disciple named Timothy was there. *Timothy* was the son of a Jewish woman who was a believer *and* a Greek father

2 who was well thought+ of by the family+ at Lystra and Iconium.

3 Paul wanted+ *Timothy* to go with him, *so* he took him *to be* circumcised because of the Jews who were in that area,+ for they all knew that his father was a Greek.

4 As they went through the cities, they delivered *to* them the decrees to *be* kept that had been ordained by the apostles and elders in Jerusalem.

5 *In this way* the assemblies+ *of believers* were established in the faith, and *they* increased in number daily.

6 When they went throughout Phrygia
and the region of Galatia, *they* were
forbidden by the Holy Spirit to proclaim+
the Word in Asia.
7 After they came to Mysia, they tried+
to go into Bithynia, but the Spirit did not
allow+ them *to go*.
8 *So* they passed by Mysia and went to
Troas.
9 *Then* a vision appeared to Paul in the
night *in which* a man of Macedonia
begged+ him saying: Come over to
Macedonia and help us.
10 After seeing the vision, we immediately
endeavored to go to Macedonia, assuredly gathering that the Lord had called
us to proclaim+ the Gospel to them.
11 Therefore sailing+ from Troas, we
went with a straight course to
Samothracia and the next *day* to Neapolis.
12 From there+ *we went* to Philippi, which
is the chief city in that part of Macedonia
and a colony. We stayed+ in that city *for*
several+ days.
13 On the Sabbath, we went out of the
city by a river side *and* prayed, as was
our custom,+ and we sat down and
spoke to the women *there*.
14 A certain woman named Lydia, a
seller of purple from the city of Thyatira,
who worshiped God, heard *us*. The Lord
opened *her* heart *so* that she *was very*
attentive+ *to* the things that Paul said.
15 Therefore she and *all of* her household
were baptized *and* she begged+ *us* saying: If you have judged me to be faithful
to the Lord, come to my house and stay+
there. And *so* she convinced+ us.
16 *Now,* it came to pass, as we went to
prayer, *that* a certain girl+ possessed
with a spirit of divination met us. *This
girl* brought her masters much gain by
soothsaying.
17 The *girl* followed Paul and us and cried
out saying: These men are servants of the
most high God who show the way of
salvation to us.
18 She did this *for* many days. But Paul,
being grieved, turned and said to the
spirit: I command you in the name of
Jesus Christ to come out of her. And *the
spirit* came out *of the girl* that same hour.
19 When *the girl's* masters saw that their
hope of gains was gone, they caught
Paul and Silas and took+ them to the
marketplace to the rulers.
20 *They* took+ them to the highest officials+
saying:-These men, being Jews, exceedingly trouble our city.
21 *They* teach customs that are not lawful
for us to receive or observe *since we are*
Romans.
22 *Therefore* the crowd+ rose up against
them *and* the highest officials+ tore+ off
their clothes and commanded *that they be*
beaten.
23 After they laid many whippings+ on
them, they cast *them* into prison, *and*
charged the jailer to keep them secured.+
24 Having received *this* charge, *he* threw+
them into the inner prison and fastened
their feet in the stocks.
25 At midnight Paul and Silas prayed and
sang praises to God *so that all* the *other*
prisoners heard them.
26 Suddenly there was a great earthquake
so that the foundations of the prison
were shaken. Immediately all the doors
were opened, and everyone's chains+
were loosed.
27 *When* the keeper of the prison awoke
out of his sleep and saw the prison doors
open, he drew out his sword and would
have killed himself, supposing that the
prisoners had fled.
28 But Paul cried *out* with a loud voice
saying: Do yourself no harm, for we are
all here.
29 *So the jailer* called for a light, got up,+
came trembling, and fell down before
Paul and Silas.
30 *Then he* brought them out and said:
Sirs, what must I do to be saved?
31 They said: Believe on the Lord Jesus
Christ and you will be saved, *you* and
your *entire* household.+
32 They spoke the Word of the Lord to
him and to all who were in his house.
33 *Then the jailer* took them, *at* that same
hour of the night, and washed *their*
wounds+ *and* he and all his *family* were
baptized immediately.+

34 Then he took them into his house,
sat food+ before them, and rejoiced,
believing in God *along* with all *the rest*
of his household.
35 When it was day, the highest officials+
sent the sergeants saying: Let those men go.
36 The keeper of the prison *then* reported+
this to Paul, saying: The highest
officials+ have sent *instructions* to let
you go. Therefore, *you may* now leave+
and go in peace.
37 But Paul said to them: They have
beaten us openly uncondemned, being
Romans, and have cast *us* into prison.
Now do they thrust us out privately+?
No truly,+ but let them come themselves and fetch us out.
38 The sergeants reported+ these words
to the highest officials+ *and* they *became*
very fearful when they heard that *Paul*
and Silas were Roman *citizens*.
39 *So the officials then personally* came and
begged+ them and brought *them* out and
asked+ *them* to leave+ their city.
40 *Then Paul and Silas* left the prison and
went+ *to* Lydia's *house*. When they saw
the family,+ they comforted them, and
then departed.

Acts Chapter 17

1 After *Paul and Silas* passed through
Amphipolis and Apollonia, they came
to Thessalonica where was a synagogue
of the Jews.
2 *Keeping* his *usual* custom,+ Paul went in
to them and *for* three Sabbath days *he*
reasoned with them from the Scriptures.
3 *He* opened *the Scripture* and showed+
them that *it was* necessary+ *for* Christ
to suffer and rise again from the dead
And he said: This Jesus I proclaim+ to
you, is Christ.
4 Some of them believed and joined+
with Paul and Silas, *including* a large+
number+ of the devout Greeks and not
a few of the prominent+ women.
5 But the Jews who did not believe *were*
moved with envy. *So they* took *some*
evil+ fellows *who could be* bought+ and
gathered a mob+ and set all the city in an
uproar. *Then they* assaulted the house of
Jason and sought to bring out *Paul and*
Silas to the people.
6 When *the mob* did not find them, they
dragged+ Jason and certain brothers to
the rulers of the city, crying *out*: Those
who have turned the world upside down
have *now* come here also.
7 *And* Jason has received *them*. They all
do *things that are* contrary to the decrees
of Caesar *by* saying that there is another
king, *one called* Jesus.
8 This troubled the people and the rulers
of the city, when they heard these things.
9 *So* when they had taken security from
Jason and from the others, they let
them go.
10 The family+ immediately sent Paul
and Silas away by night to Berea. *Upon*
arriving,+ *they* went into the synagogue
of the Jews.
11 These *Jews* were more noble than those
in Thessalonica, in that they received the
Word with all readiness of mind and
they searched the Scriptures daily *to see*
if those things *claimed* were so.
12 Therefore many of these *Jews* believed *as well as many* prominent+ Greek
women and not a few *Greek* men.
13 But when the Jews of Thessalonica
learned+ that the Word of God was
proclaimed+ by Paul at Berea, they
came there also and stirred up the people.
14 Then immediately the family+ urged+
Paul to go *on his* way by sea. But Silas
and Timothy stayed *at Berea*.
15 *Those* who escorted+ Paul took+ him
to Athens. *And then, after* receiving *in-*
structions for Silas and Timothy to come
to *Paul* with all speed, they departed.
16 While Paul waited for them in Athens,
his spirit was stirred in him when he saw
the city wholly given to idolatry.
17 Therefore he contended+ with the Jews
and religious+ people in the synagogue
and in the market daily with *those* who
met with him.
18 Then certain Epicurean and Stoick
philosophers confronted+ him and said:
What is this babbler saying? Others
said: He seems to be a proposer+ of

strange gods, because he proclaimed[+]
Jesus and the resurrection to them.
19 *So* they took him to *the* Areopagus
saying: We *would like to* know what this
new doctrine is of which you speak?
20 For you bring certain strange things to
our ears. Therefore, we would *like to*
know what these things mean.
21 For all the Athenians and strangers
there spent their time doing nothing else
but to tell or hear *about* some new thing.
22 So Paul stood in the midst of Mars' hill
and said: *You* men of Athens, I perceive
that in all things you are too superstitious.
23 For as I passed by and saw[+] *the objects
of* your worship,[+] I saw[+] an altar with
this inscription: *To the* Unknown God.
Therefore, I *now* declare to you *the God
whom* you worship *as* unknown.
24 God who made the world and everything[+] in it, since He is Lord of heaven
and earth, does not dwell in temples
made by *human* hands.
25 Neither *is* any worship *or service* needed
from human[+] hands. For *God* gives all
life and breath *to* all *things*.
26 *God* has made all nations of mankind
to dwell on all the face of the earth from
one blood, and *He* has determined *long
ago*[+] the times appointed and the bound-
aries[+] of their habitation.
27 *God desires* that *all mankind* should seek
the Lord. Even *hoping* perhaps[+] *that
some will* feel *His presence* and find Him,
although He is not far from each of us.
28 For in Him we live and move and have
our being. And as some of your own poets
have said: For we also are His offspring.
29 Since[+] we are the offspring of God,
we should not to think that the Godhead
is like gold or silver or stone, engraved
like art *by* man's devices.
30 The times of ignorance *in the past* God
overlooked,[+] but now *He* commands
everyone[+] everywhere to repent.
31 Because He has appointed a day in
which He will judge the world in
righteousness by *the* man whom He
has ordained. He has given assurance
to everyone[+] in that He raised *Jesus*
from the dead.
32 When they heard of the resurrection of
the dead, some mocked. Others said:
We will hear you again on this *matter*.
33 So Paul departed from among them.
34 However certain men joined[+] to him,
and believed. Among them *were*
Dionysius the Areopagite and a woman
named Damaris and others with them.

Acts Chapter 18

1 After these things Paul left[+] Athens
and went to Corinth.
2 *There, he* found a certain Jew named
Aquila, born in Pontus *and* recently[+]
come from Italy with his wife Priscilla,
because Claudius had commanded all
Jews to leave Rome. *Paul* went to them
3 because he was of the same craft. He
stayed[+] and worked[+] with them for in
their occupation they were tent makers.
4 Every Sabbath, *Paul* reasoned in the
synagogue, persuading the Jews and the
Greeks.
5 When Silas and Timothy came from
Macedonia, Paul was pressed *in the
spirit to* testify to the Jews *that* Jesus *was
indeed the* Christ.
6 When they opposed *this* and blasphemed, *Paul* shook *his* clothing[+] and
said to them: Your blood *be* upon your
own heads. I *am* clean. From now on, I
will go to the Gentiles.
7 *So* he departed from there[+] and entered
a certain *man's* house, *one* named Justus
who worshiped God *and* whose house
adjoined[+] the synagogue.
8 Crispus, the chief ruler of the synagogue *along* with all his household also
believed on the Lord. And many other
Corinthians *who* heard *also* believed and
were baptized.
9 Then the Lord spoke to Paul by a
vision at night, *saying*: Do not be afraid,
but speak *out*. Do not keep silent[+].
10 For I am with you and no one shall set
upon you to hurt you, for I have many
people in this city.
11 *Paul* continued *there for* a year and six
months, teaching the Word of God
among them.

12 *Then* when Gallio was the deputy of Achaia, the Jews, with one accord, made insurrection against Paul and brought him to the judgment seat.
13 *They* said: This *man* persuades people[+] to worship God contrary to the law.
14 When Paul was about to open *his* mouth, Gallio said to the Jews: If it were a matter of wrong or wicked lewdness, O Jews, *it* would *be* reasonable that I bear with you.
15 However, if it is *merely* a question of words and names and *of* your law, *then* you look *after it*. For I will not judge such *matters*.
16 And he drove them *away* from the judgment seat.
17 Then all the Greeks took Sosthenes, the chief ruler of the synagogue, and beat *him* before the judgment seat. But Gallio did not care *about* these things.
18 *After this*, Paul stayed *there for* many days[+] but then *he* left the family[+] and sailed to Syria *with* Priscilla and Aquila with him. *Paul* shaved[+] *his* head in Cenchrea, for he had *made* a vow.
19 He *then* went to Ephesus and left *Priscilla and Aquila* there while he himself entered the synagogue and reasoned with the Jews.
20 When they asked[+] *him* to stay[+] *a* longer time with them, he did not consent,
21 but bid them farewell saying: I must by all means keep this feast that comes in Jerusalem. But I will return to you again, if *it is* God's will. Then he sailed from Ephesus.
22 After he landed at Caesarea, he went up and greeted[+] the assembly,[+] *and then* he went down to Antioch.
23 After he had spent some time *there*, he departed and went over *all* the country of Galatia and Phrygia in order, strengthening all the disciples.
24 *Then* a certain Jew named Apollos *who was* born at Alexandria *and who was* an eloquent man *and* mighty in the Scriptures, came to Ephesus.
25 *Apollos* was *well* instructed in the way of the Lord. *He was* fervent in the spirit *and* he spoke and taught diligently the things of the Lord. *But he* only knew the baptism of John.
26 *As* he began to speak boldly in the synagogue, when Aquila and Priscilla heard *him*, they took him *aside* and expounded the way of God to him more perfectly.
27 *After that* when *Apollos* was disposed to pass into Achaia, the family[+] wrote *a letter*, exhorting the disciples to receive him. When he came, *he* helped those who had believed through grace.
28 For he mightily refuted[+] the Jews, *and that* publicly, showing by the Scriptures that Jesus was *the* Christ.

Acts Chapter 19

1 It came to pass that while Apollos was in Corinth, Paul passed through the upper region[+] *and* came to Ephesus. Finding certain disciples *there*,
2 he said to them: Have you received *the* Holy Spirit since you believed? And they said to him: We have not even heard that there is a Holy Spirit.
3 *Paul* said to them: Into what then were you baptized? They said: Into John's baptism.
4 Then Paul said: John truly[+] baptized with the baptism of repentance, saying to the people that they should believe in *the One* who would come after him, that is, in Christ Jesus.
5 When they heard *this*, they were baptized in the name of the Lord Jesus.
6 And when Paul laid *his* hands on them, the Holy Spirit came upon them and they spoke with tongues and prophesied.
7 All the men *there* numbered[+] about twelve.
8 *Then Paul* went into the synagogue and spoke boldly for three months, advocating[+] and persuading *those who heard him about* the things concerning the kingdom of God.
9 But when many *of* different[+] *persuasions* were hardened *against him* and did not believe, but spoke evil about the way *of Christ* before the multitude, *Paul* left them and separated the disciples *away*

from them, now reasoning[+] daily in the
school of Tyrannus.
10 This continued for two years, so that
all who lived[+] in Asia heard the Word
of the Lord Jesus, both Jews and Greeks.
11 And God worked[+] special miracles
through Paul's hands.
12 So *much so* that handkerchiefs and
aprons were taken[+] from *Paul's* body to
the sick and diseases left[+] them and evil
spirits went out of them.
13 Then some vagabond Jews *who were*
exorcists took *it* upon themselves to call
out the name of the Lord Jesus over *those*
who had evil spirits, saying: We beg[+]
you by Jesus whom Paul proclaims.[+]
14 There were seven sons of Sceva, a Jew
and chief of the priests, who did this.
15 But the evil spirit answered and said:
Jesus I know and Paul I know, but who
are you?
16 *Then* the man who had the evil spirit
leaped on them and overcame them and
prevailed against them so that they fled
out of that house naked and wounded.
17 All the Jews and Greeks *who* lived[+] in
Ephesus knew *about* this *so that* fear fell
on them all and the name of the Lord
Jesus was magnified.
18 Many who believed came and confessed
and reported[+] their deeds.
19 Many of those who used *curious* arts
also brought their books together and
burned them before all *people*. They
counted the value[+] of *those books* and
found *it to be* fifty thousand *pieces* of
silver.
20 Therefore, the Word of God grew
mightily and prevailed.
21 After these things were fulfilled,[+] in
his spirit, Paul *decided* to pass through
Macedonia and Achaia *and* go to
Jerusalem, saying: After I have been
there, I must also see Rome.
22 So he sent *word* to Macedonia *to* two
of *those* who *had* ministered to him,
Timothy and Erastus, but he himself
stayed in Asia for a season.
23 *At* the same time, there arose no small
stir about *this faith called* the Way *meaning
believing in Christ and His resurrection.*
24 For a certain *man* named Demetrius, a
silversmith, made silver shrines for
Diana, *and this* brought no small gain to
the craftsmen.
25 *So, Demetrius* called the workmen of
this occupation together and said: Sirs,
you know that by this craft we have our
wealth.
26 Moreover you see and hear that not
only[+] at Ephesus, but almost throughout
all Asia, this Paul has persuaded and
turned many people away, saying that
there are no gods that are made with
hands.
27 Therefore, not only is our craft in
danger of being rejected,[+] but also the
temple of the great goddess whom all *of*
Asia and the world worships could be
despised and her magnificence destroyed.
28 When they heard *this*, they were full of
anger[+] and cried out saying: Great *is*
Diana of the Ephesians.
29 *So* the whole city was filled with
confusion. *But* with one accord *the mob*
ran into the theater *and* caught Gaius and
Aristarchus *of* Macedonia *who were*
Paul's companions.
30 When Paul wanted[+] *to* go in to the
people, the disciples did not allow[+] him
to do so.
31 Some of the chiefs of Asia who were
Paul's friends, sent *word* to him asking[+]
him to not venture[+] into the theater.
32 Some therefore cried *out* one thing and
some another for the assembly was
confused. Most[+] did not *even* understand[+]
why[+] they had come together.
33 They pulled[+] Alexander out of the
crowd[+] *and* the Jews put him forward.
Alexander signaled[+] with the hand
and would have made his defense to
the people,
34 But when they knew that he was a Jew,
all with one voice cried out for two
hours: Great *is* Diana of the Ephesians.
35 Then the town clerk appeased the people
when he said: *You* men of Ephesus, what
man is there that does not understand[+]
that the city of the Ephesians is a worshiper
of the great goddess Diana and of
the *image* that fell down from Jupiter?

36 Since these things cannot be *success-*
fully spoken against, you ought to be
quiet and to do nothing rashly.
37 For you have brought these men here
who are neither robbers of assemblies+
nor blasphemers of your goddess.
38 Therefore if Demetrius and the craftsmen
who are with him have a matter against
anyone, the law is open and there are
deputies. Let them accuse+ one another.
39 And if you *have* any *other* inquiry
concerning other matters, it should+ be
determined in a lawful assembly.
40 For we are in danger of being called in
question for this day's uproar. *For* there
is no *justifiable* cause that we can give to
account for this *unruly* concourse.
41 When he had thus spoken, he dismissed the assembly.

Acts Chapter 20

1 After the uproar was stopped,+ Paul
called the disciples *to* embrace *them* and
then he left+ to go to Macedonia.
2 *Then* after he had gone through those
regions+ and given them much exhortation, he went *on* to Greece.
3 *He* stayed+ *there for* three months.
When the Jews *were* plotting+ *against*
him as he was about to sail to Syria, he
decided+ to return through Macedonia.
4 Accompanying him to Asia were
Sopater from Berea, Aristarchus and
Secundus from Thessalonica, Gaius from
Derbe, Tychicus and Trophimus from
Asia, and Timothy.
5 *All* these going before, waited for us
at Troas.
6 After *celebrating* the days of unleavened bread, we sailed from Philippi *and*
met+ them in Troas in five days *and*
stayed+ *with them* there *for* seven days.
7 On the first *day* of the week, when the
disciples came together to break bread,
Paul proclaimed+ *the Word* to them,
ready to depart on the next day, *and he*
continued his speech until midnight.
8 There were many lights in the upper
chamber where they were gathered
together.
9 In a window *sill*, a certain young man
named Eutychus sat *and* began to fall
into a deep sleep as Paul *continued*
speaking+ *for a* long *time*. *The young man*
slumped+ down in sleep, fell from the
third loft, and was taken *as* dead.
10 Paul went downstairs and fell upon
him *to* embrace him *and* said: Do not *be*
troubled, for his life is *still* in him.
11 Therefore, after *Paul* came *back*
upstairs again and broke bread and ate
and talked a long while, even until *the*
break of day, he *then* departed.
12 They took+ the young man *with them*,
very much alive, and *they* were not a little
comforted *by this*.
13 *So* we went to *the* ship and sailed to
Assos. There *we* had intended to take
Paul onto *the ship*. For he had appointed
himself to go *this far* on foot.
14 *Therefore*, when he met us in Assos,
we took him in and went *on* to Mitylene.
15 From *Assos*, we sailed *on* and the next
day came near+ Chios. The next *day* we
arrived at Samos and stayed at
Trogyllium. *And* the next *day* we came
to Miletus.
16 Paul had determined to sail by
Ephesus because he would not spend
the time in Asia. For he hurried,+ *so*
that if it were possible, he *wanted* to be
in Jerusalem *for* the day of Pentecost.
17 From Miletus, he sent *word* to Ephesus
to call *together* the elders of the assemblies.+
18 When they came to him, he said to
them: You know, from the first day that
I came to Asia, how+ I have been with
you at all times.+
19 *I have* served the Lord with all humility
of mind and with many tears and
trials+ that befell me from the plotting+
of the Jews.
20 I have kept back nothing that would be
beneficial+ *to you*. But *I* have shown
you and taught you *both* publicly and
from house to house.
21 *I have* testified to both the Jews and
also to the Greeks, *proclaiming* repentance to God and faith in our Lord
Jesus Christ.

22 *And* now behold, I *am* going bound in
the spirit to Jerusalem, not knowing
what things will befall me there.
23 Except[+] *I know* that the Holy Spirit
testifies[+] *to me* in every city saying that
chains[+] and afflictions *will* stay[+] *with* me.
24 But none of these things deter[+] me.
Nor *do* I count my life dear to myself,
so that I might finish my course with
joy, and*complete* the ministry that I have
received from the Lord Jesus: To testify
to the Gospel of the grace of God.
25 Now, behold I know that you all, among
whom I have gone proclaiming[+] the kingdom of God, will see my face no longer.[+]
26 Therefore I ask[+] you to record this day,
that I *am* pure from the blood of all *people*.
27 For I have not shunned *the responsibility*
to declare the counsel of God to all *of* you.
28 Therefore, take heed to yourselves
and to all the flock over which the Holy
Spirit has made you overseers. Feed the
assembly[+] of God that He purchased
with His own blood.
29 For I know this, that after I leave,[+]
grievous wolves will enter in among
you *and* will not spare the flock.
30 Also from *among* yourselves, *certain*
men will rise *up and* speak perverse
things to draw away disciples after
themselves.
31 Therefore watch and remember that
for three years I did not stop[+] warning
everyone night and day with tears.
32 Now family,[+] I commend you to God
and to the Word of His grace, which is
able to build you up and give you an
inheritance among all who are sanctified.
33 I have coveted no one's silver or gold
or apparel.
34 Yes, you yourselves know that these
hands have ministered to my *own* needs[+]
and *to the needs of those* who were with me.
35 I have shown you everything[+] *so* that,
laboring in this way,[+] you ought to
support the weak and remember the
words of the Lord Jesus, how He said:

It is more blessed to give
than to receive.

36 When he had thus spoken, he knelt
down and prayed with them all.
37 They all wept greatly[+] and fell on
Paul's neck and kissed him.
38 Of all the words that *Paul* spoke, *what*
caused them the most sorrow was that
they would see his face no longer.[+] But
then they accompanied him to the ship.

Acts Chapter 21

1 It came to pass, that after we left[+] them
and launched, we came with a straight
course to Coos and the *day* following to
Rhodes and from there[+] to Patara.
2 Finding a ship *that was* sailing to
Phoenicia, we went aboard and set forth.
3 When we sighted[+] Cyprus, we passed[+]
by it on the left and sailed to Syria and
landed at Tyre, for the ship was to
unload its cargo[+] there.
4 Finding disciples there, we stayed *with*
them for seven days. Through the Spirit,
they said to Paul that he should not go to
Jerusalem.
5 When we completed[+] those days,
we departed and went *on* our way.
They all accompanied[+] us with *their*
wives and children until *we were* out
of the city. *Then* we knelt down on the
shore and prayed.
6 After we left[+] each other, we boarded[+]
the ship *and* they returned home again.
7 When we finished *our* course from
Tyre, we came to Ptolemais and greeted[+]
the family[+] *there* and stayed[+] with them
for one day.
8 The next *day*, we who were in Paul's
company left[+] and went *on* to Caesarea.
There, we entered the house of Philip the
evangelist who was *one* of the seven and
stayed[+] with him.
9 *Philip* had four daughters *who were*
virgins *and who* prophesied.
10 As we continued[+] *there for* many
days, a prophet named Agabus came
from Judea.
11 When he arrived,[+] he took Paul's
belt[+] and bound his own hands and
feet and said: The Holy Spirit *has* said
this to me: *In this same way*, the Jews in

Jerusalem will bind the man who owns
this belt+ and deliver *him* into the hands
of the Gentiles.
12 When we heard these things, both we
and those in that place begged+ *Paul* to
not go to Jerusalem.
13 But Paul answered: Why do you weep
and break my heart? For I am ready not
only to be bound, but also to die in
Jerusalem for the name of the Lord Jesus.
14 When he would not be persuaded, we
stopped+ *protesting and* said: *May* the
Lord's will be done.
15 After those days we took our baggage+
and went to Jerusalem.
16 *Some* of the disciples in Caesarea also
went with us and *they* brought Mnason
from Cyprus, an old disciple with whom
we *had* lodged.
17 When we arrived+ in Jerusalem, the
family+ received us gladly.
18 The next+ *day*, Paul *and the rest of* us
went to James, and all the elders were
present.
19 After we greeted+ them, *Paul* de-
scribed+ *in* detail+ what *great* things
God had worked+ among the Gentiles
through his ministry.
20 When they heard *this*, they glorified
the Lord and said to *Paul*: You see,
brother, how many thousands of Jews
there are who believe, but they are all
zealous *for* this law *of* substance.
21 They have been told+ about you, that
you teach all the Jews who are among
the Gentiles to forsake Moses saying
that they should not circumcise *their*
children or follow+ the *traditional Jewish*
customs.
22 What should *we* do? Surely a crowd
will come together, for they will hear
that you have come.
23 Therefore do this that we say to you.
We have four men who have *taken* a vow.
24 Take them and purify yourself with
them and pay+ *the* costs+ for them *so*
that they can shave *their* heads. *Then* all
may know that those things *that have*
been told+ about+ you are nothing, but
that you yourself also walk orderly and
keep the law.
25 Concerning the Gentile believers, we
have written *and* concluded that they
observe no such things, except+ that they
keep themselves from *things* offered to
idols and from blood and from *things*
strangled and from fornication.
26 So Paul took the men and the next
day *after* purifying himself with them
he entered the temple to signify the
accomplishment of the days of purification until an offering could be offered
for everyone of them.
27 When the seven days were almost
ended, the Jews from Asia saw *Paul* in
the temple *and they* stirred up all the
people and laid hands on him.
28 *They* cried out: Men of Israel help *us*.
This is the man who teaches all *people*
everywhere *things that are* against the
people and the law and this place. Furthermore, *he* also took Greeks into the
temple and polluted this holy place.
29 For in the city Trophimus, they had
seen an Ephesian with *Paul and* they
assumed+ that *he* had taken *the Ephesian*
into the temple.
30 *Therefore* all the city was riled+ *up* and
the people ran together and took Paul
and dragged+ him out of the temple and
immediately+ shut the doors.
31 As *the mob* was about to kill *Paul*, a
message+ came to the chief captain of
the company+ *of soldiers saying* that all
Jerusalem was in an uproar.
32 *So the captain* immediately took soldiers
and centurions and ran down to them.
When they saw the chief captain and the
soldiers, they stopped+ beating Paul.
33 Then the chief captain came near and
took him and commanded *him* to be
bound with two chains. *The captain*
demanded *to know* who *Paul* was and
what he had done.
34 Some *people* in the crowd+ cried *out* one
thing *and* some another. When *the captain*
could not know *with* certainty *what the*
cause was for the tumult, he commanded
that Paul be carried into the castle.
35 When *they* came to the stairs, *Paul* was
carried+ by the soldiers *because* of the
violence of the people.

36 The crowd[+] followed after *them*,
crying *out*: Away with him.
37 As Paul was *about* to be led into the
castle, he said to the chief captain: May
I speak to you? *The captain* said: Can you
speak Greek?
38 Are you not that Egyptian who before
these days made an uproar and led four
thousand men who were murderers out
into the wilderness?
39 But Paul said: I am a Jew from Tarsus, *a*
city in Cilicia, a citizen of no mean city. I
urge you, allow me to speak to the people.
40 When *the captain* gave *Paul* permission,[+]
he stood on the stairs and signaled[+] to
the people with his hand. When there
was silence, he spoke to *them* in the
Hebrew tongue.

Acts Chapter 22

1 Men, family,[+] and fathers: Now hear
my defense to you.
2 When they heard that he spoke to them
in the Hebrew tongue, they kept *all* the
more silent. *Then* he said:
3 I am truly[+] a Jew, born in Tarsus, *a*
city in Cilicia. *I was* brought in this city
at the feet of Gamaliel, taught according
to the strict[+] *letter* of the law of the
fathers, and zealous toward God as you
all are this day.
4 *Therefore*, I persecuted this *faith known*
as The Way *even* to the death, binding
and delivering both men and women
into prisons.
5 The high priest and all of the council[+]
of elders testify[+] *to this fact*. And from
them, I received letters to the family[+]
and *I* went to Damascus to bring *those*
who were bound there to Jerusalem to
be punished.
6 It came to pass that, as I made my
journey and came near Damascus
about noon, suddenly there shone from
heaven a great light around[+] me.
7 I fell to the ground and heard a voice
saying to me: Saul, Saul, why do you
persecute me?
8 I answered: Who are you Lord? He
said to me: I am Jesus of Nazareth
whom you persecute.
9 *Those* who were with me also saw the
light and were afraid but they did not
hear the voice of Him who spoke to me.
10 I said: What shall I do, Lord? And the
Lord said to me, Arise, and go into
Damascus. There you will be told
about all the things that are appointed
for you to do.
11 When I could not see because of the
brightness[+] of that light, *I was* led by the
hand of *those* who were with me *and* I
came to Damascus.
12 *After I arrived there, a man named* Ananias,
who was a devout man according to the
law, *and who* had a good report from all
the Jews who lived[+] *there*,
13 came to me and stood *by me* and said
to me: Brother Saul, receive your
sight. And the same hour I looked up
and saw him.
14 He said: The God of our fathers has
chosen you, that you should know His
will and see that Just One and hear the
voice of His mouth.
15 For you shall be His witness to everyone[+] of what you have seen and heard.
16 *Therefore* why *do* you delay[+] now?
Arise and be baptized and wash away
your sins, calling on the name of the
Lord.
17 *Now* it came to pass, that when I had
come again to Jerusalem, as I prayed in
the temple, I went into a trance.
18 *And I* saw Him *and heard Him* say to
me: Hurry and quickly get out of
Jerusalem, for they will not receive
your testimony concerning me.
19 I said: Lord, they know that I impris-
oned and beat *some* in every synagogue
who believe in you.
20 When the blood of your martyr Stephen
was shed, I also was standing by and
consenting to his death and held[+] the
coats[+] of *those* who killed[+] him.
21 He said to me: Leave[+] *now*, for I will
send you far from here to the Gentiles.
22 They listened[+] to *Paul's* words and
then raised[+] their voices and said:
Away with such a *fellow* from the earth,
for it is not proper[+] that he should live.

23 As they cried out, *they* tore[+] off *their* clothes and threw dust into the air.

24 *Then* the chief captain commanded *that Paul* be brought into the castle and ordered[+] that he should be examined by scourging *so* that he might know why[+] they cried *out* so against him.

25 As they bound him with thongs, Paul said to the centurion who stood by: Is it lawful for you to flog[+] a man who is a Roman and *has not been* convicted[+] *of anything*?

26 When the centurion heard *that*, he went *away* and told the chief captain saying: Take heed what you do, for this man is a Roman.

27 Then the chief captain came and said to *Paul*: Tell me: Are you a Roman? He said: Yes.

28 The chief captain answered: I obtained this freedom at a great cost.[+] And Paul said: But I was born *free*.

29 Then immediately[+] *he* who had been *about to* examine *Paul* left.[+] The chief captain was also afraid after he knew that *Paul* was a Roman, because he *was the one who* had bound him.

30 On the next day, because he wanted to know for certain why *Paul* had been accused by the Jews, he released[+] him from *his* chains[+] and commanded the chief priests and all their council to appear, and *then he* brought Paul down and stood[+] him before them.

Acts Chapter 23

1 Paul looked[+] earnestly *at* the council *and* said: Men *and* family,[+] I have lived in all good conscience before God to this day.

2 Ananias the high priest Ananias *then* commanded *those* who stood by *Paul* to strike[+] him on the mouth.

3 Then Paul said to him: God will strike[+] you, *you* whitewashed[+] wall. For you sit to judge me by the law but *then* command me to be struck[+] contrary to the law?

4 *Those* who stood by said: Do you revile God's high priest?

5 Then Paul said: I did not understand,[+] family,[+] that he was the high priest. For it is written: You shall not speak evil about the ruler of your people. *Exodus 22:28*

6 But when Paul perceived that one part *of the audience* were Sadducees and the other Pharisees, he cried out in the council: Men *and* family,[+] I am a Pharisee, the son of a Pharisee. *Am* I *being* judged[+] *because of the* hope and resurrection of the dead?

7 When he said *this*, dissension arose between the Pharisees and the Sadducees and the crowd[+] was divided.

8 For the Sadducees say that there is no resurrection, neither angel nor spirit, but the Pharisees confess both.

9 *And so* a great cry arose. The scribes *who were* Pharisees rose *up* and argued[+] saying: We find no evil in this man, but if a spirit or an angel has spoken to him, let us not fight against God.

10 When this great dissension arose, the chief captain, fearing lest Paul might be pulled to pieces by them, commanded the soldiers to go down and take him by force from them and take *him* into the castle.

11 The following night, the Lord stoodby *Paul* and said: Be of good cheer, Paul. For as you have testified about me in Jerusalem, so also, you must testify[+] in Rome.

12 When it was day, some of the Jews banded together and bound themselves under a curse saying that they would neither eat nor drink until they had killed Paul.

13 More than forty *of them* made this conspiracy.

14 They came to the chief priests and elders and said: We have bound ourselves under a great curse that we will eat nothing until we have killed[+] Paul.

15 Now therefore you and the council signal[+] to the chief captain to bring *Paul* down to you tomorrow as though you want *to* question[+] *him* further.[+] And before[+] he comes near, we are ready to kill him.

16 When Paul's sister's son heard about

their plot,+ he entered the castle and
told Paul.
17 Then Paul called one of the centurions
and said: Take this young man to the
chief captain, for he has something to
tell him.
18 So *the centurion* took *the young man* to
the chief captain and said: Paul the
prisoner called me and asked+ me to
bring this young man to you. *He* has
something to say to you.
19 Then the chief captain took him by the
hand and went *with him* aside privately
and asked *him*: What is that you have to
tell me?
20 He said: The Jews have agreed to ask+
that you bring Paul down to the council
tomorrow, as though they would
question+ him further.+
21 But do not yield to them, for they *are*
plotting+ *against* him. More than forty
men have bound themselves with an
oath, that they will neither eat nor drink
until they have killed him. Now are they
ready, looking for a promise from you.
22 So the chief captain let the young man
leave+ and charged *him*: Tell no one that
you have shown these things to me.
23 *Then the captain* called two centurions
saying: Make ready two hundred soldiers
and seventy horsemen and two hundred
spearmen to go to Caesarea at nine
o'clock+ *at* night.
24 Provide *a* beast *for* Paul *to ride to* take
him safely to Felix the governor.
25 *Then* he wrote a letter in this manner.
26 *From* Claudius Lysias to the most
excellent governor Felix. Greetings.
27 This man *Paul* was taken by the Jews
and would have been killed by them. But
I came with an army and rescued him,
having understood that he was a Roman.
28 When I wanted to know the reason+
why+ they accused him, I brought him
forth into their council.
29 I perceived *him* to be accused regarding+
questions in their law, but to have
nothing laid to his charge worthy of
death or of chains.+
30 When I was told that the Jews *were*
plotting+ against this man, I immedi-
ately+ sent *him* to you and gave
instructions+ to his accusers also to
say before you what *they had* against
him. Farewell.
31 Then as it was commanded *to* them,
the soldiers took Paul by night to
Antipatris.
32 The next day, the *soldiers* left the
horsemen to go with *Paul* and *they*
returned to the castle.
33 When the *horsemen* came to Caesarea,
they delivered the epistle to the governor
and presented Paul to him.
34 When the governor read *the letter*, he
asked what province *Paul* was from.
When he understood that *he was* from
Cilicia,
35 he said: I will hear your *case* when
your accusers have also come. Then he
commanded *that Paul* be kept in Herod's
judgment hall.

Acts Chapter 24

1 After five days, Ananias the high
priest arrived+ with the elders and *with*
a certain orator *named* Tertullus, who
informed the governor *of the charges*
against Paul.
2 When he was called forth, Tertullus
began to accuse *Paul* saying: Since+ *it is*
by you, *governor*, *that* we enjoy great
quietness, and that very worthy deeds are
done to this nation by your providence,
3 we accept *this* always and in all places
with all thankfulness most noble Felix.
4 Nevertheless, *hoping* that I *may* not
be tedious to you, I ask+ that by your
patience+ you *might* hear a few words
from us.
5 For we have found this man *Paul to be*
a pestilent *fellow*, a mover of sedition
among all the Jews throughout the world,
and a ringleader of the sect of the
Nazarenes.
6 He has gone about profaning the
temple. *So* we took *him* and would have
judged *him* according to our law.
7 But the chief captain Lysias came and
with great violence took *him* away out of
our hands.

8 *He* commanded *us, Paul's* accusers, to
come to you. By examining him yourself, *you will* know about all the things
about which we accuse him.
9 The Jews *all* agreed[+] *by* saying that
these things were so.
10 Then, the governor signaled[+] for Paul
to speak, *and he* answered: Since[+] I know
that you have been a judge in this nation
for many years, I gladly answer for myself.
11 *So* you may understand, it *has been*
twelve days since I went to Jerusalem to
worship.
12 They *did* not find me in the temple
disputing with anyone. Nor *did anyone*
find me stirring[+] up people in the synagogues or in the city.
13 Neither can they prove the things
about which they now accuse me.
14 But I confess this to you: That *in*
following[+] The Way, which they call *a*
heresy, I also worship the God of my
fathers *and I* believe everything[+] that is
written in the law and in the prophets.
15 I have hope in God, as *do all* who
accept[+] this, that there will be a
resurrection of the dead, both of the
righteous[+] and unrighteous.[+]
16 In this *hope* I strive[+] to always have a
conscience void of offense toward God
and *toward* men.
17 Now after many years I came to bring
alms to my nation and offerings.
18 At that time,[+] certain Jews from Asia
found me purified in the temple *and* not
with *a* mob[+] or tumult.
19 *Those people* ought to have been here
before you *to* object if they had something against me.
20 Or else let these *accusers* say *so* if they
found any evil doing in me while I stood
before the council.
21 *It is* for this one sound[+] that I cried *out*
while standing among them, touching *on*
the resurrection of the dead, *that* I am
called in *for* questioning by you this day.
22 When Felix heard these things, having
straighter[+] knowledge about *the* way *from*
Paul, he deferred *the matter* and said: When
Lysias the chief captain comes down, I
will *further* consider[+] your matter.
23 *Then Felix* commanded a centurion to
keep Paul and to let *him* have liberty and
that he should not forbid any of his
acquaintances to minister or come to him.
24 After several[+] days, Felix came with
his wife Drusilla, who was a Jew,[+] *and*
he sent for Paul and *wanted to* hear *from*
him concerning faith in Christ.
25 As *Paul* spoke[+] about righteousness,
temperance, and judgment to come,
Felix trembled and answered: Go away
for this time. When I have a convenient
season, I will call for you.
26 *Felix* also hoped that Paul might give
him money *so* that he could release him.
Therefore he sent for *Paul* more often
and conversed[+] with him.
27 But after two years, Porcius Festus
came into Felix' office[+] *and* Felix,
wanting[+] to show the Jews a favor,[+] left
Paul bound.

Acts Chapter 25

1 Now when Festus came to the province, after three days he went up[+] from
Caesarea to Jerusalem.
2 Then the high priest and the chief of
the Jews informed *Festus* about Paul and
begged[+] him
3 *for a* favor, *asking Festus* to send *Paul* to
Jerusalem *so they could* wait along the
way to kill him.
4 But Festus answered that Paul should
be kept at Caesarea and that he himself
would soon[+] go[+] *there.*
5 Therefore *Festus* said: Let *those*
among you who are able go with *me*
and accuse this man *to see* if there is
any wickedness in him.
6 After he stayed[+] *there* among them *for*
ten days, he went down to Caesarea.
The next day sitting on the judgment
seat, *he* commanded Paul to be brought.
7 When *Paul* came *in,* the Jews who came
down from Jerusalem stood around[+] and
made many grievous complaints against
Paul that they could not prove.
8 When *Paul* answered for himself, *he said:*
I have not offended *anyone in* anything at
all, not against the law of the Jews or

against the temple or against Caesar.
9 But Festus, wanting[+] to do the Jews a
favor,[+] answered Paul and said: Will
you go up to Jerusalem and be judged by
me there about these things?
10 Then Paul said: I stand at Caesar's
judgment seat where I ought to be
judged. I have done no wrong to the
Jews, as you very well know.
11 For if I am an offender or have committed anything worthy of death, I do not
refuse to die. But if none of these things
are *true* of which these *Jews* accuse me,
no one *should be* able to deliver me to
them. I appeal to Caesar.
12 Then Festus, when he had conferred
with the council, answered: *Since* you
have appealed to Caesar, to Caesar you
shall go.
13 After several[+] days, King Agrippa and
Bernice came to Caesarea to greet[+] Festus.
14 When they had been there many days,
Festus described[+] Paul's case[+] to the
king saying: There is a certain man *who
was* left in prison[+] by Felix.
15 When I was in Jerusalem, the chief
priests and the elders of the Jews informed *me* about him *and* wanted[+] *a*
judgment against him.
16 I answered them, *by saying*: It is not the
Roman way[+] to deliver anyone to die
before *the one* who is accused has the
accusers face to face with license to
answer for himself concerning the crime
laid against him.
17 Therefore when they came here, without any delay, on the *very* next day I sat
on the judgment seat and commanded
the man to be brought forth.
18 When the accusers stood up, they
brought no accusation of such things as
I supposed.
19 But from their own superstition *they*
had certain questions against him and
about one *called* Jesus, who was dead,
but whom Paul affirmed to be alive.
20 Because I *was* doubtful about such
questions, I asked *Paul* if he would go to
Jerusalem and be judged there about
these matters.
21 But when Paul appealed to be heard by
Augustus, I commanded him to be kept
until I might send him to Caesar.
22 Then Agrippa said to Festus: I would
also *like to* hear the man myself. Tomorrow, *Festus* said, you shall hear him.
23 The next day, when Agrippa and
Bernice came with great pomp and
entered the place of hearing *along* with
the chief captains and principal men of
the city, at Festus' commandment Paul
was brought forth.
24 Festus said: King Agrippa and everyone[+] here present with us: You see this
man about whom all the multitude of Jews
have petitioned[+] me, both at Jerusalem
and *also* here, crying *out* that he should
not live any longer.
25 But when I found that he had committed nothing worthy of death and that he
himself appealed to Augustus, I decided[+]
to send him *there*.
26 *However*, I have no certain thing to
write *about him* to my lord *Caesar*. Therefore I have brought him forth before
you, and especially before you, O king
Agrippa, *so* that after *you have* examined
him, I might have something to write.
27 For it seems unreasonable to me to
send a prisoner and not *send* with *him a*
significant[+] *description* of the crimes *laid*
against him.

Acts Chapter 26

1 Then Agrippa said to Paul: You are
permitted to speak for yourself. Then
Paul stretched forth his hand and
answered for himself.
2 I think myself blessed,[+] king Agrippa,
because I shall answer for myself this day
before you, touching *upon* all the things
about which I am accused by the Jews.
3 Especially *because I know* you to be
expert in all *of the* customs and questions
that are *debated* among the Jews. Therefore I urge you to hear me patiently.
4 From my youth, my life from the
very beginning was formed[+] among
my own nation in Jerusalem. The
Jews all know *this*.
5 *They all* knew me from the beginning.

If they would testify, *they would say* that
I lived following[+] the strictest[+] sect of
our religion as a Pharisee.
6 *Yet* now I stand and am judged for the hope
of the promise made to our fathers by God.
7 For this *promise* our twelve tribes
earnestly[+] served *God* day and night,
hoping to attain[+] it. *It is* because[+] *of this*
hope, King Agrippa, *that* I am accused
by the Jews.
8 Why should it be thought incredible
that God could raise the dead?
9 I myself truly[+] thought that I ought to
do many things contrary to the name of
Jesus of Nazareth.
10 And I *actually* did these things in
Jerusalem. Having received authority
from the chief priests, I shut up many of
the saints in prison. When they were put
to death, I gave my voice against *them*.
11 I often punished them in all the synagogues and compelled *them* to blaspheme. Being exceedingly furious[+]
against them, I persecuted *them* even to
outlying[+] cities.
12 But then, as I went to Damascus with
authority and commission from the chief
priests,
13 At midday, O king, I saw a light from
heaven on the way. *It was* brighter than
the sun *and* shining *all* around[+] me.
Those traveling[+] with me also *saw it*.
14 When we all fell to the ground,[+] I
heard a voice speaking to me and saying
in the Hebrew tongue: Saul, Saul, why
do you persecute me? *It is* hard for you
to kick against the pricks.
15 I said: Who are you, Lord? He said: I
am Jesus whom you persecute.
16 But rise and stand up on your feet. For
I have appeared to you for this purpose,
to make you a minister and a witness
both of these things that you have seen
and of those things in which I will
appear to you.
17 *I will* deliver you from the people
and *from* the Gentiles, to whom now I
send you,
18 to open their eyes *and* to turn *them*
from darkness to light and *from* the
authority[+] of Satan to God *so* that they
may receive forgiveness of sins and
inheritance among *those* who are sanctified by faith that is in me.
19 Therefore, O King Agrippa, I was not
disobedient to the heavenly vision.
20 But *I* declared[+] *it* first to those in
Damascus and in Jerusalem and throughout all the borders[+] of Judea, and *then* to
the Gentiles *so* that they could repent
and turn to God and do works worthy[+]
of repentance.
21 For these causes the Jews caught me in
the temple and went about to kill *me*.
22 Therefore, having obtained help from
God, I continue to this day, witnessing
both to small and great saying no other
things than what the prophets and Moses
said would come:
23 That Christ would suffer *and* that He
would be the first who would rise from
the dead and show light to the people
and to the Gentiles.
24 As he thus spoke for himself, Festus
said with a loud voice: Paul, you are
beside yourself. *Too* much learning has
made you mad.
25 But *Paul* said: I am not mad, most
noble Festus, but *I* speak forth the words
of truth and soberness.
26 For the king knows *all* about these
things. Before him, I *can* speak freely.
For I am persuaded that none of these
things are hidden from him. For this
thing was not done *hidden* in a corner.
27 King Agrippa, do you believe the
prophets? I know that you believe.
28 Then Agrippa said to Paul: You
almost persuade me to be a Christian.
29 *Then* Paul said: I wish[+] to God that not
only you, but also all who hear me this
day, were both almost and entirely[+] as
I am, except these chains.[+]
30 When he had thus spoken, the king
rose up, and the governor and Bernice
and *those* who sat with them.
31 After they had gone aside, they talked
among themselves saying: This man does
nothing worthy of death or of chains.[+]
32 Then Agrippa said to Festus: This
man might have been released[+] if he had
not appealed to Caesar.

Acts Chapter 27

1 When they decided+ that we would sail to Italy, they delivered Paul and certain other prisoners to *one* named Julius, a centurion of Augustus' company+ *of soldiers*.

2 *After* entering a ship from Adramyttium, we launched, intending+ to sail passed+ the borders+ of Asia. Aristarchus, a Macedonian from Thessalonica was with us.

3 The next *day* we stopped+ *briefly* at Sidon. Julius treated Paul courteously and gave *him* liberty to go to his friends to refresh himself.

4 When we launched from there,+ we sailed under Cyprus because the winds were against+ *us*.

5 After we sailed over the sea *near* Cilicia and Pamphylia, we came to Myra, *a city* of Lycia.

6 There, the centurion found a ship from Alexandria sailing to Italy *and* he put us on it.

7 When we had sailed slowly *for* many days and barely+ came near+ to Cnidus *because* the wind did not allow+ us *closer*, we *then* sailed under Crete near+ Salmone.

8 Barely+ passing *by* it, *we* came to a place called The Fair Havens near the city *of* Lasea.

9 After+ much time had passed and sailing was now dangerous because the fast *conditions* had past, Paul cautioned *them*.

10 *He* said to them: Sirs, I perceive that this voyage will be with much injury+ and damage, not only to the ship and cargo,+ but also to our lives.

11 Nevertheless, the centurion believed the master and the owner of the ship more than the things that Paul said.

12 And, because the harbor+ was not well suited+ to winter in, most+ advised *them* to leave+ from there+ if they could by any means make+ *it* to Phoenix to winter *there. The* harbor+ in Crete faces+ to *both* the southwest and northwest.

13 *Therefore* when the south wind blew softly, they supposed that this suited+ *their* purpose *so* they left+ *there and* sailed close by Crete.

14 But not long after, a tempestuous wind called Euroclydon arose *like a hurricane* against *the ship*.

15 When the ship was caught and could not bear up into the wind, we let *it* run adrift.+

16 *As we* ran under an island called Clauda, we had much work *to do* by the lifeboat

17 that was used to help undergird the ship. But, fearing lest they might fall into the quicksands, *they* struck sail and *thus* were driven *along*.

18 Being exceedingly tossed by the storm,+ the next *day* they lightened the ship.

19 *On* the third *day*, we cast out the ship's tackle with our own hands.

20 For many days, neither sun nor stars appeared and *as* no small storm+ lay on *us*, all hope that we might be saved was taken away.

21 Then, after long abstinence, Paul stood forth in the midst of them and said: Sirs, you should have listened+ to me and not sailed+ from Crete and *you would not* have received+ this harm and loss.

22 *But* now I exhort you to be of good cheer, for there will be no loss of *any man's* life among you, but *only* the ship *will be lost*.

23 For an angel of God, whose I am and whom I serve, stood by me this night

24 saying: Do not be afraid Paul. You must be brought before Caesar. And behold, God is giving *to* you all who *are* sailing with you.

25 Therefore sirs, be of good cheer, for I believe God, that it will *indeed* be as it was told *to* me.

26 However, we must *first* be cast onto a certain island.

27 Therefore, when the fourteenth night came, as we were driven up and down in *the* Adriatic *sea*, about midnight the ship's men thought+ that they were drawing near to some country.

28 *So they* sounded *the depth* and found *it to be* twenty fathoms. After they went a little further, they sounded again and found *it to be* fifteen fathoms.

29 Then fearing lest we might fall upon rocks, they cast four anchors out of the stern, and wished for daylight.

30 As the ship's men were about to flee out of the ship, they let down the lifeboat under the pretense+ that they were casting anchors out of the bow+ *of the* ship.

31 Paul said to the centurion and to the soldiers, Unless+ these *men* stay+ in the ship, you cannot be saved.

32 Then the soldiers cut the ropes to the lifeboat and let it fall.

33 *Then* as day was coming, Paul begged+ *them* all to take *some* food+ saying: This is the fourteenth day that you have expectantly+ continued fasting *and* taken nothing *to eat*.

34 Therefore I beg+ you to take *some* food.+ For this is *so that* you *can be* saved.+ For *not one* hair shall fall from the head of any of you.

35 After *Paul* had spoken this, he took bread and gave thanks to God in presence of them all. When he had broken *it*, he began to eat.

36 Then they were all of good cheer and they also took *some* food.+

37 In all, there were two hundred *and* seventy six souls on the ship.

38 When they had eaten enough, they lightened the ship *by* casting out the wheat *that was left* into the sea.

39 When it was daylight, they did not recognize+ the land, but they discovered a certain creek with a shore into which they were of a mind+ to drive+ in the ship, if possible.

40 After they had taken away+ the anchors, they committed *themselves* to the sea. *Then they* loosened the rudder ropes,+ hoisted+ up the mainsail to the wind, and headed+ toward shore.

41 *They* fell into a place where two seas met *and* ran the ship aground. The fore part stuck fast and remained immovable but the stern+ was broken by the violence of the waves.

42 The soldiers' counsel was to kill the prisoners, lest any of them should swim out and escape.

43 But the centurion wanted to save Paul *so he* kept them from *their* purpose. *He* commanded that *those* who could swim should cast *themselves* first *into the sea* and get to land.

44 The rest *followed*, some on boards and some on *broken pieces* of the ship. And so it came to pass that they all escaped safely to land.

Acts Chapter 28

1 After they escaped, they learned+ that the island was called Malta.

2 The natives+ showed us no little kindness. They started+ a fire and accepted+ everyone because of the rain and cold.

3 When Paul gathered a bundle of sticks and laid *them* on the fire, a came viper out of the heat and fastened on his hand.

4 When the natives+ saw the *venomous* beast hang on his hand, they said among themselves: No doubt this man is a murderer *and* though he has escaped the sea, yet vengeance does not allow+ *him* to live.

5 *But Paul* shook the beast off *and* into the fire and felt no harm.

6 When they looked *at the place* where he should have swollen, *if not* suddenly fallen down dead, after they had looked *for* a great while and saw no harm had come to him, they changed their minds and said that he was a god.

7 In that same area+ was the home+ of the chief man of the island whose name was Publius. He received us courteously and lodged us *for* three days.

8 *Now* it came to pass that the father of Publius lay sick with a fever and dysentery. Paul went to him, prayed, laid his hands on him, and healed him.

9 After this, others on the island who had diseases also came *to Paul* and were healed.

10 *Therefore* they honored us with many honors *and* when we departed, they provided+ *for us* such things as were necessary.

11 After three months we left[+] in a ship from Alexandria that had wintered *there* on that island.[+] *That ship's* sign was Castor and Pollux.

12 *Upon* landing at Syracuse, we stayed[+] *there for* three days.

13 From there[+] we fetched a compass and came to Rhegium. After one day *there*, the south wind blew, and the next day we went to Puteoli.

14 There, we found family[+] who invited[+] us to stay[+] with them seven days. Then, we went toward Rome.

15 When the family[+] there heard about us, they came *from* as far *away* as *the* Appii Forum and *the* Three Taverns to meet us. When Paul saw *them*, he thanked God and was encouraged.

16 When we came to Rome, the centurion delivered the prisoners to the captain of the guard. But Paul was allowed[+] to live[+] by himself with a soldier to guard[+] him.

17 Now it came to pass that after three days, Paul called the chief of the Jews together. When they had come together, he said to them: Men *and* family,[+] though I have committed no *wrong* against the people or customs of our fathers, yet I was delivered *as a* prisoner from Jerusalem into the hands of the Romans.

18 After they examined me, *they* would have let *me* go because there was no *just* cause *to put* me to death.

19 But when the Jews spoke against *me*, I was compelled[+] to appeal to Caesar, *because* my nation did not have any[+] *just* accusation *against me*.

20 For this reason[+] therefore I have called for you to see *you* and to speak with *you*. *It is* because of the hope of Israel *that* I am bound with this chain.

21 They said to him: We did not receive *any* letters from Judea concerning you, nor *did* any of the family[+] who came *here* report[+] or speak of any harm *by* you.

22 But we desire to hear your thoughts concerning this sect. For we know that *people* everywhere are speaking against it.

23 *So* they appointed a day *and* many came to *hear* him at *his* lodging. From morning until evening, he testified and expounded *about* the kingdom of God *to* persuade them about Jesus from both the law of Moses and *from* the prophets.

24 Some believed the things that he said and some did not believe.

25 When they did not agree among themselves, they left[+] after Paul spoke one *final* word: Through the prophet Isaiah the Holy Spirit spoke well to our fathers

26 saying: Go to this people and say: Hearing, you will hear and not understand. Seeing, you will see and not perceive. *Matthew 13:14*

27 For the hearts of these people are calloused[+] and their ears are dull of hearing and they have closed their eyes, lest they should see with *their* eyes and hear with *their* ears and understand with *their* heart and be converted and *I would* heal them. *Matthew 13:15*

28 Therefore, let it be known to you that the salvation of God has been sent to the Gentiles and they will hear it.

29 After *Paul* said these words, the Jews left[+] and had a great debate[+] among themselves.

30 Paul then lived[+] *for* two whole years in his own rented[+] house and welcomed[+] all who came to him.

31 *He* proclaimed[+] the kingdom of God and taught those things that pertain[+] *to* the Lord Jesus Christ with all confidence *and* no one forbid him.

Romans Chapter 1

1 *From* Paul, a servant of Jesus Christ, called *to be* an apostle *and* separated to the Gospel of God.

2 *God* promised *this Gospel* before,[+] through His prophets in the Holy Scriptures.

3 *This Gospel* concerns His Son Jesus Christ, our Lord, who was made from the seed of David according to the flesh. *John 7:42*

4 *Jesus was* declared *to be* the Son of God, with power according to the spirit of holiness, from[+] the resurrection from the dead.

5 From *Him* we have received grace and
apostleship for obedience to the faith
among all the nations, for His name.
6 You also are called by Jesus Christ *to*
be among *the nations*.
7 To all who are in Rome, loved by
God, *and* called *to be* saints. Grace to
you and peace from God our Father and
Lord Jesus Christ.
8 First *of all*, I thank my God through
Jesus Christ for you all. Your faith is
spoken of throughout the whole world.
9 For God is my witness, whom I serve
in my spirit in the Gospel of His Son:
Without ceasing, I make mention of you
always in my prayers,
10 asking[+] if now *or* when I might have
a prosperous *journey*, by the will of God,
to come to you.
11 For I long to see you *so* that I may
impart to you *some* spiritual gift to
which you may be established:
12 That is, comforted together with
you through the mutual faith of both
you and me.
13 Now I do not want you to lack
understanding,[+] family.[+] Often times
I intended[+] to come to you *so* that I
might have *some* fruit among you
also, even as among other nations.[+]
But until now, *I* was prevented.[+]
14 I am obligated[+] to both the Greeks and
the Barbarians, to both the wise and the
unwise.
15 So, *with all that is* in me, I am ready to
proclaim[+] the Gospel to you who are in
Rome also.
16 For I am not ashamed of the Gospel of
Christ. For it is the power of God unto
salvation for everyone who believes. Both
to *the* Jew, first, and also to *the* Greek.

17 For the righteousness of God is
revealed from *believing* faith to faith
fully persuaded. As it is written: The
righteous[+] shall live by faith. *Hab. 2:4*

18 For the wrath of God is revealed
from heaven against all *the* ungodly
and unrighteous who hold *back* the
truth by unrighteousness.

19 Because what may be known of
God is revealed[+] within them, for
God has shown *it* to them.

20 For the invisible things of Him
from the creation of the world are
clearly seen *and* understood through
the things that are made, *even* His
eternal power and Godhead, *so*
unbelievers are without excuse.

21 Because, *even though* they knew God,
they did not glorify *Him* as God, nor
were *they* thankful. But *they* became
vain in their imaginations and their
foolish hearts were darkened.
22 Professing themselves to be wise, they
became fools
23 and changed the glory of the incorruptible God into an image made like
corruptible man and birds and four
footed *beasts* and creeping things.
24 Therefore, God gave them up to
uncleanness in the lusts of their hearts,
to dishonor their bodies between themselves.
25 *They* changed the truth of God into a lie
and worshiped and served the creature
more than the Creator who is blessed
forever. Amen.
26 For this reason,[+] God gave them up to
vile passions.[+] For even their women
did change the natural use into what is
against nature.
27 Likewise the men also abandoned[+]
natural joining[+] *together* with a woman
and burned in their lust toward one
another, men with men, doing[+] shame-
ful[+] *things* and receiving in themselves
the fitting[+] repayment[+] for their error.
28 And accordingly,[+] since[+] they did not
like to acknowledge[+] God, God gave
them over to a reprobate mind, to do
those things that are not proper.[+]
29 *Therefore,* being filled with all
unrighteousness, fornication, wickedness, covetousness, *and* maliciousness,
they were also full of envy, murder,
strife,[+] deceit, *and* ill will.[+] *And they*
were whisperers, *Matthew 15:19*

30 backbiters, haters of God, despiteful,
proud, boasters, inventors of evil things,
disobedient to parents,
31 without understanding, covenant
breakers, *given to* unnatural[+] affections,
unforgiving,[+] *and* unmerciful.
32 *Yet even* knowing the judgment of God,
that *those* who commit such things are
worthy of death, *they* not only do them,
but *also* consent[+] to *those* who do them.

Romans Chapter 2

1 Therefore you are inexcusable,
people,[+] whoever you are who judge.
For *in those things* in which you judge
another, you condemn yourself. For
you who judge do the same things.
2 But we are sure that the judgment of
God is according to truth against *those*
who commit such things.
3 Do you think this, *you* people who
judge *those* who do such things and do
the same, that you shall escape the
judgment of God?
4 Or do you despise the riches of His
goodness and forbearance and longsuffering, not understanding[+] that the
goodness of God leads you to repentance?
5 But according[+] to your hardness and
impenitent heart, *you* treasure up to
yourself wrath in the day of wrath and
revelation for

> the righteous judgment of God
> 6 will render to everyone[+]
> according to their deeds:
> *Matthew 16:27*
> 7 To *those* who,
> by patient continuance
> in well doing, seek for glory
> and honor and immortality,
> eternal life. *Proverbs 11:23*

8 But to *those* who are contentious and
do not obey the truth, but obey
unrighteousness, indignation and wrath,
Proverbs 11:23
9 tribulation and anguish upon every
soul of people who do evil. Of the Jew
first and also of the Gentile. *Proverbs 11:23*
10 But glory, honor, and peace, to everyone[+] who works good. To the Jew first
and also to the Gentile.
11 For there is no partiality[+] with God.
12 For all[+] *who* have sinned without law
will also perish without law, and as
many as have sinned in the law shall be
judged by the law.
13 For *it is* not the hearers of the law *who
are* righteous[+] before God, but the doers
of the law shall be justified.
14 For when the Gentiles who do not
have the law, do by nature the things
contained in the law, they, not having
the law, are a law to themselves.
15 This shows the work of the law written
in their hearts, their conscience also bearing
witness and *their* thoughts *in* the meanwhile accusing or else excusing one another
16 in the day when God will judge the
inner secrets of people's *hearts* by Jesus
Christ according to my Gospel.
17 Behold you *who* are called a Jew and rest
in the law and make your boast of God,
18 *you who* know *His* will and approve the
things that are more excellent, being
instructed out of the law,
19 *you who* are confident that you yourself are a guide to the blind, a light to
those who are in darkness,
20 an instructor of the foolish, a teacher
of babes, *you* who have the form of
knowledge and of the truth in the law.
21 Therefore you who teach another,
do you not teach yourself? You who
preach *that* people[+] should not steal,
do you steal?
22 You who say a man should not commit
adultery, do you commit adultery?
You who abhor idols, do you commit
sacrilege?
23 You who make your boast of the law,
do you dishonor God through breaking
the law?
24 For the name of God is blasphemed
among the Gentiles through you, as it is
written. *Isaiah 52:5*
25 For circumcision truly[+] benefits[+] if
you keep the law. But if you are a breaker
of the law, *then* your circumcision is
made uncircumcision.

26 Therefore if *those of* the uncircumcision
keep the righteousness of the law, shall
not their uncircumcision be counted for
circumcision?
27 Shall not *those of the* uncircumcision
which is by nature, if they fulfill the
law, judge you, who by the letter and
circumcision transgress the law?
28 For they are not outwardly Jews. *But*
neither *is* circumcision in the flesh *an*
outward *matter*.
29 But *they are* Jews who are *so* inwardly.
True circumcision *is* of the heart, in the
spirit, *and* not in the letter. Their praise
is not of men, but of God.

Romans Chapter 3

1 What advantage then has the Jew? Or
what benefit+ *is there* in circumcision?
2 Much *in* every way. Chiefly because, to
them were committed the oracles of God.
3 For what if some did not believe?
Shall their unbelief make the faith of
God without effect?
4 *That* cannot be.+ Yes, let God be true
but everyone *else* a liar. As it is written:
That you might be justified in your
sayings and might overcome when you
are judged. *Psalm 51:4*
5 But if our unrighteousness commend the
righteousness of God, what shall we say?
Is God unrighteous who takes vengeance?
Paul says, aside: I speak as a man.
6 *It* cannot be+ *that God would be unrighteous*.
For then how shall God judge the world?
7 For if the truth of God has more
abounded through my lie to His glory,
then why am I yet also judged as a sinner?
8 Not *rather*, as we *have been slanderously*
accused,+ and as some have affirmed
that we say: Let us do evil *so* that good
may come. Their judgment+ is just.
9 What then? Are we better *than they*?
No, in no way.+ For we have before
proved both Jews and Gentiles, that they
are all under sin.
10 As it is written: There are none righteous, no not one. *Psalm 14:3*
11 There are none who understand. There
are none who seek after God. *Psalm 14:2*
12 They have all gone out of the way and
they together have become unprofitable.
There are none who do good. No not one.
Psalm 14:1
13 Their throats *are* an open tomb.+ With
their tongues they have used deceit. The
poison of asps *is* under their lips. *Psalm 5:9*
14 Their mouth *is* full of cursing and
bitterness. *Psalm 10:7*
15 Their feet *are* swift to shed blood.
Isaiah 59:7
16 Destruction and misery *are* in their
ways. *Isaiah 59:7*
17 They have not known the way of
peace. *Isaiah 59:8*
18 There is no fear of God before their
eyes. *Psalm 36:1*
19 Now we know what things the law
declares. It says to *those* who are under
the law that every mouth may be stopped
and all the world may become guilty
before God.
20 Therefore by the deeds of the law no
flesh will be justified in His sight. For
by the law *is* the knowledge of sin.
21 But now the righteousness of God
without the law is revealed,+ being
witnessed by the law and the prophets.
22 The righteousness of God *comes* by
faith *in* Jesus Christ to all and upon all
who believe. For there is no difference.

23 For all have sinned
and come short
of the glory of God.

24 *All are* being justified freely by His
grace through the redemption that is in
Christ Jesus.
25 God has set *Jesus* forth *to be* a *means of*
reconciliation+ through faith in His
blood, to declare His righteousness for
the remission of sins that are past,
through the forbearance of God,
26 to declare His righteousness at this
time *so* that He might be just and the
justifier of *those* who believe in Jesus.
27 Where *is* boasting then? It is excluded.
By what law? Of works? No, but by the
law of faith.
28 Therefore we conclude that a person+

is justified by faith without the deeds of the law.

29 *Is God* the God of the Jews only? *Is He* not also of the Gentiles? Yes, of the Gentiles also.

30 Seeing *it is* one God who will justify the circumcision by faith and *the* uncircumcision through faith,

31 do we then make void the law through faith? *That* cannot be.[+] Yes *rather*, we establish the law.

Romans Chapter 4

1 What shall we say then that Abraham, our father as pertaining to the flesh, has found?

2 For if Abraham were justified by works, *then* he has *something in which* to rejoice,[+] but not before God.

3 For what do the Scriptures say? Abraham believed God and it was counted to him for righteousness. *Genesis 15:6*

4 Now to *those* who work, the reward is not counted[+] as grace, but as debt.

5 But to *those* who do not work, but believe in Him who justifies the ungodly, their faith is counted for righteousness.

6 Even as David also described the blessedness of those[+] to whom God credits[+] righteousness without works,

7 *he said*: Blessed *are* those whose iniquities are forgiven and whose sins are covered. *Psalm 32:1*

8 Blessed *are* those[+] whom the Lord does not make accountable[+] *for their* sin. *Psalm 32:2*

9 *Is* this blessedness, then, *only* upon the circumcision, or upon the uncircumcision also? For we say that faith was credited[+] to Abraham as righteousness.

10 How was it then credited[+]? When he was in circumcision or in uncircumcision? Not in circumcision, but in uncircumcision.

11 He received the sign of circumcision, a seal of the righteousness of the faith *he had while still* uncircumcised *so* that he might be the father of all who believe, *even* the uncircumcised, *so* that righteousness might be credited[+] to them also,

12 and the father of circumcision to *those* who are not of the circumcision only, but also *to those* who walk in the steps of that faith of our father Abraham, which *he had while he was still* uncircumcised.

13 For the promise, that he would be the heir of the world, *was* not to Abraham or to his seed through the law, but through the righteousness of faith.

14 For if *only those* who are of the law *are* heirs, *then* faith is made void and the promise *is* made of no effect.

15 Because the law works wrath. For where no law is, *there is* no transgression.

16 Therefore *it is* by faith, *and* that by *God's* grace, *that* the promise is assured[+] to all descendants,[+] not only to those who are of the law, but also to those who are of the faith of Abraham who is the father of us all.

17 As *it is* written: *I have* made you the father of many nations. *For you* believed God who gives life[+] *to* the dead and calls the not *existing into* what is *existing*. *Genesis 17:5*

18 Who against hope believed in hope that he might become the father of many nations according to what *God had* spoken: So shall your seed be. *Genesis 15:5*

19 Not being weak in faith, *Abraham* did not consider his own body already[+] dead when he was about a hundred years old, nor the deadness of Sarah's womb.

20 He did not stagger at the promise of God through unbelief. But *he* was strong in faith, giving glory to God,

21 being fully persuaded that what *God* had promised, He was also able to perform.

22 Therefore it was credited[+] to him for righteousness. *Genesis 15:6*

23 Now this was not written for *Abraham's* sake alone, that it was credited[+] to him.

24 But also for us to whom it shall be credited,[+] if we believe in Him who raised up Jesus our Lord from the dead,

25 who was delivered for our transgressions[+] and was raised again for our justification.

Romans Chapter 5

1 Therefore, being justified by faith, we
have peace with God through our Lord
Jesus Christ.
2 And through *Jesus*, we have access by
faith to this grace in which we stand.
And *we* rejoice in *the* hope of the glory
of God.
3 Not only *this*, but we rejoice+ in
tribulations also, knowing that

> tribulation produces+ patience,
> 4 patience *produces* experience,
> and experience *produces* hope.

5 And *it is* hope, not shame, *so* that the
love of God is shed abroad in our hearts
by the Holy Spirit who is given to us.
6 For when we were yet without strength,
in due time Christ died for the ungodly.
7 For scarcely will one die for a righteous
man. Yet perhaps+ for a good man some
would even dare to die.

> 8 But God commends His love
> toward us, in that,
> while we were yet sinners,
> Christ died for us.
> *Isaiah 53:5, John 3:16*

9 Much more then, now being justified
by His blood, we will be saved from
wrath through Him.
10 For if, when we were enemies, we
were reconciled to God by the death of
His Son, much more, being reconciled,
we will be saved by His life.
11 Not only *this*, but we also rejoice+ in
God through our Lord Jesus Christ from
whom we have now received atonement.
12 Therefore, as by one man sin entered
the world and death by sin, so death *is*
passed upon all people+ because+ all
have sinned.
13 For until the law, sin was in the world,
but sin is not chargeable+ when there is
no law.
14 Nevertheless, death reigned from
Adam until Moses, even over *those* who
had not sinned after the manner+ of the
transgression of Adam, who is symbolic+
of *Him who was* to come.
15 But the gift *is* not like the transgres-
sion+ *of Adam*. For if, through the
transgression+ of one, many are dead,
much more the grace of God and the gift
by grace, through one man, Jesus Christ,
has abounded to many.
16 The gift *is* not like *what came by* the one
who sinned. For the judgment *was* by
one to condemnation, but the free gift *is*
for many transgressions+ to justification.
17 For if by the transgression+ of one
death reigned through+ *that* one, *then*
much more shall *those* who receive
abundance of grace and the gift of
righteousness reign in life through+ one:
Jesus Christ.
18 Therefore, as by the transgression+ of
one *judgment came* upon all mankind+ to
condemnation, even so by the righteousness of one *the free gift came* upon
all people+ to justification of life.
19 For as by one man's disobedience
many were made sinners, so *also* by the
obedience of one many will be made
righteous.
20 Moreover the law entered *so* that the
transgression+ might abound. But where sin
abounded, grace did much more abound,
21 *so* that as sin has reigned to death, even
so might grace reign through righteousness
to eternal life by Jesus Christ our Lord.

Romans Chapter 6

1 What shall we say then? Shall we
continue in sin *so* that grace may abound?
2 *That* cannot be.+ How shall we who
are dead to sin, live any longer in it?
3 Do you not know that as many of us as
were baptized into Jesus Christ were
baptized into His death?
4 Therefore we are buried with Him by
baptism into death *so* that, as Christ was
raised up from the dead by the glory of
the Father, even so we also should walk
in newness of life.
5 For if we have been planted together
in the likeness of His death, *then* we will

also be *in the likeness* of *His* resurrection.
6 Know this: That our old self[+] is
crucified with *Him so* that the body of
sin might be destroyed, *so* that from
now on we would not serve sin.
7 For *those* who are dead are freed
from sin.
8 Now if we are dead with Christ, *then*
we believe that we will also live with
Him.
9 *We* know that Christ, being raised
from the dead, dies no longer.[+] Death
no longer[+] has dominion over Him.
10 For in that He died, He died to sin once.
But in that He lives, He lives to God.
11 Likewise count[+] yourselves to be dead
indeed to sin but alive to God through
Jesus Christ our Lord.
12 Therefore do not let sin reign in your
mortal body *so* that you obey it in its
lusts.
13 Do not submit[+] your members *to be*
instruments of unrighteousness to sin.
But submit[+] yourselves to God, as *people*
who are alive from the dead. *Make* your
members instruments of righteousness
to God.
14 For sin will not have dominion over
you, for you are not under the law, but
under grace.
15 What then? Shall we sin because we
are not under the law but under grace?
That cannot be.[+]
16 Do you not know that to whomever
you submit[+] yourselves *as* servants to
obey, you are *indeed* servants of whomever you obey: Whether sin unto death
or obedience unto righteousness?
17 But thanks *be* to God that *even though*
you were the servants of sin, you have
obeyed from the heart the example[+] of
doctrine that was delivered *to* you.
18 Therefore, being *set* free from sin,
you became servants of righteousness.
19 I speak after the manner of men because of the weakness[+] of your flesh.
For as you have yielded your members *as* servants to uncleanness and to
iniquity unto iniquity, even so now
submit[+] your members *to be* servants to
righteousness unto holiness.
20 For when you were the servants of sin,
you were free from righteousness.
21 What fruit did you have then in those
things about which you are now ashamed?
For the end of those things *is* death.
22 But now, being made free from sin
and *having* become servants to God, you
have your fruit to holiness, and the end:
eternal[+] life.

> 23 For the wages of sin *is* death,
> but the gift of God *is* eternal life
> through Jesus Christ our Lord.
> *Proverbs 11:19*

Romans Chapter 7

1 Do you not know, family,[+] for I speak
to *those* who know the law, that the law
has dominion over people[+] as long as
they live?
2 For the woman who has a husband is
bound by the law to *her* husband as long
as he lives. But if the husband is dead,
she is loosed from the law of *her*
husband.
3 So then if while *her* husband lives, she
is married to another man, *then* she shall
be called an adulteress. But if her
husband is dead, she is free from that
law, so she is no adulteress *even* though
she is married to another man.
4 Therefore my family,[+] you also have
become dead to the law by the body of
Christ *so* that you should be married to
another, *even* to *Christ* who is raised
from the dead, *so* that we would bring
forth fruit to God.
5 For when we were in the flesh, the
motions of sins *as exposed* by the law,
worked in our members to bring forth
fruit unto death.
6 But now we are delivered from the
law, being dead *to that* in which we
were held *so* that we might serve in
newness of spirit and not *in* the oldness
of the letter.
7 What shall we say then? *Is* the law sin?
That cannot be.[+] No, I would not have
known *about* sin, except[+] by the law.

For I would not have known *about* lust,
except the law said: You shall not covet.
8 But sin, taking occasion by the commandment, produced+ in me all kinds+
of abnormal appetites.+ For without the
law, sin *was* dead.
9 For I was alive without the law once.
But when the commandment came, sin
revived, and I died.
10 and found+ that the commandment that
was *intended* for life, *could lead* to death.
11 For sin, taking occasion by the commandment, deceived me and by it,
killed+ *me*.
12 Therefore the law *is* holy and the
commandment holy and just and good.
13 Then *was* what *is* good *a cause of*
death to me? *That* cannot be.+ But sin,
so that it might appear *as* sin, produced+
death in me by what is good, *so* that sin,
by the commandment, might become
exceedingly sinful.
14 For we know that the law is spiritual,
but I am worldly,+ sold under sin.
15 For what I do, I allow not. For what I
would *do*, that I do not. But what I hate,
that do I.
16 Then if I do what I would not *approve*,
I consent to the law that *it is* good.
17 Now then it is no longer+ I *myself*
doing it, but sin that dwells in me.
18 For I know that good does not dwell in
me, that is in my flesh. For to will *to do*
good is present within me but *how* to
perform what is good I do not find.
19 For the good that I want+ *to do*, I do not
do. But the evil that I do not *want to do*,
that I do.
20 Now if I do what I would not *want to*
do, *then* it is no longer+ I *myself* doing it,
but sin that dwells in me.
21 I find then a law: That when I would
want to do good, evil is present with me.
22 For I delight in the law of God
according+ *to* the inward man.
23 But I see another law in my members,
warring against the law of my mind and
bringing me into captivity to the law of
sin that is *lurking* in my members.
24 O wretched man that I am. Who shall
deliver me from the body of this death?
25 I thank God through Jesus Christ our
Lord. So then with the mind I myself
serve the law of God, but with the flesh
the law of sin.

Romans Chapter 8

> 1 Now *there is* no condemnation
> to *those* who are in Christ Jesus,
> who do not walk according+
> *to* the flesh but according+
> *to* the Spirit. *John 3:18*

2 For the law of the Spirit of life in
Christ Jesus has made me free from the
law of sin and death.
3 For what the law could not do, in that
it was weak through the flesh, God *by*
sending His own Son in the likeness of
sinful flesh and for sin, condemned sin
in the flesh,
4 *so* that the righteousness of the law
might be fulfilled in us, who do not walk
according+ *to* the flesh, but according+
to the Spirit.
5 For *those* who are after the flesh do
mind the things of the flesh. But *those*
who are after the Spirit *mind* the things
of the Spirit.
6 To be worldly+ minded *is* death. But
to be spiritually minded *is* life and
peace.
7 Because the worldly+ mind *is* enmity
against God, for it is not subject to the
law of God, nor indeed can *it* be.
8 So then, *those* who are in the flesh
cannot please God.
9 But you are not in the flesh, but in the
Spirit, if indeed+ the Spirit of God
dwells in you. Now if anyone does not
have the Spirit of Christ, they are not His.
10 If Christ *is* in you, *then* the body *is* dead
because of sin but the Spirit *is* life
because of righteousness.
11 But if the Spirit of Him who raised up
Jesus from the dead dwells in you, *then*
He who raised up Christ from the dead
will also give life+ *to* your mortal bodies
by His Spirit who dwells in you.
12 Therefore family,+ we are debtors,
not to the flesh to live after the flesh,

13 for if you live after the flesh you shall die.
But if you, through the Spirit, put to death+
the deeds of the body, you shall live.
14 For all+ *who* are led by the Spirit of
God are the children+ of God.
15 For you have not received the spirit of
bondage again to fear, but you have
received the Spirit of adoption through
whom we cry *out*: Abba Father.
16 The Spirit bears witness with our
spirit that we are the children of God.
17 If *we are* children, then *we are also*
heirs: Heirs of God and joint heirs with
Christ. If indeed+ we suffer with *Him so*
that we may also be glorified together.
18 For I reckon that the sufferings of this
present time *are* not worthy *to be compared*
with the glory that will be revealed in us.
19 For the earnest expectation of the
creation+ waits for the manifestation of
the children+ of God.
20 For the creation+ was made subject to
vanity, not willingly, but by reason of
Him who has subjected *it* in hope.
21 Because the creation+ itself will
also be delivered from the bondage of
corruption into the glorious liberty of
the children of God.
22 For we know that the whole creation
groans and labors+ in pain together
until now.
23 Not only *they*, but *we* ourselves also,
who have the first fruits of the Spirit,
even we ourselves groan within ourselves, waiting for the adoption, the
redemption of our body.
24 For we are *being* saved by hope. But
hope that is seen is not hope. For what
anyone *already* sees, why would they
still+ hope for *it*?
25 But if we hope for what we do not see,
then with patience we wait for *it*.
26 Likewise the Spirit also helps our
weaknesses.+ For we do not know how
to pray as we should. But the Spirit
intercedes for us with groanings more
profound+ *than words*.
27 *He* who searches the hearts knows the
mind of the Spirit because He makes
intercession for the saints according to
the will of God.

28 We know that
all things work together for good
to *those* who love God,
to *those* who are called
according to *His* purpose.
Matthew 6:33

29 For whom He did foreknow, He also
predestined *to be* conformed to the
image of His Son *so* that He might be the
firstborn among many others.+
30 Moreover *those* whom He predestined,
He also called. *Those* whom He called,
He also justified. *And those* whom He
justified, He also glorified.
31 What shall we then say to these things?

If God *is* for us,
who *can be* against us?

32 He did not spare His own Son, but
gave+ Him up for us all. How shall He not
with Him also freely give all things *to* us?
33 Who will lay anything to the charge of
God's elect? *It is* God who justifies.
34 Who condemns *us*? *It is* Christ who
died, and more *important* is risen again,
who is at the right hand of God and who
also makes intercession for us.
35 Who shall separate us from the love of
Christ? *Shall* tribulation or distress or
persecution or famine or nakedness or
peril or sword?
36 As it is written: For your sake we are
killed all the day long. We are accounted
as sheep for the slaughter. *Psalm 44:22*
37 No, in all these things we are more than
conquerors through Him who loved us.
38 For I am persuaded that

neither death nor life
nor angels nor principalities
nor powers nor things present
nor things to come
39 nor height nor depth
nor any other creature
will be able to separate us
from the love of God that is
in Christ Jesus our Lord.

Romans Chapter 9

1 I speak the truth in Christ. I do not lie.
My conscience *is* also bearing witness to
me in the Holy Spirit
2 that I have great heaviness and continual sorrow in my heart.
3 For I could wish that *I* myself were
accursed from Christ for *the sake of* my
family+ *and* my relatives+ according to
the flesh
4 who are Israelites to whom *was given*
the adoption and the glory and the
covenants and the giving of the law and
the service *of God* and the promises
5 whose *are* the fathers, and of whom,
as concerning the flesh, Christ who is
over all, God blessed forever. Amen.
6 Not as though the Word of God has
taken no effect. For they *are* not all
Israel who are from Israel.
7 Nor *are they*, because they are *from* the
seed of Abraham, all children. But in
Isaac shall your seed be called. *Genesis 21:12*
8 That is *to say*: Those *who are* children
of the flesh *are* not children of God. But
the children of the promise are counted
to *be* the seed.
9 For this *was* the word of promise: At
this time I will come and Sarah will have
a son. *Genesis 17:21*
10 Not only *that*, but Rebecca also conceived by one, by our father Isaac.
11 For *the children* not yet born nor having
done any good or evil, that the purpose of
God according to election might stand, not
of works, but of Him who calls,
12 it was said to her: The elder shall serve
the younger. *Genesis 25:23*
13 As it is written: Jacob I have loved, but
Esau I have hated. *Malachi 1:2*
14 What shall we say then? *Is there* unrighteousness with God? *That* cannot be.+
15 For He said to Moses: I will have
mercy on whom I will have mercy, and
I will have compassion on whom I will
have compassion. *Exodus 33:19*
16 So then, *it is* not of him who wills or
of him who runs, but of God who shows
mercy. *Exodus 33:19*
17 For the Scriptures said to Pharaoh:
Even for this same purpose I have
raised you up *so* that I might show my
power in you and *so* that my name
might be declared throughout all the
earth. *Exodus 9:16*
18 Therefore *God* has mercy on whomever He will *have mercy* and He *also*
hardens whomever He will.
19 Then you will say to me: Why does
He yet find fault? For who has resisted
His will?
20 Indeed,+ people,+ who are you to
reply against God? Shall the thing
formed say to the one who formed *it*:
Why have you made me thus?
21 Does the potter not have authority+
over the clay, of the same lump to make
one vessel to honor and another to
dishonor?
22 *What* if God, willing to show *His* wrath
and to make His power known, endured
with much longsuffering vessels of wrath
fitted for destruction?
23 Then He might make known the riches
of His glory on the vessels of mercy He
prepared for glory,
24 *even* us, whom He has called, not only
of the Jews, but also of the Gentiles?
25 As He also said in Hosea: I will call
them my people who were not my
people and *call* her beloved who was
not beloved. *Hosea 2:23*
26 It shall come to pass *that* in the place
where it was said to them: You *are* not
my people, there they shall be called the
children of the living God. *Hosea 1:10*
27 Isaiah also cried *out* concerning Israel:
Though the number of the children of
Israel be as the sand of the sea, a
remnant will be saved. *Isaiah 10:22*
28 For He will finish the work and cut *it*
short in righteousness, because the Lord
will make a short work upon the earth.
Matthew 24:22
29 As Isaiah said before: Except the Lord
of Sabaoth had left us a seed, we *would
have* been like Sodom and been made
like Gomorrah. *Isaiah 1:9*
30 What shall we say then? That the
Gentiles, who did not follow after

righteousness, have attained righteousness, even the righteousness that is by faith,

31 but Israel, which followed after the law of righteousness, has not attained to the law of righteousness.

32 Why? Because *it was* not by faith but by the works of the law. For they stumbled at that stumbling stone. *Isaiah 8:14*

33 As it is written: Behold I lay in Zion+ a stumbling stone and rock of offense. Whoever believes in Him will not be ashamed. *Isaiah 28:16*

Romans Chapter 10

1 Family,+ my heart's desire and prayer to God for Israel is that they might be saved.

2 For I testify+ that they have a zeal for God, but not according to knowledge.

3 For they, being ignorant about God's righteousness and going about to establish their own righteousness, have not submitted themselves to the righteousness of God.

4 For Christ *is* the end of the law for righteousness to everyone who believes.

5 For Moses described the righteousness that is *attained* by *obedience to* the law: That those who do those things shall live by them. *Leviticus 18:5*

6 But the righteousness of faith speak in this way: Do not say in your heart: Who shall ascend into heaven? *For* that is to bring Christ down *from above*. *Deuteronomy 30:12*

7 Or *do not say*: Who shall descend into the deep? *For* that is to bring Christ up from the dead. *Deuteronomy 30:13*

8 But what does it say? The Word is near you, *even* in your mouth and in your heart. That is the Word of faith we proclaim+: *Deuteronomy 30:14*

9 If you confess with your mouth the Lord Jesus and believe in your heart that God has raised Him from the dead, you will be saved. *Matthew 10:32*

10 For with their hearts, people+ believe unto righteousness, *and* with their mouths confession is made unto salvation.

11 For the Scriptures declare: Whoever believes in Him will not be ashamed. *Isaiah 28:16*

12 For there is no difference between the Jew and the Greek. For the same Lord over all is rich toward all who call upon Him.

13 For whoever will call upon the name of the Lord will be saved. *Joel 2:32*

14 How then will they call on Him in whom they have not believed? And how will they believe in Him of whom they have not heard? And how will they hear without *someone* proclaiming *the Word*?

15 And how will they proclaim+ *the Word* unless they are sent? As it is written: How beautiful are the feet of *those* who proclaim+ the Gospel of peace and bring glad tidings of good things. *Isaiah 52:7*

16 But they have not all obeyed the Gospel. For Isaiah says: Lord, who has believed our report? *Isaiah 53:1*

17 So then, faith *comes* by hearing and hearing by the Word of God.

18 But I say: Have they not heard? Yes truly,+ the sound of their *voices* went into all the earth and their words to the ends of the world. *Psalm 19:4*

19 But I say: Did Israel not know? First Moses says: I will provoke you to jealousy by *those who are* no people *and* by a foolish nation I will anger you. *Deuteronomy 32:21*

20 Isaiah boldly said: I was found by *those* who did not seek me. I was revealed+ to *those* who did not ask for me. *Isaiah 65:1*

21 But to Israel He says: All day long I have stretched forth my hands to a disobedient and rebellious+ people. *Isaiah 65:2*

Romans Chapter 11

1 I say then: Has God cast away His people? *That* cannot be.+ For I also am an Israelite, of the seed of Abraham, *of* the tribe of Benjamin.

2 God has not cast away His people whom He foreknew. Do you not know+ what the Scripture says about Elijah?

How He makes intercession to God against Israel saying:

3 Lord, they have killed your prophets and torn[+] down your altars. I am left alone and *now* they seek my life. *1 Kings 19:10*

4 But what does the answer of God say to him? I have reserved to myself seven thousand men who have not bowed the knee to Baal. *1 Kings 19:18*

5 Even so then, at this present time also, there is a remnant according to the election of grace.

6 If by grace, then *is it* no longer[+] of works. Otherwise grace is no longer[+] grace. But if *it is* from works, then is it no longer[+] grace. Otherwise work is no longer[+] work.

7 What then? Israel has not obtained what it sought.[+] Except the elect[+] obtained it and the rest were blinded.

8 As it is written: God has given the spirit of slumber *to* them, eyes that *do* not see and ears that *do* not hear, *even* to this day. *Isaiah 29:10*

9 And David said: Let their table be made a snare and a trap and a stumbling block and a repayment[+] to them. *Psalm 69:22*

10 Let their eyes be darkened *so* that they may not see and bow down their back always. *Psalm 69:23*

11 I say then: Have they stumbled *so* that they should fall? *That* cannot be.[+] But *rather* through their transgressions,[+] salvation *has come* to the Gentiles to provoke them to jealousy.

12 Now if their transgressions[+] *bring about* the riches of the world, and the diminishing of them *bring* riches to the Gentiles, how much more *shall* their fullness *be*?

13 For I speak to you Gentiles, inasmuch as I am the apostle to the Gentiles *and* I delight[+] in serving[+] *you*.

14 If by any means I may provoke to jealousy[+] *those who are of* my *own* flesh and *thereby* rescue[+] some of them.

15 For if the casting away of them *produce* the reconciling of the world, what *will* the receiving *of them be*, but life from the dead?

16 For if the first fruit *is* holy, the lump *is* also *holy*. If the root *is* holy, so *are* the branches.

17 If some of the branches are broken off, and you, being a wild olive tree, were grafted in among them, and with them partake of the root and fatness of the olive tree,

18 do not boast against the branches. But if you boast, *remember* you do not bear the root, but the root *bears* you.

19 Then you may say: The branches were broken off *so* that I might be grafted in.

20 Well, *it was* because of unbelief *that* they were broken off, and by faith *that* you stand. Do not be high minded, but fear.

21 For if God did not spare the natural branches, *take heed* lest He also not spare you.

22 Behold therefore the goodness and *the* severity of God. Severity on *those* who fell, but goodness toward you if you continue in *His* goodness. Otherwise you also will be cut off.

23 They also, if they do not abide still in unbelief, will be grafted in. For God is able to graft them in again.

24 For if you were cut out of the olive tree that is wild by nature and were grafted into a good olive tree, contrary to nature, *then* how much more shall these who are the natural *branches* be grafted *back* into their own olive tree?

25 For I would not, family,[+] want you to be ignorant of this mystery, lest you should be wise in your own conceits: That, in part, blindness is happened to Israel until the fullness of the Gentiles has come in.

26 So, all Israel will be saved. As it is written: There shall come out of Zion[+] the Deliverer, and turn ungodliness away from Jacob. *Isaiah 59:20*

27 For this *is* my covenant to them, when I shall take away their sins. *Isaiah 27:9*

28 As concerning the Gospel, *they are* enemies for your sakes. But concerning the elect,[+] *they are* beloved for the fathers' sakes.

29 For the gifts and calling of God *are* not to be repented.[+]

30 For as you in times past have not believed God, yet now *you* have received+ mercy through their unbelief.
31 Now these also have not believed *so* that through your mercy they also may receive+ mercy.
32 For God has determined+ them all *to be* in unbelief *so* that He might have mercy upon *them* all.
33 O the depth of the riches in both the wisdom and knowledge of God. How unsearchable *are* His judgments and His ways past finding out.
34 For who has known the mind of the Lord? Or who has been His counselor? *Isaiah 40:13*
35 Or who has first given to Him and it shall be repaid+ to them again? *Job 41:11*
36 For from Him and through Him and to Him *are* all things. To Him *be* glory forever. Amen.

Romans Chapter 12

1 Therefore I urge+ you family,+ by the mercies of God to present your bodies*as* a living sacrifice, holy *and* acceptable to God, *as* your reasonable service.

2 Do not be conformed to this world.
But be transformed
by the renewing of your mind
so that you may prove
what *is* that good and acceptable
and perfect will of God.

3 For through the grace given to me, I say to everyone+:

Do not think *of yourselves*+
more highly than you+ ought to
think, but think soberly,
as God has divided+ to everyone+
a measure of faith.

4 For as we have many members in one body, and all members do not have the same work+ *to do*,
5 so *also* we, *being* many, are one body in Christ, and everyone members one of *one* another.
6 But *we* have different gifts according to the grace that is given to us. If+ *our gift is* prophecy, *let us prophesy* according to the proportion of faith.
7 Or *if* ministry, in ministering. Or *those* who teach, in teaching.
8 Or *those* who exhort, in exhortation. *Those* who give, *let them do it* with simplicity. *Those* who rule, with diligence. *Those* who show mercy, with cheerfulness.

9 *Let* love be
without dissimulation.
Abhor what is evil.
Cleave to what is good.
10 *Be* kindly affectionate+
to one another, with brotherly love,
in honor preferring one another.

11 *Do* not *be* lazy+ in diligence.+ *But be* fervent in spirit in the time+ of serving.
12 Rejoice in hope. *Be* patient in tribulation. Continue *steadfastly* in prayer.
13 Distribute to the necessity of *the* saints. *And be* given to hospitality.
14 Bless *those* who persecute you. Bless and do not curse. *Matthew 05:44*
15 Rejoice with *those* who do rejoice and weep with *those* who weep.
16 *Be* of the same mind toward one another. Do not mind high things, but condescend to people+ of low estate. Do not be wise in your own conceits. *Proverbs 3:7*
17 Repay+ evil for evil to no one. *Rather* provide *what is* honest in the sight of everyone.+ *Matthew 5:39*
18 If possible, as much as lies in you, live peaceably with everyone.+ *Proverbs 12:18*
19 Beloved, do not avenge yourselves, but *rather* yield+ *the* place *of* wrath *to God*. For it is written: Vengeance *is* mine. I will repay, says the Lord. *Deuteronomy 32:35, Proverbs 20:22*
20 Therefore, if your enemy *is* hungry, feed him. If he *is* thirsty, give him *a* drink. For in so doing you will heap coals of fire on his head. *Proverbs 25:21*
21 Do not be overcome by evil, but overcome evil with good.

Romans Chapter 13

1 Let every soul be subject to the higher
authorities[+] *and powers*. For there is no
authority[+] *or power* but *what comes*
from[+] God. The authorities that exist[+]
are ordained by God.
2 Therefore, whoever resists authorities[+] *and powers*, resists the ordinance of
God and *those* who resist will receive
judgment[+] upon themselves.
3 For rulers are not a terror to good
works, but to evil. *So*, do you want[+] to
be unafraid of the authorities[+]? *Then* do
what is good and you will have praise
from *them*.
4 For they are ministers of God to you
for good. But if you do what is evil, *then*
be afraid. For they do not bear the
sword in vain. They are ministers of
God and avengers[+] to *execute* wrath
upon *those* who do evil.
5 Therefore *you* need to be subject *to*
them, not only because[+] of *fear of their*
wrath, but also for conscience sake.
6 *It is* for this reason[+] *that* you pay
tribute, also. For they are God's ministers, attending continually upon this
very thing.
7 Therefore, render to all their dues:
Tribute to whom tribute *is due*. Custom
to whom custom. Fear to whom fear.
Honor to whom honor.

8 Owe no one anything,
but to love one another.
For *those* who love *one* another
have fulfilled the law. *John 13:34*

9 For these *commandments*: You shall
not commit adultery, you shall not kill,
you shall not steal, you shall not bear
false witness, you shall not covet, *and* if
there is any other commandment, *all* are
briefly summarized[+] in this saying:
You shall love your neighbor as yourself. *Matthew 19:18,19, Exodus 20:13-17*
10 *True* love works no ill toward one's
neighbor. Therefore *true* love *is* the
fulfilling of the law.
11 Also, knowing the time, *know* that now
is the time to awake out of sleep, for now
our salvation *is* nearer than when we
first believed.
12 The night is far spent. The day is *very*
near.[+] Therefore, let us cast off the
works of darkness and let us put on the
armor of light.

13 Let us walk honestly, as in the day.
Not in rioting and drunkenness.
Not in chambering and wantonness.
Not in strife and envying.

14 But put on the Lord Jesus Christ and
do not make provision for the flesh, to
fulfill the lusts *thereof*.

Romans Chapter 14

1 Receive *those* who are weak in the
faith, *but* not to doubtful disputations.
2 For some believe that they may eat
everything. Others, who are weak, eat
only herbs.
3 Do not let *those* who eat despise *those*
who do not eat. Do not let *those* who do
not eat judge *those* who eat. For God has
received them.
4 Who are you to judge another's
servants? To their own masters they
stand or fall. Yes, they shall be held[+]
up, for God is able to make them stand.
5 One person[+] esteems one day above
another. Others esteem every day *alike*.
Let everyone[+] be fully persuaded in
their own mind.
6 *Those* who regard the day, regard *it* to
the Lord. *Those* who do not regard the
day, *it is* to the Lord *that* they do not
regard*it*. *Those* who eat, eat to the Lord,
for they give God thanks. *Those* who do
not eat, *it is* to the Lord *that* they do not
eat, and give God thanks.
7 For none of us lives to ourselves, and
no one dies to themselves.
8 For if we live, we live to the Lord *and*
if we die, we die to the Lord. Therefore,
whether we live or die, we are the Lord's.
9 For to this end Christ both died and
rose and revived *so* that He might be

Lord of both the dead and *the* living.
10 But why do you judge your brother?
Or why do you belittle[+] your brother?
For we shall all stand before the judgment
seat of Christ.
11 For it is written: *As* I live, says the Lord,
every knee shall bow to me, and every
tongue shall confess to God. *Isaiah 45:23*
12 So then everyone of us shall give
account of themselves to God.
13 Therefore, let us not judge one another
any more. But judge this instead[+]: That
no one put a stumbling block or an
occasion to fall in another's way.
14 I know and am persuaded by the Lord
Jesus, that *there is* nothing unclean of
itself. But to *those* who consider[+] anything to be unclean, to them *it is* unclean.
15 But if another[+] is grieved because of
your food,[+] *then* you are not walking *in*
true love. Do not destroy one for whom
Christ died because of your food.[+]
16 Do not let your good be evil spoken of.
17 For the kingdom of God is not food[+]
and drink, but righteousness and peace
and joy in the Holy Spirit.
18 For *those* who serve Christ in these
things *are* acceptable to God and
approved by mankind.[+]

19 Therefore, let us follow
after the things that make for peace
and things with which
one may edify another.

20 Do not destroy the work of God for
the sake of food.[+] All things indeed *are*
pure, but evil for that person[+] who
stumbles[+] by eating.
21 *It is* good to not eat flesh or drink wine
or *do anything* by which another[+]
stumbles or is offended *and caused to sin*
or is made weak.
22 Do you have faith? Have *it* to yourself
before God. Blessed *are those* who do
not condemn themselves in what they
allow.
23 *Those* who doubt are damned if they
eat because *they do* not *eat* in faith. For
whatever *is* not of faith is sin.

Romans Chapter 15

1 We who are strong ought to bear the
infirmities of the weak and not *live* to
please ourselves.
2 Let everyone of us please *their* neighbor for *their* good to edification.
3 For even Christ did not please Himself, but as it is written: The reproaches
of *those* who reproached you fell on me.
Psalm 69:9
4 For whatever things were written previously[+] were written for our learning
so that we, through patience and comfort
of the Scriptures, might have hope.
5 Now the God of patience and consolation grant you to be like minded toward
one another according to Christ Jesus
6 *so* that you may with one mind *and* one
mouth glorify the God and Father *of* our
Lord Jesus Christ.
7 Therefore receive one another as Christ
also received us, to the glory of God.
8 Now I say that Jesus Christ was a
minister of the circumcision for the
truth of God to confirm the promises
made to the fathers
9 *so* that the Gentiles might glorify God
for *His* mercy. As it is written: For this
reason[+] I will confess to you among the
Gentiles and sing to your name. *Psalm 18:49*
10 Again he said: Rejoice you Gentiles,
with His people. *Deuteronomy 32:43*
11 And again: Praise the Lord all you
Gentiles. Praise[+] Him, all you people.
Psalm 117:1
12 Again, *as* Isaiah said: There will be a
root of Jesse who will rise to reign over
the Gentiles. The Gentiles will trust in
Him. *Isaiah 11:10*
13 Now the God of hope fill you with all
joy and peace in believing *so* that you
may abound in hope through the power
of the Holy Spirit.
14 I myself am also persuaded about you,
my family,[+] that you also are full of
goodness, filled with all knowledge,
and able to admonish one another.
15 Nevertheless, family,[+] I have written
more boldly to you in some sort, as

putting you in mind, because of the
grace that is given to me from God,
16 that I should be the minister of Jesus
Christ to the Gentiles, ministering the
Gospel of God *so* that the offering up of
the Gentiles might be acceptable, being
sanctified by the Holy Spirit.
17 Therefore, I have reason+ to rejoice+
through Jesus Christ in those things that
pertain to God.
18 For I do not dare to speak *about*
anything *other than* what Christ accom-
plished+ *using* me to *make the* Gentiles
obedient, by word and deed,
19 through mighty signs and wonders by
the power of the Spirit of God so that,
from Jerusalem and *all* around+ to
Illyricum, I have fully proclaimed+ the
Gospel of Christ.
20 And so, I have endeavored+ to pro-
claim+ the Gospel, not where Christ
was *already* named, lest I should build
upon another's foundation,
21 but as it is written: To whom He was not
spoken of, they shall see. *Those* who have
not heard shall understand. *Isaiah 52:15*
22 For this cause also I have been much
hindered from coming to you.
23 But now, having no more place *to go*
in these parts, and having a great desire
these many years to come to you,
24 whenever I take my journey into Spain,
I will come to you. For I trust to see
you on my journey, and to be brought to
you on my way there, if I *may* be some-
what filled by your *company* first.
25 But *for* now I *am* going to Jerusalem to
minister to the saints *there*.
26 For it has pleased those of Macedonia
and Achaia to make a certain contribu-
tion for the poor saints who are at
Jerusalem.
27 It has truly+ pleased them. They are
indebted to them. For if the Gentiles
have been made partakers of their
spiritual things, *then it* is their duty
also to minister to them in *their needs*
in the flesh.+
28 Therefore, when I have performed
this and have sealed this fruit to them, I
will come to you *on the way* to Spain.
29 I am sure that when I come to you, I
will come in the fullness of the blessing
of the Gospel of Christ.
30 Now I urge you, family,+ for the sake
of the Lord Jesus Christ and for the love
of the Spirit, that you strive together
with me in *your* prayers to God for me
31 *so* that I may be delivered from *those*
who do not believe in Judea, *so* that my
service for Jerusalem may be accepted
by the saints,
32 *and so* that I may come to you with joy
by the will of God and may be refreshed
with you.
33 Now the God of peace *be* with you all.
Amen.

Romans Chapter 16

1 I commend to you Phebe our sister,
who is a servant of the assembly+ at
Cenchrea.
2 Receive her in the Lord, as becomes
saints, and assist her in whatever business
she has need of you. For she has been a
helper+ of many and of me also.
3 Greet Priscilla and Aquila, my helpers
in Christ Jesus
4 who have laid down their own necks
for my life. Not only *do* I give thanks to
them, but so *do* all the assemblies+ of
the Gentiles.
5 Likewise *greet* the assembly+ that is
in their house. Greet+ my beloved
Epaenetus, who is the first fruits of
Achaia to Christ.
6 Greet Mary, who bestowed much
labor on us.
7 Greet+ Andronicus and Junia, my
relatives+ and my fellow prisoners who
are of note among the apostles *and* who
also were in Christ before me.
8 Greet Amplias my beloved in the Lord.
9 Greet+ Urbane, our helper in Christ,
and Stachys my beloved.
10 Greet+ Apelles *who is* approved in
Christ. Greet+ *those* who are of *the*
household of Aristobulus.
11 Greet Herodion, my kinsman. Greet
those who are of the *household* of
Narcissus who are in the Lord.

12 Greet+ Tryphena and Tryphosa who
labor in the Lord. Greet+ the beloved
Persis who labored much in the Lord.
13 Greet+ Rufus, chosen in the Lord, and
his mother and mine.
14 Greet+ Asyncritus, Phlegon, Hermas,
Patrobas, Hermes, and the *members of*
the family+ who are with them.
15 Greet+ Philologus and Julia, Nereus
and his sister, Olympas, and all the
saints who are with them.
16 Greet+ one another with a holy kiss.
The assemblies+ of Christ *all* greet+ you.
17 Now I urge you, family+: Note+ *those*
who cause divisions and offenses
contrary to the doctrine you have learned.
Avoid them.
18 For such *people* do not serve our Lord
Jesus Christ, but their own belly. By
good *sounding* words and *a pretense of*
speaking blessings+ *they* deceive the
hearts of the simple,
19 for your obedience has become known+
to everyone.+ Therefore, I rejoice+ about
you. But yet, I would have you *be* wise to
what is good and simple concerning evil.
20 The God of peace will bruise Satan
under your feet soon.+ The grace of our
Lord Jesus Christ *be* with you. Amen.
21 Timothy my fellow worker and Lucius
and Jason and Sosipater, my relatives,+
greet+ you.
22 I Tertius who wrote *this* epistle greet+
you in the Lord.
23 Gaius, my host, and of the whole
assembly+ greets+ you. Erastus the
chamberlain of the city greets+ you, and
also Quartus, a brother.
24 The grace of our Lord Jesus Christ
be with you all. Amen.
25 Now unto Him who has the power to
strengthen+ you according to my
Gospel and *my* proclaiming+ of Jesus
Christ according to the revelation of the
mystery *that was previously* silent+ *since*
time+ began
26 but is now revealed+ by the Scriptures
of the prophets *and* according to the
commandment of the eternal+ God *to*
make *this* known to all nations for the
obedience of faith:
27 To God only wise, *be* glory through
Jesus Christ forever. Amen.

This epistle was written at Corinth and was sent to the Romans by Phebe, a servant of the church at Cenchrea.

1 Corinthians Chapter 1

1 *From* Paul, called *to be* an apostle of
Jesus Christ through the will of God,
and *from* Sosthenes *our* brother.
2 To the assembly+ of God at Corinth.
To *those* who are sanctified in Christ
Jesus *and* called *to be* saints, *along* with
everyone in every place who calls upon
the name of Jesus Christ our Lord, both
their *Lord* and ours.
3 Grace to you and peace from God our
Father and Lord Jesus Christ.
4 I thank my God always for you, for the
grace of God that is given *to* you by
Jesus Christ,
5 *knowing* that in everything you are
enriched by Him, in all utterance and *in*
all knowledge,
6 even as the testimony of Christ was
confirmed in you,
7 so that you are not lacking+ in any gift
while waiting for the coming of our Lord
Jesus Christ.
8 And *Christ* will confirm you to the end
so that you may be blameless in the day of
our Lord Jesus Christ.
9 God *is* faithful *and* you were called by
Him into fellowship with His Son Jesus
Christ our Lord.
10 Now I urge you, family,+ by the name
of our Lord Jesus Christ, that you all
speak the same thing and *that* there be
no divisions among you, but *that* you

be perfectly joined together
in the same mind
and in the same judgment.

11 For it has been declared to me about
you, my family,+ by those *who are of*
the house of Chloe, that there are
contentions among you. *Proverbs 6:19*
12 Now I say this, *noting* that each of you

says: I am of Paul, or I of Apollos or I
of Cephas or I of Christ.
13 Is Christ divided? Was Paul crucified
for you or were you baptized in the
name of Paul?
14 I thank God that I baptized none of you
except[+] Crispus and Gaius,
15 lest anyone should say that I had
baptized in my own name.
16 I also baptized the household of
Stephanas, *but* besides *that*, I do not
know if I baptized any others.
17 For Christ did not send me to baptize,
but to proclaim[+] the Gospel. *Yet* not
with *the* wisdom of words, lest the cross
of Christ should be made of no effect.
18 For the proclaiming[+] of the cross is
foolishness to *those* who *will* perish. But
to *those of* us who are being saved it is
the power of God.
19 For it is written: I will destroy the
wisdom of the wise and bring to nothing the
understanding of the prudent. *Isaiah 29:14*
20 Where *are* the wise? Where *is* the
scribe? Where *is* the disputer of this
world? Has God not made the wisdom
of this world foolishness?
21 Because, in the wisdom of God, the world
would not know *or understand* God through
human wisdom. *Instead,* it pleased God to
save *those* who *would* believe *through* the
simpleness[+] of proclaiming[+] *the Word.*
22 For the Jews require a sign and the
Greeks seek after wisdom.
23 But we proclaim[+] Christ crucified. To
the Jews *He is* a stumbling block and to
the Gentiles *He is* foolishness.
24 But to *those* who are called, both Jews
and Greeks, Christ *is* the power of God
and the wisdom of God.
25 Because the foolishness of God is
wiser than men, and the weakness of
God is stronger than men.
26 For you see *in* your *being* called,
family,[+] that not many wise according[+]
to the flesh, not many mighty, *and* not
many noble *are called.*
27 But God has chosen the foolish things
of the world to confound the wise. God
has chosen the weak things of the world
to confound the things that are mighty.
28 God has chosen *the* lowly[+] of the
world and the despised and things that
are not *mighty and noble*, *in order* to bring
to nothing the things that are *thought by
the world to be mighty and noble*,
29 *so* that no flesh would boast[+] in His
presence.
30 But from Him, you are in Christ Jesus
who by God was made wisdom and
righteousness and sanctification and
redemption to us,
31 *so* that, as it is written: *Those* who
would boast,[+] let them boast[+] *only* in the
Lord. *Psalm 105:3*

1 Corinthians Chapter 2

1 When I came to you, family,[+] I did not
come with excellent speech or wisdom,
declaring to you the testimony of God.
2 For I determined to not know anything
among you except Jesus Christ, and
Him crucified.
3 I was with you in weakness and fear
and much trembling.
4 My speech and my proclaiming[+] *was*
not with enticing words of man's
wisdom, but in demonstration of the
Spirit and of power,
5 *so* that your faith would not stand on the
wisdom of men, but in the power of God.
6 However we speak wisdom among
those who are perfect, but *it is* not the
wisdom of this world or of the princes
of this world who come to nothing.
7 But we speak the wisdom *that* God hid
in mystery. *And* God predetermined[+]
all this for our glory before the world
began.
8 None of the princes of this world
understood[+] this. For if they had understood *it*, they would not have crucified
the Lord of glory.
9 But as it is written: Eye has not seen
nor ear heard nor has *it* entered the
heart of mankind,[+] the things that God
has prepared for *those* who love Him.
Isaiah 64:4
10 But God has revealed *them* to us by His
Spirit, for the Spirit searches all things.
Yes, the deep things of God.

11 For who understands[+] the things of
mankind,[+] except[+] the spirit within
them? Likewise, no one understands the
things of God but the Spirit of God.
12 Now we have not received the spirit of
the world, but the Spirit of God, *so* that
we might know the things that are freely
given to us by God.
13 *We* do not speak in the words taught
by the wisdom of mankind, but *in words*
taught *by the* Holy Spirit, *considering*
and comparing spiritual *concepts with*
spiritual *words*.

> 14 For natural man
> does not comprehend[+]
> the things of the Spirit of God,
> for they are foolishness to them.
> Neither can they know *them*,
> because they are
> spiritually discerned.

15 But *those* who are spiritual judge all
things. Yet they themselves are judged
by no one.
16 For who has known the mind of the
Lord, that they might *presume to* instruct
Him? But we have the mind of Christ.
Isaiah 40:13,14

1 Corinthians Chapter 3

1 Family,[+] I have not spoken to you as
to spiritual *people*, but as to worldly[+]
people, *even* as to babes in Christ.
2 I have fed you with milk and not with
solid food.[+] Because until now,[+] you
have not been able *to bear it*, nor are you
able now.
3 For you are still[+] worldly.[+] For among
you *there is* envying and strife and
divisions. Are you not *still* worldly[+]
and walking in fleshly[+] *desires*?
4 For while one says: I am of Paul, and
another: I *am* of Apollos. Are you not
worldly[+]?
5 Who then is Paul and who *is* Apollos,
but ministers through whom you believed,
even as the Lord gave to everyone[+]?
6 I have planted and Apollos watered.
But God gave the increase.
7 So then, *those* who plant are not anything *special*, nor are *those* who water.
But *it is* God who gives the increase.
8 Now *those* who plant and *those* who
water are one. Everyone will receive
their own reward according to their own
labor.
9 For we are laborers together with
God. You are God's husbandry. *You are*
God's building.
10 According to the grace of God that is
given to me as a wise master builder, I
have laid the foundation and another
builds *upon it*. But let everyone[+] take
heed how they build.
11 For no other foundation can anyone
lay than the *one already* laid, *and* that is
Jesus Christ.
12 Now if anyone builds upon this
foundation: Gold, silver, precious
stones, wood, hay, *or* stubble,
13 everyone's work will be revealed.[+]
For the *judgment* day will declare it
because it will be revealed by fire.

> Fire will test[+]
> everyone's[+] work
> *to see* of what sort it is.

14 If anyone's work builds *something that*
will last,[+] *they* will receive a reward.
15 If anyone's work shall be burned *up*,
then they will suffer loss, but they
themselves will be saved, even though
through fire.
16 Do you not know that you are the
temple of God and *that* the Spirit of God
dwells in you?
17 If anyone defiles the temple of God,
God will destroy them. For the temple of God
is holy *and* you are *one of those temples*.
18 Let no one deceive themselves. If
anyone among you seems to be wise in
this world, let them become a fool *so*
that they may become wise.
19 For the wisdom of this world is
foolishness with God. For it is written:
He frustrates[+] the wise in their own
craftiness. *Job 5:13*
20 Again, The Lord knows the thoughts
of the wise, that they are vain. *Psalm 94:11*

21 Therefore let no one boast[+] in mankind.[+] For all things are yours.
22 Whether Paul or Apollos or Cephas or
the world or life or death or things
present or things to come: All are yours
23 and you are Christ's and Christ *is*
God's.

1 Corinthians Chapter 4

1 Let mankind[+] count us as ministers of
Christ and stewards of the mysteries of
God.
2 Now, it is required in stewards that
they be found faithful.
3 As for me, it is a very small thing that
I should be judged by you or by the
judgment of mankind.[+] Nor do I judge
myself.
4 For I know nothing in myself, and *it is*
not in this *that* I am justified, but *it* is
the Lord who will judge me.
5 Therefore, do not judge anything
before the time, until the Lord comes
who will bring to light the hidden things
of darkness and reveal[+] the counsels of
the hearts. Then shall everyone[+] have
praise from God.
6 Now family,[+] I have applied these
things to myself and *to* Apollos *as an*
example for you *so* that you might learn
from us to not think *that you know* more
than what has been written. None of you
should be puffed up against one another.
7 For who makes you different *from*
another? And what do you have that you
did not receive? Now if you received *it*,
then why do you boast[+] as if you had not
received *it*?
8 Now you are full. Now you are rich.
You have reigned as kings without us. I
wish[+] to God *that* you did reign *so* that
we might also reign with you.
9 For I think that God has set us forth as
apostles last appointed to death. For we
are made a spectacle to the world and to
angels and to people.[+]
10 We *are* fools for Christ's sake, but you
are wise in Christ. We *are* weak, but
you *are* strong. You *are* honored, but
we *are* despised.
11 Even to this present hour we both
hunger and thirst and are naked and are
buffeted and have no certain dwelling
place.
12 *We* labor working with our own hands.
Being reviled, we bless. Being persecuted, we suffer it.
13 Being defamed, we entreat. We are
made like the filth of the world *and* the
rubbish[+] of all things to this day.
14 I do not write these things to shame
you, but as my beloved children,[+] I
warn *you*.
15 For though you have ten thousand
instructors in Christ, yet *you do* not
have many fathers. For in Christ Jesus
I have fathered[+] you through the Gospel.
16 Therefore I urge[+] you: Be followers
of me.
17 For this reason[+] I have sent Timothy
to you. *He* is my beloved son and faithful
in the Lord. He will remind you about
my way *of life* in Christ as I teach everywhere in every assembly.[+]
18 Now some *of you* are puffed up as
though I would not come to you.
19 But I will come to you soon,[+] if the
Lord will *allow it*, and *then I* will know,
not the speech of *those* who are puffed
up, but the power.
20 For the kingdom of God *is* not in *mere*
words but in power.
21 What will you *have me do*? Shall I come
to you with a rod or in love and *in* the
spirit of meekness?

1 Corinthians Chapter 5

1 It is commonly reported *that there is*
fornication among you, and such fornication as is not even[+] named among
the Gentiles: That one should have his
father's wife.
2 And you are puffed up, instead[+] of
mourning *so* that *the one* who has done this
deed might be taken *out* from among you.
3 For truly,[+] *even though* I am absent in
body, but present in *the* spirit, *I* have
already judged *this* as though I were
present, *concerning the one* who has done
this deed.

4 In the name of our Lord Jesus Christ,
when you are gathered together, and my
spirit *with you*, with the power of our
Lord Jesus Christ,
5 deliver such a one to Satan for the
destruction of the flesh *so* that the
spirit might be saved in the day of the
Lord Jesus.
6 Your boasting+ *is* not good. Do you
not know that a little leaven permeates+
the whole lump?
7 Therefore, purge out the old leaven *so*
that you may be a new lump, as you are,
unleavened. For Christ our Passover is
sacrificed for us.
8 Therefore let us keep the feast, not
with old leaven or with the leaven of
malice and wickedness, but with the
unleavened *bread* of sincerity and truth.
9 I wrote to you in an epistle to not *keep*
company with fornicators.
10 Yet *that does* not *mean* entirely+ *isolated*
from the fornicators of this world or
from the covetous or extortioners or
from idolaters. For then you must need
to go out of the world.

11 But now I have written to you to not
keep company *with them* if anyone
who is called a believer+ is a fornicator or covetous or an idolater or a
railer or a drunkard or an extortioner.
Do not *even* eat with such a one.
12 Should I judge *those* who are
outside+ *the faith*? *No.* But do you not
judge *those* who are within?

13 God judges *those* who are outside.+
Therefore, put away from among yourselves that wicked person.

1 Corinthians Chapter 6

1 Dare any of you, having a matter
against another, go to law before the
unrighteous+ and not before the saints?
Matthew 5:25
2 Do you not know that the saints will
judge the world? And if the world will
be judged by you, are you unworthy to
judge the smallest matters?
3 Do you not know that we will judge
angels? How much more *then, the* things
that pertain to this life?
4 *So* then, if you have judgments of
things pertaining to this life, set them to
judge who are least esteemed in the
assembly.+
5 I speak *this* to your shame. Is it so that
there is not a wise person+ among you?
Not one who is able to judge between
believers+?
6 But believer+ goes to law with believer,+ and that before unbelievers.
7 Now therefore, there is utterly a fault
among you because you go to law with
one another. Why do you not instead+
just accept+ *the* wrong? Why do you not
instead+ *allow yourselves to* be defrauded?
8 No. You do wrong and defraud, and
that *among* believers.+

9 Do you not know that the unrighteous will not inherit the kingdom of
God? Do not be deceived. Neither
fornicators nor idolaters nor adulterers nor effeminate *persons* nor
defilers+ of themselves
10 nor thieves nor covetous nor drunks
nor revilers nor extortioners will
inherit the kingdom of God.

11 Such were some of you. But *now* you
are washed. But *now* you are sanctified.
But *now* you are justified in the name
of the Lord Jesus and by the Spirit of
our God.
12 All things are lawful to me. But all
things are not expedient. All things are
lawful for me. But I will not be brought
under the power of anything.
13 Food+ for the belly and the belly for
food.+ But God will destroy both it and
them. Now the body *is* not for fornication, but for the Lord. And the Lord for
the body.
14 God has both raised up the Lord and
will also raise up us by His own power.
15 Do you not know that your bodies are
the members of Christ? Shall I then take
the members of Christ and make *them* the
members of a harlot? *That* cannot be.+

16 What? Do you not know that anyone who is joined to a harlot becomes[+] one body *with them*? For two, He says, shall be one flesh. *Matthew 19:5*

17 But *those* who are joined to the Lord are one *in* spirit *with Him*.

18 Flee fornication. Every *other* sin that anyone does is outside[+] the body. But *those* who commit fornication sin against their own bodies.

19 What? Do you not know that your body is the temple of the Holy Spirit in you, whom you have *received* from God? You are not your own.

20 You are bought with a price. Therefore glorify God in your body and in your spirit, which are God's.

1 Corinthians Chapter 7

1 Now concerning the things about which you wrote to me: *It is* good *for a* man *and* woman not to touch.

2 But because of *the temptation of* fornication, let every man have his own wife and let every woman have her own husband.

3 Let the husband render to the wife due benevolence. Likewise also *let* the wife to the husband.

4 The wife does not have authority[+] over her own body, but the husband. Likewise also the husband does not have authority[+] over his own body, but the wife.

5 Do not deprive[+] one another, except *it be* with consent for a time *so* that you may give yourselves to fasting and prayer. *Then* come together again *so* that Satan will not tempt you for your inability to restrain.[+]

6 But I say this as a permission *and* not as a commandment.

7 For I would *prefer* that all mankind[+] was even as I myself. But everyone[+] has their proper gift from God: One after this manner, and another after that.

8 Therefore, I say to the unmarried and *to* widows, it is good for them if they remain even as I *am*.

9 However, if they cannot restrain[+] *themselves*, *then* let them marry. For it is better to marry than to burn *with passion*.

10 To the married I charge,[+] not I but the Lord: Do not let *a* wife separate[+] from *her* husband.

11 But if she separate,[+] let her remain unmarried or be reconciled to *her* husband. And do not let *a* husband put away *his* wife.

12 But to the rest I, not the Lord, speak: If any brother has a wife who does not believe and she is pleased to live[+] with him, *then* let him not put her away.

13 And if a woman has a husband who does not believe and he is pleased to dwell with her, *then* let her not leave him.

14 For the unbelieving husband is sanctified by the wife. And the unbelieving wife is sanctified by the husband. Otherwise,[+] your children would be *considered* unclean, but now they are holy.

15 But if the unbelieving depart, let them go.[+] A brother or a sister is not under bondage in such *cases*, but God has called us to peace.

16 For how do you know, O wife, if you *might* save *your* husband? Or how do you know, O man, if you *might* save *your* wife?

17 But as God has distributed to everyone[+] *and* as the Lord has called everyone, so let them walk. And so I *also* ordain in all *the* assemblies.[+]

18 Was anyone called *after* being circumcised? *Then* let them not become uncircumcised. Has anyone been called *while yet* in uncircumcision? *Then* let them not be circumcised.

19 Circumcision is nothing and uncircumcision is nothing, but keep the commandments of God.

20 Let everyone[+] abide in the same calling in which they were called.

21 Were you called *while* a servant? Do not be concerned[+] about it. But if you may be made free, *then* use *that* instead.[+]

22 For *those* who are called in the Lord, *while being* servants, are the Lord's free[+] *people*. And likewise *those* who are called, *being* free, are Christ's servants.

23 You are bought with a price. Do not become the servants of men.

24 Family,[+] let each one[+] abide with God in *that state* in which they were called.

25 Now concerning virgins I have no commandment from the Lord. Yet I *will* give
my judgment as one who has received+
mercy from the Lord to be faithful.
26 I suppose therefore that this *assessment*
is good for the present conditions,+ that
it is good for a man to *remain as he* is.
27 Are you bound to a wife? Do not seek
to be loosed. Are you loosed from a
wife? Do not seek a wife.
28 But if you have married, you have not
sinned and if a virgin marries, she has
not sinned. But such will have trouble in
the flesh and I *would* spare you *of that*.
29 But this I say, family+: The time *is*
short. It remains, that *those* who have
wives *should* be as though they had none
30 and *those* who weep as *though they* did
not weep and *those* who rejoice as *though*
they did not rejoice and *those* who buy as
though they did not possess *things*
31 and *those* who use this world as not
misusing+ *it*. For the fashion of this
world passes away.
32 But I would have you to be *free from*
anxious cares.+ *Those* who are unmarried
care *about* the things of the Lord *and*
how to please the Lord. *Matthew 6:25*
33 But *those* who are married care *about*
the things of the world *such as* how to
please *a* wife.
34 *And there is a* difference between a wife
and a virgin. The unmarried care about
the things of the Lord, to be holy in both
body and in spirit. But *the* married care
about the things of the world, *such as*
how to please *a* husband.
35 I say this for your own benefit.+ Not *so*
that I might cast a snare upon you, but for
what is desirable+ and *so* that you may
attend upon the Lord without distraction.
36 But if anyone thinks *that they might*
behave improperly+ *with regard* to
preserving virginity, *and* if *they are* beyond
the appropriate age, and so it ought to be,
then let them do what they will *for* they
do not sin *if* they marry.
37 Nevertheless, one does well who
stands steadfast in their heart, having
no necessity, but having authority+ over
their own will and having decreed in
their heart to preserve+ virginity.
38 So then, one who enters+ into marriage
does well. But one who does not enter+
into marriage does better.
39 A wife is bound by the law as long as
her husband lives. But if her husband
dies, she is at liberty to be married to
whomever she will, *yet* only in the Lord.
40 But in my judgment, she *will be* happier
if she remains+ *unmarried*, and I think
that I have the Spirit of God.

1 Corinthians Chapter 8

1 Now concerning+ things offered to
idols, we know that we all have knowledge, *yet* knowledge puffs up. But *true*
love edifies.
2 If anyone thinks that they know anything, they know nothing yet as they
ought to know.
3 But if anyone *truly* loves God, *then*
they are *also* known by Him.
4 Therefore, as concerning the eating of
those things that are offered in sacrifice
to idols, we know that an idol *is* nothing
in the world and that *there is* no other
God but one.
5 For though there are *some* who are
called gods, whether in heaven or in
earth, as there are many *so called* gods
and many lords,
6 yet to us *there is only* one God who *is the*
Father, from whom everything *has come*,
and we *are* His. And *there is* one Lord
Jesus Christ through whom everything
has come. And we *have come* through Him.
7 However everyone+ does not *yet* have
this understanding.+ But some still+
have a concern+ *about* sacrifices offered
to idols, and their conscience, being
weak, *would thus be* defiled.
8 But food+ does not commend us to
God. For if we eat we are not better, nor
if we do not eat are we worse.
9 But take heed lest by any means this
liberty of yours becomes a stumbling
block to *those* who are weak.
10 For if anyone sees you who have
understanding+ sit to eat+ in the idol's
temple, will not the conscience of *those*

who are weak be made bold+ to eat
those things that are offered to idols?
11 And *so* through your knowledge, will
you cause the weak brother for whom
Christ *also* died *to* perish?
12 When you sin against the family+ and
wound their weak conscience, you sin
against Christ.
13 Therefore if *certain* foods+ cause+
another to sin, I will not eat *such* flesh
ever,+ lest I offend another *and cause*
them to sin.

1 Corinthians Chapter 9

1 Am I not an apostle? Am I not free?
Have I not seen Jesus Christ our Lord?
Are you not *the fruit of* my work in the
Lord?
2 If I am not an apostle to others, yet
doubtless I am to you. For you are the
seal of my apostleship in the Lord.
3 *Therefore* my answer to *those* who
examine me is this:
4 Do we not have authority+ to eat and
to drink?
5 Do we not have authority+ to go
around+ *with* a sister *or* a wife, as well
as *the* other apostles and the brothers of
the Lord and Cephas?
6 Or *is it* only Barnabas and I *who* do
not have authority+ to forgo+ *temporal*
work *in order to minister*.
7 Who ever+ soldiers+ at his own ex-
pense+? Who plants a vineyard and does
not eat of its fruit? Or who feeds a flock
and does not eat of the milk of the flock?
8 Do I say these things as a man? Or
does the law not say the same also?
9 For it is written in the law of Moses:
You shall not muzzle the mouth of the
ox that treads out the corn. Does God
care about oxen? *Deuteronomy 25:4*
10 Or does He say *this* entirely+ for our
sakes? *No doubt this* is written for our
sakes *so* that *those* who plow should
plow in hope, *and those* who thresh in
hope should be partakers of their hope.
11 If we have sown spiritual things to
you, *is it* a great thing *to you* if we reap
some of your worldly+ things?
12 If others are partakers of *this* authority+
over you, *should* we not *just as* much+?
Nevertheless we have not used this
authority,+ but *we* suffer all things lest
we should hinder the Gospel of Christ.
13 Do you not know that *those* who
minister about holy things live *from*
the things of the temple? And *those*
who attend+ at the altar are partakers
of the altar?
14 Even so, the Lord has ordained that
those who proclaim+ the Gospel should
live from *the fruit of* the Gospel.
15 But I have used none of these things.
Nor have I written these things *so* that it
should be so done for me. For *it is* better
for me to die than that anyone should
make my rejoicing+ void.
16 For although I proclaim+ the Gospel,
I have nothing to boast+ about, for *this*
necessity is laid upon me. Yes, woe is
me if I do not proclaim+ the Gospel.
17 For if I do this willingly, I *will* have a
reward *in it*. But *even* if *it was* not
willingly, the administration+ *of the*
Gospel is entrusted+ to me.
18 What is my reward then? *Truly*+ it is
that when I proclaim+ the Gospel, I may
make the Gospel of Christ without charge
so that I do not abuse my authority+ in
the Gospel.
19 For though I am free from all *people*,
yet I have made myself *a* servant to all
so that I might gain *that many* more.
20 To the Jews I became like a Jew *so* that
I might gain the Jews. To *those* who are
under the law *I became* as *though* under
the law *so* that I might gain *those* who are
under the law.
21 To those outside+ *the* law *I became* as
though I was outside+ *the* law. Not out-
side+ *of* God's law, but *under* the law of
Christ, *so* that *I might* gain *those who are*
outside+ *the* law.
22 To the weak I became weak *so* that I
might gain the weak. I have become+ all
things to all *people so* that I might by all
means rescue+ some.
23 I do this for the sake of the Gospel *so*
that I might be *a* partaker of it with *you*.
24 Do you not know that *those* who run in

a race all run, but one receives the
prize? *Therefore,* run so that you may
obtain *it*.
25 Everyone+ who strives *for victory* is
temperate in all things. Now some+
strive to obtain a worldly+ crown. But
we do it to obtain an incorruptible *crown*.
26 Therefore, I so run, *but* not with un-
certainty. I do not fight as one who beats
the air *aimlessly*.
27 But I keep my body under *control* and
bring *it* into subjection, lest by any
means, when I have proclaimed+ *the*
Word to others, I myself should become
a reprobate.+

1 Corinthians Chapter 10

1 Now I do not want you to be ignorant,
family.+ All *of* our fathers were under
the cloud and all passed through the sea.
2 *They* were all baptized into Moses in
the cloud and in the sea.
3 *They* all ate the same spiritual food.+
4 *They* all drank the same spiritual drink.
For they drank of that spiritual Rock
that followed them *and* that Rock was
Christ.
5 But God was not well pleased with
many of them. For they were over-
thrown in the wilderness.
6 Now these things are our examples to
the intent we should not lust after evil
things as they lusted.
7 Do not be idolaters as some of them
were. As it is written: The people sat
down to eat and drink and rose up to
play. *Exodus 32:6*
8 Do not let us commit fornication as
some of them committed and in one day
twenty three thousand fell.
9 Do not let us test+ Christ as some of
them tested+ *God* and were destroyed by
serpents.
10 Do not complain+ as some of them
complained+ and were destroyed by the
Destroyer.
11 Now all these things happened to them
for examples *to us*. They were written
for our admonition. *For* upon *us* the end
of the world has come.
12 Therefore let *those* who think *that* they
stand take heed lest they fall.

> 13 There has no trial+ taken you but
> such as is common to man. But God
> *is* faithful. *He* will not allow+ you to
> be tested+ beyond+ what you are
> able *to withstand*. But *He* will, with
> the trial,+ also make a way to escape
> *so* that you may be able to bear *it*.

14 Therefore my beloved, flee from
idolatry.
15 I speak as to wise men. Judge what
I say.
16 The cup of blessing that we bless, is it
not the communion of the blood of
Christ? The bread that we break, is it not
the communion of the body of Christ?
17 For we, *being* many, are one bread *and*
one body. For we are all partakers of
that one bread.
18 Behold Israel according+ to the flesh.
Are not *those* who eat of the sacrifices
partakers of the altar?
19 What shall I say, then? That the idol is
anything or what is offered in sacrifice
to idols is anything?
20 Rather, I *say* that the things that the
Gentiles sacrifice, they sacrifice to
demons+ and not to God. I would not
allow that you should have fellowship
with demons.+
21 You cannot drink the cup of the Lord
and the cup of demons.+ You cannot be
partakers of the Lord's table and of the
table of demons.+
22 Do we provoke the Lord to jealousy?
Are we stronger than He?
23 All things are lawful for me, but all
things are not expedient. All things are
lawful for me, but all things do not edify.
24 Let no one seek their own, but *let* each
one+ *seek* other's *well being*.
25 Whatever is sold in the market,+ eat *it*
asking no question for conscience sake.
26 For the earth *is* the Lord's and the
fullness thereof. *Psalm 24:1*
27 If any of *those* who do not believe
invite+ you *to a feast* and you are inclined+
to go, *then* eat whatever is set before

you, asking no questions for conscience
sake.
28 But if anyone says to you: This was
offered *in sacrifice* to an idol, *then* do not
eat *it* because of that *one who* declared[+]
this and *for their* conscience. For the
earth *is* the Lord's and the fullness
thereof. *Psalm 24:1*
29 *By* conscience, I do not speak *of* your
own but of others'. For why is my
liberty judged by another's conscience?
30 For if by grace I am a partaker, *then*
why am I blasphemed[+] for that for
which I give thanks?
31 Therefore, if you eat or drink or whatever you do, do all to the glory of God.
32 Do not offend[+] *anyone*, not *the* Jews or
the Gentiles or those called[+] by God.
33 *Do* even as *I do*. Please all *people* in
all *things*, not seeking my own benefit[+]
but the *benefit* of many *so* that they
may be saved.

1 Corinthians Chapter 11

1 Be followers of me, even as I also *am*
of Christ.
2 Now I praise you, family,[+] that you
remember me in everything[+] and keep
the traditions[+] as I delivered *them* to you.
3 And I want you to know that *for* every
man the head is Christ. And *the* head
for woman *is* man. And *the* head *for*
Christ *is* God.
4 Every man praying or prophesying,
having *his* head covered, dishonors
his head.
5 But every woman who prays or proph-
esies with *her* head uncovered dishonors
her head. For that is one and the same
as if she were shaven.
6 For if the woman is not covered, *then*
let her *head* also be sheared.[+] But if it is
a shame for a woman to be sheared or
shaved *then* let her be covered.
7 For a man indeed should not cover
his head, since[+] he is the image and
glory of God. But the woman is the
glory of the man.
8 For the man is not from the woman,
but the woman from the man.
9 Nor was the man created for the
woman, but the woman for the man.
10 For this reason[+] the woman ought to
have authority[+] over[+] *her* head because
of the angels.
11 Nevertheless man *is* not *complete*
without woman nor woman *complete*
without man in the Lord.
12 For as the woman *is* from the man, so
also *is* the man from the woman. But
everything[+] *is* from God.
13 Judge within yourselves: Is it fitting[+]
that a woman pray to God uncovered?
14 Does not even nature itself teach you that
if a man has long hair, it is a shame to him?
15 But if a woman has long hair, it is a
glory to her, for *her* hair is given *to* her
for a covering.
16 But if anyone seems to be contentious,
we have no such custom *and* not *in* the
assemblies[+] of God.
17 Now in this I declare that I do not
praise *you because* you come together
not for the better but for the worse.
18 For first of all, when you come together
in the assembly,[+] I hear that there are
divisions among you, and I partly
believe it.
19 For there must also be heresies among
you *so* that *those* who are approved may
be revealed[+] among you.
20 Therefore, when you come together in
one place, *it* is not to eat the Lord's
supper.
21 For in eating, everyone takes their
own supper before *others*, one hungry
and another drunk.
22 What? Do you not have houses *in
which* to eat and to drink? Or *do you*
despise the assembly[+] of God and *put to*
shame *those* who do not have *very much*?
What shall I say to you? Shall I praise
you in this? I do not praise *you*.
23 For I have received from the Lord
what also I delivered to you: That the
Lord Jesus, *on* the *same* night in which
He was betrayed, took bread
24 and when He had given thanks, He
broke *it* and said: Take, eat. This is my
body, broken for you. Do this in
remembrance of me. *John 6:53*

25 In the same manner also *He took* the
cup after supper+ and said: This cup is
the new covenant+ in my blood. Do this,
as often as you drink, in remembrance
of me.
26 For as often as you eat this bread
and drink this cup, you proclaim+
remembrance of the death of the Lord,
until He comes.
27 Therefore, whoever eats this bread and
drinks *this* cup of the Lord unworthily,
shall be guilty of the body and blood of
the Lord.
28 But let everyone+ examine themselves
and accordingly+ eat of the bread and
drink of the cup.
29 For *those* who eat and drink unworthily,
eat and drink judgment+ unto themselves
for not discerning the Lord's body.
30 For this reason+ many *are* weak and
sickly among you, and many sleep.
31 For if we would judge ourselves, *then*
we would not be judged.
32 But when we are judged, we are
disciplined+ by the Lord *so* that we *will*
not be condemned with the world.
33 Therefore my family,+ when you come
together to eat, wait+ for one another.
34 If any *are* hungry, *let them* eat at home
so that you do not come together to
condemnation. And the rest I will set in
order when I come.

1 Corinthians Chapter 12

1 Now concerning spiritual *gifts*, family,+ I do not want you to be ignorant.
2 You know that you were Gentiles,
carried away to these speechless+ idols,
even as you were led.
3 Therefore I give you to understand
that no one speaking by the Spirit of God
calls Jesus accursed. No one can say that
Jesus *is* Lord, but by the Holy Spirit.
4 Now there are diversities of gifts but
the same Spirit.
5 There are differences of administra-
tions but the same Lord.
6 There are diversities of operations but
it is the same God who works all in all.
7 But the manifestation of the Spirit is
given to everyone+ to *receive its* benefit.+
8 For to one, from the Spirit, is given
the word of wisdom. To another, the
word of knowledge from the same Spirit.
9 To another, faith from the same Spirit.
To another, the gifts of healing from the
same Spirit.
10 To another, the working of miracles.
To another, prophecy. To another,
discerning of spirits. To another, *different*+ kinds of tongues. To another,
the interpretation of tongues.
11 But all these *gifts* operate+ *through* one
and the same Spirit, dividing to every-
one+ individually+ as He will.
12 For as the body is one and has many
members, and all the members of that
one body, being many, are one body, so
it is also *with* Christ.
13 For by one Spirit we are all baptized
into one body. Whether *we are* Jews or
Gentiles. Whether *we are* slaves+ or
free. All have been made to drink from
one Spirit.
14 For the body is not one member, but
many.
15 If the foot says: Because I am not the
hand I am not of the body, is it therefore
not of the body?
16 If the ear says: Because I am not the
eye I am not of the body, is it therefore
not of the body?
17 If the whole body *was* an eye, where
is hearing? If the whole *was* hearing,
where *is* smelling?
18 But now God has placed+ everyone of
the members in the body as it has
pleased Him.
19 If they were all one member, where *is*
the body?
20 But now *there are* many members, but
in one body.
21 The eye cannot say to the hand: I have
no need of you. Nor again the head to
the feet: I have no need of you.
22 No, much more those members of the
body that seem to be more feeble, are
necessary.
23 And those *members* of the body that we
think to be less honorable, upon these
we bestow more abundant honor. Our

unattractive[+] *parts* have more abundant
attractiveness.[+]
24 For our attractive[+] *parts* have no need.
But God has tempered the body together,
giving more abundant honor to that *part*
which lacked
25 *so* that there should be no division[+] in
the body, but *so that* the members should
have the same care for one another.
26 If one member suffers, *then* all the
members suffer with it. Or *if* one
member is honored, *then* all the members
rejoice with it.
27 Now you are the body of Christ and
members in particular.
28 God has placed[+] some in the assembly[+]
thus: First apostles, second prophets,
third teachers. After that miracles, then
gifts of healings, helps, governments,
and diversities of tongues.
29 *Are* all apostles? *Are* all prophets? *Are*
all teachers? *Are* all workers of miracles?
30 Do all have the gifts of healing? Do all
speak with tongues? Do all interpret?
31 Zealously[+] *desire* the better gifts. *And*
yet I *will* show you a more excellent way.

1 Corinthians Chapter 13

1 If[+] I speak with the tongues of men
and of angels but do not have *true* love,
I become *like* sounding brass or a
tinkling cymbal.
2 And if[+] I have *the gift of* prophecy and
understand all mysteries and all knowledge, and though I have all faith so that
I could remove mountains, but do not
have *true* love, I am nothing.
3 And if[+] I bestow all my goods to feed
the poor and though I give my body to
be burned, but do not have *true* love,
nothing *is* gained.[+] Matthew 9:13

4 *True* love *patiently* suffers long *and*
is kind. *True* love does not envy.
True love does not vaunt itself *and*
is not puffed up. Matthew 5:44
5 *It* does not behave shamefully.[+] *It*
does not seek *its* own *way*. *It* is not
easily provoked. *And* it does not
think evil. Matthew 5:22
6 *True love* does not rejoice in iniquity,
but rejoices in the truth. Matthew 5:8
7 *True love* bears all things, believes
all things, hopes all things, *and*
endures all things. Matthew 10:22
8 *True* love never fails.

But where *there are* prophecies, they
will fail. Where *there are* tongues, they
will cease. Where *there is* knowledge, it
will vanish away. John 15:9
9 For we know in part and we prophesy
in part.
10 But when what is perfect has come,
then what is in part will be done away.
11 When I was a child, I spoke as a child.
I understood as a child. I thought as a
child. But when I became a man, I put
away childish things.
12 For now we see through a glass darkly,
but then face to face. Now I know in
part, but then I shall know even as also
I am known.
13 Now abide faith, hope, *and true* love,
these three. But the greatest of these *is*
true love.

1 Corinthians Chapter 14

1 Pursue[+] *true* love zealously[+] and *desire*
the spiritual *gifts*, especially[+] that of
prophecy.
2 For *those* who speak in an *unknown*
tongue do not speak to people[+] but to
God. For no one understands *them*. However in the spirit *they* speak mysteries.
3 But *those* who prophesy speak to
people[+] *for* edification, exhortation, and
comfort.
4 *Those* who speak in tongues edify
themselves. But *those* who prophesy
edify the assembly.[+]
5 I would *have* you all speak with tongues,
but more[+] that you prophesied. For
those who prophesy *are* greater than
those who speak with tongues, unless
they interpret *so* that the assembly[+]
receives edification.
6 Now family,[+] if I come to you
speaking with tongues, what will I

benefit+ you? Unless+ I speak to you
either by revelation or by knowledge or
by prophesying or by doctrine?
7 Even *when* things without life *are*
giving sound, whether *it be a* pipe or
harp, unless they give a distinction in
the sounds, how will it be known what
is piped or harped?
8 For if the trumpet gives an uncertain
sound, who will prepare themselves for
battle?
9 So likewise you, unless+ you utter
words easy to be understood by the
tongue, how will it be known what is
spoken? For *otherwise* you speak into
the air.
10 There are many kinds of voices in the
world and none of them *is* without
distinctive+ *character*.
11 Therefore, if I do not know the
meaning of the voice, I will be to *those*
who speak a barbarian and *those* who
speak *will be* a barbarian to me.
12 Even so you, since+ you are zealous
for spiritual *gifts*, seek *them so* that you
may excel in edifying the assembly.+
13 Therefore, let *those* who speak in an
unknown tongue pray that they may
interpret.
14 For if I pray in an *unknown* tongue, my
spirit prays, but my understanding is
unfruitful.
15 What is it *to be* then? I will pray with
the spirit and I will pray with understanding also. I will sing with the spirit
and I will sing with understanding also.
16 Otherwise+ when you bless with the
spirit, how will *those* who occupy the
room of the uninformed+ say Amen at
your giving of thanks, since they do not
understand what you say?
17 For you truly+ give thanks well, but
the other is not edified.
18 I thank my God *that* I speak with
tongues more than all *of* you.
19 Yet in the assembly+ I would rather
speak five words with my understanding, *so* that *by my voice* I might teach
others also, than ten thousand words in
an *unknown* tongue.
20 Family,+ do not be children in *your*
understanding. However in malice,
be children. But in understanding, be
mature.+
21 In the law it is written: With other
tongues and other lips I will speak to this
people. And yet for all that, they will not
hear me, says the Lord. *Isaiah 28:11*
22 Therefore tongues are for a sign, not
to *those* who believe, but to *those* who
do not believe. But prophesying does
not *serve those* who do not believe, but
those who believe.
23 Therefore if the whole assembly+ has
come together into one place and all
speak with tongues, and *those who are*
uninformed+ or unbelievers come in,
will they not say that you are mad?
24 But if all prophesy and *some* who do
not believe or *who are* uninformed+
come in, they will be convinced by all
and judged by all.
25 Thus are the secrets of their hearts
revealed.+ So falling down on *their* face
they will worship God and report that
God is truly in you.
26 How is it *to be* then, family+? When
you come together, everyone of you has
a psalm, a doctrine, a tongue, a revelation, *and* an interpretation. And let all
things be done for edifying.
27 If any speak in a tongue, *allow* two or
at the most three, in succession,+ and
with one *to* interpret.
28 But if there is no interpreter, keep
silence in the assembly,+ *each* speaking
to themselves and to God.
29 Allow two or three prophets to speak
and the others discern.+
30 If *anything* is revealed to another who
sits by, let the first *remain* silent.+
31 For against+ one *in error*, you may all
prophesy *so* that all may learn and all
may be exhorted.+
32 For+ the spirits of the prophets are
subject to the prophets.

33 For God is not
the author of confusion,
but of peace,

as in all assemblies+ of the saints.

34 Let your women keep silence in the
assemblies.[+] For it is not permitted
for them to speak, but to be under
obedience as the law also says.
35 If they will learn anything, let them
ask their husbands at home. For it is
a shame for women to speak in the
assembly.[+]
36 *What?* Did the Word of God originate[+]
from you? Or did it come to you only?
37 If anyone thinks themselves to be a
prophet or spiritual, let them acknowledge that the things that I write to you
are the commandments of the Lord.
38 But if anyone is ignorant, let them be
ignorant.
39 Therefore family,[+] zealously[+] *desire*
to prophesy. And do not forbid *anyone*
to speak with tongues.
40 Let all things be done decently and in
order.

1 Corinthians Chapter 15

1 Family,[+] I *now* declare to you the
Gospel that I *have already* proclaimed[+]
to you and which you have received and
in which you stand
2 *and* by which you are also being saved,
if you keep in memory what I *have*
proclaimed[+] to you, unless you have
believed in vain. *Psalm 119:11*
3 For I delivered to you first of all what
I also received: That Christ died for our
sins according to the Scriptures, *Isaiah 53:5*
4 that He was buried and that He rose
again the third day, according to the
Scriptures, *Psalm 68:18*
5 that He was seen by Cephas *and* then
by the twelve.
6 After that, He was seen by more than
five hundred *of the* family[+] at once, of
whom the greater part remain to this
present *time*. But some have fallen asleep.
7 After that, He was seen by James *and*
then by all the apostles.
8 Last of all, He was seen by me also, as
one unnaturally[+] born.
9 For I am the least of the apostles, not
even suitable[+] to be called an apostle
because I persecuted the assembly[+] of God.
10 But by the grace of God, I am what I
am. His grace to me was not in vain, but
I labored more abundantly than all of
them. Yet not I, but *it was* the grace of
God with me.
11 Therefore whether *it were* I or they,
we thus proclaim[+] *the Word*, and you
thus believed.
12 Now if Christ is proclaimed,[+] that He
rose from the dead, how *do* some among
you say that there is no resurrection of
the dead?
13 But if there is no resurrection of the
dead, then Christ is not risen.
14 And if Christ is not risen, then our
proclaiming[+] *is in* vain and your faith *is*
also vain.
15 Yes, and we are found false witnesses
of God because we have testified of God
that He raised up Christ, whom He did
not raise up if *it* be so that the dead do
not rise.
16 For if the dead do not rise, then Christ
is not raised.
17 And if Christ is not raised, *then* your
faith *is* vain *and* you are yet in your sins.
18 Then also those who fell asleep in
Christ perished.
19 If *it is* only in this life *that* we have hope
in Christ, *then* we, of all people, are
most miserable.
20 But now Christ is risen from the dead
and become the first fruits of *those* who
slept.
21 For since death *came* by man, *Adam*,
then the resurrection of the dead also
came by man, *Jesus Christ*.
22 For *just* as in Adam all die, even so in
Christ shall all be made alive.
23 But everyone[+] in their own order:
Christ the first fruits, and afterward
those who are Christ's at His coming.
24 Then the end *will come*, when *Jesus*
will have delivered up the kingdom to
our God and Father, *and* when He will
have put down all rule and all authority
and power.
25 For *Christ* must reign until He has put
all enemies under His feet.
26 *And* the last enemy *to be* destroyed
is death.

27 For He has put all things *in subjection*
under His feet. But when it is said that
all things are put *in subjection* under *Him*,
it is obvious+ *that He is* excepted who
put all things under Him. *Psalm 8:6*
28 For when all things have been subdued
to Him, then the Son will Himself also
be subject to *God* who put all things
under Him *so* that God may be all in all.
29 Otherwise+ what shall those do who
are baptized for the dead, if the dead do
not rise at all? Why then are they
baptized for the dead?
30 And why do we stand in jeopardy
every hour?
31 Every day, *I risk* dying. Our rejoicing
is in having Christ Jesus our Lord.
32 If according+ to the *way* of men I have
fought with beasts at Ephesus, *then* what
benefit+ *is* it *to* me. If the dead are not
raised, *then* let us eat and drink for tomorrow we die. *Isaiah 22:13*
33 Do not be deceived. Evil companions+
corrupt good behavior.+
34 Awaken to righteousness and do not
sin. For some do not have the knowledge of God. I speak *this* to your shame.
35 But someone will say: How are the
dead raised up? And with what body do
they come?
36 *You* fool. What you sow is not given
life+ unless+ it dies.
37 What you sow *is this*: You do not sow
the body that will be, but bare grain. It
may be+ of wheat or of some other *grain*.
38 But God gives it a body as it pleases
Him, and to every seed its own body.
39 All flesh *is* not the same flesh. *There*
is one *kind of* flesh for men, another
flesh for beasts, another for fish, *and*
another for birds.
40 *There are* also celestial bodies and
terrestrial bodies, and the glory of the
celestial *is* one and the *glory* of the
terrestrial *is* another.
41 *There is* one glory of the sun and
another glory of the moon and another
glory of the stars. For *one* star differs
from *another* star in glory.
42 So also *is* the resurrection of the dead.
It is sown in corruption *and* it is raised
in incorruptibility.+
43 It is sown in dishonor. It is raised in
glory. It is sown in weakness. It is raised
in power.
44 It is sown *as* a natural body. It is raised
as a spiritual body. There is a natural
body and there is a spiritual body.
45 So it is written: The first man, Adam,
was made a living soul. *And* the last
Adam *was made* a life giving+ spirit.
Genesis 2:7
46 However the first was not spiritual but
the natural. Then *afterward came* the
spiritual.
47 The first man *came* out of the earth,
made of dust.+ The second man *came as*
the Lord out of heaven.
48 Just as *God made the first man out of*
the earth,+ of such also *are all* those
made out of the earth. And just as one+
was heavenly, of such also *is* heavenly
regeneration.
49 As we have borne the image of the
earthly, we will also bear the image of
the heavenly.
50 Now family,+ I say this: That flesh
and blood cannot inherit the kingdom
of God. Nor does corruption inherit
incorruptibility.+
51 Behold I *will* tell+ you a mystery: We
will not all sleep, but we will all be
changed.
52 In a moment. In the twinkling of an
eye. At the last trumpet. For a trumpet
will sound and the dead will be raised
incorruptible, and we will be changed.
53 For this corruptible *being* must put on
incorruptibility+ and this mortal *must*
put on immortality.
54 So when this corruptible shall have put
on incorruptibility+ and this mortal shall
have put on immortality, then shall *it*
be brought to pass that saying that is
written: Death is swallowed up in victory.
Isaiah 25:8
55 O death, where *is* your sting? O grave,
where *is* your victory?
56 The sting of death *is* sin and the
strength of sin *is* the law.
57 But thanks *be* to God who gives us the
victory through our Lord Jesus Christ.

58 Therefore my beloved+:

> Be steadfast, immovable,
> always abounding
> in the work of the Lord,
> because+ you know
> that your labor in the Lord
> is not in vain. *Matthew 4:10*

1 Corinthians Chapter 16

1 Now concerning the collection for the saints, as I have directed+ the assemblies+ of Galatia, so also you *should* do.
2 Every+ first *of the* week, let everyone of you put+ *aside* in store, as *God* has prospered, *so* that there *need* be no collections+ when I come.
3 When I come, whomever you approve by *your* letters, I will send to take+ your liberal *gifts* to Jerusalem.
4 If it is fitting+ that I go also, *then* they shall go with me.
5 Now I will come to you when I pass through Macedonia, for I do pass through Macedonia.
6 It may be that I will stay+ and winter with you *so* that you may *then* take+ me on my journey wherever I go.
7 For I will not see you now, on the way, but I trust to stay+ a while with you, if the Lord permits.
8 But I will stay+ at Ephesus until Pentecost.
9 For a great and effective door is opened to me but *there are* many adversaries.
10 Now if Timothy comes, see that he may be with you without fear. For he works the work of the Lord, as I also *do*.
11 Therefore let no one despise him, but conduct him forth in peace *so* that he may come to me. For I look for him with the brothers.
12 Concerning *our* brother Apollos, I greatly desired him to come to you with the brothers. But his will was not at all to come at this time, but he will come when he has convenient time.
13 Watch. Stand fast in the faith. Be courageous.+ Be strong.
14 Let all things be done with *true* love.
15 I urge you, family.+ You know the house of Stephanas, that it is *the* first fruit of Achaia, and *that* they have applied+ themselves to the ministry of the saints.
16 *See* that you submit yourselves to such *as them* and to everyone who helps with *us* and labors.
17 I am glad for the coming of Stephanas and Fortunatus and Achaicus, for what you were lacking, they supplied.
18 They have refreshed my spirit and yours. Therefore acknowledge *those* who are such.
19 The assemblies+ of Asia greet+ you. Aquila and Priscilla greet+ you much in the Lord, *along* with the assembly+ that is in their house.
20 All the family+ greet you. Greet one another with a holy kiss.
21 The salutation of Paul *I make* with my own hand.
22 If anyone does not delight+ *in* the Lord Jesus Christ, let them be accursed.+ Maranatha. *Oh Lord come.*
23 The grace of our Lord Jesus Christ *be* with you.
24 My love *be* with you all in Christ Jesus. Amen.

The first epistle to the Corinthians was transcribed at Philippi by Stephanas, Fortunatus, Achaicus, and Timothy.

2 Corinthians Chapter 1

1 *From* Paul, an apostle of Jesus Christ by the will of God, and Timothy *our* brother. To the assembly+ of God at Corinth with all the saints who are in all *of* Achaia.
2 Grace to you and peace from God our Father and Lord Jesus Christ.
3 Blessed *is* the God and Father *of* our Lord Jesus Christ, the Father of mercies and the God of all comfort.
4 *He* comforts us in all our tribulation *so* that we may be able to comfort *those* who are in any trouble with the *same* comfort with which we ourselves are comforted by God.

5 For *just* as the sufferings of Christ
abound in us, so also our consolation
abounds through Christ.
6 If we are afflicted, *it is* for your
consolation and salvation, which is
effective in enduring the same sufferings that we also suffer. Or if we are
comforted, *that also is* for your consolation and salvation.
7 Our hope in you *is* steadfast, knowing
that as you are partakers of the sufferings,
so also *you will be partakers* of the
consolation.
8 For we would not, family,+ have you
uninformed+ about our trouble that came
to us in Asia. We were pressed out of
measure, beyond strength, so that we
despaired even of life.
9 But we have *already* had the judgment+
of death within ourselves, *so* that we
would not trust in ourselves but in God
who raises the dead.
10 *He* delivered us from so great a death,
and *He still* does deliver. *And* we trust
that He will *even* yet deliver *us*.
11 You also labor+ together for us by
prayer, *so* that thanks may be given by
many on our behalf for the gifts *bestowed*
upon us by *so* many people.
12 This is the reason for our rejoicing:
The testimony of our conscience is that
we have had our conversation and
conduct in the world, and especially+
toward you, in simplicity and godly
sincerity and not with fleshly wisdom,
but *simply* by the grace of God.
13 For we write no other things to you
than what you read or acknowledge. I
trust you will acknowledge *this* even to
the end.
14 And, as you have acknowledged us in
part *so* that we are your *means of* rejoicing, even so you also *will be* ours in the
day of the Lord Jesus.
15 In this confidence, I was of a mind+ to
come to you before *so* that you might
have a second benefit.
16 *I intended* to pass by you to *on the way*
to Macedonia, and to come again to you
out of Macedonia and be brought by you
on my way to Judea.
17 When I was thus minded, did I use
lightness *to decide*? Or are the things
that I purpose done according to the
flesh *so* that there might be *an uncertain*
yes yes and no no?
18 *As* God *is* true, our word to you was
not *an uncertain* yes and no.
19 For the Son of God, Jesus Christ who
was proclaimed+ among you by us, *both*
by me and *by* Silvanus and Timothy,
was not yes and no, but in Him *it* was
consistently yes.
20 For all the promises of God in Him
are yes, and in Him Amen, for the glory
of God through us.
21 Now He who establishes us with you
in Christ and has anointed us, *is* God.
22 *He* has also sealed us and given *us* the
Spirit *as* the guarantee+ in our hearts.
23 But I call upon God to testify+ upon
my soul, that *it was to* spare you *that* I
did not yet come to Corinth.
24 Not that we have dominion over your
faith, but *we* are helpers of your joy.
For *it is* by faith *that* you stand.

2 Corinthians Chapter 2

1 I determined within myself that I would
not come to you again in sorrow.+
2 For if I grieve+ you, then who will
make me glad, if not those who *might*
otherwise be grieved by me?
3 I wrote this to you lest when I came, I
might have sorrow from those *in* whom
I ought to rejoice. *But I* have confidence
in you all that my joy is *in* all of you *also*.
4 For out of much suffering+ and anguish
of heart, I wrote to you with many tears.
Not *so* that you would be grieved, but *so*
that you might know the love that I have
for you more abundantly.
5 But if any have caused grief, *it is* not me
that they have grieved, but in part *it is* all
of you, *so* that I may not be overcharged.
6 Sufficient to such a one *is* this rebuke,+
which *has been expressed* by many.
7 On the contrary, you *should* instead+
forgive and comfort, lest perhaps such
a one be swallowed up with too much
sorrow.

8 Therefore I urge you to confirm *your* love toward them.

9 *It was* for this *purpose* also that I wrote *to you*, *so* that I might know the proof of you, if you are obedient in everything.[+]

10 To *those* whom you forgive anything, I also *forgive*. For if I have forgiven anything, it is for your sakes that I have forgiven it in the person of Christ.

11 *We do this* lest Satan should get an advantage over us. For we are not ignorant about his devices.

12 Furthermore, when I came to Troas to *proclaim*[+] Christ's Gospel, a door was opened to me by the Lord.

13 I had no rest in my spirit because I did not find my brother Titus. But upon leaving them, I went from there[+] to Macedonia.

14 Now thanks *be* to God who always causes us to triumph in Christ and reveals[+] the savor of His knowledge through us in every place.

15 For we are to God a sweet savor of Christ in *those* who are being saved, and *even* in those *who are* perishing.

16 To the one, *we are* the savor of death to death. To the other, the savor of life to life. And who *is* sufficient for these things?

17 For we are not like many who corrupt the Word of God. But from sincerity and as from God in the sight of God, we speak in Christ.

2 Corinthians Chapter 3

1 Do we begin again to commend ourselves? Or do we need, as some *others*, epistles of commendation to you, or *letters* of commendation from you?

2 You are our epistle written in our hearts, known and read by everyone.[+]

3 *You are* manifestly declared to be the epistle of Christ ministered by us, not written with ink but with the Spirit of the living God. Not in tables of stone, but in fleshy tables of the heart.

4 Such trust do we have through Christ toward God.

5 Not that we are sufficient in ourselves to think anything of ourselves, but our sufficiency *is* from God.

6 *God* has also made us able ministers of the new covenant.[+] Not of the letter, but of the spirit. For the letter kills, but the spirit gives life.

7 But if the administration of death written *and* engraved[+] in stones was glorious, so *much so* that the children of Israel could not steadfastly behold the face of Moses for the glory of his countenance, which *glory* was to be done away,

8 *then* how shall the administration of the spirit not be rather *more* glorious?

9 For if the administration of condemnation *is* glory, *then* much more does the administration of righteousness exceed in glory.

10 For even what was made glorious had no glory in this respect, by reason of the glory that excels.

11 For if what is done away *was* glorious, *even* much moreso *is* what remains glorious.

12 Therefore, seeing that we have such hope, we use great plainness of speech.

13 *We are* not like Moses, *who* put a veil over his face *so* that the children of Israel could not steadfastly look to the end of what is abolished.

14 But their minds were blinded. For until this day, the same veil remains. *It is* not taken away in the reading of the old covenant,[+] but *the veil* is done away in Christ.

15 Even to this day when Moses is read, the veil is upon their hearts.

16 Nevertheless, when it shall turn to the Lord, the veil will be taken away.

17 Now the Lord is that Spirit, and where the Spirit of the Lord *is*, there *is* liberty.

18 But with *an* open face beholding the glory of the Lord as in a mirror,[+] we are all changed by the Spirit of the Lord into the same image, from glory *shining upon us* to glory *reflected in us*.

2 Corinthians Chapter 4

1 Therefore, since we have this ministry, as
we have received mercy, we do not faint.
2 But *we* have renounced the hidden things
of dishonesty, not walking in craftiness or
handling the Word of God deceitfully, but
by *the* manifestation of the truth *we*
commend ourselves to everyone's[+]
conscience in the sight of God.
3 But if our Gospel is hid, it is hid to
those who are lost.
4 The god of this world has blinded the
minds of *those* who do not believe, lest
the light of the glorious Gospel of Christ,
who is the image of God, should shine
forth to them.
5 For we do not proclaim[+] ourselves,
but Christ Jesus the Lord. *We are* your
servants for Jesus' sake.
6 For God, who commanded the light to
shine out of darkness, has shown in our
hearts the light of the knowledge of the
glory of God, in the face of Jesus Christ.
7 But we have this treasure in earthen
vessels *so* that the excellency of the
power may be of God and not of us.
8 *We are* troubled on every side, yet not
distressed. *We are* perplexed but not in
despair.
9 *We are* persecuted but not forsaken,
cast down but not destroyed.
10 *We* always bear the dying of the Lord
Jesus in the body *so* that the life of Jesus
might be revealed[+] in our body.
11 For we who live are always *being*
delivered to death for Jesus' sake *so* that
the life of Jesus might also be revealed[+]
in our mortal flesh.
12 So then, death is working in us, but
life in you.
13 We have the same spirit of faith. As it
is written: I believed and therefore I
have spoken. We also believe, and therefore speak, *Psalm 116:10*
14 knowing that He who raised up the
Lord Jesus will also raise us up by Jesus
and present *us* with you.
15 For all things *are* for your sakes, *so*
that the abundant grace might, through
the thanksgiving of many, abound[+] to
the glory of God.
16 For this reason,[+] we do not faint, but
though our outward person *may* perish,
yet the inward is renewed day by day.
17 For our light suffering,[+] which is but
for a moment, works for us a far more
exceeding *and* eternal weight of glory.
18 We do not look at the things that are
seen, but at the things that are not
seen. For the things that are seen *are*
temporal. But the things that are not
seen *are* eternal.

2 Corinthians Chapter 5

1 We know that if our earthly house *in*
this tabernacle is destroyed,[+] we have
another building from God. *It is* a house
not made with hands, *but* eternal in the
heavens.
2 In this we groan, earnestly desiring to
be clothed with our house that is from
heaven.
3 Indeed,[+] being *thus* clothed, we will
not be found naked.
4 For *we* who are in *this temporary* tabernacle groan, being burdened. Not that
we wish to be unclothed, but clothed upon
so that mortality might be swallowed up
by life.
5 Now *He* who has prepared[+] us for this
is God. *And He* has also given to us the
guarantee[+] of the Spirit.
6 Therefore *we are* always confident,
knowing that while we are at home in
the body, we are absent from the Lord.
7 For we walk by faith *and* not by sight.
8 We are confident, *I say*, and willing
instead[+] to be absent from the body and
to be present with the Lord.
9 Therefore we labor *so* that, whether
present or absent, we may be accepted
by Him.
10 For we must all appear before the
judgment seat of Christ *so* that everyone
may receive the things *done* in body,
according to what they have done,
whether good or bad.
11 Therefore, knowing the terror of the
Lord, we persuade people.[+] And we are

revealed+ to God. I trust also *that we*
are revealed+ in your consciences.
12 For we do not commend ourselves to
you again. But *we* give you occasion to
rejoice+ on our behalf *so* that you may
have something to *answer to those* who
glory in *outward* appearance and not in
their hearts.
13 For if we are beside ourselves, *it is for*
God. Or if we are sober, *it is* for you.
14 For the love of Christ compels+ us.
Because we have concluded this: That if
one died for all, then all *are destined* to die.
15 *Jesus* died for all *so* that *those* who live
would no longer live for themselves but
for Him who died for them and rose
again.
16 Therefore, from now on we *will* know
no one in the flesh. Yes, though we have
known Christ in the flesh, yet from now
on we know *Him that way* no longer.+
17 Therefore if any *are* in Christ, *they are*
a new creation.+ Old things are passed
away. Behold all things are become
new.
18 All things *are* from God who has
reconciled us to Himself by Jesus Christ
and has given to us the ministry of
reconciliation.
19 As God was, in Christ, reconciling the
world to Himself, not imputing their
trespasses to them, *He* has committed to
us the Word of reconciliation.
20 Therefore, we are ambassadors for
Christ. As God has exhorted+ *you*
through us, we urge+ *you* in Christ's
place+: Be reconciled to God.
21 For *God* made *Jesus* who knew no sin
to be sin for us *so* that we might be made
the righteousness of God in Him.

2 Corinthians Chapter 6

1 *As* workers together *with Christ*, *we*
exhort+ *you* also *so* that you do not
receive the grace of God in vain.
2 For He says: I have heard you in a time
accepted, and in the day of salvation I
have helped+ you. Behold now *is* the
accepted time. Behold now *is* the day of
salvation. *Isaiah 49:8*
3 *We* give no offense in anything *so* that
the ministry *will* not be blamed.
4 But in everything+ *we* prove ourselves
as ministers of God: In much patience, in
sufferings,+ in necessities, in distresses,
5 in whippings,+ in imprisonments, in
tumults, in labors, in sleepless+ *nights*,
in fasting,
6 *and* by pureness, by knowledge, by
longsuffering, by kindness, by the Holy
Spirit, by sincere+ love,
7 by the Word of Truth, by the power of
God, by the armor of righteousness at
the right hand and at the left,
8 by honor and dishonor, by evil report
and good report, as *called* deceivers and
yet true,
9 as unknown and *yet* well known, as
dying and *yet* behold we live, as chastened
but not killed,
10 as in sorrow yet always rejoicing, as
poor yet making many rich, as having
nothing and *yet* possessing everything.+
11 O Corinthians. Our mouth is open to
bless you. Our heart is enlarged.
12 You are not constrained+ by us, but
you are constrained in your own innermost being.+
13 But I urge+ you children to respond+
the same *as us*: with enlarged *hearts*.
14 Do not be unequally yoked together
with unbelievers. For what fellowship
has righteousness with unrighteousness?
And what communion has light with
darkness?
15 What concord has Christ with Belial?
Or what part have *those* who believe
with an infidel?
16 What agreement has the temple of
God with idols? For you are the temple
of the living God. As God said: I will
dwell among them and walk among
them. I will be their God and they shall
be my people. *Exodus 29:45, Leviticus 26:12*
17 Therefore come out from among them
and be separate, says the Lord. Do not
touch the unclean *and* I will receive you
Isaiah 52:11, Numbers 16:21
18 *and* I will be a Father to you and you
shall be my sons and daughters, says the
Lord Almighty. *2 Samuel 7:14*

2 Corinthians Chapter 7

1 Therefore, having these promises, beloved, let us cleanse ourselves from all filthiness of the flesh and spirit, perfecting holiness in the fear of God.

2 Receive us. We have wronged no one. We have corrupted no one. We have defrauded no one.

3 I do not speak *this* to condemn *you*, for I have said before that you are in our hearts to live and die with *you*.

4 Great *is* my boldness of speech toward you. Great *is* my rejoicing[+] in you. I am filled with comfort. I am exceedingly joyful in all our tribulation.

5 For when we had come to Macedonia, our flesh had no rest, but we were troubled on every side. Fighting *on the* outside,[+] fearful *on the* inside.[+]

6 Nevertheless God who comforts *those* who are cast down, comforted us by the coming of Titus.

7 Not only by his coming, but by the consolation with which he was comforted by you. When he told us *about* your earnest desire, your mourning, *and* your fervent mind toward me, I rejoiced *all* the more.

8 For though I made you sorry with a letter, I do not repent, though I did repent *at first*. For I perceive that the same epistle made you sorry, although *that was* only for a season.

9 Now I rejoice, not that you were made sorry, but that you sorrowed unto repentance. For you were made sorry in a godly manner *so* that you might receive no damage from us in anything.

10 For godly sorrow produces[+] repentance unto salvation *and that is* not to be regretted.[+] But the sorrow of the world produces[+] death.

11 For behold this: That you sorrowed according[+] *to* God *and* what diligence[+] it produced[+] in you, *what* answers,[+] *what* indignation, *what* fear, *what* intense[+] desire, *what* zeal, *what* vindication.[+] In everything[+] you have proved[+] yourselves to be clear in this matter.

12 Therefore, although I wrote to you, *it was* not for *the one* who did wrong nor for *the one* who suffered wrong, but *so* that our care for you in the sight of God might be evident[+] to you.

13 Therefore we were comforted in your comfort. Yes, and we rejoiced[+] exceedingly more over the joy of Titus because his spirit was refreshed by you all.

14 For if I have boasted to him about you in anything, I am not ashamed. But as we spoke everything[+] to you in truth, even so our boasting, which *I did* before Titus, is found *to be* truth.

15 His inward affection is more abundant toward you as he remembers the obedience of you all *and* how you received him with fear and trembling.

16 Therefore I rejoice that I *can* have confidence in you in everything.[+]

2 Corinthians Chapter 8

1 Family,[+] understand[+] the grace of God *that has been* bestowed in the assemblies[+] of Macedonia.

2 In a great trial of suffering,[+] the abundance of their joy and their deep poverty abounded to the riches of their liberality.

3 I testify[+] to *their* power. Yes and *they were* willing *even* beyond *their* power.

4 With much encouragement[+] *they* urged[+] us to receive *their* gracious[+] *gift* in fellowship to serve the saints.

5 And not *only this*, according *as we* had hoped, but *they* themselves gave first to the Lord and to us, by the will of God.

6 In *view of* this, we urged[+] Titus, that as he had begun, so also he would finish with you *in* the *same* grace.

7 Therefore, as you abound in everything[+]: *In* faith and utterance and knowledge and all diligence and *in* your love to us, *see* that you abound in this grace also.

8 I do not speak *this* as a commandment, but by the diligent[+] *example* of others also proving the sincerity of your love.

9 For you know the grace of our Lord Jesus Christ, that although He was rich, yet for your sakes He became

poor *so* that through His poverty you
might be rich.
10 In this *example* I give *you my* advice.
For this is beneficial+ for you who have
already begun, not only to do *these things*,
but also to have been *so* willing *to do*
them, even before a year ago.
11 Now therefore, perform the doing. As
there was a ready will, so *may there be* a
performance also out of what you have.
12 For if there is first a willing mind, *it is*
accepted according to what one has *and*
not according to what one does not have.
13 For *I* do not *mean* that others be eased
and you burdened.
14 But *in the interest* of equality in this
present time, *may* your abundance be *a*
supply for their deficiency+ *so* that their
abundance *may* also be *a supply* for your
deficiency *later*.
15 As it is written: *Those* who *had gathered*
much had nothing over, and *those* who
had gathered little had no lack. *Exodus 16:18*
16 But thanks *be* to God who put the
same earnest care into the heart of
Titus for you.
17 For indeed, he accepted the exhortation. But being diligent,+ he went to
you of his own accord.
18 We sent with him that brother whose
praise in the Gospel *has gone* throughout
all the assemblies.+
19 Not only *that*, but *he* was also chosen
by the assemblies+ to travel with us *in*
this grace *that is* administered by us to
the glory of the Lord and *to show* your
readiness *to serve*.
20 *We are exercising* caution+ *so* that no
one should blame us *in the way* in which
this abundance is administered by us.
21 *We are* providing for honest things, not
only in the sight of the Lord, but also in
the sight of *people*.
22 We have sent our brother with them,
one whom we have repeatedly+ proved
diligent in many things, but now much
more diligent, *reflecting* upon the great
confidence that *I have* in you.
23 If *any ask* about Titus, *he is* my partner
and fellow helper concerning you. Or *if*
they ask about our brothers, *they are* the
messengers from the assemblies+ *and*
the glory of Christ.
24 Therefore show to them and before
the assemblies+ the proof of your love
and of our rejoicing+ in you.

2 Corinthians Chapter 9

1 Concerning the ministering to the
saints, it is superfluous for me to write
to you.
2 For I know the forwardness of your
mind, for which I boast about you to
those of Macedonia, that Achaia was
ready a year ago. Your zeal has provoked
very many.
3 Yet I have sent the brothers *so* that our
rejoicing+ in you might not be in vain in
some respect, *but so* that you *may indeed*
be ready, as *has been* said.
4 Lest *perhaps* if they of Macedonia
come with me and find you unprepared,
we should not be ashamed that we spoke
with such confident boasting *about* you.
5 Therefore I thought it necessary to
exhort the family+ *so* that they would
go to you before and make up your
gift of blessing+ that you previously+
announced+ beforehand *so* that it might
be ready as *a* blessing+ and not as
covetousness.
6 *Those* who sow sparingly will also reap
sparingly and *those* who sow bountifully
will also reap bountifully,
7 everyone *giving* as they purpose in
their hearts, not complaining+ or *out* of
necessity.

God loves a cheerful giver.
8 God *is* able to make
all grace abound to you
so that you always have sufficient
and abound in every good work.

9 As it is written: He has dispersed
abroad. He has given to the poor. His
righteousness remains forever. *Psalm 112:9*
10 Now He who supplies+ seed to the
sower and bread for *your* food, *may He*
also multiply your seed sown and increase the fruits of your righteousness.

11 *May you* be enriched in everything to
all bountifulness, *thereby* causing us
even greater thanksgiving to God.
12 For the administration of this service
not only supplies the needs[+] of the
saints, but is abundantly *overflowing* also
in many thanksgivings to God.
13 Through the experience of this service,
God *is* glorified *by* submissiveness[+]
that proclaims the Gospel of Christ *by*
giving[+] to Him and to all.
14 And their prayer for you longs *for* you *to*
have the exceeding grace of God upon you.
15 Thanks *be* to God for His indescrib-
able[+] gift.

2 Corinthians Chapter 10

1 Now I Paul urge you with the meekness and gentleness of Christ. In *your*
presence *I am* small[+] among you, but
being absent *I* am bold toward you.
2 But I exhort[+] *you*, that I may not be bold
when I am present with that confidence,
with which I think to be bold against
some, who think of us as if we walked
according to the flesh.
3 For though we walk in the flesh, we do
not war after the flesh.
4 For the weapons of our warfare *are*
not worldly,[+] but mighty through God
to the pulling down of strong holds,
5 casting down imaginations and every
high thing that exalts itself against the
knowledge of God, bringing into captivity every thought to the obedience
of Christ, *and*
6 having in a readiness to revenge all
disobedience when your obedience is
fulfilled.
7 Are you looking at things according to
their outward appearance? If any trust
themselves that they are Christ's *then* let
them think *about* this again: As they *are*
Christ's, so also *are* we Christ's.
8 For *even* though I boast more about
the authority that the Lord has given
to us for edification, and not for your
destruction, I should not be ashamed.
9 May *it* not seem as if I would terrify
you by *my* letters.
10 For they say letters *are* weighty and
powerful, but bodily presence weak and
speech contemptible.
11 *Rather* let one think that as we are in
word by letters when we are absent,
such *will we be* also in deed when we are
present.
12 For we dare not make ourselves of the
number or compare ourselves with some
who commend themselves. Those who
measure themselves by themselves and
comparing themselves among themselves, are not wise.
13 But we will not boast of things without
measure, but *rather* according to the
measure of the rule that God has
distributed to us, a measure to reach
even to you.
14 For we do not stretch ourselves
beyond *our measure* as though we did
not reach to you, for we have come as
far as to you also in *proclaiming*[+] the
Gospel of Christ.
15 *We are* not boasting of things without
measure. *But our measure is not* from
other men's labors, but having hope
that when your faith is increased, we
shall be abundantly enlarged by you
according to our rule.
16 *We desire* to proclaim[+] the Gospel in
the *regions* beyond you, *and* not to boast
in another man's line of things made
ready to our hand.
17 But whoever rejoices,[+] let *them*
rejoice[+] in the Lord.
18 For *it is* not *those* who commend
themselves *who* are approved, but *those*
whom the Lord commends. *Proverbs 27:2*

2 Corinthians Chapter 11

1 I wish[+] you could bear with me a little
in *my* folly and *just* endure.
2 For I am jealous over you with godly
jealousy, for I have pledged[+] you to one
husband *so* that I may present *you as* a
chaste virgin to Christ.
3 But I fear, lest by any means, as the
serpent deceived[+] Eve through his deceit,[+]
so your minds could become corrupted
away from the simplicity that is in Christ.

4 For if one comes proclaiming+ another
Jesus whom we have not proclaimed,+
or *if* you receive another spirit, not
the same as you had received or another
Gospel not *the same* as you had accepted,
you might well bear with *it*.
5 For *I* consider+ *that I am* no less+
useful than the very chief apostles.
6 Though *I am* unrefined+ in speech,
I am not *lacking* in knowledge, but in
all things, thoroughly revealed+
among you.
7 Have I committed an offense in abas-
ing myself *so* that you might be exalted,
because I have freely proclaimed+ the
Gospel of God to you?
8 I robbed other assemblies,+ taking
wages *from them*, to serve you.
9 When I was present with you and *in*
need,+ I was chargeable to no one.
For what I was lacking, the family+
from Macedonia supplied. In everything,+ I have kept myself from being
burdensome to you, and *so* I will keep
myself.
10 As the truth of Christ is in me, no one
in the regions of Achaia shall stop me
from boastful+ *rejoicing*.
11 Why? Because I do not love you? God
knows *I do*.
12 But I will *continue to* do what I do *so*
that I may cut off the occasion from
those who desire occasion *to* glory *in* that
in which they may be found even as we.
13 For such *are* false apostles, deceitful
workers, transforming themselves into
the apostles of Christ.
14 No marvel, for Satan himself is
transformed into an angel of light.
15 Therefore *it is* no great thing if his
ministers also *seem to* be transformed as
the ministers of righteousness. Their
end shall be according to their works.
16 I say again, Let no one think me a fool.
Or otherwise, *just* receive me as a fool
so that I may boast a little.
17 What I speak, I do not speak according+
to the Lord, but foolishly, in this
confident boasting.
18 Seeing that many glory after the flesh,
I glory also.
19 For *you* endure+ fools gladly, since
you *yourselves* are wise.
20 For you suffer, if *someone* brings you
into bondage, or devours *you*, or takes
something from you, or exalts themselves,
or strikes+ you on the face.
21 *I am* ashamed+ to say that *sometimes*
we were weak. However, whenever
anyone *else* is bold *even* foolishly, *I am*
bold, also.
22 Are they Hebrews? So *am* I. Are they
Israelites? So *am* I. Are they the seed of
Abraham? So *am* I.
23 Are they ministers of Christ? *Now* I
speak like a fool. I *am even* more in labor,
in whippings+ above measure, in prison
more frequently, often *near* death.
24 From the Jews, five times I received
forty *lashes*, less one.
25 Three *times* I was beaten with rods.
Once was I stoned. Three times I
suffered shipwreck. A night and a day
I have been in the deep.
26 *In* journeys often, *in* perils of waters,
in perils of robbers, *in* perils by *my own*
countrymen, *in* perils by the heathen, *in*
perils in the city, *in* perils in the wilderness, *in* perils in the sea, *in* perils
among false brothers.
27 In weariness and painfulness, in
watchings often, in hunger and thirst, in
fastings often, in cold and nakedness.
28 Beside those things that come upon me
daily from the outside, *I have* the care of
all the assemblies.+
29 Who is weak and I am not weak?
Who is offended *and caused to sin* and
I do not burn?
30 If I need to boast,+ I will boast about
those things *that reveal* my weaknesses.+
31 The God and Father *of* our Lord Jesus
Christ who is blessed forever, knows
that I do not lie.
32 In Damascus the governor under
Aretas the king kept the city of the
Damascenes with a garrison, desirous
to apprehend me.
33 But I was let down in a basket
through a window by the wall and
escaped his hands.

2 Corinthians Chapter 12

1 It is *surely* not beneficial for me to
boast.+ *Instead*, I will come to *the* visions
and revelations of the Lord.
2 About fourteen years ago, I knew a
man in Christ *who had been* caught up to
the third heaven. I do not know whether
this was in the body or out of the body.
Only God knows *that*.
3 But I did know such a man. *Again*,
whether *this was* in body or out of body,
I do not know. God knows.
4 He was caught up into paradise and
heard indescribable+ words that are not
lawful for a man to utter.
5 Of such a one I will boastfully+
rejoice. Yet of myself I will not boast,
except in my infirmities.
6 For though I would desire to boast,+ I
shall not be a fool. But I will speak the
truth. But *now* I hesitate,+ lest anyone
should think more+ of me than what is
seen or heard from me.
7 Lest I be exalted above measure
through the abundance of revelations, a
thorn in the flesh was given to me, a
messenger of Satan to buffet me, lest I
be exalted above measure.
8 Three times, I begged+ the Lord that
this might depart from me.
9 He said to me:

> My grace is sufficient for you.
> For my strength is made perfect
> in weakness.

Therefore I will most gladly rejoice+ in
my infirmities *so* that the power of
Christ may rest upon me.
10 Therefore I take pleasure in infirmities,
in reproaches, in necessities, in persecutions, in distresses for Christ's sake,
for when I am weak, then am I strong.
11 I am made+ a fool *by my* boasting.+
You have compelled me. I ought to have
been commended by you. For I am not
lacking behind the very chief apostles,
even though I am nothing.
12 Truly the signs of an apostle were
produced+ among you in all patience, in
signs, and wonders, and mighty deeds.
13 For what is it in which you were
inferior to other assemblies,+ except
that I was not a burden to you? Forgive
me *for* this wrong.
14 Behold *now for* the third time I am
ready to come to you. I will not be a
burden to you. For I do not seek *what is*
yours, but you. For children should not
need to lay up *reserves* for parents, but
parents for the children.
15 I will very gladly spend and be spent
for you. Though the more abundantly I
love you, the less I *seem to* be loved.
16 But so be it. I did not burden you.
However being crafty, guile caught you.
17 Did I make a gain from you by any of
those I sent to you?
18 I encouraged+ Titus and sent a brother
with *him*. Did Titus make a gain from
you? Did we not walk in the same spirit?
Did we not *walk* in the same steps?
19 Again, do you think that we excuse
ourselves to you? We speak before God
in Christ, but *we do* all things, beloved,
for your edification.
20 For I fear lest when I come, *that* I will
not find you as I wish+ *you would be*, and
that I will be found *by* you as you would
not *wish*, lest *there be* debates, envyings,
wraths, strifes, backbitings, whisperings,
swellings, tumults;
21 *and* lest, when I come again, my God
will humble me among you, and I shall
mourn+ for many who have sinned and
not repented of the uncleanness and
fornication and filthiness+ that they have
committed.

2 Corinthians Chapter 13

1 This *now, is* the third *time that* I am
coming to you. By the mouth of two or
three witnesses, every word shall be
established. *Matthew 18:16*
2 I *have* told you before, and *now I am*
forewarning+ you a second time as
though I were present *with you*. Being
absent *from you* now, I *am* writing to
those who have sinned before+ and to all

others *to say* that if I come again, I will not spare *you*.

3 Since you seek proof in me, *I am* speaking of Christ who is not weak toward you, but is mighty in you.

4 For though *Christ* was crucified through weakness, yet He lives by the power of God. For we also are weak in Him, but we shall live with Him by the power of God toward you.

> 5 Examine yourselves
> *to see* if you are in the faith.
> Prove yourselves.
> Do you yourselves not know
> that Jesus Christ is in you,
> unless+ you are reprobates.

6 But I trust that you will know that we are not reprobates.

7 Now I pray to God that you do no evil. Not *so* that we *may* appear *as* approved, but *so* that you would do what is honest, *even* if we are rejected.+

8 For we can do nothing against the truth, but *only* for the truth.

9 We are glad when we are weak and you are strong. This also we wish, *even* your perfection.

10 Therefore, being absent *from you*, I write these things *to you* lest *by* being present I should use sharp *words* according to the authority+ that the Lord has given *to* me for edification and not for destruction.

11 Finally, family+: Farewell. Be perfect. Be of good comfort.

> Be of one mind. Live in peace,
> and the God of love and peace
> will be with you.

12 Greet one another with a holy kiss.

13 All the saints greet+ you.

14 The grace of the Lord Jesus Christ and the love of God and the communion of the Holy Spirit *be* with you all. Amen.

The second epistle to the Corinthians was transcribed at Philippi, a city of Macedonia, by Titus and Lucas.

Galatians Chapter 1

1 *From* Paul, an apostle, not of men nor by man, but by Jesus Christ and God the Father who raised Him from the dead,

2 and *from* all the family+ who are with me. To the assemblies+ of Galatia.

3 Grace to you and peace from God *the* Father and our Lord Jesus Christ

4 who gave Himself for our sins *so* that He might deliver us from this present evil world, according to the will of our God and Father,

5 to whom *be* glory forever and ever. Amen.

6 I marvel that you so quickly+ turned+ *away* from Him who called you into the grace of Christ, to a different+ Gospel.

7 There is not another *valid Gospel*. Yet there are some who trouble you and would pervert the Gospel of Christ.

8 But if we or an angel from heaven proclaim+ any Gospel to you, *different* than what we have *already* proclaimed+ to you, *let them* be accursed.

9 As we have said before, I now say again: If anyone+ proclaims+ any Gospel to you other than what you have *already* received, *let them* be accursed.

10 For do I now persuade men, or God? Or do I seek to please men? For if I yet pleased men, I should not be the servant of Christ.

11 But I certify *to* you, family,+ that the Gospel that was proclaimed+ by me is not from man.

12 For I did not receive it from man, nor was I taught *it by man*. But *it came to me* by the revelation of Jesus Christ.

13 For you have heard about my conversation *and conduct* in *the* past, in Judaism.+ *You know* that I excessively+ persecuted the assembly+ of God beyond measure, and ravaged+ it.

14 And *I* advanced+ in the Jews' religion beyond+ many *of* my peers+ in my own nation, being more exceedingly zealous of the traditions of my fathers.

15 But when it pleased God, who separated me from my mother's womb and called *me* by His grace,

16 to reveal His Son in me *so* that I might proclaim[+] Him among the heathen, immediately I conferred, not with flesh and blood,

17 nor did I go up to Jerusalem to *those* who were apostles before me, but I went to Arabia. *Then, I* returned again to Damascus.

18 Then after three years, I went to Jerusalem to see Peter and stayed[+] with him fifteen days.

19 But I did not see the other apostles, except[+] James the brother of the Lord.

20 Now behold what I write to you. Before God, I do not lie.

21 Then, I went into the regions of Syria and Cilicia.

22 I was unknown, in person,[+] to the assemblies[+] of Judea that were in Christ.

23 But they had heard only *this*: That *he* who once[+] persecuted us, now proclaims[+] the faith that he once ravaged.[+]

24 And they glorified God in me.

Galatians Chapter 2

1 Fourteen years later,[+] I again went to Jerusalem with Barnabas and *also* took Titus with *me*.

2 I went according to *the* revelation *I received* and communicated to them the Gospel that I proclaim[+] among the Gentiles. But *I spoke* privately to those of *lofty* reputation, lest by any means I should be running or had run, in vain.

3 But *even* Titus who was with me, being Greek, was not compelled to be circumcised.

4 *Even though* false brothers came[+] *in* secretly[+] to spy out our liberty that we have in Christ Jesus *so* that they might bring us into bondage.

5 We did not yield[+] in subjection *to them*, even for an hour, *so* that the truth of the Gospel might continue with you.

6 But from those thought[+] to be somebody[+] *important*, what they were makes no difference[+] to me. God does not receive *one* person *above another*. To me *also*, those of *lofty* reputation[+] conveyed[+] nothing *special*.

7 On the contrary, *they* saw that the Gospel *to* the uncircumcision was committed to me *just* as *the Gospel to* the circumcision *was* to Peter.

8 For He who worked[+] *in* Peter for apostleship *to* the circumcision *also* worked[+] *in* me for the Gentiles.

9 When James, Cephas, and John, who seemed to be pillars, perceived the grace that was given to me, they gave to me and *to* Barnabas the right hand of fellowship *so* that we *might go* to the Gentiles[+] and they to the circumcision.

10 Only *they urged* that we remember the poor, which I also was diligent[+] to do.

11 However, when Peter came to Antioch, I challenged[+] him to *his* face, because he was to be blamed.

12 Because, before certain *ones* came from James, *Peter* ate with the Gentiles. But when they came, he withdrew and separated himself, fearing those of the circumcision.

13 The other Jews also *joined in putting on a false* pretense[+] with *Peter* so that Barnabas was also carried away with their hypocrisy.[+]

14 When I saw that they did not walk uprightly according to the truth of the Gospel, I said to Peter before *them* all: If you, being a Jew, live after the manner of Gentiles and not like the Jews, *then* why do you compel the Gentiles to live like the Jews?

15 By nature, we *are* Jews and not sinners from the Gentiles.

16 *We* know that a man is not justified by the works of the law, but by faith *in* Jesus Christ. We have believed in Jesus Christ *so* that we might be justified by faith *in* Christ and not by the works of the law. For no flesh will be justified by the works of the law.

17 But if, while we seek to be justified by Christ, we ourselves are also found sinners, *is* Christ therefore a minister of sin? *That* cannot be.[+]

18 For if I build again the things that I *had* destroyed, *then* I make myself a transgressor.

19 For through *the* law, I died *to the* law
so that I might live *for* God.
20 *I* have been crucified *with* Christ, *and*
yet[+] I live. *However, it is* no longer I, but
Christ living in me. And *the life* that I
now live in the flesh, I live by faith *in* the
Son of God who loved me and gave
Himself for me.
21 I do not reject[+] the grace of God. For
if righteousness *is* through *the* law, then
Christ died in vain.

Galatians Chapter 3

1 O foolish Galatians, who has bewitched
you to not obey the truth? Before *your*
eyes, Jesus Christ was set forth *and*
crucified among you.
2 This only would I learn from you: Did
you receive the Spirit from works of the
law or by hearing of faith?
3 Are you so foolish? Having begun in
the Spirit, are you now made perfect by
the flesh?
4 Have you suffered so many things in
vain? If *it was* in vain.
5 Therefore, *does* He who supplies[+] the
Spirit to you and works miracles among
you *do it* by works of the law or by
hearing of faith?
6 As Abraham believed God, it was credited[+] to him as righteousness. *Genesis 15:6*
7 Know, therefore, that *those* who are of
faith, the same are the children of
Abraham.
8 The Scripture, foreseeing that God
would justify the heathen through faith,
proclaimed[+] the Gospel to Abraham
before, *saying*: In you, all the nations
will be blessed. *Genesis 12:3*
9 So, *those* who are of faith are *being*
blessed with the faith[+] *of* Abraham.
10 For all[+] *who* endure[+] by works of the
law are under a curse. For it is written:
Cursed *is* everyone who does not
continue in all things that are written
in the book of the law, to do them.
Deuteronomy 27:26
11 However[+] *it is* evident that no one is
justified by the law in the sight of God.
For the righteous[+] shall live by faith.
12 However,[+] law is not by faith. But,
those of mankind[+] who make them shall
live in them. *Leviticus 18:5*
13 Christ has redeemed us from the curse
of the law *by* becoming[+] cursed for us.
For it is written: Cursed *is* everyone
who hangs on a tree. *Deuteronomy 21:23*
14 *This occurred so* that the blessing of
Abraham might come to the Gentiles
through Jesus Christ, *so* that we might
receive the promise of the Spirit
through faith.
15 Family,[+] *I am* speaking after the manner of men. Even so, no one *can* nullify[+]
or add to a man's confirmed covenant.
16 Now the promises were made to
Abraham and *to* his seed. He did not
say: And to seeds, as of many, but as of
one. And *specifically* to your seed, who
is Christ.
17 I say this: The covenant *pertaining* to
Christ was confirmed before by God.
The law that *came into* being[+] four
hundred and thirty years later,[+] cannot
nullify[+] *it so* that it would make the
promise of no effect.
18 For if the inheritance *is* from the law,
then it is no longer[+] from *the* promise.
But God gave *it* to Abraham by promise.
19 Why then *was* the law *given*? It was
added because of transgressions, until
the seed should come *for* whom the
promise was made. *It was* ordained in
the hand *of a* mediator by angels.
20 But the mediator is not *the* one *who
made the promise*, but God is.
21 Then *is* the law against the promises of
God? *That* cannot be.[+] For if a law had
been given that was able to give life,
then truly[+] righteousness could have
been *achieved* by law.
22 But the Scripture established[+] all things
under sin *so* that the promise of Jesus
Christ might be given by faith to *those*
who believe.
23 But before faith came, under law we
were guarded[+] *while* closed[+] to the faith
that was about to be revealed.
24 Therefore the law was our tutor[+] *to
bring us* to Christ *so* that we might be
justified by faith.

25 But after faith has come, we are no longer under an instructor.+

> 26 You are all children of God
> by faith in Christ Jesus.

27 For all+ *who* have been baptized into Christ have put on Christ.

28 There is neither Jew nor Greek. There is neither bond nor free. There is neither male nor female. For you are all one in Christ Jesus.

29 And if you *are* Christ's, then you are Abraham's seed and heirs according to the promise.

Galatians Chapter 4

1 Now I say: For as long a time as an heir is a child, *there* is no difference+ *from* a servant, *even though that heir* will be lord *over* all.

2 But *a child* is under tutors and guardians+ until the *time* appointed *by* the father.

3 And so when we were children, we were *held* in bondage under the elements of the world.

4 But when the fullness of time came, God sent forth His Son, made from a woman *and* made under *the* law, *Genesis 3:15*

5 to redeem *those* who were under *the* law *so* that we might receive adoption.

6 But because *you* are children+ *of God*, God has sent forth the Spirit of His Son into your hearts, crying *out*: Abba Father.

7 Therefore you are no longer+ a servant, but a child+ *of God*. And as a child+ *of God*, also an heir of God through Christ.

8 However, when you did not know God, you were in bondage+ to *those* who are not by nature gods.

9 But now, having known God, or rather having been known by God, how *can you* turn again to the weak and contemptible+ elements, to which you *seem to* desire to be in bondage again?

10 You observe days and months and times and years.

11 I am afraid *for* you, lest *somehow* I have labored for you in vain.

12 Family,+ I urge you: Be as I *am*. For I *am* like you. You have not wronged+ me at all.

13 You know how, *even* through *my* weakness+ in the flesh, I proclaimed+ the Gospel to you *from* the first.

14 And you did not despise or reject *me for* my trials+ in my flesh, but *you* received me like an angel of God, *even* as Christ Jesus.

15 What then was *the source of* your blessedness? For I testify+ that, if *it had been* possible, you would have plucked out your own eyes and given them to me.

16 Have I become your enemy because I speak the truth to you?

17 *Certain things* zealously affect you, *but* not *for* good. But *rather* they desire+ that you be zealous+ *for them* to draw+ you *away*.

18 *It is* good to be zealous in good *things* always, and not only when I am present with you.

19 My little children *for* whom I labor+ again until Christ be formed in you,

20 I desire to be present with you now and to change my voice. For I stand in doubt *about* you.

21 Tell me, you who desire to be under the law: Do you not hear the law?

22 For it is written: Abraham had two sons. One by a servant+ *woman*. The other by a free woman. *Genesis 21:10*

23 But one was born of the servant+ woman by the flesh. And one of the free woman through the promise.

24 This is an allegory. For these are *representative of* the two covenants: One from Mount Sinai that brings forth+ bondage is Hagar.

25 Hagar is *representative of* Mount Sinai in Arabia and corresponds+ to Jerusalem now, and *she* is in bondage with her children.

26 But *the* Jerusalem *that is* above is free *and* this is the mother of us all.

27 For it is written: Rejoice, *you* barren who do not bear. Break forth and cry *out*, you who do not labor+ *in childbirth*. For the desolate has many more children than she who has a husband. *Isaiah 54:1*

28 Now we, family,+ are children of *the* promise *just* as Isaac was.

29 But *just* as one born by the flesh persecuted one *born* by the Spirit, so also *is it* now.

30 Nevertheless, what does the Scripture say? Cast out the servant+ woman and her son. For the son of the servant+ woman will not be *the* heir with the son of the free woman. *Genesis 21:10, John 8:35*

31 So then, family,+ we are not children of the servant+ woman, but of the free.

Galatians Chapter 5

1 Stand fast therefore in the liberty with which Christ has made us free, and do not become entangled again with the yoke of bondage.

2 Behold I Paul say to you, that if you become+ circumcised *out of obedience to the law*, Christ will *bring* you no benefit.+

3 For I testify again to everyone+ who is *thus* circumcised, that *in so doing* one becomes+ obligated+ to do the whole law.

4 Whoever *among you* are *endeavoring to be* justified within the law are deprived+ of any benefit+ from Christ. *Rather, such as these* have fallen from grace.

5 For we, through the Spirit, by faith, wait for the hope of righteousness.

6 For in Christ Jesus, neither circumcision nor uncircumcision avails anything, but *only* faith working through love.

7 You have run well. Who hindered you *and caused you* to not obey the truth?

8 This persuasion does not *come* from Him who calls you.

9 A little leaven leavens the whole lump.

10 I have confidence in you through the Lord, that you will not be otherwise minded. But whoever has troubled you will bear the judgment, whoever it may be.

11 But I, family,+ if I still proclaim+ circumcision, *then* why do I still suffer persecution *from the Jews*? Then the offense of the cross has ceased.

12 I wish+ *those* who trouble you were cut off.

13 For, family,+ you have been called to liberty. Only do not *use* liberty for an occasion *for weakness in* the flesh, but by love serve one another.

14 For the whole+ law is fulfilled in one word, in this: Love your neighbor as yourself. *Matthew 19:19*

15 But if you bite and devour one another, take heed *so* that you are not consumed by one another.

16 *This* I say then: Walk in the Spirit and you will not fulfill the lust of the flesh.

17 For the flesh lusts against the Spirit, and the Spirit against the flesh. These are contrary the one to the other so that you cannot do the things that you should do.

18 But if you are led by the Spirit *then* you are not under the law.

19 Now the works of the flesh are revealed+ as *these*: Adultery, fornication, uncleanness, filthiness,+ *Matthew 15:19*

20 idolatry, witchcraft, hatred, contentiousness,+ jealousy,+ wrath, strife, rebellion,+ heresies,

21 envies, murders, drunkenness, riots,+ and such like. I told you about *all* this before *and* as I have also told *you* in time past: *Those* who do such things will not inherit the kingdom of God.

> 22 But the fruit of the Spirit is love, joy, peace, longsuffering, gentleness, goodness, faith,
> 23 meekness, *and* temperance.

There is no law against these things.

24 *Those* who are Christ's have crucified the flesh with its passions+ and lusts.

25 If we live in the Spirit, let us also walk in the Spirit.

26 Let us not be *overtaken by selfcentered* pride,+ provoking one another, *or* envying one another.

Galatians Chapter 6

1 Family,+ if someone+ is overtaken in a fault, you who are spiritual *ought to try to* restore such a one in the spirit of meekness, considering yourself, lest you also be tested.+ *Matthew 18:15*

2 Bear one another's burdens and thereby[+] fulfill the law of Christ.

3 For if anyone thinks themselves to be something when they are nothing, they deceive themselves.

4 But let everyone[+] prove their own work and then they will have rejoicing in themselves alone and not in another.

5 For everyone[+] shall bear their own burden.

6 Let *those* who are taught in the Word share with *those* who teach in all good things.

7 Do not be deceived. God is not mocked.

> For whatever anyone sows,
> that they shall also reap.

8 For *those* who sow to their flesh will reap corruption from the flesh. But *those* who sow to the Spirit will reap eternal[+] life from the Spirit. *Proverbs 11:18*

9 Let us not be weary in well doing. For in due season we will reap, if we do not faint.

10 Therefore, as we have opportunity, let us do good to everyone.[+] Especially to *those* who are of the household of faith. *Proverbs 3:27*

11 See *in* what large letters I have written to you with my own hand.

12 As many as desire to make a fair appearance[+] in the flesh, they constrain you to be circumcised. *But this is* only so that they might not suffer persecution for the cross of Christ.

13 For they themselves who are circumcised do not keep the law, but *they* desire to have you circumcised *so* that they might boast[+] in your flesh.

14 But *as for* me, *may it* not be[+] that I should boast[+] *in anything* except[+] in the cross of our Lord Jesus Christ through whom, to me, the world has been crucified and I to the world.

15 For in Christ Jesus neither circumcision nor uncircumcision avails anything, but *only being* a new creation[+] *in Christ.*

16 And *to* as many as walk according to this rule: Peace *be* upon them and mercy, and upon the Israel of God.

17 From now on, let no one trouble me. For I bear in my body the marks of the Lord Jesus.

18 Family,[+] the grace of our Lord Jesus Christ *be* with your spirit. Amen.

This epistle was written at Rome.

Ephesians Chapter 1

1 *From* Paul, an apostle of Jesus Christ by the will of God. To the saints at Ephesus and to the faithful in Christ Jesus.

2 Grace to you and peace from God our Father and Lord Jesus Christ.

3 Blessed *is* the God and Father *of* our Lord Jesus Christ who has blessed us with all spiritual blessings in heavenly *places*, in Christ.

4 He chose us *to be* in Him before *the* foundation of *the* world *so* that we should be holy and without blame before Him in love.

5 *He* predestined us for adoption through Jesus Christ to Himself, according to the good pleasure of His will,

6 to the praise of the glory of His grace, in which He has made us accepted in the Beloved.

7 In *Jesus*, we have redemption through His blood *and* the forgiveness of sins according to the riches of His grace

8 that He has *made to* abound to us in all wisdom and prudence.

9 He has made the mystery of His will known to us, according to His good pleasure that He purposed in Himself,

10 *so* that in the administration[+] of the fullness of times He might gather together in one all things in Christ, both *those* in heaven and *those* on earth, *all gathered* in Him.

11 *For* in *Jesus*, we also have obtained an inheritance, being predestined according to the purpose of Him who works all things after the counsel of His own will,

12 *so* that we who first trusted in Christ should be to the praise of His glory.

13 You also *trusted* in *Him* after you heard the Word of Truth, the Gospel of your salvation. In *Him* also, after you

believed, you were sealed with the Holy Spirit of promise.

14 *The Holy Spirit* is the guarantee[+] of our inheritance until the redemption of the purchased possession, to the praise of His glory.

15 Therefore I also, after I heard of your faith in the Lord Jesus and love to all the saints,

16 did not cease to give thanks for you, making mention of you in my prayers,

17 *and asking* that the God *of* our Lord Jesus Christ, the Father of glory, might give *to* you the spirit of wisdom and revelation in the knowledge of Him.

18 *I also ask that* the eyes of your understanding be enlightened *so* that you might know what is the hope of His calling and what *are* the riches of the glory of His inheritance in the saints,

19 what *is* the exceeding greatness of His power toward us who believe, according to the working of His mighty power

20 that He worked[+] in Christ when He raised Him from the dead and seated *Him* at His own right hand in the heavenly *places*,

21 far above all principality and authority[+] and power and dominion and every name that is named, not only in this world, but also in what is to come.

22 *God* has put all *things* under His feet and gave Him *to be* the head over all *things* to the assembly[+]

23 that is His body, the fullness of Him who fills all in all.

Ephesians Chapter 2

1 *In the past,* you were[+] dead in trespasses and sins.

2 *In the past,* you walked according to the course of this world, according to the prince of the power of the air, the spirit that now works in the children of disobedience.

3 *In the past,* we all had our conversation *and conduct* in the lusts of our flesh, fulfilling the desires of the flesh and of the mind. *We* were, by nature, the children of wrath, even as others.

4 But God *is* rich in mercy because of His great love with which He loved us.

5 Even when we were dead in sins, *He* gave us life[+] with Christ. By grace, you are *being* saved.

6 *He* has raised *us* up together and made *us* sit together in heavenly *places* in Christ Jesus,

7 *so* that in the ages to come He might show the exceeding riches of His grace in *His* kindness toward us through Christ Jesus.

> 8 For *it is* by grace *that* you are
> *being* saved through faith,
> and that not of yourselves.
> *It is* the gift of God.
> 9 *It is* not of works,
> lest anyone should boast.

10 For we are His workmanship, created in Christ Jesus to *do the* good works that God has before ordained *so* that we should walk in them.

11 Therefore remember that you *were*, in time past, Gentiles in the flesh *and* called uncircumcision by *those* who are called the circumcision in the flesh made by hands.

12 At that time, you were without Christ, being aliens from the commonwealth of Israel and strangers from the covenants of promise, having no hope, and without God in the world.

13 But now in Christ Jesus, you who sometimes were far off, are made near by the blood of Christ.

14 For He is our peace, who made both one and broke down the middle wall of partition *between us*.

15 *He* abolished, in His flesh, the enmity, the law of commandments *contained* in ordinances, to make in Himself one new man *out* of two, *thereby* making peace,

16 *so* that He might reconcile both to God in one body by the cross, having slain the enmity thereby.

17 *He* came and proclaimed[+] peace to you who were far off and to *those* who were near.

18 For through Him we both have access

to the Father by one Spirit.
19 Now therefore, you are no longer
strangers and foreigners, but fellow
citizens with the saints, and of the
household of God.
20 *You* are being built upon the foundation
of the apostles and prophets, Jesus Christ
Himself being the chief corner *stone*.
21 In *Jesus*, all the building fitly framed
together grows to a holy temple in the
Lord.
22 In *Jesus*, you are also built together for
a habitation of God through the Spirit.

Ephesians Chapter 3

1 For this reason,+ I Paul, *am* the
prisoner of Jesus Christ for you Gentiles.
2 *Now* indeed, you have heard of the
administration+ of the grace of God that
was given *to* me for you.
3 By revelation, *God* made the mystery
known to me, as I wrote before+ in a
few words.
4 When you read *this*, you may understand my knowledge in the mystery of
Christ.
5 In other ages, *this* was not made
known to the children+ of mankind+
as it is now revealed to His holy
apostles and prophets by the Spirit.
6 *But now* the Gentiles can be fellow
heirs and of the same body and
partakers of His promise in Christ by
the Gospel.
7 For this, I was made a minister
according to the gift of the grace of God.
This was given to me by the effective
working of His power.
8 This grace has been given to me, *one*
who is less than the least of all saints, *so*
that I might proclaim+ the unsearchable
riches of Christ among the Gentiles,
9 to make all see what *is* the fellowship
of the mystery, which from the beginning of the world has been hid in God
who created all things by Jesus Christ.
10 *This* to the intent that now the manifold
wisdom of God might be *made* known by
the assembly+ to the principalities and
powers in heavenly *places*,
11 according to the eternal purpose that
He purposed in Christ Jesus our Lord.
12 In *Him* we have boldness and access
with confidence through faith in Him.
13 Therefore, I urge+ that you not faint
at my tribulations for you, which is
your glory.
14 For this reason,+ I bow my knees to
the Father *of* our Lord Jesus Christ,
15 after whom the whole family in heaven
and earth is named,
16 *so* that He would grant *to* you, according to the riches of His glory, to be
inwardly+ strengthened with might by
His Spirit,
17 *so* that Christ may dwell in your hearts
by faith, *and so* that you, being rooted
and grounded in love,
18 might be able to comprehend with all
saints what *is* the breadth and length and
depth and height *of His love*:
19 To know the love of Christ that
surpasses+ knowledge *so* that you might
be filled with all the fullness of God.
20 Now unto Him who is able to do
exceedingly abundant above all that we
ask or think according to the power that
works in us,
21 unto Him *be* glory in the assembly+ by
Christ Jesus throughout all ages, world
without end. Amen.

Ephesians Chapter 4

1 Therefore I, the prisoner of the Lord,
urge you to walk worthy of the vocation
into which you are called,
2 with all lowliness and meekness *and*
with longsuffering, forbearing one
another in love.
3 Endeavor to keep the unity of the
Spirit in the bond of peace.
4 *There is* one body and one Spirit, even
as you are called in one hope of your
calling.
5 One Lord, one faith, one baptism.
6 One God and Father of all, who *is*
above all and through all and in you all.
7 But to everyone of us, grace is given
according to the measure of the gift of
Christ.

8 Therefore He said: When He ascended
up on high, He led captivity captive and
gave gifts to people.+ *Psalm 68:18*
9 *Knowing* that He ascended, what is *to*
be understood but that He also descended
first into the lower parts of the earth?
10 He who descended is the same also
who ascended up far above all heavens
so that He might fill all things.
11 He gave some *to be* apostles, some *to*
be prophets, some *to be* evangelists, *and*
some *to be* pastors and teachers
12 for the perfecting of the saints, for the
work of the ministry, *and* for the edifying of the body of Christ,
13 until we all come in the unity of the
faith and in the knowledge of the Son of
God to a perfect man, to the measure of
the stature of the fullness of Christ.
14 *Therefore* we *must* no longer+ be *like*
children tossed to and fro and carried
away+ with every wind of doctrine, by
the sleight *and* cunning craftiness of
those who lie in wait to deceive.
15 But *we must* speak the truth in love *and*
grow up into *Him* who is the head,
Christ, in all things.
16 Through *Christ*, the whole body *is* fitly
joined together and connected+ by what
every joint supplies. Accordingly, the
effective working together+ of every part
increases the body edifying itself in love.
17 Therefore this I say and testify in the
Lord: You *must* no longer+ walk as
other Gentiles walk, in the vanity of
their mind,
18 having the understanding darkened,
and being alienated from the life of God
through the ignorance that is in them,
because of the blindness of their heart.
19 Being past feeling, they have given
themselves over to filthiness,+ to work
all uncleanness with greediness.
20 But you have not so learned Christ.
21 If indeed+ you have heard Him and
have been taught by Him, as the truth is
in Jesus,
22 then you *will* put off the old self,+
concerning the former conversation *and*
conduct that is corrupt according to the
deceitful lusts,
23 and be renewed in the spirit of your
mind,
24 and put on the new man, which, after
God, is created in righteousness and
true holiness.
25 Therefore put away lying. Everyone+
must speak truth with their neighbor.
For we are members of one another.
26 *If you* become+ angry, do not sin. Do
not let the sun go down upon your
wrath. *Psalm 37:8*
27 Do not give place to the devil.
28 Let *those* who stole, steal no longer.+
But rather let them labor, working with
their hands *in* the things that are good *so*
that they may have *sufficient* to give to
those who *have* needs. *Proverbs 21:26*

29 Do not let corrupt communication
proceed out of your mouth,
but what is good to the use
of edifying *so* that it may
minister grace to the hearers.
Matthew 12:35

30 Do not grieve the Holy Spirit of God,
by whom you are sealed to the day of
redemption.

31 Let all bitterness, wrath,
anger, clamor, and evil speaking
be put away from you,
along with all malice.
32 Be kind to one another,
tenderhearted,
forgiving one another,
even as God for Christ's sake
has forgiven you.

Ephesians Chapter 5

1 Therefore, be followers of God, as
dear children.
2 Walk in love as Christ also has loved
us and has given Himself for us, an
offering and a sacrifice to God for a
sweet smelling savor.
3 Do not let fornication and all uncleanness or covetousness be named among
you *even* once, as becomes saints.

4 *Do not allow* filthiness or foolish
talking or jesting, which is not
proper,+ but rather give thanks.
5 For this you know: That no fornicator+
or unclean person or covetous person
who is an idolater has any inheritance in
the kingdom of Christ and of God.
6 Let no one deceive you with vain
words. For because of these things the
wrath of God *will* come upon the children of disobedience.
7 Therefore do not be partakers with
them.
8 For you were sometimes darkness.
But now *you are* light in the Lord. Walk
as children of light.
9 For the fruit of the Spirit *is* in all
goodness and righteousness and truth,
10 proving what is acceptable *and pleasing* to the Lord.
11 Do not have fellowship with the
unfruitful works of darkness, but rather
admonish+ *them*.
12 For it is a shame to even speak of those
things that are done by them in secret.
13 But all *who* are admonished+ by the
light are revealed.+ For whatever
reveals+ *truth and error* is light.
14 Therefore He says: Awake, you who
sleep. Arise from the dead, and Christ
will give you light. *Isaiah 60:1*
15 See then that you walk circumspectly,
not as fools, but as wise. *Proverbs 15:21*
16 Redeem the time, because the days
are evil.
17 Therefore do not be unwise but understand what the will of the Lord *is*.
18 Do not be drunk with wine in which is
excess, but be filled with the Spirit.
19 Speak to yourselves in psalms and
hymns and spiritual songs, singing and
making melody in your heart to the
Lord.
20 Always give thanks for all things to
God the Father in the name *of* our Lord
Jesus Christ.
21 Submit yourselves to one another in
the fear of God.
22 Wives, submit yourselves to your own
husbands, as to the Lord.
23 For the husband is the head of the
wife, even as Christ is the head of the
church, and He is the Savior of the body.
24 Therefore as the assembly+ is subject
to Christ, so *let* the wives *be* to their
own husbands in everything.
25 Husbands love your wives, even as
Christ also loved the assembly+ and
gave Himself for it,
26 *so* that He might sanctify and cleanse it
with the washing of water by the Word,
27 *so* that He might present it to Himself
a glorious assembly,+ not having spot or
wrinkle or any such thing, but *so* that it
should be holy and without blemish.
28 So *also* men ought to love their wives
as their own bodies. He who loves his
wife loves himself.
29 For no one ever yet hated their own
flesh, but nourishes and cherishes it,
even as the Lord *nourishes and cherishes*
the church.
30 For we are members of His body, of
His flesh, and of His bones.
31 For this reason+ a man shall leave his
father and mother and shall be joined to
his wife and they two shall be one flesh.
Matthew 19:5
32 This is a great mystery, but I speak
concerning Christ and the church.
33 Nevertheless, let everyone of you in
particular so love his wife, even as
himself. And the wife *see* that she
reverence *her* husband.

Ephesians Chapter 6

1 Children, obey your parents in the
Lord, for this is right.
2 Honor your father and mother,
which is the first commandment with *a*
promise, *Matthew 15:4*
3 *so* that it may be well with you and you
may live long on the earth. *Exodus 20:12*
4 And you fathers: Do not provoke your
children to anger,+ but bring them up in
the nurture and admonition of the Lord.
Proverbs 22:6
5 Servants, be obedient to *those* who are
your masters according to the flesh, with
fear and trembling, in singleness of
your heart, as to Christ.

6 Not for appearance[+] *sake*, as pleasing people,[+] but as the servants of Christ, doing the will of God from the heart.
7 With good will, do *your* service as to the Lord and not to people.[+]
8 Know that whatever good thing anyone does, they will receive the same from the Lord, whether *they are* bond or free.
9 And you masters: Do the same things to them, forgoing[+] threatening, knowing that your Master also is in heaven, and there is no partiality[+] with Him.
10 Finally, my family,[+] be strong in the Lord and in the power of His might.
11 Put on the whole armor of God *so* that you may be able to stand against the traps[+] of the devil.
12 For we do not wrestle against flesh and blood but against principalities, against powers, against the rulers of the darkness of this world, *and* against spiritual wickedness in high *places*.
13 Therefore, take up[+] the whole armor of God *so* that you may be able to stand against[+] *evil* in the evil day. And having done all *you can*, stand *firm*.
14 Therefore stand, having your waist[+] belted[+] *strong* with truth, and having on the breastplate of righteousness,
15 and your feet shod with the preparation of the Gospel of peace.
16 Above all, take the shield of faith with which you will be able to quench all the fiery darts of the wicked.
17 And take the helmet of salvation and the sword of the Spirit, which is the Word of God,
18 praying always with all prayer and supplication in the Spirit and watching to this with all perseverance and supplication for all the saints.
19 *Pray also* for me *so* that utterance may be given to me *so* that I may open my mouth boldly to make known the mystery of the Gospel,
20 for which I am an ambassador in chains[+] *so* that *even* in that *state*, I may speak boldly as I ought to speak.
21 *So* that you may also know my affairs *and* how I am doing, Tychicus, a beloved brother and faithful minister in the Lord, will make everything[+] known to you.
22 I have sent *him* to you for the same purpose, *so* that you might know our affairs and *so that* he might comfort your hearts.
23 Peace to the family[+] and love in faith, from God *our* Father and Lord Jesus Christ.
24 Grace to all who love our Lord Jesus Christ in sincerity. Amen.

This epistle was transcribed at Rome by Tychicus.

Philippians Chapter 1

1 *From* Paul and Timothy, servants of Jesus Christ. To all the saints in Christ Jesus who are at Philippi, with the bishops and deacons.
2 Grace to you and peace from God our Father and Lord Jesus Christ.
3 I thank my God upon every remembrance of you.
4 Always, in every prayer of mine for you all, *I* ask[+] with joy
5 for your fellowship in the Gospel, from the first day until now.
6 *I* am confident of this: That

> He who has begun
> a good work in you
> will perform *it*
> until the day of Jesus Christ.

7 It is right[+] for me to think this of you all, because I have you in my heart. Inasmuch as both in my chains[+] and in the defense and confirmation of the Gospel, you are all partakers *with* me *of* grace.
8 For God is my witness,[+] how greatly I long for you all in the tender[+] *mercies* of Jesus Christ.
9 This I pray: That your love may abound yet more and more in knowledge and *in* all judgment,
10 *so* that you may approve things that are excellent *and so* that you may be sincere and without offense until the day of Christ.

11 Be filled with the fruit of righteousness that *comes* through Jesus Christ, to
the glory and praise of God.
12 I want you to understand, family,+
that the things *that have happened* to
me have turned+ out instead+ to the
advancement+ of the Gospel,
13 so that my chains+ in Christ are known+
in all the palace and in all other *places*.
14 Many of the family+ in the Lord,
growing+ more confident *because of* my
chains,+ are much more bold to speak
the Word without fear.
15 Indeed, some proclaim+ Christ from
envy and strife, but some also from
good will.
16 *Those* who proclaim+ Christ from
contention *and* not sincerely *are* supposing to add suffering+ to my chains.+
17 But the others *do so* out of love, knowing that I am set for the defense of the
Gospel.
18 What then? Even so,+ *in* every way,
whether in pretence or in truth, Christ is
proclaimed,+ and I rejoice in this. Yes,
and I will *continue to* rejoice.
19 For I know that this will turn to my
salvation through your prayer and the
supply of the Spirit of Jesus Christ.
20 According to my earnest expectation
and hope, I will be ashamed in nothing.
But with all boldness, now, as always,
Christ shall be magnified in my body,
whether by life or by death.
21 For to me, to live *is* Christ and to die
is gain.
22 If I live in the flesh, this *is* the fruit of
my labor. Yet I do not know+ what I
shall choose.
23 For I am in a strait between+ two
desires. Having a desire to depart and to
be with Christ, which is far better.
24 Nevertheless, *desiring* to remain+ in
the flesh *is* more necessary+ for you.
25 *But I* have this confidence: I know
that I shall remain+ and continue with
you all for your advancement+ and
joy of faith,
26 *so* that your rejoicing may be more
abundant in Jesus Christ for me by my
coming to you again.
27 Only *let your* conversation *and conduct*
be worthy+ of the Gospel of Christ, *so*
that whether I come and see you or else
must be absent, I may hear that you stand
fast in one spirit, with one mind striving
together for the faith of the Gospel.
28 Do not be frightened+ by your
adversaries. That will be, to them, an
evidence of *their* damnation,+ and of
your salvation, and that from God.
29 For it is given to you, on the behalf of
Christ, to not only believe in Him, but
also to suffer for His sake.
30 *You may* have conflicts *just* as you saw
in mine and now hear *about* in mine.

Philippians Chapter 2

1 Therefore, if *there be* any consolation
in Christ, if any comfort in love, if any
fellowship of the Spirit, if any tender+
mercies,
2 fulfill my joy: That you

be like minded,
having the same love,
being of one accord *and* of one mind.
3 *Let* nothing *be done* through strife
or *selfcentered* pride,+
but in lowliness of mind
let each esteem others
better than themselves.

4 Do not consider+ *only those* things of
your own+ *concern* but also the things of
others.
5 Let this mind be in you, which was
also in Christ Jesus.
6 *Christ* being in the form of God did not
think it robbery to be equal with God.
7 But *He* made Himself of no reputation
and took upon Himself+ the form of a
servant and was made in the likeness
of men.
8 And being found in fashion as a man,
Christ humbled Himself and became
obedient unto death, even the death of
the cross.
9 Therefore God also has highly exalted
Him and given Him a name that is above
every name,

10 *so* that at the name of Jesus, every
knee should bow, of *things* in heaven
and *things* in *the* earth and *things* under
the earth.
11 Every tongue should confess that
Jesus Christ *is* Lord, to the glory of
God the Father.
12 Therefore my beloved, as you have
always obeyed, not as in my presence
only but now much more in my absence,
work out your own salvation with fear
and trembling.
13 For it is God who works in you both to
will and to do of *His* good pleasure.
14 Do all things without complaining and
disputing
15 *so* that you may be blameless and
harmless, the children[+] of God, without
rebuke, in the midst of a crooked and
perverse nation, among whom you shine
as lights in the world.
16 Hold forth the Word of life *so* that I may
rejoice in the day of Christ, *so* that I
have not run in vain nor labored in vain.
17 Yes, and if I be offered upon the
sacrifice and service of your faith, I
have joy and rejoice with you all.
18 For the same cause also, you *should*
have joy and rejoice with me.
19 But I trust in the Lord Jesus to send
Timothy to you soon[+] *so* that I may also
be of good comfort when I know your
condition.[+]
20 For I have no one like minded who
will naturally care for your condition.[+]
21 For all seek their own *objectives*, not
the things that are Jesus Christ's.
22 But you know the proof of Him, that,
like a son with *his* father, *Timothy* has
served with me in the Gospel.
23 Therefore I hope to send him *to you*
immediately,[+] as soon as I see how it
will go with me.
24 But I trust in the Lord that I myself will
also come *to you* soon.[+]
25 Yet I supposed it necessary to send
Epaphroditus to you, my brother,
companion in labor, and fellow soldier,
but your messenger and one[+] who
ministered to my wants.
26 For he longed after you all and was
full of sorrow[+] because you had heard
that he had been sick.
27 For indeed he was sick, near death.
But God had mercy on him. Not on him
only, but on me also, lest I should have
sorrow upon sorrow.
28 I sent him therefore *all* the more carefully *so* that, when you see him again,
you may rejoice and *so* that I may be less
sorrowful.
29 Therefore, receive him in the Lord
with all gladness. Hold such *as him* in
high reputation.
30 Because of the work of Christ, he was
near death, not regarding his *own* life, *in*
order to supply your lack of service
toward me.

Philippians Chapter 3

1 Finally my family[+]: Rejoice in the
Lord. To write the same things to you
is indeed not grievous to me. But for you
it is safe.
2 Beware of dogs. Beware of evil
workers. Beware of division.[+]
3 For we are the circumcision, who
worship God in the spirit and rejoice in
Christ Jesus and have no confidence in
the flesh.
4 Though I might also have confidence
in the flesh. If anyone[+] *else* thinks that
they have reason[+] *to* trust in the flesh, I
have more.
5 *I was* circumcised *on* the eighth day, of
the stock of Israel, *of* the tribe of
Benjamin, a Hebrew of the Hebrews,
and concerning the law, a Pharisee.
6 *As* concerning zeal, *I was* persecuting
the church. *As* touching the righteousness that is in the law, *I was* blameless.
7 But what things were gain to me, those
I counted loss for *the sake of* Christ.
8 Yes doubtless. And I count all things
but loss for the excellency of the
knowledge of Christ Jesus my Lord
for whom I have suffered the loss of
all things and do count them *but* dung
so that I may win Christ
9 and be found in Him. *For I do* not
have *any* righteousness *of* my own

from *obedience to* the law, but *only*
through faith in Christ, righteousness
from God by faith.
10 *so* that I may know Him and the power
of His resurrection and the fellowship
of His sufferings, being made con-
formable to His death.
11 If by any means I might attain to the
resurrection of the dead,
12 not as though I had already attained or
had already *become* perfect, but I follow
after *so* that I may attain[+] that for which
I am claimed[+] by Christ Jesus.
13 Family,[+] I do not count myself to have
attained[+] *everything*, but *this* one thing *I*
do: Forgetting those things that are
behind and reaching forth to those things
that are before,
14 I press toward the mark for the prize of
the high calling of God in Christ Jesus.
15 Therefore let us, as many as be
perfect, be thus minded. If, in anything,
you are otherwise minded, God will
reveal this to you.
16 Nevertheless, in what we have already
attained, let us walk by the same rule.
Let us mind the same thing.
17 Family,[+] be followers together *with*
me. Note[+] *those* who walk *in this way*, as
you have us for an example.
18 For many walk, of whom I have
often told you, and now *I* tell you
weeping, *that they are* the enemies of
the cross of Christ.
19 Their end *will be* destruction. Their
God *is their* belly. And *those* who mind
earthly things glory in their shame.
20 For our conversation *and conduct* is in
heaven. From there we also look for the
Savior, the Lord Jesus Christ
21 who will change our vile body *so*
that it may be fashioned like His
glorious body, according to the work
by which He is able even to subdue all
things to Himself.

Philippians Chapter 4

1 Therefore my family,[+] beloved and
longed for, my joy and crown, so stand
fast in the Lord, *my* beloved.
2 I urge[+] Euodias and Syntyche that
they be of the same mind in the Lord.
3 I entreat you also, *my* true yokefellow:
Help those women who labored with me
in the Gospel *and* with Clement also and
with my other fellow laborers whose
names *are* in the Book of Life.

4 Rejoice in the Lord always.
And again I say: Rejoice.
Matthew 5:12
5 Let your moderation
be known to everyone.[+]
The Lord *is very* near.[+]
Luke 12:15
6 Do not be anxious[+] about[+] anything,
but in everything by prayer
and supplication with thanksgiving
let your requests
be made known to God.
Matthew 6:25
7 And the peace of God
that surpasses[+] all understanding
will keep your hearts and minds
through Christ Jesus. *John 14:27*

8 Finally family[+]: Whatever things
are true, whatever things *are* honest,
whatever things *are* righteous,[+]
whatever things *are* pure, whatever
things *are* lovely, whatever things
are of good report, if *there be* any
virtue and if *there be* any praise,
think on these things. *Matthew 5:8*

9 Do those things that you have both
learned and received and heard and
seen in me, and the God of peace will
be with you.
10 But I rejoiced in the Lord greatly that
now at the last your care for me has
flourished again in which you were also
careful but you lacked opportunity.
11 Not that I speak in respect of want, for
I have learned, in whatever state I am,
there to be content.
12 I know both how to be humbled[+] and
I know how to abound. Everywhere and
in all things I am instructed both to be
full and to be hungry, both to abound
and to suffer need.

13 I can do all things
through Christ
who strengthens me.

14 Nevertheless, you have done well *in*
that you shared+ in my suffering.+
15 Now you Philippians also know, that
in the beginning of the Gospel, when I
departed from Macedonia, no assembly+
shared+ with me as concerning giving
and receiving, but only you.
16 For even in Thessalonica, you sent
once and again to my necessity.
17 Not because I desire a gift, but I desire
fruit that may abound to your account.
18 But I have everything+ *I need* and
abound. I am full, having received from
Epaphroditus the things *that were sent*
from you. An aroma+ of a sweet
smell, a sacrifice acceptable, well
pleasing to God.

19 God will supply all you need
according to His riches in glory
by Christ Jesus.

20 Now to God our Father, *be* glory
forever and ever. Amen.
21 Greet+ every saint in Christ Jesus.
The family+ who are with me greet you.
22 All the saints greet+ you, chiefly *those*
who are of Caesar's household.
23 The grace of our Lord Jesus Christ
be with you all. Amen.

This epistle was transcribed at Rome by Epaphroditus.

Colossians Chapter 1

1 *From* Paul, an apostle of Jesus Christ
by the will of God, and Timothy *our*
brother.
2 To the saints and faithful believers+ in
Christ who are at Colosse. Grace to you
and peace from God our Father and
Lord Jesus Christ.
3 We give thanks *to our* God and Father
and our Lord Jesus Christ, praying for
you continually.+
4 We have heard of your faith in Christ
Jesus and of the love *that you have* for
all the saints.
5 Hope *is* laid up for you in heaven.
You heard about this before, in the
Word of Truth, in the Gospel
6 that has come to you, as to all the
world. *It* brings forth fruit, as *it has* in
you since the day you heard *of it* and
knew the grace of God in truth.
7 *Just* as you learned from Epaphras,
our dear fellow servant who is a faithful
minister of Christ for you.
8 *He* also declared to us your love in the
Spirit.
9 For this reason,+ since the day we heard
about this, we have not stopped+ praying
for you and desiring that you might be
filled with the knowledge of His will in all
wisdom and spiritual understanding,
10 *so* that you might walk worthy of the
Lord to all pleasing, being fruitful in
every good work and increasing in the
knowledge of God,
11 strengthened with all might according
to His glorious power, to all patience
and longsuffering with joyfulness.
12 Give thanks to the Father who has
made us suitable+ to be partakers of the
inheritance of the saints in light.
13 *God* has delivered us from the power
of darkness and translated *us* into the
kingdom of His dear Son.
14 In *Him*, we have redemption through
His blood, *even* the forgiveness of sins.
15 *He* is the *very* image of the invisible
God, the firstborn of all creation.+
16 By Him, all things were created, that
are in heaven and that are in earth,
visible and invisible, whether *they be*
thrones or dominions or principalities
or powers. All things were created by
Him and for Him.
17 He is before all things and by Him all
things consist.
18 He is the head of the body, the
assembly.+ He is *the* beginning, the
firstborn from the dead, *so* that in all
things He might have preeminence.
19 For it pleased *the Father* that all
fullness should dwell in Him.

20 And by Him, having made peace
through the blood of His cross, to
reconcile all things to Himself. By Him,
I say, whether *they be* things in earth or
things in heaven.
21 And you, who were at one time
alienated and enemies in *your* mind by
wicked works, yet now He has reconciled
22 in the body of His flesh through death,
to present you holy and blameless[+] and
unreprovable in His sight.
23 Continue in the faith, grounded and
settled and not moved away from the
hope of the Gospel that you have heard
as *it is* proclaimed[+] to all creation[+]
under heaven. For this, I Paul am made
a minister.
24 Now *I* rejoice in my sufferings for
you, and fill up what is lacking[+] through
the sufferings[+] of Christ in my *own*
flesh, for the sake of His body, which is
the *whole* assembly[+] *of believers*.
25 I have become[+] a minister according
to the administration[+] of God. *This
assignment was* given to me *for* you, to
fulfill the Word of God.
26 The mystery *that had been* hidden for
ages and for generations is now revealed[+] to His saints.
27 To *His saints*, God wants[+] *to* make
known the riches of the glory of this
mystery among the Gentiles. *It* is Christ
in you, the hope of glory
28 whom we proclaim,[+] warning everyone[+] and teaching everyone[+] in all
wisdom *so* that we may present everyone[+] perfect in Christ Jesus.
29 To *this cause* I also labor, striving
according to His working, which works
in me mightily.

Colossians Chapter 2

1 I wish[+] that you knew what great
conflict I have *endured* for you, and *for*
those at Laodicea and *for* all[+] *who* have
not *even* seen my face in the flesh,
2 *so* that their hearts might be comforted,
being knit together in love and *enjoying*
all *the* riches of the full assurance of
understanding, *even* to the acknowledg-
ment of the mystery of God, and of the
Father and of Christ
3 in whom all the treasures of wisdom
and knowledge are hid.
4 I say *all* this, lest anyone should deceive[+] you with enticing words.
5 For *even* though I *may* be absent in
the flesh, yet am I with you in the
spirit, rejoicing[+] and beholding your
order and the steadfastness of your
faith in Christ.

6 Therefore, as you have
received Christ Jesus the Lord,
so also walk in Him.
7 *Be* rooted and built up in Him
and established in the faith,
as you have been taught,
abounding therein
with thanksgiving.

8 Beware lest anyone spoil you through
philosophy and vain deceit, after the
traditions of men *and* after the things[+]
of the world, and not after Christ.
9 For in Him dwells all the fullness of
the Godhead bodily.
10 You are complete in Him who is the
head of all principalities and authorities[+]
and powers.
11 In *Him* also you are circumcised with
the circumcision made without hands,
in putting off the body of the sins of the
flesh by the circumcision of Christ.
12 *You were* buried with Him in baptism,
in which you are also risen with *Him*
through faith in the operation of God
who has raised Him from the dead.
13 And *to* you, being dead in your sins
and in the uncircumcision of your flesh,
He has given life[+] together with Him,
having forgiven you *for* all trespasses,
14 blotting out the handwriting of ordinances that was against us, which was
contrary to us. *He* took it out of the way,
nailing it to His cross.
15 *And* having spoiled principalities and
powers, He made a show of them openly,
triumphing over them in it.
16 Therefore, do not let anyone judge
you in food[+] or in drink or in respect of

a holy day or of the new moon or of the
Sabbath *days*.
17 *These* are a shadow of things to come.
But the body *is* of Christ.
18 Do not let anyone deceive[+] you into
selfwilled[+] humility *of your own pretense*
and worshiping angels, intruding into
things that have not been seen *but* vainly
puffed up by the fleshly mind,
19 not holding *fast* the Head from which
all the body, by joints and bands having
nourishment ministered *to them* and
knit together, increases *by* the increase
of God.
20 Therefore, if you are dead with Christ
from the things[+] of the world, *then* why,
as though living in the world, are you
subject to ordinances:
21 Do not touch. Do not taste. Do not
handle.
22 All *this* is *subject* to corruption according *to* the use, commandments, and
doctrines of men.
23 *These* things indeed have the appearance[+] of wisdom in selfwilled[+] worship
and humility and neglecting of the body
but they are not of any honor for *they*
satisfy the flesh.

Colossians Chapter 3

1 If you then are risen with Christ, seek
those things that are above, where Christ
sits at the right hand of God.
2 Set your affection on things above, not
on things on the earth.
3 For you are dead, and your life is hid
with Christ in God.
4 When Christ, *who is* our life, appears,
then you will also appear with Him in
glory.
5 Therefore, put to death[+] your members
which are upon the earth: fornication,
uncleanness, inordinate affection, evil
abnormal appetites,[+] and covetousness,
which is idolatry.
6 Because of these things, the wrath of
God will come upon the children of
disobedience.
7 You also walked in *these things for* some
time, when you lived among[+] them.
8 But now you also put off all these:
Anger, wrath, malice, blasphemy, *and*
filthy communication out of your mouth.
9 Do not lie to one another, since you
have put off the old self[+] with its *self
centered* deeds.
10 *You* have put on the new *quality of
character* that is renewed in knowledge
after the image of Him who created *the
new person that you now are*.
11 *Now* there is neither Greek nor Jew,
circumcision nor uncircumcision,
Barbarian, Scythian, bond *nor* free.
But Christ *is* all and in all.
12 Therefore, as the elect of God, holy
and beloved, put on a heart[+] of mercies,
kindness, humbleness of mind,
meekness, *and* longsuffering.
13 Forbear one another and forgive one
another. If anyone has a quarrel against
another,[+] *just* as Christ forgave you, so
also you *do likewise*.
14 Above all these things *put on true* love,
which is the bond of perfection.[+]
15 Let the peace of God rule in your
hearts, to which you also are called in
one body. Be thankful.
16 Let the Word of Christ dwell in you
richly in all wisdom. Teach and admonish
one another in psalms and hymns and
spiritual songs, singing with grace in
your hearts to the Lord.
17 Whatever you do in word or deed, *do*
all in the name of the Lord Jesus, giving
thanks to God and Father by Him.
18 Wives, submit yourselves to your own
husbands as it is proper[+] in the Lord.
19 Husbands, love *your* wives and do not
be bitter against them.
20 Children, obey *your* parents in everything.
For this is well pleasing to the Lord.
21 Fathers, do not provoke your children
to anger, lest they become[+] discouraged.
22 Servants obey *your* masters in everything according to the flesh. Not for
appearance,[+] as pleasing people,[+] but
in singleness of heart, fearing God.

23 Whatever you do,
do *it* heartily as to the Lord
and not to people.[+]

24Know that from the Lord you will receive the reward of the inheritance, for you serve the Lord Christ.
25But *those* who do wrong will receive *accordingly* for the wrongs they have done. There will be no partiality[+] *shown*.

Colossians Chapter 4

1 Masters, give to *your* servants what is just and equal, knowing that you also have a Master in heaven.
2 Continue in prayer, watching in it with thanksgiving.
3 Pray for us also, that God would open a door of utterance for us to speak the mystery of Christ, for which I am also in chains,[+]
4 *so* that I might make it manifest, as I ought to speak.
5 Walk in wisdom toward *those* who are outside,[+] redeeming the time.
6 Let your speech always *be* with grace *and* seasoned with salt *so* that you may know how you ought to answer everyone.[+]
7 Tychicus, *who is* a beloved brother and a faithful minister and fellow servant in the Lord, will declare to you everything concerning my condition.[+]
8 I have sent *him* to you for that purpose, *and so* that he might know your condition[+] and comfort your hearts.
9 *Along* with Onesimus, a faithful and beloved brother who is *one* of you, they will make known to you all things that *are being done* here.
10Aristarchus, my fellow prisoner, greets[+] you, *along with* Mark whose cousin *is* Barnabas. Concerning[+] *Mark*, you have received instructions,[+] *that* if he comes to you, *you are to* receive him.
11Also Jesus who is called Justus *sends greetings*. *All of them* are of *the* circumcision *and* they alone[+] *are my* fellow workers for the kingdom of God who have been a comfort to me.
12Epaphras who is of you, a servant of Christ, greets[+] you. *He is* always laboring fervently for you in prayers *so* that you may stand perfect and complete in all the will of God.
13For I testify[+] that he has a great zeal for you and *for* those *who are* in Laodicea and *for* those in Hierapolis.
14Luke, the beloved physician, and Demas greet you.
15Greet[+] the family[+] who are in Laodicea and Nymphas and the assembly[+] in his house.
16When this epistle is read among you, cause *it* to be read in the assembly[+] of the Laodiceans also, *so* that you likewise *might* read the *epistle* from Laodicea.
17Say to Archippus: Take heed to the ministry you have received in the Lord *so* that you fulfill it.
18*I* Paul, *now close with* the salutation of my own hand. Remember my chains. Grace *be* with you. Amen.

This epistle was transcribed at Rome by Tychicus and Onesimus.

1 Thessalonians Chapter 1

1 *From* Paul, Silvanus, and Timothy. To the assembly[+] of the Thessalonians in God *the* Father and Lord Jesus Christ. Grace to you and peace from God our Father and Lord Jesus Christ.
2 We always give thanks to God for you all, making mention of you in our prayers.
3 *We* remember without ceasing your work of faith and labor of love and patient hope in our Lord Jesus Christ, in the sight of our Father God.
4 *We* know, beloved family,[+] *that* you were chosen[+] by God.
5 For our Gospel did not come to you in word only, but also in power and in *the* Holy Spirit and in much assurance, as you know what *kind of people* we were among you for your sake.
6 You became followers of us and of the Lord, having received the Word with joy in the Holy Spirit, *even* in much suffering,[+]
7 so that you became[+] examples to all who believe in Macedonia and Achaia.
8 For *it was* from you *that* the Word of the Lord sounded forth,[+] not only in

Macedonia and Achaia, but also in
every place *where* your faith toward God
was widely+ spread, so that we did not
need *to* say anything.
9 For *they* themselves declared+ *to* us
what *an* entrance+ we had to you and
how you turned to God from idols, to
serve the living and true God
10 and to wait for His Son from heaven,
whom He raised from the dead: Jesus,
who delivers us from the wrath to come.

1 Thessalonians Chapter 2

1 For *you* yourselves know, family,+ that
our entrance in to you was not in vain.
2 But *even after* we had suffered and
were shamefully treated at Philippi, as
you know, we were bold in our God to
speak the Gospel of God to you, *even* in
much contention.
3 For our exhortation *was* not from
error+ nor of uncleanness, nor in
deceitfulness.+
4 But as we were allowed by God to be
entrusted+ with the Gospel, even so we
speak. Not as pleasing men, but God,
who proves+ our hearts.
5 For as you know, we did not at any
time use flattering words or a cloak of
covetousness. God *is our* witness.
6 We did not seek glory from people or
from you or from others, *even though* as
apostles of Christ we could have *placed*
a burden *on you*.
7 But we were gentle among you, *just* as
a nurse cherishes her children.
8 So, *because of our* deep affection for
you, we were willing to have imparted
to you, not only the Gospel of God, but
also our *very* own souls, because you
were *so* dear to us.
9 For you remember, family,+ our labor
and toil,+ for working+ night and day to
not be a burden+ to any of you, we
proclaimed+ the Gospel of God to you.
10 You *are our* witnesses, and God *also*,
how holy+ and righteously+ and
blamelessly+ we behaved ourselves
among you who believe.
11 As you know how we exhorted and
comforted and charged everyone of you,
as a father *does* his *own* children,
12 *so* that you would walk worthy of God
who has called you to His kingdom
and glory.
13 For this reason+ also, we thank God
without ceasing. Because, *even though*
you received the Word of God that you
heard from us, you did not receive *it as*
the word of men, but as it is in truth, the
Word of God that works effectively in
you who believe.
14 For you, family,+ became followers of
the assemblies+ of God in Judea that are in
Christ Jesus. For you also have suffered
like things from your own countrymen,
even as they *have* from the Jews.
15 *For the Jews* killed their own prophets
and the Lord Jesus and *they* persecuted
us. They do not please God and *they* are
contrary to all people,+
16 forbidding us to speak to the Gentiles
so that they might be saved, *thus* to fill up
their sins always. But the wrath *of God* is
coming upon them to the uttermost.
17 But we, family,+ being taken from
you for a short time in presence *though*
not in heart, have endeavored *all* the
more abundantly *and* with great desire,
to see you *in* person.+
18 Therefore, we, even I Paul, would
have come to you once and again, but
Satan hindered us.
19 For what *is* our hope or joy or crown
of rejoicing? *Is it* not *to see* you in the
presence of our Lord Jesus Christ at His
coming?
20 For you are our glory and joy.

1 Thessalonians Chapter 3

1 When we could no longer endure+
waiting, we thought it good to be left
alone at Athens,
2 and sent Timothy, our brother and
servant+ of God and our fellow laborer in
the Gospel of Christ, to establish you and
to comfort you concerning your faith,
3 *so* that no one would be moved by
these afflictions. For *you* yourselves
know that we are appointed to this.

4 For truly[+] when we were with you,
we told you before that we would suffer
tribulation, even as it has come to pass
and you know *it*.
5 For this reason,[+] when I could no
longer endure[+] *waiting*, I sent to know
the condition of your faith, lest by some
means the tempter had tempted you and
our labor had been in vain.
6 But now, Timothy has come to us
from you and brought us good tidings of
your faith and *true* love. *He tells us* that
you have a good remembrance of us
always *and* greatly desire to see us, as
we also *desire to see* you.
7 Therefore family,[+] we were comforted
over you in all our affliction and
distress by your faith.
8 For now we live, if you stand fast in
the Lord.
9 For what thanks can we render to God
again for you, for all the joy with
which we rejoice[+] for your sakes
before our God.
10 Night and day *we* pray exceedingly that
we might see you *in* person[+] and might
perfect what is lacking in your faith.
11 Now *may* God Himself, our Father
and our Lord Jesus Christ direct our
way to you.
12 *And may* the Lord make you to increase
and abound in love toward one another
and toward all *people*, even as we *do*
toward you,
13 to the end *that* He may strengthen[+] your
hearts *to be* blameless[+] in holiness before
our God and Father at the coming *of* our
Lord Jesus Christ with all His saints.

1 Thessalonians Chapter 4

1 Furthermore then, we urge and exhort
you family,[+] by the Lord Jesus, that as
you have received *instruction* from us *as
to* how you ought to walk and please
God, that you should abound more *in this*.
2 For you know what instructions[+] we
gave you by the Lord Jesus.
3 For this is the will of God *for* your
sanctification: That you should abstain
from fornication.
4 Everyone of you should know how to
possess their own vessels in sanctification
and honor,
5 not in the lust of abnormal appetites[+]
like the Gentiles who do not know God,
6 *so* that no one goes beyond and defrauds
another in *any* matter. Because the Lord
is the avenger of all such, as we also
have forewarned you and testified.
7 For God has not called us to uncleanness,
but to holiness.
8 Therefore, *those* who despise do not
despise people,[+] but God who has also
given His Holy Spirit to us.
9 But concerning brotherly love, you do
not need me *to* write to you. For you
yourselves are taught by God to love one
another.
10 Indeed, you *already* do this toward all
the family[+] who are in all Macedonia.
But we urge you, family,[+] that you
increase more and more.
11 *Earnestly* endeavor[+] to be quiet and
to do your own *things* and to work
with your own hands as we have
instructed[+] you
12 *so* that you may walk honestly toward
those who are outside[+] *of the faith* and *so
that* you may lack nothing.
13 But I do not want you to lack understanding[+]
family,[+] concerning *those* who
are asleep, *so* that you are not grieved[+]
as others *are* who have no hope.
14 For if we believe that Jesus died and
rose again, *then* so also will God bring
those who sleep in Jesus with Him.
15 For this we say to you by the Word of
the Lord: That we who are alive *and*
remain until the coming of the Lord will
not precede[+] *those* who are asleep.
16 For the Lord Himself will descend
from heaven with a shout, with the
voice of the archangel, and with the
trumpet of God. *And* the dead in Christ
will arise first.
17 Then we who are alive *and* remain will
be caught up together with them in the
clouds to meet the Lord in the air. Thus
we will be forever[+] with the Lord.
18 Therefore, comfort one another with
these words.

1 Thessalonians Chapter 5

1 Family,[+] you have no need that I
write to you about the times and the
seasons.
2 For *you* yourselves know perfectly
well that the day of the Lord will come
like a thief in the night.
3 For when they say: Peace and safety,
then sudden destruction *will* come upon
them like labor[+] upon a woman with
child. And they will not escape.
4 But you, family,[+] are not in darkness
so that that day should overtake you like
a thief.
5 You are all children of light and
children of the day. We are not of the
night or darkness.
6 Therefore let us not sleep as others *do*,
but let us watch and be sober.
7 For *those* who sleep, sleep in the night.
And *those* who get drunk, *get* drunk in
the night.
8 But let us who are of the day be sober,
putting on the breastplate of faith, and
love *and* for a helmet, the hope of
salvation.
9 For God has not appointed us to wrath,
but to obtain salvation through our Lord
Jesus Christ.
10 *Jesus* died for us *so* that, whether we
are awake or asleep, we should live
together with Him.
11 Therefore, comfort yourselves together and edify one another, *just* as you
are *already* doing.
12 We urge you family,[+] to know *those*
who labor among you and are over you
in the Lord and admonish you.
13 Esteem them very highly in love for
the sake of their work. *And* be at peace
among yourselves.
14 Now we exhort you family[+]: Warn
those who are unruly, comfort the
feebleminded, support the weak, *and*
be patient toward all *people*.
15 See that no one renders evil for evil
to anyone,[+] but always[+] follow what
is good, both among yourselves and
toward all *people*.
16 Rejoice forever.
17 Pray without ceasing.
18 In everything, give thanks. For this is
the will of God in Christ Jesus concerning you.
19 Do not quench the Spirit.
20 Do not despise prophecies.

21 Prove all things.
Hold fast what is good.

22 Abstain from all appearance of evil.
23 The God of peace Himself will sanctify
you wholly *so that* your whole spirit
and soul and body *will* be preserved
blameless for the coming *of* our Lord
Jesus Christ.
24 He who calls you *is* faithful and *He*
will perform[+] *it*.
25 Family,[+] pray for us.
26 Greet all the family[+] with a holy kiss.
27 I charge you by the Lord that this
epistle be read to all the holy family.[+]
28 The grace of our Lord Jesus Christ *be*
with you. Amen.

This first epistle to the Thessalonians was written at Athens.

2 Thessalonians Chapter 1

1 *From* Paul, Silvanus, and Timothy. To
the assembly[+] of the Thessalonians in
God our Father and the Lord Jesus
Christ.
2 Grace to you and peace from God our
Father and Lord Jesus Christ.
3 We are bound to thank God for you
always, family,[+] as it is right[+] *to do*.
Because your faith grows exceedingly,
and the *true* love of everyone of you all
toward each other abounds
4 so that we ourselves rejoice[+] in you in
the assemblies[+] of God for your patience
and faith in all your persecutions and
tribulations that you endure.
5 *This is* a revealed[+] evidence[+] of the
righteous judgment of God for you to be
counted worthy of the kingdom of God
for which you also suffer.
6 If *it is* to be the righteousness of God

to repay[+] tribulation to *those* who
oppress[+] you,
7 and *to give* you who are oppressed[+]
rest with us when the Lord Jesus shall
be revealed from heaven with His
mighty angels,
8 *then* in flaming fire, *He* will take vengeance on *those* who do not know God
and who do not obey the Gospel of our
Lord Jesus Christ.
9 *They* will be punished with everlasting
destruction, *taken away* from the presence of the Lord and from the glory of
His power.
10 In that day, He will come to be
glorified in His saints and to be admired
by all who believe because our testimony among you was believed.
11 Therefore, we always pray for you,
also, that our God would count you
worthy of *this* calling and fulfill all the
good pleasure of *His* goodness and the
work of faith with power
12 *so* that the name of our Lord Jesus
Christ may be glorified in you and you
in Him, according to the grace of our
God and Lord Jesus Christ.

2 Thessalonians Chapter 2

1 Now we urge you, family,[+] *regarding*
the coming of our Lord Jesus Christ and
our gathering to Him,
2 that you not be soon shaken in mind or
troubled, not by spirit or by word or by
letter as from us, *regarding the fact* that
the day of Christ is *very* near.[+]
3 Let no one deceive you by any means.
For *that day will not come* until[+] there
first come a falling away, and the man
of sin, the son of damnation,[+] becomes
revealed.
4 *That man will* oppose *God* and exalt
himself above all *that is* called God or is
worshiped as God, so that he sits in the
temple of God, showing himself *in a*
pretense that he is God.
5 Do you not remember that I told you
about these things while I was still[+]
with you?
6 And now you know what *it is that* is
holding[+] *back* for *that man* to be revealed
in his time.
7 For the mystery of iniquity is already
working. *It is* only *being* restrained[+] now
until *the restraint is* taken out of the way.
8 Then that wicked *one* will be revealed,
whom the Lord will consume with the
breath[+] of His mouth and nullify[+] with
the brightness of His coming.
9 *That wicked one* whose coming is according[+] *to* the work of Satan with all power
and signs and false[+] wonders
10 and with every unrighteous deceit in
those who perish because they did not
receive the love of the truth *so* that they
might be saved.
11 Because[+] of this, God will send *a* strong
delusion upon them for[+] believing a lie
12 *so* that all who did not believe the truth
but *took* pleasure in unrighteousness
might be damned.
13 But we are bound to give thanks to
God always for you, family,[+] beloved
of the Lord. Because from the beginning, God has chosen you to *receive*
salvation through sanctification of the
Spirit and belief *of the* truth.
14 To this, He called you *through* our
proclaiming of the Gospel to *the* obtaining
of *the* glory of our Lord Jesus Christ.
15 Therefore family[+]: Stand fast and
hold the traditions you have been taught,
whether by Word or *by* our epistle.
16 Now our Lord Jesus Christ Himself
and God our Father who has loved us
and given *us* everlasting consolation and
good hope through grace
17 comfort your hearts and strengthen[+]
you in every good word and work.

2 Thessalonians Chapter 3

1 Finally, family,[+] pray for us: That the
Word of the Lord may have *free* course
and be glorified, even as *it is* with you.
2 *Pray* that we may be delivered from
unreasonable and wicked men, for all
do not have faith.
3 But the Lord is faithful, who will
strengthen[+] you and keep *you* from evil.
4 We have confidence in the Lord

touching you, that you both do and will
continue to do the things that we charged+
you *to do.*

> 5 *May* the Lord direct your hearts
> in the love of God
> and in waiting patiently for Christ.

6 Now we charge+ you family,+ in the
name of our Lord Jesus Christ, that you
withdraw yourselves from every *member*
of the family+ who walks disorderly and
not according+ to the tradition received
from us.
7 For *you* yourselves know how you
ought to follow us. For we did not
behave ourselves disorderly among you.
8 Nor did we eat anyone's bread for
nothing. But *we* worked+ with labor and
toil+ night and day *so* that we might not
be a burden+ to any of you,
9 not because we do not have authority,+
but to make ourselves an example to you
to follow us.
10 For even when we were with you, we
instructed+ you that if any would not
work, neither should *they* eat.
11 For we hear *that* some among you are
walking disorderly *and* not working at
all, but are busybodies.
12 Now *those* who are such we instruct+ and
exhort by our Lord Jesus Christ to work
with quietness and eat their own bread.
13 But family,+ do not be weary in well
doing.
14 If anyone does not obey our word by
this epistle, note that person and have no
company with them *so* that they may be
ashamed.
15 Yet do not count *them* as an enemy, but
admonish *them* as a *member of the* family.+
16 Now the Lord of peace Himself give
you peace always, by all means. The
Lord *be* with you all.
17 The salutation Paul by my own hand is
my signature+ on every epistle I write.
18 The grace of our Lord Jesus Christ
be with you all. Amen.

The second epistle to the Thessalonians was written at Athens.

1 Timothy Chapter 1

1 *From* Paul, an apostle of Jesus Christ
by the commandment of God our Savior
and Lord Jesus Christ *who is* our hope.
2 To Timothy, *my* own son in the faith:
Grace, mercy, *and* peace from God our
Father and Jesus Christ our Lord.
3 I urged+ you to remain+ at Ephesus *when*
I went to Macedonia *so* that you might
charge them to teach no other doctrine
4 *and to* not give heed to fables and
endless genealogies that bring+ questions
rather than godly edifying in faith.
5 Now the objective+ of this instruction+
is *true* love out of a pure heart and a good
conscience and sincere+ faith.
6 *Yet* some have erred+ *by* turning aside
to vain talking.+
7 *They* desire to be teachers of the law,
but they do not understand what they are
saying or what they affirm.
8 Now we know that the law *is* good if
it is used lawfully,
9 Know this: That the law is not made
for the righteous, but *for the* lawless and
disobedient, ungodly sinners, unholy
and worldly,+ murderers of fathers and
mothers *and all* murderers,+
10 *for* fornicators,+ *for those who* defile
themselves, *for* slave traders,+ liars,
perjurers, and any other *thing* that is
contrary to sound teaching.+
11 *This is* according to the glorious Gospel
of the blessed God that was committed
to my trust.
12 I thank Christ Jesus our Lord who has
enabled me because He counted me
faithful to put *me* into the ministry.
13 *Because* before, *I* was a blasphemer,
a persecutor, and injurious *to others*.
But I received+ mercy because I did *it*
ignorantly in unbelief.
14 The grace of our Lord was exceedingly
abundant with the faith and love that are
in Christ Jesus.
15 This *is* a faithful saying and worthy
of all acceptance: That Christ Jesus
came into the world to save sinners,
of whom I am chief.

16 However for this purpose+ I received+
mercy, *so* that in me first Jesus Christ
might show forth all longsuffering as a
pattern to *those* who would hereafter
believe in Him for eternal+ life.
17 Now to the King eternal, immortal,
invisible, the only wise God, *be* honor
and glory forever and ever. Amen.
18 This charge I commit to you, son
Timothy, according to the earlier+
prophecies about you, *so* that by them
you might fight+ a good warfare,
19 holding faith and a good conscience.
For some have put away *their conscience*
so as to make *their* faith shipwreck.
20 *Among them* are Hymenaeus and
Alexander whom I have delivered to
Satan *so* that they may learn to not
blaspheme.

1 Timothy Chapter 2

1 *I* urge+ *you*, therefore, first *of* all: Make
supplications, prayers, intercessions,
and thanksgiving for everyone,
2 *including* for kings and all who are in
authority, *so* that we may lead a quiet
and peaceable life in all godliness and
honesty.
3 For this *is* good and acceptable in the
sight of God our Savior
4 who desires+ all people+ to be saved
and to come to the knowledge of the truth.

> 5 For *there is* one God
> and one mediator
> between God and mankind+:
> the man Christ Jesus

6 who gave Himself *as* a ransom for
all *with the* testimony *of this to come* in
due time.
7 To this *purpose*, I am ordained a
preacher and an apostle. I speak the
truth in Christ. *As* a teacher of the
Gentiles in faith and truth+ *I* do not lie.
8 Therefore, I desire+ that people+
everywhere pray, lifting up holy
hands, without wrath and doubting.
9 In like manner also, *I urge* that women
adorn themselves in modest apparel,
with humility+ and moderation,+ not
with *elaborately* braided hair or gold or
pearls or costly array,
10 but *with* what becomes women professing godliness: With good works.
11 Let the woman learn in silence with all
subjection.
12 I do not allow+ women to teach or
usurp authority over men, but to be in
quietness.+
13 For Adam was formed first, then Eve.
14 Adam was not deceived, but the woman,
being deceived, went into transgression.
15 Nevertheless *women* will be saved in
child bearing if they continue in faith and
true love and holiness with moderation.+

1 Timothy Chapter 3

1 This *is* a true saying: If a man desires
the office of bishop, he desires a good
work.
2 A bishop then must be blameless, the
husband of one wife, vigilant, sober, of
good behavior, given to hospitality, *able*
to teach,
3 not given to wine, no striker, *and* not
greedy of filthy gain,+ but patient, not a
brawler, *and* not covetous.
4 *He must be* one who governs+ his own
house well, having his children in
subjection with all gravity.
5 For if a man does not know how to
govern+ his own house, *then* how can he
take care of the assembly+ of God?
6 *He must* not *be* a novice, lest being
lifted up with pride he *may* fall into the
condemnation of the devil.
7 Moreover, he must have a good report
from *those* who are outside+ *of the faith*,
lest he fall into reproach and the snare of
the devil.
8 Likewise, deacons *must be* honest,+
not double tongued, not given to much
wine, *and* not greedy for filthy gain.+
9 *They must* hold the mystery of the faith
in a pure conscience.
10 Also, let these *candidates* be proved,
first. Then let them serve+ *after* being
found blameless.
11 Even so *their* wives *must also be* honest,+

not slanderers, sober, *and* faithful in
all things.
12 Deacons *must be* husbands of one wife,
governing[+] their children and their own
houses well.
13 For *those* who have served[+] well in the
office of a deacon acquire[+] a good degree
for themselves and much boldness in
faith in Christ Jesus.
14 I write these things to you hoping to
come to you soon.[+]
15 But if I *am* delayed[+] *then by this* you
will know how you ought to behave
yourself in the house of God, which is
the assembly[+] of the living God, the
pillar and base[+] of the truth.
16 *We* confess[+] *that* the mystery of godliness is great *indeed*. God was revealed[+]
in the flesh, justified by the Spirit, seen
by angels, proclaimed[+] to the Gentiles,
believed in the world, *and* received up
in glory. *John 1:14*

1 Timothy Chapter 4

1 Now the Spirit speaks expressly that in
the latter times some will depart from
the faith, giving heed to seducing spirits
and doctrines of demons.[+]
2 *Some will* speak lies in hypocrisy, having
their conscience seared with a hot iron.
3 *Some will* forbid to marry *and require*
you to abstain from *certain* foods[+] that
God has created to be received with
thanksgiving by *those* who believe and
know the truth.
4 Every creature *created by* God *is* good,
and nothing *is* to be refused if it is
received with thanksgiving,
5 for it is sanctified by the Word of God
and prayer.
6 If you remind the family[+] about these
things, you will be a good servant[+] of
Jesus Christ, nourished with the words
of faith and good doctrine that you have
closely followed.[+]
7 But refuse the worldly[+] and old wives'
fables, and *instead* exercise yourself
toward godliness.
8 For bodily exercise is of little benefit.[+]
But godliness is beneficial[+] for everything,[+] having *both* the promise of life
now and *eternal life* to come.
9 This *is* a faithful saying and worthy of
all acceptance.
10 And for this, we labor and suffer
reproach because we trust in the living
God who is the Savior of everyone,[+]
especially believers.[+]
11 Prescribe[+] and teach these things.
12 Do not let anyone despise your youth.
But be an example *to* the believers, in
word, in conversation *and conduct*, in
true love, in spirit, in faith, *and* in purity.
13 Until I come, give attention[+] to
reading, to exhortation, *and* to doctrine.
14 Do not neglect the gift that is in you,
which was given *to* you by prophecy
with laying on of hands by the elders.[+]
15 Meditate upon these things. Give
yourself wholly to them *so* that your
advancement[+] *may be* evident[+] to
everyone.
16 Take heed to yourself and to the doctrine. Continue in them, for in doing
this both *you* yourself and *those* who
hear you will be saved.

1 Timothy Chapter 5

1 Do not rebuke an elder, but exhort[+]
him as a father. *Exhort* the younger men
as family,[+]
2 the elder women as mothers, *and* the
younger *women* as sisters, with all purity.
3 Honor widows who truly[+] are widows.
4 But if any widow has children or
nephews, let them learn to show piety at
home first, and to reciprocate[+] *care for*
their parents. For that is good and
acceptable before God.
5 Now *one who is* truly[+] a widow and
desolate trusts in God and continues in
supplications and prayers night and day.
6 But *one who* lives in pleasure is dead
while she lives.
7 *Give* instruction[+] in these *matters so*
that *all* may be blameless.
8 But if any do not provide for their
own, and especially for those of their
own house, *then* they have denied the
faith and are worse than an infidel.

9 Do not let a widow be taken into the
number *for assistance who is* less *than* sixty
years *old*, having been the wife of one man,
10 and *who is* well reported for *her* good
works: *For example:* If she has brought
up children, if she has lodged strangers,
if she has washed the feet of the saints,
if she has relieved the afflicted, *and* if she
has diligently followed every good work.
11 But refuse the younger widows. For
when they have begun to grow[+] wanton
against Christ, they will *want to* marry.
12 *In this, they will receive* judgment,[+]
because they have cast off their first faith.
13 And with all this, they learn *to be* idle,
wandering about from house to house.
Not only idle, but tattlers also and
busybodies, speaking things that they
should not. *Proverbs 11:13*
14 Therefore, I will that the younger
women marry, bear children, guide the
house, *and* give no occasion to the
adversary to speak reproachfully.
15 For some are already turned aside
after Satan.
16 If any man or woman who is a believer
has widows *in their family*, let them
relieve them and not let the assembly[+]
be burdened[+] *so* that it may relieve *those*
who are truly[+] widows.
17 Let the elders who govern[+] well be
counted worthy of double honor,
especially *those* who labor in the Word
and doctrine.
18 For the Scriptures declare: You shall
not muzzle the ox that treads out the
corn. And: The laborer *is* worthy of his
reward. *Deuteronomy 25:4*
19 Do not receive an accusation against
an elder unless[+] *it is* from two or three
witnesses.
20 Rebuke *those* who sin, before everyone,[+] *so* that others may also *have* fear.
21 I charge *you* before *our* God and Lord
Jesus Christ and the elect angels, that
you observe these things without
preferring one before another, doing
nothing by partiality.
22 Do not lay hands too quickly[+] on
anyone, nor be a partaker in the sins of
others. Keep yourself pure.
23 Do not drink *polluted* water, but use a
little wine for your stomach and your
frequent[+] infirmities.
24 The sins of some men are *clearly*
revealed[+] before *they go* to judgment,
and some follow after.
25 Likewise also, the good works *of some*
are *clearly* evident,[+] but *those* that are
otherwise cannot be hid.

1 Timothy Chapter 6

1 As many servants as are under *the*
yoke *should* count their own masters
worthy of all honor *so* that the name of
God and *His* doctrine *is* not blasphemed.
2 *Those* who have believing masters *must*
not despise *them* because they are family.[+]
But rather, do *them* service because they
are faithful and beloved partakers of the
benefit. Teach and exhort these things.
3 If anyone teaches otherwise and does
not consent to wholesome words, *even*
the words of our Lord Jesus Christ and
to the doctrine according to godliness,
4 *then* they are proud *and* know nothing.
Rather, *they have* sick[+] *minds full* of
questions and strifes of words from
which comes envy, strife, reviling,[+]
evil accusations,[+]
5 *and* perverse disputings by people of
corrupt minds and destitute of the truth
who suppose that gain is godliness. Withdraw yourself from such.
6 But godliness with contentment is
great gain.
7 For we brought nothing into *this* world
and it is certain we can carry nothing out.
8 Having food and clothing,[+] let us be
content with that.
9 *Those* who desire[+] to be rich fall into
temptation and a snare and *into* many
foolish and hurtful lusts that drown
people in destruction and damnation.[+]

10 The love of money
is the root of all evil.
While some *have* coveted after *it*,
they have erred from the faith
and pierced themselves through
with many sorrows.

11 But you, O people[+] of God, flee *from*
these things. Follow after righteousness,
godliness, faith, love, patience, *and*
meekness.
12 Fight the good fight of faith. Lay hold
on eternal life to which you are also
called and have professed a good
profession before many witnesses.
13 I charge you in the sight of God who
quickens all things, and *before* Christ
Jesus who witnessed a good confession
before Pontius Pilate,
14 that you keep the commandment without spot *and* unrebukable until the
appearing of our Lord Jesus Christ.
15 He will show, in *due* time, *who is* the
blessed and only Potentate, the King of
kings, and Lord of lords.
16 *He* alone has immortality, dwelling in
light unapproachable,[+] whom no one
has seen nor can see. To *Him be* honor
and power everlasting. Amen.
17 Charge *those* who are rich in this
world, that they not be high minded nor
trust in uncertain riches, but *only* in the
living God who gives us richly all things
to enjoy.
18 *Do this so* that they *may* do good, *so* that
they be rich in good works, ready to
distribute, willing to share,[+]
19 laying up in store for themselves a
good foundation against the time to
come *so* that they may lay hold on
eternal life.
20 O Timothy, keep what is committed to
your trust. Avoid worldly[+] *and* vain
babblings and *the* oppositions of
science, falsely so called.
21 *By* professing *these things*, some have
erred concerning the faith. Grace *be*
with you. Amen.

The first epistle to Timothy was written at Laodicea, which is the chief city of Phrygia Pacatiana.

2 Timothy Chapter 1

1 *From* Paul, an apostle of Jesus Christ
by the will of God, according to the
promise of life that is in Christ Jesus.
2 To Timothy, *my* beloved son: Grace,
mercy, *and* peace from God *the* Father
and Christ Jesus our Lord.
3 I *am* thankful to God, whom I serve
from *my* forefathers' *example* with *a* pure
conscience, as I remember you in my
prayers night and day without ceasing.
4 *I* greatly desire to see you *so* that I may
be filled with joy. *I* remember[+] your tears
5 *and* I remember the sincere[+] faith that
is in you that lived[+] first in your grand-
mother Lois and *in* your mother Eunice.
And I am persuaded that *it is* in you also.
6 Therefore I remind[+] you to stir up the
gift of God that is in you by the laying[+]
on of my hands.
7 For God has not given us the spirit of
fear, but of power and love and a sound
mind.
8 Therefore, do not be ashamed of the
testimony of our Lord nor of me His
prisoner. But endure[+] the hardships[+]
that come with the Gospel according to
the power of God.
9 *He* saves[+] us and calls[+] *us* with a holy
calling, not according to our works, but
according to His own purpose and grace
that was given *to* us in Christ Jesus
before the world began.
10 But now, *it* is revealed[+] by the appearing of our Savior Jesus Christ who has
abolished death and has brought life and
immortality to light through the Gospel.
11 To this *purpose* I am appointed a
preacher and an apostle and a teacher of
the Gentiles.
12 *It is* for this reason[+] *that* I also suffer
these things. Nevertheless, I am not
ashamed. For I know whom I have
believed and *I* am persuaded that He is
able to keep what I have committed to
Him against that day.
13 Hold fast the example[+] of sound words
that you have heard from me, in the faith
and love that are in Christ Jesus.
14 Keep *safe* that good deposit[+] that was
entrusted[+] to you by the Holy Spirit who
dwells in us.
15 You know this, that all who are in Asia
turned away from me, *among* whom are
Phygellus and Hermogenes.

16 *May* the Lord give mercy to the house
of Onesiphorus, for he often refreshed
me and was not ashamed of my chains.
17 When he was in Rome, he diligently
sought and found me.
18 *May* the Lord grant *to* him to find
mercy from the Lord in that day, *for*
you know how well he served+ me at
Ephesus.

2 Timothy Chapter 2

1 Therefore my son, be strong in the
grace that is in Christ Jesus.
2 Entrust+ the things that you heard
from me among many witnesses to
faithful men who will be able to teach
others also.
3 Therefore, you *must* endure hardship+
as a good soldier of Jesus Christ.
4 No warrior+ *becomes* entangled with
the affairs of *this* life, *so* that *the one who*
chose the soldier might be pleased.
5 If anyone competes+ *in something*, *they*
cannot be crowned *as a winner* unless+
they competed+ lawfully.
6 *Moreover,* the grower+ who labors
must be *the* first partaker of the fruits.
7 Consider what I say. *May* the Lord
give you understanding in everything.+
8 Remember that Jesus Christ, *who was*
from the seed of David, was raised from
the dead, according to my *understanding*
of the Gospel.
9 In *proclaiming* this, I suffer hardship+
like an evil doer, *even* to chains.+ But
the Word of God is not bound.
10 Therefore I endure all things for the
sake of the elect *so* that they may also
obtain the salvation that is in Christ
Jesus, with eternal glory.
11 *This is* a faithful saying. For if we have
died with *Him*, *then* we will also live
with *Him*. Romans 6:5
12 If we suffer, we will also reign with
Him. *But* if we deny *Him*, *then* He will
also deny us. Matthew 10:33
13 If we do not believe, *Jesus* remains+
faithful, *nevertheless*. He cannot deny
Himself.
14 Remind *everyone* about these things,
charging *them* before the Lord that they
not argue+ over words to no benefit+ *or*
to the subverting of the hearers.

15 Study to show yourself
approved to God, a worker+ who
does not need to be ashamed,
rightly dividing the Word of truth.

16 Shun worldly+ *and* vain babblings.
For they will increase to more ungodliness.
17 Their word will spread+ like cancer.+
Consider Hymenaeus and Philetus
18 who, concerning the truth, have erred
by saying that the resurrection is already
past. *This* overthrows the faith of some.
19 Nevertheless, the foundation of God
stands sure, having this seal: The Lord
knows *those* who are His. And: Let
everyone who names the name of Christ
depart from iniquity.
20 But in a great house there are not only
vessels of gold and of silver, but also of
wood and of earth. Some to honor, and
some to dishonor.
21 Therefore, if anyone purges themselves from these *wicked things*, *they* will
be a vessel to honor, sanctified and
fitting+ for the master's use *and* prepared
for every good work.

22 Flee youthful lusts. But follow
righteousness, faith, *true* love, *and*
peace with *all* who call on the Lord
out of a pure heart.

23 Avoid foolish and uninstructive+
questions, knowing that they pro-
voke+ strife.

24 The servant of the Lord must not
strive, but *must* be gentle toward everyone,+ *able* to teach, patient,
25 in meekness instructing *those* who
oppose *so that* perhaps+ God will give
them repentance to the acknowledging
of the truth.
26 *Thus* they might awaken+ out of the
snare of the devil, *after* being taken
captive by him to *do* his will.

2 Timothy Chapter 3

1 Know this also: That in the last days,
perilous times will come.
2 For people[+] will be lovers of themselves, covetous, boasters, proud,
blasphemers, disobedient to parents,
unthankful, unholy,
3 without affection, unforgiving,[+]
false accusers, unrestrained,[+] fierce,
hateful,[+]
4 disloyal,[+] headstrong,[+] arrogant,[+]
and lovers of pleasure rather[+] than
lovers of God.
5 *They* have a form of piety,[+] but deny
the power of it. Turn away from these.
6 For *among* them are *some* who enter[+]
into houses and lead *into* captivity
naive[+] women burdened[+] with sins, led
away with many different[+] lusts.
7 *They are* ever learning, but never able
to come to knowledge of truth.
8 *Just* as Jannes and Jambres opposed[+]
Moses, so do these also resist the truth.
They are people[+] of corrupt minds,
reprobate concerning the faith.
9 But they will progress[+] no further, for
their folly will be revealed[+] to everyone,[+] as it was *with Jannes and Jambres*.
10 You, however, have fully known my
doctrine, manner of life, purpose, faith,
longsuffering, *true* love, patience,
11 persecutions, *and* afflictions that
came to me at Antioch, at Iconium,
and at Lystra. What persecutions I
endured. But out of *them* all the Lord
delivered me.
12 Yes, and all who live godly *lives* in
Christ Jesus will suffer persecution.
13 But evil men and imposters[+] will
grow[1] worse and worse, deceiving and
being deceived.
14 But you *must* continue in the things that
you have learned and have been assured
of, knowing from whom you have
learned *them*.
15 From childhood you have known the
holy Scriptures that are able to make
you wise unto salvation through faith in
Christ Jesus.

> 16 All Scripture
> *is* given by inspiration of God
> and *is* beneficial[+] for doctrine,
> for proof,[+] for correction, *and*
> for instruction in righteousness,

17 *so* that God's people may become
perfect, thoroughly equipped to all
good works.

2 Timothy Chapter 4

1 I charge *you*, therefore, before God
and the Lord Jesus Christ who will
judge the living[+] and the dead at His
appearing and His kingdom:

> 2 Proclaim[+] the Word.
> Be attentive[+] *to duty*
> in season *and* out of season.

Prove,[+] rebuke, *and* exhort with all
longsuffering and doctrine.
3 For the time will come when they will
not endure sound doctrine, but according to their own lusts, they look[+] for
teachers to satisfy[+] their hearing.
4 They turn away *their* ears from the
truth and are turned to fables.
5 But you *must* watch in all things,
endure afflictions, do the work of an
evangelist, *and* make full proof of your
ministry.
6 For I am now ready to be offered and
the time of my departure is *very* near.[+]
7 I have fought a good fight. I have
finished *my* course. *And* I have kept
the faith.
8 Hereafter, there is a crown of righteousness laid up for me, which the
Lord, the righteous judge, will give *to*
me on that day. And not only to me, but
also to all who love His appearing.
9 Be diligent to come to me soon.[+]
10 For Demas has forsaken me, having
loved this present world. *He* has departed
to Thessalonica, Crescens to Galatia,
and Titus to Dalmatia.
11 Only Luke is with me. *Therefore* bring
Mark with you, for he is useful[+] to me
for *this* ministry.

12 I have sent Tychicus to Ephesus.
13 When you come, bring the cloak that
I left at Troas with Carpus, and the
books, especially the parchments.
14 Alexander the coppersmith did much
evil *to* me. The Lord *will* reward him
according to his works.
15 You beware+ of him also, for he has
greatly opposed+ our words.
16 In my first defense,+ no one stood
with me, but everyone+ left+ me. *I pray
that this* will not be charged to them.
17 Nevertheless, the Lord stood with me
and strengthened me *so* that, by me, the
proclaiming+ might be fully known and
all the Gentiles might hear. I was
delivered out of the mouth of the lion.
18 The Lord will deliver me from every
evil work and will preserve *me* to His
heavenly kingdom. *To Him be the* glory
forever and ever. Amen.
19 Greet+ Priscilla and Aquila and the
household of Onesiphorus.
20 Erastus stayed+ at Corinth, but I have
left Trophimus at Miletum sick.
21 Be diligent to come before winter.
Eubulus greets you, and Pudens and
Linus and Claudia and all the family.+
22 The Lord Jesus Christ *be* with your
spirit. Grace *be* with you. Amen.

The second epistle to Timothy, who was ordained the first bishop of the church of the Ephesians, was written at Rome when Paul was brought before Nero the second time.

Titus Chapter 1

1 *From* Paul, a servant of God and an
apostle of Jesus Christ according to the
faith of God's elect and knowledge of
the truth in godliness,
2 in *the* hope of eternal life, which God,
who cannot lie, promised before the
world began.
3 *He* has in due times manifested His
Word through proclaiming+ *it*. *And it* is
committed to me according to the
commandment of God our Savior.
4 To Titus, *my* own son after the common
faith: Grace, mercy, *and* peace from
God *our* Father and Lord Jesus Christ
our Savior.
5 For this reason,+ I left you in Crete *so*
that you should set in order the things
that are wanting and ordain elders in
every city as I had appointed you *to do*,
6 if any are blameless, the husband of
one wife, *and* have faithful children
who are not accused of excesses+ or
unruly *rebellion*.
7 For bishops must be blameless as the
stewards of God. Not selfwilled. Not
soon angry. Not given to wine. No
striker. Not given to filthy gain.+
8 But a lover of hospitality. A lover of
good people.+ Sober, just, holy, *and*
temperate.
9 *They must* hold fast the faithful Word as
they have been taught *so* that they may
be able, by sound doctrine, both to
exhort and to convince *those* who doubt.+
10 For there are many unruly and vain
talkers and deceivers, especially *among*
those of the circumcision.
11 *Their* mouths must be stopped. Some+
subvert whole houses, teaching things
that they should not, for *the* sake *of*
filthy lucre.
12 One of them, *one* of their own prophets
said: The Cretians *are* always liars,
evil beasts, *and* slow bellies.
13 This witness is true. Therefore rebuke
them sharply *so* that they may become
sound in the faith,
14 not giving heed to Jewish fables and
commandments of men who turn from
the truth.
15 Unto the pure, everything+ *is* pure.
But to *those* who are defiled and
unbelieving nothing *is* pure. Even their
minds and conscience are defiled.
16 They profess that they know God.
But in works, they deny *Him*, being
abominable and disobedient and reprobate to every good work.

Titus Chapter 2

1 Speak the things that become sound
doctrine,
2 *so* that older+ men become sober,

honest,+ temperate, sound in faith, in *true* love, *and* in patience.

3 Likewise *speak to* the older+ women *so* that *they become* in behavior as becomes holiness. Not false accusers. Not given to much wine. Teachers of good things,

4 *so* that they may teach the young women to be sober, to love their husbands, to love their children,

5 *to be* discreet, chaste, keepers at home, good, *and* obedient to their own husbands *so* that the Word of God is not blasphemed.

6 Likewise, exhort *the* young men to be sober minded.

7 In all things, show *in* yourself a pattern of good works in doctrine, uncorruptness, gravity, sincerity,

8 and sound speech. None *of this* can be condemned. *Therefore*, *those* who are contrary may be ashamed and have no evil thing to say about you.

9 *Exhort* servants to be obedient to their own masters *and* to please *them* well in all *things*, not contradicting+ *them*,

10 not stealing+ *from them*, but showing all good fidelity *so* that they may adorn the doctrine of God our Savior in everything.

11 For the grace of God who brings salvation has appeared to everyone,+

12 teaching us to deny ungodliness and worldly lusts *and* live soberly, righteously, and godly in this present world,

13 looking for that blessed hope and the glorious appearing of the great God and our Savior Jesus Christ

14 who gave Himself for us *so* that He might redeem us from all iniquity and purify *for* Himself a unique+ people, zealous *for* good works.

15 Speak and exhort these things and rebuke with all authority. Let no one despise you.

Titus Chapter 3

1 Remind+ *people* to be subject to rulers+ and authorities,+ to obey highest officials,+ to be ready to every good work,

2 speaking evil of no one *and* not to be brawlers, *but to be* gentle, showing meekness to everyone.+

3 For we ourselves also were sometimes foolish, disobedient, deceived, serving many different+ lusts and pleasures, living in malice and envy, hateful, *and* hating one another.

4 But after the kindness and love of our Savior God toward mankind+ appeared,

5 *we saw that it was* not by works of righteousness that we practice+ but according to His mercy *that* He saves+ us, by the washing of regeneration and renewing of the Holy Spirit

6 that He shed on us abundantly through Jesus Christ our Savior,

7 *so* that being justified by His grace, we should be made heirs according to the hope of eternal life.

8 *This is* a faithful saying and these things I urge+ that you affirm constantly *so* that *those* who have believed in God might be careful to maintain good works. These things are good and beneficial+ to people.+

9 But avoid foolish questions and genealogies and contentions and fighting+ about the law. For they are vain and not beneficial.+ *Proverbs 17:14*

10 Reject anyone who is *still* a heretic, after the first and second admonition. *Matthew 18:17*

11 Know that anyone like that is subverted and sins *and is* condemned by themselves.

12 When I send Artemas or Tychicus to you, be diligent to come to me at Nicopolis, for I have decided+ to winter there.

13 Send+ Zenas the lawyer and Apollos diligently on their journey *so* that nothing *will* be lacking+ to them.

14 Let our *people* also learn to maintain good works for necessary uses *so* that they *will* not be unfruitful.

15 All who are with me greet+ you. Greet *those* who delight+ *in* us in the faith. Grace *be* with you all. Amen.

This epistle was written at Nicopolis in Macedonia to Titus who was ordained the first bishop of the church of the Cretians.

Philemon Chapter 1

1 *From* Paul, a prisoner of Jesus Christ,
and Timothy *our* brother. To Philemon
our beloved and fellow laborer.
2 And to *our* beloved Apphia and Archippus our fellow soldier and to the
assembly[+] in your house.
3 Grace to you and peace from God our
Father and Lord Jesus Christ.
4 I thank my God, making mention of
you always in my prayers,
5 hearing of your love and faith that you
have toward the Lord Jesus and toward
all *the* saints.

6 May the communication of your
faith become effective by acknowledging every good thing that is in
you in Christ Jesus.

7 For we have great joy and consolation
in your love, because the hearts[+] of the
saints are refreshed by you, brother.
8 Therefore, *even* though I could be very[+]
bold in Christ to command[+] you *to do*
what is proper,[+]
9 *now,* because[+] of love, I appeal[+] *to you*
as Paul the aged and now also a prisoner
of Jesus Christ.
10 I appeal[+] *to* you for my son Onesimus
whom I fathered[+] *while* in my chains.[+]
11 In times past, *he* was not beneficial[+]
to you. But now *he is* beneficial[+] to you
and to me.
12 *Therefore* I am sending *him* back *to you.*
Receive him as my own heart.[+]
13 I would have retained him with me *so*
that in your place[+] he might have ministered to me in the bonds of the Gospel.
14 But without your agreement[+] I would
not do anything, *so* that your good[+]
works would not be from obligation,[+]
but willingly.
15 For perhaps this was the reason[+] he
departed for a season, *so* that you might
receive him forever.
16 Now, not as a servant, but above a
servant *as* a beloved brother, especially
to me but how much more to you, both
in the flesh and in the Lord?
17 Therefore if you count me a partner,
then receive him as *you would receive* me.
18 If he has wronged you or owes *you*
anything,[+] put that on my account.
19 I Paul have written *this* with my own
hand: I will repay. *In* that, I do not say
to you how *much* you owe to me, even
your own self besides.
20 Yes brother, let me have joy of you
in the Lord. Refresh my heart[+] in the
Lord.
21 Having confidence in your obedience,
I wrote to you knowing that you will also
do more than I say.
22 But with the same prepare a lodging
for me also. For I trust that through your
prayers I will be given to you.
23 Greet[+] Epaphras, my fellow prisoner
in Christ Jesus.
24 *Also* Mark, Aristarchus, Demas, *and*
Lucas, my fellow laborers.
25 The grace of our Lord Jesus Christ *be*
with your spirit. Amen.

This epistle was transcribed at Rome by Onesimus a servant.

Hebrews Chapter 1

1 At various[+] times and in many different[+] ways[+] in the past, God spoke to the
fathers through[+] the prophets.
2 *Now,* in these last days *He has* spoken
to us through[+] *His* Son whom He has
appointed heir of all things *and* by
whom also He made the worlds.
3 *The Son,* being the brightness of *God's*
glory and the express image of His
person and upholding all things by the
Word of His power, when He had by
Himself purged our sins, sat down at the
right hand of the Majesty on high.
4 He, being made so much better than
the angels, has by inheritance obtained
a more excellent name than they.
5 For to which of the angels did *God* say
at any time: You are my Son. This day
I have begotten you? And again: I will
be to Him a Father and He shall be to me
a Son? *Psalm 2:7, 2 Samuel 7:14*

6 Moreover,[+] when He brought in *His*
firstborn[+] into the world, He said: Let
all the angels of God worship Him.
7 And as to the angels He says: Who
makes His angels spirits and His ministers a flame of fire? *Psalm 104:4*
8 But to the Son *He says*: Your throne,
O God, *is* forever and ever. A scepter of
righteousness *is* the scepter of your
kingdom. *Psalm 45:6*
9 You have loved righteousness and
hated iniquity. Therefore God, your
God, has anointed you with the oil of
gladness above your fellows. *Psalm 45:7*
10 And you Lord, in the beginning, have
laid the foundation of the earth. The
heavens are the works of your hands.
Psalm 102:25
11 They will perish, but you *will* remain.
They will all grow[+] old as a garment
does. *Psalm 102:26*
12 Like a robe,[+] you will fold them up
and they will be changed. But you are
the same and your years will not fail.
Psalm 102:27
13 But to which of the angels did He at
any time say: Sit at my right hand until
I make your enemies your footstool?
Psalm 110:1
14 Are they not all ministering spirits,
sent forth to minister for *those* who will
be heirs of salvation?

Hebrews Chapter 2

1 Therefore we ought to give more
earnest heed to the things that we have
heard, lest at any time we should let
them slip *away*.
2 For if the word spoken by angels was
steadfast and every transgression and
disobedience received a just repayment[+]
of reward,
3 *then* how shall we escape, *if we* neglect
so great *a* salvation, which at first began
to be spoken by the Lord and was
confirmed to us by *those* who heard *Him*.
4 God also testified[+] *about this*, both with
signs and wonders and with many
different[+] miracles and gifts of the Holy
Spirit according to His will.
5 For He has not put the world to come,
about which we speak, in subjection to
the angels.
6 But in a certain place, one testified
saying: What is mankind[+] that you are
mindful of them? Or the children of
mankind[+] that you visit them? *Psalm 8:4*
7 You made mankind[+] a little lower
than the angels. You crowned them with
glory and honor and set them over the
works of your hands. *Psalm 8:5*
8 You have put all things in subjection
under their feet. For in that He put
everything in subjection under them,
He left nothing *that is* not put under
them. But now we do not yet see everything *that is* put under them. *Psalm 8:6*
9 But we *do* see Jesus, who was made a
little lower than the angels for the suffering of death *and* crowned with glory
and honor *so* that He, by the grace of
God, would taste death for everyone.[+]
10 For it was fitting[+] *for* Him, for whom
everything *was made* and by whom everything *was made* in bringing many
children[+] to glory to make the Captain
of their Salvation perfect through sufferings.
11 For both He who sanctifies and *those*
who are sanctified *are* all of one, for
which reason[+] He is not ashamed to call
them family,[+]
12 saying: I will declare your name to my
family.[+] In the midst of the assembly[+]
I will sing praise to you. *Psalm 22:22*
13 And again: I will put my trust in Him.
And again: Behold, I Am,[+] and *behold*
the children that God has given *to* me.
2 Samuel 22:3, Isaiah 8:18
14 Since[+] the children are partakers of
flesh and blood, He also Himself
likewise took part of the same *so* that
through death He might destroy him
who had the power of death, that is
the devil,
15 and deliver *those* who, through fear of
death, were all their lifetime subject to
bondage.
16 For truly[+] He did not take upon *Himself the nature of* angels, but He took
upon *Himself* the seed of Abraham.

17 Therefore, in all things it was essential+
for Him to be made like mankind+ *so*
that He might be a merciful and faithful
high priest in things *pertaining* to God,
to make reconciliation for the sins of
the people.
18 For in that He Himself has suffered,
being tempted, He is able to help+ *those*
who are tempted.

Hebrews Chapter 3

1 Therefore holy believers,+ partakers
of the heavenly calling, consider the
Apostle and High Priest of our profession: Christ Jesus.
2 He was faithful to *God* who appointed
Him, as also Moses *was faithful* in all
God's house.
3 For this *Jesus* was counted worthy of
more glory than Moses, inasmuch as He
who has built the house has more honor
than the house.
4 For every house is built by someone,
but He who built all things *is* God.
5 Moses truly+ *was* faithful in all *God's*
house as a servant, for a testimony of
those things that were to be spoken *later.*
6 But Christ *is faithful* as a Son over His
own house, whose house we are if we
hold fast the confidence and the rejoicing of the hope, firm to the end.
7 Therefore, as the Holy Spirit says:
Today, if you will, hear His voice.
Psalm 95:7
8 Do not harden your hearts as in the
rebellion+ in the day of trials+ in the
wilderness *Psalm 95:8*
9 when your fathers tested+ me, proved
me, and saw my works *for* forty years.
Psalm 95:9
10 Therefore, I was grieved with that
generation and said: They always err in
their heart *because* they have not known
my ways. *Psalm 95:10*
11 So I swore in my wrath: They shall not
enter into my rest. *Psalm 95:11*
12 Take heed, family,+ lest there be in
any of you an evil heart of unbelief in
departing from the living God.
13 But exhort one another daily while it is
called today, lest any of you be hardened through the deceitfulness of sin.
14 For we are made partakers of Christ if
we hold the beginning of our confidence
steadfast to the end.
15 In *this* it is said: Today, if you will,
hear His voice. Do not harden your
hearts as in the rebellion.+ *Psalm 95:7,8*
16 For some, when they had heard, did
provoke, however not all who came out
of Egypt by Moses.
17 But with whom was *God* grieved *for*
forty years? *Was it* not with *those* who
had sinned, whose carcasses fell in the
wilderness?
18 And to whom did He swear *that* they
would not enter into His rest, but to *those*
who did not believe?
19 So we see that they could not enter in
because of unbelief.

Hebrews Chapter 4

1 Therefore, let us fear lest being left a
promise of entering into His rest, any of
you might+ come short of it.
2 For the Gospel was proclaimed+ to us
as well as to them, but the Word pro-
claimed+ did not benefit+ them, not being
mixed with faith in *those* who heard *it*.
3 For *only* we who have believed do
enter into rest. As He said: As I have
sworn in my wrath: They shall not+
enter into my rest. *Even* though the
works were finished from the foundation of the world. *Psalm 95:11*
4 For He spoke in a certain place of the
seventh *day* in this way: And God rested
on the seventh day from all His works.
Genesis 2:2
5 And in this again: They shall not+
enter into my rest. *Psalm 95:11*
6 Therefore it remains *for* some to enter
into it. Those to whom it was first
proclaimed+ did not enter in because of
unbelief.
7 Again, He specifies+ a certain day,
saying in David: Today. After so long a
time, it is *still* said: Today, if you will,
hear His voice. Do not harden your
hearts. *Psalm 95:7,8*

8 For if Joshua+ had given them rest, *it* would not have been spoken about another after those days.

9 Therefore, there remains a rest to the people of God.

10 For *those* who have entered rest have also stopped+ from their own works, as God *did* from His.

11 Therefore, let us labor to enter that rest, lest anyone fall after the same example of unbelief.

> 12 The Word of God *is* quick and powerful and sharper than any two edged sword, piercing even to the dividing apart+ of soul and spirit and of the joints and marrow. *It is* a discerner of the thoughts and intents of the heart.

13 Nor is there any creature that is not revealed+ in His sight. But everything+ *is* naked and opened to the eyes of Him with whom we have to do. *Matthew 10:26*

14 Since+ we have a Great High Priest who is passed into the heavens, Jesus the Son of God, let us hold fast *our* profession.

15 For we do not have a high priest who cannot be touched with the feeling of our weaknesses,+ but *He* was in all points tempted as *we are, yet* without sin.

16 Let us therefore come boldly to the throne of grace *so* that we may receive+ mercy and find grace to help in time of need.

Hebrews Chapter 5

1 For every high priest taken from among men is ordained by men in things *pertaining* to God *so* that he may offer both gifts and sacrifices for sins.

2 *He* has compassion on the uninformed+ and on *those* who are erring,+ because he himself is also surrounded+ with infirmity.

3 For this+ reason, he should+ *make an* offering+ for sins for the people as for himself.

4 No one takes this honor unto himself, but *only* one who is called by God as Aaron *was*.

5 So also Christ did not glorify Himself to be made a high priest, but *God* said to Him: You are my Son. Today I have fathered+ you. *Psalm 2:7*

6 As He said also in another *place*: You *are* a priest forever after the order of Melchisedec. *Psalm 110:4*

7 In the days of His flesh, when *Christ* had offered up prayers and supplications with strong crying and tears to *God the Father* who was able to save Him from death, *He* was heard because+ He revered+ *God*.

8 *Even* though He was *the* Son, He learned obedience through+ the things that He suffered.

9 And being made perfect, He became the Author of Eternal Salvation to all who obey Him.

10 *Christ was* called by God *to be* High Priest after the order of Melchisedec. *Psalm 110:4*

11 About *Him* we have many things to say *that are* hard to explain+ because+ you are dull of hearing.

12 By this time you ought to be teachers *yet* you have need of one *to* teach you *again* the first principles of the oracles of God, and *you* have become *in* need of having milk and not solid+ food.+

13 For all who take milk *are* unskillful in the Word of righteousness, for *they* are babes.

14 But solid+ food+ belongs to *those* who are of full age, *those* who by reason of use have their senses exercised to discern both good and evil.

Hebrews Chapter 6

1 Therefore, leaving the first+ *principles* of the doctrine of Christ, let us go on to perfection, not laying again the foundation of repentance from dead works and of faith toward God,

2 of the doctrine of baptisms and of laying on of hands and of resurrection of the dead and of eternal judgment.

3 This we will do, if God permits.

4 For *it is* impossible for *those* who were once enlightened and have tasted of the heavenly gift and were made partakers of the Holy Spirit

5 and have tasted the good Word of God and the powers of the world to come,

6 if they shall fall away, to renew them again to repentance, since they themselves crucify the Son of God *all over again* and put *Him* to an open shame.

7 For the earth that drinks in the rain that often comes upon it and brings forth herbs fit[+] for those by whom it is dressed, receives blessing from God.

8 But *the land* that bears thorns and briers *is* rejected and *is* near to *being* cursed, *and* the end of that *is* to be burned.

9 But, beloved, we are persuaded *of* better things about you, things that accompany salvation. And *it is about* that, we speak.

10 For God *is* not unrighteous to forget your work and labor of love that you have shown toward His name in that you have ministered to the saints and *still* do minister to *them*.

11 We desire that everyone of you show the same diligence to the full assurance of hope to the end.

> 12 Do not be lazy,[+]
> but *be* followers of *those* who,
> through faith and patience,
> inherit the promises.

13 For when God made *His* promise to Abraham, because He could swear by no greater, He swore by Himself.

14 *He* said: Surely blessing I will bless you and multiplying I will multiply you.
Genesis 22:17

15 Therefore, after *Abraham* had patiently endured, he obtained the promise.

16 For indeed,[+] men swear with a great oath to confirm an end to all their strife.

17 In this, God *was* willing, more abundantly, to show to the heirs of promise the unchangeableness[+] of His counsel *and He* confirmed *it* by an oath.

18 *Now*, by two unchangeable[+] things in which *it was* impossible for God to lie, we have a strong consolation, *those of us* who have fled for refuge to lay hold upon the hope set before us.

19 *In this hope* we have an anchor for the soul *that is* both sure and steadfast and enters into that *area* within the veil.

20 There, the forerunner has entered for us: Jesus, made a high priest forever after the order of Melchisedec.

Hebrews Chapter 7

1 For this Melchisedec, king of Salem *and* priest of the most high God, met Abraham returning from the slaughter of the kings and blessed him.

2 Abraham gave a tenth *part* of all *the spoils* to *Melchisedec. For Melchisedec* was known[+] first as the King of righteousness and after that also as King of Salem, which is King of peace.

3 *Melchisedec was* without father, without mother, *and* without *family* history,[+] having no *known* beginning of days nor end of life, but *he was made as one* resembling[+] the Son of God, abiding as a priest without end.[+]

4 Now consider how great this man *was*, to whom even the patriarch Abraham gave a tenth of the spoils.

5 Truly[+] *those* who are of the sons of Levi, who receive the office of the priesthood, have a commandment to take tithes from the people according to the law, that is from their family,[+] though they have come out of the loins of Abraham.

6 But *Melchisedec*, whose genealogy[+] is not counted from them, received tithes from Abraham and blessed him who had the promises.

7 *Now* without any[+] contradiction, the lesser was blessed by the greater.[+]

8 Here, men who die *as mere mortals* receive tithes. But there, *one received tithes* of whom it is witnessed that he lives.

9 And, if I may say so, Levi who receives tithes, also paid tithes in Abraham.

10 For *Levi* was still in the loins of his father *Abraham* when Melchisedec met him.
11 Therefore if perfection were *attained* through the Levitical priesthood under which the people received the law, *then* what further need *was there* that another priest should rise *up* after the order of Melchisedec and not be called after the order of Aaron?
12 For the priesthood being changed, makes+ *it* necessary also *for* a change *in* the law.
13 For He about whom these things are spoken belongs+ to another tribe from which no man has given attention+ at the altar.
14 For *it is* evident that our Lord arose+ out of Judah, *and* Moses spoke nothing about that tribe concerning priesthood.
15 It is yet far more evident, because after the likeness+ of Melchisedec there arises another priest
16 who is made, not after the law of a worldly+ commandment, but after the power of an endless life.
17 For He testifies: You *are* a priest forever after the order of Melchisedec. *Psalm 110:4*
18 For there is truly+ a nullifying+ of the commandment going before for the weakness and unprofitableness of it.
19 For the law made nothing perfect. But the bringing in of a better hope *did*. By this, we draw near to God.
20 *It was* not without an oath *that He was made priest*.
21 For those priests were made without an oath. But this *priest was made* with an oath by *God* who said to Him: The Lord swore and will not repent: You *are* a priest forever after the order of Melchisedec. *Psalm 110:4*
22 By so much was Jesus made a guarantee+ of a better covenant.+
23 Truly, there had been many priests, because they were not allowed+ to continue because of death.
24 But this *one* continues forever because He has an unchangeable priesthood.
25 Therefore, He is able also to save them to the uttermost who come to God through Him since+ He lives continually+ to make intercession for them.
26 For such a high priest came *to* us *who is* holy, harmless, undefiled, separate from sinners, and made higher than the heavens.
27 *Jesus* does not need to offer sacrifices daily as the high priests, first for His own sins and then for the people's. For this He did once, when He offered up Himself.
28 For the law makes men high priests who have weaknesses.+ But the word of the oath, which *came* after+ the law, *made* the Son consecrated forever.

Hebrews Chapter 8

1 Now, *here is a* summary of the things being spoken: We have such a high priest, who is set at the right hand of the throne of the Majesty in the Heavens.
2 *He is* a minister of the sanctuary and of the true tabernacle that the Lord built,+ and not man.
3 For every high priest is ordained to offer gifts and sacrifices. Therefore *it is* necessary that this man have something to offer, also.
4 For if He were on earth, He would not be a priest, since there are priests who offer gifts according to the law,
5 who serve *the* example and shadow of heavenly things, as Moses was admonished by God when he was about to make the tabernacle. For He said: See *that* you make all things according to the pattern shown to you on the mountain. *Exodus 25:40*
6 But now He has obtained a more excellent ministry, as He is also the mediator of a better covenant established upon better promises.
7 For if that first were faultless, *then* no place would *have been* sought *for the* second.
8 Because *in* finding fault *with* them, He says: Behold the days are coming, says the Lord, when I will make a new covenant with the house of Israel and with the house of Judah, *Jeremiah 31:31*

9 not according to the covenant that I made with their fathers in the day when I took them by the hand to lead them out of the land of Egypt. Because they did not continue in my covenant, I ignored+ them, says the Lord. *Jeremiah 31:32*

10 For this *is* the covenant that I will make with the house of Israel after those days, says the Lord: I will put my laws into their mind and write them in their hearts. I will be to them God. And they shall be my people. *Jeremiah 31:33*

11 They shall not teach every+ neighbor and every+ brother saying: Know the Lord. For everyone will know me, from the least to the greatest. *Jeremiah 31:34*

12 For I will be merciful to their unrighteousness and their sins and their iniquities I will remember no longer.+ *Jeremiah 31:34*

13 In that He said: A new, He has made the first old. Now what *is* decaying and growing+ old *is* ready to vanish away.

Hebrews Chapter 9

1 Truly+ then, the first *covenant* also had ordinances of divine service and a worldly sanctuary.

2 In the first tabernacle, *there was* a table prepared *with* a candlestick and show-bread *in an area* called the sanctuary.

3 Then, after the second veil, *was* the tabernacle called the Holiest of all.

4 It had the golden censer and the ark of the covenant overlaid *all* around+ with gold. In it *was* the golden pot that had manna and Aaron's rod that budded and the tables of the covenant.

5 Over it *were* the cherubims of glory shadowing the mercy seat. About this, we cannot now speak in detail.+

6 Now when these things were thus ordained, the priests always went into the first tabernacle *to* accomplish the service *of God*.

7 But into the second, the high priest *went* alone once every year, *and* not without blood that he offered for himself and *for* the errors of the people.

8 This signified, *by* the Holy Spirit, that the way into the holiest of all was not yet revealed+ while the first tabernacle was yet standing.

9 This *was* symbolic+ for the time then present in which both gifts and sacrifices were offered that could not make *those* who did the service perfect, as pertaining to the conscience.

10 *For it concerned* only food+ and drink and many different+ washings and worldly+ ordinances imposed *on them* until the time of reformation.

11 But Christ came*as* a high priest of good things to come, by a greater and more perfect tabernacle not made with hands. That is to say, not of this building.

12 *It is* not by the blood of goats and calves, but by His own blood *that* He entered once *for all* into the holy place, *thereby* obtaining eternal redemption *for us*.

13 For if the blood of bulls and goats and the ashes of a heifer sprinkling the unclean sanctifies to the purifying of the flesh,

14 how much more shall the blood of Christ, who, through the eternal Spirit offered Himself without spot to God, purge your conscience from dead works to serve the living God?

15 For this reason,+ *Christ* is the mediator of the new covenant+ *so* that, by means of death for the redemption of the transgressions *that were* under the first covenant,+ *those* who are called might receive the promise of eternal inheritance.

16 For where a testament *is*, there must, of necessity, also be the death of the testator.

17 For a testament *is* of force after one+ is dead. Otherwise, it is of no strength at all while the testator lives.

18 Therefore, the first *covenant* was not dedicated without blood.

19 For when Moses had spoken every precept to all the people according to the law, he took the blood of calves and goats with water and scarlet wool and a hyssop *branch* and sprinkled both the book and all the people,

20 saying: This *is* the blood of the

covenant+ that God commanded+ to you. *Exodus 24:7-8, Matthew 26:28*

21 Moreover he sprinkled with blood both the tabernacle and all the vessels of the ministry.

22 Almost all things are, by the law, purged with blood. Without *the* shedding of blood, *there* is no remission.

23 Therefore *it was* necessary that the patterns of things in the heavens should be purified with these, but the heavenly things themselves with better sacrifices than these.

24 For Christ has not entered the holy places made with hands, *that are* symbolic+ of the true. But into heaven itself *He* now appears in the presence of God for us.

25 Nor *was it* that He should offer Himself often, as the high priest enters into the holy place every year with blood of others.

26 For then He must often have suffered since the foundation of the world. But now once in the end of the world He has appeared to put away sin by the sacrifice of Himself.

27 As it is appointed to *all* humans+ once to die and after that judgment,

28 so *also* Christ was offered once to bear the sins of many, *and to* appear second, without *bearing* sins, to those who wait *for* Him for salvation.

Hebrews Chapter 10

1 For the law, having *only* a shadow of *the* good things to come *and* not the very image of those things, can never, with those sacrifices that they offered year by year continually, make those *who* come to that perfect.

2 For then would they not have stopped+ being offered? Because the worshipers, once purged, would have had no more conscience of sins.

3 But in those *sacrifices, there is* a remembrance of sins *made* again every year.

4 For *it is* not possible that the blood of bulls and of goats should take away sins.

5 Therefore, when *Christ* came into the world, He said: Sacrifice and offering you did not desire,+ but you have prepared a body *for* me. *Psalm 40:6*

6 In burnt offerings and *sacrifices* for sin you have had no pleasure. *Malachi 1:10*

7 Then I said: Behold, I *have* come. *As* it is written in the pages+ of the book about me: *I delight* to do your will, O God. *Psalm 40:7,8*

8 Above saying: Sacrifice and offering and burnt offerings and *offering* for sin you would not *desire* nor have pleasure *in*, such as were offered according to the law, *Matthew 9:13*

9 *He* then said: Behold, I come to do your will O God. *In this,* He takes away the first *so* that He may establish the second.

10 By this will we are sanctified through the offering of the body of Jesus Christ once *for all*.

11 Every priest stands daily ministering and repeatedly+ offering the same sacrifices that can never take away sins.

12 But after *Jesus* had offered one sacrifice for sins forever, He sat down at the right hand of God,

13 thereafter waiting+ *expectantly* until His enemies be made His footstool.

14 For by one offering He has perfected forever *those* who are sanctified.

15 The Holy Spirit is also a witness to us. For after He had said before:

16 This *is* the covenant that I will make with them after those days, says the Lord: I will put my laws into their hearts, and in their minds I will write them. *Jeremiah 31:33*

17 Their sins and iniquities I will remember no longer.+ *Jeremiah 31:34*

18 Now where remission of these *sins is, there is* no more *need for sacrificial* offering for sin.

19 Therefore family,+ having boldness to enter into the holiest by the blood of Jesus,

20 by a new and living way that He has consecrated for us through the veil, that is to say His flesh,

21 *having* a high priest over the house of God:

22 Let us draw near with a true heart in
full assurance of faith, having our hearts
sprinkled from an evil conscience and
our bodies washed with pure water.
23 Let us hold fast the profession of *our*
faith without wavering. For He who
promised *is* faithful.
24 Let us consider one another to provoke
one another to love and to good works.
25 *Let us* not forsake the assembling of
ourselves together, as the manner of
some *is*, but exhort *one another*. So much
the more, as you see the day approaching.
26 For if we sin willfully after we have
received the knowledge of the truth,
there remains no more sacrifice for
sins.
27 But *there will be* a certain fearful
expectation[+] of judgment and fiery
indignation that will devour the adversaries.
28 *Those* who despised Moses' law died
without mercy under *the testimony of* two
or three witnesses.
29 Of how much greater[+] punishment do
you suppose one[+] shall be thought
worthy who has trampled[+] the Son of
God under foot and has counted the
blood of the covenant with which they
were sanctified an unholy thing and has
done dishonor[+] to the Spirit of grace?
30 For we know Him who said: Vengeance *belongs* to me. I will repay,[+]
says the Lord. And again: The Lord will
judge His people. *Deuteronomy 32:35-36*
31 *It is* a fearful thing to fall into the hands
of the living God.
32 But remember the former days in
which, after you were enlightened,[+]
you endured a great fight of afflictions.
33 Partly while you were made a subject
of stares[+] both by reproaches and
afflictions and partly while you became
companions of *those* who were abiding[+]
in them.
34 For you had compassion for me in my
chains[+] and took joyfully the spoiling of
your goods, knowing in yourselves that
you have in heaven a better and an
enduring substance.
35 Therefore do not cast away your
confidence that has great repayment[+] of
reward.
36 For you have need of patience *so* that
after you have done the will of God, you
might receive the promise.
37 For *it will be* only[+] a little while and
He who is coming will *indeed* come and
will not delay.[+] *Habakkuk 2:3, John 16:16*
38 Now the just shall live by faith. But if
anyone draws back, my soul will not
delight[+] in them. *Habakkuk 2:4*
39 We are not drawing back to damnation,[+] but *we have* faith[+] *in* the saving
of the soul.

Hebrews Chapter 11

> 1 Faith is the substance
> of things hoped for,
> the evidence of things not seen.

2 For by it the elders obtained a good
report.
3 Through faith we understand that the
worlds were framed by the Word of
God, so that things that are seen were
not made of things that do appear.
4 By faith Abel offered to God a more
excellent sacrifice than Cain. By this,
he obtained *a* witness that he was righteous, God testifying of his gifts. By it
he, being dead, yet speaks.
5 By faith Enoch was translated *so* that
he would not see death. *He* was not
found because God had translated him.
For before his translation, he had this
testimony: That he pleased God.

> 6 Without faith *it is* impossible to
> please *God*. For *those* who come to
> God must believe that He is and
> *that* He is a rewarder of *those* who
> diligently seek Him.

7 By faith Noah, being warned by God
of things not yet seen, moved with fear
and prepared an ark for the saving of his
house. In this, he condemned the world
and became *an* heir of the righteousness
that *comes* by faith.
8 By faith Abraham, when he was called

to go to a place that he would later[+] receive as an inheritance, obeyed. He went, not knowing where he was going.

9 By faith he sojourned to the land of promise, as *in* a strange country, dwelling in tabernacles with Isaac and Jacob, the heirs with him of the same promise.

10 He was looking for the city having foundations, whose builder and maker *is* God.

11 Through faith Sarah herself also received strength to conceive seed and gave birth[+] when she was past *child-bearing* age, because she judged Him faithful who had promised.

12 Therefore there arose,[+] even from one as good as dead, *many descendants* like the multitude of stars in the sky and innumerable as the sand on the sea shore.

13 These all died in faith, not having received the promises, but having seen them a far *distance away*. *They* were persuaded about *them* and embraced *them* and confessed that they were strangers and sojourners[+] on the earth.

14 For *those* who say such things declare plainly that they are seeking a homeland.[+]

15 Truly, if they had been mindful of that *country* from where they came, they might have had opportunity to have returned.

16 But now they desire a better *country*, that is a heavenly *homeland*. Therefore, God is not ashamed to be called their God for He has prepared a city for them.

17 By faith Abraham, when he was tested,[+] offered up Isaac. He who had received the promises offered up his only begotten *son*.

18 It was said of him that in Isaac your descendants[+] shall be called *forth*. *Genesis 21:12*

19 *Abraham* concluded[+] that God *was* able to raise *anyone* up, even from the dead. And in this, he also received a *prophetic* example.[+]

20 By faith Isaac blessed Jacob and Esau concerning things to come.

21 By faith Jacob, when he was dying, blessed both the sons of Joseph, and *he still* worshiped, *even leaning* on the top of his staff.

22 By faith Joseph, when he died, made mention of the departing of the children of Israel and gave instructions[+] concerning his bones.

23 By faith Moses, when he was born, was hid *for* three months by his parents because they saw *he was* a beautiful[+] child. They were not afraid of the king's edict.[+]

24 By faith Moses, when he had come of age,[+] refused to be called the son of Pharaoh's daughter.

25 *He* chose rather to suffer affliction with the people of God, than to enjoy the pleasures of sin for a season.

26 *He* esteemed the reproach of Christ greater riches than the treasures in Egypt. For he had respect for the repayment[+] of the reward.

27 By faith he left[+] Egypt, not fearing the wrath of the king. For seeing the invisible, he endured.

28 Through faith he kept the Passover and the sprinkling of blood, lest he who destroyed the firstborn should touch them.

29 By faith they passed through the Red sea as on dry *land*. When the Egyptians tried[+] to do *that, they* were drowned.

30 By faith the walls of Jericho fell down after they were surrounded[+] about seven days.

31 By faith the harlot Rahab did not perish with *those* who did not believe when she had received the spies with peace.

32 What more shall I say? For time would fail me to tell of Gideon and Barak and Samson and Jephthae, *of* David and Samuel and *of all* the prophets.

33 Through faith *they* subdued kingdoms, worked[+] righteousness, obtained promises, stopped the mouths of lions,

34 quenched the violence of fire, *and* escaped the edge of the sword. Out of weakness *they* were made strong, grew[+] valiant in fight, *and* turned the armies of the aliens to flight.

35 Women received their dead raised to
life again. Others were tortured, not
accepting deliverance *so* that they might
obtain a better resurrection.
36 Others received+ trials by *cruel* mock-
ings and scourgings *and* even+ chains+
and imprisonment.
37 They were stoned, sawn apart,+
tested,+ *and* slain with the sword. They
wandered about in sheepskins and goat
skins, being destitute, afflicted, *and*
tormented.
38 The world was not worthy of them.
They wandered in deserts and mountains and *in* dens and caves in the earth.
39 *And yet* all of them, *even* having obtained a good report through faith, did
not receive the promise.
40 God anticipated+ something better for
us *so* that, without us, *everything would
not be* fulfilled.+

Hebrews Chapter 12

1 Therefore, since we also are surrounded+
with so great a cloud of witnesses, let us
lay aside every weight and the sin that
does so easily beset *us*, and let us run the
race that is set before us with patience,
2 looking to Jesus, the Author and
Finisher of *our* faith. *He*, for the joy
that was set before Him, endured the
cross, despising the shame, and *He* is
now set down at the right hand of the
throne of God.
3 Consider Him who endured such
contradictions of sinners against Himself, lest you be wearied and faint in
your minds.
4 You have not yet resisted to *the point
of* blood *in* striving against sin.
5 You have forgotten the exhortation
that speaks to you as to children: My
child, do not despise the discipline+ of
the Lord nor faint when you are rebuked
by Him. *Proverbs 3:11*
6 For *those* the Lord loves, He chastens
and *He* disciplines+ every child whom
He receives. *Proverbs 3:12*
7 If you endure discipline,+ God deals
with you as *His own* children.+ For who
is *the* child whom the father does not
discipline+?
8 But if you are without chastisement, of
which all are partakers, then you are
illegitimate+ *children* and not children
of the Father.
9 Furthermore we have had fathers in
the flesh who corrected *us* and we gave
them reverence. Shall we not much
rather be in subjection to the Father of
spirits and live?
10 For indeed+ they chastened *us* for a
few days as they think+ *best*. But He
chastens for *our own* benefit+ *so* that *we*
might be partakers of His holiness.
11 Now, no discipline+ for the present
seems to be joyous, but grievous.
Nevertheless afterward it yields the
peaceable fruit of righteousness to
those who are exercised thereby.
12 Therefore lift up the hands that hang
down and the feeble knees.
13 Make straight paths for your feet, lest
what is lame be turned out of the way.
But rather, let it be healed.

14 Follow peace with all *people*,
and holiness without which
no one will see the Lord.

15 Watch+ diligently
lest anyone fail of the grace of God
and lest any root of bitterness
spring up *and* trouble *you*.
For by that+ many become defiled.

16 *Watch*, lest there *be* any fornicator or
worldly+ person like Esau who, for one
serving+ of food,+ sold his birthright.
17 For you know that afterward, when he
would have inherited the blessing, he
was rejected, for he found no place of
repentance, though he sought it carefully with tears.
18 For you have not come to the mountain being touched and burned with fire
and blackness and darkness and storm+
19 and sound of trumpet and voice of
words *at* which *those* who heard *it*
begged that the word not be spoken to
them any more.

20 For they could not endure what was commanded. And if any beast touched that mountain, it *was to* be stoned or thrust through with a dart. *Exodus 19:12,13*

21 So terrible was the sight *that* Moses said: I fear and quake exceedingly.

22 But you have come to Mount Zion,[+] to the city of the living God, the heavenly Jerusalem, and to an innumerable company of angels.

23 *You have come* to the general assembly and *to the* assembly[+] of the firstborn who are registered[+] in heaven and to God the Judge of all and to the spirits of righteous[+] people made perfect.

24 *You have come* to Jesus, the Mediator of the new covenant and to the blood of sprinkling that speaks better than Abel.

25 See that you do not refuse *the one* who speaks *to you*. For if *those* who refused *Jesus* who spoke on earth did not escape, *then* much more *will we not escape* if we turn away from Him who *speaks* from heaven.

26 *His* voice then shook the earth. But now He has promised, saying: Yet once more I *will* shake not only the earth, but also heaven. *Haggai 2:6*

27 And this yet once more signifies the removing of the things that *shall be* shaken *apart so* that the things that cannot be shaken *may* remain.

28 We *will* receive a kingdom which cannot be moved. Therefore, let us have grace by which we may serve God acceptably, with reverence and godly fear.

29 For our God *is* a consuming fire.

Hebrews Chapter 13

1 Let brotherly love continue.

2 Do not be forgetful to entertain strangers. For thereby some have entertained angels unexpectedly.[+]

3 Remember *those* who are in chains,[+] as *though you were* bound with them. *Remember those* who suffer adversity, as *though* being yourselves also in *their* body.

4 *Let* marriage *be* honorable in every *way* and the *marriage* bed undefiled. God will judge fornicators[+] and adulterers.

> 5 *Let your* conversation *and conduct*
> *be* without covetousness.
> *Be* content
> with such things as you have.
> For He has said:
> I will never leave you
> nor forsake you. *John 14:18*

6 Therefore, we may boldly say: The Lord *is* my helper and I will not fear what mankind[+] will do to me. *Psalm 118:6*

7 Remember *those* who have the rule over you *and those* who have spoken the Word of God to you. Follow *their* faith, considering the example[+] of *their* conversation *and conduct*.

> 8 Jesus Christ *is* the same
> yesterday and today and forever.
> *Malachi 3:6*

9 Do not be carried away[+] with many different[+] and strange doctrines. For *it is* good that the heart be established with grace *and* not with food[+] *laws* that have not benefited[+] *those* who have been preoccupied[+] with them.

10 We have an altar from which those who serve the tabernacle have no right to eat.

11 For the bodies of those beasts whose blood is brought into the sanctuary by the high priest for sin, are burned outside[+] the camp.

12 Therefore Jesus also, *so* that He might sanctify the people with His own blood, suffered outside[+] the gate.

13 Therefore, let us go forth to Him outside[+] the camp, bearing His reproach.

14 For here we have no continuing city. But we seek one *that is* to come.

15 Therefore through Him, let us offer the sacrifice of praise to God continually. That is, the fruit of *our* lips giving thanks to His name.

16 Do not forget to do good and to share.[+] For with such sacrifices God is well pleased.

17Obey *those* who have the rule over you
and submit yourselves *to them*. For they
watch *out* for your souls as *those* who
must give account. *Obey them so* that
they may do it with joy and not with
grief. For that *is* not beneficial+ for you.
18Pray for us. For we trust we have a
good conscience, in all things willing to
live honestly.
19But I urge+ *you* rather to do this *so* that
I may be restored to you *all* the sooner.
20Now *may* the God of peace who brought
our Lord Jesus *up* from the dead, that
great shepherd of the sheep, through the
blood of the everlasting covenant,
21make you perfect in every good work
to do His will, working in you what is
well pleasing in His sight, through Jesus
Christ, to whom *be* glory forever and
ever. Amen.
22I urge you family+: Endure+ the word
of exhortation. For I have written *this
letter* to you in few words.
23Know that *our* brother Timothy is
released,+ with whom, if he come soon,+
I will see you.
24Greet+ all who have the rule over you
and all the saints. Those from Italy
greet+ you.
25Grace be with you all. Amen.

This epistle was written by Timothy in Italy.

James Chapter 1

1 *From* James, a servant of God and of
the Lord Jesus Christ. To the twelve
tribes that are scattered: Greetings.
2 My family,+

count it all joy
when you fall into
many different+ trials.+

3 Know that the testing+ of your faith
works patience.
4 And let patience have *its* perfect
work *so* that you may be perfect and
complete,+ lacking+ in nothing.

5 If any of you lack wisdom, *then*
ask God who gives to everyone
liberally and does not upbraid,
and *it* will be given. *Matthew 7:7*
6 But ask in faith, not wavering.
For *those* who waver are like a
wave of the sea driven with the
wind and tossed.
7 For do not suppose that one+ *who
is wavering* will receive anything
from the Lord.
8 A double minded person+ *is* unstable in all their ways.

9 Let those+ of low degree rejoice in
their elevation,+
10 and *let* the rich *rejoice* in being humbled.+
Because, like the flower *of the* grass,
they will pass away.
11For the sun rises with a burning heat
and withers the grass, and its flower
falls and the grace of the fashion of it
perishes. So also will the rich fade away
in their ways.
12Blessed *are those* who *patiently* endure trials.+ For when they are proved,+
they will receive the crown of life that
the Lord has promised to *those* who
love Him.
13Let no one say, when tempted, I am
tempted by God. For God cannot be
tempted with evil, nor does He tempt
anyone.
14But everyone+ is tempted when drawn
away by lust and enticed.
15Then when lust has conceived, it
brings forth sin. And sin, when it is
finished, brings forth death.
16Do not err my beloved.+

17 Every good gift and every perfect
gift is from above and comes down
from the Father of lights with whom
there is no variableness nor shadow
of turning. *Malachi 3:6*

18Of His own will *God* brought+ us *forth*
with the Word of Truth *so* that we would
be a kind of first fruits of His creatures.
19Therefore my beloved,+ let everyone+

Be swift to hear,
slow to speak,
and slow to anger.+
Matthew 12:36, Proverbs 10:19, Proverbs 14:9

20 For anger+ does not produce+ the
righteousness of God.
21 Therefore, put away+ all filthiness
and superfluity of naughtiness. *Instead,*
receive with meekness, the engrafted
Word that is able to save your souls.
22 But *then* be doers of the Word, and not
hearers only, deceiving yourselves.
23 For if any are hearers of the Word and
not doers, they are like those beholding
their natural face in a mirror.+
24 For they behold themselves and *then*
go away and immediately+ forget what
kind+ of person they are.
25 But whoever looks into the perfect law
of liberty and continues *therein*, not
being a forgetful hearer but a doer of the
work, shall be blessed in their deeds.
26 If any among you seem to be religious
and do not bridle their tongue but
deceive their own hearts, their religion
is vain.
27 Pure religion, undefiled before God
the Father is this: To visit the fatherless
and widows in their affliction *and* keep
oneself unspotted from the world.

James Chapter 2

1 My family,+ do not have the faith of
our Lord Jesus Christ, *the Lord* of glory,
with *deferential* respect of persons.
2 For *one* man *may* come into your
assembly with gold rings *and wearing*
fine+ apparel, and a poor man *may* also
come in *wearing* vile clothing.+
3 *If* you look+ *with deferential respect*
upon the one who wears fine+ apparel
and say to him: Sit here in a good place,
and then say to the poor: Stand *over* there
or sit here under my footstool,
4 then are you not *showing* partiality
among+ yourselves and becoming judges
with evil thoughts?
5 Listen+ my beloved+: Has God not
chosen the poor of this world *to be* rich
in faith and heirs of the kingdom that He
has promised to *those* who love Him?
6 But *by acting deferentially,* you have
despised the poor. Do not rich men
oppress you and draw you before the
judgment seats?
7 Do they not blaspheme that worthy
name by which you are called?
8 If you fulfill the royal law according
to the Scripture: You shall love your
neighbor as yourself, *then* you do well.
Matthew 19:19
9 But if you *show* partiality+ to *certain*
persons, you commit sin and are
convicted+ by the law as transgressors.
10 For whoever keeps the whole law and
yet offends in one *point* is guilty of all.
11 For He who said: Do not commit
adultery, also said: Do not kill. Now if
you commit no adultery, yet if you kill,
then you have become a transgressor of
the law.
12 So speak and do as *those* who shall be
judged by the law of liberty.
13 For there will be judgment without
mercy for *those* who have not shown
mercy, and rejoicing over merciful
judgment.
14 My family,+ what *is the* benefit+ if
someone says they have faith but *they* do
not have works? Can faith save them?
15 If a brother or sister is naked and
destitute of daily food,
16 and one of you says to them: Go+ in
peace, be warm and filled, but you do
not give them those things that are
necessary+ for the body, what benefit
are your words?
17 So faith, if it does not *also* have works,
is dead, being alone.
18 Someone+ may say: You have faith
and I have works. *But I say,* show me
your faith without your works, and I
will show you my faith by my works.
19 You believe that *there* is one God *and*
you do well *to thus believe*. And the
demons+ *also* believe and tremble.
20 But will you know *this*, O vain person+:
That faith without works is dead.
21 Was not Abraham our father justified

by works when he had offered his son
Isaac upon the altar?
22 See how faith worked+ with his works,
and by works faith was made perfect?
23 *In this,* the Scripture was fulfilled that
says: Abraham believed God and it was
credited+ to him as righteousness and he
was called the Friend of God. *Genesis 15:6*
24 You see then, that by works a man is
justified, and not by faith only.
25 Likewise also was not Rahab the harlot
justified by works when she received
the messengers and sent *them* out
another way?
26 For *just* as the body without the
spirit is dead, so also faith without
works is dead.

James Chapter 3

1 My family,+ not many *of you should*
be teachers,+ knowing that we *who are*
will receive greater judgment.+
2 For in many things we all offend. If
anyone does not offend in word, *then*
they *are* perfect *and* able also to bridle
the whole body. *Proverbs 13:3*
3 Behold, we put bits in the horses'
mouths *so* that they will obey us, and
thus we turn their whole body.
4 Behold the ships, also. Although *they*
are so large+ and driven by fierce winds,
yet are they turned with a very small
rudder,+ *to* whatever course+ *the* one
who steers wills *it to go.*
5 Even so, the tongue is a little member
and boasts great things. Behold how
great a matter a little fire kindles.
Matthew 12:35
6 The tongue *can set on* fire a *whole*
world of iniquity. Thus is the tongue
set among our members *so* that it *can*
defile the whole body and set on fire the
course of nature. And, it is set on fire
by Hell. *Proverbs 16:27*
7 For every kind of beast and bird and
serpent and *sea* creature can be subdued+
and has been subdued+ by mankind.
8 However no one is able to subdue+ the
tongue of an unruly+ evil+ person full of
deadly poison. *Proverbs 16:28*
9 With *the tongue one can* bless God the
Father and with *the tongue one can* curse
men who are made in the likeness+ of
God.
10 Out of the same mouth proceed blessing and cursing. My family,+ these
things should not be.
11 Does a fountain send forth sweet and
bitter at the same place?
12 Can the fig tree, my family,+ produce+
olives? Or *can* a vine *produce* figs?
Likewise,+ no fountain *can* yield both
salt water and fresh.
13 Who *is* wise and endowed+ with knowledge among you? Let them show their
works out of a good conversation *and*
conduct, with meekness of wisdom.
14 However, if you have bitter envying
and strife in your hearts, do not boast+
and lie against the truth.
15 This *false* wisdom does not descend
from above, but *it is* earthly, sensual,
and devilish.
16 For where *there is* envy and strife,
there *is* confusion and every evil work.
Proverbs 10:12

17 But the wisdom that is from above
is first pure, then peaceable, gentle,
and yielding,+ full of mercy and
good fruits, without partiality, and
without hypocrisy.
18 The fruit of righteousness is sown
in peace by *those* who make peace.

James Chapter 4

1 From where *do* wars and fighting
arise among you? *Is it* not + from your
lusts that war within+ you?
2 You lust and do not have. You kill and
desire to have and cannot obtain. You
fight and war, yet you do not have
because you do not ask.
3 You ask and do not receive because
you ask amiss *so* that you may consume
upon your lusts.
4 *You* adulterers and adulteresses: Do
you not know that attachment+ *to the*
pleasures of the world is enmity with
God? Therefore, whoever chooses+ to

be attached[+] *to the pleasures* of the world
is *thereby* made[+] an enemy of God.
5 Do you suppose[+] that the Scripture
says *in* vain: The *natural* spirit that
lives[+] in us lusts to envy. *Genesis 6:5*
6 But *God* gives more grace. Therefore
it says: God resists the proud but gives
grace to the humble. *Proverbs 4:34*
7 Therefore, submit yourselves to
God. Resist the devil and he will flee
from you.
8 Draw near to God and He will draw
near to you. Cleanse *your* hands, *you*
sinners. Purify *your* hearts, *you* double
minded.
9 Be afflicted and mourn and weep. Let
your laughter be turned to mourning and
your joy to sorrow.[+]
10 Humble yourselves in the sight of the
Lord and He will lift you up.
11 Do not speak evil about one another,
family.[+] *Those* who speak evil of *their*
family[+] and judge their family,[+] speak
evil of the law and judge the law. But if
you judge the law, you are not a doer of
the law, but a judge.
12 There is one lawgiver who is able to
save and to destroy. Who are you that
you judge another?
13 Come[+] now, you who say: Today or
tomorrow we will go into some[+] city
and continue there a year and buy and
sell and get gain.
14 You do not know what *will be* tomorrow, for what *is* your life? It is but a
vapor that appears for a little time and
then vanishes away.
15 You *ought* to say: If the Lord is willing
and we live, *we may* do this or that.
16 But now you rejoice in your boasting,
however all such rejoicing is evil.
17 Therefore to *those* who know to do
good and do not do *it*, to them it is sin.

James Chapter 5

1 Come[+] now, *you* rich men: Weep and
howl for your miseries that shall come
upon *you*.
2 Your riches are corrupted and your
garments are moth eaten.
3 Your gold and silver are corroded[+]
and their rust will be a witness against
you and will eat your flesh as *though* it
were fire *because* you have *piled up*
treasure for the last days.
4 Behold the wages[+] of the laborers
who harvested[+] your fields, which you
kept back by fraud, cries *out*, and the
cries of *those* who harvested[+] have
entered the ears of the Lord of Sabaoth.
5 You have lived in pleasure on the earth
and been wanton. You have nourished
your hearts, as in a day of slaughter.
6 You have condemned *and* killed the
just, *and* they have not resisted you.
7 Therefore be patient, family,[+] for the
coming of the Lord. Behold the grower[+]
waits for the precious fruit of the earth
and has long patience for it until it
receives *the* early and *the* latter rain.
8 You be patient also. Strengthen[+] your
hearts. For the coming of the Lord
draws near.
9 Do not complain[+] against one another,
family,[+] lest you be condemned.
Behold, the judge stands before the door.
10 My family,[+] take the prophets who
have spoken in the name of the Lord as
an example of suffering affliction and
patience.
11 Behold, we count *those* who endure
blessed.[+] You have heard of the patience
of Job and have seen the end of the Lord,
that the Lord is full of pity and tender
mercy.
12 But above all things, my family,[+] do
not swear by heaven or by the earth or
by any other oath. But let your yes be
yes and *your* no, no. Lest you fall into
condemnation. *Matthew 5:37*
13 Are any among you suffering[+]? Let
them pray. Are any merry? Let them
sing psalms.
14 Are any sick among you? Let them
call for the elders of the assembly[+] and
let *the elders* pray over them, anointing
them with oil in the name of the Lord.
15 The prayer of faith will save the sick
and the Lord will raise them up. If
they have committed sins, they will
be forgiven.

16 Confess *your* faults to one another
and pray for one another *so* that you
may be healed. The effective+
fervent prayer of a righteous person+
avails much. *Proverbs 15:29*

17 Elijah was a man subject to passions
just as we are, and he prayed earnestly
that it might not rain and it did not
rain on the earth for three years and
six months.
18 *Then* he prayed again and the heaven
gave rain and the earth brought forth
her fruit.
19 Family, + if any of you do err from the
truth, and one convert them,
20 know this: that *those* who convert
sinners from the error of their ways,
save souls from death and cover+ *a*
multitude of sins. *Proverbs 11:30*

1 Peter Chapter 1

1 *From* Peter, an apostle of Jesus Christ.
To the sojourners+ scattered throughout
Pontus, Galatia, Cappadocia, Asia, and
Bithynia.
2 *You have been elected* according to the
foreknowledge of God *the* Father,
through sanctification by the *Holy* Spirit,
unto obedience and *the* sprinkling of
the blood of Jesus Christ. Grace *to* you
and peace *be* multiplied.
3 Blessed *is* the God and Father *of* our
Lord Jesus Christ. According to His
abundant mercy *He has made us* born+
again to a living+ hope through *the*
resurrection of Jesus Christ from the
dead,
4 to an inheritance incorruptible, undefiled, and that does not fade away,
reserved in heaven for you
5 who are kept by the power of God
through faith unto salvation, ready to be
revealed in the last time.
6 In this, you greatly rejoice. Although
now, for a season if need be, you are in
sorrow+ through *many* different+ trials.+
7 Because+ the proving+ of your faith *is*
much more precious than gold that
perishes. Though *it be* tested+ by fire,
may it be found to praise and honor and
glory, at the appearing of Jesus Christ.
8 *Even though you* have not seen *Him*, you
love *Him. Even* though you do not see
Him now, yet *you* believe *and* rejoice
with unspeakable joy and *expressions*
of glory,
9 receiving the end of your faith, the
salvation of *your* souls.
10 Regarding+ this salvation, the prophets
have inquired and searched diligently.
They prophesied about the grace *that*
would come to you,
11 searching *by* what *means* or *in* what
season of time the Spirit of Christ in
them was declaring, + when He testified
beforehand *about* the sufferings of
Christ and the glory that would follow.
12 It was revealed to *them*, that *it was* not
to themselves, but to us *that* they
ministered the things that are now
reported to you by *those* who have
proclaimed+ the Gospel to you with the
Holy Spirit sent down from heaven.
Even the angels desire to look into *these*
things.
13 Therefore, gird up the loins of your
mind. Be sober. And hope to the end for
the grace that is to be brought to you at
the revelation of Jesus Christ.
14 Be+ obedient children, not fashioning
yourselves according to the former lusts
in your ignorance.
15 But as He who has called you is holy,
so you *must* be holy in all kinds+ of
conversation *and conduct*.
16 Because it is written: Be holy, for I am
holy. *Leviticus 11:44*
17 If you call on the Father who judges
without partiality+ according to
everyone's+ work, *then* pass the time of
your sojourning *here* in fear.
18 For+ you know that *it was* not with
corruptible things *like* silver and gold
that you were redeemed from your vain
conversation *and conduct that you re-*
ceived by tradition from your fathers.
19 But *it was* with the precious blood of
Christ, as of a lamb without blemish and
without spot.

20 Truly+ He was foreordained before
the foundation of the world, but was
revealed+ in these last times for you.
21 Through Him *you* believe in God who
raised Him up from the dead and gave
Him glory *so* that your faith and hope
might be in God.
22 Your souls are purified by obedience
to the truth through the Spirit *and* to
sincere+ affection+ for the family.+
Love one another fervently with a
pure heart.
23 Be born again, not of corruptible seed
but of incorruptible, by the Word of
God who lives and abides forever.
24 For all flesh *is* like grass, and all the
glory of man is like the flower of grass:
The grass withers and its flower falls
away. *Isaiah 40:7*
25 But the Word of the Lord endures
forever. And this is the Word pro-
claimed+ *as Gospel* to you. *Isaiah 40:8*

1 Peter Chapter 2

1 Therefore, laying aside all malice and
all deceitfulness+ and hypocrisies and
envies and all evil speaking,
2 like newborn babes, desire the sincere
milk of the Word *so* that you may grow
thereby,
3 if *you* have tasted that goodness+ *of
the* Lord.
4 Come to *Jesus as to* a living stone,
rejected+ indeed by men, but chosen by
God *and* precious.
5 You also, as living+ stones, are *being*
built up *as* a spiritual house, a holy
priesthood, to offer up spiritual sacrifices, acceptable to God by Jesus Christ.
6 Therefore also, it is contained in the
Scripture: Behold I lay in Zion+ a chief
corner stone, chosen+ *and* precious, and
those who believe in Him will not be
ashamed.+ *Isaiah 28:16*
7 Therefore, to you who believe, *He is*
precious. But to *those* who are disobedient: The stone that the builders
rejected+ has become the chief+ corner-
stone,+ *Psalm 118:22*
8 a stone of stumbling and a rock of
offense. *Those* who stumble at the Word
are disobedient to *what* they also were
appointed. *Isaiah 8:14*
9 But you *are* a chosen generation, a
royal priesthood, a holy nation, a unique+
people. You should show forth the
praises of Him who has called you out
of darkness into His marvelous light.
10 In time past, *these were* not a people.
But now *they are* the people of God.
Previously, they had not received+ mercy.
But now, *they* have received+ mercy.
11 Beloved, I urge+ *you* as strangers and
sojourners+: Abstain from fleshly lusts
that war against the soul.
12 Have your conversation *and conduct*
honest among the Gentiles *so* that, *even*
if they speak against you as evildoers,
they may, by *your* good works that they
shall behold, glorify God in the day of
visitation.
13 Submit yourselves to every ordinance
of mankind+ for the Lord's sake, whether+
to the king as *the* supreme *ruler*
14 or to governors as to *those* who are
sent by *the king* for the punishment of
evildoers and for the praise of *those*
who do well.
15 For this is the will of God: That by
doing well, you may put to silence the
ignorance of foolish men.
16 As free *in the Lord* do not use *your*
liberty as a cover+ for maliciousness,
but *use it* as servants of God.
17 Honor all *people*. Love the family.+
Fear God. Honor the king.
18 Servants, *be* subject to *your* masters
with all fear. Not only to the good and
gentle, but also to the ornery.
19 For this *is* grace+: If a person,+ for
conscience toward God, endures grief
and wrongful suffering.
20 For what glory *is it*, if, when you are
buffeted for your faults, you take it
patiently? But if, when you do well and
suffer *for it*, you take it patiently, this *is*
acceptable with God.
21 For even to this you were called.
Because Christ also suffered for us,
leaving an example *for* us, *so that* you
should follow His steps.

22 He did not sin, nor was *any* deceitfulness[+] found in His mouth. *Isaiah 53:9*
23 When He was reviled, He did not
revile in return.[+] When He suffered, He
did not threaten. But *He* committed *Himself* to *the One* who judges righteously.
24 *Jesus* Himself bore our sins in His own
body on the tree *so* that we, being dead
to sins, should live to righteousness. By
His stripes you were healed. *Isaiah 53:5*
25 For you were like sheep going astray.
But now *you* are returned to the Shepherd and Bishop of your souls.

1 Peter Chapter 3

1 Likewise, you wives, *be* in subjection
to your own husbands *so* that if any do
not obey the Word, they may also, *even*
without the Word, be won by the
conversation *and conduct* of the wives,
2 while they behold your chaste conversation *and conduct coupled* with fear.
3 Do not *stress* the outward adorning of
glamorous[+] hair and luxurious[+] gold
and showy[+] apparel.
4 But *emphasize* the hidden *qualities* of
the heart, in the incorruptible *adornment*
of a meek and quiet spirit that is, in the
sight of God, of great value.[+]
5 For in this way,[+] the holy women *of
long ago* who trusted in God, adorned
themselves, being subject to their own
husbands,
6 like Sarah obeyed Abraham, calling
him lord. You become *like her* children
when you give honor *in this way and* not
out of fear[+] or terror.[+]
7 Likewise, you husbands live with your
wife with understanding,[+] honoring *her*
as a delicate[+] vessel and as being heirs
together of the grace of life, *so* that your
prayers *will* not be hindered.
8 Finally, *be* all of one mind, having
compassion for one another. *Be* affec-
tionate[+] as family.[+] *Be* compassionate.[+]
Be courteous.
9 Do not render evil for evil or reviling[+]
for reviling.[+] But instead[+] *give* blessing. Know that you are called to this *so*
that you should inherit a blessing.
10 For *those* who will *their* lives to love
and to see good days, *must* refrain
their tongue from evil and their lips to
not speak deceitfulness.[+] *Psalm 34:12-13,
Proverbs 21:23*
11 Avoid[+] evil and do good. Seek peace
and follow[+] it. *Psalm 34:14*
12 For the eyes of the Lord *are* over the
righteous and His ears *are open* to
their prayers. But the face of the Lord
is against *those* who do evil. *Psalm 34:15,16
John 9:31*
13 Who will harm you if you are followers
of what is good?
14 But if you suffer for righteousness'
sake, *be* blessed.[+] Do not be afraid of
their terror or be troubled. *Matthew 5:10
Isaiah 8:12*
15 But sanctify the Lord God in your
hearts. *Be* ready always to *give* an
answer to everyone[+] who asks you the
reason for the hope that is in you. *And do
so* with meekness and fear. *Proverbs 15:28*
16 Have a good conscience *so* that, *even*
though they speak evil about you, as
evildoers, *those* who falsely accuse your
good conversation *and conduct* in Christ
may be ashamed.
17 For *it is* better that you suffer for doing
well than for doing evil, if that is the will
of God.
18 For Christ also once suffered for sins:
The righteous[+] for the unrighteous[+] *so*
that He might bring us to God, being put
to death in the flesh, but given life[+] by
the Spirit.
19 *And* by *the Spirit* He also went to the
spirits in prison and proclaimed[+] *the
Word.*
20 When[+] *people* were disobedient, when
the longsuffering God once waited, in
the days of Noah while the ark was
being prepared, into it, a few, that is
eight souls, were saved by water.
21 *That was* an illustration[+] of what baptism also does now *to* save us. Not the
putting away of the filth of the flesh, but
the answer of a good conscience toward
God through[+] the resurrection of Jesus
Christ.
22 *Jesus* has gone into heaven and is at the

right hand of God and *all the* angels and
authorities and powers are made subject
to Him.

1 Peter Chapter 4

1 Since[+] Christ has suffered for us in the
flesh, arm yourselves likewise with the
same mind. For *those* who have suffered
in the flesh stop[+] sinning,
2 *so* that they will no longer live the rest
of *their* time in the flesh *giving in* to the
lusts of men, but to the will of God.
3 For *in* the past times of *our* life *it may
have been* sufficient[+] *for* us to have
worked[+] the will of the Gentiles, when
we walked in filthiness,[+] lusts, excess
of wine, riots,[+] wild parties,[+] and
abominable idolatries.
4 *Those caught* in that think it strange that
you do not run with *them* to the same
excesses of rioting, *and they* speak evil
of *you*.
5 *They* will give account to Him who is
ready to judge the living[+] and the dead.
6 Because *it was* for this reason[+] the
Gospel was proclaimed[+] also to *those*
who are dead, *so* that they might be
judged according to men in the flesh but
live according to God in the spirit.
7 But the end of all things is *very* near.[+]
Therefore, be sober and watch in prayer.
8 Above all things, have fervent *true* love
among yourselves. For *true* love will
cover *the* multitude *of* sins. *Proverbs 10:12*
9 Use hospitality to one another without
complaining.[+]
10 As everyone has received the gift,
even so minister the same to one another
as good stewards of the manifold grace
of God.
11 If anyone speaks, *let them speak* as the
oracles of God. If anyone ministers, *let
them do it* by the ability that God gives *so*
that in all things God may be glorified
through Jesus Christ, to whom be praise
and dominion forever and ever. Amen.
12 Beloved, do not think it strange
concerning the fiery trial that is to try
you, as though some strange thing
happened to you.
13 But rejoice in that you are partakers of
Christ's sufferings *so* that, when His
glory shall be revealed, you may be glad
also with exceeding joy.
14 If you are reproached for the name of
Christ, *be* blessed.[+] For the spirit of
glory and of God rests upon you. On
their part, He is blasphemed, but on
your part He is glorified.
15 But let none of you suffer as a murderer
or *as* a thief or *as* an evildoer or as a
busybody in other people's affairs.[+]
16 Yet if *anyone suffers* as a Christian, let
them not be ashamed, but let them
glorify God on this behalf.
17 For the time *is coming* that judgment
must begin at the house of God. If *it begins*
first with us, what will the end *be* for *those*
who do not obey the Gospel of God?
18 If the righteous scarcely be saved,
where will the ungodly and the sinner
appear? *Proverbs 11:31*
19 Therefore, let *those* who suffer according to the will of God commit the
keeping of their souls in well doing, as
to a faithful Creator.

1 Peter Chapter 5

1 I exhort the elders who are among you.
I also am an elder and a witness of the
sufferings of Christ and also a partaker of
the glory that will be revealed.
2 Feed the flock of God that is among
you. Take responsibility *for it*, not by
constraint, but willingly. Not for filthy
gain[+] but from a ready mind.
3 Do not be like lords over *God's*
heritage, but be examples to the flock.
4 When the chief Shepherd appears,
you will receive a crown of glory that
does not fade away.
5 Likewise, you younger *ones* submit
yourselves to the elders. Yes, all *of you
should* be subject to one another and be
clothed with humility. For God resists
the proud and gives grace to the humble.
Proverbs 3:34
6 Therefore, humble yourselves under
the mighty hand of God *so* that He may
exalt you in due time.

7 Cast all your care upon Him, for He
cares for you.
8 Be sober. Be vigilant. Because your
adversary the devil walks around[+]
like[+] a roaring lion seeking whom he
may devour.
9 Resist *the devil and be* steadfast in the
faith, knowing that the same afflictions
are accomplished in your family[+] that
are in the world.
10 But the God of all grace who has called
us to His eternal glory by Christ Jesus,
will, after you have suffered a while,
make you perfect. *He will* establish,[+]
strengthen, *and* settle *you*.
11 To *God be* glory and dominion forever
and ever. Amen.
12 By *the hand of* Silvanus, a faithful
brother to you, as I deduce,[+] *so* I have
written briefly, exhorting and testifying
that this is the true grace of God in
which you stand.
13 The *assembly* at Babylon *who were*
elected together with *you*, greet[+] you.
So does my son Mark.
14 Greet one another with a kiss of *true*
love. Peace *be* with you all who are in
Christ Jesus. Amen.

2 Peter Chapter 1

1 *From* Simon Peter, a servant and apostle
of Jesus Christ. To *those* who have
obtained like precious faith with us
through the righteousness of our God
and Savior Jesus Christ.
2 Grace and peace be multiplied to you in
the knowledge of God and Jesus our Lord.
3 By His divine power *He* has given
everything[+] to us that *pertains* to life and
godliness, through the knowledge of Him
who has called us to glory and virtue.
4 By this exceedingly great and precious
promises are given to us *so* that by these
you might be partakers of the divine
nature, having escaped the corruption
that is in the world through lust.
5 Also by this, giving all diligence,
add to your faith virtue *and* to virtue
knowledge,
6 to knowledge temperance *and* to temperance patience, to patience godliness
7 *and* to godliness, brotherly kindness.
And to brotherly kindness, *add true* love.
8 For if these things are in you and
abound *in you*, *then* they *will* not make
you barren or unfruitful in the knowledge of our Lord Jesus Christ.
9 But *those* who lack these things are
blind *and* cannot see *and* have forgotten
the purging of their old sins.
10 Therefore family,[+] rather *than this*, be
diligent to make your calling and election
sure. For if you do these things, you will
never fall.
11 For *in* this *way* you will be abundantly
supplied[+] an entrance into the everlasting kingdom of our Lord and Savior
Jesus Christ.
12 Therefore, I will not neglect[+] to remind
you about these things, *even* though you
already know *them* and *have already been*
established in the present truth.
13 *Yes,* I consider[+] it *proper*, as long as I
am in this tabernacle, to stir you up by
reminding you,
14 knowing that *very* soon[+] I must put off
this my *temporary* tabernacle, as our
Lord Jesus Christ has shown me.
15 Moreover, I will endeavor *in this, so*
that after my departure[+] you may be
able to always remember these things.
16 For we have not followed cunningly
devised fables when we made known to
you the power and coming of our Lord
Jesus Christ. But *we* were eyewitnesses
of His majesty.
17 For He received honor and glory from
God the Father when there came such a
voice to Him from the *most* excellent
glory: This is my beloved Son in whom
I am well pleased.
18 We heard this voice from heaven when
we were with Him on the holy mountain.
19 We also have a more sure word of
prophecy to which you *will* do well to
take heed, as to a light that shines in a
dark place, until the day dawns and the
Day Star arises in your hearts.
20 Know this first: That no prophecy
in the Scriptures is of any private
interpretation.

21 For *true* prophecy has not come *forth at any* time by the will of man, but holy men of God spoke *as they were* moved by the Holy Spirit.

2 Peter Chapter 2

1 But there were also false prophets among the people, even as there will be false teachers among you. *They* will privately[+] bring in damnable heresies, even denying the *Lord and* Master who bought them, *thereby* bringing swift destruction upon themselves.

2 Many will follow their *exceedingly* deadly[+] ways *because* through them, the way of truth will be blasphemed[+] *and slandered*.

3 Through covetousness *and* with deceptive[+] words they will exploit[+] you. *For* them, the judgment of long ago[+] is not idle.[+] Their damnation does not slumber.

4 For God did not spare the angels who sinned but cast *them* down to Hell and delivered *them* into chains of darkness to be reserved to judgment.

5 *He* did not spare the old world, but saved Noah the eighth *from Adam*, a preacher of righteousness, *by* bringing in the flood upon the world of the ungodly.

6 And *He* turned the cities of Sodom and Gomorrah into ashes *to* condemn *them* with an overthrow. *In doing this, He* made an example to *those* who might later live ungodly *lives*.

7 *He* delivered righteous[+] Lot *who was* oppressed[+] with the filthy conversation *and conduct* of the wicked.

8 For *He* saw and heard that righteous *man* living[+] among them, *his* righteous soul tormented[+] day after day with *their* unlawful deeds.

9 The Lord knows how to deliver the godly out of trials[+] and reserve the unrighteous[+] to the day of judgment to be punished,

10 but chiefly *those* who walk after the flesh in the lust of uncleanness and despise government. They are presumptuous, selfwilled, *and* not afraid to speak evil of the glory.[+]

11 Angels, however, who are greater in power and might, do not bring a reviling[+] accusation against them before the Lord.

12 But these, as natural brute beasts, are made to be taken and destroyed. *They* speak evil about things they do not understand *and they* will utterly perish in their own corruption.

13 *They* will receive the reward of unrighteousness *as those* who count it pleasure to riot in the daytime. *They are* spots and blemishes, sporting themselves with their own deceitfulness while they feast with you.

14 *They* have eyes full of adultery and cannot stop[+] sinning, deceiving[+] unstable souls. They have hearts exercised with covetous practices. *They are* cursed children

15 who have forsaken the right way and are gone astray, following the way of Balaam *the son* of Bosor, who loved the wages of unrighteousness

16 but was rebuked for his iniquity. The speechless[+] donkey[+] spoke with a man's voice *and* stopped[+] the madness of the *corrupt* prophet.

17 These are wells without water, clouds that are carried with a storm[+] for whom the mist of darkness is reserved forever.

18 They speak great swelling *words* of vanity to entice[+] into the lusts of the flesh *by* wantonness *those* who had escaped from *those* who live in error.

19 While they promise them liberty, they themselves are the servants of corruption. For anyone *who has been* overcome *by sin* is brought in bondage.

20 For if, after they have escaped the pollutions of the world through the knowledge of the Lord and Savior Jesus Christ, they are again entangled therein and overcome, *then* the latter end is worse for them than the beginning.

21 For it would have been better for them to have not known the way of righteousness than, after they have known *it*, to turn *away* from the holy commandment delivered to them.

22 But what happens to them is true to the *old* proverb: The dog returns to its own vomit again and the sow that was washed *returns* to wallowing in the mire.
Proverbs 26:11

2 Peter Chapter 3

1 Now, beloved, I write this second epistle to you, in *both of which* I *hope to* stir you up to remember *to have* a pure mind

2 *and so* that you may be mindful of the words that were spoken before by the holy prophets and of the commandments of *our* Lord and Savior *as proclaimed* by us, the apostles.

3 Know this first: That in the last days, there will come scoffers, walking after their own lusts.

4 *They will* say: Where is the promise of His coming? For since the fathers fell asleep, everything[+] continues as *it was* from the beginning of creation.

5 For this they are willingly ignorant that the heavens were *made* by the Word of God long ago[+] and the earth *came forth* out of *the* water and *still* stands in the water.

6 And the world *as it was* then, overflowed with water *and* perished.

7 But the Word *of God* has kept the heavens and the earth in store *and they are* reserved *for* fire *until* the day of judgment and damnation[+] of *all* ungodly people.[+]

8 But, beloved, do not be ignorant about this one thing: That with the Lord, one day *is* as a thousand years, and a thousand years as one day.

9 The Lord is not slack concerning His promise, as some men count slackness. But *He* is longsuffering toward us, not willing that any should perish, but that all should come to repentance.

10 The day of the Lord will come like a thief in the night in which the heavens will pass away with a great noise and the elements will melt with fervent heat and the earth also and *all* the works therein will be burned up.

11 *Seeing* then *that* all these things shall be destroyed,[+] what manner *of persons* ought you to be in *all* holy conversation *and conduct* and godliness?

12 *Should you not be* looking for and hastening to the coming of the day of God in which the heavens being on fire will be destroyed[+] and the elements will melt with fervent heat?

13 Nevertheless, according to His promise, we look for new heavens and a new earth in which righteousness will live.[+]

14 Therefore beloved, since you look for such things, be diligent *so* that you may be found by Him in peace, without spot and blameless.

15 And *know* that the longsuffering *of* our Lord *is for* salvation, *just* as our beloved brother Paul has also written to you, according to the wisdom given to him.

16 In all *his* epistles, *Paul* also spoke about these things. *Some* things among them are hard to understand, which *cause those* who are uneducated[+] and unstable *to* wrestle, as *they do* also *with* other Scriptures, to their own destruction.

17 Therefore, beloved, since[+] you knew *these things* before, beware lest you also, being led away with the error of the wicked, fall from your own steadfastness.

18 Grow in grace and *in* the knowledge of our Lord and Savior Jesus Christ. To Him *be* glory both now and forever. Amen.

1 John Chapter 1

1 That which was from the beginning, which we have heard, which we have seen with our eyes, which we have looked upon and our hands have touched[+] *is*[+] the Word of life.

2 For the life was revealed[+] and we have seen *it* and testify[+] and *we are now* showing you the eternal life that was with the Father and was revealed[+] to us.

3 What we have seen and heard we declare to you *so* that you also may have fellowship with us. Truly our fellowship *is* with the Father and with His Son Jesus Christ.

4 We write these things to you *so* that your joy may be full.

5 This then is the message we have heard from Him and declare to you: That God is light and in Him is no darkness at all.

6 If we say that we have fellowship with Him and walk in darkness, *then* we lie and do not live[+] *by* the truth.

7 But if we walk in the light as He is in the light, *then* we have fellowship with one another and the blood of Jesus Christ His Son cleanses us from all sin.

8 If we say that we have no sin, we deceive ourselves and the truth is not in us. *Proverbs 28:13*

9 *But* if we confess our sins, *then* He is faithful and just to forgive us *for our* sins and to cleanse us from all unrighteousness. *Proverbs 28:13*

10 If we say that we have not sinned, we make Him a liar and His Word is not in us.

1 John Chapter 2

1 My little children, I write these things to you *so* that you do not sin. And if anyone sins, we have an advocate with the Father: Jesus Christ the Righteous.

2 He is the *means of* reconciliation[+] for our sins, and not only for ours, but also for *the sins of* the whole world.

3 By this we know that we know Him: If we keep His commandments.

4 *Those* who say: I know Him but do not keep His commandments are liars and the truth is not in them.

5 But whoever keeps His Word, truly[+] the love of God is perfected in them, *and* by this[+] we know that we are in Him.

6 *Those* who say *that they* abide in Him should[+] *also* walk in the same way as He walked.

7 Believers,[+] I do not write a new commandment to you, but an old commandment that you have had from the beginning. The old commandment is the Word that you have heard from the beginning.

8 *Then* again, a new commandment I write to you: Which thing is true in Him and in you. Because the darkness is past and the true light now shines.

9 *Those* who say they are in the light and *yet* hate others[+] are still in darkness.

> 10 *Those* who love *one* another[+] abide in the light and there is no occasion for stumbling in them.
>
> 11 But *those* who hate *one* another[+] are in darkness and walk in darkness and do not know where they are going, because darkness has blinded their eyes.

12 I write to you little children because your sins are forgiven for His name's sake.

13 I write to you fathers because you have known Him *who is* from the beginning. I write to you young men because you have overcome the wicked. I write to you little children because you have known the Father.

14 I have written to you fathers because you have known Him *who is* from the beginning. I have written to you young men because you are strong and the Word of God abides in you and you have overcome the wicked.

15 Do not love the world or the things *that are* in the world. If anyone loves the world, the love of the Father is not in them.

16 For all that *is* in the world, the lust of the flesh and the lust of the eyes and the pride of life, is not of the Father, but is of the world.

17 The world is passing away, and the lust thereof, but *those* who do the will of God *will* live[+] forever.

18 Little children, it is the last hour.[+] As you have heard that antichrist is coming, even now there are many antichrists. And by this we know that it is the last hour.[+]

19 *Many* have gone out from among us, but they were not *a part* of us. For if they had been *a part* of us, *then no doubt* they would have continued with us. But *they went out so* that it might be revealed[+] that they were not all *a part* of us.

20 But you have an anointing[+] from the
Holy One and *therefore* you understand[+]
everything.[+]
21 I have not written to you because
you do not know the truth, but because
you *do* know it and *know* that no lie is
of the truth.
22 Who is a liar but *one* who denies that
Jesus is the Christ? *One* who denies the
Father and the Son is antichrist.
23 Whoever denies the Son does not have
the Father. *But those who confess the Son
have the Father also.*
24 Therefore, let what you have heard
from the beginning abide in you. If what
you have heard from the beginning
remains in you, *then* you also will continue in the Son and in the Father.
25 And this is the promise: That He has
promised us eternal life.
26 I have written these *things* to you
concerning *those* who *try to* deceive[+]
you.
27 But the anointing you have received
from Him lives[+] in you and you do
not need anyone *else to* teach you. But
as the same anointing teaches you
about everything and is truth and is no
lie, even as it has taught you, you shall
abide in Him.
28 Now little children: Abide in Him *so*
that when He shall appear we may have
confidence and not be ashamed before
Him at His coming.
29 If you know that He is righteous, *then*
you know that everyone who does righteousness is born of Him.

1 John Chapter 3

1 Behold what manner of love the Father
has bestowed upon us, that we should be
called the children[+] of God. Therefore
the world does not know us because it
did not know Him.
2 Beloved, we are now the children[+] of
God and it does not yet appear what we
shall become. But we know that when
He appears, we will be like Him. For
we shall see Him as He is.
3 Everyone[+] who has this hope in Him
purifies themselves, even as He is pure.
4 Whoever commits sin, transgresses
the law also. For sin is the transgression
of the law.
5 You know that He was manifested to
take away our sins, and in Him *there* is
no sin.
6 Whoever abides in Him does not sin.
Whoever sins has not seen Him or
known Him.
7 Little children, let no one deceive you.
Those who do righteousness are righteous, even as He is righteous.
8 *Those* who commit sin are of the devil,
for the devil sins from the beginning.
For this purpose, the Son of God was
manifested *so* that He might destroy the
works of the devil.
9 Whoever is born of God does not
commit sin, for His seed remains in
them. They cannot sin, because they are
born of God.

10 In this the children of God are
revealed,[+] and *also* the children of
the devil: Whoever does not do
righteousness is not of God, nor *are
those* who do not *truly* love others.[+]
11 For this is the message that you
heard from the beginning: That we
should love one another.

12 Not like Cain *who* was wicked and
killed[+] his brother. Why did he kill[+]
him? Because his own works were evil
and his brother's *were* righteous.
13 Do not marvel, my family,[+] if the
world hates you.
14 We know that we have passed from
death to life because we love others.[+]
Those who do not love others[+] abide
in death.
15 Whoever hates their brother is a
murderer. You know that no murderer
has eternal life abiding in them.
16 By this we perceive the *true* love *of
God*, that He laid down His life for us.
And we *therefore* ought to *be willing to*
lay down *our* lives for others.[+]
17 But whoever has this world's goods
and sees others[+] have needs and *yet*

shuts up their heart+ *of compassion* from
them, *then* how does the love of God live
in them?
[18]My little children, let us not love in
word or in tongue *only*, but in deed and
in truth.
[19]By this, we know that we are of the
truth and *by this we* will assure our hearts
before Him.
[20]For if our *own* heart condemns us, God
is greater than our heart and *He* knows
everything.+
[21]Beloved, if our heart does not condemn us, *then* we *can* have confidence
toward God.
[22]Whatever we ask, we receive from
Him because we keep His commandments and do those things that are
pleasing in His sight.
[23]This is His commandment: That we
should believe in the name of His Son
Jesus Christ and love one another, as He
gave us *this* commandment.
[24]*Those* who keep His commandments
live in Him and He in them. By this, we
know that He abides in us: By the Spirit
whom He has given us.

1 John Chapter 4

[1] Beloved, do not believe every spirit,
but test+ the spirits *to see* if they are of
God. Because many false prophets have
gone out into the world.
[2] By this, you know the Spirit of God:
Every spirit that confesses that Jesus
Christ has come in the flesh is from
God.
[3] Every spirit that does not confess that
Jesus Christ has come in the flesh is not
of God. This is the *spirit* of antichrist
that you have heard would come. Even
now it is already in the world.
[4] Little children, you are of God and
have overcome them. Because greater
is *He* who *is* in you than *he* who *is* in the
world.
[5] They are of the world. Therefore they
speak of the world and the world hears
them.
[6] We are of God. *Those* who know God
hear us. Anyone who is not of God does
not hear us. By this, we know the spirit
of truth and the spirit of error.

[7] Beloved, let us love one another.
For *true* love is from God.
Everyone who loves
is born of God and knows God.

[8] *Those* who do not love do not know
God, for God is love.
[9] In this, the love of God was revealed+
to us: That God sent His Only Begotten
Son into the world *so* that through Him
we might live.
[10]Herein is love: Not that we loved God,
but that He loved us and sent His Son
to be the *means of* reconciliation+ for
our sins.
[11]Beloved, if God so loved us, *then* we
should+ also love one another.

[12] No one has seen God at any time.
But if we love one another,
then God lives in us
and His love is perfected in us.

[13]By this we know that we live in Him
and He in us: That He has given us His
Spirit.
[14]We have seen and testify that the
Father sent the Son *to be* the Savior of
the world.
[15]Whoever confesses that Jesus is the
Son of God, *reveals that* God lives in
them and they *live* in God.
[16]We have known and believed the love
that God has toward us. God is love.
Those who abide in love, abide in God
and God *is* in them.
[17]Herein is our love made perfect, that
we may have boldness in the day of
judgment. Because, as He is, so are we
in this world.

[18] There is no fear in love,
but perfect love casts out fear.
Because fear has torment.
Those who fear
are not made perfect in love.

19 We love Him because He first loved us.

20 If anyone says: I love God, and hates others,+ they are a liar. For how can *those* who do not love others+ whom they have seen, love God whom they have not seen?

21 This commandment we have from Him: That *those* who love God love others+ also.

1 John Chapter 5

1 Whoever believes that Jesus is the Christ is born of God. Everyone who loves *God* who fathered+ *us all* also loves *those* who are fathered+ by Him.

2 By this we know that we love the children of God: When we love God and keep His commandments.

> 3 For this is the love of God: That we keep His commandments.

His commandments are not grievous. *John 14:15*

4 For whatever is born of God overcomes the world. This is the victory that overcomes the world: Our faith.

5 Who are *those* who overcome the world but *those* who believe that Jesus is the Son of God?

6 This is *the One* who came by water and blood: Jesus Christ. Not by water only, but by water and blood. And it is the Spirit who bears witness, because the Spirit is truth.

7 For there are three who bear witness+ in heaven: The Father, the Word, and the Holy Spirit. And these three are one.

8 There are three who bear witness on earth: The Spirit, the water, and the blood. And these three agree in one.

9 If we receive the witness of men, the witness of God is greater. For this is the witness of God that He has testified about His Son.

10 *Those* who believe in the Son of God have the witness within themselves. *Those* who do not believe God, have made Him a liar because they do not believe the record that God gave of His Son.

11 This is the record: That God has given eternal life to us, and this life is in His Son.

12 *Those* who have the Son have life. *Those* who do not have the Son of God do not have life.

> 13 I have written these things to you who believe in the name of the Son of God *so* that you may know that you have eternal life and *so* that you may believe in the name of the Son of God.

14 *Now* this is the confidence that we have in Him: That if we ask anything according to His will, He hears us.

15 And if we know that He hears us, whatever we ask, *then* we know that we *shall* have the petitions that we desired of Him.

16 If anyone sees another sin a sin *that is* not unto death, they should ask and He will give life to *those* who do not *commit* sin *that leads* to death. *Yet* there is a sin *that is* to death and I do not say that you shall pray for this.

17 All unrighteousness is sin, *but* there is sin *that is* not unto death.

18 We know that whoever is born of God does not sin, but *those* who are fathered+ by God keep themselves and the wicked does not touch them.

19 *And* we know that we are of God. *But* the whole world lies in wickedness.

20 We know that the Son of God has come and given us an understanding *so* that we may know Him who is true and *so that* we are in Him who is true, in His Son Jesus Christ. This is the true God and eternal life.

21 Little children, keep yourselves from idols. Amen.

2 John Chapter 1

1 *From John* the elder. To the elect lady and her children whom I love in the truth. Not only I but also all who have known the truth.

2 For the sake of the truth that lives in us
and shall be with us forever.
3 Grace be with you, mercy, *and* peace,
from God the Father and from *the* Lord
Jesus Christ, the Son of the Father, in
truth and love.
4 I rejoiced greatly that I have found of
your children walking in truth as we
received commandment from the Father.
5 Now I appeal+ *to* you, lady, not as
though I wrote a new commandment to
you, but *one* we have had from the beginning: *to* love one another.
6 And this is love: That we walk after
His commandments. *And* this is the commandment: That as you have heard from
the beginning, you should walk in it.
7 For many deceivers have entered the
world who do not confess that Jesus
Christ has come in the flesh. This is the
deceiver and the antichrist.
8 Look to yourselves *so* that we do not
lose those things *for* which we have
worked,+ but *so* that we receive a full
reward.
9 *For* everyone who transgresses and
does not abide in the doctrine of Christ,
does not have God *within them. But those*
who abide in the doctrine of Christ have
both the Father and the Son.
10 If anyone comes to you and does not
bring this doctrine, do not receive them
into *your* house or bid them *cordial*
greetings.+
11 For *those* who bid them *cordial* greet-
ings+ are partakers of their evil deeds.
12 *Although I* have many things to write
to you, I would not *write* with paper and
ink, but I trust to come to you and speak
face to face *so* that our joy may be full.
13 The children of your elect sister greet
you. Amen.

3 John Chapter 1

1 *From John* the elder. To the beloved
Gaius whom I love in the truth.
2 Beloved, I wish above all things that
you may prosper and be in health, even
as your soul prospers.
3 For I rejoiced greatly when the family+
came and testified of the truth that is in
you, even as you walk in the truth.
4 I have no greater joy than to hear that
my children walk in truth.
5 Beloved, you do faithfully whatever
you do for the family+ and for strangers.
6 *For they* have testified+ of your *true*
love before the assembly.+ *If* you bring
them forward on their journey in a godly
way, you will do well.
7 *It was* for *His* name *that* they went
forth, taking nothing from the Gentiles.
8 Therefore, we ought to receive such
people so that we might be *their* fellow
helpers for the truth.
9 I wrote to the assembly,+ but
Diotrephes, who *takes* pleasure+ in
having preeminence among them, does
not receive us.
10 Therefore if I come, I will remember
his deeds that he does, babbling+ against
us with malicious words. And not
content with that, neither does he himself receive the family+ and *he* forbids
those who would, and casts *them* out of
the assembly.+

11 Beloved, do not follow what is
evil, but what is good. *Those* who do
good are of God. But *those* who do
evil have not seen God.

12 Demetrius has good report from
everyone and from the truth itself. Yes,
and we *also* testify+ and you know that
our testimony+ is true.
13 I had many things to write, but I will
not write to you with pen and ink.
14 But I trust *that* I will see you soon+ and
we will speak face to face. Peace to you.
Our friends greet+ you. Greet the friends
by name.

Jude Chapter 1

1 *From* Jude, the servant of Jesus Christ
and brother of James. To *those* who are
sanctified by God the Father, preserved
in Jesus Christ, *and* called.

2 Mercy to you, and peace and love be
multiplied.
3 Beloved, when I gave all diligence to
write to you of the common salvation, it
was necessary[+] for me to write to you
and exhort*you* that you should earnestly
contend for the faith that was once
delivered to the saints.
4 For certain men crept in unexpectedly,[+] who were long ago[+] written[+] *off*
as ungodly men, turning the grace of our
God into filthiness[+] and denying the
only Lord God and our Lord Jesus
Christ.
5 Therefore I remind you, though you
once knew this, that the Lord, having
saved the people out of the land of
Egypt, afterward destroyed *those* who
did not believe.
6 The angels who did not keep their first
estate but left their own habitation, He
has reserved in everlasting chains under
darkness until[+] the judgment of the
great day.
7 Even as Sodom and Gomorrah and the
cities around them in like manner, giving
themselves over to fornication and
going after strange flesh, are set forth
for an example, suffering the vengeance
of eternal fire.
8 Likewise also these dreamers defile
the flesh, despise the dominion, and
speak evil of the glory.[+]
9 Yet Michael the archangel, when con-
tending with the devil *as* he disputed
about the body of Moses, did not dare[+]
to bring a reviling[+] accusation against
him but said: The Lord rebuke you.
10 But these *ungodly men* speak evil about
things that they do not understand,[+] but
what they understand[+] *in a* natural *sense,*
as brute beasts, in those things they
corrupt themselves.
11 Woe to them. For they have gone in
the way of Cain and run greedily after
the error of Balaam for reward and
perished in the rebellion[+] of Korah.
12 These *ungodly men* are spots in your
love feasts when they feast with you,
feeding themselves without fear. *They*
are clouds without water carried about
by winds, rotten[+] trees without fruit,
twice dead *and* uprooted,[+]
13 raging waves of the sea foaming out
their own shame, wandering stars to
whom is reserved the blackness of darkness forever.
14 Enoch, the seventh from Adam, also
prophesied about them saying: Behold
the Lord comes with ten thousands of
His saints
15 to execute judgment upon everyone
and convict[+] all who are ungodly among
them for all their ungodly deeds they
have ungodly committed and for all the
harsh[+] *words* that ungodly sinners have
spoken against Him.
16 These *ungodly people* are complainers[+]
and faultfinders[+] walking after their
lusts. Their mouths speak great swelling *words* in admiration of people *to gain*
favor[+] *and* benefit.[+]
17 But beloved, remember the words that
were spoken before by the apostles of
our Lord Jesus Christ.
18 They told you that there would be
mockers in the last *of* time who would
walk after their own ungodly lusts.
19 These are *the ones* who who set *them-*
selves apart[+] *as* sensual *persons*, not
having the Spirit.
20 But you, beloved, building up yourselves on your most holy faith, praying
in the Holy Spirit,
21 keep yourselves in the love of God,
looking for the mercy of our Lord Jesus
Christ to eternal life.
22 On some have compassion, making a
difference.
23 Others save with fear, pulling *them* out
of the fire, hating even the garment
spotted by the flesh.
24 Now to Him who is able to keep you
from falling and to present *you* faultless
before the presence of His glory with
exceeding joy,
25 to the only wise God our Savior *be*
glory and majesty, dominion and power,
both now and ever. Amen.

The Revelation Chapter 1

1 *The* Revelation *of* Jesus Christ *that* was
given *by the One* who *is* God to show His
servants *those* things that must soon+
come to pass. He sent *this* communication+
through His angel to His servant John.
2 *John* testified+ *about* the Word of God
and the testimony *of* Jesus Christ and
about all *the* things that he saw.
3 Blessed *are those* who read and who
hear the words of this prophecy and
keep those things that are written *here*.
For the time *is very* near.+
4 *From* John, to the seven assemblies+ *of*
believers in Asia. Grace to you and peace
from Him who is and who was and who
is to come, and from the seven spirits
who are before His throne.
5 From Jesus Christ *who is* the faithful
witness, the firstborn+ of the dead, and
the prince of the kings of the earth. To
Him who loves us and washes us from
our sins by His own blood,
6 and makes us kings and priests to God
and His Father, to Him *be* glory and
dominion forever and ever. Amen.
7 Behold, He *will* come after+ clouds and
every eye will see Him, *even* those who
pierced Him. All families+ of the earth will
mourn+ because of Him. Even so, Amen.
8 I am the Alpha and the Omega: *The*
beginning and *the* end, says the Lord
who is and who was and who *is* to come,
the Almighty.
9 I John, your brother and companion in
tribulation and in the kingdom and
patience of Jesus Christ, was on the island
called Patmos because of the Word of
God and testimony of Jesus Christ.
10 *I* became in the Spirit on the Lord's
day and heard a great voice behind me,
sounding like+ *that* of a trumpet.
11 *The voice* said: I am Alpha and Omega,
the first and the last. What you see,
write in a book and send *it* to the seven
assemblies+ *of believers* in Asia: To
Ephesus, to Smyrna, to Pergamos, to
Thyatira, to Sardis, to Philadelphia, and
to Laodicea.
12 I turned to see the voice that spoke to
me and I saw seven golden candlesticks.
13 In the midst of the seven candlesticks
was one like the Son of man, clothed
with a garment down to the foot and
belted+ about the chest+ with a golden
belt.+
14 His head and hair *were* white like
wool, as white as snow. His eyes *were*
like a flame of fire.
15 His feet *were* like fine brass as though
they burned in a furnace. His voice *was*
like the sound of many waters.
16 In His right hand He *held* seven stars.
A sharp, two edged sword came *forth*
out of His mouth, and His countenance
was like the sun shine in *its* power.+
17 When I saw Him, I fell at His feet as
though dead. But *then* He laid His right
hand on me, saying to me: Do not be
afraid. I Am The First and The Last.
18 *As one* living, I became dead, and
behold I am *now* alive forever and ever.
Amen. And *I* have the keys *to* Hell and
to death.
19 Write *down* the things that you have
just seen and the things that are *now*
before you and *the* things that are about to
come to pass.
20 The mystery of the seven stars that
you saw in my right hand and the seven
golden candlesticks: The seven stars are
the angels of the seven assemblies.+
The seven candlesticks that you saw are
the seven assemblies+.

The Revelation Chapter 2

1 To the angel of the assembly+ *of*
believers in Ephesus write: These things
says He who holds the seven stars in His
right hand *and* walks in the midst of the
seven golden candlesticks:
2 I know your works and your labor and
your patience and how you cannot bear
those who are evil. You have tested+
those who say they are apostles and are
not and have found them *to be* liars.
3 *You* have carried+ *the load* and *endured*
with patience and for my name's sake
you have labored and have not fainted.

4 Nevertheless I have *something* against you because you have left your first love.

5 Remember therefore from where you have fallen and repent and do the first works. Or else I will come to you quickly and remove your candlestick out of its place, unless you repent.

6 But you have this *right*: That you hate the deeds of the Nicolaitans *who commit fornication*, which I also hate.

7 *Those* who have an ear, let them hear what the Spirit is saying to the assemblies.[+] To *those* who overcome I will give *the reward* to eat from the tree of life that is in the midst of the paradise of God.

8 To the angel of the assembly[+] in Smyrna write: The First and The Last who was dead and is *now* alive says these things:

9 I know your works and tribulation and poverty. Yet you are *really* rich. *I know* the blasphemy of *those* who say they are Jews and are not, but *are of* the synagogue of Satan.

10 Do not fear *any* of the things that you *must* suffer. Behold the devil will cast *some* of you into prison *so* that you may be tested[+] *and* have tribulation *for* ten days. *But* be faithful *even* to death and I will give you a crown of life.

11 Let *those* who have an ear hear what the Spirit *is* saying to the assemblies.[+] *Those* who overcome will not be hurt by the second death.

12 To the angel of the assembly[+] in Pergamos write: These things says He who has the sharp sword with two edges.

13 I know your works and where you live, *even* where Satan's throne[+] *is*. You hold fast *to* my name and have not denied faith*in* me, even in those days in which my faithful martyr Antipas was slain where Satan lives among you.

14 But I have a few things against you because you have *some* there who hold *to* the doctrine of Balaam who taught Balac to cast a stumbling block before the children of Israel *and* to eat things sacrificed to idols and to commit fornication.

15 You also have *some* who hold the doctrine of the Nicolaitans, which I hate.

16 *Therefore* repent. For if *you* do not, I will come to you quickly and fight against them with the sword of my mouth.

17 Let *those* who have an ear hear what the Spirit *is* saying to the assemblies.[+] To *those* who overcome I will give *the reward* to eat of the hidden manna and *I* will give them a white stone and in the stone a new name written that no one knows except[+] *those* who receive *it*.

18 To the angel of the assembly[+] in Thyatira write: The Son of God who has eyes like a flame of fire and feet like fine brass says these things:

19 I know your works, *your* love and service, your faith and patience, and *that* your last works *are* more than the first.

20 Nevertheless I have a few things against you because you allow[+] that woman Jezebel who calls herself a prophetess to teach and seduce my servants to commit fornication and to eat things sacrificed to idols.

21 I gave her time[+] to repent of her fornication, but she did not repent.

22 Behold I will cast her into bed and *those* who commit adultery with her into great tribulation unless they repent of their deeds.

23 I will kill her children with death. All the assemblies[+] will know that I Am He who searches the reins and hearts. I will give to everyone of you according to your works.

24 But I say to you and to the rest in Thyatira, *to* as many as do not have this doctrine and who have not known the depths of Satan as they speak, I will put no other burden on you.

25 Hold fast what you have until I come.

26 To those who overcome and keep my works to the end I will give authority[+] over the nations,

27 to rule them with a rod of iron. *Just* like the vessels *that* the potter breaks, so also *will they* receive *judgment* from[+] my Father.

28 I will give them The Morning Star.
29 Let *those* who have an ear hear what
the Spirit *is* saying to the assemblies+.

The Revelation Chapter 3

1 To the angel of the assembly+ in
Sardis write: These things says He who
has the seven spirits of God and the
seven stars. I know your works, that you
have a name that *says that* you *are* alive,
but *really, you* are dead.
2 Be watchful and strengthen the things
that remain, that are ready to die. For
I have not found your works perfect
before God.
3 Remember therefore what you have
received and heard, and hold fast and
repent. If you do not watch, I will come
upon you like a thief and you will not
know *at* what hour I will come upon you.
4 You have a few names even in Sardis
who have not defiled their garments.
They shall walk with me in white, for
they are worthy.
5 *Those* who overcome will be clothed in
white clothing.+ I will not blot out their
names out of the Book of Life, but I will
confess their names before my Father
and before His angels.
6 Let *those* who have an ear hear what
the Spirit *is* saying to the assemblies+.
7 To the angel of the assembly+ in
Philadelphia write: These things says
He who is holy, He who is true, He who
has the key of David, He who opens and
no one shuts, and shuts and no one
opens.
8 I know your works. Behold I have set
before you an open door and no one can
shut it. For you have a little strength and
have kept my Word and have not denied
my name.
9 Behold I will make those of the synagogue of Satan who say they are Jews
and are not, but lie, behold I will make
them to come and worship before your
feet and to know that I have loved you.
10 Because you have kept the Word of
my patience, I will also keep you from
the hour of trials+ that is about to come
upon all the world, to try *those* who live
upon the earth.
11 Behold I *will* come quickly. Hold fast
what you have *so* that no one *will* take
away your crown.
12 *Those* who overcome I will make a
pillar in the temple of my God and they
shall go out no longer.+ I will write
upon them the name of my God and the
name of the city of my God, *the* new
Jerusalem that comes down out of heaven
from my God. *I will write upon them* my
new name.
13 Let *those* who have an ear hear what
the Spirit *is* saying to the assemblies+.
14 To the angel of the assembly+ of the
Laodiceans write: The Amen, The Faithful and True Witness, The Beginning of
the Creation of God says these things:
15 I know your works, that you are
neither cold nor hot. I would *prefer that*
you were *either* cold or hot.
16 *However* because you are lukewarm
and neither cold nor hot, I will spew you
out of my mouth.
17 Because you say: I am rich and
increased with goods and have need
of nothing, *you* do not understand+
that you are wretched and miserable
and poor and blind and naked.
18 I counsel you to buy from me gold
tested+ in the fire, *so* that you may be
rich. And *buy from me* white clothing+
so that you may be clothed *properly* and
so that the shame of your nakedness does
not appear. And anoint your eyes with
salve+ *so* that you may see.
19 For as many as I love, I rebuke and
discipline.+ Therefore be zealous and
repent.

20 Behold
I stand at the door and knock.
If anyone *will* hear my voice
and open the door,
I will come in to them
and dine+ with them
and they with me.

21 To *those* who overcome I will grant to
sit with me in my throne, even as I also
overcame and am set down with my
Father in His throne.
22 Let *those* who have an ear hear what
the Spirit *is* saying to the assemblies[+].

The Revelation Chapter 4

1 After this I looked and behold a door
was opened in heaven. The first voice
that I heard *was* like a trumpet speaking
with me *and* saying: Come up here and
I will show you things *that* must be
fulfilled after this.
2 Immediately, I became[+] in the spirit
and behold, a throne was set in heaven
and *one* was sitting on the throne.
3 He who sat *there* was like a jasper and
a ruby[+] stone in appearance. And a
rainbow *was all* around[+] the throne, like
an emerald in appearance.
4 *All* around[+] the throne *were* twenty four
seats *and* on the seats I saw twenty four elders
sitting. *They were* clothed in white clothing[+] *and* had gold crowns on their heads.
5 Lightning, thunder, and voices came
forth[+] out of the throne and seven lamps
of fire *representing* the seven spirits of
God *were* burning before the throne.
6 Before the throne *was* a sea of glass
like crystal. In the midst of the throne and
all around[+] the throne *were* four beasts
full of eyes *both* in front[+] and behind.
7 The first beast *was* like a lion. The
second beast like a calf. The third beast
had a face like a man. And the fourth
beast *was* like a flying eagle.
8 The four beasts each had six wings
around *them* and *they were* full of eyes
within. They did not rest day and night
saying: Holy, holy, holy, Lord God
Almighty who was and is and is to come.
9 When the beasts give glory and honor
and thanks to Him who sits upon the
throne *and* who lives forever and ever,
10 the twenty four elders fall down
before Him who sits upon the throne
and *they* worship Him who lives forever
and ever and cast their crowns before
the throne saying:
11 You are worthy, O Lord, to receive
glory and honor and power. For you
have created all things and for your
will[+] they are and *they* were created.

The Revelation Chapter 5

1 And then I saw in the right *hand of God*
sitting on His throne a scroll written *both*
inside and *on the* backside *and* sealed
with seven seals.
2 And I saw a strong angel proclaiming
with a loud voice: Who is worthy to
open the scroll and loosen its seals?
3 No one in heaven or on the earth or
under the earth was able to open the
scroll or look upon it.
4 I wept many *tears* because no one was
found worthy to open and read the scroll
or *even* to look upon it.
5 One of the elders said to me: Do not
weep. Behold the Lion of the tribe of
Judah, the Root of David has prevailed to
open the scroll and loosen its seven seals.
6 I observed[+] and saw in the midst of the
throne and *among* the four beasts and in
the midst of the elders, stood a Lamb
that had been slain. *But now He* had
seven horns and seven eyes that are the
seven spirits of God sent forth into all
the earth.
7 He came and took the scroll out of the
right *hand of the one* who sat upon the
throne.
8 And when He had taken the scroll, the
four beasts and twenty four elders fell
down before the Lamb. Each of them had
harps and golden vials full of fragrances,[+]
which are the prayers of saints.
9 They sang a new song saying: You are
worthy to take the scroll and open its seals
for you were slain and *thereby* redeemed
us to God by your blood out of every
family,[+] tongue, people, and nation.
10 *You* have made us kings and priests to
reign upon the earth.
11 Then I saw[+] and heard the voice of
many angels *all* around[+] the throne.
The number of beasts and elders was
ten thousand times ten thousand, and
thousands of thousands.

12 With a loud voice, *they were all* saying:
Worthy is the Lamb who was slain to
receive power and riches and wisdom
and strength and honor and glory and
blessing.
13 Every creature in heaven and on the
earth and under the earth and such as
are in the sea and all who are in them,
I heard saying: Blessing and honor
and glory and power *be* to Him who *is*
upon the throne, and to the Lamb,
forever and ever.
14 The four beasts said: Amen. And the
twenty four elders fell down and worshiped Him who lives forever and ever.

The Revelation Chapter 6

1 When the Lamb opened one of the
seals, I saw and heard, as *though* it were
the noise of thunder, one of the four
beasts saying: Come and see.
2 *Then I looked* and behold I saw a white
horse and He who sat upon it had a bow.
A crown was given to Him and He went
forth conquering and to conquer.
3 When *the Lamb* opened the second
seal, I heard the second beast say: Come
and see.
4 *Then* another horse *that was* red went
out. *Power* was given to *the one* who sat
upon it to take peace from the earth *so*
that *people* would kill one another. A
great sword was given to him.
5 When *the Lamb* opened the third seal,
I heard the third beast say: Come and
see. And I observed+ and saw+ a black
horse and *the one* who sat upon it had a
pair of balances in his hand.
6 Then I heard a voice in the midst of the
four beasts say: A measure of wheat for
a penny and three measures of barley
for a penny. *See that* you do not hurt the
oil and the wine.
7 When *the Lamb* opened the fourth seal,
I heard the voice of the fourth beast say:
Come and see.
8 I looked and behold *I saw* a pale horse
and his name who sat upon it was Death,
and Hell followed with him. Power was
given to them over a fourth of the earth,
to kill with sword and with hunger and
with death and with the beasts of the
earth.
9 When *the Lamb* opened the fifth seal, I
saw under the altar the souls of *those*
who had been slain for the Word of God
and for the testimony that they held.
10 They cried *out* with a loud voice saying:
How long, O Lord, holy and true, will
you not judge and avenge our blood
upon *those* who live on the earth?
11 White robes were given to everyone of
them and it was said to them that they
should rest for yet a little season *longer*
until their fellow servants and their
family+ who would also be killed as
they *had been*, should be fulfilled.
12 When *the Lamb* opened the sixth seal,
I looked+ and behold there was a great
earthquake. The sun became *as* black as
sackcloth *made* of hair and the moon
became *the color of* blood.
13 The stars of heaven fell to the earth
like a fig tree casts *off* untimely figs
when shaken by a mighty wind.
14 The heavens disappeared+ like *writing*
on a scroll when it is rolled together. All
the mountains and islands were moved
out of their places.
15 *All* the kings of the earth and *all* the
great men and rich men and chief
captains and mighty men and every
servant+ and free man hid themselves
in the dens and in the rocks of the
mountains.
16 *They all* said to the mountains and
rocks: Fall on us and hide us from the
face of Him who sits on the throne and
from the wrath of the Lamb.
17 For the great day of His wrath has
come *and* who shall be able to stand?

The Revelation Chapter 7

1 After these things, I saw four angels
standing at the four corners of the earth,
holding *back* the four winds of the earth
so that the wind would not blow on the
earth or on the sea or on any tree.
2 Then I saw another angel with the seal
of the living God ascending from the east.

He cried *out* with a loud voice to the four
angels who had been given *authority* to
hurt the earth and the sea,
3 saying: Do not hurt the earth or the sea
or the trees until we have *placed a* seal on
the foreheads *of* the servants of our God.
4 I heard the number of *those* who were
sealed *and there were* a hundred *and*
forty four thousand from all the tribes
of the children of Israel.
5 From the tribe of Judah twelve thousand *were* sealed. From the tribe of
Reuben twelve thousand *were* sealed.
From the tribe of Gad twelve thousand
were sealed.
6 From the tribe of Asher twelve thousand *were* sealed. From the tribe of
Nepthalim twelve thousand *were* sealed.
From the tribe of Manasseh twelve
thousand *were* sealed.
7 From the tribe of Simeon twelve
thousand *were* sealed. From the tribe of
Levi twelve thousand *were* sealed.
From the tribe of Issachar twelve
thousand *were* sealed.
8 From the tribe of Zabulon twelve
thousand *were* sealed. From the tribe of
Joseph twelve thousand *were* sealed.
From the tribe of Benjamin twelve
thousand *were* sealed.
9 After this, lo and behold, a great multitude that no one could number of all
nations and families+ and people and
tongues *of the earth* stood before the throne
and before the Lamb, clothed with white
robes and *with* palms in their hands.
10 *They all* cried *out* with a loud voice
saying: Salvation *is by* our God who sits
upon the throne, and by the Lamb.
11 All the angels stood around+ the throne,
and the elders and the four beasts fell
before the throne on their faces and
worshiped God,
12 saying: Amen. Blessing and glory and
wisdom and thanksgiving and honor and
power and might *be* to our God forever
and ever. Amen.
13 One of the elders answered, saying
to me: Who are these who are arrayed
in white robes? And from where did
they come?
14 I said to him: Sir, you know. And he
said to me: These are the ones who have
come out of great tribulation and have
washed their robes and made them white
by the blood of the Lamb.
15 Therefore, they are before the throne
of God and serve Him day and night in
His temple. And He who sits on the
throne will live among them.
16 They will no longer hunger or thirst
anymore. Nor will the sun blaze+ on
them. Nor *will they suffer* any heat.
17 For the Lamb who is in the midst of the
throne will feed them and lead them to
fountains of living water *and* God will
wipe away all tears from their eyes.

The Revelation Chapter 8

1 When *the Lamb* opened the seventh
seal, there was silence in heaven *for*
about half an hour.
2 Then I saw the seven angels standing
before God *and* seven trumpets were
given to them.
3 Another angel came and stood at the
altar with a golden censer *and* much
incense was given to him *so* that he
could offer *it* with the prayers of all
saints upon the golden altar that was
before the throne.
4 The smoke of the incense *that came*
with the prayers of the saints ascended
up from the angel's hand to God.
5 Then the angel filled the censer with
fire from the alter and cast *it* onto the
earth and there were voices and thunder
and lightning and a *great* earthquake.
6 The seven angels with the seven
trumpets *then* prepared to sound.
7 The first angel sounded and hail and
fire mingled with blood were cast *down*
upon the earth. One third of *all the* trees
and all *of* the green grass was burned up.
8 The second angel sounded and *it was* as
though a great mountain burning with
fire was cast into the sea and one third
of the sea became *like* blood.
9 One third of *all* the creatures living in
the sea died *and* one third of *all* ships
were destroyed.

10 The third angel sounded and a great
star fell from heaven burning like a
lamp and falling upon a third of *all* the
rivers and fountains of waters.
11 The name of this star was Wormwood
and one third of the waters *that it fell upon*
became wormwood *poisoned*. Many
people[+] died because the waters were
made bitter *with poison*.
12 The fourth angel sounded and one
third of the sun and moon and stars were
struck[+] so *that* one third of them were
darkened. *Therefore* for one third of
each day and night *the sun, moon, and*
stars did not shine.
13 *Then* I saw[+] and heard an angel flying
through the midst of heaven saying with
a loud voice: Woe, woe, woe, to the
inhabitants of the earth because[+] of the
other voices of the trumpets of the three
angels that are yet to sound.

The Revelation Chapter 9

1 The fifth angel sounded and I saw a
star fall from heaven to the earth, and
the key to the bottomless pit was given
to him.
2 He opened the bottomless pit and smoke
like *that* from a great furnace rose *up* out
of the pit, and the sun and air were
darkened by the smoke from the pit.
3 Out of the smoke, locusts *covered* the
earth and were given power like the
power of scorpions upon the earth.
4 They were commanded*to* not hurt the
earth or any green thing or any tree, but
only those people[+] who did not have the
seal of God on their foreheads.
5 *The locusts* were given *instructions* that
they should not kill *the* people,[+] butthat
they should be tormented *for* five
months. The torment *was to be* like the
torment of a scorpion when it strikes.
6 In those days, people[+] will seek death,
but will not find it. *They* will desire to
die, but death will flee from them.
7 The shapes of the locusts *were* like
horses prepared for battle. On their
heads were gold crowns and their faces
were like the faces of men.
8 They had hair like women's hair and
teeth like a lion's.
9 They had breastplates like iron and the
sound of their wings *was* like the sound
of chariots with many horses running to
battle.
10 They had tails like scorpions with
stingers in their tails to hurt people[+] *for*
five months.
11 They had a king over them, the angel
of the bottomless pit, whose name in
Hebrew *is* Abaddon and in Greek is
Apollyon.
12 *After all this,* one woe is past and behold,
there are two more woes *to come*.
13 The sixth angel sounded and I heard a
voice from the four horns of the golden
altar that is before God.
14 *God* said to the sixth angel with a
trumpet: *Let* loose the four angels who
are bound in the great river Euphrates.
15 So the four angels were released.[+]
They had been prepared for *this* hour and
day and month and year to slay one third
of *all* mankind.[+]
16 The number of the army of the horsemen *was* two hundred million[+] and I
heard their number.
17 Then in the vision I saw the horses and
those who sat on them. *They* had breastplates of fire, hyacinth,[+] and brimstone.
The heads of the horses *were* like the
heads of lions, and fire, smoke, and
brimstone came[+] out of their mouths.
18 By these three *plagues*, a third of all
mankind were killed: by the fire, the
smoke, and the brimstone that came out
of their mouths.
19 For their power[+] was in their mouth and
in their tails. For their tails *were* like serpents with heads that *caused great* pain.[+]
20 The rest of mankind[+] that was not
killed by these plagues still[+] did not
repent of *worshiping* the works of their
hands. *They did not stop* worshiping demons[+] and idols of gold, silver, brass,
stone, and wood that can neither see nor
hear nor walk.
21 Nor did they repent of their murders,
sorceries, fornications, or thefts.

The Revelation Chapter 10

1 I then saw another mighty angel come down from heaven, clothed with a cloud. There was a rainbow on his head and his face *shone* as *though* it were the sun, and his feet were like pillars of fire.

2 He had a little book open in his hand, and he placed[+] his right foot on the sea and *his* left *foot* on the earth.

3 *He* cried *out* with a loud voice like a lion's roar. When he cried *out*, seven thunders uttered their voices.

4 After the seven thunders uttered their voices, I was about to write when I heard a voice from heaven saying to me: Seal up those things that the seven thunders uttered and do not write them.

5 Then the angel that I saw standing upon the sea and upon the earth lifted up his hand to heaven.

6 He swore by *God* who lives forever and ever and who created heaven and earth and the sea and everything that is in them, that time shall not be *further delayed*.

7 But in the days when the voice of the seventh angel shall begin to sound, the mystery of God will be finished, *just* as He declared to His servants the prophets.

8 Then the voice that I heard from heaven spoke to me again and said: Go *and* take the little book that is open in the hand of the angel who is standing upon the sea and upon the earth.

9 I went to the angel and said to him: Give me the little book. He said to me: Take *it* and eat it up. It will make your belly bitter, but it will be sweet as honey in your mouth.

10 I took the little book out of the angel's hand and ate it up. It was as sweet as honey in my mouth, but as soon as I had eaten it, my belly was bitter.

11 He said to me: You must prophesy again before many peoples, nations, tongues, and kings.

The Revelation Chapter 11

1 Then a reed like rod was given to me and the angel standing *there* said: Rise and measure the temple of God and the altar and *those* who worship there.

2 But leave out and do not measure the court that is outside[+] the temple for it is given to the Gentiles and they shall tread the holy city under foot *for* forty two months.

3 I will give *power* to my two witnesses and they shall prophesy for a thousand two hundred and sixty days, clothed in sackcloth.

4 These *two witnesses* are *the* two olive trees and two candlesticks standing before the God of the earth. *Zechariah 4:2-12*

5 If anyone *tries to* hurt them, fire will come[+] out of their mouth and devour their enemies. If anyone *tries to* hurt them, they must be killed in the same way.

6 These *two witnesses* have *the* power to shut *up* heaven *so* that it will not rain during the days of their prophecy. *They* have power over *the* waters to turn them to blood and to strike[+] the earth with all *kinds of* plagues as often as they will *it to be done*.

7 When they have finished their testimony, the beast will ascend out of the bottomless pit to make war against them and overcome them and kill them.

8 Their dead bodies *will lie* in the street of the great city that is spiritually called Sodom and Egypt, where our Lord was also *in essence* crucified.

9 *All* the people and families[+] and tongues and nations will see their dead bodies *for* three and a half days but will not allow[+] their bodies to be put into graves.

10 Then *those* who live on the earth will rejoice and make merry and send gifts to each other because these two prophets tormented *those* who lived[+] on the earth.

11 After three and a half days, the spirit of life from God entered them and they stood up on their feet, and great fear fell upon *all* who saw them.

12 Then they *all* they heard a great voice
from heaven say to *the two witnesses*:
Come up here. And their enemies saw[+]
them *as* they ascended up to heaven in a
cloud.
13 *In* that same hour, there was a great
earthquake and a tenth part of the city
fell and seven thousand people[+] were
killed.[+] *Those who* remained[+] were
frightened[+] and gave glory to the God of
heaven.
14 *Now* the second woe is past *and* behold
the third woe is quickly coming.
15 The seventh angel sounded and there
were great voices in heaven saying: The
kingdoms of this world *now* become *the
kingdom* of our Lord and of His Christ
and He shall reign forever and ever.
16 *Then* the twenty four elders who sat on
their seats before God fell face *down* and
worshiped God
17 saying: We give you thanks, O Lord
God Almighty, who is and was and is to
come, because you have *now* taken *up*
your great power to reign.
18 The nations were angry, but *now* your
wrath has come. And the time *has come*
for the dead to be judged and to give
rewards to your servants the prophets
and to the saints and to *those* who fear
your name, great and small, *and* to
destroy *those* who have destroyed the
earth.
19 Then the temple of God was opened in
heaven and the ark of His covenant[+]
appeared[+] with lightning and voices and
thunder and an earthquake and great
hail.

The Revelation Chapter 12

1 Then a great wonder appeared in
heaven: A woman clothed with the sun,
the moon under her feet, and a crown
with twelve stars on her head.
2 *Being* in labor[+] with child, *she* cried
out in pain to give birth.
3 Then another wonder appeared in
heaven: Behold, a great dragon with
seven heads, ten horns, and seven crowns
upon its heads.
4 Its tail drew *together* a third of *all* the
stars of heaven and cast them to the
earth. Then the dragon stood before the
woman who was ready to give birth,[+] to
devour her child as soon as it was born.
5 *After the woman* brought *forth* a man
child to guide[+] all *the* nations with a rod
of iron, her child was caught up to God
and *to* His throne.
6 The woman *then* fled into the wilderness *to* a place prepared for her by God
who would care[+] for her *there* for a
thousand two hundred *and* sixty days.
7 *Then* there was a *great* war in heaven.
Michael and his angels fought against
the dragon *and* the dragon fought *back*,
but his angels
8 did not prevail. *There was* no place for
them in heaven any more.
9 The great dragon *known as* the old
serpent, the Devil, and Satan, *the* deceiver of the whole world, was cast out
onto the earth, and his angels were cast
out with him.
10 Then I heard a loud voice in heaven
say: Now, salvation and strength and
the kingdom of God and the authority[+]
of His Christ have come. For the
accuser of our family[+] who accused
them before our God day and night has
now been cast down.
11 *Believers* overcame *Satan* by the blood
of the Lamb and by the word of their
testimony, not loving their *own* lives to
the death.
12 Therefore rejoice *O* heavens and you
who live in them. Woe to the inhabitants
of the earth and of the sea. For the devil
has come down to you with great wrath,
because he knows that he has only[+] a
short time.
13 When the dragon saw that he was cast
down to the earth, he persecuted the
woman who brought forth the man *child*.
14 But the woman was given two wings
of a great eagle *so* that she could fly to
the wilderness, to her place where she
she would be nourished *and protected* from
the presence[+] of the serpent for a time
and times and half a time.
15 Then the serpent thrust[+] water out of

his mouth like a flood after the woman
so that he might *try to* cause her to be
carried away by the flood.
16 But the earth helped the woman. It
opened up its mouth and swallowed up
the flood that the dragon had thrust out
of its mouth.
17 Then the dragon was angry[+] with the
woman and went to make war with the
remnant of her seed who keep the
commandments of God and have the
testimony of Jesus Christ.

The Revelation Chapter 13

1 Then standing on the sand of the
seashore, I saw a beast rise up out of the
sea with seven heads and ten horns. On
his horns were ten crowns and on his
heads a blasphemous name.
2 The beast that I saw was like a leopard.
His feet were like *those* of a bear and his
mouth like a lion's. The dragon gave
him his power, his throne,[+] and great
authority.
3 I saw *that* one of his heads *was*
mortally[+] wounded but *then* the wound
was healed and all the world marveled[+]
over the beast.
4 *So the people* worshiped the dragon that
gave authority[+] to the beast and they
worshiped the beast saying: Who *is*
like the beast? Who is able to make
war with him?
5 *The beast* was given a mouth to speak
great things and blasphemies, and he
was given power to continue *for* forty
two months.
6 So he opened his mouth in blasphemy
against God, to blaspheme His name
and His tabernacle and *those* who live in
heaven.
7 He was given *the ability* to make war
with the saints and overcome them *with*
power over all families,[+] tongues, and
nations.
8 All who live on the earth will worship
the beast, except not *those* whose names
are written in the Book of Life by the
Lamb *who was* slain. *His* from the
foundation of the world.
9 If anyone has an ear, let them hear.
10 *Those* who lead into captivity shall go
into captivity. *Those* who kill by the
sword must be killed by the sword. Here
is the patience and the faith of the saints.
11 Then I saw[+] another beast coming up
out of the earth with two horns like a
lamb but speaking like a dragon.
12 *This beast* exercises all the authority[+]
of the first beast before him, and *he*
causes *all* the earth and *those* who live
there to worship the first beast whose
deadly wound was healed.
13 He does great wonders, *even* causing[+]
fire to come down from heaven to earth
in the sight of men.
14 And *he* deceives *those* who live on the
earth by *performing* miracles that he is
given[+] the power to do in the sight of the
beast. *Then he* tells *those* who live on the
earth that they should make an image to
the beast that had been *mortally* wounded
by a sword, but *yet* lived.
15 *The second beast* had power to give life
to the image of the beast *so* that the
image of the beast could both speak and
cause all[+] *who* would not worship the
image of the beast to be killed.
16 *This beast* causes all, both small and
great, rich and poor, free and bond, to
receive a mark in their right hand or in
their foreheads,
17 *so* that no one may buy or sell except[+]
those who have the mark or the name of
the beast or the number of his name.
18 Here is wisdom: Let *those* who have
understanding count the number of the
beast, for it is the number of a man, and
his number *is* six hundred *and* sixty six.

The Revelation Chapter 14

1 Then I looked and behold, a Lamb
stood on Mount Zion,[+] and with Him a
hundred *and* forty four thousand, *all*
having His Father's name written in
their foreheads.
2 I heard a voice from heaven like the
sound of many *rushing* waters and like
the sound of great thunder. I also heard
the sound of harpists playing[+] their harps.

3 They sang a new song before the throne and before the four beasts and the elders. No one could learn that song but the hundred *and* forty four thousand who were redeemed from the earth.

4 These are the *ones* who were not defiled with women, for they are virgins. These are the *ones* who follow the Lamb wherever He goes. These were redeemed from among men, *being* the first fruits to God and to the Lamb.

5 No deceitfulness+ was found in their mouth for they are without fault before the throne of God.

6 Then I saw another angel flying in the midst of heaven and proclaiming+ the everlasting Gospel to *all* who live on the earth, to every nation, family,+ tongue, and people.

7 With a loud voice, *he* said: Fear God and give glory to Him, for the hour of His judgment has come. Worship *the one* who made heaven and earth and the sea and the fountains of waters.

8 Another angel followed, saying: Babylon has fallen. That great city has fallen because she made all nations drink the wine of wrath *caused by* her fornication.

9 If anyone worships the beast and his image and receives *the beast's* mark in their forehead or in their hand,

10 the same shall drink the wine of God's wrath that will be poured *full* strength+ into the cup of His indignation. They will be tormented with fire and brimstone in the presence of the holy angels and in the presence of the Lamb.

11 The smoke from their torment will ascend up forever and ever. Those who worship the beast and his image and whoever receives the mark of his name will have no rest day or night.

> 12 Here the patience
> of the saints *is revealed*
> in keeping the commandments
> of God and faith *in* Jesus.

13 Then I heard a voice from heaven saying to me: Write *this*: Blessed *are* the dead who die in the Lord from now on. Yes, says the Spirit. *So* that they may rest from their labors, their works follow them.

14 And then I looked and saw a white cloud and the Son of man sitting on the cloud. On His head, he had a golden crown, and in His hand a sharp sickle.

15 Then another angel came out of the temple, crying *out* with a loud voice to *the one* who sat on the cloud: Thrust in your sickle and reap, for the time to reap has come, for the harvest of the earth is ripe.

16 So *the one* who sat on the cloud thrust His sickle across+ the earth and reaped *the harvest from* the earth.

17 Then another angel came out of the temple in heaven. He also had a sharp sickle.

18 And *still* another angel came out from the altar. *This one* had authority+ over fire. *He* cried *out* with a loud cry to the one who had the sharp sickle saying: Thrust in your sharp sickle and gather the clusters of vines from the earth, for her grapes are fully ripe.

19 So the angel thrust his sickle across+ the earth and gathered the vines and cast *them* into the great wine press of the wrath of God.

20 The wine press was *then* trod+ outside+ the city and blood came out of the wine press, even *up* to the horse's bridles for two hundred miles.+

The Revelation Chapter 15

1 Then I saw another great and marvelous sign in heaven: Seven angels *appeared* with the seven last plagues and the wrath of God is fulfilled+ by them.

2 I saw *what appeared to be* a sea of glass mingled with fire. *Those* who overcame+ the beast, his image, his mark, *and* the number of his name, stand on the sea of glass with harps from God.

3 They sing the song of Moses, the servant of God, and the song of the Lamb saying: Great and marvelous *are* your works, Lord God Almighty. Just

and true *are* your ways *O* King of *all* *that is* holy.+

4 Who shall not fear you, O Lord, and glorify your name? For *only you* alone+ *are* holy. All nations will come and worship before you. for your righteousness+ is *clearly* seen.+

5 After that, I saw+ *that* the temple of the tabernacle of the testimony in heaven was opened.

6 The seven angels clothed in pure white and girded with golden belts+ came out of the temple with the seven plagues.

7 One of the four beasts gave to the seven angels the seven golden vials filled with the wrath of God who lives forever and ever.

8 The temple was filled with smoke from the glory of God and from His power. No one was able to enter into the temple until the seven plagues of the seven angels were fulfilled.

The Revelation Chapter 16

1 Then I heard a great voice out of the temple saying to the seven angels: Go and pour out the vials of the wrath of God upon the earth.

2 The first *angel* poured out his vial on the earth and an evil+ and grievious sore fell on *those* who had the mark of the beast and *on those* who worshiped his image.

3 The second angel poured out his vial on the sea and it became like the blood of a dead *man* and every soul living in the sea died.

4 The third angel poured out his vial on the rivers and fountains of waters and they became blood.

5 I heard the angel of the waters say: You are righteous, O Lord, who is and was and shall be, because you have judged *in this* manner.+

6 For they have shed the blood of saints and prophets, and you have given them blood to drink, *which is* a worthy *judgment*.

7 Then I heard another *voice* from the altar say: So *be it* Lord God Almighty, your judgments *are* true and righteous.

8 The fourth angel poured out his vial on the sun and it was given power to scorch mankind+ with fire.

9 *Therefore* great heat scorched mankind+ and *they* cursed+ the name of God who has authority+ over these plagues, but they did not repent to give Him glory.

10 The fifth angel poured out his vial on the throne+ of the beast and his kingdom was filled with darkness and they gnawed their tongues with pain.

11 *They* cursed+ the God of heaven because of their pain and sores, and *they* did not repent of their deeds.

12 The sixth angel poured out his vial on the great river Euphrates and its water was dried up *so* that the way for the kings of the east would be prepared.

13 Then I saw three unclean spirits like frogs *come* out of the mouth of the dragon, out of the mouth of the beast, and out of the mouth of the false prophet.

14 These are the spirits of demons+ working *pretended* miracles. *They* go to *all* the kings of the earth and of the whole world to gather them *together* for the *final* battle of that great day of God the Almighty.

15 *The Lord said:* Behold I will come like a thief, *unexpected*. Blessed *are those* who watch and keep their garments *ready*, lest they walk naked and in shame. *Matthew 25:13*

16 Then *the spirits* gathered them together to a place called Armageddon in Hebrew.

17 The seventh angel poured his vial into the air and a great voice came out of the temple in heaven from the throne saying: It is done.

18 Then there were voices, thunder, lightning and a great earthquake. Such a great *and* mighty earthquake had not *previously occurred* since mankind+ *came* upon the earth.

19 The great city was *broken* into three parts and the cities of the nations fell. And *then* God remembered to give the great Babylon the cup *filled with* the wine of the fierceness of His wrath.

20 Every island fled away and mountains *just* disappeared.+

21 Great hail with *stones* the weight of a talent fell from heaven onto mankind.+ People+ cursed+ God because the plague of hail was *so* exceedingly great.

The Revelation Chapter 17

1 Then one of the seven angels who had the seven vials came and talked with me. He said: Come here and I will show you the judgment of the great whore who sits on many waters.

2 Kings of the earth have committed fornication with her and the inhabitants of the earth have been made drunk with the wine of her fornication.

3 *The angel* then carried me away in the spirit into the wilderness. There, I saw a woman sitting on a scarlet colored beast with seven heads and ten horns and filled with blasphemous names.

4 The woman was arrayed in purple and scarlet color, and decked with gold and precious stones and pearls. She had a golden cup in her hand full of abominations and filth from her fornication.

5 The name written on her forehead *was*: Mystery Babylon the great, the mother of harlots and abominations of the earth.

6 I saw *that* the woman *was* drunk with the blood of the saints and with the blood of Jesus' martyrs and I wondered with great amazement.+

7 The angel said to me: Why did you marvel? I will tell you the mystery of the woman and of the beast with seven heads and ten horns that carries her.

8 The beast that you saw was *of one kind*, is not *now the same*, but will *again* ascend from the bottomless pit and go into damnation.+ *Those* who live on the earth whose names were not written in the Book of Life from the foundation of the world will wonder when they behold the beast that was *of one kind*, is not *now the same*, and yet is.

9 Here, the mind must+ have understanding+: The seven heads are the seven mountains on which the woman sits.

10 There are seven kings. Five have fallen, one is *still there*, *and* the other has not yet come. When he comes, he must continue *for* a short time.+

11 The beast that was *of one kind*, and is not *now the same*, will also *become an* eighth after+ the seven, and *then he will go* into damnation.+

12 The ten horns that you saw are ten kings who have received no kingdom yet, but *they* have received authority+ as kings *for* one hour with the beast.

13 They are of one mind and *therefore* give their authority+ and strength to the beast.

14 These *kings* will make war with the Lamb, but the Lamb will overcome them. For He is Lord of lords and King of kings. *Those* who are with Him *are* called and chosen and faithful.

15 Then *the angel* said to me: The waters that you saw where the whore sits are peoples and multitudes and nations and tongues.

16 The ten horns that you saw on the beast will hate the whore and will make her desolate and naked and will eat her flesh and burn her with fire.

17 For God has put *it* in their hearts to fulfill His will and to agree to give their kingdoms to the beast until *all of* God's words are fulfilled.

18 The woman you saw is that great city that reigns over the kings of the earth.

The Revelation Chapter 18

1 After *all* these things, I saw *another* angel come down from heaven with *such* great power that the earth was illuminated+ with his glory.

2 He cried *out* mightily with a strong voice saying: Babylon the great has fallen, *yes* fallen. *It* has become the habitation of demons+ and prison+ *for* every unclean+ spirit and prison+ *for* every unclean and hated bird. *Isaiah 21:9*

3 For all nations have drunk of the wine of the wrath of her fornication. The kings of the earth have committed fornication with her and the merchants

of the earth have grown+ rich through
the abundance of her delicacies.
4 Then I heard another voice from heaven
saying: Come *away* from her my people
so that you will not be partakers of her
sins and *so* that you will not receive her
plagues.
5 For her sins have reached to heaven
and God has remembered her iniquities.
6 Reward her even as she rewarded
you and double to her. *Give her* double
according to her works in the cup *that*
she has filled, fill her double.
7 *Consider* how much she has glorified
herself and lived deliciously, *and* give
her that much torment and sorrow. For
she said in her heart: I sit *as* a queen.
I am no widow. I shall see no sorrow.
8 Therefore, *all* her plagues shall come
in one day: death, mourning, and
famine. She shall be utterly burned
with fire. For the Lord God who judges
her *is* strong.
9 The kings of the earth who have
committed fornication and lived deliciously with her will wail and mourn+
for her when they see the smoke from
her burning.
10 *They will* stand a far *distance away* for
fear of her torment saying: Alas, alas
that great city Babylon, that mighty
city. In one hour, your judgment has
come.
11 The merchants of the earth will weep
and mourn over her, for no one buys
their merchandise any more.
12 *Their* merchandise *included* gold and
silver, precious stones and pearls, fine
linen in purple, silk and scarlet, all *kinds*
of fragrant+ wood, all kinds+ of ivory
vessels, all kinds+ *of* vessels in precious
wood, brass, iron, and marble,
13 cinnamon, fragrances,+ ointments,
frankincense, wine, oil, fine flour,
wheat, beasts, sheep, horses, chariots,
slaves, and people's *very* souls.
14 The fruits that your soul lusted after
are gone+ from you. All *the* things
that were dainty and fine+ are gone+
from you. You shall no longer find
them at all.
15 The merchants of *all* these things who
were made rich by her will stand a far
distance away for fear of her torment,
weeping, and wailing.
16 *They will* say: Alas, alas, *for* that great
city that was clothed in fine linen,
purple and scarlet, and decked with
gold, precious stones, and pearls.
17 For in one hour such+ great riches
have come to nothing. Every ship master
and all the company in ships and sailors
and all+ *who* trade by sea, stood at a far
distance away.
18 *They all* cried *out* when they saw the
smoke from her burning, saying: What
city is like this great city.
19 They threw+ dust on their heads and
cried *out*, weeping and wailing, saying:
Alas, alas, that great city in which all
who had ships in the sea were made rich
by her wealth,+ in one hour she is made
desolate.
20 Rejoice over her *demise*, *O* heaven and
holy apostles and prophets. For God has
avenged you on her.
21 Then a mighty angel took up a stone
like a great millstone and cast *it* into the
sea saying: Thus with violence that
great city Babylon *is* thrown down, no
longer+ to be found at all.
22 The voices of harpists, musicians,
pipers, and trumpeters will no longer+
be heard in you at all. No craftsman of
any *kind of* craft will be found in you any
more. The sound of a millstone will no
longer+ be heard in you at all.
23 The light of a candle will no longer+
shine in you at all. The voices of brides
and grooms will no longer+ be heard in
you at all. Your merchants were the
great men of the earth, *but* all *the* nations
were deceived by your sorceries.
24 *The* blood of prophets, saints, and all
who have been slain on the earth *by her*
order is found in *Babylon*.

The Revelation Chapter 19

1 After these things, I heard a great
voice of many people in heaven saying:
Alleluia. Salvation, glory, honor, and

power *belong* to the Lord our God.
2 His judgments *are* true and righteous.
For He has judged the great whore who
corrupted the earth with her fornication,
and *He* has avenged the blood of His
servants at her hand.
3 Again they said: Alleluia. And her
smoke rose up forever and ever.
4 The twenty four elders and the four
beasts fell down and worshiped God
who sat on the throne saying: Amen.
Alleluia.
5 Then a voice came from the throne
saying: Praise our God all *of* you *who are*
His servants and you who fear Him,
both small and great.
6 I heard the voice of a great multitude
like the voice of many waters and like
the voice of mighty thunder saying:
Alleluia, for the Lord God omnipotent
reigns.
7 Let us be glad and rejoice and give
honor to Him, for the marriage of the
Lamb has come and His wife has made
herself ready.
8 To her was granted that she should be
arrayed in fine linen, clean and white.
For fine linen is *to affirm* the righteousness of saints.
9 *The angel* said to me: Write *this*: Blessed
are those who are called to the marriage
supper of the Lamb. And *then* he said to
me: These are the true sayings of God.
10 I fell *down* at *the angel's* feet to worship
him, but he said to me: See *that you do*
not, *for* I am your fellow servant and
one of your family[+] who has the
testimony of Jesus. Worship *only* God.
For the testimony of Jesus is the spirit
of prophecy.
11 Then I saw heaven open and behold, *I*
saw a white horse and *the one* who sat on
it called Faithful and True. In righteousness, He judges and makes war.
12 His eyes *were* like a flame of fire and
on His head *were* many crowns. *And* He
had a name written *on Himself* that no
one but He Himself knew.
13 He *was* clothed with a robe[+] dipped in
blood, and

His name is called
The Word of God.

14 The armies in heaven followed Him
on white horses, clothed in fine linen,
white and clean.
15 Out of His mouth, a sharp sword *came*
forth to strike[+] the nations. He will rule
them with a rod of iron and tread the
wine press with the fierceness and wrath
of Almighty God.
16 On *His* robe[+] and on His thigh He has
this name written: King of kings and
Lord of lords.
17 Then I saw an angel standing in the
sun. He cried *out* with a loud voice to all
the birds[+] that fly in the midst of heaven:
Come and gather yourselves together
for the supper of the great God.
18 Thus *the birds shall* eat the flesh of
kings and the flesh of captains and the
flesh of mighty men and the flesh of
horses and of *those* who sit on them and
the flesh of all *men, both* free and bond,
both small and great.
19 Then I saw the beast and the kings of
the earth and their armies gathered
together to make war against *the Lord*
who sat on the *white* horse and against
His army.
20 The beast was taken *captive* and with
him the false prophet who worked[+]
pretended miracles. By them, *the false*
prophet deceived *those* who had received
the mark of the beast and *those* who
worshiped his image. Therefore, these
two were *both* cast alive into the lake of
fire burning with brimstone.
21 The rest[+] were killed[+] by the sword of
the Lord who sat on the *white* horse,
whose *sword* came[+] *forth* out of His
mouth. And all the birds[+] were filled
with their flesh.

The Revelation Chapter 20

1 I then saw an angel come down from
heaven with the key to the bottomless pit
and a great chain in his hand.
2 He laid hold on the dragon, that old

serpent who is the Devil or Satan, and bound him *for* a thousand years.

3 *Then the Lord* cast *Satan* into the bottomless pit and shut him up and set a seal on him *so* that he could no longer[+] deceive the nations until the thousand years would be fulfilled. After that, *Satan* must be loosed *again for* a short[+] time.

4 Then I saw thrones and sitting on them and giving judgment were those souls *who had been* beheaded for their testimony[+] *for* Jesus and for the Word of God. They had not worshiped the beast or his image nor received *his* mark on their foreheads or in their hands, *and therefore* they *would* live and reign with Christ *for* a thousand years.

5 But the rest of the dead would not live again until the thousand years were finished. This *is* the first resurrection.

6 Blessed and holy *are those* who have a part in the first resurrection. The second death will have no authority[+] over them, but they shall be priests of God and of Christ and shall reign with Him *for* a thousand years.

7 When the thousand years have expired, Satan will be released[+] from his prison.

8 *He* will go out to deceive *all* the nations in the four corners[+] of the earth, Gog and Magog, to gather them together for battle. The number of them *is* like *grains of* sand on the seashore.[+]

9 The *enemy* went across[+] the breadth of the earth and surrounded[+] the camp of the saints and the beloved city. And then fire came down from God in heaven and consumed[+] them.

10 The devil who had deceived them was cast into the lake of fire and brimstone where the beast and the false prophet *are*, and *where they* will be tormented day and night forever and ever.

11 Then I saw a great white throne and *the Lord* who sat on it. Heaven and earth fled away from *His* face and no place was found for them.

12 I saw the dead, small and great, stand before God and the books were opened. Then another *book called* the Book of Life was opened and the dead were judged out of those things that were written in the books, according to their works.

13 The sea gave up the dead that were in it. Death and Hell delivered up the dead that were in them. Everyone[+] was judged according to their works.

14 Then death and Hell were cast into the lake of fire, *and* this is the second death.

> 15 Anyone *whose name*
> *was* not found written
> in the Book of Life
> was cast into the lake of fire.

The Revelation Chapter 21

1 Now I saw a new heaven and a new earth. For the first heaven and the first earth had passed away and there was no more sea.

2 Then I John saw the holy city, the new Jerusalem, coming down from God out of heaven, prepared as a bride adorned for her husband.

3 I heard a great voice out of heaven saying: Behold the tabernacle of God *is* with men and He will live with them and they shall be His people and God Himself will be with them *and be* their God.

4 And God will wipe away all tears from their eyes. There will be no more death nor sorrow nor crying nor any more pain. For the former things are *now* passed away.

5 Then *the Lord God* who sat upon the throne said: Behold, I make everything new. And He said to me: Write *this down*, for these words are true and faithful.

6 And He said to me: It is done. I am Alpha and Omega, the beginning and the end. I will give to *those* who are thirsty from the fountain of the water of life freely.

7 *Those* who overcome will inherit everything. I will be their God and they will be my children.

8 But the fearful and unbelieving and the abominable and murderers and fornicators+ and sorcerers and idolaters and all liars will have their part in the lake that burns with fire and brimstone. *For* that is the second death.

9 Then one of the seven angels who had the seven vials filled with the seven last plagues came to me and talked with me saying: Come here, I will show you the bride, the wife *of* the Lamb.

10 He carried me away in the spirit to a great and high mountain and showed me that great city, the holy Jerusalem, descending out of heaven from God.

11 Its light *radiated* with the glory of God like a most precious stone, like crystal clear jasper.

12 *It* had a great, high wall *with* twelve gates and twelve angels at the gates and *the names* of the twelve tribes of the children of Israel written on them.

13 *There were* three gates on the east, three gates on the north, three gates on the south, *and* three gates on the west.

14 The wall of the city had twelve foundations and on them *were* the names of the twelve apostles of the Lamb.

15 *The angel* who talked with me had a golden reed to measure the city and its gates and its walls.

16 The city lay foursquare with its length *equally* as long as its breadth. He measured the city with the reed, *and it was* fifteen hundred miles.+ Its length, breadth, and height *were all* equal.

17 He measured the wall *as one* hundred *and* forty four cubits, *or 216 feet, according to the* human+ measure *used by* the angel.

18 The wall was made+ *of* jasper and the city *was* pure gold as clear as glass.

19 The foundations of the wall of the city *were* adorned+ with all kinds+ of precious stones. The first foundation *was* jasper, the second sapphire, the third quartz,+ the fourth an emerald,

20 the fifth onyx,+ the sixth ruby,+ the seventh golden topaz+ the eighth beryl, the ninth green topaz, the tenth *green* agate,+ the eleventh *blue* hyacinth,+ *and* the twelfth an amethyst.

21 The twelve gates *were* twelve pearls. Each gate was *made* of one pearl. And the street of the city *was* pure gold as *though* it were transparent glass.

22 But no temple could be seen there, for the Lord God Almighty Himself is the temple and the Lamb.

23 The city had no need for the sun or the moon to shine there, for the glory of God illuminated+ it, and the Lamb *is* its light.

24 The nations of *those* who are saved will walk in this light and the kings of the earth will bring their glory and honor into it.

25 Its gates will not be shut *any* day and there will not be *any* night there.

26 And *the Lord* will bring the glory and honor of the nations, *all true believers*, into it.

27 But none+ who defile or work abominations or lie shall enter into it. Only *those* whose *names* are written in the Lamb's Book of Life *shall enter*.

The Revelation Chapter 22

1 *The angel* then showed me a river of the pure water of life as bright+ as crystal, *flowing* forth+ from the throne of God and the Lamb.

2 In the midst *between* the street *on* this+ *side* and the river *on* that+ *side was a* tree of life producing+ twelve fruits, yielding fruit each month, and the leaves of the tree *were* for the healing the nations.

3 All curses will no longer exist+ *there*. But the throne of God and of the Lamb will exist+ there and His servants will serve Him.

4 *True believers* will see His face and His name *will be* on their foreheads.

5 There will be no night there and no need for any lamp+ or sunlight. Because the Lord God will enlighten+ them and they will reign forever and ever.

6 *The angel* said to me: These sayings *are* faithful and true. The Lord God of the holy prophets sent His angel to show to His servants the things that must soon+ be done.

[7] *And the Lord said:* Behold I am coming quickly. Blessed *are those* who keep the words+ of the prophecy of this book.
[8] I John saw *all* these things and heard *them*. And when I had heard and seen, I fell down to worship before the feet of the angel who showed these things to me.
[9] But he said to me: See *that you do* not *do this*. For I am your fellow servant and of your family+ the prophets and of *those* who keep the words of this book*to* worship God.
[10]He said to me: Do not seal *up* the words of the prophecy of this book, for the time is *very* near.+
[11]*Those* who are unjust, let them be unjust still. *Those* who are filthy, let them be filthy still. *Those* who are righteous, let them be righteous still. *Those* who are holy, let them be holy still.
[12]*And the Lord said:*

Behold I am coming quickly
and my reward *is* with me
to give *to* everyone+
according *to* their work.

[13]I am Alpha and Omega, The Beginning and The End, The First and The Last.
[14]Blessed *are those* who do His commandments *so* that they may have *the* right to the tree of life and *to* enter into the city through the gates.
[15]For outside+ *are* dogs and sorcerers and fornicators+ and murderers and idolaters and everyone who delights+ *in* and commits+ a lie.
[16]*Then the Lord said:* I Jesus have sent my angel to testify to you these things in the assemblies.+ I am the Root and the offspring of David, The Bright and Morning Star.
[17]The Spirit and the bride say: Come. Let *those* who hear say: Come.

Let *those* who are thirsty come.
And whoever will, let them take
from the water of life freely.

[18] For I testify to everyone+ who hears the words of the prophecy of this book: If anyone shall add to these things, God will add to them the plagues that are written in this book.
[19] And if anyone takes away words from this book *of* prophecy, God will take away their part from the Book of Life and *from* the holy city and *from* the *rewards* written in this book.
[20]*The Lord* who testifies *to* these things says: Surely I come quickly. Amen. Even so, come Lord Jesus.
[21]The grace of our Lord Jesus Christ *be* with you all. Amen.

What choice have you made?

Do you realize that your eternal destiny will be determined by whatever choice you make? You have the option to choose to believe in God ***and*** believe His Word and follow Him...or to just go your own way and do your own thing, disregarding God's Word. Whatever you choose will determine the consequences and the reward that you will receive for all of eternity.

God loves you. He wants your life to be filled with love, joy, peace, and all the fruit of the Spirit here and now during your brief journey through this temporary life. And, He wants to give you the gift of eternal life. It's up to you to decide if you want to accept His offer, or reject it. On the last page of this book is an invitation that you can accept or reject. The choice is yours.

A Treasure of Old Testament Wisdom

The Old Testament is a treasure of history and prophecy, all of which points forward to that day when the Word of God Himself appeared in the flesh to speak directly to mankind.

The Old Testament describes God's creation of the world, declares His sovereignty, and documents His interaction with the human race from the creation of the first man and woman through the accounts of each individual that God appointed to communicate His messages to various target audiences over many centuries of human history.

While there is much wisdom encompassed within the 610,000 words in the Old Testament, most of it is revealed through illustrative case histories rather than by direct statements of declarative instructions and declarations of universal truth.

Other than the Ten Commandments, most of the other "commandments," "statutes," "ordinances," "laws," and "decrees" that the prophets declared as God's spokesmen were clearly intended for very specific target audiences and for very specific times, places, and circumstances.

Following is a representative selection of Old Testament verses that are featured in the book, ***The Most Essential Truth in the Bible***.

---

1 Genesis

1:1 In the beginning God created the heaven and the earth.

1:27 God *also* created mankind+ in His *own* image … He created them *as* male and female.

2:2 On the seventh day, God ended His work that He had made, and He rested on the seventh day from all His work that He had made.

2:7 *When* the Lord formed man *from* the dust of the ground, *He* breathed the breath of life into his nostrils and man became a living soul.

2:15-17 The Lord put man into the Garden
of Eden to dress it and to keep it. 16 And
He commanded the man, saying: Of
every tree in the garden you may freely
eat, 17 but from the tree of the knowledge of good and evil, you shall not eat.
For in the day that you eat of it, you will
surely die.

2:18 The Lord God said: *It is* not good that a man should be alone. I will make a help meet for him.

2:24 Therefore shall a man leave his father and his mother and be joined+ to his wife and they shall be one flesh.

3:1-5 Now the serpent was more subtle
than any beast of the field that the Lord
God had made, and he said to the
woman: Has God said you shall not eat
of every tree of the garden? 2 The
woman said to the serpent: We may eat
from the fruit of the trees of the garden,
3 except from the fruit of the tree in the
midst of the garden, *for* God said: You
shall not eat from it nor shall you touch
it, or else you will die.

4 The serpent said to the woman: You will not die, 5 for God knows that in the day *that* you eat from it, your eyes will be opened and you*yourselves* will be like gods, knowing good and evil.

3:6-7 *Therefore,* when the woman saw that the tree *was* good for food and pleasing to the eyes and desired to make *one* wise, she took *some* of the fruit and ate and gave *it* to her husband with her and he ate; 7 and their eyes were opened and they knew that they *were* naked. *So* they knit+ fig leaves together and made aprons *to cover* themselves.

3:8-13 When Adam and his wife heard the voice of the Lord God walking in the garden, they hid themselves from *His* presence … 11 *God said:* Have you *disobeyed me and* eaten from the tree that I commanded that you should not eat? 12 *Adam* said: The woman that you gave me, gave me *fruit from* the tree and I did eat. 13 The Lord God said to the woman: What have you done? The woman said: The serpent beguiled me and I did eat.

3:16-17 *The Lord* said to the woman: *Because you have done this,* I will greatly multiply your sorrow in your conception. In sorrow you shall bring forth children and your desire *shall be* to your husband and he shall rule over you. 17 *Then* to Adam He said: Because you have listened+ to the voice of your wife and have eaten from the tree that I commanded you saying: You shall not eat from it, cursed *is* the ground for your sake. In sorrow shall you eat *from* it all the days of your life.

3:23 Therefore the Lord banished+ mankind+ out of the garden of Eden …

6:5-7 *Later, when* God saw *all* the wickedness *on the earth* … 6 He regretted+ that He had made mankind+ … *all the rebellion* grieved Him … 7 and the Lord said, I will destroy mankind+ from the face of the earth.

6:8 However, *one righteous man,* Noah, found grace in the eyes of the Lord … *and God saved Noah and his family* …

9:1 God blessed Noah and his sons and said to them: Be fruitful and multiply and replenish the earth.

17:2-21 *Later still, God said to another righteous man, Abraham:* I will make my covenant between me and you and will multiply you exceedingly.
4 My covenant *is* with you and you shall be a father of many nations.
7 I will establish my covenant between me and you and your descendants+ after you for an everlasting covenant, to be God to you and to your descendants after you.

18:18 Abraham will surely become a great and mighty nation and all the nations of the earth will be blessed through him.

21:5 Abraham was a hundred years old when his son Isaac was born.

22:18 In your descendants, + all nations of the earth will be blessed because you have obeyed my voice.

24:1-4 *When* Abraham was old … 2 *he* said to his eldest servant … 4 go to my country, to my kindred, and take a wife for my son Isaac.

24:67 Isaac took Rebekah into his mother's tent and she became his wife … and he loved her …

25:23 The Lord said to *Rebekah*: Two nations *are* in your womb and two kinds+ of people shall be separated from your bowels, and *one* people shall be stronger than *the other* people, and the elder shall serve the younger.

2 Exodus

20:1-17 *The Ten Commandments as found in these verses are presented on page 5 of this book.*

34:14 You shall worship no other god because the Lord, whose name *is* Jealous, *is* a jealous God.

3 Leviticus

18:5 You shall keep my statutes and my judgments: which, if anyone does, they shall live in them: I *am* the Lord.

19:18 You shall not avenge nor bear any grudge against the children of your people, but *rather* you shall love your neighbor as yourself: I *am* the Lord.

4 Numbers

6:24-26 The Lord bless you and keep you. The Lord make his face shine upon you and be gracious to you. The Lord lift up His countenance upon you and give you peace.

5 Deuteronomy

1:11 The Lord God of your fathers *will* make you a thousand times as many more as you *are now*, and *He will* bless you *just* as He has promised.

4:2 You shall not add to the word which I command you, neither diminish *anything* from it, so that you may keep the commandments of the Lord your God which I command you.

6:5-7 You shall love the Lord your God with all your heart and with all your soul and with all your might. 6 These words which I command you shall be in your heart. 7 You shall teach them diligently … and shall talk of them *daily* …

6:16 You shall not tempt the Lord your God …

8:3 … mankind+ does not live by bread only, but by every *word*+ that proceeds out of the mouth of the Lord does mankind+ live.

10:12 What does the Lord require of you, but to fear the Lord your God, to walk in all His ways, and to love Him and to serve the Lord your God with all your heart and with all your soul …

10:20 You shall fear the Lord your God. You shall serve Him and to Him shall you cleave and swear by His name.

6 Joshua

1:8 … you shall meditate *in the Word* day and night+ …

22:5 … love the Lord your God and walk in all His ways and keep His commandments and cleave to Him and serve Him with all your heart and with all your soul.

24:15 … as for me and my house, we will serve the Lord.

7 Judges

8:23 Gideon said, I will not rule over you and neither shall my son rule over you, but the Lord shall rule over you.

8 Ruth

2:12 *May* the Lord repay+ you and a full reward be given to you by the Lord God of Israel under whose wing you trust.

9 1 Samuel

15:22-23 Does the Lord have *as great a* delight in burnt offerings and sacrifices, as in obeying the voice of the Lord? Behold, to obey *is* better than sacrifice, *and* to hearken *is better* than the fat of rams. 23 For rebellion *is as bad as* the sin of witchcraft, and stubbornness *as bad as* iniquity and idolatry. Because you have rejected the Word of the Lord, He has also rejected you …

16:7 *The Lord* does not *see things* as man sees things. For man looks at the outward appearance, but the Lord looks at the heart.

10 2 Samuel

22:4 I will call upon the Lord *who is* worthy to be praised. So shall I be saved from my enemies.

11 1 Kings

3:9 Give your servant an understanding heart to judge your people, so that I may discern between good and evil …

[12] 2 Kings

19:15 … You are God *and* you alone of all the kingdoms of the earth. *For* you have made the heavens and the earth.

[13] 1 Chronicles

16:8 Give thanks unto the Lord. Call upon His name. Make known His deeds among the people.

16:10-12 Glory in the holy name of the Lord. Let the heart of *those* who seek the Lord rejoice. 11 Seek the Lord and His strength *and* seek His face continually. 12 Remember the marvelous works that He has done, His wonders and the judgments of His mouth.

29:12 *All* riches and honor *come* from the Lord. He reigns over everything. *All* power and might are in His hand *alone* and *it is* in His hand *alone* to make greatness and to give strength.

[14] 2 Chronicles

7:14 If my people who are called by my name will humble themselves and pray and seek my face and turn from their wicked ways, then I will hear from heaven and *I* will forgive their sin and heal their land.

14:11 … Help us, O Lord our God, for we rest on you and in your name we go against the multitude. O Lord, you *are* our God. Do not let *evil* men prevail against you.

36:16 They mocked the messengers of God and despised His words and misused his prophets until the wrath of the Lord arose against His people until *there was* no remedy.

[15] Ezra

7:10 Ezra prepared his heart to seek the law of the Lord, and to do *it*, and to teach statutes and judgments in Israel.

[16] Nehemiah

8:10 … the joy of the Lord is your strength.

[17] Esther

1:19-20 Let there be a royal commandment from the king … that *if the* queen+ refuses+ to come before the king, then let the king give her royal estate to another who is better than she. 20 And when the king's decree is published throughout his empire, all the wives shall give their husbands honor, both to great and small.

4:16 Gather *everyone* together *to* fast *and pray* for me *for* three days … and *then* if I perish, I perish.

[18] Job

22:22 Receive the law from His mouth and lay up His words in your heart.

[19] Psalms

1:1-6 Blessed *is* the man who does not walk in the counsel of the ungodly or stand in the way of sinners or sit in the seat of the scornful. 2 But his delight *is* in the law of the Lord and in His law does he meditate day and night. 3 He shall be like a tree planted by the rivers of water that brings forth fruit in its season. His leaf shall not wither and whatever he does shall prosper. 4 The ungodly *are* not like that, but *rather they are* like chaff that the wind blows+ away. 5 Therefore the ungodly shall not stand in the judgment, nor *shall* sinners *stand* in the congregation of the righteous. 6 For the Lord knows the ways of the righteous, but the ways of the ungodly shall perish.

18:2 The Lord *is* my rock and my fortress, my deliverer, my God *and* my strength in whom I will trust. *He is* my buckler, the horn of my salvation *and* my high tower.

19:14 Let the words of my mouth and the meditation of my heart be acceptable in your sight, O Lord, my strength, and my redeemer.

23:1-6 The Lord *is* my shepherd, I shall not want. 2 He makes me to lie down in green pastures. He leads me beside the still waters. 3 He restores my soul. He leads me in the paths of righteousness for His name's sake. 4 Yes, *even* though I walk through the valley of the shadow of death, I will fear no evil. For you *are* with me. Your rod and your staff comfort me. 5 You prepare a table before me in the presence of my enemies. You anoint my head with oil. My cup overflows+. 6 Surely goodness and mercy will follow me all the days of my life, and I will dwell in the house of the Lord forever.

27:4 One *thing* I have desired of the Lord that will I seek after: that I may dwell in the house of the Lord all the days of my life, to behold the beauty of the Lord and to inquire in His temple.

31:23 Love the Lord, all you His saints, *for* the Lord preserves the faithful ...

34:3 O magnify the Lord with me and let us exalt His name together.

34:4 Delight yourself in the Lord and He will give you the desires of your heart.

37:11 The meek shall inherit the earth and delight themselves in the abundance of peace.

27:14 Wait on the Lord. Be of good courage and He will strengthen your heart.

46:1 God *is* our refuge and strength, a very present help in trouble.

46:10 *The Lord God has said:* Be still and know that I am God.

51:10 Create in me a clean heart O God and renew a right spirit within me.

61:2 From the ends of the earth, when my heart is overwhelmed, I will cry *out* to you: Lead me to the rock *that* is higher than I.

62:5 My soul waits only upon God, for my expectation *is* from Him.

62:11 God has spoken once *and* twice I have heard this: that *all* power *belongs* to God.

84:5 Blessed *are all*+ whose strength *is* in *God* ...

84:11 The Lord God *is* a sun and *a* shield. He gives grace and glory. No good *thing* will He withhold from those who walk uprightly.

107:9 He satisfies the longing soul and fills the hungry soul with goodness.

119:11 I have hid your Word in my heart so that I might not sin against you.

119:105 Your Word *is* a lamp unto my feet and a light unto my path.

145:20 The Lord preserves all who love Him, but He will destroy all the wicked.

147:3-5 He heals the broken in heart and binds up their wounds. 4 He tells the number of the stars. He calls them all by name. 5 Great *is* our Lord and of great power. His understanding *is* infinite.

20 Proverbs

1:7 The fear of the Lord *is* the beginning of knowledge. But fools despise wisdom and instruction.

3:5-6 Trust in the Lord with all your heart and do not lean on your own understanding. 6 In all your ways acknowledge Him and He will direct your paths.

3:12 *Those* whom the Lord loves, He corrects ...

6:16-19 Six *things* the Lord hates ... seven are an abomination to Him ...

17 a proud look, a lying tongue, hands that shed innocent blood,

18 a heart devising wicked imaginations, swift running to mischief,

19 a false witness ... and one who sows discord among the family+.

Proverbs *(continued)*

8:17 I love those who love me, and those who seek me early will find me.

8:32-33 Listen+ ... for blessed *are those who* keep my ways. 33 Listen to instruction and be wise and do not refuse it.

9:9-10 Give *instruction* to the wise and they will be wiser. Teach the just and they will increase in learning. 10 The fear of the Lord *is* the beginning of wisdom ...

10:11-12 The mouth of a righteous *person is* a well of life. But violence covers the mouths of the wicked. 12 Hatred stirs up strifes, but love covers all sins.

10:19 In a multitude of words, sin is not absent+. But those who refrain their lips *are* wise.

10:27-28 The fear of the Lord prolongs days, but the years of the wicked shall be shortened. 28 The hope of the righteous *shall be* gladness, but the expectation of the wicked shall perish.

11:13 A talebearer reveals secrets, but one who is of a faithful spirit conceals the matter.

11:14 Where no counsel *is*, the people fall, but in the multitude of counselors *there is* safety.

11:17 The merciful do good to their own soul. But *those who are* cruel trouble their own flesh.

11:19 Righteousness *is* to life. *Those* who pursue evil *pursue it* to their own death.

11:22 A pretty+ woman without discretion *is like* a jewel of gold in a pig's+ snout.

11:23 The desire of the righteous *is* good. The expectation of the wicked *is* wrath.

11:28 *Those* who trust in riches will fall, but the righteous will flourish ...

11:29 *Those* who trouble their own house will inherit the wind. The fool *will become a* servant to the wise of heart.

11:30 The fruit of the righteous *is* a tree of life. One who wins souls *is* wise.

12:2 A good *person* obtains *the* favor of the Lord, but *the Lord* will condemn those of wicked devices.

12:4 A virtuous woman *is* a crown to her husband, but one who makes ashamed *is* like rottenness in the bones.

12:15 The way of fools *is* right in their own eyes, but one who heeds+ counsel *is* wise.

12:16 A fool's wrath is quickly+ known, but a prudent *person* covers shame.

12:22 Lying lips *are an* abomination to the Lord, but those who deal truly *are* His delight.

12:25 Heaviness in the heart makes one stoop, but a good word makes one glad.

13:7 There are *some* who make themselves rich yet *have* nothing, and *some who* make themselves poor who *have* great riches.

13:10 Contention comes from pride, but from the well advised *comes* wisdom.

13:11 Wealth *gotten* by vanity will diminish, but one who gathers by labor will increase.

13:13 Whoever despises the Word will be destroyed, but one who fears the commandment will be rewarded.

13:18 Poverty and shame *come to* those who refuse instruction, but those who regard reproof will be honored.

14:9 Fools mock at sin. But among the righteous *there is* favor.

14:29 *One who is* slow to wrath *is* of great understanding, but *one who is* hasty of spirit exalts folly.

15:1 A soft answer turns away wrath, but grievous words stir up anger.

15:2 The tongue of the wise use knowledge rightly, but the mouths of fools pour out foolishness.

15:3 The eyes of the Lord *are* in every place, beholding the evil and the good.

15:22 Without counsel purposes are disappointed. But in the multitude of counselors *purposes* are established.

15:29 The Lord *is* far from the wicked. But He hears the prayers of the righteous.

15:31-33 The ear that hears the reproof of life abides among the wise. 32 *Those* who refuse instruction despise their own soul. But *those* who hear *and heed* reproof gain+ understanding. 33 The fear of the Lord *is* the instruction of wisdom and before honor *is* humility.

16:3 Commit your work to the Lord and your thoughts will be established.

16:7 When *one's* ways please the Lord, they make even their enemies to be at peace with them.

16:18 Pride *goes* before destruction and a haughty spirit before a fall.

16:20 One who handles a matter wisely will find good, and whoever trusts in the Lord *will be* blessed+.

16:27 An ungodly person+ digs up evil and in their lips *are* like a burning fire.

16:28 A contrary+ person+ sows strife and a whisperer separates chief friends.

16:32 *One who is* slow to anger *is* better than the mighty ...

17:9 Those who cover a transgression seek love, but those who repeat a matter separate friends.

17:17 A friend loves at all times ...

17:22 A merry heart does good *like* a medicine, but a broken spirit dries the bones.

17:27-28 Those who have knowledge spare their words. A man of understanding is of an excellent spirit. 28 Even a fool is considered wise when he remains silent.+ Those who keep their mouths closed *are esteemed* to have understanding.

18:10 The name of the Lord *is* a strong tower. The righteous run into it and are safe.

18:21 Death and life *are* in the power of the tongue ...

18:22 *Whoever* finds a wife finds *something* good and obtains *the* favor of the Lord.

19:5 A false witness will not be unpunished. *One who* speaks lies will not escape.

19:11 Discretion defers anger. *It is to one's* credit+ to pass over a transgression.

19:20 Hear counsel and receive instruction *so* that you may be wise in the latter end.

20:3 *It is* an honor to cease from strife, but every fool will *continue* meddling.

20:18 *Every* purpose is established by *wise* counsel ...

21:19 It is better to dwell in the wilderness than with a contentious, angry woman

21:23 Whoever keeps the mouth and the tongue *still* keeps the soul from trouble.

22:1 A *good* name *is* better+ to be chosen than great riches ...

22:6 Train up children in the way they should go and when they are old, they will not depart from it.

22:24 Do not make make a friendship with an angry person+.

22:26 Do not be a cosigner+ for the debts of others.

23:7 For as one thinks in their heart, so *are* they. Eat and drink, one *may* say to you. But their heart *is* not with you.

23:9 Do not speak in the ears of fools, for they will despise the wisdom ...

24:11 If you forbear to deliver *those who are* drawn to death and *those who are* ready to be slain.

24:26 ... kiss *the* lips that give a right answer *or a forthright response*.

25:6 Do not put yourself forth in the presence of the king and do not stand in the place of *those who are* great.

25:11 A word fitly spoken *is like* apples of gold in pictures of silver.

25:21-22 If your enemy is hungry, give them bread to eat. If they are thirsty, give them water to drink. 22 For *thereby* you heap coals of fire upon their head, and the Lord will reward you.

26:4 Do not answer a fool according to his folly, lest you also be like them.

26:20 Where no wood is, the fire goes out, so where *there is* no talebearer, strife ceases.

27:2 Let others praise you, not your own mouth ...

27:5 Open rebuke *is* better than secret love.

27:12 A prudent *person* foresees the evil *and* hides. The simple continue+ on *and* are punished.

27:15 A continual dropping in a very rainy day and a contentious woman are alike.

27:17 Iron sharpens iron. So *also* a friend+ sharpens the countenance of a friend.

28:6 Better *are* the poor who walk in uprightness than *those* perverse *in their* ways, *even if they are* rich.

28:25 Those who are of a proud heart stir up strife, but those who put their trust in the Lord shall be made whole+.

28:26 Those who trust in their own hearts are fools ...

29:18 Where *there is* no vision, people perish. But one who keeps the law *is* blessed+.

29:23 A person's pride will bring them low, but honor will uphold the humble in spirit.

> 30:5 Every Word of God *is* pure.
> He *is* a shield to those
> who put their trust in Him.

21 Ecclesiastes

8:11 *The* sentence against an evil work is not executed speedily, therefore the hearts of the sons of men is fully set in them to do evil.

9:9 Live joyfully with the wife whom you love all the days of *your* life …

10:1 Dead flies cause the ointment of the apothecary to send forth a stinking smell.+ *So does* a little folly *to one who* has a reputation for wisdom *and* honor.

22 Song of Solomon

8:7 Many waters cannot quench love, neither can the floods drown it …

23 Isaiah

8:12 … do not fear nor be afraid.

26:3 You *Lord,* will keep in perfect peace *the* mind stayed on you *by* trusting in you …

30:18 … The Lord *is* a God of judgment. Blessed *are* all who wait for Him.

32:17 The work of righteousness shall be peace, and the effect of righteousness *will be* quietness and assurance forever.

40:8 The grass withers, the flower fades, but the Word of God will stand forever.

40:31 Those who wait upon the Lord shall renew *their* strength. They shall mount up with wings like eagles. They shall run and not be weary. They shall walk and not faint.

41:10 Do not be afraid for I *am* with you. Do not be dismayed for I *am* your God. I will strengthen you. Yes, I will help you. Yes, I will uphold you with the right hand of my righteousness.

49:15-16 … *Others* may forget *you* but will I not forget you. 16 I have engraved you upon the palms of *my* hands.

53:5 He *was* wounded for our transgressions. *He was* bruised for our iniquities. The chastisement of our peace *was* upon Him. And with His stripes we are healed.

55:11 So shall my Word be that goes forth out of my mouth. It will not return to me void, but it will accomplish that which I please and it will prosper *in those purposes* to which I send it.

61:3 *I will give to them* beauty for ashes, the oil of joy for mourning, *and* the garment of praise for the spirit of heaviness *so* that they might be called trees of righteousness, the planting of the Lord, *so* that He might be glorified.

63:9 In all their affliction He was afflicted and the angel of His presence saved them. In His love and in His pity He redeemed them and He bore them and carried them all the days of old.

24 Jeremiah

3:1 If a man *shall* put away his wife … and she becomes another man's, shall he *ever* return to her again? Is that land not greatly polluted?

15:16 I found your words and consumed+ them and your Word became+ the joy and rejoicing of my heart. For *now* I am called by your name, O Lord God of hosts.

29:8 For thus says the Lord of hosts, the God of Israel: Do not let prophets and diviners among you deceive you …

29:11 For I know the thoughts that I think toward you, saith the Lord, thoughts of peace, and not of evil, to give you an expected end.

29:13 You shall seek me and find *me* when you search for me with all your heart.

31:3 The Lord has appeared to me *saying*, I have loved you with an everlasting love. Therefore, with lovingkindness have I drawn you.

31:25 I have satiated the weary soul and replenished every sorrowful soul.

32:17 Ah Lord God. Behold, you have made the heaven and the earth by your great power and your outstretched arm. There is nothing too hard for you.

25 Lamentations

3:22-23 *It is because of* the Lord's mercies that we are not consumed, because His compassions do not fail. 23 *They are* new every morning. Great *is* your faithfulness.

3:25 The Lord *is* good to those who wait for Him, to the soul *that* seeks Him.

26 Ezekiel

36:26 I will give you a new heart and I will put a new spirit in you.

27 Daniel

9:4 … God keeps the covenant and *shows* mercy to those who love Him and to those who keep His commandments.

28 Hosea

2:19 I will betroth you to me forever … in righteousness and in judgment and in loving kindness and in mercies.

6:6 I desire mercy and not sacrifice and knowledge of God more than burnt offerings.

29 Joel

2:32 Whoever shall call upon the name of the Lord shall be delivered …

30 Amos

5:15 Hate the evil and love the good

31 Obadiah

1:12 You should not look *down* on your brother, neither should you rejoice … in their destruction …

32 Jonah

2:2 I cried *out* to the Lord because+ of my affliction and He heard me

33 Micah

6:8 He has shown you what *is* good. And what does the Lord require of you, but to do justly and to love mercy and to walk humbly with your God?

34 Nahum

1:7 The Lord *is* good, a strong hold in the day of trouble, and He knows those who trust in Him.

35 Habakkuk

2:4 *The* souls *of those who* are lifted up are not upright in them. But the just shall live by faith.

3:19 The Lord is my strength … He will make me to walk in high places …

36 Zephaniah

3:17 The Lord your God in the midst of you *is* mighty. He will save you. He will rejoice over you with joy

37 Haggai

2:8 The silver *is* mine and the gold *is* mine, says the Lord of hosts.

38 Zechariah

4:6 Not by might nor by power but by my spirit, says the Lord of hosts.

39 Malachi

2:16 The Lord … hates divorce+ … therefore take heed… *so* that you do not deal treacherously.

3:6 I *am* the Lord.
I do not change …

AV7

Features & Benefits

AV7 is an accurate literal translation, not a paraphrase. This is important because non-literal Bible versions often incorporate interpretive words and paraphrasing that may not be accurate but may instead reflect subjective ideas, opinions, and doctrinal distinctives.

AV7 uses easy-to-read present-day English. It was compiled by a computerized system that uses seven levels of processing to translate original language sources into grammatically correct English, preserving the literal translation accuracy of the trustworthy sources.

AV7 replaces the obsolete and archaic words and phrases that are used in the traditional 1611 English text with direct-equivalent present-day English words and phrases, using translation tables that identify and explain compilation details, word-for-word and phrase by phrase.

AV7 corrects previous grammatical and translation errors and provides exhaustive documentation to explain the corrections.

AV7 uses *reduced-size italics* to identify words that have been added interpolatively to improve the readability and clarity of the text.

AV7 uses superscript pluses⁺ as key-word flags to unobtrusively identify significant word revisions and to prompt readers to investigate corresponding word-studies.

AV7 replaces non-essential masculine gender presentation style with more accurate gender-inclusive wording. For example, inaccurate wording such as "he that" is revised to "those who" where applicable.

AV7 uses identity clarification revision to replace confusing pronoun sequences with proper nouns or descriptive titles in italics to clarify who is speaking with whom: For example, "he said to him" might be replaced by "*Jesus* said to him" where applicable.

AV7 is supported by exhaustive documentation to explain every aspect and detail of its compilation and presentation.

How the **AV*7*** *text was compiled*

AV7* = *A*uthorized *V*ersion + *7

AV7 is a computer-generated, updated, and enhanced presentation of the Bible that closely follows the traditional 1611 English text commonly known as "The Authorized Version" or "King James Version" or "KJV" but with acknowledged errors corrected and with thousands of archaic words and phrases replaced by their direct equivalent, present-day English words and phrasing.

The 1611 English compilation stood, virtually unchallenged, as the most widely accepted English translation of the Bible for more than 300 years. It acquired the title "Authorized Version" by acclaim, although it was never formally authorized by any official body. Today, the 1611 text continues to be a valuable benchmark against which to test and compare the accuracy of other versions of the Bible.

AV7 gives new meaning to the title "Authorized Version" because, unlike the many "All Rights Reserved" copyright restricted Bible versions and paraphrases in print today, ***AV7*** is authorized to be freely copied and distributed for any non-commercial purpose.

AV7 is compiled without using any paraphrasing or so-called "dynamic-equivalent" or "thought-for-thought" renderings such as have become common in many Bible versions. Instead …

AV7 is compiled by an automated system that is able to perform translations directly from Greek and Hebrew original language sources into word-for-word, direct equivalent English. The resulting literal translation is then fine-tuned through seven levels of processing to produce an accurate yet easy-to-read, present-day English text.

In the example below, on line 1 is the Greek source text for John 3:8. On line 2 is an interlinear transliterated representation of the Greek. On line 3 is a literal, word-for-word English translation of each Greek word using mostly 1611 English words and spellings:

1.	το	πνευμα	οπου	θελει	πνει	και	την	φωνην	αυτου
2.	to	pneuma	opou	qelei	pnei	kai	thn	fwnhn	autou
3.	the	wind	where [it]	will*	bloweth	and	the	sound [of]	it*

1.	ακουεις	αλλ	ουκ	οιδας	ποθεν	ερχεται	και	που	υπαγει
2.	akoueiV	all	ouk	oidaV	poqen	ercetai	kai	pou	upagei
3.	hearest	but	not	know*	whence	cometh	and	where	goeth

1.	ουτως	εστιν	πας	ο	γεγεννημενος	εκ	του	πνευματος
2.	outwV	estin	paV	o	gegennhmenoV	ek	tou	pneumatoV
3.	so	is	every[one]	who [is]	born	of	the	spirit

Limited space here does not permit a complete explanation of all of the sophisticated processing used in ***AV7*** compilation. The words shown with asterisks in the example above have alternate renderings that ***AV7*** processing uses to replicate the following *traditional* "KJV" text:

> The wind bloweth where it listeth, and thou hearest the sound thereof, but canst not tell whence it cometh, and whither it goeth: so is every one that is born of the Spirit.

Multiple additional translation tables include the following:

BEFORE		AFTER
bloweth	....	blows
listeth	....	will+
thou	....	you
hearest	....	hear
thereof	....	of it
canst not	....	[you] cannot
whence	....	from where
cometh	....	comes
whither	....	where
goeth	....	goes
so is	....	So [it] is [with]
every one that	....	everyone who

When all seven ***AV7*** translation tables are applied, this is the result:

> The wind blows where it will+ and you hear the sound of it, but *you* cannot tell from where it comes and where it goes. So *it* is *with* everyone who is born of the Spirit.

AV7 compilation is much more complex than indicated in this overview, but this provides a brief description of the process. Following are the seven stages of computer processing ***AV7*** uses to convert the Bible's original language source texts into the result shown above:

Stage 1 translates Greek and Hebrew to the literal English equivalent
Stage 2 converts literal English to a traditional 1611 English equivalent
Stage 3 converts archaic Olde English text to present-day English, replacing obsolete and archaic words, spelling, and syntax
Stage 4 corrects known grammatical and translation errors
Stage 5 adds technical enhancements into the master source files
Stage 6 incorporates many textual refinements to fine-tune the presentation
Stage 7 encodes the text for print font styles, sizes, and custom features

Additional information about the ***AV7*** translation and compilation system can be found at this Internet address: www.***AV7***.org

The case for literal accuracy.

Prove all things.
Hold fast what is good.
1 Thessalonians 5:21

People often ask: "Why are there so many different versions of the Bible, and which one is the best and most trustworthy?"

There are four basic answers to the first part of this question — two good reasons and two reasons that can be a cause for concern.

Reason #1: To translate the Bible into common languages. Since the Bible was originally written in Hebrew and Greek, it has been necessary to translate it into contemporary languages that people understand. The Bible has been translated into more languages than any other book.

Reason #2: To update obsolete and archaic language. The English language has undergone significant changes over centuries of time, and so it is beneficial to replace outdated words, grammar, and phrasing with literally accurate, direct equivalent words and grammatically correct phrasing in order to make the Bible easier to read and understand.

Reason #3: To promote private interpretations. Regrettably, some versions of the Bible have been compiled to promote the private interpretations and doctrines of various groups.

Reason #4: For commercial objectives. Some proprietary versions of the Bible have been sponsored and published by various commercial firms.

Since there can never be more than one version of the truth, ideally there should be only one version of the Bible in any given language. And yet, non-literal-translation paraphrases of the Bible can sometimes be helpful to first time readers. Any version of the Bible that helps people to know God and encourages them to learn and understand more about God's purpose and plan for their lives, serves a useful purpose.

However, it is important to make a very clear distinction between literal truth and subjective interpretation. Everyone who would like to understand God's Word better and grow in faith will do well to compare whatever version they consider using to an accurate literal translation.

Just as a ship or airplane that is only a fraction of a degree off course can end up hundreds of miles away from its intended destination, so also following interpretations that are not literally accurate can lead to serious error. The following explanation includes a few examples:

First, it is important to note that ***AV7*** is *not* a new version of the Bible. Rather, ***AV7*** is a new *presentation* of the traditional English translation that has stood the test of time for nearly 400 years.

The first English translation of the Bible began with work done by William Wycliffe in 1385 A.D. and by William Tyndale in 1536 A.D. Between 1603 and 1611 A.D., a team of 50 scholars compiled a further developed English text based largely on Wycliffe and Tyndale's work. But even after that, the English text first published in 1611 was further revised and improved many times between 1611 and 1769 A.D. That text became almost universally recognized as the most trustworthy English translation.

Even so, while there are few significant errors in this traditional English text, there are some renderings that are curious and not literally accurate. For example, in Acts 12:4, the Greek word πασχα, which is correctly translated as "passover" in 26 other places, is incorrectly translated as "Easter" in this verse. Another translation error is the colloquial expression "God forbid" that appears, incorrectly, 15 times in the traditional English text. The correct translation of the Greek source, μη γενοιτο, is "not be" or "*may it* not be." So, these are a just a few examples of errors in the traditional English translation that are corrected in ***AV7***.

More serious problems occur when paraphrases take great liberty in changing the literal Word of God to say something quite different than an accurate literal translation. Compare the Greek, literal, 1611, ***AV7***, and three currently popular versions below for the verse Luke 21:19:

Greek	εν	τη	υπομονη	υμων	κτησασθε	τας	ψυχας	υμων
literal	in	the	patience	you	possess	the	souls	you
1611	In	your	patience		possess ye	your	souls	
AV7	In	your	patience,		possess	your	souls	
(x)	By standing firm you will save yourselves							
(y)	By standing firm you will gain life							
(z)	By your endurance you will gain your lives							

As you can see, the ***AV7*** rendering exactly follows the literal word-for-word and the traditional 1611 English translation. Version "x" is a radically different interpretation. One must ask, is it really possible for anyone to "save themselves"? Versions "y" and "z" are paraphrases that suggest a very different interpretation and understanding than the literal. These same versions (x, y, and z) all translate υπομονη as "patience" in dozens of other places, but here change the meaning to "endurance" or "standing firm." One must question why.

Study to show yourself approved to God,
a worker+ who does not need to be ashamed,
rightly dividing the Word of Truth.
2 Timothy 2:15

A Cordial Invitation

to join the family of God

Do you know that ***God loves you***
and that He wants you and everyone you care about
to be filled with love, joy, peace,
patience, gentleness, goodness,
and faith that will encourage and inspire you?

All you need to do
to become a member of God's family
is ***read or listen*** to the Word of God and ***believe*** Him.

That is all… He will do the rest.

You do not have to join any particular church
or follow any special religious doctrine
based on man-made rules.
You do not have to pay any dues or fees.
And you do not have to participate
in any special ceremonies or secret rituals.

If you will ***just read the most essential truths*** in the Bible
you will see how easy it is to receive the free gifts
of abundant life for today and eternal life
after your temporary life on earth comes to an end.

But you must understand
that God's greatest blessings are given
only to those who ***choose*** to believe in Him
and believe Him *(believe His Word)*
and who make a resolute decision
to join His family and follow Him.

The good news is that this is very easy to do.
God never intended for reading and believing His Word
to be confusing or complicated.

Repent. For the kingdom of heaven is very near.
Matthew 4:17

Those who believe and are baptized will be saved,
but those who do not believe will be damned.
Mark 16:16